John Dewey
and Confucian Thought

SUNY series in Chinese Philosophy and Culture
Roger T. Ames, editor

John Dewey and Confucian Thought

Experiments in Intra-cultural Philosophy

Volume Two

Jim Behuniak

Front cover: Roofline image taken by John Dewey in China.

Back cover: Image of John Dewey (Peking, July 5, 1921), courtesy of the Morris Library, Special Collections Research Center, Southern Illinois University Carbondale.

Published by State University of New York Press, Albany

© 2019 State University of New York

All rights reserved

No part of this book may be used or reproduced in any manner whatsoever without written permission. No part of this book may be stored in a retrieval system or transmitted in any form or by any means including electronic, electrostatic, magnetic tape, mechanical, photocopying, recording, or otherwise without the prior permission in writing of the publisher.

For information, contact State University of New York Press, Albany, NY
www.sunypress.edu

Library of Congress Cataloging-in-Publication Data

Names: Behuniak, James, author.
Title: John Dewey and Confucian thought / Jim Behuniak.
Description: Albany : State University of New York Press, [2019] | Series: Experiments in intra-cultural philosophy ; Volume two | Series: SUNY series in Chinese philosophy and culture. | Includes bibliographical references and index.
Identifiers: LCCN 2018033272 | ISBN 9781438474472 (hardcover : alk. paper) | ISBN 9781438474465 (pbk. : alk. paper) | ISBN 9781438474489 (ebook)
Subjects: LCSH: Dewey, John, 1859–1952—Knowledge—Philosophy, Confucian. | Dewey, John, 1859–1952—Travel—China. | Philosophy, Confucian. | Philosophy, Chinese. | Philosophy, Comparative. | East and West.
Classification: LCC B945.D44 B39 2019 | DDC 191—dc23
LC record available at https://lccn.loc.gov/2018033272

10 9 8 7 6 5 4 3 2 1

For Anton

Contents

List of Illustrations	ix
Interlude	xi
Dewey's Chinese Dinners	xi

Part I

1. John Dewey and Intra-cultural Naturalism	3
Dissolving the Blank Slate	3
Humanism and Intra-cultural Philosophy	12
Continuity and Common Sense	16
Culture and the "Return Wave"	26
Cultural Relations and Reconstruction	33
2. Education and Tradition	43
Learning (*xue* 學) and Personhood	43
Dewey Arrives in China	53
Education and Its Reach	60
Learning and Thinking	67
The *Dao* 道 of Tradition	77
3. Custom and Reconstruction	85
Breakthroughs in China	85
Li 禮 and Custom	91
Toward a "Social Philosophy," Part One	99
Custom and Reflection	109
Ren 仁 and Human Association	115

4. Pluralism and Democracy — 123
  Democracy vs. The Melting Pot — 123
  Guojia 國家 and the "Great Community" — 132
  Three Complimentary Studies — 139
  Toward a "Social Philosophy," Part Two — 146
  Dewey Leaves China — 159

Part II

5. Roles and Exemplars — 169
  The *Analects* as Virtue Ethics — 169
  Exemplarism and the Denotative Method — 178
  Role Ethics and Human Nature — 184
  Hitting the Mark (*zhong* 中) — 190
  Morality is Social — 198

6. Humans and Nature — 207
  Naturalizing Heaven — 207
  Spiritualizing Nature — 212
  Understanding Human Nature — 219
  The Goodness (*shan* 善) of Human Nature — 230
  Nature and Normality — 237

7. Harmony and Growth — 243
  Family and Human Nature — 243
  The Norm of Harmony (*he* 和) — 251
  The Meaning of Growth — 256
  Family Experience and Non-Dualism — 264
  Culture and Adaptation — 272

8. Integration and Religiousness — 281
  Integration (*cheng* 誠) and Adjustment — 281
  Recovering the Forfeiture — 288
  Ideals and the Actual — 294
  Communion and the Human Spirit — 301
  Returning to China — 310

Notes — 323

Works Cited — 373

Index — 391

Illustrations

Figure 0.1 Business card of the original "Shanghai Café," date unknown. xii

Figure 1.1 John Dewey and family arrive in Honolulu on January 17, 1951. 32

Figure 2.1 John Dewey's photograph of Confucius' tomb in Qufu, Shandong, which he visited on July 13, 1921. The inscription on the stele reads "The Sage of Great Cultural Accomplishment." 49

Figure 2.2 Dewey in Beijing with his friend, Grace Wu, who ran a small school for girls from underprivileged families and helped to raise money to support them. According to Lucy Dewey, "She is certainly one of the saints of the earth." 63

Figure 3.1 Chinese caption reads (Right to Left), "Jiangsu Education Department Welcomes Dr. and Mrs. Dewey from the United States, Photo Taken May 10, 1920." 96

Figure 5.1 *John Dewey*, by Edwin B. Child, 1929. This painting, featuring Dewey with a statue of a Chinese sage, hangs in the Dewey Memorial Lounge on the campus of the University of Vermont. 202

Figure 7.1 One of several photographs in John Dewey's collection depicting the young people he encountered while travelling in China. 258

Figure 8.1   Tao Xingzhi wearing the traditional Chinese clothing that he had come to prefer, date unknown.   297

Figure 8.2   John Dewey in 1946 sitting under a Chinese scroll in his Manhattan apartment. This was the year that Dewey hoped to make his return trip to China.   313

Interlude

> Dewey is still in China—learning, I hope, from the Chinese.
>
> —Lewis Mumford to Patrick Geddes, May 5, 1921

Dewey's Chinese Dinners

Tucked under the elevated local tracks at Broadway and 125th Street in Manhattan, Shanghai Café opened its doors in 1949. It was the first non-Cantonese Chinese restaurant to open in New York and remains widely remembered as one of the best Chinese restaurants that the city has ever seen.[1] Shanghai Café would be the first of many eateries to open near Columbia University by chefs who fled China in the years immediately following the Communist revolution.[2] By that time, the Cantonese were so well established in Chinatown that it was difficult for immigrants from other Chinese regions to gain a foothold in the district.[3] Thus, in the last few years of Dewey's life, the area around Columbia became a hub for what were then known as "Mandarin" restaurants—basically any *non*-Cantonese Chinese cuisine.

Gradually, the Shanghai Café on Broadway and 125th came to be known as the "Old Shanghai Café" to distinguish it from its eponymous competitors. Dewey and his family dined there every Sunday night and Sing-nan Fen often joined them. Lawrence Cremin, one of Fen's classmates at Teacher's College, came to join these dinners by accident. As he explains:

> Fen asked me quite unexpectedly one evening whether I would be willing to deliver a package for him to the Dewey apartment on my way home, and I said of course I would . . . I went on up and rang the bell and Mrs. Dewey came to the door and graciously accepted the package and asked whether I would like to meet Professor Dewey. I said it would be a privilege and was

promptly ushered into the study, where Dewey was pecking away at an ancient typewriter, using two fingers. He looked up, smiled, greeted me warmly, said he was working on an article dealing with the improvement in his concept of interaction that the term "transaction" made possible, and then asked quite bluntly, "What do you think, Mr. Cremin?" It was one of those occasions when the lips move but the words have trouble coming out. The words did come, and the point is [that] we had a lively conversation for about a half-hour, in which at the age of twenty-three I was treated as an absolute equal . . . I shall never forget it.

From then on, Cremin was on the "Invite" list for Dewey's Chinese dinners. "I must tell you," writes Cremin, "that whatever the emphasis on the social and communal in Dewey's writings, it was rampant individualism in that Chinese restaurant." Eating was the main event, and Dewey did not defer to his underlings. "I may be the only person living who learned to use chopsticks fighting over fried rice with John Dewey," reckons Cremin.[4]

Dewey became adept at using chopsticks during his Asia trip, while also solidifying his affection for Chinese food. Prior to leaving San Francisco for Asia, he and Alice put in the requisite preparations. "Last Friday we went to Chinatown again for dinner so that Papa and Mama could get used to using chopsticks," Sabino Dewey relates to Lucy. They are "doing fine," he reports—

Figure 0.1. Business card of the original "Shanghai Café," date unknown. Image source: https://www.chowhound.com/post/remember-shanghai-cafe-126th-broadway-196905#photo=1060802.

"the food they don't have to get used to it, as they are quite crazy about it."[5] Before his Chinese audiences, Dewey would display his usual modesty: "I have to pay so much attention to the way I hold my chopsticks that sometimes I hardly know what I am eating."[6] But he had mastered the technique well enough. "We have learned to eat with chopsticks very well," Alice wrote from Japan, "and it is not a bad way."[7]

Dewey's first letter from China is all about food. "I will tell you something of what we had to eat," he writes to his children. "On the table were little pieces of sliced ham, the famous preserved eggs which taste like hard boiled eggs and look like dark colored jelly, and little dishes of sweet shrimps, etc." So the description begins. "We had chicken and duck and pigeon and veal and pigeon eggs in soup and fish and little oysters . . . nice little vegetables and bamboo sprouts mixed in with the others, and we had shrimps cooked and sharks fin and bird's nest." So it rolls to its conclusion: "For dessert we had little cakes made of bean paste filled with almond paste and other sweets."[8]

One month later, there would be the following to report: "I am going right on getting fat on delicious Chinese food."[9] When Dewey travelled ahead to Nanjing in the spring of 1920, his daughter Lucy asked him not to "eat up all the food in Nanjing before we get there."[10] Dewey, however, was packing it in. About halfway through his visit, he confessed to his children: "I never confided in you how fat I got, 170 when I tried the scales last some months ago." This was portly for his modest frame. To keep things under control, Dewey "resolved upon walking daily."[11] He did whatever he needed to do to retain his eating habits. When he travelled to Hunan province, he was again blown away by what he was being fed—"Only Chinese food, I'm glad to say. Darn good cooking at that."[12]

So the founding of the People's Republic of China in 1949 would have one salutary effect on Dewey's life: it allowed him to end his days in New York surrounded by excellent Chinese food. He did not let the opportunity pass. Dewey was always eating in some Chinese restaurant or another. He once ran into Hu Shih's son in a Chinese restaurant,[13] he took new friends to Chinese restaurants,[14] and if one wished to get face-time with Dewey a promising tactic was to note to him "that you and your niece like to dine occasionally at a Chinese restaurant on 49th Street. May I ask you and your niece to be my guests?"[15] Lovers of Chinese food can relate. Fine cuisine is one of the myriad ways in which cultures take what is basically a common biological requirement—in this case, *eating*—and elevate it through human intelligence and creativity. China achieves this as well as any culture in the world.

Like every cultural showcase, fine cuisine emerges against the background of a shared human nature. Stemming from our earliest forest diets, humans have always had a preference for sugars and acids, cravings that we continue to share with the great apes. When our ancestors moved into open terrain, tastes expanded accordingly, with the most dramatic changes in dietary versatility and taste occurring in hominids between 4.4 and 2.3 million years ago.[16] Alongside other sense capacities, taste is genetic—passed down in our DNA. Generally speaking, modern humans share the same range of tastes and preferences, but no two gustatory profiles are exactly alike. The wildcard appears to be bitterness.[17] While receptor cells for sweet (*tian* 甜), salty (*xian* 鹹), sour (*suan* 酸), and spicy (*la* 辣) in the human taste buds are fairly uniform, the set of compounds involved in bitterness (*ku* 苦) are large and structurally diverse, involving around twenty-five specific taste receptor genes.[18] Such structural complexity owes to the crucial role that bitterness plays in evolution. Bitter compounds trigger an "electrochemical cascade in the brain." This storm is experienced as "distaste," an innate warning system that helps to keep toxins from entering the body. Researchers are still unable to trace the subtle ways in which bitterness receptors augment or diminish the activity of partner receptor cells when specific chemicals are released upon specific palates. The connections are too complex to map. Thus, as the old saying goes, "There is no accounting for taste." Indeed, even one's own perceptions of taste fluctuate with various physiological factors: anticipatory metabolic responses, states of illness and health, nutritional deficiencies, pregnancy, and other factors can affect the way things taste.[19]

Nevertheless, humans gather around the table to share what is by and large a common pleasure in artfully prepared food. Taste is only part of it. On the strictly metabolic level, our bodies require the same carbohydrates, proteins, sugars, and amino acids that other animal bodies require. We convert these into raw energy and through transduction use the nutrients to replace damaged cells. Unlike that of many other animals, human metabolism is normally running at maximum capacity. The reason is that 16 percent of our basal metabolism is allocated to our brains, whereas the average mammal allocates only 3 percent. This makes us unusual, because in the economy of life, animals are under selection pressure to be as dumb as they can get away with.[20] But Nature (*tian* 天) is no dummy. Since our brains have grown so costly, they must be naturally good at something—and *really* good. As Mencius suggests, there is nothing alien or unnatural about human brain functions (a.k.a. *xin* 心). Through them, we realize our natures (*xing* 性) and serve the cosmos in the process.[21] Through such natural endowments we forge relationships, communicate, engage in ritualized behavior, create art and music, and prepare the delectable *xiaolongbao* 小籠包 that Dewey enjoyed on Sunday evenings at the "Old Shanghai Café." Appreciating the continuity (*yi* 一) of such experiences with the rest of Nature (*tian*) will be the central theme in the present volume.

This volume follows the same conventions as the last. Again, when quotations of any kind go uncited, they are from the same source cited in the next footnote in the same paragraph. Also, in Dewey's "China lectures," I have taken the liberty of rendering his language gender-neutral. I also substitute the word "Chinese" for Dewey's more antiquated term "Oriental" whenever it is clear that Dewey is referring to something specifically Chinese. Such in-text substitutions appear in brackets. Chinese names appear in the Romanziation system most appropriate. All Chinese translations are my own unless otherwise noted. For other conventions, please refer back to volume one.

Some of what follows has appeared in alternate forms elsewhere. Chapter 2, section 1 draws from Behuniak (2008) and chapter 5, section 4 reformulates Behuniak (2011). See "Works Cited" for more information. I thank Open Court and Wiley-Blackwell for permissions accordingly. I also wish to thank, once again, everyone mentioned in the "Prelude" to volume one.

VOLUME TWO

Part I

1

John Dewey and Intra-cultural Naturalism

> When we speak of human nature we do not refer to the idle logomachies about the inherent goodness or innately evil nature of humans, but rather to objective study of observable human behavior and scientifically derived hypotheses about its changing trends . . . On the basis of these findings we devise our approaches to and methods for solving human problems.
>
> —John Dewey, National Peking University, November 1919

Dissolving the Blank Slate

Confucius taught that, "Human beings are similar in their natures, but vary with respect to their cultural practices (*xi* 習)."[1] In this, the Master was essentially correct. It is also said that Confucius formulated no doctrine (*yan* 言) about our natures.[2] In this, the Master was equally wise. Given the sheer number of shared human traits, coherent doctrines of "human nature" (*renxing* 人性) can only be assembled selectively, and once taken up into verbal formulation (*yan* 言) they are destined to become instruments of culture as much as any account of human nature. This is what happens in China, most famously in debates over whether human nature is "good" (*shan* 善) or "bad" (*e* 惡).

Such "idle logomachies," as Dewey calls them, work well in introductory Philosophy courses, but we know that the facts are not that simple. As Donald E. Brown argues (not un-controversially), there are at least hundreds of human traits that "comprise those features of culture, society, language, behavior, and psyche for which there are no known exception."[3] Brown's list includes: conflict, play, music, weapons, revenge, jokes, envy, rape, empathy, insults, hope, dominance/submission, cooperation, pride, sexual attraction, ethnocentrism, morality, male coalitional violence, gift giving, economic inequality, retaliation, fear of snakes, and the list goes on.[4] From such a list, one might classify a "good" or "bad" set of traits and call that "human nature" on solid empirical grounds ("classification," and "good/bad distinctions," by the way, are also on Brown's list of universals). The more important point is that, as soon as such theories (*yan* 言) become objects of debate, the discussion becomes more about the desirability of certain cultural practices than it does about any shared human nature. Dewey thought that it was important to have such debates. Empirical facts about human nature, he believed, were necessary to make them more intelligent (*ming* 明).

The present chapter explores how our shared human nature relates to intra-cultural philosophy specifically. Chapter 1 of the previous volume, *John Dewey and Daoist Thought*, developed intra-cultural philosophy as an alternative to the more conventional notion of "comparative philosophy." The argument there was that philosophy is genetic-functional in nature—both situated *in* a culture as well as being the critical and constructive mode *of* that culture. Thus, philosophical assertions, comparisons, and inquiries are always culturally situated. This being the case, philosophical comparisons are never made from some standpoint *outside* of culture, meaning that intra-cultural engagements are necessarily "interwoven in a vast variety of ways in the historico-cultural process."[5] Dewey's inaugural essay in *Philosophy East and West*, "On Philosophical Synthesis," indicates not only where he thought global philosophy should go as a result, but also where he was going with his own philosophy—engaged as he was in a transition between "experience" and "culture." As fate would have it, Dewey's declining health prevented him from fully completing his "cultural turn" and articulating an intra-cultural philosophy of his own.

That turn, however, was not as abrupt as it might seem. As early as 1938, within the pages of *Logic: A Theory of Inquiry*, Dewey had his preliminary theory of culture already in place. Thus, in its broader context, Dewey's statement in *Philosophy East and West* is part of a final, culminating insight that marked his final period. In order to appreciate this, one can begin with 1938's *Logic*, follow Dewey's thinking up through the 1940s (as he wrote and then lost his masterwork, *Unmodern Philosophy*), and then terminate with his visit to Hawai`i in 1951. In tracing this trajectory, the present chapter will serve as a companion to the opening chapter of volume one. The latter considered the difference between intra-cultural philosophy and comparative philosophy primarily from a methodological standpoint. The present chapter focuses more on how intra-cultural philosophy relates to Dewey's late period cultural naturalism. For as Sing-nan Fen notes, it was because Dewey's outlook was "naturalistic [that] his philosophy was cut out to be intercultural" and "had the potentiality of transcending the so-called Western tradition."[6] In what follows, we examine how this is so.

We can begin by distinguishing Dewey's "cultural" approach from its so-called "postmodern" alternative. Since intra-cultural philosophy is genetic-functional in nature, i.e., always *in* and *of* a particular culture, it would be reasonable to ask whether intra-cultural philosophers are destined in all cases to reduce other cultures to their own cultural categories. As intra-cultural philosophers, are we not trapped within our own "prison houses of culture," with no direct access to other cultures unmediated by our own sociocultural situations? If this is so, then it might make our approach similar to that of the "postmodern relativist," a figure whom Edward Slingerland associates with the following philosophical tendencies:

> [An] approach to the study of culture that assumes that humans are fundamentally linguistic-cultural beings, and that our experience of the world is therefore mediated by language and/or culture *all the way down*. That is, we have no direct cognitive access to reality, and things in the world are meaningful to us only through the filter of linguistically or culturally mediated preconceptions. Inevitable corollaries of this stance are a strong linguistic-cultural relativism, epistemological skepticism, and a "blank slate" view of human nature: we are nothing until inscribed by the discourse into which we are socialized, and therefore nothing significant about the way in which we think or act is a direct result of our biological endowment.[7]

Slingerland's concerns echo those expressed by Steven Pinker in his work, *The Blank Slate: The Modern Denial of Human Nature*, which also projects the "postmodern" as one who vehemently rejects "the possibility of meaning, knowledge, progress, and shared cultural values," basing their ideas on "a false theory of human psychology, the Blank Slate," thus maintaining that "[everything] in perceptual experience is a learned social construction."[8]

Philosophers who align themselves with Dewey read Pinker's *The Blank Slate* with a mixture of consent and befuddlement. Our *consent* lies in the fact that Dewey also accepts the reality of shared human traits and values. As he says, "There is a constitution common to all normal individuals. They have the same hands, organs, dimensions, senses, affections, passions; they are fed with the same foods, hurt by the same weapons, subject to the same diseases, healed by the same remedies, warmed and cooled by the same variations in climate."[9] The environment presents human experience with a common set of conditions: e.g., "that certain things are foods, that they are to be found in certain places, that water drowns, fire burns, that sharp points penetrate and cut, that heavy things fall unless supported, that there is a certain regularity in the changes of night and day and the alternation of hot and cold, wet and dry."[10] Dewey rejects "blank slate" theories because they "slur over the fact that the environment involves a personal sharing in common experiences."[11] He regards blank slate empiricism to be an "anachronism [given] the demonstration of the number and variety [of] instinctive non-acquired tendencies."[12]

Our *befuddlement* lies in the fact that Pinker can write a 400+ page book on this topic and not mention Dewey even once. Given Pinker's historical account, this is an egregious oversight. In the twentieth century, he argues, "behaviorist minimalism" eclipsed William James' "rich psychology," while the cultural reductionism of anthropologists such as Margaret Mead and Ruth Benedict, for whom "culture is autonomous from biology," replaced the more balanced approach of their teacher, Franz Boas.[13] Both statements are true. James and Boas, however, were major influences on Dewey, and under such influences Dewey (who was more prolific than James and Boas combined) spent half a century developing the kind of biologically grounded theory of culture that Pinker says we must now begin to formulate.[14]

Throughout his writings, Dewey never once doubts the presence of shared, native, pre-linguistic instincts and functions in the human experience. His main point is always that *biological heredity does not predetermine future use*, and on this he remains remarkably consistent. Heredity, as Dewey sees it, "means neither more nor less than the original endowment of an individual." To regard such an endowment as predetermining future use is a "misuse of the idea of heredity." For Dewey, environment always has a role to play in settling the eventual expression of one's native tendencies. The human being, for instance, is endowed at birth with the equipment for speaking language—but "if the sounds which he makes occur in a medium of persons speaking the Chinese language, the activities which make like sounds will be selected and coordinated."[15]

Along more philosophical lines, Dewey focuses on breaking down the "Nature/Culture" dualism altogether, arguing that the operations of the former are always continuous with their expressions in the latter. "It is at least as true," he writes, "that the state of culture determines the order and arrangement of native tendencies as that human nature produces any particular set or system of social phenomena so as to obtain satisfaction for itself." He continues: "These statements do not signify that biological heredity and native individual differences are of no importance. They signify that as they operate within a given social form, they are shaped and take effect *within* that particular form."[16] For Dewey, our shared biological background is what makes culture possible, serving as the operative *limit* to our cultural situations. "Otherwise," he says, "everything would go wrong—higgledy-piggledy that is."[17]

While it is true that mental and linguistic features uniquely characterize all cultural-level experiences, such features do not go "all the way down" as they would for the so-called "postmodern relativist." For Dewey, biological-level experiences such as "hunger," and he expands this list to include "fear, sexual love, gregariousness, sympathy, parental love, love of bossing and of being ordered about, imitation, etc.," do not express elements or forces that are "psychic or mental in their first intention." In first accounting for such experiences, one turns to "physics, chemistry and physiology rather than to psychology." The result of such analysis reveals not the variability of our natural tendencies (or *xing* 性) but the contingent status of their cultural expressions. In the case of something like fear, there is no single *psychological* species of that emotion, no "one fear having diverse manifestations," Dewey writes. There are different kinds of fear, and there are diverse sociocultural triggers for fear-like experiences. Empirical observation reveals, however, that they "all have certain physical organic acts in common—those of organic shrinkage, gestures of hesitation and retreat."[18]

Such common physiological operations are taken up differently in different sociocultural situations. The same can be said for faculties such as memory, attention, and perception, the objects of which are developed in a social environment. Thus, as Dewey observes, "The faculty of memory is developed in one way in China, and in another way in the United States."[19] Accordingly, such operations become valued differently. The experience of fear in moment "X," for instance, might be regarded as intelligent in some societies but cowardly in others. Lunar eclipses were objects of dread in premodern societies, whereas today most people feel fortunate to witness one. So, while the basic physiology of "fear" in humans is the same, occasions for fear and its cultural expression become diversified as human communities evolve. As Mark Johnson observes, "Although cultures will share many values because of commonalities of our bodies and the recurring features of the environments we inhabit, *value pluralism* is an inescapable fact of the human condition."[20] Another way of saying this is to repeat what Confucius already said: "Human beings are similar in their natures (*xing* 性), but vary with respect to their cultural practices (*xi* 習)."[21]

Dewey's classic statement on the relationship between biological- and cultural-level experiences appears in his *Logic: The Theory of Inquiry*. It is here that Dewey introduces the phrase "cultural naturalism" to describe his position. The central term in Dewey's treatment is *continuity*. "The idea of continuity is not self-explanatory," he writes—"its meaning excludes complete rupture on one side and mere repetition of identities on the other; it precludes reduction of the 'higher' to the 'lower' just as it precludes complete breaks and gaps. The growth and development of any living organism from seed to maturity illustrates the meaning of continuity." In Dewey's nondualistic and nonreductive approach, "rational [or human-level] operations *grow out of* organic activities, without being identical with that from which they emerge."[22]

Thus understood, culture constitutes neither break nor gap within nature. Rather, it constitutes the growth of complexity *within* nature, a growth that results in properties non-identical to those exhibited prior to its development. While the development of culture at the species-level correlates to emergent properties in human brain function over several millions of years, Dewey suggests that the principle of continuity exhibited in its growth is the same principle as that observed in the evolution of any living species that exhibits new functions and properties over time. Dewey's objective, in the *Logic* and elsewhere, is to overcome the association of nature with the purely physical, and to establish that culture is equally natural in that it both *conditions* and is *conditioned by* that which is purely physical. As he puts it, his position is that "mental phenomena represent life-functions of a physiological order transformed by interaction with social conditions involving language and its cultural products."[23]

The challenge is to render this position coherent without succumbing to either dualism or reductionism. "To a very large extent," Dewey writes, "the ways in which human beings respond even to physical conditions are influenced by their cultural environment." In such environments, he explains, "physical conditions are modified by the complex of customs, traditions, occupations, interests and purposes which envelop them." Dewey is not suggesting that human beings cannot experience the purely physical, "but the occasions in which a human being responds to things as merely physical in purely physical ways are comparatively rare." Here, he offers the examples of jumping at a sudden noise, withdrawing one's hand at the feeling of heat, and our "animal-like basking in sunshine" (alluded to in chapter 7 of volume one). Such a list could be extended indefinitely. The point is that such "raw" experiences are normally taken up on the plane of human meaning as soon as they register as experiences. It is the *rusty old truck* that suddenly backfires, the *chain restaurant coffee* that burns my hand, and the *well-earned vacation* that makes basking in the sunshine so grand. Who really knows how often the *purely* physical is experienced? Dewey imagines that one would have to observe a person all day to determine which experiences are purely physical and which are enveloped in cultural meaning. His guess is that, "the result would show how thoroughly saturated behavior is with conditions and factors that are of cultural origin and import."[24]

The drafts of Dewey's lost manuscript indicate that his thinking in the 1940s remained consistent with *Logic: The Theory of Inquiry*. Important developments, however, can be observed both in the 1949 "Re-Introduction" to *Experience and Nature* and in the aforementioned manuscript. In the 1949 "Re-Introduction," Dewey further explains his decision to replace the term "experience" with "culture" as follows: "The limitation of the expression 'experience and nature' is overcome by the more generalized statement that the *standing problem* of Western philosophy throughout its entire history has been the connection-and-distinction of what on one side is regarded as *human* and on the other side as *natural*."[25]

This is a key statement, because the bilateral relation of "connection-and-distinction" between *human*-level phenomena and *natural*-level phenomena is what "culture" finally comes to mean for Dewey. The hyphen in the phrase "connection-and-distinction," as Dewey sees it, is something that "stands for inherent connection, in *both* directions, between what the two terms stand for."[26] Culture would come to replace "experience" because the latter word, in Dewey's estimation, remained tainted by "the spirit of the post-medieval period," where it represented the "human" element of philosophical subject matter in contrast to an ostensible "natural" element. The assumption that "experience," so understood, provides a "sure standard of judgment by which to determine the status of everything else," explains why "[modern] philosophies purporting to be philosophies of experience [were] so unable to deal effectively with experience." By foregrounding "culture," i.e., the life-functions that operate in ongoing "connection-and-distinction" between the human-and-natural, Dewey hoped to prevent erroneous conceptions of "experience" from being read into his position. The move was meant to *preserve* what experience actually stood for in Dewey's thinking.

The switch, he thought, would help to liberate philosophy from its parochial association with early modern forms of "experience" and to re-envision it as an activity inclusive of cultural-level experience and its diversity. This is how it was to serve within the larger framework of the "cultural turn." The present term "intra-cultural" is meant to register the fact that philosophical activity, while comprehensive as human activity within shared conditions, is always culturally situated and thus variable. As Dewey explains:

> To hold that the scope of philosophy is comprehensive, inclusive, in the sense that philosophy, whatever the time and place, is always concerned with the *connection-and-distinction* of the *human* and the *natural*, is in effect to deny that it is comprehensive in the sense that it is identical in content at all times and places. It is to deny that the scope of philosophy can be stated in terms once and for all as it could be if philosophy were independent of time and place . . . entirely unaffected by the changes in human events, including those that occur in the science of nature as well as in other cultural activities and conditions, aesthetic, industrial, political, etc.[27]

Philosophy, as a genetic-functional activity situated *within* a culture as well as being the critical and constructive mode *of* that culture, changes focus as cultural conditions evolve. Rather than risk the misunderstanding that philosophy deals in some perennial way with reconstructing human-level experience *vis-à-vis* an external "nature," Dewey decided to just drop the word "experience" and replace it with "culture," thus underscoring the evolving nature of philosophy *and* experience within the framework of his cultural naturalism.

This was an important shift in vocabulary, but not a revolution in core thinking. The touchstones would remain continuity and nondualism, with the "great harm" being done when distinctions "entirely genetic-functional" were "erected into a difference of kinds of existence." This would remain Dewey's approach in his lost manuscript. While illustrating the nature of the "Material/Ideal" distinction, for instance, Dewey summarizes his final position as follows: "[The main point] is that culture, by and in its own nature, is a union of qualities and traits which, when discriminated in inquiry and discourse, are respectively called material and non-material."[28] This is another way of saying that "culture" stands for the underlying continuity of elements that we identify as exclusively "human" or "natural" in specialized discourse.

In the tenth and longest chapter, "Mind and Body," Dewey provides an extensive account of what in *Experience and Nature* is called the "body-mind," only now considered within a larger sociocultural context. As Pierre Steiner observes, readers "will not find [in this chapter] *totally new* elements concerning the status of mental phenomena in Dewey's philosophy."[29] What was to be Dewey's final statement on "body-mind" remains consistent with what he wrote in earlier treatments, only now he places even more stress on the sociocultural factors. In describing the continuity between mental and physical phases of experience, Dewey now notes that: "the 'monism' involved is not of a metaphysical sort but consists simply of recognition that the phenomena in question are behavioral in nature," which is to say they are socioculturally situated as "life-functions."[30]

This, again, is a significant statement for Dewey. Recall that he intends for "life-functions" to serve as a comprehending category that includes both the physical "body" as well as the extra-physical "self." As we learned in chapter 7 of volume one, Dewey considered the absence of such a single, comprehensive term to be an intellectual travesty; for the category that eludes us stands precisely for "human life." As we then saw, the Chinese term *shen* 身 can stand for "body," "self," and "person" all at the same time. Dewey complains, however, that in English, "we have no word by which to name mind-body in a unified wholeness of operation. For if we said 'human life' few would recognize that it is precisely the unity of mind and body in action to which we were referring."[31]

With respect to "human life," culture (and thus philosophy) for Dewey represents ongoing activities concerned with the "connection-and-distinction" between things human (e.g., "minds") and natural (e.g., "bodies") always in response to special problems or other social purposes. Over the course of such operations, there is no ontological distinction between *human*-level and *natural*-level phenomena. Only functional distinctions obtain. But now, every functional distinction indicates a sociocultural situation. Thus, Dewey writes:

> It follows that the subject matter of philosophy is social when it uses such words as "mind," "mental," "sensations," "ideas" . . . [that when] used in analysis and description, stand for life-activities or behavioral events in which the environmental interacting partner can be said to be *physical* only in consequence of an analysis in which qualifying social conditions are deliberately dropped out, because of the nature of the special problem then and there dealt with.

The principle that there is no "mental" without a deliberate, social decision to drop out what is "physical" applies both ways. For as Dewey adds: "The very notion of a 'world' which is physical and nothing but physical is itself a product of social factors."[32]

While arriving at this position, Dewey also arrives at what is perhaps his keenest insight into Chinese philosophy. In his unfinished drafts of the 1949 "Re-Introduction," he suggests that the Chinese tradition is better positioned to understand the continuity of the "human" and the "natural" by virtue of having already identified and overcome "the constant and unifying problem of Western philosophy throughout its whole career," namely "the relation [by] way of distinction-and-connection of what at a given period and in a given area has been taken [up as] *natural* on one side and as *human* on the other."[33] Dewey writes:

> [This] is not intended to exclude [Chinese] philosophy from the scope of the statement about the enduring and unifying problem of philosophy as it develops at different times in diverse cultural areas. As a matter of fact, it is my impression that those who created [Chinese] philosophy have been [more] steadily aware that the problem with which they were concerned is of the kind just stated than have the Westerners, who have been so preoccupied with the then-and-there urgent phase of the problem as not to have seen the forest because of the trees right about them.[34]

Dewey is remarkably astute in observing this. As explained in volume one, the "continuity between Nature and the human" (*tianrenheyi* 天人合一) will emerge as a key assumption in Confucian thought. It would go on to become perhaps *the* central tenet in the tradition and will account for many of the parallels between Dewey's thought and Confucian thinking explored in this volume.

In the final analysis, Dewey's postulation of "culture" as coextensive with human "life-functions" provides a way around "Mind/Body" dualism without reductionism. Remember—"philosophy" represents the genetic-functional activity in which the "connection-and-distinction" between humans and nature comes up for discussion *at all*. There *is* no ontological distinction between the two—they are *continuous* (*yi* 一). Culture *is* nature. Every time "Culture/Nature" distinctions are made they are functional, not ontological. Thus, Dewey is not in any "blank slate" or "postmodern" camp. For positing sets of "connections-and-distinctions" within the human-nature continuum does not involve the denial of our common "human nature"—in fact, *it affirms it*. After all, as Donald E. Brown points out, the act of making "Culture/Nature" distinctions is itself a human universal.[35]

Humanism and Intra-cultural Philosophy

Retaining as it does a realist component, Dewey's cultural naturalism is consistent with what William James labels "humanism." For James, reality is "what truths have to take account of." James never doubts that "reality 'independent' of human thinking" plays a role in our experience—he only maintains that it is a "thing very hard to find" because "what we say about reality . . . depends on the perspective into which we throw it. The *that* of it is its own; but the *what* depends on the *which*; and the *which* depends on *us*." Reality is what is given, but it is also what is *taken up* into language and thought. As James explains: "We humanly make an *addition* to some sensible reality, and that reality tolerates the addition." Once these additions are made, it is difficult to "weed out the human contribution."[36]

Again, for Dewey, physiological processes such as fear have genuine standing in reality; but once they are taken up in sociocultural activity, it is hard to know where "nature" ends and where the "human" begins. Physiological responses associated with "anger," for instance, serve an attack and defense function in nonhuman animals, but in the human world such a function is "as meaningless as a gust of wind on a mud puddle apart from [the] direction given it by the presence of other persons." Within different sociocultural contexts, such raw physiological responses become "a smoldering sullenness, an annoying interruption, a peevish irritation, a murderous revenge, a blazing indignation."[37] In the case of human anger, where is the "Human/Nature" line drawn? Or, as James frames the question, does the river make its banks or do the banks make the river? "Just as impossible may it be to separate the real from the human factors in the growth of our cognitive experience," James submits.[38]

As we saw in chapter 6 of volume one, the *Zhuangzi* suggests that "knowing what Nature (*tian* 天) does and what the Human (*ren* 人) does is the optimal standpoint" for human beings.[39] Dewey would agree. He understands that the animal body performs myriad operations, and that "we are not aware of the qualities of many or most of these acts." Meanwhile, "meanings acquired in connection with the use of tools and of language exercise a profound influence upon organic feelings."[40] As James says, it may be impossible to clearly parse the human and natural in cognitive experience, primarily because the former element is so predominate in cognition. In his lost manuscript, Dewey recognizes "the decisive effect of *social* environment" upon human sensory experience, and acknowledges "how completely what are regarded as merely physical stimuli are transformed by the social setting in which they arise and operate." He also recognizes the "extreme difference" between an actual experience with direct sensual character and "a quality that is called *sensory* because of analysis undertaken for a purpose."[41]

Dewey just leaves this difference standing. We *have* the first sensation, and we can *discuss* the second. This is not the "postmodern relativist" position, because discussion does not go "all the way down," as Edward Slingerland says. Remember—Dewey appeals to his own body-practice, the Alexander technique, in discussing some of the purely *physical* aspects of his own experience, and he describes the physiological aspects of things like anger and fear in his own realist terms: "They denote *ways of behavior*."[42] While it is difficult to capture such realities "raw" in language, nothing *but* such realities ever manage to get captured. There is no dualism here, and no reductionism—Dewey positively affirms the continuity between minds-and-bodies and humans-and-nature.

Dewey's cultural naturalism thus opens broad avenues for intra-cultural philosophy, enabling substantive "Sameness/Difference" distinctions to be made for a variety of purposes in specific inquiries. While cultures might determine and value the "connection-and-distinction" between humans-and-nature, minds-and-bodies, etc. differently, cultural experience proceeds within a shared reality characterized by the principle of continuity (*yi* 一). Hence, there is nothing preventing the philosopher from one culture from moving across situations in a genetic-functional mode, reflecting on her own connections-and-distinctions, until she arrives at the standpoint of another culture. This is not like trying to understand what it's like to be a bat. One will encounter conceptual obstacles and uncommon assumptions along the way, but there are no insurmountable chasms—no radical incommensurabilities.

In many ways, the process of cross-cultural understanding is like that of cross-personal understanding. The big difference, however, is that there will always be *one* insurmountable gap in cross-personal understanding. As James puts it, "Each of us dichotomizes the Kosmos in a different place."[43] One can never fully experience what it is like to *be* another person. Radical pluralism here is the rule. There is nothing, however, that it is like to *be* a culture. To the reflective understanding, culture is known as an object and this does not violate its essence. Through patient and persistent inquiry, one can and does come to know other cultures better as matrices of "connections-and-distinctions" between humans-and-nature, minds-and-bodies, etc., with all their varied expressions and valuations.

The human commonalities (*xing* 性) that become expressed in diverse cultural practices (*xi* 習) might be thought of in terms of the "vague field" that David L. Hall and Roger T. Ames discuss in their methodological writings. Recall that Hall and Ames suggest that cultural systems are related to one another against an indeterminate background. Such a background, as they see it, is not a standing ground of perennial human meanings, but rather a "vague field of significances open to articulation for this or that purpose, but existing primarily *in potentia*." Such a "productively vague" theory of culture understands cultural differences as "local distortions of a general field which is itself without specifiable boundary conditions," but allows for "a vague complex of significances [to be] focused in accordance with a variety of interests."[44]

Hall and Ames' position is sometimes misunderstood. Certain critiques of it are plainly mistaken.[45] Still, given that Hall and Ames chart their course through the straits of sameness and difference, the ideal of *not* lapsing into cultural essentialism is not perfectly realized—but such is the nature of making comparisons. As Dewey reminds us in his inaugural essay in *Philosophy East and West*, cultural terms are not "block-like" objects but rather "interwoven in a vast variety of ways" within a matrix of "complexities, differences, and ramifying inter-relationships."[46] Again, Dewey was prepared to inaugurate a new term to describe this emerging vision—*Togetherness*—but he lost the manuscript in which he would have made the suggestion.[47] Intra-cultural philosophy picks up where Dewey left off, providing a basis for cross-cultural philosophy that is sensitive both to the vague background furnished by cross-cultural universals (i.e., human nature) and to the culturally situated nature of philosophy as a genetic-functional activity. Once recast in the broader framework of intra-cultural philosophy, the paradoxes and transgressions of comparative philosophy are mitigated, and its outcomes, while enabled by real similarities and differences, are understood primarily in terms of the contexts in which they are situated.

Such contexts are cultural and thus "human." Unlike William James, however, Dewey resists describing his position as "humanism." One problem, Dewey explains, is that "humanism is a portmanteau word. A great many incongruous meanings have been packed into it."[48] The word is typically contrasted with "naturalism" or with the natural sciences, thus making "humanism" into the "conviction that spiritual and ideal values are of supreme rank in the makeup of reality, and that these values are most adequately expressed in the great or classic achievements of humanity in literature and art—especially literature."[49]

As such, "humanism" adopts various guises on both the cultural left and the cultural right. On the one hand, it is the conceptual precursor to what Edward Slingerland and Steven Pinker call "postmodernism"—the seeming disregard for biological "nature" in favor of the products of human language (or "texts") that go "all the way down." On the other hand, "humanism" becomes the framework for cultural conservatives to fortify the "canon" against the encroachment of an increasingly secular "naturalism." Irving Babbitt and Paul Elmer More, two conservative Harvard philologists, formulate what they call "New Humanism" accordingly. In their 1929 work, *Humanism and America*, they erect a sharp "Human/Nature" dualism and place the entirety of human value and meaning on the former side.[50]

Dewey responds to Babbitt and More in his 1930 article, "What Humanism Means to Me." Rejecting their "New Humanism" as "negative" and "anti-naturalistic," Dewey explains that "in an age like our own, any philosophy which sets off [humans] from nature, and which condemns science as a foe to higher interests cannot, it is safe to predict, become productive." Dewey's positive conclusion is that "what Humanism means to me is *an expansion, not a contraction, of human life, an expansion of which nature and the science of nature are made the willing servants of human good.*"[51] Dewey regards the "Spiritual/Material" dualism to be "the greatest dualism which now weighs humanity down," and he looks forward to a time when the "vexatious and wasteful conflict between naturalism and humanism is terminated."[52] Dewey long hoped to discover a "common background or matrix" in which humanistic and naturalistic interests were unified—one in which "the tracing of their respective differentiations from this community of origin [would] not become a separation" but would secure "the possibility of fruitful interaction between them whenever desired."[53] While turning to "life-functions" and the "connection-and-distinction" between humans-and-nature in the 1940s, Dewey realized that "culture" was precisely that common background or matrix.

So, Dewey had good reason to avoid the term "humanism." Were he to label his standpoint "humanism" he would risk evoking the dualism that he was trying to overcome. He did sign the "Humanist Manifesto" in 1933 out of sympathy for its rejection of supernatural religion, but he did not thereby mean to identify his own position with its definition of "humanism."[54] Corliss Lamont pressed Dewey to openly describe his philosophy as "humanism," but Dewey demurred, concerned that the term suggested the "virtual isolation of [the human] from the rest of nature." As Dewey explained to Lamont, "I have come to think of my own position as cultural or humanistic naturalism—Naturalism, properly interpreted seems to me a more adequate term than humanism."[55] Lamont pressed on. "I still think [humanism] is a better word . . . [naturalism] is certainly confusing to the average person, who considers a Naturalist one who, like John Burroughs, makes a specialty of birds and flowers."[56] Dewey stood firm. "I don't see that I have anything to add to what I wrote you the other day. I note that you prefer the word Humanism as a name for my philosophy . . . I suppose I must be the judge in the case of my own philosophy."[57]

Dewey saw the specter of Slingerland's "postmodern relativist" already on the horizon, and he anticipated by decades the crisis that C. P. Snow would describe in his 1959 work, *The Two Cultures*. As Dewey writes: "The philosophic dualism between [the human] and nature is reflected in the division of studies between the naturalistic and the humanistic, with a tendency to reduce the latter to the literary records of the past."[58] The severance of humanistic studies from the natural sciences, as Dewey saw it, only furthers the "tragic split" that prevents culture from reaching its fullest potential.[59] Dewey resists trends in the Humanities that would deepen the rift—whether these came from the cultural left or the cultural right. He also steers clear of such trends in Cultural Anthropology. He maintains, for instance, that Ruth Benedict's brand of "cultural-solipsism" only exacerbates "*the* problem in philosophical communication," and he had no inclination to follow its lead.[60]

Continuity and Common Sense

Dewey's "cultural naturalism" now comes into view. Human culture, as well as cultural difference, is continuous with nonhuman nature—it *is* nature in one of its manifold expressions. Just as diverse forms of organic life are localized descendants from a common ancestor, diverse cultural practices (*xi* 習) are localized developments from a common source: a largely shared set of psycho-physiological dispositions (*xing* 性) that come from Nature (*tian* 天). Early Confucianism, broadly speaking, assumes the same.

With respect to the cultural diversity that it generates, human nature is an exceedingly *vague* background. Its content includes *ways of behaving* that trace back hundreds of millions of years and can only be observed "raw" through specific technological operations. "Anger," for instance, stems from precortical activity centered in the amygdala that triggers the release of neurotransmitters increasing blood pressure, heart rate, and muscular tension. Structurally, this is a universal human trait. Thus, when St. Paul says, "Be angry but do not sin, do not let the sun go down on your anger," everyone can relate. Such vague universal traits provide underground bridges that preclude cultural incommensurability while allowing for broad cultural differences. Human nature, thus understood, does not need to descend from any supernatural "God" or "Heaven." Instead, the human mind-and-body is an adaptive mechanism coextensive with Nature (*tian* 天), one that is ideally suited to cope with a statistical composite of selection pressures that *Homo sapiens* faced during its evolutionary history.

How old, or how new, are different aspects of human nature? This is an empirical question and difficult to answer with precision. Leda Cosmides and John Tooby maintain that the human mind is largely a "Stone-Age" product, formed during the 99%+ of our history living in hunter-gathering societies.[61] Others, like Stephen M. Downes, argue that not all human cognitive habits were secured during the Pleistocene epoch—some are older, some are newer, and such adaptations vary in flexibility.[62] What evolutionary psychologists tend to agree on, however, is that "William James was right" about the genesis of common sense. As Cosmides and Tooby observe, "James' view of the mind, which was ignored for much of the 20th century, is being vindicated today by evolutionary psychologists."[63]

The next step is to understand what this means for intra-cultural philosophy. Dewey follows James in foregrounding how "common sense" serves as the baseline against which "connections-and-distinctions" within culture are made. In order to see how progress in intra-cultural philosophy is possible, it needs to be understood how "common sense" is both the subject matter of intra-cultural philosophical inquiry and its prerequisite. This complex function needs to be better understood.

"Common sense" has a long and complicated history. Here, we focus on its development within classical American philosophy. In his lecture, "Pragmatism and Common Sense," James argues that there are three sources of human understanding: common sense, science, and philosophy. Among these, common sense is the most primitive. It consists of evolutionary inheritances, or "indelible tokens of events in our race-history." As James writes, "Our ancestors may at certain moments have struck into ways of thinking which they might conceivably not have found. But once they did so, and after the fact, the inheritance continues." This is the feature that aligns James with modern evolutionary psychology. For as he states: "My thesis now is this, that *our fundamental ways of thinking about things are discoveries of exceedingly remote ancestors, which have been able to preserve themselves throughout the experience of all subsequent time.* They form one great stage of equilibrium in the human mind's development, the stage of *common sense*." The commonsense notions that James has in mind are core intuitions such as "things," "kinds," "minds," "bodies," and "causal influences."[64]

As products of evolution, there are two things that can be said about such notions. First, they are contingent. Commonsense categories might have been different had they not worked so well in coordinating transactions between the human species and its environment. "Were we lobsters, or bees," James explains, "it might be that our organization would have led to our using quite different modes [of thinking]."[65] Second, our core intuitions are now virtually inescapable as native instincts, for having "first fitted; and then from fact to fact [having] *spread*, until all language rested on them . . . we are now incapable of thinking naturally in any other terms." James actually underestimates the depth to which some commonsense notions have their "innings" in the brain, guessing that "young children and the inferior animals" have no general tendency to apprehend "things." As he explains: "A baby's rattle drops out of his hand, but the baby does not look for it . . . same with dogs. Out of sight, out of mind, with them."[66] It is now understood, however, that object permanence is apprehended very early in human development and that it crosses species boundaries.[67]

Common sense, according to James, becomes consolidated in pre-reflective experience long before it emerges into reflection. As it emerges, it comes under the scrutiny of philosophical and scientific understandings that "burst the bounds of common sense." Here, cultural variation is the rule. Zhuangzi, Descartes, Einstein, the Buddha, Democritus, Darwin, Advaita Vedānta, the *Book of Changes*—these represent just some of the ways in which "things," "kinds," "minds," "bodies," and "causes" are reconstructed through human inquiry. Just as the Buddha knew that his approach to things "went against the stream" (*paṭisotagāmi*), science and philosophy tend to be critical with respect to established habits of thought. With the arrival of science and philosophy, says James, "havoc is made of everything" for common sense.[68] Dewey thought this dynamic was so important that his lost 1947 manuscript was initially intended to be a popular text on the relationship between common sense, science, and philosophy.[69] Accordingly, when he undertook the 1949 "Re-Introduction" to *Experience and Nature*, the relationship between these terms became its centerpiece.

Dewey's thoughts on this topic trace back to 1938's *Logic: The Theory of Inquiry*. It is in this work that he explains that the phrase "common sense" has two meanings. The first is "sagacity": the power to "discriminate the factors that are relevant and important in significance in given situations." In this context, we speak of "sound practical sense" within a given cultural group.[70] The second meaning is that which James discusses, i.e., the common sense of "instinctive beliefs": intuitions that are "*common* in the sense of being widely, if not universally, accepted." In this context, "we speak of the *deliverances* of common sense as if they were a body of settled truths."[71]

Dewey understands common sense in the first respect to be *culturally specific*, and in the second respect to be *culturally universal*. As he suggests: "It is possible today, along with our knowledge of the enormous difference that characterize various cultures, to find some unified deposit of activities and of meanings in the 'common sense and feeling of [*humankind*].'" Dewey's list of universal notions that "dominate common sense in every period" is similar to James' own. Dewey's list goes as follows:

1) "Things" in a stable world, "designated by common nouns in general use."

2) "Natural Kinds," which are "overwhelming from the standpoint of common sense."

3) "Teleological Ends," which control ideas, beliefs, and judgments "in every culture."

4) "Ranks and Hierarchies," that grade things "low and high," "base and noble," etc.[72]

Dewey also mentions "color and light" as deliverances of common sense, variously taken up into cultural experience, and he identifies the distinction between the "ordinary and extraordinary" to be a human universal. His concern in all such instances is with identifying "certain traits of all pre-philosophic beliefs, traits which form the common matrix out of which emerged all the world's philosophies, Asiatic as well as European."[73]

Like James, Dewey maintains that science and philosophy challenge the standing of common sense. The degree to which such reflection is *critical* results in cultural differences with respect to the status of commonsense intuitions. For instance, by refining and securing certain articles of common sense in its logic and metaphysics (e.g., teleological ends, essential natures, etc.) Greek-medieval philosophy "precluded the possibility of the reaction of science back into common sense."⁷⁴ As long as science was largely directed by common sense, it met with little resistance and returned only modest results. Thus, as Dewey reminds us, "[The] conclusions of Greek science . . . were much closer to the objects of everyday experience than are the objects of present scientific thought."⁷⁵ From the standpoint of modern science, it was clear that the modest progress of Greek-medieval science was precisely a result of its *too*-close relationship to common sense. Thus, articles of common sense such as the "final cause" were eradicated from the natural sciences in the modern period. As a result, new instrumentalities were opened and new forms of inquiry enabled.

What thus became required, however, was a new logic based not on Greek-medieval common sense but on ideas that can better accommodate the "two-way movement between common sense and science." This new logic never materialized, so Dewey undertook its development in his 1938 *Logic*. The work was premised on the fact that "common sense" can and does change in response to scientific, technological, and other cultural advancements. As Dewey thus observes: "Common sense in respect to both its content of ideas and beliefs, and its methods of procedure, is anything but a constant." As he writes: "One has only to note the enormous differences in the contents and methods of common sense in modes of life that are respectively dominantly nomadic, agricultural, and industrial."⁷⁶

Had Dewey not forwarded *two* working definitions of "common sense"—one *universal* and one *culturally specific*—this statement would be difficult to square with the idea that there is a "unified deposit" of activities and meanings that characterize the "common sense and feeling" of human beings tracing back to Paleolithic times. Remember, this is the common sense that for William James has its "innings" in the brain already. The question now becomes: *What is the relationship between the "common sense" that is universal to the species and the "common sense" that is culturally specific, i.e. "anything but a constant"?* In *Logic: The Theory of Inquiry*, Dewey leaves the answer ambiguous (in fact, he doesn't even ask the question), likely because he knew that a dualism lurked in its formulation. As his thinking evolves throughout the 1940s, a nondualistic answer gradually emerges. It is one that goes hand-in-hand with his "cultural turn," and thus helps to set the agenda for what is here called intra-cultural philosophy.

Presenting this answer, however, is not as simple as pointing to select passages in Dewey's published works. His unpublished (and belabored) attempts to compose the "Re-Introduction" to *Experience and Nature* suggest that Dewey *had* the answer but he didn't know how to present it. Analysis got the better of him. In helping Dewey along, I propose revisiting a neglected corner of the Greek-medieval tradition. John Scotus Eriugena (c. 810–c. 880) understands "analysis" in a unique and subtle way. "*Analytike* comes from the verb '*analuo*' which means 'I resolve' or 'I return,'" writes John. Accordingly, "*Analytike* is used in connection with the return of the division of the forms to the origin of that division."[77] In this spirit, let us generate an analytic distinction to assist Dewey in getting his late-period insight across; and then, let us "return" through such analysis to what is continuous in nature. Let us here posit a sharp "Universal/Culture-Specific" distinction.

Note that, with this distinction, "comparative philosophy" is instantly enabled. The "Universal/Culture-Specific" distinction tracks onto the "Sameness/Difference" distinction observed in chapter 1 of volume one. What is *universal* is the "Same," and what is *culturally specific* is the "Different." The uneasy co-presence of these features is what gives rise to what Zhang Xianglong calls the "comparison paradox."[78] But no matter—as Zhang says, we make comparisons despite this paradox. So let us erect a framework in which to make our comparisons. The "common sense" that is common to humankind is the "Same," so let us call it "*universal* common sense." Meanwhile, the "common sense" that is peculiar to specific cultures is the "Different." So let us call it "*culture-specific* common sense."

This distinction enables us to establish the *tertium* necessary to make various observations. For instance, the manner in which any reflective thinker takes up *universal* common sense invariably modifies its form. The *universal* common sense intuition of "thing," for example, is more primitive than Aristotle's refined category of substance (*ousia*), which qualifies as *culture-specific* common sense for the Greek-medieval thinker. "Things," as Dewey says, are "far from being the metaphysical substance or logical entity of philosophy" as distilled in the writings of Aristotle and his followers. First and foremost, "things," suggests Dewey, are for *universal* common sense always located within doing-and-undergoing as "parties in life-transactions." The clearest expression of the *universal* common sense notion of "things," he submits, is when children take things up as, "what you do so-and-so with," thereby uniting "things" with the *events* in which they are implicated.[79] As Dewey argues in *Experience and Nature*, "[*universal*] common sense has no great occasion to distinguish between bare events and objects; objects being events-with-meanings."[80] In this respect, the Chinese notion of *shi* 事 (thing/event) might be somewhat closer than substance (*ousia*) to what Dewey regards as the *universal* common sense notion of "thing." Such relative proximity, however, does not mean that *shi* is not also an article of *culture-specific* common sense, one with its own history of reflective use and development in Chinese culture.

In making this suggestion, the point to recognize is that Greek substance (*ousia*) and Chinese *shi* 事 are each *culture-specific* common sense variations of a more primitive, prelinguistic article of *universal* common sense, one that has its "innings" in the brain already. Accordingly, every human language has a term for "thing," and the meaning of such terms retains continuity with the "thing" of our prereflective *universal* common sense. Each term, however, also acquires distinct cultural associations in becoming *culture-specific* common sense. The same can be said for other items on Dewey's list. Belief in "natural kinds," for instance, "is overwhelming from the standpoint of [*universal*] common sense."[81] From an evolutionary perspective, identifying plants and animals according to their "kind" has given the human species a survival advantage, and all humans inherit such a *universal* common sense. Susan Gelman's work on "essentialism" in early childhood supports this hypothesis.[82]

Different cultural groups, however, come to explain the origin and criteria for "kinds" differently and organize things into non-identical categories in keeping with localized *culture-specific* common sense. As we saw in chapter 2 of volume one, Chinese thinkers tend to classify plants and animals into types (*lei* 類) according to where they live and how they transact with other things through resonant influences (*ganying* 感應). Such thinking in adult populations diminishes the influence of our universal essentialist intuitions. Chinese common sense, in this particular case, appears to be more "evolved" than Aristotelian common sense, which remains more closely aligned to the untutored intuitions of children. Chinese and Aristotelian commonsense notions, however, each retain some degree of continuity with the *universal* common sense about "kinds" while also evolving somewhere beyond it. As long as science and philosophy continue to operate within culture, such evolution will continue.

Methodologically speaking, this means that articles of *culture-specific* common sense, e.g., the Greek-medieval ideas of species (*eidos*) and the Chinese ideas of *lei* 類, are comparable but highly unlikely to be identical. Like any two descendants from a common ancestor, they tend naturally to diverge within their respective habitats. However, "as is the way with evolutions generally," as Dewey suggests, "[something] of the old, and often much of it, survives within or alongside the new."[83] Ultimately, such continuity (*yi* 一) enables the comparative philosopher to detect points of "Sameness/Difference" within their continua. To such continua, John Scotus Eriugena's "*Analytike*" beckons us to return.

The comparative philosopher, however, is slow to return—she cannot get free from the "Sameness/Difference" distinction and thus overlooks the basis upon which her comparisons are being made. She fails to see that it is the genetic-functional continuities *within* "common sense" trajectories that are operational, not the "Continuity/Discontinuity" *between* them. The comparative philosopher is *already* culturally located in one or another "stream" of common sense. Everyone is. The *tertium quids* of our comparative judgments are established from *within* such streams; and as Ralph Weber argues, they are generally not reflected on. Such ad hoc comparative frameworks are always vulnerable. They have nowhere near the sophistication of the refined scientific instruments that might establish actual baselines in nature. Thus, one launches a cultural comparison, and a fellow "comparative philosopher" proceeds to shoot it down—like an endless contest in skeet shooting, "this" reading vs. "that" reading. Intra-cultural philosophy hopes to chart a course around this dynamic.

The intra-cultural stance is assumed once John's "return" is made complete. We have posited the "Universal/Culture-Specific" distinction in order to parse what Dewey had to say about "common sense" in his 1938 treatment. In order to understand his final position, however, this dualism needs to be collapsed and genetic-functional continuity (*yi* 一) restored. This is where "culture" comes into play. For like philosophy, common sense also has a "double status" as genetic-functional in nature: both preceding inquiry and furnishing its objects.[84] Its operative status is always that of the "quart bowl" in which objects are determined and inferences made.[85] Common sense, thus understood, receives its final treatment in 1948's *Knowing and the Known*, where its twofold nature becomes continuous *via* its analysis as "*trans*-actional" and as explicitly expressive of human "life-activities." This treatment is consistent with both the "connection-and-distinction" mode of inquiry reflected in the 1949 "Re-Introduction," and the general turn toward "life-activities" as it appears in the lost draft of the "Experience as Life-Function" chapter and elsewhere. Typing with two fingers, this is what Dewey was trying to work out when Lawrence Cremin stopped by to deliver the package from Sing-nan Fen. "What do you think, Mr. Cremin?" asked Dewey.[86] This was going to be the last major installment in Dewey's mature philosophy, but it was one that would never achieve its full articulation as a component in his "cultural turn."

Let us attempt to recover such an application. "The discussion that follows," Dewey writes in *Knowing and the Known*, "is appropriately introduced by saying that both common sense and science are to be treated as transactions."[87] Dewey and Bentley present the "*trans*-activity" of organism-in-environment as *the* irreducible mode of natural occurrence. They justify this approach in light of contemporary findings in physics and the biological sciences. Observation in the mode of "*trans*-activity" is distinct from more standard analyses in the modes of "self-activity" or "inter-activity" (the former being inquiry with respect to powers that operate independently and the latter with respect to causal connections between them). Contemporary physics and biology reveal to us the degree to which such standard analyses rely on substance-oriented abstractions that do not track on to the underlying dynamics of the natural world. Observations in the mode of "*trans*-activity" aim for analyses closer to the world that science discloses. As the authors explain, transactional observation proceeds "without final attribution to 'elements' or other presumptively detachable or independent 'entities,' 'essences,' or 'realities,' and without isolation of presumptively detachable 'relations' from such detachable 'elements.'"[88] In other words, transactions do not have "parts" that are entirely separable ontologically. Here as in Nature (or *tian* 天), continuity (*yi* 一) is the rule.

As a tool in reflecting upon common sense, it appears now that the "Universal/Culture-Specific" distinction serves as a heuristic device that enables inquiry into modes that Dewey and Bentley call "self-action" and "inter-action," but it obscures inquiry into the more primary mode of "*trans*-action." Here's how. Common sense, as a subject matter, can indeed be organized in such a way that ontological and epistemological inquiries are made into how a primitive stratum of *universal* common sense (i.e., the "Sameness" element) "self-acts" upon or "inter-acts" with subsequent expressions of *culture-specific* common sense (i.e., the "Difference" element). Such analyses seem natural enough within the rubric of "comparative philosophy," wherein postulations approximating *universal* common sense become the *tertium quids* enabling notions like substance (*ousia*) and *shi* 事 to be compared. This, however, is not the line of inquiry one pursues with respect to common sense in its natural operation. Common sense is precisely the cognitive mode that stands for "direct active participation in the transactions of living" *prior* to such dualistic analyses. Common sense *as* common sense can never be adequately parsed and observed in "self-action" or "inter-action," but only in "*trans*-action." Common sense always indexes a whole, lived situation—one in which organism-and-environment exhibit an achieved equilibrium. This is how common sense becomes "common sense" in the first place. Dewey's final treatment thus begins and ends with "life-activities" as the locus of common sense in action. Intra-cultural philosophy intends to base its operations within this living context.

Dewey does not mean to foreclose inquiries into "self-action" and "inter-action." These are standard operations in bringing problematic situations to resolution. Thus, he still offers us his two definitions of common sense: the general senses and feelings that "impinge upon the feeling and wit of all [humankind]" (i.e., *universal* common sense), and "good sound practical sense" in a given community (i.e., *culture-specific* common sense). Acknowledging that these two terms do enter into traditional epistemological and ontological inquiries, Dewey notes that the former is sometimes spoken of as "objective" and the latter as "subjective." His intention, however, is to finally overcome this dualism and to locate common sense squarely and explicitly in the realm of *trans*-action. After all, no community or mind engages the world in terms that are strictly "subjective" or "objective" in nature. Life doesn't work that way. As Dewey writes: "The everyday affairs of a community constitute the *life* characteristics of that community, and only these common life-activities can engage the general or common wits and feelings of its members."[89]

Common sense in its most primary mode evolves alongside other life-functions as transactions between organisms-and-environment. As such, there is no distinction between *universal* (or "objective") common sense and *culture-specific* (or "subjective") common sense in its natural state. When common sense is existentially expressed in the *life* of a culture, community, or individual, continuity (*yi* 一) is the rule. As Dewey suggests, common sense in actual operation is "guiltless of the division between objective reality and subjective events" and thus swings free from the "Universal/Culture-Specific" distinction here introduced.[90]

Intra-cultural philosophy means to re-center "life-activity" as the *primary* context that actually shapes our inquiries into the "connection-and-distinction" between the numberless points that might be taken up into "Sameness/Difference" inquiries in the matrix of culture. There is ample room for comparative philosophy in this regard, so long as it recognizes its *own* basis in common sense and realizes its purposes accordingly. Dewey advises that all philosophers must "take seriously the concerns, cares, affairs, etc., of common sense" since they are transactions constituted by "the indissoluble *active* union of human and non-human factors." Human concerns, both "intellectual and emotional," are never "independent of and isolated from" the primary concerns of common sense. They "belong to and are possessed by the one final practical affair," he writes: "the state and course of life as a body of transactions."[91]

Common sense is thus at the center of human experience—while science and philosophy, comparative or otherwise, depend on its being there in order to operate at all. "Without systematic attention to [common sense] 'science' cannot exist," writes Dewey; and without common sense, philosophy is "deprived of footing to stand on as well as a field of application."[92] Recall that philosophy, as genetic-functional, is both situated *in* a culture as well as being the critical and constructive mode *of* that culture, resulting in the reconstruction of experience. Science, for Dewey, likewise grows out of the "direct problems and methods of common sense," and then returns "into the latter in a way that enormously refines, expands and liberates the contents and the agencies at the disposal of common sense."[93] Once Dewey understood that "culture" was the medium through which this happened, everything started coming together. The clock, however, was running out.

Culture and the "Return Wave"

The years leading up to Dewey's 1951 trip to Hawai'i were tough on his health but invigorating for his thought. Six months after writing "Common Sense and Science," the tenth chapter in *Knowing and the Known*, Dewey engaged in correspondence with the sociologist, Jack Lamb. He relates his enthusiasm for his latest ideas. "Since the beginnings of science . . . there has been a steady *return wave* of science . . . back into 'common sense,'" Dewey scribbles. This *return wave* is "thoroughly ambivalent—not a single item thoroughly good and probably not one thoroughly bad"—but in just this respect, he writes, it is "the key to the state of the world." As he approached his ninetieth year, Dewey was feeling intellectually reborn. As he closes his letter to Lamb: "Until fairly recently, my philosophizing had been tentative. I felt in general [that] I was on the right track, but didn't go beyond that. Now I know I have something. I feel that if I had more strength and were younger I'd start a campaign with the young and say, 'try it'—put *that* in your pipe and smoke it."[94]

What Dewey had in his pouch was something fresh, but with a classic flavor. In "Common Sense and Science," he had portrayed the genetic-functional character of science in its usual terms, but then he identified a problem that had long occupied him: "[One] very important *consequence* of science is to obtain human mastery over nature. That fact is identical with the 'return wave' that is emphasized. The trouble is that the view back of the quotation [i.e., that "Science is the means of obtaining practical mastery over nature through understanding it."] ignores entirely the kind of human *uses* to which 'mastery' is put."[95] This problem concerns the relation of "science and common sense with each other," but it is not one that is to be taken up in any traditional epistemological sense by "attempting to determine which of the two is the 'truer' representative of 'reality.'" That is simply the wrong question to ask.[96] The "*return* of scientific method and conclusions into the concerns of daily life is purely factual, descriptive," Dewey notes. The important issues that arise between science and common sense are not epistemological or ontological. They are *moral*. "The *problem*," Dewey observes, "concerns the possibility of giving direction to this return-wave so as to minimize evil consequences and to intensify and extend good consequences, and, if possible, to find out how such return is to be accomplished." Such functions would help to define the future role of philosophy. For if philosophy "surrenders concern with pursuit of Reality (which it does not seem to be successful in catching), it is hard to see what concern it can take for its distinctive care and occupation save that of an attempt to meet the need just indicated."[97]

This further clarifies Dewey's concern with philosophical ideas that are "out of gear" with current scientific conceptions. Philosophy's pursuit of "Reality," as Dewey suggests, never had much chance of resulting in any lasting consensus. Scientific methods and technologies have now rightfully taken over this domain, meaning that philosophers no longer need to concern themselves with *phusis*. Its obligations to *nomos*, however, have not diminished. The modern philosopher must be concerned as Francis Bacon was, with "IDOLIS ANIMI HUMANI NATIVIS ET ADVENTITIIS."[98] Regardless of where they lodge on the plenum of common sense, the idols of our own natures, biographies, vocabularies, and systems need to be reflected upon critically in light of emerging evidence that comes to us from the natural sciences. Bacon teaches that this is the Christian thing to do, and by stressing that the undertaking is *moral* rather than epistemological or ontological Dewey concurs. Dewey long admired Bacon as the true spirit of European modernity: the champion of critical reconstruction and the "prophet of new tendencies."[99] But only as Dewey began to understand the "return wave" of science in the broader context of his "cultural turn" did he feel that his own philosophical vision was becoming unified in that spirit.

Dewey's late-period enthusiasm continues into another set of letters with the sociologist, Kurt Wolff. He explains to Wolff that the "return wave" is an idea that "covers everything in the present world as far as that is distinctly *modern*." He informs Wolff that his current efforts are to "treat philosophy as a concern—its distinctive concern being precisely with this return of processes and materials originating in *knowing* [in the sciences] . . . In other words, philosophy should be a set of working hypotheses for *moral* valuations."[100] Wolff writes to confirm his understanding of Dewey's position. "Your diagnosis of our time tells you that the 'return wave' of science is an important element of this time because, among other effects, of its social implications. Therefore you consider it as an important job of philosophy to take care of this phenomena."[101] Wolff's understanding is correct. As the "return wave" of the natural sciences steadily re-makes the world, philosophy's role is to monitor that world and to attend to the social consequences of being "out of gear" with it. "The philosopher's concern as I see it is a *moral* concern," Dewey tells Wolff. "What is to be done about—or with—the factual situation? The best ascertainment of the latter seems to be the business of the scientists."[102]

These exchanges have Dewey thinking anew about the nature of philosophy. Dewey explains to Wolff that, as he now understands it, philosophy is a form of art rather than a science:

> Every art does something: the study of *what* to do—and the *how* is part of the what—becomes more and more important the more complex and extensive the situation about or with which something needs to be done. I don't believe philosophy is *scientia*

> *scientiarum* or *a* science at all—but it would seem to be the most inclusive of the arts as respects the study of what measures to take—not to the actual doing of which is the business of everybody not specially of any one group or class. Today I take it the prime business of engineers is with the *study* part of what others are to *do*, including study and proposals of better ways of doing. I'd rank philosophy as properly an engineering art with respect to human affairs; in other words as Theory of Morals—in case that word isn't past saving.

Dewey summarizes his new vision of philosophy in three points: (1) "We *have* to do something whether we wish to or not," (2) "It would seem advisable that our doings be as intelligent as possible," thus, (3) there needs to be "a systematic study with respect to the art with greatest generality or inclusiveness"—i.e., philosophy.[103]

During these 1948 exchanges, Dewey was at various stages in the completion of two articles, "Has Philosophy a Future?" and "Philosophy's Future in Our Scientific Age."[104] One year had passed since the loss of his 1947 manuscript, and these articles reflect the next iteration of those ideas. Dewey explains that philosophical systems have traditionally concerned themselves with *inclusive* subject matter—"Being," "Reality," "Nature," and the like—and that these topics had been regarded as somehow "marked off" from any concerns or affairs that were distinctly human. Such moves established the conditions for dispassionate epistemological inquiry. The future of philosophy, Dewey writes, now lies in turning things "the other way around and about." Philosophies, in fact, have *always* been responses to challenges and problems faced by human beings in specific cultural contexts—i.e., "they have always been human in the ends they served." Today, we live in "One World," he notes, and our problems are myriad and shared. Moreover, we live in a world in which advances in science and technology are so rapid that they have outpaced both traditional philosophies and common sense.[105] Such advances are "ambiguous and double-faced," Dewey explains. They are (as we saw in chapter 7 of volume one), neither positive nor negative. Technologies bring forth new problems and new solutions. Philosophy has so far met the consequences of science and technology inadequately—with approaches that are a "mixture of old and new." In the meantime, the "return wave" continues to change everything about our world. Turning things "the other way around and about" is for philosophy to "have an active share in developing points of view and outlooks which will further recognition of what is humanly at stake" given what we have come to *know* through science and technology.[106]

In turning things "the other way around and about," Dewey suggests that the time has come for philosophy to rediscover its ancient roots. "[This] turn-*about* is, after all but a *re*-turn to the view of philosophy put forward of old by Socrates. It constitutes search for the wisdom that shall be a guide of life. It marks a return to the original view of philosophy as a *moral* undertaking in the sense in which the moral and the deeply and widely human are identical."[107] Dewey's understanding is that "the special results of science are always finding their way back into the natural and social environment of daily life and modifying it." The problem, however, is that "this fact does not of itself cause the latter to be known objects."[108] Beholden as we are to various idols of the mind, material transformations that drive crises in culture are often only dimly understood or known only through instruments "out of gear" with the conditions that are actually shaping them.

Such a "turn-*about*" approach is what inspires intra-cultural philosophy. Given the recent and rapid advancement of our sciences and technologies, what Dewey describes as the "return wave" is not being managed well in American culture. Changes wrought in daily life by new instrumentalities in genetics, digital media, energy, neuroscience, etc., can hardly be productively "known" when much of the American mind remains rooted in pre-Darwinian and sometimes Bronze-age ideas about itself. Inherent contradictions are plain to see. Websites devoted to the static truth of one or another dogma pop onto our monitors thanks to the fact that engineers manipulate the electrical properties of silicon, a process that is based on the fact that objects have a band structure in which electrons exist in a combination of states at the same time. On what factual basis or according to what empirical framework does one believe that ideational objects, on the contrary, are fixed? It is the responsibility of philosophers to mediate between science and common sense in such connections. Not only must philosophy assist the latter in reconstructing itself to better reflect what science tells us; but it must also *use* common sense to identify how scientific and technological developments impact human needs and values.

As Dewey suggests, this is a return to the original Socratic function—a kind of "midwifery" that applies "all possible tests to the offspring, to determine whether the young mind is being delivered of a phantom, that is, an error, or a fertile truth."[109] Again—morally speaking, technology is neither good nor bad; and scientific theories are neither positive nor negative. Their impact on human experience, however, *does* have a moral dimension—problems and opportunities are born, and their birth is properly the concern of philosophers. Dewey's chief concern remains that "physical science has had its effect in changing social conditions. But there has been no correspondingly significant increase of intelligent understanding."[110]

This is the classic flavor of Dewey's newest smoke. The *freshness* comes from realizing that this concern operates in a genetic-functional mode within the matrix of culture. This notion was born of the confluence of two related ideas: "*trans*-action" as the mode in which "life-activities" occur, and the functions of humans-and-nature in the mode of "connection-and-distinction," such that "life-activity is not anything going on *between* one thing, the organism, and another thing, the environment, but that, *as* life-activity, it is a simple event over and across that distinction (not to say separation)."[111] Cultural activity is activity in which "connections-and-distinctions" are made between what are regarded as minds-and-bodies, humans-and-nature, etc., resulting in the constitution of particular cultures. Their diverse manifestations are interwoven within "culture" as a whole, which is the matrix of human-level experience in which such "connections-and-distinctions" occur. Accordingly, communication between individualized cultures does not evoke ontological or epistemological dualisms.[112] It is properly speaking an "over-and-across" affair rather than something that occurs "between."

In the summer of 1949, Dewey was back to work on the "Re-Introduction" to *Experience and Nature*, and trading letters with Joseph Ratner regarding the drafts. Ratner tastes the freshness of Dewey's smoke on the first puff. "You've really got it now!" he writes. "Now that you've got it, it seems so obvious. I wonder how it is I've never thought of it! Nature and *Culture* is what Nature and *Experience* mean. Culture *is* experience, in the double-barreled form in which *experience* is historically known." Ratner continues: "The transformation of the problem of 'culture' into the problem of 'experience' is a way of tying up the two. Also, in modern philosophic discussion science or scientific knowledge was not seen as a part of 'culture'—but was an independent enterprise, set over against the 'Humanities' which latter were alone 'cultural.'"[113] Ratner appreciates what Dewey is doing, and he recognizes that he has his finger on the "tragic split" that severs "human life" into isolated domains.

Dewey's "cultural turn" continues to evolve throughout the summer of 1949. He corresponds with John Graves, a Manhattan lawyer who intrigues Dewey with his philosophical ideas. Graves was working on an article that presented what he called the "operation of culture," a description of how culture interacts with the totality of human experience. Graves argues that Dewey's pragmatism "makes a better cultural anthropology than anything so far turned out by the professors of that subject."[114] Dewey appreciates Grave's suggestion and pays him back in kind. "My conclusion is that [your article] contains a greater number of observed facts of primary (and for the present, *final*) importance than any like number of pages I've ever read," Dewey writes.[115] In a letter to a friend, Dewey describes his exchange with Graves as "a fairly exciting experience, intellectually."[116] Their correspondence carries over months, Graves working on his article and Dewey laboring over his "Re-Introduction." Neither side makes much progress. "I am having the devil of a time organizing [the "Re-Introduction"]," Dewey tells Graves, "been at it fairly steadily now for eight months."[117] He also begins doubting that Graves is making much progress on his end. "I am sorry to report that Graves' attempt at a 'constructive' statement doesn't seem to measure up to his critical efforts which had led me to have great hopes of him," Dewey confesses to Ratner.[118] The Dewey-Graves correspondence soon enough fizzles out.

Nevertheless, this exchange galvanized Dewey's own thoughts on culture. Graves stressed the biological continuity of cultures in a manner that stimulated Dewey's thinking about cross-cultural communication. The operations of "humanity" and "culture" are "where we stand," Graves explained to Dewey. "We must reach 'down' in order to find the common reality by which one culture can communicate with another," he writes, which is "a damn sight better than reaching 'up' to the non-existent heavens."[119] Like Dewey, Graves was firmly of the opinion that cultural operations emerged from commonly held biological inheritances. "[I believe] that culture or the social," he wrote, "is 100% an invention utilizing previously sub-human *capacities* (purely physiological); and that *that* is the full meaning of the instrumental character or nature of culture and all its works—from reciting Keats to buying a loaf of bread."[120]

With Graves as a sounding board, Dewey struck upon the centrality of language and communication in cross-cultural experience and identified this function with philosophy itself. "There is nothing like 'thinking' (really talking)," Dewey wrote, "*over and across* instead of between [cultures]. As far as I can perceive, these two things—probably only one—are all there is to 'philosophy'—which isn't a subject but a way or road."[121] Dewey and Graves occasionally talked past one another, but Dewey expressed his gratitude to Graves for "having virtually forced me to become clearer to myself."[122] Henceforth, Dewey would have a keen interest in cross-cultural communication and an appreciation for the role of philosophy in effecting it. As he would write to Sing-nan Fen: "I am of late more acutely aware of the role of language as communication than ever before . . . it now stands out with me that language as communication across the ages, past and future and over the globe is the most important transaction in which [humans] engage."[123]

Dewey slowed down considerably in 1950, afflicted with a stubborn viral infection and other ailments. "I can't brag of making progress in any direction," he confessed to Arthur Bentley.[124] "I've been paying more attention to medicines than to ideas lately," he told Joseph Ratner.[125] Having broken new philosophical ground, Dewey saw irony in the depletion of his physical energies. "Now that I *see* that cultural transformation . . . is the key to the whole thing," he mused, "I'm not physiologically up to doing what I should have been centering on and around lo these many years."[126]

Dewey began to feel better in the autumn of 1950. In early October, he wrote his initial letter to Charles A. Moore at the University of Hawai'i, expressing support for the forthcoming journal *Philosophy East and West*.[127] A few days later, Paul Arthur Schilpp invited Dewey to contribute a short, two to four page "Reflections" piece for the new edition of *The Library of Living Philosophers*.[128] While "vacillating and uncertain," Dewey believed that he could marshal the energy to write the piece. He already had his thesis. "[In] my 'Reflections,' " he wrote, "I could point out that my central and directive interest or theme has been that philosophy's *primary* concern is with the conflicts that occur in cultural life, being to translate them into problems—that is give them a statement that can be dealt with in intellectual terms, and to indicate hypotheses by which they can be dealt with in practice." In this final statement, Dewey intended to recast his philosophy specifically in terms of the "crisis in human culture."[129]

Figure 1.1. John Dewey and family arrive in Honolulu on January 17, 1951. John Dewey collection, Special Collections Research Center, Morris Library, Southern Illinois University–Carbondale.

Schilpp set the deadline for December 31. "I have got started in writing and have an outline roughly in mind," Dewey told him.[130] The piece would be an application of the "principle of continuity," with "the primary and obvious continuity being found in the processes of culture."[131] Shortly thereafter is when Moore asked Dewey to submit original comments for the inaugural issue of *Philosophy East and West*.[132] As December progressed, Dewey's health again deteriorated. On the first of January, he wrote to Schilpp telling him that he had overestimated his recovery and that he would be unable to complete the "Reflections" piece.[133] A few days later, Dewey left for Hawai'i.

Cultural Relations and Reconstruction

It is within this context that Dewey's contribution to *Philosophy East and West* must be understood. While "On Philosophical Synthesis" is a short piece, it would end up being the last original philosophical statement that Dewey ever made.[134] This also sheds light on the "Green Ink" pages from the Halekulani resort in Waikīkī, where Dewey sketches the outline for his book on culture that would never materialize. Here, Dewey was preparing to present cultural communication as "what culture achieves . . . in process of *trans*-mission sent across and over, thereby cancelling [the] separation of organic processes-operations *qua* physical and . . . making a leap towards a *new* status—as cultural *dispositions*."[135] Again—this would have liberated intra-cultural philosophy from ontological pretention, enabling it to participate in the "fruitful development of inter-cultural relations—of which philosophy is simply one constituent part," by focusing purposefully on "*specific* philosophical relationships," within the matrix of culture, without invoking "cultural block universes."[136] By the time he docked in Honolulu, Dewey had also taken up (once again) the 1949 "Re-Introduction" with the aim of changing the "title as well as subject matter" from "experience" to "culture." It is from Hawai'i that he realizes, "I was dumb not to see the need for such a shift when the old text was written.[137]

Unfortunately, Dewey accomplished little during his stay. The tropical climate was not improving his health as planned. Upon returning to the mainland he was hospitalized in Los Angeles and underwent a blood transfusion and a surgical procedure. By the summer, he was resting at the family's wooded Maple Lodge resort in Pennsylvania. Sing-nan Fen visited the family there, discussed philosophy with Dewey, and "gained weight."[138] Fen reported to friends that Dewey had slowed down and was now "doing little or no writing or reading."[139] By the end of the summer, Dewey judged that his "working days in the sense of intellectual productivity [were] at their close."[140] He would never come to express his ideas about philosophy and intra-cultural communication. Those in Dewey's inner circle, however, recognized that Sing-nan Fen represented "the extent to which the seeds of [Dewey's] wisdom are scattering and taking root."[141] As Joseph Ratner told Dewey, Chinese thinkers are among those who "understand you best"—and Sing-nan Fen especially so.[142]

Sing-nan Fen's next article, "The Contribution of Cultural Relationism to Cultural Reconstruction" would appear in January 1952, offering insight into what the two philosophers discussed during that final summer at Maple Lodge. Fen introduces the phrase "cultural relationism," echoing Dewey's vision in *Philosophy East and West*. "In talking about cultural relationism," Fen writes, "we must realize that we are culturally related in many, many ways. Cultural relations are not of one general pattern."[143] Given that the matrix of culture is an elastic field of manifold coherences and continuities, epistemological "subjects" and "objects" do not lock permanently into fixed connections. They can be construed variably as inquiry requires. Such a view is consistent with the provisional status of inquiries into "self-action" and "inter-action" in *Knowing and the Known*.

This line of thinking dovetails with Dewey's unfinished essay: "*How, What*, and *What For* in Social Inquiry," where he is keen on developing a related insight. Modernity *should*, Dewey argues, have resulted in the realization that epistemological terms are "discriminated from and connected with one another on the basis of their functions respectively and reciprocally performed." Instead, the Greek-medieval bias in favor of static realities resulted in fixing "the inherently subjective and the inherently objective as two independently given immutable kinds of existence."[144] Once an intra-cultural (or "*transactional*") perspective is adopted, however, it becomes clear that these are context-dependent designations. As Sing-nan Fen explains, "Objectivity and subjectivity are not self-evidently discriminated. What we call objective in a narrow context can be subjective in a wider context." This is especially true when more than one culture is involved in the transaction. As Fen explains, there are matters that are "objective in the matrix of Western culture, but beyond the Western culture, let us say, in a South Pacific culture, it can quite possibly be subjective."[145]

The central question, as Dewey sees it, is *why* certain "connections-and-distinctions" are taken up and *what for* in "connection with the means-consequence function." This requires intelligent (or *ming* 明) reflection on the "consequentiality of consequences" that result from each "connection-and-distinction" made within the matrix of culture. Given that relations in the world are always changing, such knowledge cannot be cemented into place. In Daoist terms, it moves along with the "Pivot of *dao* 道"—that attitude from which various perspectives can be considered and adjustments made to accommodate the future as it arrives. As Dewey writes, "Every procedure resting upon fixed standards amounts to an automatic foreclosure of free and hence full inquiry and critical reflection. It is a mortgage against the future."[146]

Does this result in relativism? Sing-nan Fen addresses the question directly. The view of the so-called "relativist" (if such individuals exist beyond our imaginations) results from an essentially *negative* view of value. When we say, "value is relative to culture," explains Fen, the relativist understands this as an indictment against the absolute status of value *as such*. According to the relativist, since *no* value enjoys absolute status, each value is as good as any another. The pragmatic naturalist, however, maintains an essentially *positive* view of value. To say, "value is relative to culture" means that value in each cultural context is functionally absolute. This is the more empirically justified position—for every genuine value is one that is actually *held* somewhere. Thus, the problem is not that *no* value enjoys absolute status; rather, the problem is that *every* value does. Values are not downgraded because they are relative to perspective. There is *no such thing* as value without perspective. "The fallacy of cultural relativism," Fen explains, "lies in the confusion between relativism and relationism." Relationism regards each value positively: as a valuation having been performed from some perspective or another. As such, there is nothing there to deconstruct or to relativize. Each value is a *genuine value*. "Cultural relativism does not imply a relativistic theory of truth nor does it imply a relativistic theory of value," writes Fen.[147]

Dewey provides further distinctions that help to clarify the issue. As he notes, "human beings are continuously engaged in valuations." These are different, however, from what Dewey calls "valuation-propositions," which involve "propositions about valuations made in terms of their conditions and consequences." Eating lamb, for instance, might be regarded as a value in certain cultures. But is it worth the environmental consequences for China to import 27,000 tons of lamb meat from New Zealand every year? To take a stand on such a question would be a "valuation-proposition," and these can be distinguished from plain "value-*facts*." The latter are "of the nature of historical and cultural-anthropological knowledge," whereas the former are judgments measured by the standards of intelligence (*ming* 明).[148]

As Sing-nan Fen explains, "We realize that our value activities as well as our value standards are relational to our other cultural conditions. This does not imply that we cannot decide which [value-*fact*] is better and which is worse." To the contrary—understanding how value relates to a given culture is a *prerequisite* for intelligent discussion on such matters. For, "until and unless we have these conditions, circumstances, and causes under control, good is abstract and bad is uncontrollable."[149] Recognizing that "value is relative to culture" is the first step in any thoughtful adjudication of value claims. "Judgments of values," Dewey writes, "is the deliberate development of an aspectual constituent of the more direct prizings and cherishings [i.e., value-*facts*] that human beings as living creatures must and do continually engage in, and under such conditions that *at first* they are relatively 'thoughtless.'"[150] As Fen explains, the cultural-anthropological approach to values is to determine "under what concrete and specific conditions *A* is and becomes good; *B* is and becomes bad."[151] Such conditions lie within the matrix of "life-activities" to which individual cultures belong—"events of the nature of *life-processes* in general and animal life-processes in particular," Dewey explains. The field of value thus has a physical basis. "But this is a radically different matter from *reduction* to physical terms," he warns.[152]

As Mark Johnson says, even though cultures will share many values due to commonalities in biology and environment, "*value pluralism* is an inescapable fact of the human condition."[153] Why? This is simply because such ancestral, biological commonalities are too vague to provide ready-made tools to satisfy the diverse forms of value enjoyment that have evolved in particular cultures. As Sing-nan Fen neatly puts it: "Happiness as a cultural value is [not] as simple as the movement of our cheek muscles." He continues:

> We cannot establish the much desired or desirable value standard on the basis of these common human nature and/or needs, not because they do not exist, but because values are not concerned with the bare satisfaction of these needs. Rather they are concerned with the cultural ways or cultured ways through which these needs may be satisfied. Needs or common nature are biological and psychological data. Values and value standards are cultural achievements. Logically and practically, we cannot justify our cultural achievement by appealing to these raw data without falling into theoretical reductionism and practical primitivism.[154]

Such appeals also risk falling into the so-called "naturalistic fallacy." Select any subset of traits from Donald E. Brown's list of human universals: conflict, gift giving, envy, rape, empathy, morality, male coalitional violence, fear of snakes, and so on. To note that we *are* so inclined towards "X" is not an argument that we *ought* to be so inclined.

The discovery and enumeration of common human traits provides an inventory of facts with which intelligence works. These are not, however, inherently value-*propositions*. There is a discretionary phase culturally mediated before "Gift giving is desired" becomes a value-proposition and "Rape is desired" does not. Facts about human tendencies are neutral powers in such cultural developments, but along with other neutral facts they become instrumental in making intelligent (and often common) valuation-propositions. Dewey explains:

> The connection of value-*facts* with other facts forms a problem that is legitimate-plus. It is indispensable. Evaluative judgments cannot be arrived at so as to be warranted without going outside the "value field" into matters physical, physiological, anthropological, historical, socio-psychological, and so on. Only by taking facts ascertained in these subjects into account can we determine the conditions and consequences of given valuings, and without such determination "judgment" occurs only as pure myth.[155]

Thus, for instance, value-propositions regarding value-*facts* such as "lamb meat is desirable" may trace back (as Mencius suggests they do) to the biological fact that roast meat is a common pleasure for human beings.[156] As noted earlier, however, Dewey appeals to the popular essay "A Dissertation Upon Roast Pig" to argue that "the *value* of enjoyment of an object *as* an attained end is a value of something which in being an end, an outcome, stands in relation to the means of which it is a consequence."[157] Such value analysis can only be undertaken when other facts are brought into consideration. Otherwise, hedonism is the perfect philosophy. When an auxiliary set of facts is considered, it may be judged that the pleasure of roast lamb isn't worth it.

As Sing-nan Fen observes, "Dewey's classical analysis of the means-end continuum theory can be very much improved by a proper cultural-anthropological approach to our value activities."[158] This is what Dewey wished to accomplish in the final phase of his philosophical career. Unfortunately, he ran out of time. Since Dewey was unable to initiate this turn, Fen helped to sketch its groundwork in his 1952 "Cultural Relationism" article. Alongside Dewey's piece in *Philosophy East and West*, it records the last stop for the ideas that Fen and Dewey traded in their final years together. Fen's article portrays a future in which the adjustments of culture remain as open and responsive as other organic adjustments. Like any *dao* 道-activity, the process of intra-cultural communication and reconstruction would be frustrated by assertions of essentialism—be they postulations of "block-like" objects or essential "human natures" that entail their own value-propositions. "In every progressive branch of knowledge," as Dewey reminds us, "'essences' have long since given way to consideration of space-time connections [i.e., processes]. Progress of inquiry in the value-field waits upon a similar methodological change."[159]

Intra-cultural philosophy attempts to pick up where Dewey and Sing-nan Fen left off. Such an approach, Fen submits, enables us to analyze "the internal logical structure of an inquiry which warrants its genuine freedom through a constant awareness of its own cultural context."[160] Such freedom liberates philosophical inquiries, granting them *reflexivity* in recognizing the situated, provisional status of their means-end operations plus *flexibility* in modifying their ends-in-view as needs change. Sustaining such intelligence (*ming* 明)—marked by pliancy and yielding (*flexibilis* or *rouruo* 柔弱)—is crucial to advancing the *dao* 道 of one's culture. Dewey hoped for philosophy to adopt such an approach toward value inquiries generally. He regrets that well-meaning, liberal-leaning philosophers were hampering such progress by insisting on the "inherency" of values and by failing to recognize that alternative theories of value were not "relativistic" by default. Failing to advance beyond such assumptions only perpetuates outworn Greek-medieval reasoning and leaves the court open to dogmatists. We can do better. "The notion that there are such affairs as exclusively 'final' values is now the chief obstacle to making the trial," Dewey writes. "It is hardly less than a moral tragedy to find those who profess 'liberal' tenets actively aiding and abetting dogmatic absolutists."[161] Rather than becoming stuck in the "Absolutism/Relativism" dualism, intra-cultural philosophers accept their own cultural situations, respect the variability of other cultural contexts, and trust that a common stock of facts can become operational in value-related inquiries. Intelligence (*ming*) is then free to do its critical work. Intra-cultural philosophy accords with Fen in believing that, "making such freedom of inquiry possible will bring about our cultural reconstruction."[162]

The vision that Sing-nan Fen had formulated alongside Dewey did not come to be widely accepted. The Cold War had begun, and the general atmosphere became more congenial to "Either/Or" binaries than to intra-cultural communication. Plus, the analytic movement had descended upon the American academy like an arctic frost, stalling value inquiries in their tracks. The line running from Emerson through Dewey was being terminated. The broad-minded "American Scholar" was being replaced by the more narrowly defined "Anglo-American philosopher." Dewey knew that he was being sidelined, as doctoral students who followed his line of thinking were coming under attack by faculty members at Columbia.[163] In the face of such attacks, those in Dewey's circle were justifiably both outraged and dismissive. "For your effort and good will towards your profession," Joseph Ratner told Dewey, "your repayment has been that they have written you out of the 'philosophy party.' You aren't a philosopher they say. For which I say thank God—if being a philosopher is being what they are."[164]

Like Ratner, Dewey was unimpressed with the kind of positivistic analysis that was coming to dominate philosophy. While in Honolulu, he commented on the "deplorable lack of vitality" in the analytic movement—dry and unnutritious like "popcorn."[165] The zeal "to find some 'analytic' proposition as the foundation of every statement that can be validly affirmed," Dewey thought, was "reducing philosophy to a form of empty intellectual gymnastics."[166]

Dewey did not, however, display personal offense or long-term discouragement in the face of these historical developments. He was, if anything, remarkably gracious and hopeful about the future. "While I regret the conditions that [currently] exist," he wrote to Ratner, "I can say that I don't suffer from personal disappointment; in one way or another I have had as much recognition as is good for anybody." He continues:

> Of course, however, the "future of philosophy" is a much larger matter; having given a fairly long lifetime professionally to philosophy I have a sort of identification with it which makes me loath to give up all hopes. The [*ill.*] of it is that students are as a rule so dependent on their teachers that one can't have the assurance regarding the oncoming generation one would like to have. But I can't surrender the belief that here and there one will come through, and I've always been a great believer in the parable of the sowers in the [New Testament]; most of the seed falls by the wayside or on stone crop but some bears fruit—and when it does it is manifold.[167]

Dewey had hopes in the likes of Sing-nan Fen, one who might take his philosophy further than he had taken it. Perhaps somewhere better.

As interest in classical American and non-Western philosophies continues to rebound in North America, intra-cultural philosophy is well positioned to evolve from where its growth was cut short in the post-war period. Moreover, I believe that there are distinct advantages to envisioning intra-cultural activity in Chinese terms—i.e., as the *dao* 道 of culture. First and foremost, such a conception suggests its own measure of success. *Dao*-activity is optimized whenever means-and-ends achieve continuity (*yi* 一) in practice. In traditional Chinese thinking, the width of "Means/End" divergence provides an index to measure the extent of our *stupidity*—an indispensable standard for us to preserve and to use. In the human realm, conditions have the capacity to change radically and suddenly, providing ample opportunities for intelligence (*ming* 明) to fall short. Cultures, accordingly, must be steadily reconstructed, if only because they involve a constant influx of novelty. Every minute, it is estimated that 105 humans die and 250 more are born. Each culture thus sustains ever-emerging relations, the orders of which register against existing harmonies (*he* 和) and coherences (*li* 理) and produce a dynamic web of values and practices. At this stage in the human experience, such webs are too complex to navigate in the simpler terms inherited from our Greek-medieval predecessors. Philosophers in the present century need to move on.

That this evokes some cultural discord is to be expected. As Sing-nan Fen reminds us, just as "harmony and coherency are relations, frictions and tensions are relations also. In describing 'patterns of cultures,' it is therefore important to keep our eyes open to the process of disintegration as well as the process of integration within the pattern."[168] As *dao* 道-activity, the course of any given culture is both stable and precarious: adjusting both to *accommodate* the "return wave" of science and to *adapt* to new facts that call for reappraisals of operative values. Fen teaches that "[culture] will be a pure abstract notion unless we take it as the actual ongoing adjustment" among such terms.[169] When cultures fail to adjust themselves to empirical facts, disharmony and incoherence result. Philosophy goes "out of gear" and the stage is filled with a range of types: antibiotic-taking Creationists, science-denying politicians, un-reconstructed philosophers, and so on—all denizens of an errant *dao*.

Progressive-minded thinkers must work around such elements. To some degree, social mal-coordination, ineptitude, and confusion will always be with us, posing both challenges and opportunities. As Sing-nan Fen teaches, in the *dao* 道 of tradition "we must always bear in mind that cultural disintegration is not necessarily an undesirable thing. As a matter of fact, in certain specific instances we should work deliberately toward such disintegration."[170] As in any process of organic growth, agitation (*dong* 動) calls forth new phases of equilibrium (*jing* 靜). In helping cultures to grow, philosophy must agitate and reconstruct as needed.

The May Fourth Movement in China provides us with an exceptionally clear object lesson in the dynamics of cultural agitation and reconstruction. Republican-era Chinese thinkers grappled with problems stemming from the disintegration of their cultural balance—problems involving the continuity of tradition, the "return wave" of science, and social and technological change. This was no theoretical drill in social reconstruction—this was the real thing; and as fate would have it, Dewey was right in the middle of it.

Dewey's activities and experiences in China would contribute to the development of his views, especially in the areas of social and political philosophy. As Dewey later explained, his philosophical ideas always began in abstraction, but "some personal experience, through contact with individuals, groups, or (as in visits to foreign countries) peoples, was necessary to give the idea concrete significance." Dewey maintained that his philosophical insights were never that original, but his personal experiences *were*—and even a commonplace idea, he believed, would be "given a new expression when it operates through the medium of individual temperament and the peculiar, unique, incidents of an individual life."[172] By becoming part of Dewey's life, the Chinese world became a medium for his ideas, and his involvement in that world changed his thinking demonstrably.

The remainder of part I in the present volume will concern itself with Dewey's trip to China and with the philosophical connections between Dewey's philosophy and Confucian thought. The first topic will be education and tradition, followed by custom and reconstruction, and then pluralism and democracy. There is a lot to cover in the coming chapters, so my treatment will take advantage of existing research by focusing primarily on where new insights present themselves.

As an intra-cultural episode, "Dewey in China" is complex. It encompasses not only the strains of thinking that Chinese students acquired under Dewey's tutelage and how such influences played out in China, but also what Dewey learned from his students and from his own experiences with Chinese culture. While there is already excellent scholarship on the Dewey-Confucianism relation, there are "*specific* philosophical relationships" between these traditions that I hope to establish. There are also important side topics to explore, such as how Chinese students studying with Dewey and others in America became pulled into cultural debates in the American academy. Such strands I hope to restore.

We must start, however, by establishing China's cultural foundations. One does this by reconstructing the teachings of Confucius as related in the *Analects*, beginning with the topic that unites Dewey and Confucius more than any other—*education*.

2

Education and Tradition

> Teaching is not the same thing as pouring tea from a teapot into a number of cups, nor is it the same thing as shelving an accumulation of books in a bookcase. When teachers are really teaching, they are helping students to develop the ability to inquire, to understand, and to pass judgment . . . Practical education is thus the kind of education that equips students to understand the society in which they live and enables them to work intelligently for the improvement of that society.
>
> —John Dewey, Jinan, July 1921

Learning (*xue* 學) and Personhood

Dewey and Confucius belong to a small number of philosophers for whom education is absolutely central. Apart from Plato, it is difficult to think of others who belong in their class. Confucius is celebrated as China's "First Teacher" and his traditional birthday (September 28) is associated with "Teacher's Day" in much of the Chinese world. Dewey has primary, elementary, middle, and high schools named after him across the United States, and he is remembered as the "Father of Progressive Education." The philosophical legacies of Confucius and Dewey are also educational legacies, and they are recognized and celebrated as such.

For each thinker, education serves a critical function in the maintenance of human civilization. Without it, cultures would simply disappear. Education, Dewey teaches, is the lifeblood of human social life—"what nutrition and reproduction are to physiological life, education is to social life," he explains. The reason is simple: human beings are always coming and going (again, at a ratio of 250:105 per minute). This ineluctable turnover determines the necessity of education. It is the responsibility of each generation to transmit the past into the future. "This transmission," Dewey writes, "occurs by means of communication of habits of doing, thinking, and feeling from the older to the younger." Such renewal through transmission is not automatic. "Unless pains are taken to see that genuine and thorough transmission takes place," he warns, even the most civilized group "will relapse into barbarism and then into savagery."[1] As Dewey reminds his Chinese audience, "All that we call culture would disappear if we did not have education as a means to transmit it to oncoming generations."[2]

The effective transmission of a cultural tradition involves both conservative and progressive activities, and Confucius and Dewey encourage both. Since Dewey is best known as a progressive-minded thinker, his more conservative concerns are often under-represented. For Dewey however, the principles of continuity and transaction preclude any clean breaks from the past. "We live from birth to death in a world of persons and things which in large measure is what it is because of what has been done and transmitted from the past," he writes. "When this fact is ignored, experience is treated as if it were something which goes on exclusively inside an individual's body and mind."[3] Since Confucius is better known as a conservative-minded thinker, his more forward-looking concerns are often under-represented. Within the teachings of Confucius, however, there is a great deal of creative thinking. In truth, neither Dewey nor Confucius would be a paragon of education if he were exclusively "progressive" or "conservative." For it is precisely in negotiating the tension between these two elements that one encounters the dynamic of growth as it pertains to education and its purposes.

In order to understand how this dynamic works in the Confucian tradition, we need to take a sustained look at Confucius' teachings on education. One might begin with Confucius' own son, Boyu. It is recorded that Boyu was once asked if he had received any special instruction from his father. He replied that he had not. He said his father expected of him what he expected of all his students: mastery of the *Rituals* and the *Songs*. These classics were at the heart of the erudite (*ru* 儒) tradition—the essence of cultural form (*wen* 文), which is listed first among the categories under which Confucius taught.[4] The son of Confucius admitted to being lax in his studies of the classics. His father's response speaks to their importance in the curriculum. The Master said: "If you do not study the *Songs* you will be at a loss as to what to say . . . If you do not study the *Rituals*, you be at a loss as to where to stand."[5] Confucius elsewhere says that becoming a person without mastering the *Songs* is like "trying to take your stand with your face to the wall."[6]

Throughout the *Analects*, Confucius' deference to the classical tradition is clear. He claims not to be an innovator, reveres antiquity, dreams of the ancients, and identifies himself as heir to the values and institutions of the past.[7] Along with mastery of the classics, Confucius attends to formal details in areas as diverse as oral pronunciation, garment color, hunting and fishing, the timbre of court music, and the seasoning of meat.[8] Confucius understands himself to be the custodian of the Zhou tradition—and with King Wen 文 no longer among the living, Confucius maintains that the entire cultural heritage (*wen*) resides with him.[9]

Confucius desires, however, for his students to understand the rationale for his strict adherence to form. He is sensitive about being misunderstood in this regard. As he says: "In referring time and again to observing ritual-custom, how could I just be talking about gifts of jade and silk? And in referring time and again to making music, how could I just be talking about bells and drums?"[10] Confucius believes there is more to following tradition than mere congruity to established ways. Such forms serve *functions* that, in the broader picture, are of greater importance than the formal details themselves. He suggests that there are three distinct functions, each one corresponding to one area of his curriculum. First, one "arouses sensibility (*xing* 興) through the *Songs*." Second, one "becomes established (*li* 立) through the *Rituals*." Third, one "consummates oneself (*cheng* 成) through music."[11]

While there are many avenues into Confucius' philosophy of education, few serve more effectively than reflecting on these three functions. Readers of a more systematic bent will recognize why. Conceptually, the elements of arousal (*xing* 興), establishment (*li* 立), and consummation (*cheng* 成) correspond to the 1-2-3 of Chinese cosmology. Confucius' understanding of the cultivation of human personhood (*shen* 身) thus displays consistency with early Chinese thinking about order more generally. The assumption is that there is something native, spontaneous, "raw" (*zhi* 質) in the human experience (*one*) that enters into relations (*two*) and thus comes to express "patterns" (*wen* 文) that integrate productively into broader wholes (*three*). For Confucius, traditional education is meant to facilitate this. Tracing the *zhi/wen* 質文 dynamic in the *Analects* reveals the text's underlying approach to human personhood while exposing various fault lines and disagreements between interlocutors. As we will see, this dynamic also signals that harmony (*he* 和) is the normative measure that guides Confucius' philosophy. This will become clearer as we explore his three educational functions in turn: "arousing sensibility" (*xing*), "becoming established" (*li*), and "consummating oneself" (*cheng*). The resulting vision is one in which personhood is achieved through traditional education (*xue* 學) in the *Songs*, *Rituals*, and music.

Confucius cites the *Songs* more often than any other ancient source. Wondering aloud why students neglect the *Songs*, he presents the following to be the advantages of mastering them: "An apt quotation from the *Songs* can arouse sensibilities, provide insight, bring people together, and help voice complaints. It enables one to serve one's father when close to home, and to serve one's lord when far away. And through them one acquires a broad vocabulary to distinguish animals and plants."¹² The *Songs* provide the foundation, in other words, for a variety of sophisticated conversations. The prerequisite for participation in these conversations is indeed memorization. This, however, is not the sole requirement. Confucius maintains that one must register what is important in concrete situations in order to use the songs effectively. "If one can recite all three hundred songs by heart," he says, "and yet, when given responsibility to govern, fails to move things forward; or when sent as an envoy to distant quarters, is unable to engage one's counterpart, then even if one has mastered so many, what use are they?"¹³ The songs are not simply memorized for the sake of honoring the past. The songs are memorized in order to maintain a common fund of images that help to foreground what is important in the present. This focus illustrates one of the hallmarks of Confucian education: "Review the old in order to realize the new."¹⁴ Confucius regards the ability to realize the new (*zhixin* 知新) as one of the most desirable traits in his students.¹⁵

In the *Analects*, canonical songs play an important role in generating opportunities to realize such connections. Zixia, for instance, asks: "What does the song mean when it says, 'Her smiling cheeks—so radiant. Her dazzling eyes—so sharp and clear. It is the unadorned that is colored?'" The Master replies: "Color is applied to what is originally unadorned." Zixia then inquires: "Does ritual-custom (*li* 禮) itself come after?" The Master replies: "Zixia, you have stimulated my thoughts. It is only with people like you that one can discuss the *Songs*."¹⁶ In this exchange, Zixia draws on his familiarity with the *Songs* to guide the conversation in a new direction. He transforms an image from the canon into a moment of insight: this time into the relationship between cultural form (*wen* 文) and the rougher qualities (*zhi* 質) of a person. Again, this dynamic emerges as a major theme in the text.

In a similar exchange, Confucius and Zigong discuss the relationship between wealth and moral virtue. Model sayings are traded until Zigong introduces a verse. "'Like bone carved and polished; like jade cut and ground.' Is this not what you have in mind?" Confucius responds in appreciation of Zigong's ability to use a traditional song to inspire reflection and carry the conversation forward. He says: "Zigong, it is only with people like you that I can discuss the *Songs*. From what is established you realize what comes next."¹⁷ In realizing what comes next (*zhilai* 知來) a connection is made rather than found. Zigong's insight is original: he introduces an image into the discussion and thus broadens the scope of the conversation. Confucius appreciates such ingenuity. Zigong "realizes" what comes next by knowing (*zhi* 知) it in a particular context.¹⁸ He relies on the fact that the songs are productively vague—or as David Schaberg says, "intrinsically interpretable."¹⁹ Different individuals can open them to novel disambiguation in different contexts.

Confucius is said to have personally edited the *Songs*, assembling 305 canonical songs from an existing repository of three thousand. This original repository was collected from all corners of China in order to register the raw feeling and sentiments of the people. As Mark Edward Lewis explains, the songs began within ritualistic contexts in which an "entire cultic association sings in a collective first person that marks the communal nature" of an experience. Eventually, the songs become "an anonymous voice presenting an idealized account of the community's norms and actions," one that every listener recognizes as authentic.[20] Confucius recognizes that the songs convey an unassailable veracity through their raw emotive force. They feature what Schaberg calls the "uncontrolled genuineness" of a rustic purity.[21]

In the repertoire of the creative student, the *Songs* facilitate the transmission of those qualities into the present. As Confucius sees the matter, to memorize the *Songs* is to have a broad range of qualitatively *raw* experiences at one's disposal. When one draws from these experiences in articulating one's own feelings, one can be sure that what one says will fall within the compass of what is communicable to others who have similar feelings. So long as one's own sentiments remain consonant with the fund of recognizable human sentiments, one can be vigorous in expression without deviating into perversity or insignificance. As Confucius says: "Although the songs are three hundred in number, they can be covered in one expression: 'Go vigorously without swerving.'"[22] The *Songs* enable one, in other words, to arouse sensibilities (*xing* 興) that are broadly and recognizably human within one's own circumstances.

Nowhere is Confucius' embrace of traditional form more evident, however, than in his attitude toward ritual-custom (*li* 禮), for this is where "becoming established" (*li* 立) actually occurs. Here, Confucius' orthodoxy is manifest. In responding to an inquiry into how to become a person of human quality (*ren* 仁), Confucius relates the following: "If it is not *li*, look away. If it is not *li*, stop listening. If it is not *li*, remain silent. If it is not *li*, do not engage."[23] It is difficult to see how such scrupulous adherence to form could possibly result in the emergence of self-respecting persons. Confucius, however, sees no such conflict. In the same passage he says: "Becoming a person of human quality is self-originating (*youji* 由己). How could it originate from another?" The reasoning behind this needs to be understood.

Like the canonical *Songs*, ritual-custom (*li* 禮) serves to render personal expressions fitting and communicable in a social context. Thus, "exemplary persons learn broadly of cultural forms (*wen* 文), discipline this learning through observing ritual-custom (*li*), and in so doing, can remain on course without straying from it."[24] Confucius insists, however, that such refinement of character must retain continuity with one's unique qualities, such that becoming an exemplary person (*junzi* 君子) results in a well-balanced integration of the two. Thus, "When raw quality (*zhi* 質) overwhelms cultural form (*wen* 文), one is a rustic (*ye* 野). When cultural form overwhelms raw quality, one is a pedant. Only when cultural form and raw quality are combined is one an exemplary person."[25]

Despite this ideal of balance, Confucius is so wary of pedantry and hollow formalism that, when pressed, he sides with the rustic. As he says: "The first to initiate ritual and music were the rustic folk (*yeren* 野人). The exemplary persons (*junzi* 君子) came to them later. When it comes to putting ritual and music to use, I accord with those who came to them first."[26] Perhaps following this cue, there are those around Confucius who propose that the more rustic qualities (*zhi* 質) of one's personality *alone* dictate whether or not one becomes an exemplary person. Ji Zicheng suggests as much: "Exemplary persons are determined by nothing other than their raw quality (*zhi*)," he says—"what need is there for cultural form (*wen* 文)?" Zigong, representing Confucius' preference for balance in form-and-quality, delivers the rebuke: "Form (*wen*) is no different from quality (*zhi*), and quality no different from form. The skin of a tiger or leopard, shorn of its coat, is no different from the dog or sheep."[27] Form-and-quality, once blended, is *one*. The concluding trope suggests once again that cultural refinement (*wen*) in fact *promotes* the appreciation of native qualities. Without formal refinement, unique features go under-appreciated. Tigers and leopards are importantly different from dogs and sheep. Shorn of the patterns (*wen*) that emerge on their coats, however, such differences go undetected.

For Confucius, the rationale for adhering to form is that, in the absence of structures for preservation and reinforcement, genuine qualities depreciate—and at worst, they fail to be differentiated from counterfeits. The balance, however, is a delicate one. In order to be recognized as genuine, a raw quality (*zhi* 質) must find its integral fulfillment through the operation of cultural form (*wen* 文). Form alone, however, is not enough. The function of form is that it enables persons to become established (*li* 立). This does not mean simply *following* form—this means refining one's qualities *through* it.

The difference is expressed in the text. Confucius is once asked to comment on a boy from a neighboring village who comes carrying a message, a task that was complex in ritual form and normally executed by adults. Asked if he thought the boy was making progress, Confucius responds: "I have seen him sitting in places reserved for his seniors, and walking side by side with his elders. This is someone intent on growing up fast rather than on making progress."[28] In sending messages, the boy was not "becoming established" (*li* 立) through ritual-custom (*li* 禮). Rather, he was usurping a place (*wei* 位) that was reserved for those better qualified than himself. The boy was all form (*wen* 文) and no substance (*zhi* 質). Confucius would no doubt encourage

Figure 2.1. John Dewey's photograph of Confucius' tomb in Qufu, Shandong, which he visited on July 13, 1921. The inscription on the stele reads "The Sage of Great Cultural Accomplishment." John Dewey collection, Special Collections Research Center, Morris Library, Southern Illinois University—Carbondale.

the boy to continue cultivating his person, but he would remind the upstart: "Do not worry about not having a place (*wei* 位), worry about what it takes to become established (*li* 立)."[29] Here, ritual-custom serves as a means *through* which the boy can actually make progress. Such forms are thus not restrictive of human freedom; rather, they are generative of the positive freedom to achieve the cultivation and expression of one's raw abilities.

As Dewey understood, the world of sports provides useful illustrations of how form operates in self-cultivation.[30] "The aim of a football team," to paraphrase William James, "is not merely to get the ball to a certain goal. If that were so, they would simply get up on some dark night and place it there. Rather, the aim is to get it there under a set of conditions: the game's rules and the other players."[31] Formal regulations in football do not stifle creativity and personal expression. To the contrary, such constraints furnish the conditions under which these and other qualities can be developed and recognized. Without such regulations, there would be no way to showcase the raw quality (*zhi* 質) of the athlete. He or she can only excel within the constraints posed by the form (*wen* 文) of the sport. The most excellent professional athletes so exemplify the form of their sport that their unique contributions to it become indistinguishable from the sport itself.

Likewise for Confucius, "quality/form" (*zhi/wen* 質文) work together in the promotion of personal expression. However conservative he appears, Confucius does not consider one aspect more important than the other. On occasion we find him privileging the more rustic, unrefined qualities that are unique to untutored dispositions. Recall his discussion with Zixia: "Color is applied to what is originally *un*-adorned."[32] The unique qualities of the individual are never out of sight or out of mind for Confucius. In the cultivation of one's person (*xiushen* 修身), the rougher qualities (*zhi*) contribute themselves from beginning to end.

The "quality/form" dynamic that informs Confucius' thinking does not operate in a conceptual vacuum. It works in conjunction not only with the broader assumptions of Chinese natural philosophy but also with the guiding value in early Chinese thinking: harmony (*he* 和). In one of the more significant contemporary works in Chinese philosophy, Chenyang Li demonstrates the several ways in which *he* is "the most cherished ethical and social ideal in Chinese culture." Given its centrality, interpretations that misconstrue or overlook this notion tend to depart from the spirit of classical Chinese philosophy. Unfortunately, as Li explains, the term has been systematically misinterpreted in both Western and Chinese scholarship as "presupposing a fixed grand scheme of things that pre-exists in the world to which humanity has to conform."[33] Such approaches call to mind the "therapeutic" readings of Chinese philosophy, those more tender-minded options that invite us to "follow the Way" and to "accord with an ethical scheme inherent in the world."[34] In contrast to such understandings, Li argues that the ideal of harmony in Chinese thought is "deep" in nature; it is "without a pre-set order" and thus "opposed to the kind of harmony [e.g., the Pythagorean] seen as conforming to a pre-existing structure in the world."[35]

As we move forward in this volume, harmony (*he* 和) will play a central role in foregrounding how early Chinese thought provides alternatives to Greek-medieval thinking. It is important then to understand this concept in its native context. In the early Chinese corpus, harmony (*he*) is best illustrated through its association with the culinary arts, particularly with making soup. As the *Zuozhuan* 左轉 explains:

> Harmony (*he*) is similar to soup. Soup is made by adding various kinds of seasoning to water and then cooking fish and meat in

it. One mixes them all together and adjusts the flavor by adding whatever is deficient and reducing whatever is in excess. It is only by mixing together ingredients of different flavors that one is able to create a balanced, harmonized taste.[36]

Flavorful soup is constituted by the ratio of its raw ingredients. Its harmony is measured by the degree to which it succeeds in incorporating those ingredients in a good (*shan* 善) way.

Onion, for instance, is wonderful in soup; but one does not therefore add all the onion that one can find. That would disrupt the unique contributions of the other ingredients and result in disharmony. The most harmonious soup effectively showcases the unique quality (*zhi* 質) of the onion—it balances its flavor with other ingredients, thereby tempering its otherwise pungent and over-bearing taste. Here, one observes how the norm of harmony (*he* 和) relates to the functions of the *Songs* and *Rituals* in promoting personhood. Here too, there is a "raw" element that is isolated, formalized, and thus expressed in ways that temper its excesses and augment its value, thus rendering its native qualities communicable and appreciated.

One does not need to remain in the Warring States period to find illustrations of how harmony (*he* 和) works. One recent example of this ancient norm is the once popular (now legendary) Japanese television program, *Iron Chef*. Here, master chefs are challenged to prepare five dishes that showcase a single "theme" ingredient that is announced only at the time of taping. They have one hour to bring the uniqueness of this theme ingredient into harmony with whatever else is at hand, and they are judged in three categories: *taste*, *creativity*, and *presentation*. In order to win, chefs must foreground the distinct quality of this ingredient in a variety of combinations.[37] Just as Confucius is concerned with "bringing out what is aesthetically best (*mei* 美) in a person,"[38] the Iron Chef needs to bring out what is aesthetically best in an ingredient. For Confucius, what is best in a person is brought out through social relations; for the Iron Chef, what is best in an ingredient is brought out through culinary relations. In each case, what is unique is rendered communicable and becomes value-added in a larger harmony. Soup and ritual-custom, then, each function to enable the expression, register the worth, and temper the idiosyncrasy/excess of their constituents. Each promotes the healthy expression of some rough quality (*zhi* 質), giving it outlet and rendering its palatable in some refined form (*wen* 文).

That such harmonies do not correspond to preordained "schemes" is underscored in the "Ritual Instruments" (*Liqi* 禮器) chapter of the *Rituals*. Here, we are told that the unique taste of raw sugar and the unique texture of unpainted surfaces possess their raw qualities (*zhi* 質) prior to becoming ingredients in the aesthetic wholes that subsequently showcase those qualities. The same holds true, we are told, for persons who study ritual-custom (*li* 禮). "What is sweet can be brought into harmony (*he* 和), and what is bare can be brought into vibrant color. Likewise, persons who are genuine and sincere (*zhongxin* 忠信) are capable of becoming educated through ritual-custom (*li*)."[39] Just as raw sweetness precedes the dish in which it is preserved and surface quality precedes the object in which it is displayed, what is most genuine in a person precedes and becomes an ingredient in the harmonies that result from ritual forms—in other words, they *contribute* to the orders that eventually emerge.[40] Facilitating such expression is what ritual-customs are intended to do. As Master You says: "Achieving harmony (*he*) is the most important function of ritual-custom (*li*)."[41]

While Confucius adheres strictly to tradition, his mind is always on the *function* of tradition rather than on its mere perpetuation. In fact, in the refinement and expression of quality through ritual form, Confucius prioritizes the genuine expression of the quality over the formalism of the ritual. When asked what is fundamental (*ben* 本) to the practice of mourning rituals, for instance, Confucius says: "It is better to express real grief than to worry over formal details."[42] Rituals are designed to facilitate the shared expression of feelings that are *genuine*. In performing the function of harmony (*he* 和), ritual-customs operate in refining the transmission of such feelings. Like the canonical songs, ritual forms (*li* 禮) render sentiments appropriate and communicable while aiming at their adequate expression. As Ziyou remarks: "In the mourning ritual, one expresses one's grief and stops at that."[43]

The final function that traditional education serves for Confucius is "consummating oneself" (*cheng* 成). This is associated with music, and here too Confucius' deference to tradition is manifest. "When the master was with others who were singing and they sang well, he would invariably ask them to sing the piece again before joining in the harmony (*he* 和)."[44] For Confucius, to contribute one's unique voice to a harmony requires deference to the chorus of others. To contribute deferentially results in a feeling of satisfaction: one's voice is recognized and appreciated in the newly augmented order. To enter into ensemble *without* due deference causes dissonance, and this results in feelings of shame and embarrassment—one is detested for interfering with something that was otherwise going well (*shan* 善). Confucius assumes that humans desire not to experience such shame and embarrassment. By listening to the tune before joining in, Confucius illustrates again that deference to form (*wen* 文) actually *preserves* raw quality (*zhi* 質) by creating conditions in which it secures adequate expression for itself.

Confucius (unlike Dewey who, sadly, was tone deaf) was an avid lover and devoted student of music. Ensemble music represents the power to harmonize difference without a loss of individual uniqueness, and this is central to Confucius' philosophy. "Much can be realized through music," says Confucius, "if one begins by playing in unison, and then goes on to improvise with purity of tone and distinctness and flow, thereby bringing everything to consummation (*cheng* 成)."[45] The consummation (*cheng*) that comes with the achievement of harmony (*he* 和) carries with it an aesthetic unity and intensity that foregrounds the uniqueness of its parts. David L. Hall and Roger T. Ames have contributed most significantly in bringing this to our attention.[46] Whenever harmony is achieved, the uniqueness of each part finds its proper amplification. If such uniqueness disappears into the background, the result is a loss of intensity—the loss of value. In aesthetic terms, this results in a numbing sameness to which Confucius is steadfastly opposed. "Exemplary persons seek harmony (*he*) not sameness (*tong* 同)," says Confucius, "while petty persons do the opposite."[47] In adhering to form, Confucius cares most that such forms do not overwhelm the expression of what is genuine about a person. Thus, he is ever on guard against the duplicity of the counterfeit and the starched and punctilious formalism of the pedant—for these are the enemies of harmony.

Once harmony (*he* 和) is restored to Confucius' thinking, he becomes less the stern conservative and more the sophisticated aesthete who understands the subtleties of the "quality/form" (*zhi/wen* 質文) dynamic. The Master understands that harmony (*he*) is required for the achievement and expression of human significance, and securing this remains the primary aim of his philosophy. Education, for Confucius, is the key. He maintains that by properly "arousing sensibilities" (*xing* 興) through the *Songs*, "becoming established" (*li* 立) through the *Rituals*, and "consummating oneself" (*cheng* 成) through music, one achieves personhood without frivolity and secures public distinction without arrogance.[48] Wishing for his son to do the same, he admonishes Boyu to study the classics. For Confucius, there is no way to meaningfully cultivate personhood (*shen* 身) but through the instrumentalities provided by such a tradition.

Dewey Arrives in China

The Confucian tradition is 2,500 years old. Naturally, there have been deviations from the original teachings of the Master. The early twentieth century would mark a low point in the Confucian *dao* 道. As Ni Peimin explains, the term "Confucian education" had become substitutable for "outdated impractical indoctrination." As he notes, "this image is largely due to later followers' preoccupation with literacy in the Confucian classics, especially in the imperial examination system."[49] Meanwhile, "Confucian ritual" was on the verge of becoming a state religion, with conservatives stressing the importance for government officials to "kowtow to the icons of the Sage," with little reflection on how well ritual-custom (*li* 禮) actually performed its function in securing personhood.[50] Such an ossified "Confucianism" was what Dewey would encounter on his trip to China in 1919–1921.

Dewey and his wife, Alice, departed for Asia in 1919 with an invitation to visit and give lectures at National Imperial University in Tokyo. Upon learning that Dewey would be in Asia, his former students from Columbia—prominent intellectuals such as Hu Shih 胡適, Jiang Menglin 蔣夢麟, and Tao Xingzhi 陶行知—hastily arranged to receive Dewey for a brief visit to China. At the time, China was in the throes of a decades-long period of social and political upheaval. Taking time to understand this historical background is vital to appreciating the context and significance of Dewey's visit.

China's predicament traced back at least to the Second Opium War (1856–1860), when its defeat resulted in humiliating treaty agreements conceding broad commercial privileges, territories, and missionary freedoms to European powers. In response to such incursions, there was a growing demand that Qing officials modernize Chinese institutions and defenses. Progress was slow, and with China's subsequent defeat in the Sino-Japanese war (1894–1895), calls for modernization became intensified. Increasingly, the assimilation of Western ideas, institutions, and technologies was seen as critical to preventing the dismemberment of China by rival imperialist powers. There was no broad agreement, however, about how to proceed with reforms. In 1898, the Qing court inaugurated the "Hundred Days of Reform" but that was quickly aborted. Several of its measures, however, would be enacted in the coming years, including one major reform that rendered Dewey's visit especially relevant: the 1905 abolishment of the imperial exam system (*keju* 科舉).

Chinese imperial exams traced back at least to the Han Dynasty. Their function as the sole means for aspiring bureaucrats to enter into government service, however, was not formalized until the Tang dynasty (618–907 CE). While undergoing modification and occasional suspension over its long history, the system proved to be a remarkably sturdy institution and lent considerable stability to Chinese culture. The content of the exams included some "practical" arts such as civil law, geography, and military strategy, but the primary goal was to ensure complete mastery of the Confucian classics, including those texts that Confucius had admonished his own son to master.

By the Qing dynasty, imperial examinations were being administered under the most austere conditions, ones that Confucius could hardly have imagined. Candidates would enter tiny cubicles with only the barest necessities provided and would remain inside for up to 72 hours. They prepared answers in the notoriously exacting style of the "Eight-Legged Essay," requiring verbatim quotations from classical sources in a tightly stipulated format.⁵¹ Early in their visit, John and Alice Dewey were invited to tour what remained of these examination halls. The Dewey children received the following description: "We visited the old examinations halls which are now being torn down. These are the cells, about 25,000 in number, where the candidates for degrees used to be shut up during the examination period . . . No one could approach them from the outside for any reasons."⁵² Dewey would suggest to his Chinese audiences that such "examination compartments" symbolized the compartmentalization of education itself, the tendency to "isolate learners from the environment in which they live."⁵³ Retiring the imperial exam system was critical to moving Chinese culture forward. Its discontinuation, however, opened up a cultural vacuum. Fundamental questions about the structure and purpose of Chinese education needed to be asked. The time had come to change course, but there was no clear consensus about where to go.

While Qing officialdom heeded calls for modernization, events at the end of the nineteenth-century had already outpaced their efforts to steer the situation. The "Boxer Rebellion" (1899–1901)—a violent uprising against foreign commercial interests and Christian missionaries in China—found the Qing court stuck between entrenched foreign powers whose material assistance it wanted and a fanatically patriotic population whose loyalty it needed. Officials were split on how to respond to the uprising, with horrific atrocities being committed on both sides. Eventually, the court sided with the Boxers and declared war on all foreign powers. In response, Japan, Russia, the British Empire, France, the United States, Germany, Italy, and Austria-Hungary formed an "eight nation alliance" against the allied Qing and Boxer armies. Fearing mass casualties and its own dissolution, the Qing court relented and signed the "Boxer Protocol," again granting disproportionate concessions to foreign governments, the most significant being $335 million in indemnities to be paid to the eight nations over 39 years.

There would be one salutary outcome. An overage of $11 million paid to the United States would be negotiated back in 1909 as the "Boxer Indemnity Fund," providing merit-based scholarships for Chinese students studying in the United States.⁵⁴ Hu Shih received a Boxer scholarship, allowing him to study with Dewey at Columbia. Boxer funds would also be directed toward other educational initiatives: e.g., the establishment of Tsinghua 清華 College (now Qinghua University) in 1911, and the establishment of the China Institute in New York City in 1926. As mentioned in the "Prelude" to volume one, this is the oldest nonprofit in the United States devoted to China and it was cofounded by John Dewey.

The Qing dynasty collapsed in 1911, replaced by the Republic of China with a new central government led provisionally by Dr. Sun Yat-sen. Born in southern China and raised in Hawai`i, Sun returned to China in the 1890s to help organize a reform movement and petition the Qing government with his proposals. Rebuked, he left China to begin his career as a revolutionary fugitive and agitator against the Manchu court. He would eventually be heralded as the "Father of the Country" (*Guofu* 國父) and remains revered by all Chinese. Dewey was invited to have dinner with Sun in Shanghai just eleven days after his arrival. Dewey came away from their meeting duly impressed. Dr. Sun, Dewey reported, "is a philosopher."[55]

The newly established Republic, however, hardly resolved the challenges that China faced; and in certain ways, it only exacerbated them. The years directly following the fall of the Qing dynasty did not go smoothly. Sun Yat-sen would clash with his general, Yuan Shikai, who was granted presidency of the Republic but declared himself "Emperor" (*huangdi* 皇帝) instead. The fragmentation and infighting that ensued laid the foundation for a period of warlord militarism, foreclosing the possibility that the Republic would be easily unified under a single banner. Naturally, the sudden demise of the longest surviving dynastic system in history left China dislocated and adrift. By this time, students who had left China to study abroad had returned home to assume leadership roles in debating the future of their homeland. Dewey's students were among these numbers.

Among all of Dewey's students, Hu Shih is the one most closely identified with Dewey's visit to China. Hu Shih began his American education at Cornell in 1910, more than one year before the Qing dynasty came to an end. His interests gradually turned to philosophy, but the objective idealism fashionable in Ithaca at the time held little attraction for him. In the summer of 1915, he read "with great eagerness, all the works of Dewey" who henceforth became, in Hu's words, the "guiding principle of my life and thought and the foundation of my own philosophy."[56] There was much in Dewey for the young Hu to identify with. Hu was an avowed Darwinist, influenced along with his contemporaries by Yen Fu's 嚴復 translation of T. H. Huxley's *Evolution and Ethics*. He was also deeply influenced by the humanism of the neo-Confucian thinker, Wang Yangming 王陽明 (1472–1529). Like Dewey, Wang believed in the "continuity of knowledge-and-action" (*zhixingheyi* 知行合一) and stressed the need for human beings to progressively "investigate things" (*gewu* 格物) in order to optimize knowledge and rectify affairs in the world. It was not unusual for such Chinese students, inspired by Wang Yangming, to eventually find their way to Dewey.

Dewey's persistent, but gradualist approach to social progress also appealed to Hu Shih. In the summer of 1915, as Hu was preparing to leave

Cornell for Columbia, Dewey delivered a talk in Chicago entitled "Human Progress." The piece would later appear simply as "Progress." It is a somber piece, as the talk was delivered on June 2, 1915—two days after German Zeppelins began aerial bombings over London's suburbs. "Some people will see only irony in a discussion of progress at the present time," Dewey begins. He then explains, however, that such discouragement presents an opportunity to rethink the meaning of "progress," finally divorcing it from nineteenth-century European notions of assured, uninterrupted improvement. According to such wishful thinking, all change is progress and all newness is better. This only "confuses rapidity of change with advance," when in fact, "rapid change of conditions affords an *opportunity* for progress, but is not itself progress." Progress depends not simply on change, Dewey argues, "but on the direction which human beings deliberately give that change." The fact that progress is not automatic—i.e., metaphysically guaranteed by some "cosmic sanction"—means that it must be realized step-by-step through human intelligence or not at all. "It is not a wholesale matter," Dewey writes, "but a retail job, to be contracted for and executed in sections."[57]

This idea deeply resonated with Hu Shih as he contemplated affairs in his homeland. As late as 1959, at the Third East-West Philosophers' Conference in Honolulu, Hu would return to Dewey's 1916 essay in critiquing communist thinkers who believed in "total and cataclysmic revolution, which will bring about wholesale progress overnight."[58] As his "China lectures" indicate, Dewey also favored a gradualist approach to addressing problems in China. In chapter 3 of this volume, we will see how this made Dewey and Hu relative moderates in the midst of more "conservative" and "radical" elements in early Republican China.

This shared approach, however, did not mean that Hu Shih and Dewey saw eye-to-eye on China's future. Their eventual differences were foreshadowed in Hu's 1917 PhD dissertation, *The Development of the Logical Method in China*, which was supervised by Dewey at Columbia. The argument motivating the work was that "the revival of the non-Confucian schools [in Chinese philosophy] is absolutely necessary because it is in these schools that we may hope to find the congenial soil in which to transplant the best products of occidental philosophy and science." The work proceeds with detailed and often fine summaries of each major philosophical school in pre-Qin China—a survey from which Dewey surely learned a great deal. Hu's presentation of Confucianism, however, was idiosyncratic. In what is initially an orthodox move, Hu identifies the underlying purpose of Confucian teachings with the rectification of names (*zhengming* 正名), the standardization of meanings required for any community to thrive. Then, however, he identifies the objects of Confucian "names" (*ming* 名) with "ideas" (*xiang* 象) in the *Book of Changes*. This Confucian conception of "ideas," Hu submits, was basically Aristotelian: they were "the 'formal causes' of things and institutions."[59]

Against this unusual reading of Confucianism, Hu Shih highlights features of several non-Confucian schools that he argues better anticipate modern Western ideas—Mohism's "pragmatic method," Daoism's "theory of evolution," and Legalism's "notion of progress," for instance. The resulting narrative becomes the inverse of the Western narrative. Whereas Aristotelian outlooks in the West succumbed to *modernity* with the rise of the Enlightenment, modern ideas in China succumbed to *premodern essentialism* with the rise of State Confucianism. Philosophical stagnation in China was thus inevitable, and as Hu informs his readers: "Confucianism is long dead" as a philosophy.[60]

For thinkers of Hu Shih's generation, such sentiments were broadly held, forcefully articulated, and widely circulated. In 1915, the magazine *La Jeunesse* (*Xinqingnian* 新青年) became the main forum in which to debate the causes of China's problems, and it provided a platform for advancing the so-called "New Culture Movement." "New Culture" advocates argued, to various degrees, for the rejection of traditional Confucian thought and the adoption of more "Western" and "scientific" ideas. In January 1919, four months before Dewey's arrival in China, the founding editor of *La Jeunesse*, Chen Duxiu 陳獨秀, published his famous article calling upon "Mr. Confucius" to give way to "Mr. Democracy" and "Mr. Science," thus proclaiming that "only these two gentleman can save China from the political, moral, academic, and intellectual darkness in which it finds itself."[61] It was at this critical juncture that Dewey's visit to China was arranged.

Naturally, Dewey was not received impartially. For reformers, he represented "Mr. Science" and "Mr. Democracy." In their eyes, he had come to further the "New Culture" agenda while helping to dismantle traditional Confucian institutions. In anticipation of his visit, an entire issue of the journal *New Education* (*Xinjiaoyu* 新教育) was devoted to Dewey's philosophy and its importance to the reformist agenda, with several of his students contributing essays.[62] As Tsuin-chen Ou relates, Dewey's Chinese students were thoroughly persuaded that "the old Confucian-centered culture and tradition had to be critically examined and changed," and that Dewey "embodied the new thought [and] represented a new hope for intellectual enlightenment and guidance."[63] Little did Dewey know, but he was expected to serve as a reliable instrument against all things Confucian.

With impeccable timing, Dewey arrived in Shanghai on May 1, 1919. The following day, Hu Shih marked the commencement of Dewey's visit with an introductory lecture to an audience of over one thousand people.[64] Two days later, the May Fourth uprising in Beijing broke out with thousands of students and intellectuals assembling in Tiananmen Square to protest China's unfair treatment in the Versailles treaty. Days of unrest followed. Student demonstrators descended on the residence of the Minister of Foreign Affairs, which was set on fire. Demonstrators were arrested and beaten, and students across the city went on strike and were joined by sympathetic workers and merchants.[65] Dewey arrived in the capital on June 1. The scene was electric. He was promptly recruited on behalf of the reformist movement. Cai Yuanpei 蔡元培, then acting President of Peking University, came to describe Dewey's role as follows: "Confucius said respect the emperor, but the learned doctor [Dewey] advocates democracy. Confucius said females are burdensome, but the learned doctor advocates equal rights for men and women. Confucius said transmit but do not create, but the learned doctor advocates creativity."[66] Thus Dewey and his philosophy were positioned at center stage. His letters relate how absorbed he was in the historical moment in which he was suddenly cast—one that Dewey described as "the most enthralling drama now anywhere enacting."[67]

As weeks turned to months, Dewey decided that he needed to remain in China for an extended period of time. In his requests for an additional year leave from Columbia University, he describes living in China as the "most interesting and intellectually the most profitable thing I've ever done."[68] In the end, Dewey would spend two years, two months, and ten days in China, visiting eleven provinces and delivering nearly two hundred public talks and lectures. This opportunity gave him more than just a chance to share his philosophy—it enabled him to learn from experiences unlike any that he ever had. After only three months in Japan and one month in China, Dewey wrote to his children, "[Your mother and I] agreed yesterday that never in our lives had we begun to learn so much as in the last four months. And in the last month particularly, there is almost too much food to be digestible."[69] Nine days later he observed: "For a country that is regarded at home as stagnant and unchanging, there is certainly something doing [here]. This is the world's greatest kaleidoscope."[70]

Dewey entered into this kaleidoscope by delivering a series of lectures that were translated into Chinese and widely distributed. His "China lectures" covered a range of topics: education, art, industry, social problems, politics, logic, intellectual history, and more. Dewey's lectures on education were the most impactful. Early in his visit, he delivered a series of sixteen lectures entitled "The Philosophy of Education" at National Peking University. These would be published along with another sixteen lecture series on "Social and Political Philosophy," also delivered in Beijing. By 1921, there were 100,000 copies of these lectures in circulation.[71] In his inaugural lecture of the first series, Dewey outlined three issues that he argued would be central to educational reform in China:

First: How can we provide for the majority of people to have access to education, rather than having it restricted to an elite? That is, how can we popularize education, and make it universal? *Second:* How can we bring about a balance between literary education and education for ordinary human activities? *Third:* How can we make school truly conservative—that is, on the one hand, enable it to conserve and transmit the best of our traditional cultural heritage, and, on the other, to cultivate personalities that can successfully cope with their environment?[72]

Since Confucius also concerns himself with such issues, the three remaining sections of this chapter will consider each of them in turn.

Education and Its Reach

In the Chinese tradition, Confucius is recognized as a pioneer in expanding access to education. Prior to his teaching career, education was largely a matter of private tutorials. Students were normally the sons of nobility—destined already to become government officials. Confucius' own students, on the contrary, came from every walk of life.[73] Overturning what was then traditional custom, Confucius declared that, "In education, there are no social classes."[74] While Confucius never secures an official post from which to leverage widespread reform along these lines, he advocates for such measures in his teachings.

Confucius' socioeconomic vision is one that today we would call "progressive." For him, the only thing that takes priority over education is economic welfare. When asked what one could do for the teeming masses, the Master answers: "Make them prosperous." When asked what could be done once they were prosperous, he answers: "Educate them."[75] Given that learning starts not in school but in the home, economic welfare must take precedence. As Mencius argues, "When people lack constant livelihoods, they lack constant hearts and minds (*xin* 心)."[76] If the material conditions of family life are unstable, it is more difficult for its members to benefit from education. This is not because education itself will be costly—for as Confucius suggests, tuition should be set at whatever rate the student can afford, even if this amounts to a "package of cured meat."[77] Instead, it is because establishing the wherewithal, the support, and the time for education is more difficult when hardship prevails.[78]

Unfortunately, while Confucius advocates providing each social class with access to education, the Confucian tradition has failed for most of its history to extend education and other avenues of personhood to women. In her exemplary study of Confucianism and women, Li-Hsiang Lisa Rosenlee explains that a constellation of Confucian customs and values have conspired against women. As she explains, "The familial virtue of filial piety, ancestor worship, and the continuity of the family line work as a theoretical, ethical ground to justify and sustain social practices—most noticeably concubinage, child bride/servants, and female infanticide."[79] This is not to suggest that women failed to make considerable contributions to Chinese culture in spite of such conditions. Rosenlee demonstrates the opposite. The traditional idea, however, that women were supposed to operate in the inside realm (*nei* 內) of home/family while men operated in the outside realm (*wai* 外) of society/politics restricted such influence.

As often happens in early Chinese thought (we saw this in our review of rival anthropologies in chapter 7 of volume one), transgressions of gendered role assignments trigger the animalization trope. Recall that, for Confucians like Xunzi, animals divide into "male and female" (*pinmu* 牝牡) but not "man and woman" (*nannü* 男女).[80] The latter categories are reliant on the ability to make social distinctions, and such distinctions are what differentiate humans from animals. "Man and Woman" are names (*ming* 名) given to social roles (*fen* 分) constructed to delineate expectations in a "human" (*ren* 人) world. Once this world becomes confused, then humans revert to being animals.[81] Thus, in order to remain "human," men and women need to retain their separate and distinct roles—or so such thinking goes. While such an approach is not as disreputable as the kind of essentialist thinking one finds in Aristotle,[82] it can become fortified all the same and thus resistant to intelligent reconstruction.

There are plenty of ways for Confucianism to rebound from this. As David L. Hall and Roger T. Ames observe, the sexism that infects Confucianism is not a "dualistic" sexism but a "correlative" sexism, wherein gender traits identified as "feminine" are encompassed within the scope of exemplary personhood (*junzi* 君子)—the problem then being that "females have historically not been allowed to be persons."[83] Given the nature of Confucian values, this is readily seen to be internally incoherent. Joanne D. Birdwhistell demonstrates how, in Confucian philosophy, the virtues of motherhood are abstracted from their natural context and appropriated as "virtues" for male rulers, who unlike females are then permitted to become "Parents to the People" (*renminzhifumu* 人民之父母).[84] Such cultural errors are grave in practice, but philosophically they are easily corrected.

Recognizing that Confucianism is an adaptable, living tradition, Rosenlee provides a viable roadmap for "Confucian feminism." The problem, she says, is that "the Confucian project of self-cultivation and the ideal of *junzi* 君子

["exemplary person"] although they are not gender specific in their moral content, are nevertheless beyond the reach of women as gendered beings of *nei* 內 ["the inner realm"]."[85] Once this mistake is made plain and corrected, the *junzi* ideal as it appears in texts like the *Analects* and the *Mencius* can be enlisted to *rectify* the problem of Confucian sexism. Facilitating this in the Western academy, however, remains a challenge. The twenty-first century begins, unfortunately, with a significant setback for such a project: complete English translations of the *Analects* and the *Mencius* that revert to using the gendered term "Gentleman" as the sole translation for *junzi*.[86]

The May Fourth Movement in China saw significant advancements in women's rights. *La Jeunesse*, according to one contemporary writer, played a major role in the "achievement of a life of independent personality" for Chinese women.[87] The so-called "Woman Problem" (*funüwenti* 婦女問題) implicated several customs and encompassed a range of substantive issues: the family system, marriage, divorce, children, chastity, suffrage, and suicide. The latter topic rose to prominence as essayists (including the young Mao Zedong) composed penetrating and disturbing biographical accounts of female suicides, vividly bringing the struggles of women to social consciousness.[88]

One of the untold stories of Dewey's time in China is the extent to which his wife and daughter worked on behalf of women's rights in China. Alice and Lucy delivered numerous talks on the education of women and on the history of the women's rights movement while they were there, talks that have only recently returned to circulation.[89] Alice was vocal about the shortage of women attending John's lectures, and she was unafraid to speak directly to provincial governors about the need to expand women's education. She spoke with women and girls who confided in her their difficulties, and she was known to occasionally pay the tuition of girls in need.[90] John Dewey had long advocated for the rights of women, and in China he did not relent. He spoke on behalf of equal pay and, stressing the continuity between old and new, maintained that, "women should have the kind of education that fits them to be contributing members of society and useful and intelligent citizens, as well as good wives and mothers."[91]

Hu Shih's commitment to women's issues in China was equally strong, and it had been initially sparked while he was studying in the United States. Hu relates that, shortly after arriving in New York, he came across a number of women making speeches on behalf of women's rights on the street corner. He spotted Dewey there, and figured that the philosopher must have been passing by. When the speeches were over, however, Dewey "got into the car and drove off with all the women." Hu realized at that moment, much to his surprise, that Dewey was assisting with their campaign. This was eye opening for him.[92] In China, Hu would go on to become a major advocate for the

Figure 2.2. Dewey in Beijing with his friend, Grace Wu, who ran a small school for girls from underprivileged families and helped to raise money to support them. According to Lucy Dewey, "She is certainly one of the saints of the earth." John Dewey collection, Special Collections Research Center, Morris Library, Southern Illinois University–Carbondale.

social emancipation of women through the broadening of educational and other opportunities.[93]

Of all Republican-era reforms, however, the one most responsible for expanding access to education was the replacement of classical Chinese (guwen 古文) with vernacular Chinese (baihua 白話) as the written language in China's schools. Hu Shih was directly responsible for this reform, which became the centerpiece of a larger "Literary Revolution" during the period. The speed with which this reform came about is remarkable given the weight of tradition in this area of Chinese culture. How did it happen?

The imperial exam system had been terminated in 1905, but the language of instruction in education remained classical Chinese—a dead language whose use, apart from classical learning, was in official communications between regions with different dialects. Over the course of Chinese history, there had been literary works that were written in more informal styles, but the bulk of Chinese learning, and the entirety of the classical corpus, was preserved in the classical language. At the time of the 1911 revolution, the vast majority of people in China were illiterate, as classical Chinese was not a spoken language and thus impractical to learn. There were discussions ongoing in China about how to rectify the situation. One common suggestion was to use some form of written vernacular for useful periodicals, newspapers, simple instructions, etc. while reserving the classical language for education and governance. No consensus, however, had been reached.

As Hu Shih would later explain, "The solution to this problem came from the dormitories in the American universities."[94] While still at Cornell, Hu began to formulate his own solution to the language problem. He proposed simply replacing classical Chinese with a written form of the vernacular for all purposes—educational, practical, and literary. He had communicated this idea to some of his Boxer Scholarship friends, including Mei Guangdi 梅光迪 who received from Hu a poem in the vernacular expressing his sentiment that, "*The coming of a new tide is unstoppable, and it is time for the literary revolution.*"[95] Hu's friends gathered in the summer of 1915 in Ithaca to discuss the issue. This was the summer in which Dewey delivered his "Progress" talk in Chicago and during which Hu, having recently discovered Dewey, was preparing to move to Columbia for the upcoming semester. Mei Guangdi was on a parallel trajectory in the opposite ideological direction. He had recently discovered the "New Humanism" of the conservative Harvard philologist Irving Babbitt and was in the process of transferring from Northwestern to Harvard for the upcoming semester. (Recall that Dewey would lock horns with Babbitt after the latter wrote *Humanism and America* with Paul Elmer More in 1929). Mei stopped in Ithaca for the meeting with Hu on his way to Cambridge.

The disparate experiences of Hu Shih and Mei Guangdi reflect enduring fissures in the American mind—fissures that would further stimulate disagreements among intellectuals in early Republican China. To see how this is so, Mei's mindset needs to be understood. Mei was rare among his American cohorts. Prior to its termination in 1905, he had actually passed through the first level of the imperial exam system to become a person of "distinguished talent" (*xiucai* 秀才).[96] Under the old system, this would have granted him certain rights and privileges. It did not take him long to discover, however, that in the United States this accomplishment counted for nothing. In part, this is what attracted Mei to Babbitt's "New Humanism," which celebrated the hierarchical ranking of classical learning over the seemingly rudderless egalitarianism of Dewey's "progressive education."

Needless to say, Mei Guangdi and Hu Shih would come to disagree on language reform and much else. Mei found Hu's vernacular (*baihua* 白話) poetry, for instance, to be a "complete failure."[97] In fact, Hu's peers were at first largely skeptical of his proposals to reform the Chinese language. As Hu remembers, "With the exception of a Chinese girl in Vassar College, all my literary friends in the American universities were opposed to this outrageous theory of mine."⁹⁸ (That Vassar girl was Chen Hengzhe 陳衡哲, who would go on to become a prominent vernacular author and China's first female university professor). Undeterred, Hu Shih penned essays in support of language reform during 1916–1917 while studying with Dewey at Columbia. These articles were published and widely read in *La Jeunesse*. They were persuasive pieces, for by the time Hu returned to China the literary revolution was in full swing and he was already its leader.⁹⁹

When Dewey arrived in China, it was not difficult for him to get behind the reform. "Some people, no doubt, think it presumptuous of me to make such comments as these about the Chinese language since I am a foreigner and since I have been in China for such a short time," he explains. "But my observations since I have been here have convinced me that China can never have universal education unless the language is reformed."¹⁰⁰ Dewey thought that language reform, in fact, was more important than the adoption of a new constitution.¹⁰¹ The proposal worked its way through official channels, and by 1920 it was decided that primary school textbooks would be written in vernacular Chinese in 1921 and that by 1922 elementary and secondary school textbooks would follow.¹⁰² Dewey weighed in on the announcement. "I was pleased to read in the newspaper the other day that the Chinese National Education Conference had passed a resolution favoring the adoption of textbooks written in the spoken language of China," he said. "Although I am not as familiar with conditions in China as I should like to be, I believe that the use of the spoken language of the people in textbooks should prove to be one of the greatest steps forward that you could take."¹⁰³

So, does such a "progressive" reform amount to a repudiation of Confucianism or to a twentieth-century reconstruction? Where would Confucius have been on this issue? Certainly, securing the means to expand education would meet with his approval—but do such reforms not jeopardize the status of traditional learning (*xue* 學)? In pushing for reform, Hu Shih wished to elevate the "vulgar" language of the common people and to create a new literature, one that was "written in the living tongue of a living people," and thus "capable of expressing the real feelings, thoughts, inspirations, and aspirations of a growing nation."¹⁰⁴ Hu argued correctly that, for Confucius, it was the more rustic, vernacular flavor of the *Songs* that made them so worthy of the classical canon in the first place.¹⁰⁵ Remember—*this* was the text at the center of Confucius' curriculum. It is cited more than any other ancient source in the *Analects*. The Master admired this text precisely for its rustic purity and accessibility. So, the question really comes down to this: *Is the creation (zuo 作) of new songs, literature, poetry and arts warranted from a Confucian perspective?*

Conservatives say "no" and they have their evidence ready: the Master said he "transmits (*shu* 述) but does not create (*zuo* 作)."[106] This, however, is a weak position. As we have seen, the word "create" in early China is closely related to the historical sages. This is a point that Sor-hoon Tan is keen to make in her discussion of this issue.[107] In the *Rituals* we read, "One who creates (*zuo*) is called a sage (*sheng* 聖). One who transmits (*shu*) is called intelligent (*ming* 明). An intelligent sage is one who both transmits and creates."[108] Since Confucius explicitly denies being a "sage," it makes perfect sense that he would claim not to be a creator.[109] This does not mean, however, that he is opposed to creation altogether or on principle. There is nothing in the *Analects* to suggest that "intelligent sages" (*mingsheng* 明聖) would not be needed in the future. Indeed, texts like the *Mencius* express anxious anticipation of their coming. To suggest that Confucius regarded 305 songs to be the alpha and omega of all meaning is both textually unwarranted and a rather uncharitable reading. The fact that Confucius "transmits" but does not "create" means only that *he* is not a creator—not that he is altogether *against* creativity. Besides, as Tan suggests, one should remember that Confucius was a thinker who tended to downplay his own virtues. "Confucius' apparent denial of his own creativity," she writes, "may attest more to his modesty than to a neglect of creativity."[110]

With respect to the "literary revolution" specifically, Hu Shih did not see it as a "radical" act that departed from Chinese tradition. In his writings, he reconstructs in some detail the cyclical emergence and transmutation of vernacular styles in China over the years and how such cycles galvanized Chinese letters. For Hu, the twentieth-century "literary revolution" was but another stage in "twenty centuries of historical evolution." Such "revolutions" are not abrupt departures from tradition, because "all revolutions have a background of historical evolution, all have their roots in the past." The difference between "revolution" and "evolution," as Hu sees it, is simply a matter of time. "Where a change takes place rapidly, we call it a revolution; where it takes place slowly and there is the imperceptible progression of history, then we call it evolution." In the broader context of tradition, "revolution" and "evolution" amount to the same thing: stages in the constant interplay between transmission (*shu* 述) and creation (*zuo* 作).[111]

In any case, the question of whether Confucianism allows for the creation of new entries into its canon is a moot point because, of course, it does. Important texts like the *Mencius* (*Mengzi* 孟子), *Focusing the Familiar* (*Zhongyong* 中庸), *The Classic of Family Reverence* (*Xiaojing* 孝經), and *The Great Learning* (*Daxue* 大學), *The Classic of Music* (*Yueji* 樂記), and *The Five Practices* (*Wuxing* 五行) were all composed after the death of Confucius.

Learning and Thinking

For Confucius, exemplary persons (*junzi* 君子) are achieved in a fusion of the more formal elements represented by cultural patterns (*wen* 文) and the more idiosyncratic elements represented by raw qualities (*zhi* 質). Understanding how these elements intersect in value-added harmonies (*he* 和) is essential to understanding not only Confucius' teachings but also classical Chinese philosophy more generally. With respect to the aim of these volumes, early Chinese thinking provides conceptual resources that might serve in reconstructing our current value inquiries. As we saw in chapter 8 of volume one, "inherent value" is a notion that invokes a range of traits that are "out of gear" with scientific understandings. Harmony (*he*), however, does not require such intellectual forfeitures. Like an onion without soup, raw quality (*zhi*) does not have *inherent* value prior to becoming integrated in some larger whole. Again—onions are wonderful in a soup, but one does not then go to the kitchen to eat all the onions. The onion is good (*shan* 善) *in* the soup, such that the value sustained in the harmony registers as value-added to the onion. The onion accrues more value in the soup than it does isolated from its fellow ingredients. Such an axiology exhibits the kind of "relationism" that Dewey and Sing-nan Fen regarded as crucial to rethinking value.

Such thinking is critical to any adequate understanding of Confucian philosophy. Confucius believes that human worth can only be achieved *in relation* to others in patterns of togetherness sustained through ritual-custom (*li* 禮). Apart from such formal arrangements, there is little chance that individuals will register as significant. The challenge that harmony (*he* 和) presents as a normative ideal is that of facilitating the *optimal* expression of raw qualities (*zhi* 質) in formal patterns (*wen* 文) that render their inclusion most valuable. This can be done better or worse—*better* when more ingredients express more of their qualities, and *worse* when fewer ingredients express fewer. As Chenyang Li explains, such a metric does not track on to any "fixed grand scheme of things that pre-exists." In fact, postulating such a "grand scheme" impedes harmony by assuming that its emerging constituents (i.e., the always-incoming ratio of 250:105) will slavishly conform to a preexisting order regardless of what raw qualities (*zhi*) they happen to possess.

Confucius' pedagogical teachings hinge on the tension between these more formal and more idiosyncratic elements. There is, no doubt, a premium placed on classical learning (*xue* 學). But there is also a premium placed on thinking it through (*si* 思). Learning and thinking, Confucius explains, cannot be severed without deleterious results. "Learning without thinking leads to perplexity, and thinking without learning leads to danger."[112] Dewey had plenty of opportunities to comment on the pitfalls of the former tendency while in China. On the eve of the May Fourth Movement (literally, May 3, 1919), Dewey spoke to an audience in Shanghai about classical studies during the European Renaissance, explaining that, "When traditional education relied so excessively on rote memory, and neglected the development of thinking, the act of teaching was not unlike the manner in which a mother bird feeds her young, regurgitating the predigested food and pouring it into the gaping beaks of her fledglings. This sort of education is fatal to individuality."[113]

Dewey might have used late-imperial Confucianism itself as an example of such rote learning, but he was always careful not to criticize Chinese traditions directly before his Chinese audiences. Lecturing in the southeastern city of Fuzhou in June of 1921, twenty-five months into his visit, he still approached the topic indirectly. "I have not been in China very long," he explains, "but I am told that almost everywhere students memorize and recite the Chinese classics without having even a remote understanding of their meaning."[114] Rather than being overtly dismissive of the imperial exam system and its legacy, Dewey puts a positive spin on it. "The ancient Chinese examination system for government officials," he tells an audience in Shanxi province "is evidence to me of the fact that the Chinese have attached greater value than any other people to education." Thus, if progressive reforms do take hold, "these methods should be even more fruitful in China than in the United States, provided, of course, that teachers rise to the opportunity."[115]

Since Confucius is more on the "conservative" side of the spectrum, his warnings against excessive thinking (si 思) tend to be most remembered. Upon hearing that one of his students was thinking about things three times before acting, the Master remarks: "Twice is enough." He also relates that once he went a whole day lost in thought, without eating or sleeping, only to realize that his time would have been better spent learning (xue 學).[116] For Confucius, as Edward Slingerland observes, "rather than attempt to pointlessly reflect on one's own, the accumulated wisdom of the classics should form the very basis of one's thinking."[117] As a basis for thinking, however, the classics are not *inert*—Confucius is quite clear about this. If one memorizes all 305 songs by heart but cannot mobilize them effectively in dealing with specific situations, then "what good are they?"[118] Dewey relates the same to his audience in Shanghai. Too many students, he says, "find themselves limited to their textbooks, instead of finding in these books the key to richer and more meaningful living . . . if they cannot *use* their knowledge to enable them to understand the life of their society and to contribute to its improvement, their schooling is a waste of their time and of the money which supported the school."[119]

This recalls again that great hallmark of Confucian education: "Reviewing the old in order to realize the new."[120] Such creative initiative is central to Confucian pedagogy. As the Master says: "If upon showing students one corner of a square they do not come back with the other three, I am not repeating the exercise."[121] Confucius did not expect students to learn the classics by heart and simply repeat what they had learned. Instead, he expected them to take whatever they had learned and to expand its meanings into the present. This is what it means to "review the old in order to realize the new." As Dewey relates in his "Philosophy of Education" lectures in Beijing, "We must not forget that the main reason we want to conserve and teach the culture of the past is that we need to relive it, to infuse life into it, and make it applicable to present-day social situations and conditions." If we fail to do so, says Dewey, "we are getting nothing out of our ancestors' investment."[122]

As we will see in chapter 3, Dewey's "China lectures" forge a middle way between so-called "conservative" and "radical" options in cultural affairs. This "third way" amounts to the path of intelligent reconstruction. Intelligent reconstruction entails both preserving the learning the past (*xue* 學) and reflecting on its uses and consequences (*si* 思). As Dewey says, "Our common sense and our everyday observation tell us that the problems of human life cannot be solved either by completely discarding our habits, customs, and institutions, or by doggedly hanging on to them and resisting all efforts to modify and reconstruct them."[123] The same basic concern for balance underwrites the Confucian approach.

Over the years, Dewey grew sensitive to what he saw as distortions of his middle way position, both by his detractors and by some of his followers. One suspects that, if Confucius were around today, he too would be disturbed by what some of his followers have done with his carefully balanced teachings. In response to distortions of his own position, Dewey attempts in *Experience and Education* to set the record straight by dissolving the so-called "Traditional/Progressive" dualism altogether. Such "extreme opposites" are overcome, he suggests, once it is understood that traditional learning serves not as the *end* of education but as a *means* to furthering the life and vitality of a cultural tradition. The central question for education, says Dewey, is "How shall the young become acquainted with the past in such a way that the acquaintance is a potent agent in appreciation of the living present?" Dewey's answer is that present experience must be "stretched, as it were, backward," so as to "take in the past" in order to project it intelligently into the future.[124] Understanding the present is hardly possible *without* the past. Each of us, in fact, begins where Confucius begins: "Not born with knowledge; but rather, with fondness for the ancients, earnestly seeking it out."[125] This is the opposite of one who would, without knowing the past, unilaterally create (*zuo* 作) something new and more often than not reinvent the wheel.

As Confucius makes clear, he is not such a person. Instead, he is one who listens carefully to what the past has to offer and then "selects what is good" (*zeqishanzhe* 擇其善者) and "adheres to that" (*congzhi* 從之).[126] Confucius treats the past exactly as he does the present. Walking alongside his contemporaries, he also "selects what is good and adheres to that."[127] The fact that Confucius does not uncritically follow the past is frequently lost on his commentators. Ni Peimin, however, reminds us that Confucius exercises critical discretion in adhering to past traditions:

> Indeed, Confucius appeals to the past, the Zhou tradition. But he does not choose the Zhou simply because it belongs to antiquity. There were other traditions in antiquity, such as the Yin-Shang tradition, or the Xia tradition, which were both earlier than the Zhou tradition. Confucius never said that what comes from the past is right. He chooses the Zhou because the early Zhou exhibited an order, a spirit that is conducive to harmony [*he* 和].[128]

Again—in the final analysis, neither Dewey nor Confucius can be reduced to the categories of "progressive" or "conservative." Both are somewhere in between. Each appreciates the fact that education is a fusion of both learning (*xue* 學) and thinking (*si* 思). More than anything, it is their respective historical circumstances that place them on different halves of the progressive-conservative spectrum. For Dewey (and for us), the crisis of the age is that the principles that inform our cultural values and institutions are "out of gear" with empirical facts; thus, the focus is on progressive revision. For Confucius, the crisis of the age was that cultural order had devolved into chaos. There were perfectly serviceable models available with which to restore social harmony; thus, the focus was on conservative restoration. Both Dewey and Confucius retain the prerogative of "selecting what is good" from the past (and the present) and "adhering to that." Confucius finds that many Zhou practices work productively, so he accepts them. Dewey finds that our lingering Greek-medieval concepts work poorly, so he rejects them. Despite their respective historical agendas, Dewey and Confucius share a deeper philosophical affinity in their approaches.

Given how the "Conservative/Progressive" dichotomy is currently understood in the Western academy, it is difficult for us to appreciate this affinity. Indeed, there are few dichotomies more fraught with distortion, confusion, and irony than our current "Conservative/Progressive" dichotomy. This can be observed in how we tend to think of what Edward Slingerland refers to as the "postmodern relativist." One would presume, for instance, that a "conservative" virtue ethicist basing her arguments and inferences on Greek-medieval principles would hardly be considered a "postmodern relativist." Aristotle's substance ontology and his teachings about fixed essences and ends, however, are demonstrably *wrong*. The natural world is *not* as Aristotle thought it was. If such a philosopher continued to pass along such teachings un-reconstructed, bracketing out the likes of Darwin, Einstein, Faraday, et al., then she would be inflicting the same cultural damage charged to the so-called "postmodern relativist." For someone in the Humanities to actually *espouse* a system of ethics, politics, etc. that is based on scientifically disproven principles is more-or-less saying that the natural sciences do not matter to the humanist—that the Humanities swing free of such things. If this is true, then indeed "edifying discourse" goes all the way down. Thus it is the staunch "conservative," not the more progressive-minded thinker, who is the real "postmodernist."

Dewey maintains that the humanist is obliged to pay attention to the "return wave" of science and to tend to common sense accordingly, updating even our most cherished values and assumptions if need be. This is why Aristotle factors so importantly into Dewey's *Reconstruction in Philosophy*. More than any other thinker in the Western tradition, it is Aristotle who needs to be reconstructed. Dewey's appeal to science in this connection, as R. W. Sleeper explains, is not reductionism in the sense that we associate "with philosophies that embrace 'scientism' and argue that scientific method provides us with an algorithm for solving *all* our problems." Dewey never makes such claims. His concern instead is that "any philosophy which is not consistently experimental will always traffic in absolutes."[129] Thus, he insists that "we ought to look at the way of going at things that accounts for success in science," and to recognize "what the sciences can tell us about ourselves and about the environments in which we have to live out our lives." The lessons of science, both in form and content, need to circle back into our "conduct of culture," explains Sleeper, so that adjustments can be made in "the ways in which we live our moral lives as individuals."[130] This essentially *moral* dimension of the progressive outlook is the one that the conservative mind never seems to comprehend.

For over four centuries now, critiques of our Greek-medieval heritage have triggered backlash from cultural conservatives in the Western world. This reflex carries over into the so-called "culture wars" phenomena in the United States, which has severely eroded civil discourse and now threatens to undermine its democratic institutions. The first Chinese students in America were not exempt from being pulled into these skirmishes. They gravitated naturally along its fissure lines and then returned to China to continue the hostilities. Hu Shih and Mei Guangdi, given their parallel but opposite trajectories, provide a case in point.

Having disagreed with Hu Shih over language reform in Ithaca, Mei Guangdi proceeded to Harvard in the fall of 1915 to begin his tutelage under Irving Babbitt. To understand where Babbitt stands in the pantheon of American conservatism, one might begin with Russell Kirk's hagiography, "The Conservative Humanism of Irving Babbitt," written upon Dewey's death in 1952. In a rather callous move, Kirk uses the occasion to celebrate Babbitt, who had died in 1933. Kirk writes that, according to Babbitt, Dewey stood for all that was wrong with modernity: "making material production the goal and standard of human endeavor; the past is trash, the future unknowable, and present gratification the only concern of the moralist." As Kirk explains, Dewey's philosophy was popular "among that distraught crowd of the semi-educated and among people of more serious intellectual pretensions who found themselves lost in a withered world that Darwin and Faraday had severed from its roots."[131]

Indeed, faced with the challenges of modern biology and physics, Babbitt did what the conservative mind is wont to do—he sought refuge in the "higher truths" of human nature and refused, as Dewey did not, to assume the "continuity between Nature and the human" (*tianrenheyi* 天人合一) which would mean taking seriously the likes of Darwin and Faraday. As Babbitt saw it, Dewey suffered from "an advanced stage of naturalistic intoxication," causing him to reject "the enormous mass of experience that has been accumulated in both East and West," which teaches "the habits that make for moderation and good sense and decency." In Babbitt's mind, Dewey stood for the wholesale rejection of the past and thus did a profound disservice to the education of children. "From an ethical point of view," writes Babbitt, "the child has the right to be born in a cosmos, and not, as is coming more and more the case under such influences, pitchforked into chaos."[132]

Mei Guangdi's own sense that Chinese culture had become chaotic drew him naturally to Babbitt and his ideas. Moreover, Babbitt's profile was impressive. He received training both at Harvard and the Sorbonne-Paris in classical languages, including Pali and Sanskrit. By 1915, he was full professor of French and Comparative Literature at Harvard. His 1908 work, *Literature and the American College*, was among the books that deeply impacted Mei. Reflecting on the rise of science in China, Mei was inspired by the solid wall that Babbitt erected between the Humanities and the natural sciences. His dismissal of science in favor of classical learning struck him as persuasive. "We reason that science must have created a new heaven because it has so plainly created a new earth," argues Babbitt, who then adds sardonically: "We are led to think lightly of the knowledge of human nature possessed by a past [so] palpably ignorant of the laws of electricity."[133] Babbitt declares that there is a "dual nature of existence" in the universe—one law for "humans" and one law for "things."[134] Having become so enamored with "things," contends Babbitt, the modern West has lost esteem for "the ancient and permanent sense of mankind as embodied in tradition."[135]

As Babbitt saw it, Dewey contributed most malignantly in this connection. For, as Russell Kirk explains, "Veneration was dead in Dewey's universe, indiscriminate emancipation was cock of the walk."¹³⁶ Babbitt saw himself as the defender of the traditional Humanities against the encroachment of an all-consuming naturalism. "There is needed in the classics today a man who can understand the past with the result, not of loosening, but of strengthening his grasp upon the present," he writes. "The teaching of the classics thus understood could be made one of the best preparations for the practical life, and less might be heard of the stock complaint about wasting time in the study of dead languages."¹³⁷ Mei was instantly converted. As he writes: " I became for the first time aware that something might be done in China in a similar spirit to bridge over the gap [of] a ruthless and indiscriminate undermining of her cultural foundations."¹³⁸

Mei Guangdi's arrival at Harvard corresponded with Babbitt's own budding interest in Chinese thought, particularly Confucianism (he associated Daoism with "naturalism" and "primitivism"—basically *anti*-humanism).¹³⁹ Mei would become Babbitt's first Chinese disciple, the first of a number of Chinese students who found their way to Babbitt.¹⁴⁰ Thus, in the years leading up to the May Fourth Movement, there were two main centers for Boxer Indemnity students interested in humanistic studies: Dewey at Columbia, and Babbitt at Harvard—opposite hemispheres of the American mind.

At the end of the 1915 fall term, after one semester as Babbitt's student, Mei Guangdi wrote eagerly to Hu Shih who was by then studying under Dewey:

> The culture of our country is humanistic. It emphasizes moral cultivation of individuals. The goal of our culture is to nurture *junzi* 君子, the "gentleman-scholar" or humanist in Western culture. The way to nurture [the gentleman-scholar] is to overcome the individual desires inherent in human nature and to develop virtue, wisdom, and intelligence through education. A true [gentleman-scholar] is hard to find. In any given time, therefore, there are only a few [gentleman-scholars] in a society, the rest are all just ordinary people, or the profane vulgar. I personally believe that to nurture [the gentleman-scholar] remains our cultural goal today. The more [gentleman-scholars] a society has, the better it becomes. So in conclusion, Confucianism must remain the culture of our country. What do you think?¹⁴¹

Hu disagreed, and thus unraveled their friendship. Mei would go on to become one of Hu's principle adversaries when he returned to China. Along with other Chinese students who studied under Babbitt, Mei established the *Scholarly Review* (*Xueheng* 學衡) in 1922, a conservative journal that gave voice to those who opposed the "New Culture" movement. *Scholarly Review* was one of hundreds of periodicals that sprang up during this period. It was, however, one that had a built-in ceiling to its readership. Every article was written in classical Chinese (*guwen* 古文).

Dewey and Babbitt remain a study in contrasts. Each man enjoyed enormous devotion and affection from a significant number of Chinese students, and each would play some part in the debates that consumed Chinese intellectuals during the Republican era. Their ideas, however, were as different as their personal styles. Dewey spent time in China, and he learned about its culture through experience on the ground. Babbitt's connection to China was indirect. His wife, Dora May Drew, was born in Shanghai and lived there for several years while her father held a government post.[142] It is known that his wife sometimes found Babbitt "conceited," because he "professed to understand [China] as she did not." She would tell him that he had no knowledge of China because he did not know "how it looks and how it smells." Babbitt's response neatly underscores the severity of his "Mind/Body" dualism. "The five senses do not admit us to the full truth—no, nor the deep truth—about a country," he would say.[143]

The Babbitt home was adorned in exotic *Chinoiserie*. "Far Eastern disciples" treated Babbitt like a sage, and he did little to discourage the adulation. At Harvard, Mei Guangdi found his Master awe-inspiring. "The moment he entered the room, you felt the presence of a master . . . [He] set up a reign of unquestioned authority and contentment in the lecture room: there was rarely heard a dissenting voice, and heated debate was altogether unknown."[144] In the pages of *Scholarly Review*, Babbitt would be described as a cultural figure on par with the Buddha, Jesus Christ, Aristotle, and Confucius.[145] From his perch in Cambridge, Babbitt encouraged his students in China to use their journal to place a check on Dewey's influence. "I wish, by the way, you could publish notices of John Dewey's last two volumes of a kind that will expose his superficiality," Babbitt wrote to one student. "He has been exercising a bad influence in this country, and I suspect also in China."[146]

Dewey's relationship with his students took a different form. He made a different impression on them and evoked different responses in return. Max Eastman's recollections capture vividly the atmosphere of Dewey's classrooms:

> He used frequently to come into [the classroom] with his necktie out of contact with his collar, a sock down around his ankle, or a pants leg caught up into his garter. Once he came for a whole week with a large rent in his coat sleeve which caused a

flap of cloth to stick out near the shoulder like a little cherub's wing. His hair always looked as though he had combed it with a towel . . . He would come in through a side door—very promptly and with a brisk step. The briskness would last until he reached his chair, and then he would sag . . . He would look vaguely off over the heads of the class and above the windows, as though he thought he might find an idea up there along the crack between the wall and the ceiling. He always would find one.

When he spoke, Dewey plodded forward in a manner that more closely resembled thinking out loud than professing: "evolving a system of philosophy *ex tempore*," remembers Eastman, "and taking his time about it." The difference in style and attitude between Dewey and Babbitt is fully revealed in what happens next. Eastman continues:

> The process [i.e., thinking out loud] was impersonal and rather unrelated to his pupils—until one of them would ask a question. Then those glowing eyes would come down from the ceiling and shine into that pupil, and draw out from him and his innocent question intellectual wonders such as he never imagined had their seeds in his brain or bosom . . . [Dewey's] instinctive and active deference, the unqualified giving of attention to whatever anybody, no matter how dumb and humble, may have to say, is one of the rarest gifts or accomplishments of genius. He embodies in his social attitude, as Walt Whitman did in a book, the essence of democracy.[147]

Scanning his surviving syllabi, one sees that Dewey managed his classroom around questions and in a multidirectional way. In a module on the comparison between Greek and Chinese education from 1907, Dewey provides his students with nothing but questions: "What characteristics are attributed to Chinese life as a social type?" he asks. "Why were certain literary writings held so important [in China]? How does this differ from the importance attached to the Bible in our own country?" When not thinking out loud, Dewey wanted to learn alongside his students. "What are the good points involved in the fundamental importance attached to the family [in China]?" he asks—"What is the meaning of *piety* in Greek and Roman thought?"[148]

When comparing the Greek and Confucian traditions in Irving Babbitt's classroom, there was nothing for his students to think about or to discuss. No questions needed to be provided or even considered. Aristotle and Confucius were identical and Babbitt was there to tell them how.

Shortly after Dewey returned from his life-altering trip to China, Babbitt delivered the keynote address to an annual meeting of Chinese students studying in the United States. While he lacked the kind of perspective that Dewey had acquired during his time in China, Babbitt would tell the students exactly what they needed to do to address China's problems:

> The remedy, it seems to me, is not to lose touch with your own background in the name of a superficial progress, and at the same time to get into closer touch with our background beginning with the Greeks. You will find that the two backgrounds confirm one another especially on the humanistic side, and constitute together what one may term the wisdom of the ages. It seems to me regrettable that there are less than a dozen Chinese students in America today who are making a serious study of our occidental background in art and literature and philosophy. There should be at least a hundred. You should have scholars at all your more important seats of learning who could teach the Confucian *Analects* in connection with the *Ethics* of Aristotle.[149]

Fast-forward one century, and interpreting the *Analects* alongside Aristotle's ethics remains a proxy war between "conservatives" and "progressives" in the American academy. From the standpoint of intra-cultural philosophy, this is not surprising—in fact, it would be surprising if this were not the case. Each of us finds in a text what it is that interests us, and our readings reflect our broader cultural influences, values, and outlooks. Since American culture is fractured, so too is its reading of the *Analects*.

The position taken here is that, in the cultural present, it is important to utilize the Chinese tradition as a resource that provides *alternatives* to Greek-medieval thinking. It is certainly possible to entertain the Chinese tradition otherwise—that cannot be denied. It is important to recognize, however, that while transcendent orders, inherent schemes, divine plans, fixed natures, etc. may be spiritually "therapeutic," such proclivities are symptomatic of the same cognitive habits that give rise to religious fundamentalism, Creationism, climate denial, and moral dogmatism—forces that stand to destroy human civilization. The Chinese world is relatively free from such scourges, and this suggests the inadequacy not to mention undesirability of readings of the tradition that rely upon the cognitive habits implicated.

Assimilating Chinese thought as a possible alternative to our Greek-medieval options stands not only to relieve us of such "out of gear" encumbrances; it also promises to restore a range of positive virtues. Taking process-oriented concepts seriously, for instance, restores *responsibility* into the intellectual life. The comforts that we have long secured from transcendent, substance-oriented assumptions, as Dewey says, "naturally shifted a burden of responsibility that [philosophers] could not carry over to the more competent shoulders of the transcendent cause." Thus all moral questions were answerable in some "inherent scheme" that one needed only to "follow." Once such Greek-medieval notions are overcome, philosophy is compelled to become "a method of locating and interpreting the more serious of the conflicts that occur in life, and a method of projecting ways for dealing with them: a method of moral and political diagnosis and prognosis."[150] Without question, it is *easier* to be a "conservative" than a "progressive"—i.e., a Babbitt rather than a Dewey. The conservative need only gesture to the past and tell everyone to "follow it." The progressive task of intelligence (or *ming* 明) however is to determine how the past and present work together in preparing us for the *future*. This involves heavier philosophical lifting, but such work becomes relevant to the degree that it shoulders that responsibility.

The *Dao* 道 of Tradition

Dewey's teachings in China are balanced between preservation and reform. He continually encourages China to retain all that is worthy in its own heritage while selectively adopting Western approaches. On numerous occasions, he encourages his audience not to blindly imitate the West so as to avoid the West's mistakes.[151] Merely imitating Western science, he feared, would pull Chinese civilization apart. "If you do this, you run the greatest risk of getting the worst aspects of Western civilization at the risk of forfeiting what is best in your own Chinese traditions; and at the same time you will be pulling your people in two opposing directions."[152] Dewey was fully aware that China's contact with the West up to that point had been grossly imbalanced in favor of Western commercial interests. The only way forward, however, was through further cultural contact. "The only method by which China can remedy the present sad state of affairs is to speed up cultural exchange between East and West, and to select from Western culture for adaptation to Chinese conditions those aspects which give promise of compensating for the disadvantages which accrued from earlier contacts." This process, Dewey adds, "calls for men and women of wide knowledge and creative ability."[153] Like all transactions, this too must be doubled-barreled. The Chinese should "recognize that out of their heritage they can help the rest of the world be on the alert for crises in culture" and thus "contribute richly and creatively to the development of a new world culture."[154]

Hu Shih's attempt to reconcile traditional China and modern science began with his doctoral dissertation, wherein he identified pragmatic, evolutionary, and progressive ideas within various schools in ancient China.[155] He would later come to argue that precursors to the scientific method were embodied in the neo-Confucian notion of the "investigation of things" (*gewu* 格物), whereby inquiries into the coherence (*li* 理) of nature lead to what were then called "investigative expansions" (*gezhi* 格致). (*Gezhi* became the first phrase used to translate "Science" in China.)[156] While sorting through these various strands of the Chinese and Western traditions, Hu resists cultural essentialism, describing the difference between China and the West as a "difference in degree which in the course of time has amounted to a difference in kind." He also avoids traps such as the "Material/Spiritual" dualism, arguing that there is "true spirituality" even in the traditions of Western science, in its "ceaseless search for truth" and in the "rapturous and ecstatic joy which frequently rewards the patient creative researcher."[157] Like Dewey (and unlike Irving Babbitt), Hu had no intention of fortifying any "Mind/Body" or "Humanities/Science" dualism and then exalting one side over the other. This is what distinguishes him not only from the conservatives but also from the materialistic scientism of more radical thinkers like Wu Zhihui 吳稚暉 and others.[158]

While Babbitt, stationed in Cambridge, would not have known this, it was against the more unabashed materialism of figures like Wu Zhihui that the conservative's counterclaim, inspired by Babbitt—*viz.* that "Spiritual" China was superior to "Material" Western science—really found its voice. Dewey and his students had little to do with this debate. Again, Dewey spent his entire career attempting to overcome such dualisms. In return for his efforts, conservative thinkers like Russell Kirk portray Dewey as embracing a "thoroughgoing naturalism, like Diderot's and Holbach's, denying the whole realm of spiritual value: nothing exists but physical sensation, and life has no aim but physical satisfaction."[159] It is no wonder that Dewey was so skittish about using terms like "naturalism" and "humanism" to describe his approach, preferring instead some combination of the two and finally settling on "culture" to encompass both.

Again—"culture" for Dewey represents the "connection-and-distinction" between the human-and-natural in the continuity of life-activity. Dewey believes that to sharply bifurcate this continuity is the most destructive tendency in civilization. When C. P. Snow comes forth to say the same thing in his influential 1959 work, *The Two Cultures*, he anecdotally canvasses a problem that Dewey had grappled with for six decades. As Sidney Hook observes: "A half century before C. P. Snow's superficial book on *The Two Cultures* appeared, Dewey had defined the problem facing reflective citizens concerned with education as 'how we are to effect in this country a combination of a scientific and humanistic education.'" This was among the problems that China faced during Dewey's visit. According to Hook, Dewey understood that without reference to a larger "culture" that embraced what Snow calls the "*two* cultures," then humanism was "in danger of becoming precious, if not snobbish" and the natural sciences "harnessed to barbaric goals."[160] In the meantime, each side would accuse the other of behaving just so.

Because this strikes at the heart of what culture is about: the "connection-and-distinction" between the natural and the human—or as the Chinese say, the "continuity between Nature and the human" (*tianrenheyi* 天人合一), disruptions that occur in such instances tend to be culturally specific in their composition. Thus, Dewey knew that it was not his job to tell the Chinese how to solve their so-called "modernization" problem. He called instead for Chinese "men and women of wide knowledge and creative ability" to meet the challenge.[161] Just about midway though Dewey's China trip, an article appeared in *Millard's Review of the Far East* relating the truth as Dewey himself knew it. As the author writes: "Dewey cannot apply his own philosophy to Chinese life. It will require someone as close to Chinese thought as he is close to American thought to do this. He can, however, help this forward by his presence in China and by his advice to the Chinese who are hopeful and intelligent enough to undertake it."[162]

This explains why, throughout his stay, Dewey was tireless in encouraging the Chinese to build upon their own tradition. As John Herman Randall observes, it is "difficult to see how any perceptive reader could fail to discern [this]." As Randall notes, "The true traditionalist does not merely repeat the familiar shibboleths; he understands how to use tradition in facing our present problems."[163] Mei Yibao 梅貽寶, one of Dewey's Chinese students at Columbia in the 1920s (and later Professor of Philosophy at Iowa State University), recalls that it was precisely in this regard—understanding that one must "review the old in order to realize the new"[164]—that Dewey "was so in step with Chinese tradition and history that [he] was referred to by us students as the American Confucius."[165] While Dewey and Confucius indeed approach their pasts differently in light of their respective presents, each thinker understands how important it is for societies to sustain the vitality and health of tradition.

In getting at this understanding, much can be learned by reflecting on what tradition actually means in the Chinese context. The word for "tradition" in modern Chinese is *chuantong* 傳統. *Chuan* 傳 means "to transmit" and *tong* 統 is glossed in the *Shuowen* lexicon as the "strands of silk" (*ji* 紀) that hold a material together—its warp-and-weft. Thus, "tradition" suggests the transmission of strands of culture through time. As Geir Sigurðsson notes, the modern Chinese term is a neologism taken from the Japanese. There is no term in classical Chinese for "tradition." At least with respect to Confucius, Sigurðsson suggests to us that, "the word in classical Chinese that comes closest to the general English term 'tradition' is *dao* 道." As he explains, tradition is "the path on which the present arrived from the past, and which, provided we attend to its maintenance by constantly adapting it to new situations, will lead the present into the future."[166] Accordingly, when lamenting his contemporaries' disregard for the Zhou tradition, Confucius asks: "Why is it that no one goes out (*you* 由) from this *dao*?"[167]

To think of each tradition as a *dao* 道 leads to important philosophical insights. As we have seen, the function of ritual-custom (*li* 禮) is to promote harmony, i.e., to integrate form (*wen* 文) and quality (*zhi* 質) in value-added togetherness. If a particular ritual-custom fails to perform this function, then it no longer works (*xing* 行). However, if the end is sought through more coercive means, that also does not work. "Achieving harmony (*he* 和) is the most important function of ritual-custom (*li*)," but as Master You hastens to add: "When things are not working (*buxing* 不行), to realize harmony for harmony's sake without using ritual-custom to regulate it is not going to work."[169] What this means is that ritual-custom, when operating properly, *exhibits continuity between means-and-ends*. It expresses, in other words, *dao*-activity. Social destabilization occurs when ritual-customs are no longer serving as means-ends—they are no longer, as Dewey would say, instrumental-consummatory in nature. They no longer "work" (*xing*) and *dao* is thereby impeded.

Tradition in Confucianism thus sustains itself both through transmission (*shu* 述) and creation (*zuo* 作). As Yao Xinzhong explains, Confucian education is "intended to transmit in creation and to create in transmission," thus maintaining the *dao* 道 of tradition.[169] This places tremendous importance on the *continuity* of tradition. It would be difficult—in fact, unthinkable—to start a new culture from scratch. Cultural strands are already interwoven such that ritual-customs are intertwined within broader sets of habits. In fact, ritual-customs have histories that implicate even our material and biological substrata.

In part II of the present volume, this will be explored in greater detail. For now, it is enough to observe that as Peter J. Richardson and Robert Boyd argue, "The evolution of culture has led to fundamental changes in the way that our species responds to natural selection."[170] Our emotions-and-rituals, desires-and-customs, appetites-and-cuisines (not to mention our diets-and-physiques) share the same histories—and these histories defy any simple "Nature/Nurture" dualism. Thus, to start a new culture from scratch would be like removing fishes from water and expecting them to sing and dance—it defies Nature (*tian* 天) as well as the principle of continuity (*yi* 一). As Dewey explains, each cultural tradition "exists through a process of transmission quite as much as biological life." Tradition "not only continues to exist *by* transmission," says Dewey, "but it may fairly be said to exist *in* transmission."[171]

The cultural evolution of the Confucian tradition is plain to see—it has undergone continual growth and transformation for 2,500 years. In maintaining its own continuity, ritual-customs (*li* 禮) have obviously needed to change over the course of Chinese history and indeed they have. But what does our study of Confucian philosophy and the experiences of the May Fourth Movement tell us about what determines—or *ought* to determine—such changes? When do ritual-customs need to change and how?

The legalization of same-sex marriage in the United States (and in twenty other countries) provides a good example of how ritual-customs evolve and why. Modern marriage is a cherished institution, the form (*wen* 文) of which recognizes, ennobles, and expresses the special qualities (*zhi* 質) of emotion and commitment that two people feel toward one another in a socially communicable way. The harmony (*he* 和) of each marriage expresses how a particular love relationship becomes integral in a broader set of cultural, legal, and institutional coherences. Harmony (*he*), as we have seen, carries its own measure of better or worse—*better* when more ingredients express more of their qualities, and *worse* when fewer ingredients express fewer.

Human societies, to put it mildly, have lagged in recognizing that the love of same-sex couples is identical to that of opposite-sex couples and fully deserving of the ritual-custom of marriage. It is easy to see retrospectively that, by being discriminatory, the institution of marriage had functioned in some ways but not in others—for in arbitrarily excluding the qualities (*zhi* 質) of an entire class of ingredients, it fell short of expressing its own significance. Marriage that is inclusive of same-sex couples is a fuller and *better* version of the ritual-custom, which thus becomes strengthened as an institution going forward.

The strict Confucian conservative might argue that same-sex marriage could never be "Confucian" because it was never endorsed in the Zhou dynasty. Such thinking is refuted by the teachings of Confucius. Confucius recognizes that ritual-customs (*li* 禮) evolve over time and in ways that cannot be foreseen. When asked by Zizhang if one can know what ritual-customs will be like ten generations from now, Confucius responds in a clever manner. "The Yin dynasty adapted the ritual-customs of the Xia dynasty," he replies, "How they altered them can be known. The Zhou dynasty adapted the ritual-customs of the Yin dynasty. How they altered them can be known. Thus, if there is a dynasty that succeeds the Zhou, even if it is a hundred generations from now, it can be known."[172] *How*, though, can its changes be known? Obviously, they can be known only as changes in the former two instances are known—*retrospectively*. Zizhang is looking for future predictions, and Confucius isn't taking the bait. The genetic method only works in one direction. Confucius and Zizhang can know how the past became the present, evolving as it has through the Xia, the Yin, and the Zhou. Only those in a future dynasty, however, can know how that dynasty has come to be from its predecessors. So *yes*—how ritual-customs will evolve ten or a hundred generations in the future can be known—*just not by us*. Our place is the present, and the material that we work with comes from the past.

Confucius refuses to look too far ahead because grand future projections are not in keeping with *dao* 道-practice and with the more measured approach of sustaining perspicacity (*ming* 明) in the midst of transforming conditions. More often than not we find that our grand projections reveal the extent of our ignorance and/or stupidity. They only confirm, as Dewey says in China, that "the task of reorganization, of transformation, of union of old and new, is so vast, so appalling in its complexity, that neither any wholesale forecast of the future nor any simple remedy is worth the paper it is written on."[173] The work of making the future better than the past entails absorbing the past while remaining in the present, carefully "embracing the one" (*baoyi* 抱一) and "observing the small" (*jianxiao* 見小) as the process unfolds.

The ever-present task of intelligently maintaining the warp-and-weft of a cultural tradition falls to each succeeding generation. In his China lectures, Dewey uses a memorable image to describe the process of transmitting the past through present circumstances:

> [Such reconstruction] is a task not unlike that of steering a ship. The cargo (that is to say, the cultural heritage) must be so arranged that the ship can maintain an even keel and not sink to the bottom of the ocean. On the other hand, the ship must also be able to go forward and deliver its cargo where it is needed and can be used, rather than remaining tied to the dock so long that the cargo desiccates or decays. If the cargo is the heritage of our culture, the winds into which we tack are the trends of the current age. We must make sure that our ship is well laden with a cargo made up of the best that our traditions have to offer; the cargo must be well stowed so that we can get at what we need when we need it, and we must also make sure that the navigation of the ship takes the fullest advantage of the winds and currents which flow from today's and tomorrow's trends and needs.[174]

Steering the ship of culture is how the *dao* 道 of tradition proceeds. Each of us must realize that we are *on* the ship as it moves. Philosophers especially must remain mindful of their coordinates and not mistake their location for some other time or place.

In chapter 3, the degree to which Dewey came to re-think custom and tradition during his China trip will be explored. While Dewey's students were antagonistic toward late Imperial Confucianism, he soon came to realize that they were being "truer to Confucianism in attacking it." He started to understand how ritual-customs (*li* 禮) functioned in the Chinese world and came to appreciate their normative dimensions. "The breakdown in Chinese national life," Dewey realized, "is proof of their inefficiency according to the standard of Confucianism itself."[175] This resulted in a breakthrough in Dewey's own thinking. Its trajectory can be traced from before Dewey's China trip through to its conclusion, and subsequently in works such as 1927's *The Public and Its Problems* and 1930's *Individualism Old and New*. As Jessica Ching-Sze Wang argues, the extent to which Dewey was inspired to do original philosophizing in China is a topic that is generally neglected in "Dewey in China" scholarship. She alerts us that "new dimensions for future research on Dewey and China" lie in this unexplored area.[176] In chapter 3, we make fresh excursions into this territory.

3

Custom and Reconstruction

The thinking person does not fall into the trap of supposing that the old is bad and that the new is good. Instead, he or she looks at both with a critical eye, and determines what should be retained from the past, and what should be incorporated from the current of new ideas. He or she knows that both Eastern cultures and Western cultures have their strengths and their weaknesses, and that the wise thing to do is to let them supplement each other, communicate with each other, and thus bring into existence a new culture that is stronger than either of the present ones.

—John Dewey, Young Men's Christian Association, Fuzhou, June 1921

Breakthroughs in China

It is worth remembering that Dewey's long sojourn in China, his single most extensive international experience, was not planned in advance. When John and Alice Dewey left San Francisco for Japan in January 1919, they had not been preparing to go to China. Looking back decades later, Dewey relates that, "I had a wonderful two years and a half in China. I had got in a rut or the doldrums. I hadn't read up on China and went in a state of blissful ignorance with no operation of culture weighing me down—and it was literally wonderful."[1] What Dewey calls his "rut or the doldrums" was likely a confluence of his misgivings about his position during the First World War and the recent exhaustion of his philosophical reserves. He regarded his set of lectures in Japan (which resulted in 1920's *Reconstruction in Philosophy*) to be the closing of a chapter. "I tried to sum up my past in that and get rid of it for a fresh start," he says.[2] While delivering those lectures, even Dewey did not know that his "fresh start" would begin with twenty-seven months in China. The abruptness of the opportunity, not to mention its intensity, provided him with a "rebirth of intellectual enthusiasms."[3]

By Dewey's own account, he "did no philosophical reading at all" in China.[4] Instead, he composed lectures and essays that sought to address the novel and concrete demands of his surroundings. Past scholarship has focused largely on the relative success or failure of Dewey's influence on Chinese affairs. Such "Dewey in China" scholarship is vast in scope, and so is the range of opinion that it represents. The most sober assessment is probably that of John E. Smith, who writes: "It would be quite unrealistic to ask for a single, total assessment of Dewey's visit to China, whether it was successful or not, whether his influence was positive or negative."[5] Rather than enter into such debates (which are complex and largely academic) one might take notice instead of the asymmetrical bias that such scholarship exhibits. It is often overlooked that Dewey did not only *teach* his Chinese audiences while in China. He also considered himself to be a *student* and he learned a great deal while he was there.[6] As his daughter Jane relates, "Whatever the influence of Dewey upon China, his stay there had a deep and enduring influence upon him."[7] The present study remains primarily concerned with how the China experience influenced *Dewey*.

John and Alice Dewey witnessed all sides of Chinese culture—the good and the bad. They met women, "slow, rocking, hobbling," whose feet had been bound into disfigurement; they noticed women segregated "in all public gatherings;" and they marveled at the shortage of female doctors in the country.[8] Dewey was exposed to the graft and corruption that infected every level of official government, prompting him to observe wryly that, "*Status quo* is China's middle name, mostly *status* and little *quo*."[9] He met with Reginald Johnston, Scottish-born tutor to the last emperor, Puyi 溥儀, and returned with a portrait of despair. "[The boy] is waited upon by the eunuch attendants who crawl before him on their hands and knees," Dewey writes. "At the same time he is, of course, practically a prisoner, being allowed to see his father and younger brother once a month. Otherwise he has no children to play with at all."[10]

Dewey's students instructed him that all of this reflected the moribund state of the Confucian tradition. Their argument was not unsound. What is plain, however, is that Dewey did not have uncritical sympathy for every proposal of the "New Culture" movement. It was easy for him to get behind school reform, women's rights, and the language initiative; there were other proposals, however, that he was not enthusiastic about. As we have seen, he consistently stressed that China must not "copy" Western thinking but rather intelligently reconstruct its own tradition and maintain continuity with its own past. Dewey made it clear that China's new, outward-looking culture must be a new *Chinese* culture—"the evolution of a culture which will be the common possession of all humanity."[11] Such views, and the positions that they entailed, were not always well received among the more radical elements in Chinese society. Most reformers expected Dewey to be more uncompromising toward China's past. As Barry Keenan notes, Dewey's method "was in no way a wholesale rejection of tradition. In fact it was in ways explicitly conservative, as Dewey called for Chinese reformers to retain a direct connection between the past and change."[12]

As Dewey's approach became better understood, China's more strident "New Culture" reformers dismissed him for being too conservative. Dewey was critical of them in return. As he relates in a letter to Albert Barnes:

> The whole temper among the younger generation is revolutionary, they are so sick of their old institutions that they assume any change will be for the better—the more extreme and complete the change, the better. And they seem to me to have little idea of the difficulties in the way of any constructive change . . . [To] the liberals here anything is likely to be [as] true and valuable as anything else, provided only it is different . . . Since the Chinese family system for example badly needs reform, the family ought to be completely done away with [and] promiscuous relations between the sexes set up. . . .[13]

Within a month, Bertrand Russell (who remained legally married) arrived in China accompanied by his former student and mistress, Dora Black. China's leftists flocked to Russell, who they projected as a more radical alternative to Dewey. The Secretary of the Chinese Anarchist-Communist Association informed Russell that, "Dr. Dewey is successful here, but most of our students are not satisfied with his conservative theory."[14] Before long, Russell too would fail to live up to the expectations of the radicals.[15] His analytic approach, at the same time, would have no impact on the Chinese scene. Russell's methods, as Ding Zijiang explains, "were too technical, too trivial, and totally different from traditional Chinese patterns of thinking."[16]

Existing "Dewey in China" scholarship does an adequate job of exploring how Dewey's reception in China waxes and wanes during his visit. What is more difficult to trace, however, is how Dewey revised his own philosophical outlook during the same period. While he was critical of specific institutions in late Imperial Confucianism, Dewey found himself largely sympathetic with traditional Chinese thought. He was a perceptive observer of social behavior, and he came to recognize how specific patterns of behavior corresponded to long-standing Chinese traditions. The "social philosophy" that Dewey experimented with in China reflects such influences, and such elements carry through into his later works. All of this and more will be explored in the present chapter. The most distinct breakthrough in Dewey's thinking, however, and the one that contributes most to his "conservative" reputation among Chinese leftists, is his reassessment of the role that custom plays in culture. The "custom" breakthrough is where we begin.

Since Dewey did not speak Chinese, the term "custom" in his China writings reflects his general understanding of ritual-custom (*li* 禮)—a Chinese term that was not in his vocabulary. He understood perfectly well, however, that "China rests upon a network of local and voluntary associations cemented by customs."[17] He fully appreciated that "what the Chinese abundantly possess is community of life, a sense of unity of civilization, of immemorial continuity of customs and ideals."[18] Dewey was aware that there were ongoing debates over ritual-custom in the Chinese idiom, and in light of these debates he came to re-think "custom" as he understood it. As Abraham Edel and Elizabeth Flower explain, "Dewey's view of habit and custom was itself reconstructed" while he was in China, and "the change appears to have been stimulated by contact with a large-scale instance of what happens to custom in a situation of revolutionary change."[19]

What made the China experience so invigorating for Dewey was that nothing had prepared him for the dynamic he encountered. As Roberto Gronda observes, "It did not take much time [for Dewey] to realize that his conceptual framework did not fit very well [into] the Chinese situation, and that in order to properly understand the latter he had to strip off most of his habits of thought."[20] One of those habits of thought was his sometimes knee-jerk reaction against custom. One need only consult the "Custom" entry in his contributions to the 1911 *Cyclopedia of Education* to see that Dewey had regarded the relation between the individual and custom to be a "crucial problem" that needed to be solved.[21] In class lecture notes dating back to 1901, Dewey would use China as the stock example of the "reign of social custom," which meant a "society which relatively speaking is not progressing."[22] He envisioned custom as a retarding factor in the "relation of individualism and conservatism to progress," wherein China represented the "relatively stationary social type."[23]

By the time Dewey put the final touches on 1922's *Human Nature and Conduct*, his outlook on custom had changed significantly. "The choice is not between a moral authority outside custom and one within it," he writes: "It is between adopting more or less intelligent and significant customs."[24] As Dewey would observe, "The Chinese mind thinks, of course, as naturally in terms of its customs and conventions as we think in ours. We merely forget that we think in terms of customs and traditions which habituation has engrained; we fancy that we think in terms of mind, pure and simple."[25] Henceforth for Dewey, the "individual" would no longer find itself in conflict with "custom" *per se*. Nor would "custom" be something in natural tension with more reflective modes of thinking. While teaching "Ethical Theory" in 1926, Dewey explains that: "In the long warfare between custom and reason as the basis of morality, the real business of intelligence is not to put up some rival to custom, but to render custom itself more reasonable."[26] This is not how he approached this topic prior to the China visit.

Subtler breakthroughs in China set the stage for what would later become Dewey's "cultural turn." As Dewey says, his thinking had entered a "rut or the doldrums," and the China trip helped him to get out of it. One area in which Dewey's thinking had become stuck was that, to some extent, he was still operating as if modern Western civilization exhibited some kind of standard for cultural development—an assumption that was almost universally held by Western intellectuals at the time. The China experience revealed such lingering assumptions to Dewey and helped him to overcome them. "This is really 'the other side of the world' in every sense," Dewey wrote to a colleague, "and it [is] most interesting to see a culture where so many of our prepossessions are reversed."[27] Many of our "habitual Western ideas," Dewey realized, made it "impossible intelligently to describe Chinese conditions, or even grasp them intelligently." As he would relate to his readers: "The visitor spends his time learning, if he learns anything about China, *not* to think of what he sees in terms of the ideas he uses as a matter of course at home."[28] Eventually, Dewey would come to understand that these were divergent lineages of "common sense" at work. At the time, he came simply to realize that China was on its own course of cultural reconstruction, one that did not track on to any universal Western trajectory. "There will not be adoption of Western external methods for immediate practical ends [in China]," he reports, "because the Chinese genius does not lie in that direction."[29] China's future, Dewey came to realize, "can be understood only in terms of the institutions and ideas which have been worked out in its own historical evolution."[30] For China, "transformation from within" was the only way forward.[31] As Thomas D. Fallace argues, by living in China Dewey "gained a greater respect for the cultural difference of the Chinese people," and thus realized that one could "not simply place a country so vast, populous, and ancient on a single continuum of cultural development" alongside countries in the West.[32]

Dewey already understood as much theoretically. As related in chapter 6 of volume one, he argued in 1902 that, while the primitive mind establishes the "ground pattern" for more sophisticated cultural expressions, such developments were not to be explained in terms of higher or lower phases in a linear process.[33] What Dewey had *not* given much thought to, largely because he lacked the anthropological expertise and field experience to do so, was *how* and *why* specific cultures diverge as they do from a common origin. Dewey's

China-related writings made up for this deficit. As Gronda demonstrates, by locating Chinese culture in the "agrarian, agricultural" setting in which it evolved, Dewey arrives at a positive, still quite insightful account of Chinese conservatism, both in terms of its careful management of natural resources and as a response to its unique demographic realities. Dewey's attempt "to come to terms with the 'Chinese difference,'" Gronda argues, "prompted him to radicalize his thought in a direction that lead him to formulate in a more inclusive and holistic way the relations between nature and culture." Dewey, he explains, came to see cultures in more organic terms, such that "cultural aspects (philosophies of life) and natural aspects (environmental conditions) were so closely interwoven that they were impossible to disentangle."[34]

While Dewey did not, at this stage, establish a full-blown theory of "culture," the China experience afforded him insights that would later inform his theory. Dewey's China-related writings even foreshadow the intra-cultural turn that Sing-nan Fen would secure in his 1952 "Cultural Relationism" article, wherein he distinguishes cultural relationism from "the fallacy of cultural relativism."[35] Gronda notes that Dewey's China-related writings demonstrate that he "did not believe that the plurality of philosophies of life supported a relativistic account of social life," and that "the relativistic position was a too abstract description of the dynamics of intercultural interaction." At this early stage, Dewey was inclined toward cultural relationism but "did not provide any argument in favor of that view." Gronda recommends that future inquiries be directed toward determining "how much of the theoretical achievements that Dewey had reached [in China] passed into the new phase of his philosophy."[36] That is the present question.

In determining the answer, one important link is a 1921 article that Dewey wrote while in China for publication in the Japanese magazine, *Reconstruction* (*Kaizō* 改造), which was in publication from 1919 to 1955. The article is variously titled, "Some Factors in Mutual National Understanding," and "Is Eastern Culture Spiritualistic and Western Culture Materialistic?" This piece appears alongside four other articles, each of which survives only in Japanese translation.[37] The *Kaizō* article addresses, among other things, how it is that international travel educates the traveler—i.e., how intra-cultural encounters "become a real means of education, a means of insight and understanding." Dewey's focus is on how the traveler (and "the case of the traveler is taken simply as an illustration or symbol of every kind of contact") comes to observe connections-and-distinctions between spiritual-and-material in such encounters. Rather than do what Irving Babbitt had done, i.e., simply equate "Eastern" spiritual ideals with "Western" spiritual ideals, Dewey observes that there are "different standards and measures" used to determine what is "spiritual" and what is "material" in different cultural fields. It is difficult,

Dewey says, to adjust one's spiritual-material barometer when thrust into another cultural region. Since one cannot instantly penetrate into the soul of another culture, "it is precisely the material phase of a civilization which is most evident to a visitor or foreigner." Thus, it is easily assumed (as it was for many Chinese intellectuals) that the West is "materialistic" and China is "spiritual." Dewey's point is that, from a Western perspective, such an assessment might well be reversed.[38]

Tucked away in *Kaizō*, this article foreshadows important dimensions of Dewey's late-period "cultural turn." Just as the spiritual-and-material continuum represents designations contextualized within individual cultures, the "connection-and-distinction" between what is human-and-natural, mind-and-body, etc. would also register within each cultural context in the broader, interwoven matrix of culture. The "cultural traveler" traverses such a matrix not objectively but in a genetic-functional manner. How cultural objects and distinctions come to be known and related is largely a function of the technologies brought to specific inquiries along the way. Dewey had pieces of the puzzle in hand, but it would be another four decades before he fit them all together.

Li 禮 and Custom

Before returning to Dewey's philosophical activities in China, let us consider his "custom" breakthrough in more detail. Scholars of Chinese philosophy are now well along in recognizing that Dewey's philosophy resonates with Confucian thought.[39] Even Dewey's former students recognized as much and used it for their own purposes.[40] Others, however, remain unsure. May Sim, for instance, argues that there are "irreconcilable differences" between Dewey and Confucius on core issues such as tradition and the individual. As Sim sees it, Confucius believes that "the social ideal has been achieved in the Zhou *li* 禮 and all we need is to realize it," hence, "[Confucius] honors tradition and custom in ways that are totally foreign to Dewey."[41] As evidence that Dewey harbored antipathy toward custom and tradition, Sim presents Dewey in his own words: "To take the rules of the past with any literalness as criteria of judgment in the present, would be to return to the unprogressive morality of the régime of custom—to surrender the advance marked by reflective morality."[42] Given such statements, Sim concludes that Dewey would have had little tolerance for tradition-bound Confucian culture. His visit to China, in her estimation, confirms this. She notes that when asked publically what reforms he thought were needed in China, Dewey responds as follows: "My answer is that we must start by reforming the component institutions of the society. Families, schools, local governments, the central government—all these must be reformed."[43]

For insight into what such reforms would entail, Sim turns to Barry Keenan's account of what Dewey's students were proposing at the time. As Keenan reports, Dewey's students believed that "the independent dignity of each individual must be recognized." For instance, rather than endorse the "traditional deference required by the five Confucian relationships," Jiang Menglin "attacked the hierarchy of social values based on the family system that extended outward to the emperor and his officials." In place of the Confucian role-based system, Jiang "recommended that all people be treated simply as 'you,' 'he,' and 'she,' giving each person his or her inherent dignity."[44] For Sim, proposals such as these illustrate the "drastic differences" between Dewey's teachings and Confucius' on the issue of tradition and the individual. Given such differences, she argues that any Dewey-inspired reform in China would "result in a society that undermines Confucianism at its core."[45]

There are serious problems with May Sim's argument. First, she relies heavily on the 1908 *Ethics* for evidence of Dewey's antipathy toward custom and tradition. This work was written over a decade before his trip to Asia. By focusing exclusively on this work, Sim overlooks the impact that China had on Dewey's thinking. As Dewey reported to his family after meeting a school principle in Tianjin, "[The encounter] confirmed my growing idea [that] the conservatism of the Chinese [is] much more intellectual and deliberate, and less a mere routine clinging to custom, than I used to suppose."[46] Dewey's own ideas about "custom" were being revised accordingly. This helps to explain why the "régime of custom" quotation that Sim draws from the 1908 *Ethics* does not appear in the 1932 *Ethics*. The removal of this passage would have been part of the 1921 revisions made to part II of the *Ethics* while Dewey was actually living in China.[47] In other words, *the exact passage that Sim relies on to demonstrate Dewey's antipathy towards "custom" is one that he personally expunged while in China.*

As for Sim's other assertion, that any Dewey-inspired reform would introduce into Chinese society "individuals" who care nothing for the "traditional deference required by the five Confucian relationships," there are two oversights to observe. The first is obvious—one cannot equate a student's position with that of the teacher. Whatever Jiang Menglin might have believed has no bearing on Dewey's position—and besides, Jiang's views were more nuanced than Sim suggests. He made it clear that, "Those holding the new attitude never advocate for the outcast of every old convention. They only examine them critically, and try to discard the ones that are outmoded."[48] Jiang felt that his approach was consistent with core Confucian teachings about human relationships. Observing that Western influence enabled a "loosening" of family ties in China, ties that had been "partly responsible for retarding the organization of individuals into a broader society," Jiang argued that it is precisely "Confucius' teachings on proper relations," i.e., Confucianism's "special emphasis on human relations," that then "[fits] China to be a modern democratic state."[49] Properly understood, Jiang's view of the individual is not a radical rejection of Confucianism but an attempt at its reconstruction.

Sim's remaining oversight is subtler: it is to assume that Dewey *had* a firm position on the nature of the "individual" to pass along to his students at the time. As Keenan reminds us, political philosophy was only a recent interest of Dewey's in 1919. Hu Shih wanted very much for Dewey to develop a political philosophy during his stay in China.[50] Dewey's forays into the topic, however, come across as little more than a "first-draft attempt to see how well pragmatism might be applied to politics."[51] His lecture in June 1919, "Freedom, Equality, Individualism, and Education in American Democracy," for instance, critiques the notion of "rugged individualism" and suggests that "democratic individualism" might offer an alternative—but apart from the vague suggestion that the latter individuals mutually develop their potentials, there is little substance to Dewey's discussion.[52] The more radical notion, that the individual "you," "he," and "she" must be liberated from the "five Confucian relationships," does not represent any notion of the individual that Dewey held at the time, or ever. Dewey actually *feared* that an abrupt reform of the family structure in China might result in radical individualism—or what Keenan calls "uncontrolled individualism"—and he said so.[53] In his April 1920 lecture, "Desire and its Relationship to Customs and Institutions," Dewey outlines several ways in which the institution of family is both basic to social organization and a human universal.[54] As Barbara Schulte reminds us, "Dewey cautioned against eradicating traditional structures" in China where there was no intelligent consideration of the consequences.[55]

To Sim it is conceded that, when Dewey first arrived in Asia, he did not fully appreciate how "custom" and "tradition" related to the formation of individuals. This was something that he needed to learn from experience. This evolution can be traced over the first few months of his journey. Although Dewey did not have the terminology of Confucian philosophy at his disposal, living in Japan and China gave him a direct feel for how the "quality/form" (*zhi/wen* 質文) dynamic operates in Confucian cultures.

Let us begin in Japan. During their three months there, John and Alice Dewey encountered ritual-custom (*li* 禮) in its purest form. They participated in tea ceremonies, observed the performance of martial arts, and witnessed a nine-hour-long Noh play.[56] "I have an enormous respect now for the old etiquette and ceremonies regarded as physical culture," Dewey wrote to his children.[57] Wherever they went in Japan, they were treated as honored guests and received with the most formal of courtesies. Alice marveled at how stylized and exquisite such occasions were. She relates one event in great detail:

> Cushions are placed about three feet apart on three sides of the long and beautifully shaped room . . . We place ourselves after having all the guests one after another brought up . . . After each one has his table before him the mayor [the host] comes to the center of the hollow square and makes a little speech of welcome. He always tells you how sorry he is he has such a poor entertainment and that he could not do better . . . Then Papa [Dewey] does his best to make a reply, and after he sits down we lift the cover of a lovely lacquer soup bowl . . . By this time another tray of pretty lacquer is put beside you on the floor . . . two little fish browned to perfection, and trimmed with two little cakes of egg and powdered fish, very nicely rolled in cherry leaves. Every dish is a work of art in its arrangement . . . As soon as this tray is in place you see a lovely girl . . . she has in her hand a blue and white china bottle placed in a tiny lacquer coaster . . . Everybody drinks to the health of everybody else. . . .[58]

This is an abridged description of the event. In terms of detail, the account is in league with the *Etiquette and Ritual* (*Yili* 儀禮), the traditional compendium of rituals that date back to the Zhou dynasty. John and Alice Dewey came as close to experiencing the formalities of ritual form (*li*) as one is likely to get in the modern world, and they relished the experience. As Alice related to the children: "I am sorry again you cannot all share in these daily festivals which add so much to the dignity of living."[59]

After a few months, however, the formalism of Japan began to wear on them, and by the time they reached China they were happy to balance such formality (*wen* 文) with qualities a bit more rough-hewn (*zhi* 質). "The Chinese are noisy, not to say boisterous, easy-going and dirty—and quite human in general effect," Alice related.[60] John echoed her sentiment, observing that "Human nature as one meets it in China seems to be unusually human, if one may say so."[61] Alice's impression of the Japanese, "gradually sinking into perspective with distance," was that their mode of social intercourse rendered everything a "little over-made." She told her children candidly: "It is easy to see that the same qualities that make them admirable are also the ones that irritate you."[62]

In China, the Deweys were treated with equal dignity and ceremony, but they felt that the people that they met were more genuine. The Chinese, Alice observed, displayed things more in the raw. "When we visited schools [our host] did not arrange in advance because he did not want us to see a fixed up program," she wrote.[63] John's sentiments were consistent with Alice's. As he wrote of the Japanese, "Their treatment of visitors is beautiful, and they have the most artistic knack of making the visible side of everything beautiful . . . They are the greatest manipulators of the outside of things that ever lived."[64] However anecdotal and private these reflections are, they illustrate the degree to which Dewey actually *experienced* the zhi/wen 質文 dynamic during his East Asian visit—and "a strange process too, this," observes Ralph Waldo Emerson, "by which experience is converted into thought, as a mulberry leaf is converted into satin. The manufacture goes forward at all hours."[65] Dewey's thinking was being transformed. As he wrote to his children: "When I reflect on the changed aspect of our minds and on the facts we have become accustomed to gradually since coming here, I realize we have much to explain to you which now seems a matter of course."[66]

As his evolving thoughts came together, Dewey began to relate the balance between tradition and progress in China with the social conditions under which the Chinese people lived. In his article, "What Holds China Back," the connection is made. Dewey writes that the Chinese, "conservative [as] they doubtless are," are also "supple, pliant, accommodating and adaptive—neither rigid nor dull." The Japanese, he suggests, remain "somewhat formal," whereas the Chinese, "have toned down and mellowed the forms of intercourse till they no longer seem forms."[67] From a Confucian philosophical standpoint, this is high praise. Such tempering of form (*wen* 文), Dewey figures, is a reflection of the sheer length of Chinese history. "The history of this country extends over four thousand years," he notes. "Nowhere else does the earth show such a record of continuity and stability."[68]

Such a record is not obtained by standing still. As Dewey explains: "[Chinese] history is not a history of stagnation, of fixity, as we are falsely taught, but of social as well as dynastic changes. They have tried many experiments in their day."[69] What is it, then, that holds the fabric of China together? Dewey came to realize that it was "custom" itself—the tradition (*chuantong* 傳統)—always operative, yet adaptive. "The consciousness of a unity of pattern woven through the whole fabric of their existence never leaves them," Dewey writes. "To be a Chinese is not to be of a certain race nor to yield allegiance to a certain national state. It is to share with countless millions of others in certain ways of feeling and thinking, fraught with innumerable memories and expectations because of long-established modes of adjustment and intercourse."[70] Dewey had begun to realize that, rather than being some kind of impediment, the *dao* 道 of tradition sustained through ritual-custom was the *intelligence* (*ming* 明) of Chinese civilization. "China

Figure 3.1. Chinese caption reads (Right to Left), "Jiangsu Education Department Welcomes Dr. and Mrs. Dewey from the United States, Photo Taken May 10, 1920." John Dewey collection, Special Collections Research Center, Morris Library, Southern Illinois University–Carbondale.

has changed several times, moving constantly in the direction of practical utility, of ingenious adaption of means and ends," he observes. In his considered estimation, "No country whose conservatism came from sheer routine, from lack of imagination, from mental rigidity, could have maintained and extended its civilization as China has done."[71]

Dewey came to realize that ritual-custom (*li* 禮) afforded China a "high state of civilization" through its operative function as educative and socializing. "It produces civilized persons almost automatically," he observes. "For the essence of civility, or of civilization, is the ability to live consciously with others, aware of their expectations, demands and rights, of the pressure they can put upon one, while also conscious of just how far one can go in response in exerting pressure on others. The Chinese, as long as they were left undisturbed by other peoples, had all the complex elements of the social equation figured out with unparalleled exactness."[72] Regardless of what English word Dewey uses to describe this Chinese phenomenon (generally, he uses "custom"), it is the operation of *li* that he is describing.

Dewey probes into the conditions that lend themselves to such a social balance. He guesses that if there is any "single key" to understanding how the Chinese came to operate this way, it is demographic. "Many traits of the Chinese mind are the products of an extraordinary and long-continued density of populations," he observes.[73] Civilized behavior in China "came from lifelong living in the immediate presence of members of the family and clan, to whom every personal act was public and who exercised unremitting pressure of approbation and reproof."[74] There was little management of social intercourse from "on high," Dewey notes. "In the words of perhaps their oftenest quoted proverb, 'Heaven is high and the Emperor far away.' The implication is that earth is close and intimate, the family and village nearby." Meanwhile, the rule of "Heaven" (*tian* 天) in the Confucian world is of an "absentee nature." It does not purposefully *do* anything. "The Court which represented Heaven," Dewey writes, "was contented to imitate the latter's non-interference with the details and customs of life."[75] Thus, rather than mirror some divine pre-ordained "scheme," the Chinese moral character is the result of a long process of flesh-and-bone human association and experience. In Dewey's estimation, the natural restraint of the Chinese character, its moderation of extremes like "glumness and fanaticism," and its overall courtesy and cheerfulness, "are undoubted products of long-continued close face-to-face crowded existence," products of "direct face-to-face intercourse."[76]

This idea: "face-to-face," would shape Dewey's thinking for years to come. The phrase had already been used in the work of the American sociologist, Charles Horton Cooley.[77] This is the first time, however, that Dewey uses it in his own work: in connection with the lived environment of the Chinese people. Seven years later, the phrase would emerge as a centerpiece of Dewey's sociopolitical philosophy in *The Public and Its Problems*.[78]

Even among those who knew Dewey well, it is not generally recognized that it was China that inspired his adoption of this terminology. Consider the following transcript of a 1958 conversation between those in Dewey's circle as they try to determine what influenced his "face-to-face" turn:

> Herbert Schneider begins: "I don't know whether it was Robert MacIver that influenced him or Charles Horton Cooley. Cooley, I guess."
>
> Horace Kallen replies: "I should say it was his youth in Vermont that influenced him."
>
> Schneider responds: "It was the old Vermont town meeting idea and that conception of democracy that seemed to come out on top of his mind."

> James Gutmann disagrees: "But does he have any nostalgia at all for this Vermont boyhood? I see no sign of it."
>
> To which Schneider concurs: "No, he told me he left that God-forsaken country as soon as he could."
>
> John Herman Randall then concludes: "As a matter of fact, I think that face-to-face business, while it undoubtedly has overtones of town meeting and so on, that's one of the things he got from Jane Addams."[79]

With eleven people in the room, not *one* person guessed that it was exposure to Chinese culture that initiated the "face-to-face" turn in Dewey's thinking. This only underscores the extent to which the "Dewey in China" episode is regarded asymmetrically. Again, it is normally assumed that Dewey went to China only to *teach*. The truth, however, as Jessica Ching-Sze Wang tells us, is that "[Dewey's] visit to China undoubtedly stimulated his thinking, and the contours of his philosophy were expanded as a result. Having an alternative place to stand and from which to look, Dewey was able to review his ideas in a fresh light."[80]

Before proceeding further, let us pause to reflect on how such asymmetrical biases represent a systemic problem in comparative studies. As Roger T. Ames and Henry Rosemont Jr. argue, research in comparative philosophy is replete with "narrative and methodological approaches [that] are presumed to be philosophically neutral when in fact they are not."[81] According to some unwritten rule, scholars are free to observe (for instance) the "lack" of theoretical reasoning (*theoria*) in Confucius but never the "lack" of exemplary personhood (*junzi* 君子) in Aristotle. The Western side serves as the default norm. The same thinking shapes "Dewey in China" research. There are plenty of studies that track the extent to which Dewey's ideas were adopted by Chinese thinkers, but there are hardly any studies of how Chinese ideas might have helped to correct deficiencies in Dewey's own philosophy.

From the perspective of intra-cultural philosophy, such biases are not that surprising. They are, however, completely errant and unacceptable. First, they demonstrate a failure to recognize how cultural situations shape the act of comparison, and this is what intra-cultural philosophy is most intent on foregrounding. Second, they exhibit blindness to the reciprocal, transactional nature of intra-cultural contact. Such asymmetrical approaches amount to one-way analyses, when in fact every cultural encounter is a two-way street. One-way analyses may indeed be instrumental for specific purposes—but if we do not continually keep those purposes in mind, default-norm biases set in. Once this happens, intra-cultural philosophy cannot function as envisioned.

"Dewey in China" demonstrates that intra-cultural philosophical encounters are always bi-directional in nature. While Dewey indeed had an impact on China, he was simultaneously absorbing elements of Chinese thinking into his own outlook. Once the impact of China on Dewey's thinking is recognized, texts like 1922's *Human Nature and Conduct*, 1927's *The Public and Its Problems*, and 1930's *Individualism Old and New* never feel quite the same. "Dewey in China" thus provides an object lesson in how world philosophies operate—"all interwoven in a vast variety of ways in the historico-cultural process," just as Dewey says.[82] In the warp-and-weft of this particular encounter, thinkers in China sought to become less "Confucian" by hosting Dewey, while Dewey became more "Confucian" by going there.

Toward a "Social Philosophy," Part One

Tracing the impact of the China trip on Dewey's philosophy is not a straightforward exercise. Many of the ideas that Dewey seemed to "arrive" at in China already had their precursors in his earlier work. China simply galvanized them or in other ways touched their trajectories. Also, not all of Dewey's ideas in China would be immediately realized in subsequent works. For instance, based on Dewey's "China lectures" and other materials, Roberto Frega argues that, "between 1919 and 1923 Dewey was actively involved in the project of developing a social philosophy that . . . never saw the light."[83] It might be more accurate to say that Dewey's China-period "social philosophy," rather than surfacing as a unified system, splintered into separate tracks in the post-China years—some tracks continued, while others were put on hold. These tracks, I believe, might have resumed and reconnected had his "cultural turn" been fully realized. In order to assess the likelihood of this, the "social philosophy" that Dewey formulated in China needs to be reexamined.

This is now made possible thanks to a game-changing recent discovery—a set of notes for Dewey's 1919–1920 "Social and Political Philosophy" lectures in Beijing. The context for this discovery needs to be understood. Dewey delivered his "China lectures" in English with simultaneous translation into Chinese. For each lecture, Dewey produced typewritten notes. He furnished copies of these notes to his translators who recorded his lectures as he delivered them for later publication in newspapers, pamphlets, and magazines. Barry Keenan describes the process in detail:

> The procedure for interpreting Dewey's lectures into Chinese and recording them for publication in the Chinese press was established at the opening talks in Shanghai. Dewey typed brief notes of what he planned to say and gave these to his interpreters to

study before every lecture. Interpretation was done consecutively, Dewey giving about a paragraph in English, then the interpreter turning this paragraph into Chinese. At times [the translator] would stop interpreting to ask Dewey for clarification on some point, then continue the Chinese version. Recorders who took down the Chinese interpreted version were selected by the Dewey students beforehand, and they often met with Dewey after the talks to clear up their notes. The recorders edited their transcriptions of the lectures and submitted them to the interpreter to check for accuracy. *Even in the instances in which his English typescript was fairly detailed, Dewey often digressed so much from the typescript that it became no more than a reference matter for him.* The recorders' corrected notes appearing in the Chinese journals were a relatively accurate version of what Dewey actually said in China.[84]

Given the kind of digression that Keenan describes, what Dewey actually said in China was not necessarily what was in his prepared notes and *vice versa*. Unfortunately, while he gave close to 200 public talks and lectures, hardly any of Dewey's notes survived. Three or four pages were preserved in the Dewey archives. The rest were considered lost.

This changed in 2014. DePauw University historian Chiang Yung-chen, while working on a multi-volume biography of Hu Shih, stumbled upon a substantial set of Dewey's notes buried in the Hu Shih archives in Beijing. Why had these not surfaced earlier? The Hu Shih archive, located at the Institute of Modern History at the Chinese Academy of Social Sciences, was closed to researchers until the mid-1990s and then only selectively opened. Chiang requested to visit the archives in the 1990s but he was denied. Eventually, in the early 2000s, he was granted access and began to explore the collection. Dewey's notes, which did not bear his name, were stored in the "Authors Unidentifiable" Box in the foreign language materials section of the archive—not a very conspicuous place. Chiang glanced at the notes, but did not recognize them as anything that Hu had written. Since photographing materials was forbidden, he left the notes alone and moved on.

Years later, after reading more of Dewey's writings, it occurred to Chiang that those might have been Dewey's own notes in the archive. By this time, the Hu Shih Memorial in Taipei, which had proprietary rights to the materials, acquired scanned copies of nearly the entire Beijing collection. Chiang visited Taipei and was permitted to photocopy the notes. Now able to cross-reference them with Dewey's "China lectures," he discovered that what the archives held were indeed over 80 pages of Dewey's own typewritten notes for Lectures I, II, III, IV, VI, X, XI, XII, and XVI of his sixteen-part series on "Social and Political Philosophy."[85] Chiang arranged for the notes to be deposited at the Center for Dewey Studies at Carbondale and helped to arrange for their publication in 2015.[86] An academic meeting, "Re-Reading John Dewey's *Lectures in Social and Political Philosophy*," was convened in Paris in March 2016 to discuss the implications of the newly discovered materials.

What is immediately apparent is that the recovered notes do diverge from the Chinese end products, providing evidence of the kind of ad-lib digression that Keenan notes.[87] In addition, there are conceptual discrepancies between the notes and the published lectures. As Hu Shih warns us in 1919, "It is inevitable that in material so complex as these lectures on-the-spot oral interpretation and simultaneous recording should result in certain inaccuracies and inadequacies."[88] As Barry Kennan explains, procedural safeguards were put into place to minimize the most serious discrepancies. That said, Chiang Yung-chen's work on the newly recovered notes suggests that Hu was prone to altering Dewey's meanings significantly, and that his "translations were re-writes, but not translations in the conventional sense." The substance of the discrepancies between Hu's translations and Dewey's own notes suggest that Hu was sometimes "using Dewey to advance his own cultural and political agenda."[89]

There are certainly moments in which one suspects that Hu Shih is meddling with Dewey's message.[90] There is, however, simply not enough evidence to maintain that Hu systematically distorted Dewey's message repeatedly and on a large scale. As Keenan explains, there were safeguards in place to minimize the most serious discrepancies. Plus, there are instances in which Dewey's lectures (as transcribed by Hu) relate ideas that Hu would likely have expressed differently, e.g., Dewey's ubiquitous refrain that China must not "copy" the West and that it must remain true to its own history and tradition. In any event, scholars must exercise due caution and diligence with Dewey's "China lectures" as received. In their current English-language format, they are back translations—from English into Chinese and then back into English. As such, they are hardly perfect records. The Chinese documents from which they come, however, *do* represent exactly what the Chinese learned from Dewey.[91] In any case, we now have 80 pages of original notes to help us reconstruct Dewey's "social philosophy" in China.

Let us begin to look at these notes.[92] Lectures I through IV are important because they outline a unified "social philosophy" that would not, as such, be subsequently presented in Dewey's writings. The first lecture begins with a classic Dewey premise: that human-level cultural activities are continuous with precultural, natural conditions. "Breathing, eating, digesting, seeing and hearing long preceded anatomy and physiology," Dewey writes. Likewise, customs, philosophies, ideas, etc. all emerge from precultural conditions, but they also reciprocally influence the nature of those conditions. "[Such] effects after they are brought into being," Dewey writes, "get intermingled in all living forms with the causes that evolved them and modify the forces that produced them."[93]

This results in emergent sociocultural fields that as individual systems are each continuous as nature-culture circuits. Such continuity, which would become showcased in 1938's *Logic: The Theory of Inquiry*, helps to explain how cultures become "steadied, stabilized" in human groups—namely, that material conditions and social practices evolve side-by-side so that their roots become inextricably connected in a nonreducible nature-culture complex. This results in fairly durable and distinct subfields within culture that like any loci of organic growth enjoy their own histories and integrities while being continuous with neighboring fields.

Dewey's primary interest is in determining, given the nature of such fields, how one ought to approach social problems. He observes that when problems arise in such nature-culture complexes, three types of response are possible—one is optimal, but two are typical (and not always helpful). As for the latter responses, the first is "radical," in that "sudden and revolutionary change" is deemed possible for bringing about social improvements—*it is realized that something is wrong and immediate change is demanded*. The second is "conservative," in that such change is resisted while one "consecrates and justifies things as they essentially are"—*it is realized that instability is occurring and one upholds the status quo*.[94] Each of these responses, according to Dewey, fails to understand fully the integral union of natural-cultural conditions. The "radical" fails to understand that cultural change cannot be forced or accelerated in a manner that is not permitted by conditions as they stand, whereas the "conservative" fails to understand that changes in conditions do in fact require cultural habits to evolve. Each of these errant approaches is premised on a "Nature/Culture" dualism. The "radical" sees culture as pliable and swinging free from nature, something that we can instantly and voluntarily change; while the "conservative" sees culture as transcendent and fixed with respect to nature, something that by its own nature never changes.

This concludes lecture one. The second lecture takes up the third and optimal approach to social problems, which is variously called the "progressive" or simply the "intelligent" approach. This "third way" is distinct from both the "radical" and "conservative" approaches. Its purpose is understood as "to cultivate knowledge and intelligence by use of which humans may remedy particular disorders and solve particular problems."[95]

There are two hallmarks to this "third" approach. First, it does not pretend to be objective. Here, Dewey believes that it thus resumes an esteemed tradition in philosophy. "The great thing about the classic systems of philosophy," Dewey writes, "is that they thought with a purpose in view." Not content to merely observe the world, the great philosophers "tried to educe principles for the direction of life, principles to be used in judging the value of events and in projecting plans and purposes." Second, the approach is not dogmatic. It will "avoid large, general isms, and consider specific questions, using the isms simply for what light they may throw on the special need at hand." In approaching the social complex, the third way "tries to find out how *this* and *that* arrangement, custom and institution works in detail to promote happiness or misery. It aims at amelioration . . . rather than at either universal condemnation and destruction or consecration and conservatism."[96]

Thus far, Dewey's discussion is in keeping with positions that he formulated prior to his arrival in China.[97] The most striking developments come in the third and fourth lectures. In the third, Dewey renews focus on the nature-culture continuum and identifies a number of features of human nature that require outlet: "interests to be served," "impulses that have to be expressed," and "instincts that form needs to be satisfied." Such features result in "fairly universal modes of union and association." In every sociocultural field, for instance, one encounters institutions of family, economy, government, religion, education, etc. Such modes of association are universal human practices and express universal human needs. The critical social question—or the question that *enables* social criticism—is how the relative success of any social complex (e.g., *this* particular example of family organization in *this* particular society under *these* particular conditions) stands to be measured. In responding to this question, Dewey generates the following ideal:

> We can frame in imagination a picture in which there is an equal proportionate development of all these forms of associated life, where they interact freely with one another . . . where in short there is mutual stimulation and support and free passage of significant results from one to another.[98]

From here, Dewey explains that there are two factors that might disrupt such harmonies in the social complex. *First*—one mode of associated life might come to dominate other modes in a disproportionate manner, resulting in "arrests, fixations [and] rigidities." To illustrate, Dewey uses the "family" mode in China and the "economic" mode in Western societies. Each mode "tends to be central and regulative" in its respective cultural context. Granted disproportionate status, each one involves "one-sidedness and distortion of human nature—suppression of growth in some direction, exaggeration in others." Dewey presents the status of women, East and West, as an example of what can happen in such instances. In societies dominated by the "family" mode, women are prone to being regarded as "passive means of reproduction." Dewey had seen with his own eyes women in China whose feet were bound. Meanwhile, in societies dominated by the "economic" mode, women are prone to be regarded as "property" under coverture, such that "husband and wife are one and for legal purposes the husband is that one."[99] Dewey had lived to witness this as well. Remnant laws of coverture survived into the 1960s in some American states.

According to Dewey's "social philosophy," the solution to the oppression of women in China and in the United States would be formally the same; but it would differ in its particulars according to the distinct nature-culture complex in which each problem is set. Each problem involves making adjustments in the social field such that "equal proportionate development" of all modes of associated life will "interact [more] freely with one another."[100] Not *every* human good can be reduced to family relations, and not *every* human good takes the form of an economic transaction. There are specific goods that stem from each interest, but when either mode becomes over-dominate in the social system distortion and disharmony can result. Dewey's assumption is that rebalancing various modes of association helps to mitigate the excesses of any single mode—e.g., the "disproportionate value on material things" that characterizes the hyper-economic mode, and the "conservatism and inequality" that characterizes the hyper-family mode. Such rebalancings help to rectify forms of disharmony that persist in their absence.[101]

The *second* factor that disrupts the harmony of associated life in its various modes reflects the fact that none of this occurs in a vacuum. It is the "increased mobility of life," e.g., "local groups [in] closer contact with each other" and the "rapid development of industrial changes," that threaten to throw components of the social complex "out of gear."[102] In the case of China, Dewey observes that "there came the eruption of forces from the outside which were radically new, which were unprecedented, for which the social calculus provided no rules." Such forces, he explains, "were not, strictly speaking, human; they were physical forces of a strange and incalculable kind—battleships, artillery, railways, strange machines and chemicals."[103] Since the social complex is both cultural-and-material in nature, such material changes can and do disrupt the working balance of existing social customs. This is what Dewey wishes to bring into focus. As he asks: "What is really undermining the family system, which was the basis of old China? The teachings of returned students? The desire of a small number to select their own life companions, thereby breaking down parental authority; to have educated women as their wives, thereby revolutionizing China by changing the traditional status of women? *No*." Such things, Dewey argues, are "symptoms, not causes." Disruption in China implicates a range of material and scientific forces: "The railway and the factory system are undermining the family system," submits Dewey. "They will continue to do so, even if every student take the vow of eternal silence."[104]

Dewey thus establishes as the proper object of social criticism the unified matrix of material conditions and operative ritual-customs: i.e., specific, integrated fields in the nature-culture complex. Accordingly, the "third" way is best positioned to respond to social change intelligently (*ming* 明)—neither with a "radical" agenda that forces change based on some abstract "ism" (thereby ignoring the function of ritual-custom) nor with a "conservative" agenda that denies changing circumstances and thus refuses to adopt new methods (thereby ignoring material conditions). Note that, in this connection, the Chinese idioms of the "Shoot puller" and the "Stump watcher" would be emblematic of each attitude, respectively.[105]

This concludes Dewey's third lecture. The fourth lecture proceeds to describe the "social problem" as it now pertains to social philosophy. As stated, Dewey had at one time regarded the relationship between the individual and custom to be the "crucial problem" that needed to be solved.[106] Here, we find Dewey revising such a position after being exposed to Confucian patterns of behavior. Writing in the aftermath of the May Fourth protests, Dewey observed the manner in which "law" operated with respect to the students who were arrested. The students were released from jail largely, he says, because "the heads of the schools gave assurance that the students would not engage in further disorder." As Dewey notes, "To Western eyes, accustomed to the forms of regular hearings and trials, such a method seems lawless." The students were not treated as "individuals" but as part of the school group, one that evokes "the principle of corporate solidarity and responsibility which plays such a large part in Chinese consciousness."[107]

The reason that such thinking is so prevalent in China is that it traces back to Confucius, who teaches that it is more effective to govern society through the mechanisms of ritual-custom (*li* 禮) than through impersonal law (*fa* 法).[108] In the case of the students, as Dewey observes, "the moral sense of the community would have been shocked by a purely legal treatment." What this suggests is that "individuals" are not the central actors in social problems—rather, "troubles of importance are regarded as between groups," and such groups, "families, villages, clans, guilds," are better positioned to arrive at solutions than is a government that has only the tools of impersonal law at its disposal.[109] Thus, ritual-custom (*li*) is hardly in tension with the "individual" as such. Ritual-custom is instead the glue that holds groups together and that works to adjudicate problems among them without appeal to abstract "laws" (*fa*) that strip persons of their social relations and thus convert them into autonomous individuals.

Dewey recognized this as a uniquely "Chinese" approach, and it changed the way he understood the issue. "It is to be doubted whether China will ever make the complete surrender to legalism and formalism that Western nations have made," he observes. He surmises that, "This may be one of the contributions of China to the world."[110] The lesson that Dewey took from the May Fourth Movement and the patterns of behavior exhibited was that it was erroneous to state the problems of social philosophy in terms of a "conflict of society and the individual." Such "Society/Individual" dualisms tend to obscure the underlying group dynamics.

With this in mind, Dewey's fourth lecture poses two questions: (1) "How does it happen that social philosophy has become so preoccupied with a wrong conception?" And (2) "What practical difference is there between the two ways of stating and attacking social questions" (i.e., the one that proceeds according to the "Society/Individual" dualism and the one that does not)?[111]

As for the first question, conceiving social problems in terms of the "Society/Individual" dualism is a symptom of the disharmony among modes of associated life discussed in lecture three. Dewey again uses the dynamic of the women's movement as an example. When one form of a single mode of association (e.g., the Chinese "family") becomes over-dominant in the social complex, it tends to provide social sanction to the authority of a particular group, in this case, "male adults." When women and children express frustration at the social impediments that such institutional constraints present, such expressions become "an attack of licentious individualism upon the foundations of society." Such so-called "individualism" is easy for the *status quo* to marginalize. In the case of the women's movement, such social demands are reduced and dismissed, as Dewey says, to the grumblings of "a few aggressive, more or less ill-natured and disappointed women."[112]

For Dewey, however, "individualism" is *not* what is being expressed in the process of such resistance. When such groups become "rebels against society," what they are fighting for is "social reorganization, which will make the relation of the family group to scientific, literary, religious, industrial, and political groups more flexible, less frozen and rigid."[113] Feminists do not resist oppression as "individuals," but as *wives, mothers,* and *daughters* who are also *doctors, artists, business owners,* etc. with raw qualities (*zhi* 質) to contribute who are being prevented from contributing fully to the social complex. The feminist movement, East and West, is not a protest on behalf of some bare, inherent value of the "individual." Rather, it is a demand for better and fuller integration in those associations *through which* the full range of human values are showcased, ennobled, and secured in social patterns (*wen* 文).

Dewey now takes up the second question regarding the "Society/Individual" dualism: "What practical difference is there between the two ways of stating and attacking social questions?" In answering this question, Dewey outlines what he calls the "three-stage" nature of social progress. In surveying these three stages, it is helpful to make reference to a concrete example. Again, the experience of same-sex couples in the United States and more recently in Taiwan provides a useful illustration.

In the "first stage" of social progress, "there is such an equilibrium that the suppressed group or class is not aware of its suppression, it takes it as part of the established and necessary order of things." For most of American history, it was socially unacceptable to be gay. One was "in the closet" because one understood and had no real choice but to accept that there was something socially "wrong" with it. In the "second stage," there is "restlessness, discontent, because social conditions have changed enough to arouse a sense of powers which do not function, which have no definite social channel provided for their utilization."[114] This is the stage at which those who feel able "come out of the closet," declare who they are, and stand against the existing social order. At this stage, however, they tend to be labeled as "radicals" and might even self-identify as such. This attribution renders them more easily marginalized—one thinks that these must be self-gratifying "individualists" of some kind who care more about their own satisfaction than about the social order. The conservative reflex is then to portray the *status quo* as the steward of the "social order," oblivious to the fact that the current "order," having entered a state of disequilibrium, is objectively *disordered*.

In the "third stage," the demand that fuels discontent in the "second stage" succeeds in "[grouping] about itself a sufficient number of persons, so that it has social standing and repute." Its claims are then recognized as being "made in behalf of social need and welfare not in behalf of purely individualistic non-social factors."[115] This is the stage at which social discontent is recognized not as the symptom of some rampant "individualism" perpetuated by a few self-absorbed troublemakers, but as the expression of a social disharmony that suppresses in certain groups the full expression of human desires and needs. This is the stage of criticism at which social intelligence aims: identifying and helping to communicate how specific groups become marginalized through the operation of specific customs or conventions resulting in the inability of groups to express the fullness of human life.

From the standpoint of Dewey's "social philosophy," the important thing is *not* to get stuck in the "second stage," where the "Society/Individual" dualism dominates. While the emergence of this dualism is an important signal that social discord exists, it must be recognized as an operative impediment to the restoration of social harmony. Again, this dualism provides a conceptual framework in which the marginalization of oppressed groups becomes easier. The longer the "second stage" continues, the stronger the "Radical/

Conservative" narrative becomes and the more strident its tendencies. Here, social philosophers have concrete work to do. The need is to survey society, identify where conflict exists (or will exist) in the first two stages, and help to advance thinking about such problems to the "third stage." This is real, concrete work that social philosophers can do. Otherwise, our two default ways of looking at social problems tend to become entrenched: the "radical" aligns conceptually with "individualism in general," and the "conservative" aligns conceptually with "society in general."[116]

By working from *within* the nature-culture complex, progressive social philosophers look at the "social problem" through a different lens. The social field is coextensive with the natural field—one that in large measure shapes our common human desires and needs. Specific ritual-customs and institutions have specific effects in specific environments, depending on how cultural interests in general are harmonized. It would be bizarre in the extreme if the entire world were structured so as to disenfranchise one or any number of "individuals." That sounds more like *The Truman Show* than anything that has ever occurred in human history. Social disharmony disenfranchises *groups* rather than individuals, and this occurs not in a vacuum but within particular nature-culture complexes. The distinct social fields in which groups become oppressed must be understood in a genetic-functional manner—they have historical roots and operative structures that do not make solutions in one field simply transferable to another. As Dewey came to recognize, the solution to the so-called "Woman Problem" (*funüwenti* 婦女問題) during the May Fourth Movement was not necessarily going to be the same as the solution to the "Oppression of Women" in the United States. Nor will same-sex marriage in Taiwan be the same as same-sex marriage in the United States, because the ritual-custom of marriage is different in the two cultures.

As problems surface in each social field, the social philosopher thus regards local factors to be primary in the adjustment of ritual-customs in each situation. "This means an appeal to intelligence," Dewey writes. Here, "observing the small" (*jianxiao* 見小) is important. Social philosophers must detect social disharmony as it occurs (or before it occurs) and model the flexibility (*flexibilis* or *rouruo* 柔弱) required to restore (or sustain) social harmony (*he* 和). As Dewey says, we must examine "customs, conventions, institutions" so as to "keep the good and improve or do away with the worse."[117] Confucius refers to such critical sifting as "selecting what is good" (*zeqishanzhe* 擇其善者) and adhering to it.[118] Attending to the preservation of what works (*xing* 行), for Dewey, is the "path for orderly and continuous progress" in the social field.[119] This is what Confucians regard as maintaining the *dao* 道 of a tradition.

Custom and Reflection

The newly recovered notes for Dewey's "Social and Political Philosophy" lectures are important because, upon returning to America, Dewey did not consolidate his China-period "social philosophy" in any major book or publication. He did, however, assemble an extensive syllabus for a new course: "Philosophy 131–132: Social Institutions and the Study of Morals," which expanded on his "China lectures." As Roberto Frega argues, the 1923 Syllabus (which was only intended for classroom use) is "an extremely important text to understand Dewey's concern with social philosophy and a decisive one to contextualize [his "China lectures"]."[120] It is also an important document for understanding how Dewey's work in China established the groundwork for his "cultural turn" decades later.

As we have already seen, Dewey's *Kaizō* article anticipated his late-period interest in the "connection-and-distinction" between the human-and-natural—a touchstone of his final theory of culture. In the 1923 Syllabus, Dewey sets as one topic for discussion, "The distinctions and connections that exist between original human nature (often confused with the individual), and culture, or acquisitions under the influence of language and other social agencies."[121] Such concerns would not resurface in this form for another twenty-five years, when Dewey had his late-period breakthrough.[122] Once again we see that, while Dewey was clearly onto something new in the China-period, he stopped short of fully articulating it.

Why were such developments put on hold? Partly, they were suspended in order to receive fortification for future articulation. With *Experience and Nature* in 1925, Dewey would step back from "social philosophy" *per se* to establish the framework for his eventual "cultural turn," such that when his reflections on culture resurfaced they would do so within a fuller naturalistic framework. Only in Hawai`i and in retrospect did Dewey realize that it was "dumb" not to incorporate culture explicitly at the 1925 juncture.[123]

Another reason that Dewey's social philosophy was put on hold is that, upon returning to the United States, he was confronted with a new set of challenges that were too urgent to ignore. Dewey had left in 1919 under a cloud of misgivings about the First World War. With respect to events on the American scene, China provided him an ideal environment in which to withdraw, reset, and recalibrate. Back home, however, "democratic idealism," which had been associated with Wilson's "Fourteen Points," was under severe criticism. The 1920s was the decade in which "democratic realism" found its voice. Walter Lippman's 1922 work, *Public Opinion*, sided with Plato in arguing that the *hoi polloi* only knows its environment indirectly, through "fictions" and representations and are thus incapable of intelligent democratic participation. Lippman's 1925 work, *The Phantom Public*, took the argument one step further—arguing that the "public" itself is a fiction. The American populace, argues Lippman, is a diffuse mass, unreliable, slow, and incapable of formulating and sustaining genuine agency. Since Dewey's name was associated with "democratic idealism," he was compelled to defend the existence of public opinion and agency and the viability of democratic practices. The result was 1927's *The Public and Its Problems*.

Dewey's China experience would influence *The Public and Its Problems* in important ways. The first indication is that Dewey grounds the "public" in the "face-to-face relationships" that "generate a community of interests, a sharing of values, too direct and vital to occasion a need for political organization." Like the neighborly community, it is "constituted largely on the same pattern of association that is exemplified in the family. Custom and measures, improvised to meet special emergencies as they arise, suffice for its legislation."[124] All of this sounds very Confucian because it is.[125] Dewey attributes such phenomena accordingly. "For long periods of human history, especially in [China]," he writes, "the state is hardly more than a shadow thrown upon the family and neighborhood."[126] In such communities, "custom-patterns" provide the means through which individuals are formed.[127]

Dewey's phrase "custom-patterns" would be a defensible translation of the Confucian term *li* 禮, one that even captures its functional operation as *wen* 文.[128] "[Always] and everywhere customs supply the standards for personal activities," Dewey writes, "[they] are the pattern into which individual activity must weave itself."[129] Before arriving in China, Dewey understood perfectly well that "every individual has grown up, and always must grow up, in a social medium."[130] He did not, however, consistently understand "custom-patterns" as integral to the formation of individuals. During an early lecture in 1919, for instance, after he announced to his audience that he "arrived in China quite recently, and [knows] very little about either your modes of thinking or the characteristics of your society," Dewey suggests (if our records be accurate) that it would be a "mistake" to regard "custom" (translated here as *fengsu* 風俗) as the source of morality, for "customs are external to the child; they have little to do with his individual consciousness."[131] As we have seen, Dewey's thinking on the role of custom would be considerably different by 1922: "The choice is not between a moral authority outside custom and one within it," he writes— "It is between adopting more or less intelligent and significant customs."[132]

Adopting more or less intelligent and significant customs. This is what Dewey had advocated in China. Once he appreciated the role of "custom-patterns" in forming individuals, the critical work was to intelligently determine which customs lent themselves to the restoration of social harmony and which did not. Turning his attention back to the American scene, Dewey continued to ask how new technologies in production and commerce were posing challenges to "face-to-face" communities, this time in the United States. The scope of such changes were "so vast and their impact upon face-to-face associations so pervasive and unremitting that it is no exaggeration to speak of 'a new age of human relations,'" writes Dewey.[133] This new age, brought about by technological and other changes, was one that presented local communities with unprecedented variability and mobility in their "custom-patterns."

Exhibited here is the same problem and general tactic that Dewey had formulated in China. Whereas Chinese culture had previously experienced a "remarkably static equilibrium," it was now pushed into social revolution by contact with an "impatient, mobile Western world."[134] The question that Dewey brought back to America was the following: "Is it possible for local communities to be stable without being static, progressive without being merely mobile?"[135] Thinking like a progressive-minded Confucian, Dewey poses questions that were largely formulated in response to Chinese conditions and he asks them in similar terms. Like Confucius, he advocates that critical reflection (or *si* 思) coexist alongside tradition and ritual-custom—not antagonistically, but as a check. As Abraham Edel argues, "The Chinese experience suggested to Dewey that custom may in some cases be what reflection could reaffirm, the lesson that preserves rather than retards." In other words: "custom too can be released from the charge of being the drag of the past."[136]

Once again, this new approach is reflected in differences between the 1908 and 1932 editions of the *Ethics*. In the 1908 edition, custom is described in James Tufts' section as "an anchor, and a drag," and left at that.[137] Tufts' words would not be altered in the 1932 edition, but Dewey is surely responsible for the interjection that directly follows in the 1932 version: "What are the actual, concrete effects of customary morality? Does it secure peace and harmony in a society?"[138] Custom, in other words, *may* become "an anchor, and a drag," but this must be continually reassessed in light of changing conditions. Customs, for Dewey, are now indispensable in their function of securing harmony—the question is only whether or not *specific* customs are actually doing so. This is why reflective intelligence (or *si* 思) is necessary. As Dewey told his audience in Fuzhou: "It is only when our traditions and our customs fail to allow for changing conditions and get in the way of our achieving our goals that we recognize the need to alter them or abandon them."[139]

What norm measures the efficacy of ritual-customs? For Confucius, the measure is harmony (*he* 和). Social forms are *better* when they enable more varied qualities (*zhi* 質) to obtain expression, and *worse* when they enable fewer. Dewey's democratic ideal in *The Public and Its Problems*, having come to fruition alongside his own reconstruction of custom, intersects with this

Confucian ideal. For Dewey, the ideal society is one in which individual contributors enjoy their own share in the social harmony while all members of the community appreciate the contribution of one another in sustaining the value shared. As Dewey writes: "*From the standpoint of the individual, it consists in having a responsible share according to capacity in forming and directing the activities of the groups to which one belongs and in participating according to need in the values which the groups sustain. From the standpoint of the groups, it demands liberation of the potentialities of members of a group in harmony with the interests and goods which are common.*"[140] If one is intent on finding a Western equivalent of what *he* 和 signifies in Confucian social philosophy, it is hard to improve upon Dewey's ideal.

Dewey's focus on group dynamics in *The Public and Its Problems* carries over from his "Lectures on Social and Political Philosophy" in Beijing—such that it is more accurate "to think of society as being constituted of people in many sorts of groupings, rather than being made up of collections of individual persons considered as entities."[141] With respect to the "individuals" that result, David L. Hall and Roger T. Ames have pointed out that "like Dewey's understanding of the individual, the Confucian conception is dynamic, entailing a complex of social roles."[142] This is no doubt true, but from the standpoint of intra-cultural philosophy it can be stated more concretely. Dewey's notion of the "individual" in *The Public and Its Problems* is not only "like" the Confucian conception. Dewey's notion, in reality, is an amalgamated extension of that very conception, since his China-related experiences became woven into the fabric of his own social and political outlook before he arrived at his mature position.

That position, as formulated in 1930's *Individualism Old and New*, is that "assured and integrated individuality is the product of definite social relationships and publically acknowledged functions."[143] By this point, Dewey had fully assimilated the Confucian idea that "individuals" as such were *impossible* without the medium of ritual-customs (*li* 禮). This did not happen instantly. According to Abraham Edel, it would take Dewey a few years *after* the China trip to fully "fashion a moral meaning for individuality to replace the discarded general idea of individualism."[144] The so-called "lost individual," as Dewey would come to see it, is the by-product of a disintegration of customs and traditions that once gave meaning to "individuality." Such disintegration is what Dewey observed happening in China. So too, in the American context, the individual becomes lost because "the scene in which individuality is created has been transformed." America, Dewey argues, is no longer a place in which its own "individualistic" traditions work (*xing* 行). The vast frontier has been exhausted. The old pioneer tradition of the "rugged individual" has become an anachronism. In cases such as these, as Dewey says: "Traditional ideas are more than irrelevant. They are an encumbrance."¹⁴⁵ The American frontier is not coming back. Ritual-customs (*li*) intertwined with such conditions *have* to change, for they no longer give rise to viable individuals.

Again—such analysis, structurally and tactically, mirrors the kind of inquiry that Dewey was promoting in China. While many elements surely predate Dewey's visit to China, his understanding of how "custom" relates to "individualism" was specifically nourished on Chinese soil. Turning his attention back to the American scene, Dewey had a clearer sense of how sustaining the *dao* 道 of the American tradition required identifying those elements in the national character that could be reconstructed in contemporary ways. Accordingly, if the "frontier" mentality is to continue to mean anything in an ever more crowded and diversified United States, Dewey suggests that the "adventure of the individual" now turn its sights toward the "un-subdued social frontier."¹⁴⁶ This would be in keeping with conditions as they stand. As Jay Martin observes, "Dewey did not yet have a suitable name for this new integration" (that of conditions-customs-and-individuals).¹⁴⁷ After China, however, the word "harmony" gets used more and more often in his discussions. From *Individualism Old and New*:

> Individuals will re-find themselves only as their ideas and ideals are brought into harmony with the realities of the age in which they act. The task of attaining harmony is not an easy one. But it is more negative than it seems. If we could inhibit the principles and standards that are merely traditional . . . individuals might in consequence find themselves in possession of objects to which imagination and emotion would stably attach themselves.¹⁴⁸

However the influence was transmitted, Dewey's position comes to echo the basically Confucian understanding that achieving harmony (or *he* 和) is the primary function of ritual-custom (*li* 禮).¹⁴⁹ In Dewey's mind, the American situation is now marked by "the absence of harmony within the state of society."¹⁵⁰ Between the two extremes of the "Radical/Conservative" dichotomy, the intelligent (or *ming* 明) response is clear: it is to reflect on operative "custom-patterns" as they relate to existing conditions and to reconstruct the social complex such that individual lives can be most fully expressed and realized. The degree to which societies fail to do this is the degree to which they withhold human dignity from their citizens.

Sadly, we often learn this the hard way. On October 17, 2016, Jacques Camille Picoux (Bi Ansheng), artist and retired lecturer in French literature at National Taiwan University, was found deceased outside of his apartment building in Taipei. He was sixty-eight years old. He had jumped from the roof of the building. Picoux's life partner of thirty-five years, Tseng Ching-chao, had recently died after a painful battle with cancer. During Tseng's illness, Picoux faced strict visitation limits at the hospital because he and Tseng were not legally related. In fact, they were "strangers" under Taiwanese law, and as a result Tseng faced procedural hurdles in his attempt to leave his assets to Picoux. According to friends, the heartbreaking circumstances under which Tseng died were too much for Picoux to overcome. He fell into a deep depression and then took his own life.[151]

At the time of writing, Taiwan is the first and only Asian government to have legalized same-sex marriage, and much of this owes to the tragic story of Tseng and Picoux, which received extensive press coverage on the island. Public opinion in Taiwan shifted considerably in a short span of time, between 2013 (when a bill legalizing same-sex marriage failed to pass in parliamentary committee) and 2017 when it did. There has been a similarly rapid change in public opinion in the United States, with polling in the early 2000s averaging 30 to 40 percent in favor of same-sex marriage and then rising to an all-time high of 61 percent in 2016.[152]

As suggested earlier, the continuing struggles of LBGTQ communities illustrate well the "three stages" of social progress that Dewey outlines in his "China lectures." In the first stage, the oppressed disappear into what is presumed to be the "necessary order of things." In the second stage, there is "restlessness and discontent," during which the "conservative" marginalizes the so-called "radical" who wishes to change things. In the third stage, the "progressive" cuts through the "Radical/Conservative" stalemate and treats the problem in terms of the "social need and benefit" of the groups involved. As Dewey teaches, such approaches rely on intelligence (or *ming* 明) and this means making adjustments along the way—examining "customs, conventions, institutions," so as to "keep the good and improve or do away with the worse."[153] Confucian thinking provides a dynamic normative framework in which to consider how well ritual-customs (*li* 禮) work in making human lives richer and more significant.

There will always be more conservative readings of Confucianism. For those like May Sim, Confucius teaches that "the social ideal has been achieved in the Zhou *li* 禮 and all we need is to realize it."[154] Confucianism thus becomes irretrievable for us. For others like Philip J. Ivanhoe, "Heaven" (*tian* 天) has a "grand plan" with us in mind and to read Confucius otherwise raises the modern specter of "secular humanism," with its threat that "faith in classical culture would be transformed into the open-ended search for the best form of culture."[155] Such an ultra-conservative reading rests on select Greek-medieval assumptions along with a literal reading of *tian* 天-related passages in the *Analects*. More will be said about this in part II of this volume.

Such interpretations, which freeze the meanings of Confucianism into a fixed set of practices or a divinely sanctioned "grand plan" or "scheme," do not address it as a living tradition. Confucianism *lives* because what animates it is arguably the supplest normative measure in world philosophy: harmony (*he* 和). Unless Confucius had an unorthodox understanding of this ancient Chinese concept (and neither Sim nor Ivanhoe establishes that he did), then the most philosophically and hermeneutically defensible thing to do is to understand him as endorsing the process of sustaining the *dao* 道 of tradition while remaining sensitive to the moving dynamics (*dongjing* 動靜) of change. As the Master says, it is not for us to know what the next hundred generations will bring. If *dao* prevails, it will do so as it always has—by sustaining continuity between means-and-ends and adapting to cultural changes over time—preserving what works (*xing* 行), just as the ancients had done from the Xin to the Yin and the Yin to the Zhou.[156]

As will be argued in part II, the "Heaven's plan" reading of early Confucianism is quirky and has its own special demerits. For now, we simply observe that, if it is true that "Heaven has a plan for human beings," then it is impossible to determine whether or not couples like Tseng and Picoux were entitled to be married from a Confucian perspective. To assert that same-sex marriage conforms to "Heaven's plan" has as much, or as little standing as asserting that it does not. There is nothing to empirically weigh (*quan* 權) or to intelligently consider. On the contrary, harmony (*he* 和), as Chenyang Li demonstrates, is a *working* norm, one that demands intelligence (*ming* 明) precisely because it "does not admit a fixed formula, and is open-ended and continuously self-renewing." By restoring harmony (*he*) to its rightful place at the center of Confucian thinking, Li provides a more philosophically nuanced, historically accurate, and concretely useful account of the tradition—one that displays a fundamentally "practical attitude and pragmatic approach" toward problems in the social realm.[157]

Ren 仁 and Human Association

Before leaving off the present chapter, more needs to be said about another key idea in Confucian philosophy: *ren* 仁. This term is central to the teachings of Confucius, appearing over one hundred times in the *Analects*. It is also one of the most obscure terms in the text. As Ni Peimin observes, "Nowhere in the book can one find a precise definition of it, nor have translators been able to reach an agreement on any satisfying English translation."[158] Mary Bockover describes the term as "the real, objective, but nonetheless mysterious quality of moral and spiritual integrity that eludes identification."[159] Amy Olberding identifies it accordingly as at once "the most important and the most opaque" term in the *Analects*.[160] What does the term mean?

The fact that *ren* 仁 refers to habits and attitudes that make one qualitatively "human" (*ren* 人) is manifest. According to the etymology provided in the Han era *Shuowen* lexicon, the character is composed of the "human" (*ren*) along with the number "two" (*er* 二). This would underscore the relational character of traits that are deemed "human" in the tradition. The English translation of *ren* 仁 might be something like "associated humanity"—i.e. that which is cultivated when two or more humans are associated.

The term, however, is not merely descriptive—it describes how humans *ought* to live. As such, it is a virtue that is cultivated through ritual-custom (*li* 禮) and thus never in solitude.[161] "Through cultural form (*wen* 文) the exemplary person gathers friends," Confucius teaches, "and through friends associated humanity (*ren*) is supported."[162] To be *ren* is to be productively related to *other* people, and this requires that ritual-customs function as they should in the social complex. Again, the most important function of ritual-custom is to promote harmony (*he* 和).[163] This means that the raw qualities (*zhi* 質) of each person are integrated and appreciated in forms (*wen* 文) that serve to showcase their contributions. Meanwhile, each person is beneficiary of a social order that affords the positive freedom to *grow* in one's relations and thereby live a properly human life. As Dewey observes: "The deepest urge of every human being [is] to feel that he or she does count for something with other human beings and receives a recognition from them as counting for something."[164] Confucius recognizes the same basic need and his philosophy is largely focused on creating the conditions for satisfying it.

"Association," for Dewey, is a basic feature of human nature. It is hardly, however, a feature that is restricted to human activity. "Association in the sense of connection and combination is a 'law' of everything known to exist," he observes. "Nothing has been discovered which acts in entire isolation." Association is among those "mysteries of *fact*" that do not open themselves to further ontological explanation. "If there is any mystery about the matter," Dewey writes, "it is the mystery that the universe is the kind of universe [that] it is."[165] Since the world is one in which association is the rule, it makes sense that things reveal their natures in the degree to which they enter into associative transactions.

As Dewey argues in his 1928 article, "The Inclusive Philosophic Idea," every philosophical question and problem must be placed within an associative framework in order to be sensibly treated and understood. This must be done, however, empirically and with specificity. Association in general "is a wholly formal category."[166] There is nothing much to say about "association" *per se*—again, it is simply a mystery of *fact*. There is, however, an "intelligible question about human association," namely—"Not the question how individuals or singular beings come to be connected, but how they come to be connected in *just those ways* which give human communities traits so different from those which mark assemblies of electrons, unions of trees in forests, swarms of insects, herds of sheep, and constellations of stars."[167] Dewey insists that, "In such a comparison of definite types of association, the social, in its human sense, is the richest, fullest, and most delicately subtle of any mode actually experienced."[168] This rich complex of conditions, "upon which human beings associate and live together," is for Dewey "summed up in the word *culture*."[169] As such, culture is the matrix through which potentials of a seemingly miraculous depth and complexity are released, and questions about culture pertain to the kinds of associations involved in their happening.

Thus, the difficulty that we face in translating *ren* 仁 into English is the same difficulty that Confucius had when his students asked him what it was. What *single* description or example covers all the virtues of "human association"? As Roger T. Ames explains, there is no one word that covers "the broad meaning contained in *ren* that references an entire person—the cultivated moral, aesthetic, religious, intellectual, and even physical habits that are expressed in one's relations with others."[170] The term is surely limited, however, by virtue of its being normative, i.e., not descriptive of *every* mode of human association but only those that are regarded as distinctly "human" in a discretionary sense. Thus, just as types (*lei* 類) in early China are matters of discretion, *ren* is originally employed as a stative verb corresponding to the noun "human" (*ren* 人) which the aristocratic classes of the Zhou used to distinguish themselves from those who were *not* human—i.e., barbarian tribes and others who might be "civilizable by the adoption of Chinese customs" but who were, as A. C. Graham explains, "until civilized [to be] classed rather with the beasts and birds."[171] *Ren* 仁 would thus come to signify, as Arthur Waley concludes, behavior that is "'human' as opposed to 'animal'" in the sense of being *worthy* of the human, "as distinct from the behavior of the mere beast."[172]

Such behavior is expressed in practices that distinguish human behaviors from the behaviors of nonhuman animals, and this is why associated humanity (*ren* 仁) and ritual-custom (*li* 禮) are so closely integrated. In one of the sharpest rebukes in the *Analects*, for instance, Confucius disparages the errant Zaiwo for not endorsing the customary three-year mourning period on the death of one's parents. "One year is enough," says Zaiwo. Confucius criticizes his attitude as "not *ren*" (*buren* 不仁), which suggests that Zaiwo's response to the ritual-custom (*li*) is subhuman in register.[173] Humans (*ren* 人)

properly mourn for their parents—animals, however, do not. Somewhere in that fact lies the difference between humans and animals.

This raises a by-now familiar question. Within the complex of associations that enable humans to behave in "human" (*ren* 人) ways, is there a single generic feature that makes the difference? As we saw in chapter 7 of the previous volume, Xunzi suggests that language makes the difference. "What makes humans 'human,' " he argues, "lies not in being featherless bipeds, but in having the ability to make distinctions (*bian* 辨)."[174] While continuing to possess the animal body, we are fundamentally social animals with the unique ability to distinguish ourselves from other animals through social organization (*qun* 群) and the adoption of ritually delineated roles.[175] As Xunzi sees it: "When it comes to distinctions, none are more important than social roles (*fen* 分), and in establishing social roles, nothing is more important than ritual-custom (*li* 禮)."[176]

It is difficult to say whether or not Confucius subscribes to this view. As we have seen, Confucius taught that, "Human beings are similar in their natures (*xing* 性), but vary with respect to their cultural practices (*xi* 習)."[177] The Master does not volunteer any precise account of what makes us "human" (*ren* 人), leaving space for his followers (and for us) to reflect on the question. The ideal of *ren* 仁, however, would suggest that the answer lies deeper than linguistic distinctions. By not recognizing the proper mourning period for his parents, Zaiwo displays not only his obliviousness to a social role name (*ming* 名) and its semantic associations. He shows, more fundamentally, that he is incapable of *feeling* association with his parents to the depth and extent that was the "human" standard. *This* is why he is found to be *buren* 不仁. As we will see in part II, the Confucian tradition turns more decisively toward feeling (*xin* 心) as the benchmark for human-level experience in the philosophy of Mencius.

Dewey does not reduce the human difference to our ability to make distinctions (*bian* 辨) or create names (*ming* 名) *simpliciter* because for him there is something else at the "heart of language"—namely, *communication*. This, Dewey teaches, is the real means-and-end (or *dao* 道) of the human experience. Communication both "procures something wanted" and provides "an immediate enhancement of life, enjoyed for its own sake."[178] Humans associate with one another in myriad ways; but for Dewey, the "only form of association that is *truly* human . . . is the participation in meanings and goods that is effected by communication."[179]

In coming to understand what Dewey means by "communication," it is hard not to be moved by his insights. "Of all affairs, communication is the most wonderful," he writes. That something should pass from the plane of our inner experience, to be converted into a meaning that is shared with and participated in by another person, "is a wonder by the side of which transubstantiation pales." Human communication has become so ubiquitous and ordinary—such a commonplace—that we fail to recognize how miraculous it really is. "Even the dumb pang of an ache achieves significant existence when it can be designated and descanted upon," Dewey writes. "It ceases to be merely oppressive and becomes important; it gains importance, because it becomes representative; it has the dignity of an office."[180]

Simply to confide to a friend, "My elbow hurts when I bend it." Where? Right *here*. "Ah, that same thing happened to me." The world is utterly remade in such moments. Objects, meanings, and implications surface and interrelate. Sympathies, concerns, and solidarities intermingle and connect. "Language" does not capture the nature of such communion. As William James reminds us, "Each of us dichotomizes the Kosmos in a different place."[181] Yet these unbridgeable gaps feel so nearly closed when a friend comes calling to inquire, "How's your elbow today?" James asks: "What Makes a Life Significant?" The answer is simple. It is *shared experience*—our ability "to realize each other in this intense, pathetic, and important way." Where would any of us be, James asks, "were there no one willing to know us as we really are or ready to repay us for *our* insight by making recognizant return?"[182] Dewey builds upon James' vision when he reflects on the wonders of communication. It is the same fundamental truth that he expresses. Dewey puts it succinctly: "Shared experience is the greatest of human goods."[183] Period.

In its communicative function, ritual-custom (*li* 禮) can be thought of as a kind of "social grammar." Ames describes it accordingly, as the "language of body and gesture, of music and food, of roles and relationships."[184] Such social grammars allow communication to occur. In its modern form, the institution of marriage is one of the most ennobled and highly respected ritual-customs of shared human experience. At its best, Dewey suggests, marriage "is more intimate, more beautiful, and more mutually helpful, than any other form of human relationship." As he sees it, "The fact of sharing ambitions, hopes, experiences of joy and sorrow, especially of united planning and concern for the welfare and futures of children, builds up a certain community of life which is found in no other type of experience."[185] As such, marriage is a good example of how ritual-customs (*li*) enable forms of human association that lend themselves to communication on the deepest levels.

While what Dewey says about marriage is true, this has not always been the case. Marriage customs have evolved within the matrix of culture to fortify and support diverse human needs over time. As Stephanie Coontz demonstrates in her work: "For most of history it was inconceivable that people would choose their mates on the basis of something as fragile and irrational as love and then focus all their sexual, intimate, and altruistic desires on the resulting marriage." Such an idea is distinctly modern. "For thousands of years," Coontz explains, "marriage served so many economic, political, and social functions that the individual needs and wishes of its members (especially women and children) took second place."[186] This was certainly the case in traditional China.

So while the institution of marriage is a human universal, it is also widely variable and constantly evolving over time. As Dewey suggests, marriage in the West has traditionally suffered from its organization in an overly "economic" modality. Coverture was not legally challenged in the United States until 1874, when it was decided in *State vs. Oliver* that, "the old doctrine that a husband had the right to whip his wife, provided that he used a switch not larger than his thumb, is not the law in North Carolina."[187] In China, the institution has traditionally been organized within the "family" modality. Producing a male heir was its central function, and failure to do so was grounds for expelling one's wife. To this end, the practice of holding concubines became enshrined in the "Rules of the Household" (*neize* 內則) chapter of the *Rituals*.[188] Sinologists note that such practices were "a natural fallout of the family system and social structure that requires male descendants to conduct ancestor worship."[189] Given the weight of this tradition, marriages were routinely prearranged in the interests of the paternal clan. During the "New Culture" movement, women struggled against the oppressive results of such thinking and fought for the right of self-determination in marriage.[190] Despite progress in this area, the male-heir function of marriage continued unabated in Republican-era China. The practice of holding concubines, for instance, was not officially outlawed until 1949.

As the empirical facts regarding the history of marriage suggest, humans are indeed engaged in what conservatives fear most: "the open-ended search for the best form of culture." To equate this with "relativism," however, relies on what is probably the most tired pattern of thinking in the Western mind. Maintaining that things can be made *better* as conditions and sensibilities change is not "relativism." It only appears so to minds that deny that change actually happens. As Dewey says, "The idea that unless standards and rules are eternal and immutable they are not rules and criteria at all is childish."[191] Minds adjusted to the reality of change see things differently. "Change becomes significant of new possibilities and ends to be attained," writes Dewey: "it becomes prophetic of a better future."[192]

Adopting such a vision is well in keeping with the teachings of Confucius, provided that the *dao* 道 of tradition is properly understood. Reviewing the old in order to "realize the new" (*zhixin* 知新) makes little sense if nothing is new.[193] Custodians of *dao* always have one eye on the future, so that "instead of reproducing current habits, better habits shall be formed, and thus the future adult society [will] be an improvement on their own."¹⁹⁴ The key insight of Confucius is that, without "loving the ancients," such improvement is not likely to happen—in fact, it is almost certain *not* to happen.¹⁹⁵ "Not following in the footsteps of others, one does not gain entry into the inner chamber."¹⁹⁶ The Confucian ideal is to unite the "funded experience" of the past with an intelligence (*ming* 明) that looks to the future.¹⁹⁷ It is impossible to imagine entering the future without an operative tradition (*dao*)—without the experience and perspective that such continuity affords. When tradition falls away, individuals become "lost" in the present. The same thing happens, however, when tradition stands still.

As Li Chenyang says, harmony (*he* 和) in early Confucianism does not presuppose a "transcendent, static foundation," one that serves as a "pre-established order" to which particular harmonies must conform. Instead, it involves "an active process in which heterogeneous elements are brought into a mutually balancing, cooperatively enhancing, and often commonly benefitting relationship."¹⁹⁸ As such, it is corollary to that great mystery of Nature (*tian* 天)—"association." That association occurs, and that its elements become cooperatively enhancing is a datum that fits naturally into Chinese cosmology. Recall that each particular (*one*) enters into relations (*two*) and when this happens, orders emerge (*three*) in which particular traits reveal themselves as general types. Such orders achieve the one (*deyi* 得一) as units of possibility in the Great Continuum (*taiyi* 太一). Human association occurs within the same cosmological system. Human relationships are dynamic—they grow, change, can endure, and dissolve. There is no "pre-established order" to which they conform, but when they succeed they always bear the traits of unity (*yi* 一) and harmony (*he*).

As Aristotle teaches, human relationships coalesce around shared interests and experiences. Friendships endure so long as two people share a set of proclivities, and each takes reciprocal pleasure in the other's enjoyment of the same. Relationships take many forms, notes Aristotle: "Some drink together, others dice together, others join in athletic exercises and hunting, or in the study of philosophy, each class spending their days together in whatever they love most in life; for since they wish to live with their friends, they do and share in those things which give them the sense of living together."¹⁹⁹ Just as Aristotle asserts that human happiness is unthinkable without relationships, Dewey regards being in association as central to any healthy human living. As he says: "Individuals who are not bound together in associations, whether domestic, economic, religious, political, artistic, or educational are monstrosities."²⁰⁰

Dewey agrees with Aristotle that human beings are fundamentally social creatures, for whom relationships are indispensable.²⁰¹ "The notion of a state of nature in which individuals exist prior to entering into a social state," Dewey writes, is a "mythical condition."²⁰² Humans are *born* into association along with everything else. Accordingly, there is something "deep within human nature itself which pulls towards settled relationships," such that "happiness which is full of content and peace is found only in enduring ties with others, which reach to such depths that they go below the surface of conscious experience to form its undisturbed foundation."²⁰³

As Antonio S. Cua observes, when ritual-customs (*li* 禮) function properly, they serve to "delimit," "support," and "ennoble" those modes of association that enable human beings to flourish in concert with one another.²⁰⁴ In Dewey's terms, they enable *communication*. Through *li*, inchoate emotions are transmuted and shared—gratitude, joy, respect, deference, sorrow, and sympathy become not only felt but expressed. As instrumental-and-consummatory, such communication is the means-and-end (*dao* 道-activity) of the human experience. We enjoy such experience through sharing with others. "Various phases of participation by one in another's joy, sorrows, sentiments and purposes, are distinguished by the scope and depth of the objects that are held in common," Dewey writes—"from a momentary caress to continued insight and loyalty."²⁰⁵ Therein lies the essence of human significance.

The philosophies of Dewey and Confucius converge in arguing that positive effort is required to sustain the means-ends of human significance. As Dewey relates in his "Social and Political Philosophy" lectures, such phases of meaning "cannot be developed or realized except in association with others, interchange, [and through] flexible intercommunication."²⁰⁶ When ritual-customs (*li* 禮) are not functioning well, human communication is no longer enjoyed. One's raw (*zhi* 質) feelings are had in isolation, finding no adequate outlet through which to be shared and expressed. When this happens, the deeper harmonies (*he* 和) of human association condense into shallower pools of experience; a blander uniformity (*tong* 同) takes hold in which growth is retarded and ordered richness is abridged. As a result, there are fewer opportunities for significant experience to be had.

While the philosophical vocabularies of Dewey and Confucius differ, each exhibits concern with sustaining the cultural technologies that prevent this from happening. Achieving a society in which all members can communicate and realize human significance is the common goal—but it is one that presents complex challenges, and these are made especially steep in contemporary multicultural societies. We now have the conceptual tools at hand to consider some of these problems. Dewey and the Confucians each have a special term for that state in which full and moving communication is realized. Confucians call it *dao* 道 and Dewey calls it "democracy." In chapter 4, connections between these ideals will be experimented with and their pertinence to contemporary problems explored.

4

Pluralism and Democracy

> Democracy emphasizes not only free individual development . . . but also the development of associated living, the creation of a community of interests, and the cultivation of a common will . . . A society or a state can exist only on the basis of implicit common understandings and mutual communication between and among people. It is this common understanding and this mutual communication that have made social life possible.
>
> —John Dewey, National Peking Academy of Fine Arts, May 1919

Democracy vs. The Melting Pot

On Columbus Day in 1915, President Theodore Roosevelt gave a speech before the largely Irish-Catholic "Knights of Columbus" at Carnegie Hall in New York City. The topic was the emergence of so-called "hyphenated Americanism." The phrase referred to Americans who had immigrated to the United States but who still identified with their own cultural backgrounds, e.g., those who might call themselves Irish-American, Mexican-American, or Chinese-American, meaning to retain some continuity with the former term.

"There is no room in this country for hyphenated Americanism," boomed Roosevelt. "There is no such thing as a hyphenated American who is a good American. The only man who is a good American is the man who is an American and nothing else." This speech was delivered over a century ago, but it sounds like one that could be delivered by an American President today. In the opening decades of the twenty-first century, the tension between ethnicity and democracy has resurfaced at the center of political discourse in the United States and in Europe—just where it was in the opening decades of the twentieth century. The same issues that fueled two world wars: nationalism, economic protectionism, and ethnicity, have returned to center stage. The next few decades will reveal what, if anything, Western democracies have learned.

The Confucian ideal of harmony (*he* 和) speaks to our current situation, and it connects with American philosophy in important ways. As Chenyang Li suggests, however, the term has been routinely misunderstood. With respect to *wholes*, harmony does not imply any preordained "plan" or "scheme" that is imposed from above. Each harmony emerges from the constituents that succeed in making it up. Accordingly, with respect to *parts*, it is distinct from Aristotle's concept of "just proportion" among its constituents, which amounts to "equality of ratios" according to strictly mathematical considerations in the *Nicomachean Ethics*.[1] For Chinese thinkers, harmony instead implies equity (*gedeqisuo* 各得其所): "extending to each its proper due" given the circumstances that obtain and the results that follow.

Chenyang Li's work is helpful in distinguishing the elemental decisions that go into sustaining such harmonies in the social realm. As he observes, "harmony presupposes differences." This does not mean, however, that all differences are to be included. Rather, these fall into three classes: differences that we *accept*, differences that we *reject*, and differences that we *tolerate*. Such designations need to be made with respect to the dynamic coherence (*li* 理) of the whole. In the optimal scenario, we "embrace difference of the first kind," "cautiously examine and, when warranted, accept the third kind," and "strive to eliminate or minimize the second kind."[2] This is what "equity" means as a Chinese value—extending to each thing its "proper due." Generally speaking, the Chinese tradition approaches such matters differently than they are approached in the Greek-medieval tradition. In the Chinese tradition, the stress is on "weighing things up" (*quan* 權) in particular circumstances; whereas in the Greek-medieval tradition, the stress is on apprehending ratios that track onto fixed objects of knowledge.[3]

Six years prior to delivering his "hyphenated Americanism" speech, Roosevelt was in Washington for the city premier of Israel Zangwill's play, *The Melting Pot* (1905). The play, which was dedicated to President Roosevelt, portrayed itself as "The Great American Drama," an adaptation of *Romeo and Juliet* set in contemporary New York City. David, an immigrant Russian Jew, falls in love with Vera, an immigrant Russian Christian. Together, they unite as Americans to overcome the Old World prejudices that challenge their love. Naturally, they succeed. Watching as the setting sun gilds the copper flame of the torch on the Statue of Liberty, the protagonist declares: "It is the Fires of God around his Crucible! There she lays, the great Melting Pot—Listen! Can't you hear the roaring and the bubbling? There gapes her mouth, the harbor where a thousand mammoth feeders come from the ends of the world to pour in their human freight." As David proclaims: *"America is God's Crucible, the great Melting-Pot where all the races of Europe are melting and reforming . . . God is making the American!"*[4] David and Vera embrace as the curtain falls, and a burly Teddy Roosevelt could be seen protruding from his loge shouting to the playwright, "That's a great play, Mr. Zangwill. That's a great play!"[5]

Indeed, there is something beautiful and moving about the storyline. It reminds one that parochial differences between particular cultures can be overcome and deeper loyalties realized. Really—what is there not to like? Henceforth, the idea of America as a "Melting Pot" would take on a life of its own. Not, however, without some disturbing manifestations.[6]

"The theory of the Melting Pot always gave me rather a pang," Dewey confessed.[7] It grated against his aesthetic sensibilities. The idea, however, had become central in American political discourse and Dewey had to contend with it. In the years surrounding the First World War, questions about democracy and ethnicity loomed large in the United States, as did concerns about national loyalty. Dewey was critically engaged in these discussions. Having "lulled ourselves to sleep with the word 'Melting-Pot,'" he observes, "we have now turned to the word 'hyphenate' as denoting the last thing in scares with a thrill." Some were advocating compulsory military service as a means of forging a common national identity among disparate groups in the United States. Dewey rejected that idea. "My recognition of the need of agencies for creating a potent sense of a national ideal and of achieving habits which will make this sense a controlling power in action is not ungrudging," Dewey allows. "But the primary question is what *is* the national ideal, and to what kind of national service does it stand related?" To use military training to foster a national identity among diverse groups would only "reduce them to an anonymous and drilled homogeneity," he submits, "an amalgam whose uniformity would hardly go deeper than the uniforms of the soldiers."[8]

The intelligent (*ming* 明 or *dao* 道-like) approach to this problem would be to address together the means-and-end of forging a national identity. As Dewey says, "We must ask what a real nationalism, a real Americanism, is like. For unless we know our own character and purpose we are not likely to be intelligent in our selection of the means to further them."[9] The first question to ask then is what is the *distinct character* of America as we find it? It is not the "legalistic individualism" that informs our founding documents—for as Dewey reminds us: "[this] is not indigenous; it is borrowed from a foreign tradition." Moreover, as the shortcomings of classical liberalism become increasingly apparent, "many of us are consciously weaned from it." So again—*what is it that makes the American experience distinct?* "We need a new and more political Emerson," he suggests, to alert to us to our national character.[10]

America's original seer here is Walt Whitman. As Americans, we turn to him to reconnect with our national spirit. *Leaves of Grass* (1855) is a quintessentially "American" document. Instantly and almost unnervingly intimate, the poet cuddles up against the reader to recite a love song to the human race—a stream of unvarnished particulars, each human being a poem inside a poem. The teeming diversity of Whitman's New York City is delivered unabridged. "I speak the password primeval . . . I give the sign of democracy," he exclaims. "By God! I will accept nothing which all cannot have their counterpart of on the same terms."[11] This sentiment aligns with the Chinese value of equity (*gedeqisuo* 各得其所)—but it is an elusive ideal, and even Whitman wavers.[12] America is a puzzle because it evokes the age-old problems of "Whole/Part" and "One/Many." As a poem, America embraces the entirety of the human race: "I am large . . . I contain multitudes."[13] Among its multitudinous parts, however, each has its own character and biases in tension with its counterparts. Ideally, such an arrangement works. As one Whitman scholar understands it, "the first edition of *Leaves of Grass* was a utopian document," one in which cultural differences are preserved in the social landscape while also "dissolved by affirmation of the cross-fertilization" of its varied parts.[14]

Given its dynamic nature, harmony (*he* 和) is frustrated by the insistence that a single, preselected denominator underwrite or determine the whole. Wanting metaphysical guidance in this area, one naturally turns to William James. James' pluralism emerges in tension with the "One" that was popular as the "Absolute" in the monistic idealism of his day. James' key insight, which is radical in Western philosophy but rather unremarkable from an East Asian point of view, is that the "Whole/Part" and "One/Many" problems that result from monistic idealism are intractable so long as reality is regarded in static terms. "Time keeps budding into new moments," James writes, "every one of which presents a content which in its individuality never was before and will never be again."[15] With this as the starting point, "wholeness" becomes *modal*. It becomes a perpetually reconstituted feature of reality the character of which constantly changes.

This is easier to envision in Daoist terms. Since *dao* 道 is always giving birth to novelty, the moment one designates everything here (*you* 有) as a "whole" it has already changed because something new has arrived. *Now* it is a different whole, and *now* it is another. Wholeness is thus never static. Given the steady influx of novelty, things change *within* relations of coherence (*li* 理) such that "oneness" is a dynamic *way* of being. There are numberless *ways* of being "one." For James, "Things are 'with' one another in many ways, but nothing includes everything, or dominates over everything. The word 'and' trails along after every sentence."[16] In such a world, "there are innumerable modes of union," James notes. There is "neither absolute oneness nor absolute manyness," but rather "a mixture of well-definable modes of both." One-and-many are thus bound in what Dewey would eventually call *Togetherness*: "co-ordinate features of the natural world."[17]

These are core ideas in the American philosophical tradition, and they are highly original in Western thought. In fact, for all practical purposes, William James single-handedly *invents* the modern term "pluralism"—which is remarkable to consider. Given the illustrious career of this term in contemporary discourse, it is surprising that James' insights are not more often evoked. Perhaps such neglect is due to the fact that his reflections on pluralism were primarily confined to metaphysics and epistemology. James never got around to applying the notion to issues in the social and political realm. He had students, however, who did.

Horace Kallen, in his 1915 article in *The Nation*, "Democracy vs. the Melting Pot: A Study of American Nationality," formulates a truly American, pluralistic alternative to the ersatz "Melting Pot" ideal. One century later, his argument still holds up remarkably well. Kallen begins by providing a broad overview of American immigration: the economic forces that drive it, the stratification that it introduces, and how "Americanization" as the adaptation of Anglo-Saxon attitudes by other ethnic groups factors into it. His conclusion is that "Americanization," understood as the widespread adoption of Anglo-Saxon attitudes, is never going to happen—the situation is simply too complex and variable. Thus, as it stands, suggests Kallen, "America" has yet to occur. "America is a word: as a historic fact, a democratic ideal of life, it is not realized at all," he writes. The practical question then, Kallen asks, is *what kind* of society does the dominant classes in the United States really want? He observes:

> At the present time there is no dominant American mind. Our spirit is inarticulate, not a voice, but a chorus of many voices each singing a rather different tune. How to get order out of this cacophony is the question for all those who are concerned about those things which alone justify wealth and power, concerned about justice, the arts, literature, philosophy, science. What must, what *shall* this cacophony become—a unison or a harmony?
>
> As in an orchestra, every type of instrument has its specific timbre and tonality, founded in its substance and form; as every type has its appropriate theme and melody in the whole symphony, so in a society each ethnic group is the natural instrument, its spirit and culture are its theme and melody, and the harmony and dissonances and discords of them all make civilization . . . within the limits set by nature they may vary at will, and the range and the variety of the harmonies may become wider and richer and more beautiful. But the question is, do the dominant classes in America want such a society?[18]

Dewey read Kallen's article with great interest and immediately wrote to him hoping to arrange a time to meet to discuss its thesis. In a rare personal aside, Dewey shares with Kallen reflections on his own ethnic heritage in relation to the national debate:

> To put it personally: My forbears on both sides are Americans for over two hundred fifty years: they were I suppose partly English and partly Flemish in the beginning. I have some sentimental interest in the Flemish part, next to none in the English. And I cannot remember the time when I had any interest in the Anglo-Saxon talk. I want to see this country American and that means the English tradition reduced to a strain along with others. It is convenient for "Americans" to put the blame of things they don't like on the "foreigners," but I don't believe that goes very deep; it is mostly irritation at some things they don't like and an unwillingness to go below the surface. I quite agree with your orchestra idea, but upon condition we really get a symphony and not a lot of different instruments playing simultaneously. I never did care for the Melting Pot metaphor, but genuine assimilation *to one another*—not to Anglo-Saxondom—seems to be essential to an America. That each cultural section should maintain its distinctive literary and artistic traditions seems to me most desirable, but in order that it might have the more to contribute to others.[19]

"Genuine assimilation *to one another*"—this is the touchstone for Dewey's vision of a pluralistic, multi-ethnic, culturally diverse America. "To maintain that all the constituent elements, geographical, racial, cultural, in the United States should be put in the same pot and turned into a uniform and unchanging product," Dewey writes, "is distasteful." We must rather "respect those elements of diversification in cultural traits which differentiate our national life."[20]

The true nature of the American character now comes into view—"the peculiarity of *our* nationalism," Dewey writes, "is its internationalism."[21] "In our internal constitution we are actually interracial and international," he explains. "It remains to [be seen]," Dewey writes, "whether we have the courage to face this fact and the wisdom to think out the plan of action which it indicates."[22]

These are profound statements about what America means. In order to fully appreciate them, one must overcome prevailing Eurocentric conceptions of the American experience and assume a broader view. Human history in North America began with Eurasian migrations 30,000 years ago, resulting in the evolution of a patchwork of cultural groups with diverse languages and customs. The arrival of Europeans is often treated as the "beginning" of the

American experience—such that we imagine that the American character was forged in a mythical, stark encounter between "humans" (i.e., Europeans) and an untamed "wilderness." This narrative is entirely false. North America possessed a rich cultural history prior to the arrival of Europeans, and the latter's experience was shaped through its encounter with the former. While Native American cultures were nearly annihilated by European-borne diseases (populations declined by as much as 90 percent between 1492 and 1650), there was a sophisticated cultural matrix in place along the eastern seaboard when the Europeans landed. They were greeted by existing territorial claims, trade networks, multiple languages, material technologies, tribal identities, arts and customs, animosities and alliances, and so on. The "New World" was hardly a blank slate. As Scott L. Pratt argues, the "problem of origins" in American philosophy has yet to fully recognize the context in which the American mind actually took shape.

American thinkers, most famously Ralph Waldo Emerson in his "American Scholar," sought to distinguish themselves from European thinkers and to express something uniquely "American." But what was this thing? Pratt traces this indigenous "something" back to Roger Williams (1603–1683), our most famous exponent of religious liberty and defender of Native American land claims against British colonial charters. Williams learned to communicate with Native Americans and published a phrasebook, *A Key Into the Language of America* in 1643. He established relationships of trust and respect with indigenous peoples, especially with the Narragansett tribe. Against the colonial attitude of those like Cotton Mather, for whom Native Americans were future Christians at best, Williams' intra-cultural experience involved assimilating the Narragansett custom of *wunnégin* ("Welcoming Strangers") into his own Christian outlook, resulting in a concept of acceptance, friendliness, and civility unique to the American character. As Pratt demonstrates, "Williams' ideal of a plural community stands in strong contrast to Locke's notion of toleration on a number of points." Ideals that would eventually become the "common core of classical pragmatism," which Pratt identifies as "interaction, pluralism, community, and growth," resonate more strongly with *wunnégin* than with anything in classical European liberalism.[23]

While this ideal becomes diffuse in its influence and fails historically to prevent the emergence of the "colonial attitude" and the enshrinement of classical liberalism in the United States constitution, its spirit ought still to be recognized as the indigenous spirit of America. Anyone who identifies as "American," in any case, should understand this heritage and the values native to the continent. "Welcoming Strangers" is what America means.

Dewey understood, as well as anyone, that the most important agency for sustaining and transmitting such a welcoming character is a robust public education system—one that transmits America's immigrant heritage and its significance. Such liberal education is the first line of defense against those who would be enemies to America. Dewey refers to some of these agents as "the enemy within." These are "the misleaders who attempt to create disunity and hatred among Americans," those who "preach hatred and discrimination against Americans who happen to be darker skinned, speak with an accent, or share a minority faith." Such enemies "work untiringly to exaggerate racial and religious differences" and thus "do not grasp the uniqueness of America."[24] As Dewey warns: "Skillful politicians and other self-seekers have always known how to play cleverly upon patriotism, and upon ignorance of other peoples, to identify nationalism with latent hatred of other nations."[25]

For Dewey, liberal education ideally *liberates* the student from the limitation of the group biases into which he or she is born and prepares the student for the "broader environment" of America and the world. By necessity, in order to ensure continuity and core learning standards, subject matter in public education must remain relatively uniform. "The intermingling in the school of youth of different races, differing religions, and unlike customs," however, "creates for all a new and broader environment. Common subject matter accustoms all to a unity of outlook upon a broader horizon than is visible to the members of any group while it is isolated."[26]

Given recent events in American politics, it is worth hearing from Dewey at length about the role that public education plays in relation to "American nationalism." Hardly a more cogent statement could be desired:

> I want to mention only two elements in the nationalism which our education should cultivate. The first is that the American nation is itself complex and compound. Strictly speaking it is interracial and international in its make-up. It is composed of a multitude of peoples speaking different tongues, inheriting diverse traditions, cherishing varying ideals of life. This fact is basic to *our* nationalism as distinct from that of other peoples. Our national motto, "One from Many," cuts deep and extends far. It denotes a fact which doubtless adds to the difficulty of getting a genuine unity. But it also immensely enriches the possibilities of the result to be attained. No matter how loudly any one proclaims his Americanism, if he assumes that any one racial strain, any one component culture, no matter how early settled it was in our territory, or how effective it has proved in its own land, is to furnish a pattern to which all other strains and cultures are to conform, he is a traitor to an American nationalism. Our unity cannot be a homogeneous thing like that of the separate states of

Europe from which our population is drawn; it must be a unity created by drawing out and composing into a harmonious whole the best, the most characteristic which each contributing race and people has to offer.

I find that many who talk the loudest about the need of a supreme and unified Americanism of spirit really mean some special code or tradition to which they happen to be attached. They have some pet tradition which they would impose upon all. In thus measuring the scope of Americanism by some single element which enters into it they are themselves false to the spirit of America. Neither Englandism nor New-Englandism, neither Puritan nor Cavalier any more than Teuton or Slav, can do anything but furnish one note in a vast symphony.

The way to deal with hyphenism, in other words, is to welcome it, but to welcome it in the sense of extracting from each people its special good, so that it shall surrender into a common fund of wisdom and experience what it especially has to contribute. All of these surrenders and contributions taken together create the national spirit of America. The dangerous thing is for each factor to isolate itself, to try to live off its past, and then to attempt to impose itself upon other elements, or, at least, to keep itself intact and thus refuse to accept what other cultures have to offer, so as thereby to be transmuted into authentic Americanism.

In what is rightly objected to as hyphenism the hyphen has become something which separates one people from other peoples—and thereby prevents American nationalism. Such terms as Irish-American or Hebrew-American or German-American are false terms because they seem to assume something which is already in existence called America to which the other factor may be externally hitched on. The fact is the genuine American, the typical American, is himself a hyphenated character. This does not mean that he is part American, and that some foreign ingredient is then added. It means that, as I have said, he is international and interracial in his make-up. He is not American plus Pole or German. But the American is himself Pole-German-English-French-Spanish-Italian-Greek-Irish-Scandinavian-Bohemian-Jew-and so on. The point is to see to it that the hyphen connects instead of separates. And this means at least that our public schools shall teach each factor to respect every other, and shall take pains to enlighten all as to the great past contributions of every strain in our composite make-up. I wish our teaching of American history in the schools would take more account of the great waves of migration by which our land for over three centuries has been continuously built up, and make every pupil conscious of the rich breadth of our national make-up. When every pupil recognizes all the factors which have gone into our being, he will continue to prize and reverence that coming from his own past, but he will think of it as honored in being simply one factor in forming a whole, nobler and finer than itself.[27]

Such a statement leaves no ambiguity about where Dewey stands on the question of "American nationalism." Over the years, some have misunderstood his approach to public education as endorsing "Americanization" in a more uniform sense. Sidney Hook was once asked about this, and he put such readings to rest. "[The] *whole spirit* of Dewey's theory of democracy and education requires a commitment to the philosophy of cultural pluralism," Hook replies. "You can announce it from the housetops on my authority."[28]

Guojia 國家 and the Great Community

Alongside texts like *The Public and Its Problems* and *Individualism Old and New*, the Confucian dynamic of ritual-custom (*li* 禮) and harmony (*he* 和) recommends itself as a framework in which to envision the challenges of American democracy. As Dewey observes, America's (now unofficial) national motto, "From the Many, One" (*E Pluribus Unum*),[29] "cuts deep and extends far." The notion, however, that the "one" emerges from the "many" without usurping the integrity of "each" is difficult to conceptualize without the kind of process-oriented assumptions that early Chinese thinkers exhibit. (Just ask Plato's *Parmenides*.) In this respect, the Chinese notions of harmony (*he*) and coherence (*li* 理) provide indispensable conceptual tools, and they have the added benefit of being grounded in a philosophical vision that responds well to current understandings in the natural sciences.

Another feature that renders Confucian thought conversant with the natural sciences is its identification of human social orders with the family (*jia* 家), such that to speak of the "Chinese nation" is to speak of the "nation as a family" (*guojia* 國家). Naturalistically speaking, this is a proposition that appeals metaphorically to our actual instincts. Human beings are animals that exhibit family-group behaviors and display primary loyalties or partiality (*bie* 別) toward their kin. In the Warring States period, Mozi argues that such preferences are not conducive to social order and that humans would be better off replacing such preferences with impartial concern (*jianai* 兼愛).[30]

Such an argument sounds nice, but it is no match for human nature. Kin-based emotional ties are not mere accessories. Like those of other placental mammals, human parenting behaviors involve a complex set of neuropeptides covariant with evolved structures such as internal gestation, lactation, and infant attachment behavior. We are born into social groups already characterized by kin-based emotional ties. In securing the resources needed for survival, hominoid coalitions have proven capable of cooperating and developing larger emotional loyalties. But nothing—and hardly something as feeble as logical argument—is going to override the massive evolutionary history that makes us partial toward our own families. At this stage in its history, the human species is family-borne and bound—and while this is a contingent outcome of natural selection, it is not changing any time soon.

Naturally, then, the loyalties of human beings begin in the family, and as larger loyalties are cultivated they remain grounded in such filial instincts (*xiao* 孝) and grow from there. As Confucius teaches, filial piety serves as the root (*ben* 本) from which associated humanity (*ren* 仁) extends.[31] The "nation as a family" (*guojia* 國家) metaphor reminds us that there is only "one root" (*yiben* 一本) from which our larger loyalties grow, and as they are realized they most naturally model themselves on the facts and norms characteristic of the primary unit of social cohesion: *the family*. For Confucian thinkers, the family is emblematic of harmony (*he* 和) itself. Each constituent ingredient contributes to an order the worth of which is greater than the sum of its parts.

E Pluribus Unum is a similar ideal. Emerging alongside process-oriented thinking in the West, the phrase traces back to the Latin translation of Heraclitus' "Tenth Fragment," which reads: "Out of many there comes one, and out of one, many."[32] Its more direct classical source, however, is Virgil. The poet uses the phrase in his "Moretum," a poem in honor of the herb-cheese salad favored by the Romans. Moretum brings together the "many" (garlic, parsley, rue, onions, cheese, salt, coriander, vinegar, and oil) and mixes them into "one"—*E Pluribus Unum*. Thus, *"Round all the mortar doth he go at last and into one coherent ball doth bring, the different portions, that it may name and likeness of a finished salad fit."*[33]

The culinary association behind America's motto calls to mind the soup analogy that informs harmony (*he* 和) in the Chinese tradition. This culinary ideal, again, is that the raw qualities (*zhi* 質) of various ingredients are showcased in the finished whole, just as music brings together different instruments in a symphonic harmony. When this is done well (*shan* 善), the process of bringing things together forms a coherence (*li* 理) in which each constituent is appreciated. For Confucians, family is ideally such an order. It facilitates the meaningful inclusion of its members and gives expression to their unique roles in the process.³⁴ The concept of "nation as a family" (*guojia* 國家) is founded on such an ideal—even to the extent that the distinction between the "nation" and the "family" often becomes unclear in early Confucian texts, as Sor-hoon Tan demonstrates.³⁵

With respect to American nationhood, the challenge is to forge a truly multiethnic, international "family" within its borders. This involves calling forth and preserving differences. Horace Kallen sees the American nation not as a "Melting Pot" but as a "Cooking Pot" in which the mixing actually draws out different strains of human culture for inclusion in the finished product. "The institutions of the Republic," he writes, "have become the liberating cause and the background for the rise of the cultural consciousness and social autonomy" of cultural groups. "On the whole," he argues, "Americanization has not repressed nationality. Americanization has liberated nationality."³⁶

The truth of this remains an empirical question. Surely there is a vast difference between first- and third-generation Americans, with the dilution of cultural difference plain to see. Americanization thus requires, as Dewey says, a robust public commitment to its own multicultural heritage. The social, economic, and industrial forces that drive homogenization in America are not uniquely "American" forces—or so I would submit. Global capitalism threatens local cultures *everywhere*, including in the United States. The best hope for America is to reconnect with its own national spirit. To regard *E Pluribus Unum* as a process of homogenization (or *tong* 同) violates America's history as well as its deepest philosophical heritage. Harmony (*he* 和) serves as an important corrective to such misperceptions—an ancient Chinese ideal that, odd as it may sound, has the potential to remind America of what it means to achieve a more perfect union.

There is little room for Pollyannaish hyperbole in this world. I readily admit that the challenges that we face are steep. Failures in both the United States and the People's Republic of China are plain to see. This means that governments must do better. Change in this regard, however, does not originate from the top-down. As Dewey argues, the primary agency in bringing about change is *public* pressure, *public* education, and "publicity" in general. Understanding the instrumentalities involved is an important step for anyone who would assist in bringing about constructive change.

One thing that makes Dewey such a vital thinker today is that, like us, he lives in an age of rapidly changing media technologies. Dewey recognized the need to factor these changes into his philosophy. The emerging mass-media landscape that Dewey had to contend with sounds quaint to our ears: "Telegraph, telephone, and now the radio, cheap and quick mails, the printing press, capable of swift reduplication of material at low cost."³⁷ But such changes were profound in Dewey's time. Between 1920 and 1925 every state in the union acquired wireless radio broadcasting stations. The monopoly of print media was broken overnight, challenged by a more immediate and visceral electronic medium.

As we saw in chapter 7 of volume one, technologies are neither good nor bad in themselves—neither rational nor irrational. Normative claims about technologies reference the degree to which they facilitate "wholeness" between specific body-mind habits and the ends served, with particular attention paid to how *we* are being used in the process. In the case of media technologies, these functions are critically important to understand. Dewey knew that the "fourth estate" exercised "more power than the citizenry acting through recognized government channels."[38] Accordingly, there can be no separation between the wellbeing of a democracy and the health of its media. In his 1934 piece, "Radio's Influence on the Mind," Dewey describes the revolutionary medium of radio as "the most powerful instrument of social education the world has ever seen." He warns, however, that while radio has the potential to deepen human communication, it also "lends itself to propaganda in behalf of special interests."[39] Radio, Dewey notes, is among "the most powerful means of inculcating mass prejudice."[40]

These are hardly the concerns of a bygone era. Dewey lived to see federal regulations enacted to protect American airwaves from abuse, and most of us have lived to see those regulations rolled back.[41] Students of American culture know perfectly well what has occurred since: civility in political discourse began to erode soon after the deregulation in the radio domain began in the 1980s and has now plummeted to once unthinkable depths. Such moves have enabled right-wing zealots and hate-driven conspiracy theorists to command enormous listening audiences, spreading distortions and falsehoods unchecked by opposing viewpoints or legal restrictions. Dewey observed in his day the emergence of a certain "radio-conscious" or "air-minded" mental state, one that provided only a "half-conscious sense of the external ways in which our minds are formed and swayed and the superficiality and inconsistency of the result."[42] Such "air-mindedness" has returned to America in full force. More and more, Americans "know" things but they cannot remember where they learned them—and as Confucius understood, "Those who repeat things heard on the street relinquish excellence (*de* 德)."[43] Such excellence is markedly absent in American public discourse. One must believe that America is capable of reversing this condition, but not without pressure on its political class to reinstate fairness regulations in the broadcasting sector. If such deregulation was meant to be a social experiment, the results are now in—Americans are more polarized and less informed than ever.

Of course, the media landscape has completely transformed since the deregulation of radio broadcasting. There were no websites when such deregulation began. By 1995, there were 2,738 websites. Today, there are over one billion. My own generation enjoys the distinction of being the last to have straddled, as adults, two profoundly different epochs: "Analog" and "Digital." We became adults without the Internet. It is difficult at this stage to put a name on the age into which we have been thrown—the "Information Age" perhaps, or simply the "Internet Age." One thing, however, is certain: the present age will stand on par with the Bronze Age, the Iron Age, the Agricultural, and the Industrial Revolutions in terms of its ramifications for the human experience. Here at the threshold, these can only be glimpsed.

Like previous technological revolutions, our bodies-and-brains will undergo change. Excessive use of the Internet has already been linked with attention deficit hyperactivity disorder (ADHD) in children.[44] Confirmation bias has been understood for decades, but we have hardly begun to understand how the Internet fuels such biases and to what extent the medium supports or challenges the limited-effects theory. Politically and legally, we have entered uncharted waters. In terms of content, it is possible but difficult to control what occurs on the Internet. Chinese state media self-reports that *two million people* are employed by the central government to monitor the Internet, allowing for swift removal of content that is illegal or objectionable to the Chinese Communist Party.[45] In the United States (at the time of writing) no such restrictions apply. During the 2016 presidential campaign, agents hostile to American democracy—foreign and domestic—flooded the Internet with "fake news" and there was little that could be done about it. Again, we have only just begun to direct our intelligence (or *ming* 明) toward the challenges that the "Internet Age" presents.

Dewey was concerned with a parallel set of problems; and while much has changed in the intervening century, much has not. Graham Wallas was the first to systematically explore the social implications of mass media in his 1914 work, *The Great Society*. As he notes, we now find ourselves "working and thinking and feeling in relation to an environment, which, both in its world-wide extension and its intimate connection with all sides of human existence, is without precedence in the history of the world."[46] The rapid social changes witnessed by Wallas suggested to him that environmental stimuli were largely responsible for human behavior, and his work became something of a plea for intelligent social engineering.

Wallas dedicated his book to his star student, Walter Lippman. Thus, in challenging Lippman's rejection of the "public" in *The Public and Its Problems* in 1927, Dewey was simultaneously responding to Wallas' behavioristic stance in *The Great Society*. Dewey agrees with Wallas that, "we have the physical tools of communication like never before." The problem, however, is that "the thoughts and aspirations congruous with them are not communicated, and hence are not common." Without such communication, the public remains "shadowy and formless," realizing itself only "spasmodically." The key, Dewey says, is to secure the instrumentalities that convert the "Great Society" into a community. The intellectual task thus becomes to "search for conditions under which the Great Society may become the Great Community."[47]

Dewey was influenced by his experiences in China when he wrote these words. He introduces his vision of the democratic ideal accordingly. It is the society in which individual contributors enjoy their own share (or *fen* 分) in the social harmony (*he* 和) while all members of the community appreciate the contribution of one another in sustaining the value shared. "The task of democracy," writes Dewey, "is forever that of creation of a freer and more humane experience in which all share and to which all contribute."[48] Such "humane" experience in the flourishing democracy echoes the Confucian ideal of associated humanity (*ren* 仁). For Dewey, "democracy is not an *alternative* to other principles of associated life. It is the idea of community life itself."[49] While in China, Dewey observed such humanity in the "face-to-face" manner in which the Chinese people lived, prompting him to suggest that China already exhibited aspects of the democratic way of life. As he remarks in Beijing in 1920, "Although Chinese society is in some respects less fully developed than some Western societies, foreigners who come to China are impressed with the degree to which certain democratic principles pervade the whole culture."[50] Such habits were born over "long periods of human history," Dewey observes, during which the State—and "Heaven" (*tian* 天) by extension—was "hardly more than a shadow thrown upon the family and neighborhood by remote personages." Meanwhile, "the relationships of husband and wife, parent and children, older and younger children, friend and friend, are the bonds from which authority proceeds."[51] Dewey hardly needed to explain to the Chinese what they already knew—that "the problem of democracy is close to daily living, not far off in the skies."[52]

For Americans, such lessons remain to be learned from Dewey's observations. In Confucian culture, the reciprocal nature of associated humanity (*ren* 仁) characterizes social experience in each phase of its growth, from the family to the national level. For Dewey, such ideas about the reciprocity of human experience coalesce in his signature notion of "Democracy as a Way of Life."[53] Dewey's philosophy of reciprocal human relations—grounded in social "give-and-take"—develops into a notion of personhood that parallels the deepest insights of Confucian philosophy.

This development can be appreciated by tracing the phrase "give-and-take" in Dewey's writings. He begins by using the phrase to describe both the relational dynamic *in* a family and a social skill learned *from* a family.[54] The phrase is then used in *Democracy and Education*, where the "genuinely social medium" of the school is described as one in which "there is give-and-take in the building up of a common experience."[55] Shortly thereafter, Dewey makes "give-and-take" the centerpiece of his pluralistic theory of American nationalism. He writes: "The concept of uniformity and unanimity in culture is rather repellent . . . Variety *is* the spice of life, and the richness and the attractiveness of social institutions depend upon cultural diversity among separate units. In so far as people are all alike, there is no give-and-take among them. And it is better to give-and-take."[56]

In Dewey's post-China writings, this line of thinking becomes fortified and enhanced. In the 1932 *Ethics* (which Dewey revised while in China), the fact that "every member of a group stands in certain relations of give-and-take" becomes "the *basis* for customs"—now identified with the democratic ideal on its "social side." Such a function clearly displays lessons learned in China: it is "cooperation in place of coercion, voluntary sharing in a mutual process of give-and-take instead of authority imposed from above."[57]

Dewey's theory of personhood takes shape in this connection. In *The Public and Its Problems*, "give-and-take" becomes central to securing the *individual*: "To learn to be human is to develop through the give-and-take of communication an effective sense of being an individually distinct member of a community." This can only occur, however, "in face-to-face relationships by means of direct give-and-take."[58] In *Individualism Old and New*, this becomes the meaning of the *social*: "The particular interactions that compose a human society include the give-and-take of participation, of a sharing that increases, that expands and deepens, the capacity and significance of the interacting factors."[59] In his 1938 essay, "Democracy and Education in the World Today," such "give-and-take" becomes wholly *reciprocal*: "[Give-and-take] is ultimately the only method by which human beings can succeed in carrying out this experiment in which we are all engaged . . . that of living together in ways in which the life of each of us is at once profitable in the deepest sense of the word, profitable to himself and helpful in the building up of the individuality of others."[60]

For Dewey, "Democracy as a Way of Life" thus comes to represent the virtue of human association itself—that by which human significance is conferred-and-received in the "give-and-take" of living together "face-to-face." The more Dewey reflects on this dynamic, the better he comes to express the *individual-social-reciprocal* nature of human personhood. Confucians understand this dynamic as that of associated humanity (*ren* 仁).

Three Complimentary Studies

In exploring the relationship between Dewey's notion of "democracy" and Confucian thinking there is no need to reinvent the wheel. There are already excellent studies exploring their philosophical connections. Three of these, in order of release, are David L. Hall and Roger T. Ames' *Democracy of the Dead: Dewey, Confucius, and the Hope for Democracy in China* (1999), Sor-hoon Tan's *Confucian Democracy: A Deweyan Reconstruction* (2003), and Joseph Grange's *John Dewey, Confucius, and Global Philosophy* (2004). Together, these volumes succeed in establishing the empirical and theoretical basis for a convergence between Dewey's "democracy" and classical Confucianism. After exploring how these studies work together in advancing the prospects for "Confucian democracy," we will return to Dewey's newly discovered notes for the "Social and Political Philosophy" lectures in Beijing and experiment with reading them alongside these works.

The first thing these works do is to establish the complexity that surrounds the whole notion of "Confucian democracy." Hall and Ames begin by dispelling what they call the "myth" of Han 漢 identity. While China may never be the ethnically diverse "family" that America strives to become, it is not as homogenous as it might seem. The Han people are the principle ethnic group, comprising over 92 percent of the nation. What remains are some fifty-odd minority ethnic groups. Despite such imbalance, several demographic forces—regional, cultural, linguistic, and economic—conspire to "create strains on the presumed harmony of the Han Chinese."[61] Generated within this tension is a rather fervent need to define and retain "Chinese-ness" in the face of this inexorable dynamism within the population. Paramount in any consideration of political reform, then, is keeping the "core" of the culture intact.

As Sor-hoon Tan explains, however, there is considerable disagreement even here, especially when it comes to defining "Confucianism." For some, "Confucian democracy" is a contradiction in terms. Many scholars in the Chinese world maintain that Confucianism is "inherently authoritarian and incompatible with democracy." No doubt, this is how it was perceived during the May Fourth Movement, when Dewey visited. But as Tan reminds us, "different societies have practiced Confucianism differently at different times." Arguably, this has been true since its inception—there never really *was* a single "Confucianism" since the *Analects* itself is a multi-authored work compiled some generations after Confucius' death, at which time the tradition had already splintered into different schools of thought. Thus, Tan's concern is with "what Confucianism could mean now and in the future, not with what Confucianism is *essentially*." Tan thus opens the door for creative thinkers to come forward to explore how Confucianism can be reimagined through contact with Dewey's philosophy.⁶²

Through this door enters Joseph Grange. Grange establishes a series of "working connections" between Dewey's central ideas and Confucian values. As a point of departure, he identifies two important truths that inform these traditions. First, "Both Dewey and Confucius share a similar conviction: human beings must *grow* in order to become fully human." Second, "Confucius and Dewey affirm the fact that to be human is to *live together*."⁶³ It is easy to forget how important these truths really are. Pathologies unique to human beings stem from overlooking them. Confucius refers to those who disregard such truths as "small persons" (*xiaoren* 小人). Unlike exemplary persons (*junzi* 君子), there is never an instance in which small persons realize their associated humanity (*ren* 仁).⁶⁴ Thus, as Confucius suggests, their growth trajectory (*da* 達) trends downwards (*xia* 下).⁶⁵

Noting that the "individual" of classical Western liberalism is conceived in abstraction from such fundamental truths, Grange diagnoses a profound malaise in contemporary Western civilization, something that he calls the "Great Disconnect." Like Dewey, he recognizes that the Western mind is "plagued by a series of separations," obscuring the nature of what it means to be human. For Grange, "each split prevents our experience from becoming whole and continuous." His work thus helps to recover the philosophical link between Dewey's "consummatory experience," wherein means-and-ends are co-terminus, and the Chinese notion of *dao* 道. For Dewey and Confucius, these are concepts that "embrace in the widest possible terms the richest view of human existence." Both Dewey's "experience" and the Confucian *dao* are premised on the "continuity between Nature and the human" (*tianrenheyi* 天人合一), once again converging on the most fundamental truths about the human experience. "What is really here and what is really our destiny," writes Grange, "is the process of discovering new and more satisfying connections with both the natural and human environment."⁶⁶

Hall and Ames recognize that the benefits of the Dewey-Confucius encounter stand to be reciprocal, and they hope to clear away assumptions that might prevent this from being the case. Historically, for instance, there has been much consternation about the relationship between "modernization" and "Westernization" in China. It has long been recognized that Western-styled "individualism" poses a threat to China's cultural core, and this plays itself out as a tension within China's efforts to "modernize." Hall and Ames, however, in a move that has grown only more sensible since they made it, proceed to "challenge entrenched assumptions about the equation of modernization and Westernization."⁶⁷ "Modernity" is a mercurial term at best. If "modernization" means (in part) developing and implementing the latest technologies, then one wonders which side of the China-Western axis currently stands to modernize. Over the two-or-three-odd centuries that the Western world surpassed China technologically, there developed an arbitrary assumption that "modernization" fundamentally meant "Westernization." For most of human history, however, advanced technologies multiplied on the Chinese side—gun powder, printing, water mills, the blast furnace, and so on. Severing "modernization" and "Westernization" breaks the tendency to think about evolving exchanges asymmetrically.

Since cultural and technological exchange has always been bidirectional, Tan underscores that the engagement of Dewey's theory of "democracy" with the Confucian tradition is one that promises to galvanize both the Chinese and American sides.[68] "Westernization," as Hall and Ames explain, is part of an intra-cultural encounter that includes "Easternization," despite the fact that "the possibility that the West might be fundamentally shaped through its Asian encounter has yet to be entertained by most Westerners."[69]

Such a possibility adds to the potential implications of any future Confucian democracy in two ways. First, there is no reason to assume that such a democracy would mimic existing Western democracies. Second, there is no reason to assume that Western democracies would have nothing to learn from such a development. It is plain to see that contemporary American democracy is dysfunctional. Seeking revitalization through the assimilation of a "foreign" example would be wholly in keeping with the spirit of American nationalism, since the current model is already based on foreign-born principles. The possibility that China might someday provide a "Confucian" model is an intriguing prospect for those who recognize the conceptual overlap between Dewey's philosophy and Confucian thought. For as our authors contend, certain features of Confucian democracy would likely resonate well with the best-developed theory of democracy that America has, which is Dewey's. "Confucian democracy will be seen to have many similarities with the Deweyan form of communitarian thought," write Hall and Ames, and this "offers the most productive understanding of democracy for America."[70]

Here, however, there emerges some divergence among these studies. Hall and Ames, as Tan observes, "use Dewey's communitarian view to criticize liberalism in their discussion of the prospects of democracy in China." This proves to be a fruitful approach, because Dewey himself critiques classical Western liberalism based on a vision of human community that Confucianism largely shares. As Tan suggests, however, "if he were alive today, Dewey would no doubt dismiss the Liberal/Communitarian dualism as a false dichotomy, as he was wont to do with all dualisms."[71] Grange agrees, suggesting that Dewey "overcomes the old and tired dispute between the partisans of individual freedom and the advocates of strong community action," paving the way for a social philosophy in which the "Individual/Social" dualism no longer obtains.[72] Dewey's position, Tan argues, strikes a balance. Like the communitarian, Dewey "rejects the conception of self as disembodied and pre-social," but like the liberal, he "does not see the self as 'encumbered' or 'embedded' in a static or passive manner" in the social body.[73]

This methodological discrepancy is minor and does not result in materially different conclusions. All parties agree that the restoration of "community" is central to Dewey's vision of democracy and that the rights and values normally associated with classical liberalism undergo significant transformation in his treatment. As Hall and Ames argue, one primary transformation involves the relative status of "first-" and "second-generation" rights. "First-generation" rights are basically civil and political: the rights to liberty, free speech, voting, equality before the law, etc. "Second-generation" rights are economic and social: rights to housing, health care, social security, unemployment benefits, etc. As they observe, "first-generation" rights are the bedrock of most rights-based theories, while "second-generation" rights become "difficult to maintain" in societies that focus primarily on the former.[74] The distinction is easy to spot in politcal discourse. It is common for libertarian-leaning politicians and media outlets in the United States, for instance, to declare that health care is a "good, not a right," or a "privilege, not a right," and this is due to esteeming "first-generation" rights disproportionally. From a communitarian standpoint it is harder (as well as heartless) to argue that health care is "not a right."

Dewey's thinking on the topic of "rights" changes over the years, and it is possible that the China experience alters its trajectory. As Tan observes, "Though the 1908 *Ethics* makes considerable use of the concept, it all but disappears in the 1932 *Ethics*, even in the section 'Liberty of Thought and Expression' [in Section Three]." While it is unclear how and why Dewey moves away from the concept of "rights," the change occurs during the pivotal period that includes the China years.

Easier to track is the evolution of Dewey's understanding of the core values of democracy: "fraternity," "liberty," and "equality." In *The Public and Its Problems*, Dewey would come to argue that, when "isolated from communal life," such values are "hopeless abstractions."[75] Grange is eloquent in expressing what "community life" means in this context: "A community is formed when its members can identify, share, and express something in common," he writes. The profundity of this simple statement reveals itself once it is recalled that such "communication" is miraclulous from Dewey's perspective. To *truly* identify, share, and express meanings with other people is the greatest of human goods. It creates conditions for "participating, sharing, and belonging" that, as Grange reminds us, for Dewey is "the meaning of human life."[76] One must never take human community or communication for granted. These can deteriorate within the body politic—and when they do, democratic values degenerate into aberrant and impoverished versions of themselves. "Fraternity" becomes mushy sentimentalism, flag-pin grandstanding, and a sloganeering patriotism that lends itself to factionalism and confrontation. "Liberty" becomes independence from all social ties, illusory autonomy, and a kneejerk distrust of anything public. "Equality" becomes a hollow assurance of value equivalence, demands for sameness, and the reduction of all qualities to what is substitutable.

When "community life" prevails, however, these virtues are expressed differently. "Fraternity" becomes the fruit of common goods, consciously appreciated and participated in. It is the natural expression, as Hall and Ames suggest, of a lived environment in which "human beings function principally in support of things-in-common."[77] "Liberty" ceases to be freedom from all restraint, becoming as Tan says the "freedom to grow," one that can be realized only within the constraints provisioned by living with other people.[78] "Equality," as Hall and Ames explain, reverts from being an abstract, quantitative given to the "realization of a qualitative equality" among different constituents of a social order, grounded in the "unique and distinctive features of individuals."[79] It thus denotes "the unhampered share that each member of the community has in the consequences of associated action."[80] Again, this is not something that is primordially given but rather, as Tan explains, something "to be fostered deliberately by individuals acting together to change social arrangements so that they would *produce* equality."[81] Dewey appeals to the "baby in a family" to underscore that enjoying equal status "denotes effective regard for whatever is distinctive and unique in each" in the context of some concrete social organization. Equality "is not a natural possession but is a fruit of the community when its action is directed by its character as a community."[82]

That Dewey's theories of "fraternity," "liberty," and "equality" were not fully formed when he arrived in China is clear. In California, just prior to leaving for Asia, Dewey had begun experimenting with the values of liberal democracy, and his understanding was very much in flux. "Liberty" meant a "universe in which there is real uncertainty and contingency," "equality" was "construed as individuality," and "fraternity" meant "continuity."[83] His democratic thinking at this stage was hardly precise. In his opening series of lectures in Beijing, he treated these three values differently again. Dewey told his audience that, "Liberty is the individual aspect of democracy, while fraternity is the social aspect; and equality is both individual and social."[84] This would suggest (assuming Hu's transcription of Dewey's lecture is accurate) that Dewey had not completely liberated himself from the "Individual/Social" dualism at this juncture. It would be definitively overcome, however, in the

"Lectures in Social and Political Philosophy" a few months later, as Dewey setttled into China and the May Fourth Movement ran its course.

What had become clear to Dewey by the time he wrote *The Public and Its Problems* was that "fraternity," "liberty," and "equality" would manifest themselves differently according to how strongly "community life" obtains. The evidence of Chinese influence here is not definitive but it is strong. Abraham Edel outlines several ways in which Dewey's thinking on the "individual" and "society" changed between the 1908 and 1932 *Ethics*, and he considers the China experience as central to this evolution. As Edel notes, Dewey evokes Mencius in his lecture on "The Rights of Individuals" in connection with the teaching that the state has an "obligation to protect people as parents do."[85] Given its family-centric conception of the state, Dewey here observes that China might be positioned to bypass "political individualism" altogether, thus "amalgamating" two Western "steps" at once. China might even secure "individualism" and "equality" together through its own nature as a robust "fraternity."[86] Given that Dewey's own conception of these terms was changing, this must have been eye-opening for him. Considered in retrospect, if this was the moment that he realized that the status of these values change depending on the strength of the community that holds them, then it appears that Dewey's eventual view of "fraternity," "liberty," and "equality" was influenced by his exposure to Mencius.[87]

The idea is not far-fetched. While Dewey's Chinese students were generally disinclined to give him sympathetic lessons in Confucian thought, he was not without access to the classical tradition. Among Dewey's interpreters and friends in China was Meng Chih 孟治, seventy-second generation descendant of Mencius. Meng recalls that when Dewey learned of his pedigree he peppered him with questions about the Confucian *Four Books* (*sishu* 四書), which Meng could recite from memory. Dewey "seemed to think quite highly," Meng remembers, of the *Great Learning*, which underscores among other things the continuity between family and political order.[88] The *Great Learning* identifies human personhood (*shen* 身) as the root (*ben* 本) of social and political order, which radiates outward from each focal point. Since this obtains "from the Ruler all the way to the common person," the result is the sturdiest social web imaginable. As the *Great Learning* teaches:

> When the ancients wished for the world to radiate intelligence (*ming* 明) and virtue (*de* 德), they would administer their states. Wishing to administer their states, they would order their own families. Wishing to order their own families, they would cultivate their own persons (*xiushen* 修身). Wishing to cultivate their own persons, they would correctly align (*zheng* 正) their thoughts and

feelings (*xin* 心). Wishing to correctly align their thoughts and feelings, they would extend their knowledge (*zhi* 知). Wishing to extend their knowledge, they would investigate things (*gewu* 格物).[89]

It is easy to see why Dewey would be attracted to such a formula, one that Mencius relates through the common expression, "World, State, Family" (*tianxiaguojia* 天下國家). As Mencius says: "The world is rooted in the state, the state is rooted in the family, and the family is rooted in the person."[90] It is plausible that such ideas spoke to Dewey.

Dewey's idea of "democracy," in any event, clearly resonates with Confucian thinking. As Dewey says, "Democracy must begin at home, and its home is the neighborly community."[91] As Hall and Ames explain, "If there is no local or focal identity born of face-to-face encounter then the extrapolation of experience from the local to the national or international levels cannot take place. If our primary interest is in world events, the absence of a sense of connectedness can only lead to a feeling of impotence. We should begin at the local level and extend our sense of control over our local contexts to ever-broader contexts."[92]

The key here is to recognize that aligning one's thoughts and feelings through understanding (*zhi* 知) and the investigation of things (*gewu* 格物) effects the obverse of what Hall and Ames identify as the "absence of a sense of connectedness" and the "feeling of impotence." The *Great Learning* not only makes each person *focal* to sustaining social and political order, it also identifies the cultivation of personhood (*xiushen* 修身) as the key to nurturing each individual focus. Even in ancient China, one could not attend to local affairs effectively without knowing something about the world (*tianxia* 天下). This now obtains on the maximum scale. World affairs must be investigated and understood in order to think and feel (*xin* 心) in a manner adequate to the realities shaping our immediate locales.

American immigration again provides a good example. When a family of Syrian refugees arrives in my town, the private thoughts and feelings (*xin* 心) of some community members might not correctly align (*zheng* 正) with the facts surrounding this event. Ignorance of current affairs, world history, and much else, may result in some callousness or hostility. From the perspective of Confucian democracy, the *local community* is responsible for correcting such misalignments before they scale out to the national level, where they can become catastrophic. In this respect, strong public schools and community engagement remain at the core of this vision. Once one properly understands how affairs in one's own "face-to-face" community interface with the broader world, one can be entrusted to raise children, foster a national character, and contribute to the world from within one's local community. The more one investigates things (*gewu* 格物), the more one knows (*zhi* 知) how events in one's immediate community relate to larger trends and happenings.

The American spirit lives at the intersection of the local-and-global, and its nodes are everywhere. In Lewiston, Maine, for instance, there is an aging generation of French-Canadians who still speak the mother tongue. French-Canadians comprise 24 percent of Maine's population, but only 12 percent of these people speak French.[93] They maintain their heritage through the local Franco Center, which sponsors a monthly luncheon for Francophones called *Le Rencontre* ("The Gathering"). Over the last few decades, central African immigrants have been resettling in Maine, refugees from ethnic conflicts resulting from an oppressive history under Belgian occupation. These newly arrived French speakers want nothing more than to get to know their neighbors. So, they have begun showing up for lunch at *Le Rencontre*. The French-speaking community in Maine is being revitalized in the process. The older French-Canadian Mainers now find themselves helping the immigrants acclimate to their new home, and one-by-one friendships are being formed.[94]

Imagine all the intersecting strands and distant connections that bring a retired Québec native and a teenage girl from Burundi together for a French luncheon in Lewiston, Maine. *That* is America. Confucianism contributes something here because the questions that it asks and the norms it employs are general enough to apply across all times and cultures. Its central question, in fact, never changes: "How do we cultivate human persons (*xiushen* 修身) so as to sustain social harmony to an optimal degree?" The precise answer to this question changes with time and place. All that ever mattered to *any* Confucian was how to achieve harmony (*he* 和) *here and now*. Whatever falls outside of that can be left to the antiquarian. As Grange suggests: "This is the question of *ren* 仁 recast for the twenty-first century."[95]

Toward a "Social Philosophy," Part Two

Having established multiple connections between Dewey's theory of democracy and Confucian thought, let us return to the newly recovered notes for Dewey's "Social and Political Philosophy" lectures in Beijing and mix them into the present discussion. Having already considered lectures I–IV, we turn now to lectures VI, X, XI, XII, and XVI.

Unfortunately, only the first page of lecture VI, "Communication and Associated Living" survives. The opening sentence, however, encapsulates its entire message: "The supreme test of any social arrangement, custom, institution, law etc. is its relationship to promoting living together, association, intercourse, communication—exchange of feelings and ideas that makes experiences common (common, communication, community)."[96] Were one to translate this sentence into classical Chinese, it is hard to imagine *ren* 仁 not being somewhere in that sentence. Hu Shih, however, was not interested in translating Dewey's lectures into Confucian Chinese. The centerpiece of Dewey's message is "living together, association, intercourse, communication," but this is a compound for which Dewey had no single term. Hu steers clear of Confucian terminology and condenses it blandly into "living together" (*tongshenghuo* 同生活). Clopton and Ou then translate it back into "associated living."[97]

However the meanings ricochet here, if *ren* 仁 resonates anywhere in Dewey's philosophy it is within this cluster of ideas. "True social or community life," he writes, "means [*trans*-action], reciprocal influence, mutual response to the needs and claims of the other parts or partners in the combination."[98] According to Hu Shih's transcription, the lecture proceeds to contrast democratic societies with "authoritarian governments," which "do not see associated living as a relevant goal." While such régimes "may appear to be solidly grounded and strong," they are "always weaker than a government based on the values of associated living."[99] This immediately calls to mind the teachings of Mencius, who as Sor-hoon Tan reminds us is "extremely critical of hegemons."[100] The hegemon, Mencius teaches, is one who through force (*li* 力) pretends to govern through associated humanity (*ren*) but instead legitimizes his rule by the size of the state at his command. Meanwhile, the more virtuous ruler is one who governs with associated humanity (*ren*) even though his state is modest in size.[101] The former citizens look happy, but they live in fear and trepidation. The latter citizens *are* happy, because "they move in productive directions (*shan* 善) without knowing how it occurs."[102] In other words, they live in societies in which they can *grow*.

In lecture X, "The State," Dewey addresses the role of state force (*li* 力) directly. "The issue," Dewey explains, "is not between physical force on one side and moral force on the other. It is between an intelligent and constructive use of physical force and a negative, wasteful, destructive one." State force, which Dewey explains is properly more "mental" as a deterrent than "physical" as a reality, is appropriately used only as a means to preserve the "community of interest" that underwrites the moral force of the state. The fact that moral force will normally prevail without coercive force is based on two assumptions. First, it assumes the existence of "the *community of interest*" which is the sole justification of the state. Second, it assumes that all parties "have a like interest in reaching an understanding and settlement" when disagreements arise.[103] Moral force, explains Dewey, will lose its footing should either condition fail, and this is when coercive force enters the picture.

The Confucian ideal is that the state reflect the same kind of "community of interest" exhibited in the family, virtually ensuring that moral force has the chance to prevail. Filial piety (*xiao* 孝) develops naturally within the family, and when such a sensibility extends into associations at the state level, open defiance and rebellion, as Confucius suggests, become inhibited.[104] Of course, this assumes that the ruler is behaving as a *ruler*, just as concord within the family depends on the father behaving as a *father*. This explains Confucius' stress upon the rectification of names (*zhengming* 正名), which he teaches is the first thing that any polity must attend to.[105] As Hall and Ames explain, this is necessary to "prevent abuses of personal authority." As they write: "A father who does not act as a father ought not be called a 'father.' A ruler who does not act as a ruler is not deserving of the name."[106] Since the exact responsibilities associated with such terms change over time, so too must their meanings. Instances are rare, however, in which such social roles are created *sui generis*. Past experience, in the form of customs and traditions, provide us with models upon which names (*ming*) are developed.

In "The State" lecture, Dewey is cautious about equating family-borne "roles" with the power structure of the state, since when this metaphor becomes literal it amounts to a nepotism that China (and recently the United States) knows too well. The center of state control becomes "the family or clan organization, based on blood tie real or imputed," such that the state "centers mystically in a single family."[107] This is where it is important that metaphors remain metaphors. For the state to be run *like* a family does not require it to be run *by* a family. The early Confucians maintained that, while filial piety (*xiao* 孝) is a virtue that rulers must have, there is also a more charismatic quality (*de* 德) associated with true leadership that transcends family experience.

This is another area in which Confucius declined to follow the Zhou tradition. Political legitimacy in the Zhou dynasty was a family affair—King Wen 文 bequeathed power to his son, King Wu 武, who secured the dynasty and placed his brothers in charge of feudal territories. Meanwhile, the Duke of Zhou, another blood brother, served as Wu's loyal advisor. King Wu passed rule down to his own son, King Cheng 成, who passed it on to his son, King Kang 康, and so on. During Confucius' lifetime, this imperial lineage had already broken down. Rather than seek to revitalize the Zhou custom of royal succession by blood, Confucius exercised his prerogative to "select what is good" (*zeqishanzhe* 擇其善者) and reached further back into history for his model.[108] The ancient sage Shun inherited the rule of Yao over a thousand years before the Zhou, and that succession of power was noteworthy for *not* being hereditary. Shun was the lord of no house, the chief of no tribe. He was not even the head of his own family.[109] He was a relative nobody, but he possessed extraordinary filial piety and charismatic virtue. This is the ruler that Confucius admires more than any other. As Ni Peimin notes, this was a "radical departure from the accepted norm," and a clean break from Zhou practices.[110]

Again, the ideal Confucian state is one in which its citizens can *grow*. What Confucius admires most about Shun is that his virtue (*de* 德) inspired and encouraged people to cultivate their own persons without need for any coercive force. Upon cultivating themselves, social order would develop naturally with minimal effort from the ruler. Confucius explains that Shun approached governing without overt doing (*wuwei* 無為): "Embodying reverence, he took his position facing south—that is all."[111] It is hard to distinguish this ideal from that which is found in *Daodejing* Chapter 65, where governing with profound virtue (*xuande* 玄德) means going along with things as they annul (*fan* 反) their own stock of possibilities without overt guidance or interference. Perhaps there is no real difference between these visions. One must remember that "Confucianism" and "Daoism" were not sharply distinguished "schools" in the Warring States period. Confucius' theory of governing reflects a mainstream reaction to the more heavy-handed "Legalist" approach, opposition to which crossed over school affiliations.

Dewey's general approach in "The State" is not one that would have struck a Confucian thinker as highly unusual. The operations of the state, Dewey explains, must be "as constructive as possible—that in its effects upon human nature its work be fostering, cultivating, rather than restrictive and choking."[112] As Tan reminds us, "Lack of faith in the possibilities of human nature is not characteristic of early Confucianism."[113] Indeed, Dewey shares with Confucians the assumption that human beings are more than capable of developing a robust community within a political system that does little more than provide the opportunity to do so.

In lecture XI, "The Government," Dewey observes how principles of governance differ in classical Western liberalism and traditional Confucian philosophy. He explains:

> A Chinese scholar has astutely remarked that the European theory of responsible Government is based upon a belief in the inherent badness of humans, and the consequent needs of checks even upon rulers. [Meanwhile] the old Chinese theory was based upon faith in the intrinsic goodness of human nature, the orderliness and loyalty of the subjects, the wisdom and benevolence of rulers. Hence Confucian political philosophy really assumed the supremacy of moral forces, while the European philosophies—at least of the liberal school—have assumed the need of physical backing in order to prevent the immoral forces from becoming supreme.

Dewey is siding with the Confucian approach here, since his previous lecture argues for the desirability of states in which moral force prevails. His immediate concern, however, is practical. The older Confucian model had been feasible when the state really *could* relinquish significant degrees of control to "the stead inspection and judgment of [one's] own local and definite permanent group." However, with the arrival of industry, commerce, finance, railways, factories, chemicals, and so on, these "locales" are now global. "The decay of customary control means an increase of legislative and administrative control," Dewey writes. "The channels in which moral forces operate change." Dewey is hardly rejecting Confucian political philosophy here; rather, he is challenging his Chinese audience to reconstruct that tradition to meet these changed conditions. At issue is how a future Chinese government develops "new organs" adequate to the need for greater coordination and control among local groups while still preserving moral force as its governing principle.[114]

In lecture XII, "Political Liberalism," Dewey provides a condensed but quite nuanced account of the history of classical liberalism, covering Locke, Hobbes, Rousseau, the French Revolution, the British response, Utilitarianism, and the advent of republicanism. With the latter, the elements of "political democracy" are set forth. As Hall and Ames maintain, classical liberalism as such is a "Western invention," with liberal democracy as "one contingent factor."[115] Dewey's approach is similarly historical and critical. The mechanics of political democracy "have no intrinsic sacredness," Dewey writes. They are, however, "the best devices yet invented for keeping officials responsible to the public will."[116]

More pressing for Dewey is his concern with "two errors" that reside within the foundation of classical liberalism. The first is "thinking of government as a kind of necessary evil, a surrender of some rights and liberties in order to be more certain of others." The second is "supposing that the individual is an adequate judge of his own interest, and this self-interest of each may be counted upon to secure a regard for the net welfare of all."[117] Each error is based on the false premise that "association" is not essential to human nature. Classical liberals overlook what Grange identifies as one of the great insights that Dewey and the Confucians share—namely, that to be "human" means to *live together*. The "freedom" upon which classical liberalism is premised is one that, as Grange says, stands in defiance of both nature and reality—it is a "delusion that creates its own illusion."[118] Dewey proceeds to argue, accordingly, that "political democracy" alone is insufficient to secure a humane polity. Political democracy naturally "runs into the broader moral and social democracy," for without a "public, civic conscience," there can be no genuine "democracy" no matter how many times one enters the voting booth. Dewey argues that, "A public interest and *public opinion*, rather than self-interest and judgment of what is to [be] the interests of the self, must be the chief reliances of democratic government."[119]

What this suggests is that "political democracy" is impotent when not grounded in the kind of "World, State, Family" (*tianxiaguojia* 天下國家) model of concentric expansion that Confucianism advocates and that Dewey admired in texts like the *Great Learning*. Dewey describes this as a process of "extending sentiments from personal and local and family" to encompass "the welfare of the country," thus cultivating a "public conscience and civic loyalty in the broader polity."[120]

If not directly influenced by his exposure to Confucian thought, Dewey's newly discovered notes for Lectures X–XII develop a political philosophy that is clearly meant to be congruent with that tradition. Unfortunately, his notes for the next three lectures remain missing. Relying on Hu Shih's transcriptions, however, we get a good sense of what they cover. In "The Rights of the Individual" lecture, Dewey is interested in presenting a historical and theoretical overview of the idea of "rights," with the message being twofold. First, "The rights and powers we are discussing have no meaning if we choose to consider the individual apart from the society and state." Second, "The problem [of rights] has changed from that of seeking individual rights themselves to one of seeking the opportunity to exercise these rights." This is the lecture in which Dewey evokes the Confucian ideal of governing the state as "parent to the people" (*minzhifumu* 民之父母), suggesting that such a notion "can readily be modified into the concept of the protection of its citizens by a democratic government."[121] Tan provides a thorough and well-supported account of how the family (*jia* 家) ideal in Confucianism lends itself to the type of democratic community that Dewey is referring to.[122]

Lecture XIV, "Nationalism and Internationalism," underscores how transnational forces "such as science, the fine arts, literature, religion, travel, postal service, commerce, finance" now require that local communities be international in outlook. Our world is one in which a "negative kind of peace," one in which each community minds its own business, is no longer a tenable aim. Our problems and prospects are too intertwined. Dewey thus encourages us to seek after a "positive peace," one in which different nations "engage together in constructive enterprises that contribute to their common welfare." This requires the cultivation of an *intra-cultural* mindset, one in which "there will be associated living on a world-wide scale, with humankind living in a society which transcends all national and linguistic barriers."[123]

Lecture XV, "The Authority of Science," offers a preview of how Dewey's thinking resonates with Confucian anthropology—a topic that will be central to part II of the present volume. Here and in lecture XVI, Dewey addresses "the intellectual and cultural life" of the human being. He begins with two seemingly basic propositions. First, "The intellectual and spiritual aspects of life enhance the value of associated living." Second, "These aspects are in themselves the very foundations of civilization." As Dewey writes, "we know very well that human beings are something more than mere animals." While we share our bodies, physical needs, and most appetites with animals, these do not define the human (*ren* 人) experience. We must "engage in intellectual and spiritual activities" and thereby "metamorphose" our animal features and "elevate them to the level of civilization." In terms of anatomy and physiology, "there have probably been no significant alterations" in the human form for 300,000 years, Dewey surmises, but the human experience has been "immeasurably enriched" in terms of culture. This is due, Dewey suggests, to the transformative power of associated living and tradition—what Confucians call *ren* 仁 and *dao* 道.

The next topic that Dewey addresses raises an issue that we will need to pause to consider. While the human form has not changed dramatically in the last 300,000 years, our material culture *has*—and we now stand at the "crossroads of change." New technologies and material conditions have risen to challenge our long-held traditions and customs. The authority that such customs once commanded as a "system of ideas according to which we make our decisions and which controls the ways in which we act," has broken down.[124] Dewey explains to his Chinese audience that tradition and ritual-custom must now be reconstructed for the present. On what authority, however, is such reconstruction to be undertaken? Dewey's answer is contained in title of the lecture: "The Authority of Science."

But how compatible is this with Chinese thinking? In Dewey's mind, the "scientific attitude" is not an impediment blocking traditional Chinese ideas and customs from developing further; rather, it is an invitation to reconstruct those very ideas and customs. Hu Shih's then recently completed dissertation, "The Development of the Logical Method in Ancient China," might have helped to persuade Dewey that the Chinese tradition had indigenous resources to mobilize itself in becoming more "scientifically minded," and that such "methods of the West are not totally alien to the Chinese mind."[125] Not everyone would agree with Hu on this point. The entire issue, however, is fraught with disagreements over assumptions that are largely unstated. During the May Fourth Movement, the most strident anti-traditionalists assumed for a variety of reasons that modern Western scientific methods and traditional Chinese thinking were incompatible. Were they correct?

Nathan Sivin's work, especially his 1982 article (revised in 2005), "Why the Scientific Revolution Did Not Take Place in China—or Didn't It?" is critical to addressing such questions. Compared with other cultures, China's technological achievements are without question in the uppermost tier. One need only peruse Joseph Needham's series, "Science and Civilization in China" to appreciate the wealth of experiment and invention that China claims as it own. Yet, Needham asks the famous "Needham Question"—"Why did modern science not develop in China?"[126] Sivin reveals two fallacies upon which the "Needham Question" is based, fallacies concerning claims that (1) "if an important aspect of the European Scientific Revolution cannot be found [in China], the whole ensemble of fundamental changes could not have happened there," and (2) "inhibiting factors" must have "prevented" modern science from emerging from precursor states that can be identified. Such fallacies are serious errors in historical reasoning. Ultimately, the "Needham Question" suffers the logical challenge of demonstrating why *anything* didn't happen. "The question," Sivin observes, "is analogous to the question of why your name did not appear on page 3 of today's newspaper."[127]

The "inhibiting factors" fallacy is particularly distorting. It allows one to regard the presence of some phenomenon as an "obstacle" to something else, thus inviting one to neglect what that "obstacle" is positively doing. The inverse mistake is to note the absence of specific "aspects" of a certain phenomenon, thus inviting one to overlook the presence of other operations characteristic of that phenomenon. Sivin uses the Song dynasty polymatic scientist Shen Kuo 沈括 (1031–1095) as an example. His achievements in geology, mathematics, meteorology, zoology, pharmacology, etc. positioned him among the greatest scientific minds of the time. But in his writings, as Sivin notes, "there are no clear boundaries between material that fits the modern conception of science and material that doesn't." We look for specific markers of Western science in Shen Kuo, but we do not find them. Instead, we find a thinker concerned with the overlapping orders of things, someone who recognizes no difference in kind between his "scientific" undertakings and his work in the field of art criticism, especially in Chinese landscape painting (we considered Shen Kuo briefly in chapter 4 of the previous volume). Encountering Shen Kuo, one can either be blinded by the "absence" of specific markers of Western science or, as Sivin is, alert to "the relations of the sciences to other kinds of knowledge" that Shen Kuo exemplifies.[128]

The traditional approach in early Chinese science is to investigate the orders of connections among things. The core of the *Great Learning* regards such "investigation of things" (*gewu* 格物) to be at the center of personal cultivation, and hence at the center of the social and political order. Thus, there is already a premium placed on empirical observation and inquiry in the Chinese tradition. That said, the original meaning of *gewu* is quite unclear. As Daniel K. Gardner explains, the phrase "is by no means transparent, and, in fact, [it has] been understood by [early] commentators and thinkers in a variety of ways."[129]

In the twelfth-century, the Neo-Confucian Zhu Xi 朱熹 developed an influential interpretation of *gewu* 格物 that involved how the mind penetrates into the coherences (*li* 理) of things; but this reading was deeply influenced by Song metaphysics. What *gewu* means in the *Great Learning* is something of a mystery. As A. C. Graham submits, "What attracts attention is that the whole social order is conceived as depending on what seems to be an objective knowledge of things, 'arriving' at them as they are out there."[130] Graham continues: "This has often been understood as an anticipation of the scientific attitude which unfortunately failed to bear fruit."[131] Hu Shih regarded this tradition as a viable foundation for modern science in China. As he relates, "Fortunately, there is this scientific tradition which makes the Chinese feel not entirely at sea in the scientific age."[132] This does not change the history of specific practices in China and the West, but it does invite us to reconsider just how alien Dewey's "most general" sense of science really is to Chinese thinking. Arguably, it is not that strange at all.

Returning to Dewey's "The Authority of Science" lecture, he proceeds to explain that scientific authority has three hallmarks: *naturalism*, *publicity*, and *education*. These can be examined in turn. First, *naturalism*. Science, explains Dewey, "substitutes realism for the old method of speculation, and naturalism for supernaturalism." The latter substitution needs to be properly understood. Without question, one of the signature hang-ups in Western thinking is the knee-jerk assumption that "naturalism" somehow entails the evaporation of spiritual value. Cultural conservatives like Irving Babbitt believe as much. Such errors, however, must be corrected. The rejection of "supernaturalism" is almost wholly procedural. When the question of same-sex marriage, for instance, is approached with a "scientific attitude," the emphasis is placed on *fact*—inquiry "follows observation and investigation of fact with a judgment about its value." The alternative approach would be based on some "supernatural mystery." When value is furnished by "Heaven's plan" or what Christians call "God's will," there is nothing there to be investigated (*gewu* 格物). As a result, thoughts and actions "accumulate day by day without being examined . . . and people, without taking thought, move into deeper thralldom to rules which are essentially absurd."[133]

The second hallmark of science, *publicity*, is also a procedural feature. Scientific inquiries make themselves open to "public examination" and rely upon public modes of communication. This feature dovetails with the third hallmark of science, *education*. Dewey recognizes the function of education as the organ that transmits custom and tradition. This has been appreciated, he says, "since time out of mind." The question in a scientific society, however, is how to accomplish this function while also developing in people the "ability to think and to judge." As Dewey establishes at the outset of this lecture, the intellectual and spiritual aspects of associated living form the foundation of human civilization. The traditions that carry it forward, however, must be tended by critical reflection and guided by intelligence. Through this, "the quality of our social life in the future will be enhanced" and one's culture made durable.[134]

For the concluding Lecture XVI, "Intellectual Freedom," we return to Dewey's own notes. Dewey identifies the topic of this lecture as the "culmination" of the ideal factors discussed in the previous lecture. The intellectual and spiritual factors that establish the foundations of civilization *culminate* in experience that is cultural. "Culture, civilization measure the worth of social life, and civilization and culture are what they are because of ideal elements," writes Dewey. "Put in a more specific form, the actual worth of any social arrangement lies in its *educative* effect."[135]

In this context, the word "educative" is best understood in terms of its Latin origin *educare*, "drawing out." As Dewey explains, each culture is measured according to what its associated living "draws out" from the human person—"its release of thought, its nurture of the imagination, its refinement of emotions."[136] Here, what unites Dewey and Confucius as masters of *educare* also unites them as masters in the technologies of culture. As Hall and Ames explain, for Confucius, ritual-custom (*li* 禮) serves as a "body of practices for registering, developing, and displaying one's own sense of cultural importances." Ritual-customs "authorize those who participate in the life forms of the community, and the community is in turn authored by them."[137] Ritual-custom thus "educates" in a double respect, both as the subject matter of an education (*xue* 學) and as the means through which the elements of human personhood are, as Dewey says, "released," "nurtured," and "refined."

This provides further insight into why Confucius tells his son: "If you do not study the *Songs* you will be at a loss as to what to say . . . If you do not study the *Rituals*, you will be at a loss as to where to stand."[138] Becoming a person without mastering the technologies of culture is like "trying to take your stand with your face to the wall."[139] Without access to such instrumentalties, nothing of cultural value is "released," "nurtured," or "refined." Such education, as Confucius and Dewey would agree, cannot be pursued alone. "Mind lives only in communication, in give-and-take," Dewey explains in his China notes. "It has to receive from others to be stimulated; it has to give out in order that its ideas may take form and be rendered clear and articulate, coherent."[140] Thus, as Joseph Grange reiterates: "*Li* 禮 is the social grammar used by communities to convey their most important values." Culture itself amounts to "the ongoing process of finding adequate media for the expression of values important to a community and its people." For Grange, the expression and enjoyment of *meaning* is what hangs in the balance when it comes to education and to *li*. Education is the critical mechanism through which particular cultures transmit their meanings through sustaining their own ritual-customs. There is no cultural substitute for this—and no other alternative. As Grange reminds us: "A culture that cannot communicate its meanings is on the way out."[141]

This helps to explain Confucius' seriousness when speaking about the relationship between associated humanity (*ren* 仁) and ritual-custom (*li* 禮). When asked what the former virtue entails, Confucius replies: "If it is not *li*, look away. If it is not *li*, stop listening. If it is not *li*, remain silent. If it is not *li*, do not engage."[142] The message here is at least threefold. First, Confucius is reminding us that there is no safety net for one's culture. Should we *stop* observing forms of association that release and communicate the meanings of a particular culture then those meanings are no longer released or communicated. End of story. Second, Confucius suggests that there are plenty of opportunities to entertain sights, sounds, words, and actions that fall short of the proper standards of cultural meaning sustained through what Dewey identifies as its "ideal elements," intellectual and spiritual. The media through which our meanings pass is replete with *meaningless* content as well—gossip, sensations, lies, and diversions. We simply must tune such content out. Third, Confucius is saying that no one can become civilized on behalf of another person. He makes it clear in this passage that becoming *ren* is something that emerges from oneself (*youji* 由己). Each person who *fails* to participate in and contribute to the deeper meanings sustained through the technologies of culture makes the social fabric that much weaker. And to repeat: *there is no safety net*.

A proper Confucian democracy would recognize that government agencies have an obligation to *preserve* the means and to *promote* the use of cultural technologies. These technologies enable what Dewey calls "freedom of expression," in the sense "not only that society may get the advantage of every individual's contribution, but in order that the individual may have anything worth expressing."[143] Such dual motivation echoes that which Confucius relates as the rationale for mastering classics like the *Songs*.[144] Such technologies enable persons to express themselves effectively—with depth, nuance, and impact. Problems arise not only when such mediums for public expression are neglected. They can also be forcibly distorted or suppressed. Where government agencies are to blame or stand complicit in this they are failing their people.

Dewey was deeply disturbed by media trends leading up to the First World War and especially by the implications of the Espionage/Sedition Acts of 1917–1918 in the United States. In a piece entitled, "The New Paternalism," he reflects on how media coverage during the war provided a "remarkable demonstration of the guidance of the news upon which the formation of public opinion depends." The news was not only censored during the war, it was positively skewed. "One almost wonders whether the word 'news' is not destined to be replaced by the word 'propaganda'—though of course words linger after things have been transformed," Dewey writes.[145] With such events fresh in his memory, Dewey continues in his "Intellectual Freedom" lecture in China to reflect on the emergence of propaganda in the media. "This is more dangerous than censorship because it has the form of free speech," he tells his Chinese audience. "It poisons the sources of belief, the wells of truth . . . There was never a time when real knowledge of what people all over the world are doing and thinking was so badly needed as at present, and upon the whole there hasn't been a time when this information was so perverted and distorted."[146]

Dewey's point is simple and utterly relevant. The dissemination (and false attribution) of what we now call "fake news" stabs at the heart of democracy. Such distortions prevent knowledge from being communicated. From the Confucian perspective, this makes it more difficult to investigate things (*gewu* 格物) and thereby know (*zhi* 知) the world, thus preventing one from cultivating one's person (*xiushen* 修身) as a responsible citizen. So again—the health of the news media is critical to the health of any democracy. As Hall and Ames observe, the kind of education that a "Confucian democracy" requires is one that "militates against the sense of disconnectedness that is endemic in a society whose sources of information are predominantly patterned by a sensationalizing news media."[147] This, unfortunately, is largely what drives public opinion in the United States. Our media Goliaths pose tremendous challenges for local communities already ravished by their divisive effects. There is no option but to resist these forces.[148]

As we resist the forces of "fake news," we must remain mindful of what "real news" actually is. Etymologically, "news" is simply a plural form of the "new," the "news" (plural) are the "new things" (*nova*). In *The Public and Its Problems*, Dewey explains that the problem with the "news" (plural) is that they come at us "without coordination and consecutiveness," and without such continuity "events are not events, but mere occurrences, intrusions." On cable television, we receive "news alerts" when each new thing "breaks" and this holds our attention until another new thing is "just breaking." Such sensations, Dewey explains, *are not events*. They are too "isolated from their connections" to even happen. "An event," Dewey writes, "implies that out of which a happening proceeds."[149] Things always seem to be happening on cable news, but very few of these things register as *events*.

Philosophically, we should approach this on the most sophisticated level that we can. Dewey thinks carefully about what "events" actually are. As he suggests, "Slipping down a hill" is an event, but only within a larger context that includes the hill.[150] In Daoist cosmology, *dao* 道 constantly gives birth to "news" (plural), but each "new thing" (*one*) relates to everything else right away (*two*), assuming value and coherence within a more enduring set of patterns (*three*). So it is with anything that actually *happens*. The art of journalism, in its ontological sense, is to communicate some aspect of what is happening by presenting it within some clarifying *context*. This renders it known (*zhi* 知) and such knowing constitutes another happening. The same process occurs in education. As Confucius says, the educator is one who "reviews the old in order to realize the new."[151] To realize the new (*zhixin* 知新) is to secure what is "new" within the continuity of an ongoing set of meanings, thus realizing its significance to what came before and what is coming next. Good journalism, like good education, is thus ideally an *educare*—a "drawing out" that stimulates the situational awareness and felt sensibilities (*xin* 心) of those who "know" what is happening through its means.

As Dewey suggests in the "Intellectual Freedom" lecture, "[Such] activity of thought and emotion is distinctively human, and without it [the human] lives on a non-human plane."[152] To be fully human (*ren* 人) is both to *know* what is happening and to be *engaged* emotionally and intellectually in its happening. As Grange observes, this is an easily overlooked aspect of Confucius' teachings—i.e., that "Confucius demands that his disciples actually take part in what is happening." As Grange reminds us: "There is no such thing as a spectator theory of knowledge" in the Confucian tradition.[153] Similarly, there is no such thing as a "spectator theory of democracy." As Warren G. Frisina argues, the continuity between knowledge-and-action, as captured in the slogan "unity of knowledge-and-action" (*zhixingheyi* 知行合一), is one area in which Dewey and the Confucian tradition plainly overlap. In each tradition, "knowledge is a kind of action rather than the passive mental replication of the real."[154] Thus, in a Confucian democracy, as in Dewey's own, technologies must be sustained to promote the communication of knowledge in order to facilitate participation in what is actually happening.

This is why despots attack not only the news media, but also the artists. As Dewey understood, "Artists have always been the real purveyors of news, for it is not the outward happening in itself which is new, but the kindling by it of emotion, perception and appreciation."[155] Good journalism is artistic in quality precisely because it has the power to make people more humane (*ren* 仁) in outlook, helping them to think and feel (*xin* 心) things properly. The power of despots, however, comes not from fostering compassion and communication but from sowing animosity and fear. Presently, this is the primary tool by which power is secured in American politics: turning citizens against one another. But let there be no mistake—such behavior is patently *un*-American and the exact opposite of democracy in all its forms. As Dewey reminds us at the close of his "Intellectual Freedom" lecture: "*Every* individual is a center of conscious life, of happiness and suffering, of imagination and thought. This is the final principle upon which democracy rests."[156]

Dewey understood that democracies are slow to be realized. As Horace Kallen observed, America has yet to achieve its own pluralistic, multi-ethnic democracy. Today, we continue the struggle towards this ideal. It is easy to lose faith in America. Dewey, however, never lost faith in the American prospect. "Democracy will come into its own," he writes—"for democracy is a name for a life of free and enriching communication. It had its seer in Walt Whitman. It will have its consummation when free social inquiry is indissolubly wedded to the art of full and moving communication."[157]

Dewey Leaves China

"[We are] on the train on the way to Qingdao, and for the first time I feel as if we were really leaving China and I am feeling quite sentimental about it," records Dewey.[158] His final days in China were spent exploring Shandong's beautiful coastal city, built by the Germans but at that point occupied by the Japanese. He visited a movie theatre with Lucy, Alice did some last minute shopping, and they all enjoyed the lovely scenery. "No wonder the Germans are sore," Dewey remarked.[159] Qingdao was among the finest cities that they had seen in China.

Dewey would leave port knowing that he had made a difference. The "School Reform Decree" of 1922 was being finalized, a document that would lay the groundwork for a transition from the imperial exams to a more progressive educational system, thus promoting "the spirit of democratic education" in China. Dewey had contributed to the meetings in Taoyuan in 1919 that led to the drafting of its provisions.[160] The principles outlined in the 1922 Decree were as follows: "(1) To adapt the educational system to the needs of social evolution, (2) to promote the spirit of democracy, (3) to develop individuality, (4) to take the economic status of the people into special consideration, (5) to promote education for life, (6) to facilitate the spread of universal education, and (7) to make the school system flexible enough to allow for local variations."[161]

One of Dewey's students in particular, Chen Heqin 陳鶴琴, was well positioned to expand the reform movement by building upon Dewey's ideas. After earning his MA from Columbia in 1919, Chen returned to China to devote himself to early childhood education. After experimenting with Dewey's methods and conducting extensive empirical research on his own, he published major works in the 1920s on early childhood development, largely confirming Dewey theories. In 1923, Chen founded the Gulou 鼓楼 Kindergarten in Nanjing and served as its Principal. He would go on to found several other schools in eastern China.¹⁶² Chen's approach came to known as "Living Education" (*huojiaoyu* 活教育), a movement around which a number of Dewey-inspired themes converged. In 1942, Chen would establish the journal *Living Education* and in 1947 devote an entire issue to the importance of Dewey's influence in China.¹⁶³ With figures like Chen Heqin taking the lead, Dewey's influence on the reform movement felt secure.

Returning to America, Dewey wasted no time getting back into affairs—teaching, writing, and reconnecting. "You probably have stored in your brain and graven across your heart a good deal of valuable feeling about China," wrote his publisher at E. P. Dutton, eager to get a monograph on China out of Dewey.¹⁶⁴ Dewey, however, showed no interest in writing a book on China. He had already written close to three dozen articles on East Asian affairs, and he had more China-related articles in the works. Plus, he was brimming with philosophical ideas that would result in some of his finest works. After leaving China, *Human Nature and Conduct*, *Experience and Nature*, and *The Public and Its Problems* would be written in a five-year burst.

Dewey remained engaged with China in other ways. At Columbia, he was returning to the *de facto* center for Chinese students in America. By 1920, Columbia had the largest Chinese student population in the United States (123 students), and a majority of them were there to study education.¹⁶⁵ When the Columbia Faculty Club hosted a "welcome back" dinner for Dewey, he spoke encouragingly about the University's connections to the Chinese world. "The influence of students who have returned from America is strong," he told the assembled faculty, "and those from Teacher's College particularly so." He delivered a status report on women's education in China, and described the Chinese students that he had encountered on his trip. "Where American students take an interest in athletics and other forms of student activities," he explained, "the Chinese students talk, think, and act on matters relating to their country's welfare."¹⁶⁶ Dewey was lastingly impressed by this.

Among the Chinese students waiting on Dewey's return was Feng Youlan 馮友蘭. Feng had attended Dewey's lectures in Beijing before leaving for Columbia in the winter of 1919. He was eager to begin formal studies under Dewey once the philosopher returned. Feng had, however, developed some misconceptions about Dewey's approach. Even though Dewey lectured extensively on the history of Western philosophy while in China, Feng came away with the impression that all Western philosophy (before Dewey) was being "superseded and discarded" to make way for "progressivism." Feng was at Columbia to hear "Dewey teach Dewey." He was surprised to discover, however, that Dewey mostly "talked of Aristotle and Locke and the others" rather than focus on his own system.[167] Feng soon came to realize that, as a critical method, philosophical reconstruction *requires* that continuity be retained with one's own historical tradition—a feature that would distinguish Dewey's approach in the coming decades from the more a-historical approach of the analytic movement. Feng would come to embrace Dewey's broadminded and reconstructive attitude in his own treatments of Chinese philosophy. "All ideas or ideals of the past are equally to be reviewed and revalued," Feng writes, "and none of them can claim to have more authority than the others."[168]

While working together at Columbia, Dewey and Feng would occasionally discuss Chinese affairs over dinner.[169] Feng would write his dissertation, *A Comparative Study of Life Ideals*, under Dewey's supervision. The work, which was completed in 1923, was something of an East-West *tour de force*, covering the human-nature relations in major Chinese schools alongside Plato, Aristotle, Descartes, Kant, Hegel, and others.[170] At Feng's dissertation defense, Dewey pressed him primarily on method. "Shouldn't we trace the developmental *relations* among [these traditions]," Dewey asked, "instead of laying them out fanwise, alongside one another?"[171] Dewey's approach, while historically minded, was never simply historical. It was the historical *connections* between philosophies that interested him most. Such an approach, again, would influence Feng as he went on to become one of the most important Chinese historian-cum-philosophers of his generation. Feng's primary concern would become how "Chinese and Western philosophies can be complementary and how, in give-and-take, Chinese thought may contribute to a future world philosophy."[172] Dewey surely learned from Feng's dissertation a good deal about Chinese philosophy. Again, how this influenced his own thinking is unknown. His supervision of Feng's dissertation, however, covers exactly the period during which he wrote the Carus lectures that became *Experience and Nature*.[173] Jessica Ching-Sze Wang alerts us to the possibility of cross-fertilization between these projects.[174]

Dewey also enjoyed the company of Meng Chih, the descendent of Mencius. Meng arrived at Columbia to begin his own graduate studies shortly after Dewey returned. Dewey was delighted to receive his old friend. In turn, Meng was happy to receive Dewey's advice and counsel. "Dewey tended to take a broad approach," Meng remembers, "[suggesting] that I audit a number of courses or professors before settling on any particular area of research." Dewey was never one to recruit his own acolytes. Irving Babbitt, however, was a different story. Upon learning that a descendent of Mencius was at Columbia, the Harvard sage arranged for Meng to come to Cambridge to give a lecture on his ancestor's teachings. Meng was happy to oblige. Babbitt, however, could not resist the impertinence of using the occasion to malign

Dewey's influence on Chinese students at Columbia and to promote his own agenda. "During the course of discussion," Meng remembers, "[Babbitt] warned that China should be wary of the differences between Confucianism and pragmatism, and he characterized John Dewey as 'the greatest catastrophe in Western thought since Rousseau.'"[175]

As always, Dewey remained focused on what was important. The second remission of the Boxer Indemnity Fund was soon to be released. He had agreed to be a founding trustee for the "China Foundation for the Promotion of Education and Culture," which would oversee the allocation of its funds. Along with his colleague, Paul Monroe, and a former student, Kou Ping-wen 郭秉文, Dewey was beginning to think about a future "China Institute." The project would come to fruition in 1926. Meng was appointed Honorary Secretary in 1928, and he would go on to serve as its Director from 1929 through 1965. Over the course of his long service, Meng co-served as the Director of the "Chinese Educational Mission" through Qinghua University, coordinating the arrival of Chinese students in America, arranging scholarly exchanges between China and the United States, and creating opportunities for Americans to study in China. The Institute expanded its operations over the years, opening hospitality centers for visiting Chinese students and offering courses in Chinese civilization to public school teachers.[176] Dewey served as a founding member on the board, while simultaneously serving as Chair of the "National Committee for the Legal Defense of China," a committee formed to address legal hardships and discrimination faced by Chinese nationals in the United States, tracking disputes and providing defendents with adequate counsel.[177] From this point forward, the lives of Chinese people would be woven into Dewey's own.

Dewey's family, meanwhile, wove itself back into China. Lucy was in the United States for only two years before returning to China to marry a Viennese gentleman working for an American trading company stationed in Beijing and in Ulaanbaatar, Mongolia. They would be married in Shanghai in the summer of 1923. In October 1924, John and Alice Dewey's grandson, Carl, was born in Beijing—a healthy 7.7 lbs. and "the largest baby in the hospital."[178] Lucy's updates from China and Mongolia are lengthy and vividly detailed. She relates her experiences in China and Central Asia in a stream of letters that John and Alice Dewey must have cherished. The several letters that Dewey sent to China, unfortunately, have not survived. There was much reporting, however, from the Chinese side. Lucy and her new husband had plenty of friends in Beijing and they remained politically well connected. They would send Dewey details on the latest happenings in Chinese culture and politics, including information on Sun Yat-sen's health in the months before his death.[179]

While Dewey returned to teaching and writing, Alice took to helping Chinese students adjust as they arrived to study at Columbia. "It is a satisfaction to know that you are concerned about their welfare," an official from Wellesley College writes, thanking Alice for her assistance in facilitating the transfer of two Chinese students.[180] "We came here about 6 p.m. and cooked our supper," reads the resulting thank-you note. "Herewith you will find your key."[181] The Dewey's had opened their apartment to the newly arrived students. Such hospitality was well known among Chinese students at Columbia and warmly appreciated. When Dewey lost Alice to heart failure in the summer of 1927, among his condolences was to learn that she had been "the beloved mother of many Chinese students in America."[182]

Dewey's philosophical influence in China began to wane in the late 1920s as the Nationalists came to power and reorganized educational standards along more classical lines. "Dewey in China" scholarship is better positioned to trace the varied fortunes of progressive education during this tumultuous period in Chinese history.[183] The most important recent study is Gu Hongliang's work, *A Misreading of Pragmatism: The Influence of Dewey's Philosophy on Modern Chinese Philosophy*.[184] As the title suggests, many Chinese thinkers "misread" (*wudu* 誤讀) Dewey's philosophy, but not in ways that were necessasarily bad. Gu traces how Chinese thinkers variously absorbed Dewey into their own projects and outlooks in ways that were selective, creative, and constructive. In terms of intra-cultural philosophy, Dewey was "assimilated" into Chinese thinking. Dewey's ideas, in any case, were not entirely rejected even when the fortunes of progressive education turned. The Nationalist government, after all, awarded Dewey the "Blue Grand Cordon of the Order of the Jade" for his service to Chinese education in 1938.[185] Dewey always understood that China needed to determine its own path forward, and where "*Duwei* 杜威" fit into that was never really his concern. He had received from China more than he could ever return, and that deposit had become permanent in his own philosophical outlook.

One can only imagine how Dewey must have felt as he boarded the oceanliner in the port of Qingdao. He arrived in China at a professional low point, and he was leaving after two years, two months, and ten days personally and intellectually re-energized. As the SS *Shinyō Maru* cut its path at 13.5 knots across the Pacific—straight lines from Japan to San Francisco *via* Honolulu—Dewey could look ahead. His best work was yet to come.

❧

This concludes part I of volume two. We have explored topics such as education, custom, tradition, and democracy, as well as Dewey's visit to China and its influence on his thinking. We have explored the importance of ritual-custom (*li* 禮) in sustaining a world in which human-level meanings are transmitted and viable individuals are realized. As we have seen, such achievements are not possible without the operation of form (*wen* 文). This operation, however, is easily misunderstood in early Confucian philosophy. For Confucius, ritual-custom (*li*) is not designed to be eternally fixed but rather to facilitate the achievement and preservation of harmony (*he* 和).¹⁸⁶ When this function goes unrecognized, ritual-custom goes from being something organic and living to something *static* and *dead*—like petrified wood.

It is easy to miss this when reading the *Analects*. As we saw earlier, in one of its sharpest rebukes, Confucius disparages the errant Zaiwo for not endorsing the ritual-custom of the three-year mourning period on the death of his parents. "One year is enough," says Zaiwo.¹⁸⁷ Today, it is hard to imagine criticizing another person for how he or she chooses to mourn a parent, but Confucius does just that. Thus, he *must* have a single, unchanging form in mind for how this ritual-custom is to be performed—or so we think.

Amy Olberding has done some fine work in this area, alerting us to both the uniqueness of the parent-child relation and the caution that must be exercised when approaching issues of mortality in the *Analects*, framed as it is "in a context culturally and temporally distant from our own." As she notes, the challenge of understanding Confucius' injunction to mourn one's parents in a particular manner "resides in locating the sorts of judgments he believes should properly inform our sorrow." Such content needs to be understood in its native context. As Olberding points out, this is an instance in which "the material realities of [Confucius'] time operate against our own popular sentiments."¹⁸⁸ While there is undoubtedly continuity between the ancients and ourselves when it comes to how one reacts to the loss of a parent (this must, at some level, be a function of *xing* 性), the ways in which such emotions register at the cultural-level (*xi* 習) diverge as time passes and circumstances change. Ritual-customs (*li* 禮) evolve within the matrix of culture in order to sustain the effective communication of such feelings. True: Confucius insists upon restoring the mourning practices of the Zhou dynasty. He had no intention of changing such practices. He was thoroughly convinced that they were right and proper and that they worked (*xing* 行). *Nowhere*, however, does he suggest that such practices will never change. To the contrary, he suggests to Zizhang that such practices *do* change but that their historical trajectories can only be known retrospectively from some future point.¹⁸⁹

Dewey arrived in China seventy-plus generations after Confucius. At that juncture, parental funeral rituals had grown excessively elaborate and complex. Among other things, the use of moirologists (professional mourners) had become widespread, a practice that has recently rebounded in China.¹⁹⁰ The professional mourner is paid to wail sufficiently to affect emotional contagion so that everyone at the funeral starts crying—a practice that is hard to imagine Confucius endorsing.[191] About six months prior to Dewey's arrival, Hu Shih felt that he had something important to say about such practices. He arranged to give a public lecture on "Reforming Funeral Rites" in Beijing on November 27, 1918. But three days before, on November 24, he received an urgent telegram from his hometown. The news was not good. His mother had died. Hu left Beijing for is hometown in Anhui the following day. He would never deliver his prepared remarks on funeral practices.

Hu Shih would compose a new piece the following year entitled, "Reforming Funeral Rites: My Personal Experience."[192] In this essay, Hu describes in detail how he modified traditions in paying respects to his mother. Her obituary, he explains, was brief and devoid of the "empty" conventions that were routinely employed. He shortened the typically long ceremonies and eliminated practices that he felt were affected or contrived. He elected to wear the traditional mourning garments, but after five months he felt that he was ready to resume his normal attire. Confucius had indeed upbraided his contemporary, Zaiwo, for not following the prescribed ritual of mourning one's parents for three years—but 2,400 years were then separating the death of Zaiwo's parents from the death of Hu Shih's mother. It would be outlandish to insist that the same cultural rules apply. Hu sought in his own way to bring into focus what Confucius taught was fundamental (*ben* 本) to the practice of mourning rituals: to "express real grief rather than worry over formal details."[193] Hu did what he needed to do—he struck a balance between ritual formality (*wen* 文) and the unique texture (*zhi* 質) of his own emotions.

Part II of this volume will focus largely on how such balances are struck ethically and religiously in the human experience. We begin by inquiring further into the cultivation of personhood in the *Analects*—exploring how it does and does not resemble Western "virtue ethics," and how more contemporary hermeneutical approaches are improving our understanding. We also continue to develop harmony (*he* 和) as a normative measure and look further into how it informs early Confucian thinking.

The most important undertaking in the second half of this volume, however, will be to formulate and defend a naturalized reading of *tian* 天 that is able to underwrite early Confucian ethical and religious thought. Here, our featured philosopher is Mencius. Relying on Donald J. Munro's and Irene Bloom's readings for guidance, the so-called "Heaven's plan" reading of the *Mencius* championed by Philip J. Ivanhoe and others will be deconstructed and replaced. Dewey will be instrumental in the concomitant reconstruction of what *tian* comes to mean in the subsequent framework. The argument will be that, for Mencius as for Dewey, the sensibilities that inform our deepest ethical and religious experiences do not descend from a preternatural "Heaven." Rather, they are sourced deep within Nature (*tian*), such that our ethical and religious experiences reflect the continuity (*yi* 一) of human-level experiences with the broader cosmos. Restoring such continuity requires us to rescue Mencius from his Greek-medieval captivity and to return him to his native intellectual habitat: *Chinese natural philosophy.*

VOLUME TWO

Part II

5

Roles and Exemplars

Some people have argued that morality is not a matter of growth, that it is nothing more than proper conduct. When conduct is proper, they say, it is moral, even though it may be the same behavior that has prevailed throughout the history of humankind . . . If we were always to behave exactly as people before us behaved, our conduct would be mechanical and without life, like an automobile or a locomotive. How could we, in such a case, claim that our conduct was moral?

—John Dewey, National Peking University, October 1919

The *Analects* as Virtue Ethics

Let your countenance be pleasant, but in serious matters somewhat grave.
Sleep not when others speak, and sit not when others stand.
When you meet with one of greater quality than yourself, stop and retire, especially if it be a door or any straight place to give way for him to pass.
Run not in the streets; neither go too slowly nor with mouth open. Go not shaking your arms. Go not upon the toes nor in a dancing fashion.

Related here are selections from George Washington's *Rules of Civility and Decent Behavior in Company and Conversation*, etiquette tips drawn from a sixteenth-century collection that Washington received as a penmanship assignment when he was fourteen years old.[1] There are 110 entries, many of which resemble passages from Book Ten of the Confucian *Analects*. There, at the center of the *Analects*, we receive an intimate portrait of the Master. We learn that, "At court, when speaking with lower officials, he was congenial, and when speaking with higher officials, straightforward yet respectful." Also,

"While eating he would not converse, and having retired for the night he would not talk." And, "On passing through the entrance way to the duke's court, he would bow forward from the waist . . . and while in attendance, he would not stand in the middle of the entranceway."[2] One imagines that Confucius refrained from proceeding down the street "with mouth open" or in a "dancing fashion" as well. Indeed, many Book Ten behaviors sound like items that could have found their way into Washington's lesson book.

Of course, while thematically similar, they differ completely in mode of presentation. Washington's *Rules* are just that—*rules*. Meanwhile, Book Ten provides a series of *examples* set by the Master himself. Here, we observe a feature that for Western-trained philosophers signals that Confucianism more closely resembles "virtue ethics" than deontological or consequentialist ethics. Virtue ethics emphasizes the *character* of the ethical person, not the *rules* that determine such behavior or the *results* that follow. Such stipulations do not factor into a virtue-based ethics. For virtue ethicists, behavior that is virtuous is its "own reward" owing to the kind of creatures that we are. This results for Aristotle in human "flourishing" (*eudaimonia*) and for Aquinas in a kind of "blissful felicity" (*beatitudo*) in the virtuous. As Stephen C. Angle explains, virtue-ethical treatments of early Confucianism are a fairly recent phenomenon, occurring within the larger context of the rebound of virtue ethics in the Western academy.[3] Arguably, however, the Presbyterian minister and eminent Sinologist James Legge (1815–1897) established the conceptual foundation for such readings in the nineteenth century. In any event, a rich literature treating the *Analects* within this general framework has emerged since the 1980s.[4]

Bryan W. Van Norden adopts this approach, arguing that the *Analects* qualifies as a "virtue ethics" if the definition of that term is understood "thinly." His "thin" description includes the following four criteria:

1) An account of what a "flourishing" human life is like.

2) An account of what virtues contribute to leading such a life.

3) An account of how one acquires those virtues.

4) A philosophical anthropology that explains what humans are like, such that they can acquire those virtues so as to flourish in that kind of life.

The *Analects*, Van Norden argues, satisfies all four criteria. First, it presents an account of human flourishing, focusing as he observes on "participation in ritual activities, ethically informed aesthetic appreciation and intellectual activity, acting for the good of others, and generally participating in relationships with other people, especially family relationships." Second, there are a number of terms that suggest themselves as possible virtues. Examples include "humaneness" (*ren* 仁), "righteousness" (*yi* 義), "propriety" (*li* 禮), "wisdom" (*zhi* 智), "courage" (*yong* 勇), "filial piety" (*xiao* 孝), and so on. Third, there is an account of how virtue is acquired. It involves the dynamic interplay between "learning" (*xue* 學) and "thinking" (*si* 思). Fourth, it contains some understanding of human nature. Specifically, that such a nature is "inert and recalcitrant," a view that surfaces in *Analects* 1.15 where self-cultivation is likened to cutting and polishing jade. Thus having satisfied 1–4, Van Norden concludes that the *Analects* can be understood as a "virtue ethics."[5]

From the standpoint of intra-cultural philosophy, there is little doubt that the *Analects* can be understood as a virtue ethics because it already is. Numerous essays, monographs, and edited volumes all attest to this fact. Clearly, the text is readily assimilated as a virtue ethics by a number of commentators. Such assimilation occurs when scholars familiar with the Western tradition of virtue ethics locate in the *Analects* elements corresponding to Van Norden's 1–4 and proceed to read the text alongside other traditions that have similar elements, thus experimenting with problems that are set within that general paradigm. In doing such work, implicitly or explicitly, one brings texts like Aristotle's *Nicomachean Ethics* and the *Analects* together in mind as two comparable instances of "virtue ethics," which then operates as a *tertium*. This *tertium* becomes part of a cultural situation in which "*specific* philosophical relationships" are observed.[6] As established in chapter 1 of volume one, this is what the human mind does, and it results in important intra-cultural work. The only pitfall is one that we all share—namely, that the *tertium quids* informing such activities are more apparent to others than to ourselves. To those *not* interested in virtue ethics, the fact that Van Norden's 1–4 brings an external logic to the *Analects* is glaringly obvious.[7]

Like it or not, there is an iron rule in hermeneutics—*Seek and ye shall find*. Those who are looking for virtue ethics in the *Analects* tend to find it. Meanwhile, those who are *not* looking for it tend to find something else. This rule is bilateral. Ni Peimin, for instance, employs the Song-Ming notion of "artistic perfection" (*gongfu* 功夫) as a guiding framework in which to read the *Analects*.[8] From this hermeneutic perspective, the extra baggage that comes with the virtue ethics approach is noticed immediately. As Ni explains, Confucius' teachings aim at personal cultivation "in the sense of creating an excellent human life rather than in the sense of fulfilling a predetermined *telos*."[9] The latter notion, in its Greek-medieval form, is overlaid on the text *in order* to read it as a virtue ethics. Subsequent experiments then shed light on how the *Analects* does or does not respond to such an overlay.

Nothing here is inconsistent with Van Norden's own methodological position. He is not suggesting that virtue ethics is the *only* correct way to read the *Analects*. His claim instead is that "virtue ethics illuminates many interesting aspects of [the tradition] that might otherwise go unnoticed." That is beyond dispute, and the same is true of many interpretations. In this respect, Van Norden's approach is akin to intra-cultural philosophy in that he too embraces "methodological pluralism," wherein "there are a number of disciplines and methodologies that can be applied to texts in ways that are illuminating."[10]

Intra-cultural philosophers, however, are not interested in *every* reading that happens to be illuminating. Too many lights blind the eyes, and when it comes to the *Analects* there are too many lights to choose from. Usually, one is trying to *do* something with the text and looks for readings that determine whether or not it can be done. At present, we are looking for readings of Chinese philosophy that might help us to update philosophical conceptions that are "out of gear" with more scientific understandings.

For such purposes, the "virtue ethics" approach is somewhat helpful, but also problematic. Its main problem lies in the "philosophical anthropology" department. Like any moral theory, virtue ethics requires some foundation upon which to ground its claims. Deontology is grounded in "reason." Utilitarianism in "desire." Virtue ethics is traditionally grounded in "human nature," such that for Aristotle, each thing has a nature (*phusis*) that operates as an internal principle of change (*kinēsis*)—an original constitution with a built-in potential (*dunamis*) that is neither contingent nor alterable.[11] Aristotle presumes that humans possess such a nature and thus identifies the "human good" with activities "in accordance with [that nature's] virtue (*arete*)."[12] Medieval theologians assimilate Aristotle's view and provide divine reinforcement to its foundation, declaring God to be the creator of all natures. Each end (*telos*) thus becomes part of a grand scheme, such that for Aquinas, "divine goodness is the end of all things."[13] Within such a framework, "all events, even the most trifling, are disposed according to God's plan."[14] As we have seen, Dewey identifies such Greek-medieval assumptions as "out of gear" with what we currently know about the world. Yet, much of our common sense and moral reasoning remains grounded in them.

Van Norden concedes that the virtue ethical reading of the *Analects* faces challenges. Among the "thin" traits that he cites (1–4), the text provides only "the most sketchy account of philosophical anthropology."[15] This is problematic because "human nature" is precisely where the theory is supposed to be grounded. This inconvenience troubles Confucian virtue ethicists like Edward Slingerland. "Without the element of universality lent to a virtue ethic in the form of substantialist claims about human nature," he writes, "it is difficult to see how the slide into cultural relativism—which would reduce any virtue ethic to a mere 'notional' curiosity—can be checked."[16] The *Analects*, however, refuses to mitigate such concerns. The term "nature" (*xing* 性) occurs only twice in the text, and these instances provide Slingerland little reassurance. First: "Human beings are similar in their natures (*xing*), but vary with respect to their cultural practices (*xi* 習)," and second: "The Master formulated no doctrine (*yan* 言) about our natures (*xing*)."[17] The first statement, as Van Norden says, is "painfully vague," and the second suggests that Confucius intended to keep it that way.[18] Even if one were to grant that *Analects* 1.15 teaches that human nature is "inert and recalcitrant," as Van Norden suggests, this offers little assistance. A human nature that is resistant to its own "flourishing" is hardly a solid candidate for a virtue ethics. Given the lack of any obvious theory—*plus the fact that the text states explicitly that there is no theory*—"human nature" is an exceedingly weak foundation upon which to ground virtue ethics in the *Analects*. One cannot force the text to deliver what it claims not to have.

In keeping with Greek-medieval reasoning, the next step would be to bypass "human nature" and to look for its divine reinforcement in the *Analects*, grounding its alleged virtue ethics in "Heaven's plan" just as Aquinas folded Aristotelian natures into "God's plan." Philip J. Ivanhoe represents this approach. Relying on literalist readings of passages that mention *tian* 天 in the *Analects*, he generates a robust account of "Heaven's plan" in the text. Threatened by ambush, for instance, Confucius says: "Since *tian* is not going to destroy our culture, what can [these people] do to me?" For Ivanhoe, this means that Confucius "believed that he had a special role in Heaven's plan." Confucius complains that: "No one understands me . . . only *tian* understands me." This means that, "Only Heaven could really understand [Confucius]"— and this should be taken literally because, "If not omniscient, Heaven seems at least capable of understanding anything it chooses to understand." When his favorite student dies, Confucius says: "Oh, *tian* is the ruin of me!" This means for Ivanhoe that Confucius has "complete confidence that Heaven works for the best," and so on.[19]

These few passages, which are peripheral to the philosophical core of the *Analects*, can be read in various ways. A. C. Graham notes that Confucius "tends to personify" *tian* 天 when he wonders whether or not it is on his side, a point on which he is "seen to fluctuate."[20] Robert Eno regards these passages as little more than evidence that Confucius had the "ability to employ traditional religious rhetoric in order to say something about matters *other* than *tian*," since the latter performs "no significant function in [his] philosophy."[21] Franklin Perkins likewise notes that appeals to *tian* in these passages are not their point, but rather the "means toward some further point."[22] All of this leaves open the possibility that such passages are not much more than figures of speech, eulogizing, and/or pathetic fallacy.

But who really knows? Since no one can penetrate the head of Confucius, the literalist readings of *tian* 天 are incapable of either verification or refutation. They are sheer postulations. Nevertheless, Ivanhoe extrapolates boldly from them, asserting that Confucius maintains that, "Heaven has a *plan* for human beings" and it has "*arranged* things in such a manner that virtue has a direct and dramatic effect on others."[23] In the process of anchoring virtue ethics in the *Analects*, Slingerland arrives at a similar reading, declaring that: "Like many versions of traditional Western virtue ethics . . . the ethical project of Confucius was inextricably linked to a *carefully articulated theistic vision*," one that involves the "design of Heaven."[24]

There are, without question, genuine obscurities in the *Analects*. If anything is clear, however, it is that the text *itself* does not support the weight of such theistic and intelligent design inferences. Moreover, evidence drawn from the context of Warring States philosophy runs directly counter to such readings. The most proximate assessment that we have of early Confucian thought paints exactly the opposite picture: "Confucians take Heaven *not* to be intelligent (*ming* 明)," says Mozi.[25] As Chris Fraser explains, the early Confucians were regarded as impious toward "Heaven" precisely because they disregarded what Mozi sees as "humanity's proper role in the normative order of the cosmos."[26] How, then, do Ivanhoe and Slingerland arrive at understandings of early Confucianism so contrary to those more historically proximate? Again, *Seek and ye shall find* is the iron rule. Those who are looking for faith in "Heaven's plan" in the *Analects* see evidence for it and overlook evidence to the contrary and *vice versa*.

Most would agree that, with respect to *tian* 天, Confucius' conception lies somewhere between the more supernatural account that marks the advent of the Zhou dynasty and the more naturalistic account held by Xunzi. As mentioned in chapter 6 of the previous volume, ancient China enjoyed a robust religious culture and a variety of spirits were worshipped. During the Shang dynasty, religious worship coalesced around a primary deity, the "High Ancestor" (*shangdi* 上帝). This was not a Creator God, and there was no sense of "radical difference" between the spiritual and human realms.[27] With the arrival of the Zhou dynasty, the "High Ancestor" of the Shang was displaced with a more generic force that early Christian missionaries later translated into English as "Heaven" (*tian*).

During the Warring States period, the meaning of *tian* 天 was evolving from a roughly anthropomorphic deity to the impersonal forces of nature, with texts often oscillating between one conception and the other. The key moment in Chinese religious history arrives when Confucius turns away from the spirit realm toward the human-centered world. He suggests that sacrifices are more about the living than the dead.²⁸ He refuses to discuss any "supernatural" (*guai* 怪) things.²⁹ Thus, while retaining his awe and reverence for the inscrutable "Mandates of Heaven" (*tianming* 天命), he is likely referring to all *non*-supernatural forces—cosmic, social, cultural, and natural—that determine our fates. In line with this more humanistic and naturalistic orientation, Confucius directs the use of ritual-custom (*li* 禮) away from divine propitiation to focus on its social and cultural dimensions.³⁰ Again, as Michael J. Puett explains: "by decrying the instrumental use of sacrifices by ritual specialists, [he] denied the powers that were used in the Bronze Age to mollify divine forces and to make them work for the living. Instead, he urged that we simply cultivate ourselves and accept whatever the divine powers do."³¹ Confucius never *denies* that "supernatural" things exist—he simply turns his attention away from them and encourages his followers to do the same.

Locating an essentialist theory of "human nature" or an intelligent design theory of "Heaven's plan" in Confucius' teachings would indeed secure—*for us*—the Greek-medieval foundation for a Confucian virtue ethics. As a strategy for reading the *Analects*, however, this is risky. In fact, it is worse than risky. To set out looking for a pair of theories (*yan* 言) that *the text states explicitly that Confucius did not expound* has disaster written all over it. *Analects* 5.13 tells us directly: "We can hear the Master discourse on cultural refinements, but as for theorizing about human nature (*xing* 性) or about Heaven's way (*tiandao* 天道) we can never hear about those."³² That ought to settle the question. There are no theories of "human nature" in the *Analects* and there is no intelligent design theorizing.

Slingerland allows that *Analects* 5.13 presents, "something of a puzzle."³³ Ivanhoe responds by providing an extensive account of its commentarial history. His analysis shows that there is a tendency for commentators to read their own proclivities into it. Seven centuries after the death of Confucius, the Wei dynasty thinker He Yan 何晏 surmised that Confucius never talked about "human nature" or "Heaven's way" because these were "esoteric teachings" that could not be shared. As Ivanhoe explains, however, the views that inform this approach are "arguably largely of Daoist origin."³⁴ The "esoteric teachings" reading of *Analects* 5.13 is thus not very persuasive. And besides—it was Confucius himself who said: "Students, do you think that I am hiding something from you? I am not. There is nothing that I do that is not shared with you. This is who I am."³⁵ Building upon the "esoteric teachings" approach, Song dynasty Neo-Confucians Cheng Hao 程顥 and Cheng Yi 程頤 argue in different ways that "human nature" and "Heaven's way" involved for Confucius a quasi-mystical, intuitive grasp of reality beyond words. Zhu Xi expands upon such ideas within the framework of his own metaphysics.

These commentaries, however, as Ivanhoe points out, "are deeply and fundamentally influenced by Buddhist philosophy."[36]

Six centuries later, Qing dynasty scholars Dai Zhen 戴震 and Zhang Xuecheng 章學誠 criticize the Song commentaries for being "subjective" and for introducing foreign philosophical elements into the classical tradition. Zhang wishes to return to the "concrete, practical teachings of the Master." Confucius, he explains, never discusses "human nature" or "Heaven's way" because "[he] never tried to abstract the Way (*dao* 道) from its true arena: the actual, observable world. Apart from the actual world, there *was* no human nature or Way of Heaven."[37] Such commentary, one assumes, returns us as closely as possible to the original, humanistic-naturalistic teachings of Confucius. As David S. Nivison explains, Zhang maintains that for Confucius, *tian* 天 was nothing more than "the order of nature, regarded with reverence." Thus understood, "Heaven's way" is something that "commands all the respect of a religious absolute, even though it is not supernatural." Such a view, explains Nivison, would restore "an essentially religious reverence for the human moral order, yet at the same time [one] completely evolutionary and naturalistic."[38]

None of this is helping the "Heaven's plan" reading. Through analysis of the commentarial tradition, Ivanhoe indeed demonstrates that "eminent representatives of the Confucian tradition at times disagreed—often deeply" over their interpretations of the *Analects*. "A more thorough appreciation of the tradition," he concludes, "may also help contemporary interpreters avoid reading classical Chinese thinkers as if they were advocating or groping their way toward *our* view of things."[39] That sounds right, but the larger point is ambiguous. Is Ivanhoe suggesting that by properly understanding the commentarial tradition one can avoid becoming part of it? Surely, the "Heaven's plan" reading of the *Analects* is as culturally situated as any other. Indeed—to scour the text against all odds for the foundations of Western "virtue ethics" is precisely to anticipate that the text is "advocating" or "groping" its way toward our view of things. I rather take Ivanhoe's conclusion as a reminder that one should *not* expect the text to conform to our preexisting criteria (e.g., Van Norden's 1–4).

This lesson is especially important when, failing to find what one expects to find, the tradition is thought to be *lacking* in some way. May Sim, for instance, in adopting the "virtue ethics" approach, has no illusion about the strength of its foundations in the *Analects*. Aristotle, she notes, was able to "reconstruct his standards of morality by using his metaphysics," whereas "Confucius has no similar foundation for reconstructing his moral virtues." Confucius, she observes, has "no explicit theory of human nature, let alone a teleological one." Thus, "Confucianism could *benefit* from a metaphysical account."[40] Perhaps, but let us not miss the opportunity to imagine how a non-Western tradition might sustain its virtues without recourse to our own Greek-medieval expectations.

Again, it is axiomatic in intra-cultural philosophy that arguments for any reading of a tradition as remote and protean as "early Confucianism" are never only arguments about the truth and accuracy of an interpretation. They are also arguments about *importance* and *meaning*—claims about what is at stake, and why anyone should care. From the standpoint of intra-cultural philosophy, such work involves locating strains in culture that can express one's concerns and convictions effectively—communicating them through the funded experience of a tradition that still guides and inspires. If there is some other way of *doing* Chinese philosophy I have never found it. I suspect, then, that none of us wholly avoids the tendencies that Ivanhoe identifies with the commentarial tradition.

It might be better, in that case, to just accept that our own values and concerns shape our interpretations of the text. Intellectual responsibility can then be properly attributed and assumed. For truth, "comparative philosophers" should not be trading in their cultural duty as philosophers for the masquerade of greater fidelity to a text that has been opaque for twenty-five centuries. Personally as a philosopher, I'm not interested in pretending to have no purpose. I join Dewey in holding that certain lines of thinking are "out of gear" with our best scientific understandings and that such misalignments are doing us harm. My interest, accordingly, is to experiment with readings of Chinese thought that do not rely on outdated Greek-medieval assumptions. If others prefer to exercise that worldview, there is not much to do but point out its errors and deficiencies. I realize that, should Greek-medieval elements actually be operative in early Chinese thought, I am not putting myself in the best position to notice them. But as inquirers, each of us sets out from *somewhere* to do *something*.

Fortunately, contemporary research into the *Analects* provides alternatives—or better yet, supplements—to the "virtue ethics" approach that do not rely on Greek-medieval inferences. These are the "exemplarist" and the "role ethics" approaches. Methodologically, these more recent approaches have a distinct advantage over the "virtue ethics" approach. Each attempts to work from *within* the *Analects* to generate a novel ethical theory rather than coming to the text from without and testing it against existing Greek-medieval criteria (e.g., Van Norden's 1–4). This does not deactivate the iron rule of hermeneutics, but it does signal intent to understand the *Analects* on its own terms to whatever degree that is possible. I hope that whatever clarity is won through such approaches will not be obscured as I ease Dewey back into the discussion.

Exemplarism and the Denotative Method

In the winter of 1919, Dewey gave a series of lectures on "Ethics" in Beijing. In one of these lectures, he took a run at cross-cultural comparison. In his lecture, "A Comparison of Eastern Thought and Western Thought," Dewey compares the "five Confucian relations" with more "abstract" virtues in the Western ethical tradition. He notes that Confucian role-based ethics is more *concrete*, but less flexible; and that Western ethics is more *general*, but also more ambiguous. He notes that Confucian role-based ethics offers fewer freedoms, but also produces less selfishness, whereas Western individual-based ethics promises more freedoms, but also produces fewer obligations. He begins his talk by carefully explaining that he is "going to make an intellectual comparison, not a value judgment," and he succeeds in remaining admirably neutral in his analysis.[41]

Dewey draws attention to the fact that Confucian role-based ethics is "down-to-earth, definite, concrete," in that it is rooted in actual *persons*. "Everyone has a father, a son, a wife or husband, brothers, and friends," he observes, and everyone "must be either an emperor, or a government official, or a member of the populace." Meanwhile, Western virtue-based ethics are grounded in something more general. "The concepts stressed in the West are justice and benevolence, both of which are abstract, and without necessary reference to facts or events. In other words, we can say that justice and benevolence are intellectual concepts derived from study." This, however, can present some advantages. "Intellectual moral concepts are more flexible," he suggests. One might reflect upon the meaning of "benevolence" in *abstraction* from any particular person and consider how it might apply in future instances. Chinese role-based ethics, however, retains its advantage of being more *concrete*—it is grounded in exemplary persons and their relations to one another. Dewey simply notes the difference. "I do not intend to take sides," he explains, "to build up a case for the one and to downgrade the other."[42]

In his own unassuming way, Dewey anticipates what are today the two most cutting-edge approaches to Confucian ethics: the role ethical and exemplarist approaches. Amy Olberding, who represents the latter approach, is changing the way that we think about the *Analects*. Together with Linda Zagzebski, her colleague at the University of Oklahoma, Olberding argues that the Confucian *Analects* provides the richest example anywhere of a novel ethical approach: "a virtue ethics that is exemplarist in character."[43]

The idea of an "Exemplarist Virtue Theory" is one that Zagzebski arrives at through her work on Christian ethics. "Christian ethics is supposed to be focused on the imitation of Christ," she observes, "but there is rarely any attempt at a connection between the person described in the Gospels and systematic moral theology."[44] Indeed, the virtue ethics that dominates Scholastic theology stands rather coldly apart from the Gospel narratives, the lives of the saints, and the real-life experiences of admirable Christians all over the world. Why such disconnect? Zagzebski proposes that, in assessing the relationship between Christian *ethics* and Christian *lives*, one might perform a simple inversion. Christian virtues are routinely grounded in abstract definitions based on "human nature." Aquinas, for instance, defines "fortitude" as "the disposition whereby the soul is strengthened for that which is in accord with reason, against any assaults from the passions, or the toil involved by any operations."[45] Rather than grounding such virtues in the essence of "human nature," Zagzebski proposes that we ground them in the *persons* who actually embody them—just *there*, in *those* persons.

The way to understand exemplarism is through examples. Father Óscar Romero, for instance, is known for resisting a violent right-wing military in El Salvador in the 1970s, imploring soldiers to stop killing innocent civilians. He was threatened with retribution, but he would not relent. Performing the holy Sacrifice of the Mass on March 24, 1980, he took a bullet to the chest. So, do you want to know what fortitude is? Father Óscar Romero—*that* is fortitude. Be certain, however, to complete the inversion. Romero did not instantiate some abstract "fortitude" the foundation of which is located elsewhere in some generic scheme or pre-figured design. Romero *was* the fortitude. Fortitude is *that*. Our admiration for *him* opens the possibility of formulating and exploring a more generic notion of human goodness and calling it "fortitude." As Zagzebski explores the implications of this new approach, it becomes apparent that it stands to upend the way that ethical theory is generally understood. For this reason, her work has attracted plenty of attention in the field.[46]

As colleagues, Zagzebski and Olberding have been able to reflect together on how this new approach provides fresh insight into the *Analects*. Before discussing this, let us look more closely at Zagzebski's theory. One of her central aims is to establish a foundation for ethical theory that does not rely on conceptually refined, non-evaluative postulations such as "human nature" or "God's plan." Such postulations, presumed by some theorists to be central to grounding moral evaluations, are irrelevant in the vast majority of cases. Normal people make moral evaluations all the time without any thought of "human nature" or "God's plan." Feelings of admiration or aversion become approbation and disapproval pre-reflectively, prior to any theoretical knowing. There is simply an emotional response to *that* behavior and to the person who exhibits it. Accordingly, Zagzebski proposes to "anchor" our moral concepts directly in such responses.[47]

Philosophically, Zagzebski models this move on the direct reference semantics of Hilary Putnam and Saul Kripke.[48] Through direct reference, natural kind terms such as "gold" are fixed by ostension—simply by *pointing*. Gold is *that*. As a natural kind term, "gold" refers to the same kind of stuff indexed in that particular instance.[49] As Olberding notes, among the advantages of direct reference is "its obviation of the need for precise definition or elaborate conceptual schemata before the work of understanding can begin."[50] Humans have interacted with gold for at least 5,000 years. Only recently, however, has "gold" been known as 79Au with an electronegativity rating of 2.54 on the Pauling scale—and even then, few people actually know it as that. Direct reference allows us to successfully use natural kind terms like "gold" without having to generate or even share very elaborate (let alone fixed or exhaustive) descriptive schemata. Zagzebski suggests that moral knowledge works the same way. People will largely agree that Óscar Romero exhibits "fortitude" without having to consider any elaborate theoretical accounts. Here, our admiration for him proves sufficiently foundational.

At this juncture, the traditional virtue ethicist will say: "OK, but why not just *determine* what it is that makes Óscar Romero admirable, formalize that criteria, and then ground the ethics of 'fortitude' on *that*?" Well, twenty-five centuries after first asking, "What is the Good, Socrates?" it is safe to say that there are two reasons. First, try as we might, we cannot readily determine what it is that makes "good persons" good. Second, we seem to get along well enough without doing so. As Olberding observes, there is a "significant disanalogy" between things like "gold" and the "good person." While we make progress toward articulating the "species essence" of something like "gold" (a.k.a. 79Au) there is no such *obvious* progress being made in ethics.[51] Thus, we continue to rely on emotions like admiration and aversion to serve foundationally. Such emotions, however, serve us pretty well. Zagzebski suggests that their reliability is due to the fact that human beings do "share the same nature, the same emotional dispositions, and at least roughly the same physical, psychological, and social needs." If such a nature ever opens itself to better-grounded moral inquiry, then we would want "to figure out the psychological structure of wise persons," and "if there are neurological differences between wise persons and the rest of us, we would be interested in discovering that also."[52] But this may never happen.

Empirically speaking, we can still make broad and serviceable generalities about the "good life for humans." Reaching consensus on a solid, permanent foundation for "human goodness" this late in the game, however, is unlikely. Still, moral philosophy has its place. As Dewey observes: "each great system of moral thought brings to light some point of view from which the facts of our own situations are to be looked at and studied."[53] When moral problems or disagreements arise, philosophical ethics can prove useful in resolving them—but this is also true of discourse, art, narrative, or just a momentary glance and a change of heart. Nothing is instantly gained by introducing moral theories (*yan* 言) at the outset of a problem. As we saw in chapter 8 of volume one, such theories might even make matters worse. As Olberding observes, for most people (i.e., "those outside of the domain of philosophical ethics") claims of admiration or aversion "are frequently made with little recourse to any formal conceptual schemata against which the exemplar's qualities are measured and found adequate."[54] Whatever it is that moral philosophers think they are doing, the fact that moral experience takes place almost entirely on the pre-theoretical plane in the mode of direct reference is firmly established and incontrovertible.

Dewey anticipates direct reference semantics. In presenting his ethical philosophy, Gregory Fernando Pappas reminds us that the "denotative method" remains Dewey's point of departure for most of his career. "To take experience as the starting point," explains Pappas, "is simply to begin where we are, not with a theory, but with what is pre-theoretically given in the midst of our lives."[55] Again, this method—that which Thomas M. Alexander calls the "thread through the labyrinth"[56]—is first established in Dewey's 1905 article, "The Postulate of Immediate Empiricism." Here, he maintains that things "*are* what they are experienced *as*." Experience, Dewey writes, "is always of *thats*."[57] The denotative method sets out by first "finding and pointing to [such] things in the concrete contexts in which they present themselves." Subsequent inquiry can then "review the starting point when it is found necessary."[58] Direct reference is what designates subject matter at the outset of any inquiry. "Once we designate the subject matter," Pappas explains, "we then engage in inquiry proper which may include constructing theories and developing concepts."[59]

To understand this procedure the wrong-way-around, for Dewey, is to once again commit "*the* philosophical fallacy." When theoretical content is front-loaded and regarded as primary in experience, an *eventual* outcome is converted into an antecedent existence and then postulated as the *cause* that explains its eventual emergence. Again, the circularity is obvious. As Dewey explains, "The fallacy converts consequences of interactions of events into causes of the occurrence of these consequences—a reduplication which is significant as to the *importance* of the functions, but which hopelessly confuses understanding of them."[60]

Exemplarist ethics avoids this fallacy. Óscar Romero is *primary*—a concrete exemplar against which the usefulness of any subsequent theory of "fortitude" is assessed. To convert such a theory into an antecedent *cause* explaining Father Romero's fortitude is to put the cart before the horse. It overlooks the actual *context* in which Romero conducted himself. Dewey maintains that "the most pervasive fallacy of philosophic thinking goes back to [such] neglect of context."[61] "Conduct is absolutely individualized," he observes. "There is no such thing as conduct in general—conduct is *what* and *where* and *when* and *how* to the last inch."[62] For Dewey, human conduct is the irreducible foundation upon which morality rests, and such conduct is always *situated*. Moral theories, definitions, principles, etc. are *tools* that enable us to appropriate and formulate moral knowledge that originates in genuine human conduct, thus becoming "inherited instrumentalities for analyzing individual and unique situations" in the future.[63]

To reify our theoretical instruments and convert them into *causes* introduces strange practices in philosophy. Most curiously, once moral theories slide into formalism and rigidity, they become adversarial toward one another. Some philosophers then argue over them in abstraction, which is a ridiculous thing to do. Such types resemble Duke Huan in the upper (*shang* 上) part of the hall—"reading the dregs of the sages" while the Wheelwright engages in his work below (*xia* 下).[64] Remember, it is intelligence (*ming* 明) that guides the craftsman as he makes micro-adjustments in response to actual conditions as they evolve. Intelligence is what sustains the life of any theoretical "tool" that exists in use. As Dewey asks: "What can give [such a tool] the life and spirit necessary to make it other than a cramped and cramping petrification except the continued free play of intelligence upon it?"[65] *Real* exemplars (like Óscar Romero) require us to test, revise, and improve our moral instruments going forward. By keeping what is real in the foreground, "Moral life is protected from falling into formalism and rigid repetition," says Dewey. "It is rendered flexible, vital, growing."[66]

Olberding's exemplarism illuminates the *Analects* with floodlights. First, consider the obvious. While there are a number of important moral terms employed, the text is not very forthcoming with its definitions. What do terms like associated humanity (*ren* 仁), ritual propriety (*li* 禮), and appropriateness (*yi* 義) actually *mean*? Even the text's interlocutors are unsure, and when Confucius is asked to clarify he gives different answers. Meanwhile, the text is *teeming* with people—the Master, Yan Hui, Duke Jing, Zigong, Yuanrang, the Duke of Zhou, the boy from Que village, to name only a few. By my reckoning, there are 186 distinct *persons* who either appear or are made reference to in the *Analects*. Consider that number for a moment. It is an extraordinary figure. Now, perform Zagzebski's inversion. The result is nothing less than a *Gestalt* shift. Suddenly, the *Analects* is not so much about a set of abstract "virtues." It is about admirable (and not so admirable) *people*, and the manner in which their conduct and interactions with one another give rise to moral growth and reflection. Here, virtues are anchored not in "human nature" or "Heaven's plan" but in specific figures. We learn, for instance, that Zijian is an exemplary person (*junzi* 君子), Taibo is a person of excellence (*de* 德), Min Ziqian has great filial piety (*xiao* 孝), Guanzhong displays associated humanity (*ren* 仁), and Shiyu is genuine (*zhen* 真).[67] Book Five devotes itself almost entirely to registering specific moral exemplars, and beyond that the list continues.[68]

Confucius relies upon exemplars not only in referencing specific virtues, but also in prescribing a method for morally regulating one's own conduct. "When encountering persons of exceptional character, one thinks to stand shoulder to shoulder with them; and upon encountering those of little character, one looks inward and examines oneself."[69] Accordingly, the Master asserts: "Conducting myself alongside two other people, I am bound to find a teacher. Selecting what is good, I follow it. As for what is not good, I use it to reform myself."[70] The message here is clear: becoming moral requires nothing but contact with *other people*. Since additional foundations such as "human nature" or "Heaven's plan" are unnecessary, it suddenly makes perfect sense that Confucius refuses to provide them.

Objections are expected. As Edward Slingerland asks, without the element of universality granted by "human nature" or "Heaven's plan," how does such an ethics *not* result in cultural relativism?[71] Such concerns highlight the importance of the denotative method and direct reference in this approach. Notice that there are distinct philosophical assumptions that lead to the postulation of "cultural relativism" as a generic problem. First and foremost, it is assumed that right conduct correlates with cognitive privilege. Moral disagreements are regarded as conflicts between propositions that are "objectively" true or false. Resolution requires one to "know" which moral propositions are *actually true*. From such a standpoint, those who resist are thought to regard moral truth as "subjective" and are "relativists."

Dewey avoids this trap because his point of departure is different. For Dewey, there is always an operative situation in which moral conduct occurs first and last. Moral inquiry begins and ends *there*. Moral actors are never disengaged spectators who undergo "subjective" uncertainty in relation to some "objective" situation. Rather, they are involved as constituents *inside* the situation—a larger whole that actually bears the quality of uncertainty. Resolving a problematic situation involves making adjustments from *within* the situation, and some of these adjustments, functionally speaking, might be more "objective" or "subjective." Such designations, however, are derivative rather than primary. When it is assumed that moral judgment "merely apprehends and enunciates" some strictly "objective" factor, says Dewey, then "there is no *situation* which is problematic." Suddenly, "there is only a person who is in a state of subjective moral uncertainty or ignorance."[72] Once this conversion is made, the philosopher can treat the problem in terms of propositional statements. Discourse about such statements then usurps experimental inquiry. Returning to the grainy vicissitudes of the lived situation suddenly feels like a descent into "relativism." Such philosophers, as Dewey notes, refuse to "go outside the universe of discourse" and thus shut themselves out from "understanding what a 'situation,' as directly experienced" even *is*.[73]

In theory, "cultural relativism" poses a real and present danger to moral practice. Opposing value propositions on any number of issues—what to do? Cultural difference, however, is not a problem until it *becomes* a problem; and when it does, it happens in a situation. For Dewey, as Pappas explains, "even if people in moral disagreement do not share beliefs, they share the situation of unique and particular disagreement as something that is outside of discourse and without propositional content."[74] Dewey's faith in experience is ultimately a faith in our ability to weigh up (*quan* 權) situations and to resolve them in ways that are intelligent (*ming* 明). This involves, as always, restoring continuity between means-and-ends in specific ways—in other words, it means restoring *dao* 道. Accordingly, rather than locate fixed ends that are external (*wai* 外) to each situation, one considers "goods previously experienced" as possible *means* for resolving each problem as it is confronted. Such goods "are material to be surveyed and evaluated in reference to the kind of action needed in the *existing* situation." Here again, moral theories (*yan* 言), definitions, principles, etc. are useful tools, but as Dewey explains: "These standard 'prepared' propositions are not final. Though highly valuable means, they are still means for examining the existing situation and appraising what mode of action it demands. The question of their applicability in the new situation, their relevancy and weight with respect to it, may and often does lead to their being re-appraised and re-framed."[75]

Moral progress remains possible so long as actual conduct in real situations remains the foundation. But make no mistake—solving complex moral problems requires tremendous effort and imagination and there is never any guarantee of success. What *is* certain, however, is that as long as our moral convictions rest upon non-evaluative foundations like "human nature" or "Heaven's plan," moral disagreements will remain intractable and future conflicts inevitable and someday possibly catastrophic.

Role Ethics and Human Nature

More needs to be said about human nature, as its equivocation in moral discourse is common. Recall that we have already "dissolved the blank slate." As Donald E. Brown argues, there are *scores* of generic traits that humans share: conflict, play, music, weapons, revenge, jokes, envy, rape, empathy, and the list goes on. Such a hodge-podge conception of "human nature" cannot provide a foundation for morality—for it has no essential moral character. As Dewey suggests, debates over its "goodness" or "badness" are idle logomachies. Such debates do nothing more than register one's general approach to promoting or curbing select tendencies, usually with some ulterior motive. "Those who wished to justify the exercise of authority over others took a pessimistic view of the constitution of human nature," notes Dewey, while "those who wanted relief from something oppressive discovered qualities of great promise in its native makeup."[76] For thinkers who adopt a modern outlook, Brown's "human nature" is neither good nor bad—it is simply *there* to be acknowledged and worked with as datum.

The "human nature" sought by conventional virtue ethicists, however, remains something different. Based in premodern thought, it presumes that each thing has a nature (*phusis*) with a built-in potential (*dunamis*) that is neither contingent nor alterable. Such an essential "nature" provides organisms with both a directional order of growth and a structural basis for normative flourishing (*eudaimonia*). As discussed in chapter 2 of volume one, evolutionary biology requires us to rethink our understanding of such terms. First, we must abandon the old, "honorific" conception of fixed and final ends. For Dewey, organic form is a unit of organization that exhibits sequential order *only*. Goal-oriented and directional in nature, it is marked by the orderly co-adaptation of means toward a single result—*survival*, or continued *growth*. Growth, then, is the only real "end" in any organic process, precisely because it goes on in each living thing *without* end. Living things never stop growing until they *stop living*.

In reconstructing the notion of ends, Dewey builds upon Aristotle's naturalism by identifying norms that pervade life-activities most generally. While the basis for Greek-medieval teleology is undermined in Dewey's thinking, the general values of "growth" and "development" are left intact. Precluded is the possibility of grounding the "good life for humans" in some teleological essence of "human nature" *per se*. Not precluded, however, is grounding the "good life for humans" in the essence of *life itself*. This is what Dewey tries to do. Along with everything else known to exist, the life-process depends on *associations*. "There are trees which can grow only in a forest," explains Dewey. "Seeds of many plants can successfully germinate and develop only under conditions furnished by the presence of other plants . . . The life-history of an animal-cell is conditioned upon connection with what other cells are doing."[77] The same goes for humans. It is hard even to imagine what a completely isolated human being (say, raised on a deserted island) would end up being like. Given what human nature *is*, one would expect such a creature to exhibit severe pathologies. Like many "thought experiments," however, this scenario is completely unrealistic. A full-term human infant left alone on a deserted island would contain enough water and glucose to suffer for about a week. So, when Dewey says that, "Apart from the ties which bind [us] to others, [we] are nothing," he is correct.[78] Humans cannot even *become* human in isolation from other humans. So, while Confucius may be reticent on human nature (*xing* 性), the term *ren* 仁 acknowledges a basic truth. The term underscores that those characteristics that we deem "human" are irreducibly social.

With respect to human nature, the biological and social needs for association have co-evolved within the nature-culture matrix so as to blend inseparably. As a result, human nature presents us with structures, functions, and tendencies adapted to engage in associated life as social creatures. So why not make this the "foundation" for human flourishing? The answer is that human nature is a necessary but not a sufficient condition for the "good life." At least in the teachings of Confucius, the *working* norm is not "human nature" but harmony (*he* 和). Confucius does not say much about this norm, perhaps because he refuses to discuss the "Ways of Nature" (*tiandao* 天道),[79] or maybe because harmony (*he*) is already tacitly understood as a norm in early China. In any case, Confucius clearly subordinates ritual-custom (*li* 禮) to harmony (*he*) and he formulates a model of self-cultivation in which raw qualities (*zhi* 質) and form (*wen* 文) are aesthetically integrated, a notion that cannot be understood without appeal to *he* as explicated in the classical corpus. As Chenyang Li argues: harmony is *the* "desirable goal" in Confucian philosophy—"an end in itself as well as a means for human flourishing."[80]

One might say, then, that human nature provides the original material (*zhi* 質) with which to become a human being. As such, humans start out close (*jin* 近), but then "vary with respect to their cultural practices (*xi* 習)."[81] For Confucius, such variance signals the refining (*wen* 文) operations of ritual-customs (*li* 禮). Here, Dewey concurs. "Native human nature supplies the raw materials," he writes, "but custom furnishes the machinery and the designs."[82] The notion of human flourishing in the *Analects* is thus indicated in the fact that harmony is prioritized (*gui* 貴) in the operation of ritual-custom. Accordingly, to harmonize means to defer to harmonies already achieved so as to express one's individuality most effectively, like the next ingredient in the good soup—or, as Confucius suggests, the next instrument in the musical ensemble.[83] With respect to human nature, "all that we can safely say," Dewey writes, "is that human nature, like other forms of life, tends to differentiation, and this moves in the direction of the distinctively individual, and that it also tends towards combination, association."[84] For both Dewey and Confucius, *how* human beings become differentiated (through combination and association) depends on their cultural practices (*xi*). Measured according to the norm of harmony (*he* 和) such practices can be evaluated as better or worse. In harmonious societies, human flourishing has a better chance of occurring because cultural refinement (*wen* 文) and ritual-custom (*li*) are operating at their best.

So, what *is* "flourishing" for Confucius? Amy Olberding suspects that, in the absence of any teleological human nature, there is no "technical" account of flourishing in the *Analects*.⁸⁵ Bryan W. Van Norden disagrees, maintaining that a technical account of flourishing is present. He relates its basic components as follows: "participation in ritual activities, ethically informed aesthetic appreciation and intellectual activity, acting for the good of others, and generally participating in relationships with other people, especially family relationships."⁸⁶ Whether or not we bundle such values together and label them "an account of flourishing" is a second-order technicality and largely irrelevant within Confucianism. The primary question, really, is whether or not Greek-medieval "virtue ethics" best clarifies how the realization of such values is understood in the tradition.

Again—I find virtue ethics moderately insightful, but also seriously limited. Since "human nature" is off the table in the *Analects*, other approaches are needed right away to supplement its insights. Exemplarism provides a theoretical foundation in the absence of "human nature" and does a much better job than virtue ethics of pulling together different aspects of the *Analects*.⁸⁷ Role ethics offers further assistance by rendering the elements of the "good life" consistent with the norm that actually guides the tradition: harmony (*he* 和). Rather than *guessing* how virtues in the *Analects* relate to an absentee "human nature," it is more promising to start with the tradition's guiding norms and work *back* toward an understanding of the virtues. As Roger T. Ames explains, "The vocabulary that is most frequently used [in the Confucian tradition] to express the more general, aggregated sense of human flourishing orchestrated out of these interpenetrating values are 'harmonizing, harmony' (*he*) and 'centering, equilibrium, focus, balance' (*zhong* 中)."⁸⁸ These are the terms that best indicate what human flourishing means in Confucianism, and role ethics takes them as its point of departure.

The development of Confucian role ethics is a collaborative effort on the part of Roger T. Ames and Henry Rosemont Jr., one that grew out of their landmark 1998 translation of the *Analects*. In the "Introduction" to that text, they explain that from the Confucian standpoint, "We express our unique personhood—*not* individualism—by the creative ways we interact with others, as children, parents, lovers, friends, and so forth, within the constraints denoted by what is meant by 'parent,' 'lover,' 'friend,' and 'neighbor.'"⁸⁹ Their translation of *The Classic of Family Reverence* provides a focal text around which these larger ideas are arrayed—ideas about what it means to flourish as a human person (*shen* 身) in Confucian thought.

In recent years, each author has independently produced monographs exploring the nature of role ethics.⁹⁰ Their theory takes its cue from what is probably the most basic ethical premise in the *Analects*—namely, that filial piety (*xiao* 孝) is the root of associated humanity (*ren* 仁).⁹¹ The guiding question, then, is how to understand a tradition that regards family relations as the entry point for the cultivation of moral competence, an approach that differs markedly from both principle- and virtue-based ethical theories in the West. As Ames and Rosemont see it, what this premise means is that every human being is a role-bearing person *from the start*, and all subsequent personal growth occurs as a result of taking on new roles and/or having roles change. If one replaces the word "role" with "relation," there is little question that this corresponds with Nature (*tian* 天) as we currently understand it. How else would an organism grow or change but through its relations? From the standpoint of Dewey's philosophy, one of the strengths of role ethics is that it preserves continuity between organic- and human-level processes.

One important feature of role ethics, then, is that it resists postulating the discrete "individual" as the locus of social analysis. Dewey likewise rejects this construction in his "Social and Political Philosophy" lectures in Beijing. Leading up to this, Dewey knew that "individuality is not originally given but is created under the influences of associated life."[92] In Beijing, however, he observed concretely that students were regarded *as students* (during the May Fourth Movement) and that *wives, mothers, teachers*, and future *doctors* were yearning for greater social recognition, rather than bare "individuals" who happened to be female.[93] As Dewey comes to see it: "The human being is an individual because of and in relations with others. Otherwise, [he/she] is an individual only as a stick of wood is, namely, as spatially and numerically separate."[94]

Ames and Rosemont concur. In their view, substituting the generic "individual" for the individualized, role-bearing *person* is perhaps the gravest error in social reasoning. As they ask: "What is known about a person when we are told she is an 'individual,' as contrasted with 'mother'?"[95] The issue here has direct relevance to moral practice. While various levels of abstraction each have their function, apprehending individuals as *primarily* role-bearing persons retains more constitutive elements of the situations in which human conduct actually occurs. As we have seen, retaining access to "situations" is central to the *dao* 道 of resolving moral problems. "Each actual situation presents its own configuration of relations and conditions that need to be inventoried and assessed with discernment," Ames writes.[96] Adjudicating a dispute between two "individuals" can be easily done if it involves something like an accounting error. *Moral* disputes, however, tend to be more textured, and it matters greatly that they occur between bosses and employees, teachers and parents, some mothers and other mothers, elected officials and citizenry, etc. Consistent with the Confucian practice of rectifying names (*zhengming* 正名),[97] Ames and Rosemont insist that role-terms "are themselves normative standards."[98] Thus, one *must* pay attention to roles if one's moral judgments and sensibilities are to remain calibrated and reliable enough to "weigh things up" (*quan* 權) appropriately.

Role ethics and virtue ethics sometimes present themselves as adversarial readings of the Confucian tradition. Ames and Rosemont present role ethics as an alternative to virtue ethics and they critique the latter point by point. Advocates of virtue ethics, in turn, push back against role ethics. Philip J. Ivanhoe, for instance, argues that: "The various roles described by early Confucians all afford one the opportunity to develop and express a range of common *virtues*," and thus "virtues and *not* roles are the foundation of early Confucian ethics." He objects to the manner in which the "self" in role ethics "evaporates up and condenses into the matrix of one's social roles," thus ignoring "the depth and complexity of the Confucian self."[99]

In truth, this debate is only marginally about the *Analects*. Ivanhoe's reaction to role ethics takes place in a Western intellectual context, where it is fairly predictable. Hans-Georg Moeller and Paul D'Ambrosio's analysis of the sincerity/authenticity dialectic in late modern philosophy captures it perfectly.[100] Ivanhoe's resistance to Confucian role ethics is a modernist critique of an "ethics of sincerity" that awaits an agent-centered "authenticity" to compensate for its perceived shortcomings. Only briefly does Ivanhoe elaborate on the so-called "depth and complexity" that Confucian role ethics allegedly lacks, postulating only that the terms "great" (*da* 大) and "small" (*xiao* 小) in the *Analects* are used to "distinguish between the ethically authentic and inauthentic fulfillment of roles."[101] Maybe—but such an inference is based already on virtue ethics assumptions. If one adopts role ethics assumptions, then "great" and "small" reflect the breadth and depth of one's interpersonal relationships.

Henry Rosemont Jr.'s response, in turn, is refreshing. Rather than engage Ivanhoe directly, he points out that they probably have two different audiences in mind. Ivanhoe works squarely within the tradition of Western virtue ethics, whereas Rosemont wishes, he says, "to engage in dialogue with my fellow philosophers, but equally with my fellow Americans." Rosemont is simply being honest here. He drops the pretention that greater fidelity to the text is actually the point of contention between himself and Ivanhoe. We must distinguish, Rosemont writes, "between the question of whether what either Ivanhoe or I have to say is the better interpretation of Confucian writings, and the very different question of whether the positions on the self we each advance are worthy of philosophical attention on their own." From the perspective of intra-cultural philosophy, different assimilations of the *Analects* will naturally reflect different philosophical convictions. The text is not there to arbitrate between such convictions. As Rosemont points out, when it comes to choosing between a more role-based "self" and a more individual-based "self," each of these views are "eminently capable of becoming self-fulfilling prophecies," thus it follows "that our criterion for choice must be a *moral* one." While Rosemont makes it abundantly clear that, in terms of textual evidence, he does not believe that Ivanhoe is "correct in attributing as much of an individual self as he does to the Confucius of the *Analects*," he also wishes to assume responsibility for his choice to understand the text otherwise.[102]

My own sense is that role, virtue, and exemplarist ethics are not wholly incompatible readings when broadly enough construed.[103] Any treatment that would render one of these theories *wholly* incompatible with another would probably have to hypostatize something and thus generate a dualism that, for Dewey at least, would be unproductive. We need also to keep in mind that these are, after all, theories (*yan* 言). One might work better in one situation/passage, and one in another. On this point, our proponents would likely agree. Roger T. Ames and Henry Rosemont Jr. make it clear that they do not regard role ethics "to be an ultimate and self-sufficient vision of the moral life."[104] Bryan W. Van Norden, since he embraces "methodological pluralism," remains open to approaches other than virtue ethics.[105] Amy Olberding, likewise, regards exemplarism as compatible with insights generated through other approaches.[106] For intra-cultural philosophers, these theories (and others) are "tools" for understanding the *Analects*. And more importantly, they enable us to use the *Analects* as a tool for understanding ourselves.

We should also remember that theoretical analysis is not the only means by which to unlock the meanings of Confucianism. As Edward Slingerland argues, readers should begin "to take metaphor more seriously as a foundational bearer of philosophical meaning in early China."[107] Chinese philosophical discourse is rich in metaphor, and one of the best ways to get inside the tradition is to reconstruct its metaphors, getting a feel for their parts and relations and for how they relate to life in early China.

When it comes to Confucian ethics, there are few metaphors as prevalent as *archery*. The Han scholar Yang Xiong 揚雄 draws upon a long-standing tradition when he describes the entire ethical life in terms of archery: "Cultivate personal character (*xiushen* 修身) and let it be your bow. Rectify your thoughts and let them be your arrows. Establish appropriateness (*yi* 義) as your target. Settle, aim, and let the arrows fly. You are certain to hit the mark (*zhong* 中)."[108] Let us now turn from our more theoretical considerations to consider this most loaded of Confucian metaphors.

Hitting the Mark (*zhong* 中)

The *Artificer's Record* (*kaogongji* 考工記), the earliest Chinese treatise on technology, tells us that it takes a full year for bow makers (*gongren* 弓人) to assemble a bow. The wood must be cut in winter, the horn cured in spring, and the sinews prepared in summer. When these steps are completed, in autumn (when atmospheric conditions are just right) the three elements are brought together. Ideally, each bow is fashioned to match the individual archer "personally" (gong 躬), a word that is itself composed of the human person (shen 身) and the bow (gong 弓). The instrument must fit the archer's level of resolute commitment (zhi 志) and his particular physiological temperament (xueqi 血氣). Those who tend to be sluggish require a bow with greater elasticity that shoots blunter arrows, whereas one who is more quick-tempered requires a bow that is looser but shoots thinner arrows.[109] When the technology properly fits the person, the "shot" takes place in perfect unity.

Upon further analysis, however, we learn that the "shot" also involves two separable elements: skill in positioning, to ensure proper aim; and strength in discharge, to ensure that an arrow reaches its target. In terms of ethics, Mencius likens wisdom (zhi 智) to the first element and sagacity (sheng 聖) to the second. As he says:

> To begin in a sound way is a matter of wisdom. To carry a process through to the end is a matter of sagacity. Wisdom is like skill [at the beginning]. Sagacity is like strength [in carrying through]. In discharging (you 由) an arrow from a hundred paces out, arriving [at the target area] is a matter of strength. As for whether or not the arrow hits the mark (zhong 中), this is not a matter of strength.[110]

In archery, the quality of one's aim is distinct from the strength of one's release. Analogously, in ethical experience: wisdom involves having the proper "stance" to know what is ethically appropriate (yi 義), whereas "strength" indicates willingness and the effort put into realizing it. Both elements, however, can be regarded as derivative from something more primary. In archery, when an arrow is let loose, it is the *unity* of position-and-discharge that constitutes the shot itself.[111] The shot takes place as a *whole*.

Since the archery metaphor is meant to illuminate Confucian ethics, one looks for an analogous unifying notion in Confucian thought that denotes both aim-and-strength simultaneously, a notion from which the elements of "position" and "discharge" can be derived. This notion is none other than that in accord to which the bow maker originally fashions each bow, *viz.* the resolute commitment (zhi 志) of the archer. As Mencius suggests, this notion is primary in ethical experience. When asked to describe the main concern of the scholar-official, Mencius replies with this one term: *zhi*. When asked to elaborate, he says: "I mean associated humanity (ren 仁) and appropriateness (*yi* 義). . . . Associated humanity is where one is positioned. Appropriateness is the path. To be positioned in associated humanity (*juren* 居仁) and to proceed out in appropriateness (*youyi* 由義) is the sum concern of a great person."[112] For Mencius, resolute commitment (*zhi*) is the all-encompassing ethical term. It simultaneously denotes the "position" from which aims are formulated and one's ability to "discharge" them with conviction. As Mark Edward Lewis explains, the single term *zhi* denotes the entire "moral conception of personality" for early Confucians; it represents, in his words, the whole "thrust of a person's being."[113]

Not unlike Paul Tillich's notion of "ultimate concern," *zhi* 志 encompasses "two sides of a relationship," both the *concerned* and the *concern*.[114] As a holistic expression of one's ethical character, resolute commitment (*zhi*) embraces the qualities of judgment, choice, strength of intention, aspiration, and determination all at once. According to the Chinese tradition, it is impossible to feign one's *zhi*. During Zhou times, it was believed that *zhi* could be observed (*guanzhi* 觀志) in ritualistic settings such as poetry recitations.[115] In line with this tradition, Confucius assesses the quality of his disciples in how they give voice to their *zhi* (*yanqizhi* 言其志) when posed with open-ended questions.[116] Again, like Tillich's notion of "ultimate concern," *zhi* defies reduction into cognitive, emotional, or volitional elements—it represents "the unity of every element in the centered self."[117]

The archery metaphor extends institutionally into a range of practices. Traditional archery rituals provided an important means by which to assess personal character in ancient China. Serving as occasions on which to observe virtue (*guande* 觀德), these were among the most important rituals in the Zhou period.[118] Male gentry took up archery as one of the traditional "Six Arts" (*liuyi* 六藝).[119] The sport was considered so important that, on the birth of a son, a bow would be hung on the lefthand side of the door to herald his arrival into the world.[120] When it came time to recruit males for civil service, an archery contest was held to assess the personal character of each. As Mary H. Fong explains, this "Major Archery Ritual" (*dashe* 大射) was "the sole means of testing the competence of prospective government officials, literally the entrance examination to the service of the Zhou king."[121] Held twice a year, in spring and autumn, it marked the culmination of an educational "course" (*xu* 序) that spanned the early years of male education.[122] The function of archery as a culminating experience in this curriculum was so important that Mencius considers the entire "course" to be one in archery (*she* 射).[123] Thus, when philosophers like Mencius employ archery as a metaphor for ethical competence, it is with an understanding that archery is an important factor in revealing the entire "thrust" (*zhi* 志) of one's personal character.

What precisely is the *moral* content of *zhi* 志? In the archery metaphor, it represents the conviction with which the shot is let loose.[124] Mencius relates that when Master Archer Yi first taught human beings to shoot, he demanded that one's *zhi* be fully set on drawing the bowstring, and required that all subsequent students do the same.[125] The "Meaning of Archery" (*sheyi* 射義) chapter of the *Rites* locates the term accordingly: "The meaning of archery is to let loose—some say, to 'shoot.' As for letting loose, each archer lets loose his personal *zhi*."[126] As a term in ethical psychology, *zhi* contains within itself elements normally distinguished in philosophical analysis: elements such as "goal," "choice," "effort," and "motive." Cheng Chung-ying demonstrates as much in his discussion of the term:

> [*Zhi*] is a choice and decision the self makes in view or in recognition of an ideal value or a potential reality that can be achieved through one's efforts . . . [It] is furthermore a vision or a goal that can be projected into the future and pursued and actualized in time by one's efforts. As a future goal or vision, [it] is a choice of value and a choice of a form of life that one comes to embrace and identify with as one's innermost own.[127]

Thus understood, resolute commitment (*zhi*) includes within itself both the "target" at which one aims and the "effort" put into reaching it. Moreover, to take aim at a target identifies one with a "form of life" pursuant to that particular goal. *Zhi* thus resembles what Dewey describes as "motive" in his ethical writings—not that which is a drive *to* action but rather "*is* the movement of the self as a whole, a movement in which desire is integrated with an object so completely as to be chosen as a compelling end."[128]

Such commitment is made clear in the "Meaning of Archery," in which the "targets" at which one aims are identified with the roles that constitute one as a person. Thus: "One who makes of oneself a father (*weirenfuzhe* 為人父者), aims at the father target; one who makes of oneself a son, aims at the son target; one who makes of oneself a ruler, aims at the ruler target; one who makes of oneself a subject, aims at the subject target. So it is that each particular archer aims at his own personal target."[129] The target metaphor suggests that the "shooting" identified with *zhi* 志 is a holistic activity wherein means-and-ends are coterminous. In other words, the *dao* 道 of becoming a "father" requires aiming to be a father, and that of becoming a "ruler" requires aiming to be a ruler. Central to role ethics, the notion that a person is identical to his/her role-fulfilling activities finds expression in Confucius' account of the optimal community: one in which "the rulers *rule*, ministers *minister*, fathers *father*, and sons *son*."¹³⁰ For Confucians, the ideal person is one whose identity *as* a person is indistinguishable from the activities that express the social roles that one aspires to realize.

Living such roles and doing what is appropriate within them is always the ethical "target." According to the archery metaphor, *wisdom* refers to the position (*ju* 居) one assumes in order to hit the target, which also corresponds to the associated humanity (*ren* 仁) that one brings to the "shot." Meanwhile, *strength* refers to one's ability to "go the distance" in reaching the target, which also corresponds to the courage and willingness to do what is appropriate (*yi* 義) in the roles that define one's person. Together, one's "position" and "discharge" indicate the entire thrust of one's being as an ethical person. In other words, they indicate one's *zhi* 志.

The "self" suggested in the Confucian archery metaphor is commensurable with that which is found in role ethics. Moreover, the connection between resolute commitment and the adoption of roles underscores that *zhi* 志 is something deeper than mere "will," as the term is sometimes translated. As Dewey suggests, "It is *as* a parent, not just as an isolated individual, that a man or women imposes obligations on children; these grow out of the office or function the parent sustains, not out of mere personal will."¹³¹ The functions sustained through role-based relationships give content to our resolute commitments rather than the other way around. As Ames and Rosemont see it, within this matrix of roles the unique person surfaces. "Each of us is the sum of the roles we live—not 'play'—in our relationships and transactions with others," they write. "The goal of living, then, is to achieve harmony and enjoyment for oneself and for others through acting most appropriately in those roles and relations that make us uniquely what we are."¹³²

The idea that cultivating such a self is enjoyable (*le* 樂) evokes an important component of virtue ethics, namely that "virtue" is its own reward given the kind of creatures that we happen to be. If there is anything like the notion of "flourishing" (*eudaimonia*) in the Confucian tradition, it certainly connects up with our nature as relational beings, captured in the ideal of associated humanity (*ren* 仁). Again, for Dewey, there is something "deep within human nature itself which pulls towards settled relationships," such that "happiness which is full of content and peace is found only in enduring ties with others."¹³³

Dewey demonstrates, however, that such flourishing is coherent without strong teleological commitments. As he notes, Aristotle frames *eudaimonia* in teleological terms—it is that *sole* end which is "for itself and never for the sake of something else." Ever sensitive to "*the* philosophical fallacy," Dewey is cautious not to bifurcate "Means/Ends" in his discussion of human happiness. We must, Dewey allows, "make a distinction between pleasures and happiness, well-being, what Aristotle calls *eudiamonia*." But in doing so, it is not required that we posit happiness as a remote "end" that works by final causation. For Dewey, happiness "is not directly an *end* of desire and effort, in the sense of an end-in-view purposely sought for, but is rather an end-product, a necessary accompaniment, of the character which is interested in objects that are enduring and intrinsically related to an on-going and expansive nature."[134] For the Confucian, human association (*ren* 仁) is *intrinsically* related to being human. It is the "*dao* of the human" (*rendao* 人道). This is the final analysis—for as we have seen, the moment one makes the additional move of taking *dao*-activity up instrumentally, one is no longer talking about *dao*-activity. The Confucian *dao* involves cultivating a self through taking on roles and hitting the mark (*zhong* 中). It is understood that such experience brings pleasure (*le* 樂) in the doing. That's all there is to it.

The archery metaphor reflects this rather well. Like any sport, archery is something communal and designed to bring enjoyment to each of its participants. "Sport," as James W. Keating explains, is precisely activity undertaken for its own rewards:

> In essence, sport is a kind of diversion which has for its direct and immediate end fun, pleasure, and delight . . . The primary purpose of sport is not to win the match . . . but to derive pleasure from the attempt to do so and to afford pleasure to one's fellow participants in the process. . . . Sport, then, is a co-operative endeavor to maximize pleasure or joy, the immediate pleasure or joy to be found in the activity itself.[135]

Using "sport" as a metaphor for ethical experience underscores that ethical living is also the sort of activity undertaken for its own sake. It is a serious form of play, continuous with the primitive features of the "hunting vocation" discussed in chapter 6 of volume one. As such, ethical living is "concerned primarily with *wholes*" and thus a good-in-itself.[136] As Mencius makes clear, the motivation to do what is appropriate (*yi* 義) cannot be located outside (*wai* 外) of its own activity.[137] In other words, means-and-ends must remain continuous. As recognized in the virtue ethics tradition, truly ethical acts are not done out of "duty" or even because they are "virtuous." Such outside considerations divide activity into "Means/Ends," making the ethical act something one *must* or *should* do. Assuming "ends lying *outside* our activities," explains Dewey, these become "something for which we *ought* to act."[138]

The essence of sport is similarly violated the moment it becomes something that one is required or expected to do. The English word "sport" is derived from the Middle English *desport* and the Old French *desporter*, meaning precisely the release from work that is in any way laborious or mandatory.[139] Truly ethical activity, like sport, is done out of enjoyment and for its own sake. As Confucius says: "To simply recognize [what is right to do] is not as good as being fond of it, and being fond of it is not as good as enjoying it (lezhi 樂之)."[140] As Ames and Rosemont indicate, it is already true that "the most important thing in the human experience [for Confucians] is the quality of the relationships that locate one in community and constitute one as a human being."[141] The ideal, then, of the ethical "sportsman"—i.e., one who remains firmly "positioned" in associated life and hits the mark (zhong 中) by doing what is appropriate—is an extension of these existing goods. For Confucians, being ethical is "sports-like" in that the pleasure and significance that comes *with* doing it also comes *from* doing it.

By exploring the connection between archery, enjoyment (le 樂), and the continuity between means-and-ends, one comes to see how "targets" operate within Confucian ethics and the archery metaphor. This underscores what Ni Peimin notes are the "profound differences" between the early Confucians and Aristotle.[142] For Aristotle, the "highest good" is the target. Thus, as Aristotle reasons: "Will not the knowledge of it have a great influence on life? Shall we not, like archers who have a mark to aim at, be more likely to hit upon what is right?"[143] For Confucians, such thinking is an externalization (wai 外) of moral ends and thus a bifurcation of dao 道-activity. Targets are not self-standing, transcendent objects.[144] Rather, "targets" grow out of the pleasure (le) that one derives from aiming at them. Dewey concurs. "Men shoot and throw" instinctively, explains Dewey, but they soon discover that there is pleasure found in the simple act of taking aim. "Liking the activity in its acquired meaning, they not only 'take aim' when they throw instead of throwing at random, but they find or make targets at which to aim," he writes. "This is the origin and nature of 'goals' in action. They are ways of defining and deepening the meaning of activity." Thus, human beings do not shoot because targets exist. Instead, human beings set up targets so that shooting itself is made more rewarding and significant. Any target or "end," so understood, operates as a *means* of directing present activity toward significant results. To "take aim" and to "hit the target" are qualities of *activity* in its optimal mode.

The Confucian moral life now comes into focus. To hit a target at which one aims, as Dewey suggests, is "as truly the beginning of another mode of activity as it is the termination of the present one." Similarly, hitting the mark (zhong 中) in the Confucian archery metaphor refers not to a discrete act with a fixed end, but rather to a form of life that one has assumed and that one *lives*. This holistic process: taking aim, shooting, and enjoying the activity, are encompassed in the notion of resolute commitment (zhi 志). This process manifests itself in large part through the roles that one assumes—and it is rightly understood as a process and not as a series of isolated acts. To do what is appropriate as a parent, for example, *in a single instance*, is hardly the terminus of "parenthood." Parenthood instead is a process of continually aiming at parenthood. Parenting means cultivating the wisdom (*zhi* 智) and strength (*li* 力) to become and remain a good parent. The metaphorical "target" of parenting, then, operates as what Dewey calls an "end-in-view" or "aim."[145] It does not indicate a terminal end, but rather something that directs and re-directs activity in directions that are meaningful, desirable, and significant. This is how ethical "targets" operate in the Confucian archery metaphor.

As such, hitting the mark (*zhong* 中) cannot be considered apart from the concrete process of taking aim and shooting; nor can it be hypostasized and imposed as a "duty" or fixed as a terminal "end" without losing its natural status as an active good. This, as Dewey says, "puts the center of moral gravity outside the concrete processes of living."[146] The early Confucians agree. Whenever duties, virtues, or ends are over-determined and fixed outside (*wai* 外) the circuit of concrete activity, there is the risk of alienation and a resultant decay in the ethical quality of activity.

Such a situation, as Dewey sees it, unfolds as follows:

> If generation after generation were shown targets they had no part in constructing, if bows and arrows were thrust into their hands, and pressure were brought to bear upon them to keep shooting . . . some wearied soul would soon propound to willing listeners the theory that shooting was unnatural . . . that the *duty* of shooting and the *virtue* of hitting are externally imposed and fostered, and that otherwise there would be no such thing as a shooting-activity—that is, morality.[147]

Genuinely ethical behavior, as virtue ethics dictates, requires an identification of the "self" with the "target" at which one aims. It is not enough to simply be *presented* with a target in the form of a "duty." Truly ethical targets enter meaningfully into the very activity of taking aim and shooting: the holistic process that Confucians identify with *zhi* 志. Here, it is the *activity* rather than the *end* that is primary. "Strictly speaking," says Dewey, "not the target but *hitting* the target is the end-in-view; one *takes* aim by means of the target," meaning that, through the target, the shooter is "realizing his end at every stage."[148] In this way, ethical "targets" emerge alongside the realization of one's genuine aims and purposes.

An episode in the *Annals of Lü Buwei* makes a similar point about the importance of identifying oneself with a target. We learn that Liezi once hit the mark in archery and presented this to Master Guanyin. The Master asks him: "Do you realize why you hit the mark?" Liezi replies: "No." Thus, the Master said: "It is unacceptable." Liezi withdraws and practices archery for another three years. Again, he presented himself to the Master. The Master asks again: "Do you realize why you hit the mark?" Liezi replies: "Yes." The Master then says: "That is acceptable. Now maintain [this level of engagement] and do not lose it."[149]

For Confucians (*pace* Zhuangzi), just happening to hit a target does not make one a good archer. Nor, in the context of the archery metaphor, does accidentally hitting a target reveal anything about one's personal character.[150] According to the Confucians, to be a good archer one must incorporate the "target" holistically into one's activity, identifying oneself with the "aim" and the "shot" taken. Only then does one realize the meaning and significance of the whole "shooting" enterprise, and only then does the shooting become enjoyable (*le* 樂) and thus revealing of character. As Dewey says: "There is nothing in which a person so completely reveals himself as in the things which he judges enjoyable and desirable."[151] The Confucian archery metaphor concurs.

Morality is Social

For the Western reader, it is a bit odd to think of archery in terms of our association with other people. Western antiquity, after all, is replete with "stories of superlative marksmanship on the part of *individuals*," ancient heroes such as Agamemnon and Ulysses were great archers; and then there are individuals such as William Tell and Robin Hood, who displayed marvelous feats of marksmanship.[152] Western traditions do not suggest that there is any constituent *need* for other people in order to register one's skill as a marksman (the example of William Tell having to shoot an apple off his son's head notwithstanding).[153] The Chinese archery tradition, however, is different. The Chinese archery contest was an event that took place in full observance of ritual-custom (*li* 禮), and as such it was not about lone individuals trying to hit targets in a display of their privately owned gifts. Archery was an elaborate, highly stylized affair, the details of which contribute to a more adequate understanding of archery as a metaphor in the Confucian mind. According to some accounts, Confucius himself would stage archery contests.[154] By the time of Mencius, however, it would appear that the remnant, ritualistic wing of the erudite (*ru* 儒) tradition had evaporated, and along with it went the Zhou-inspired contests. Still, the archery metaphor remains a conceptual extension of ideals embodied in the original practice, so that practice deserves our consideration.

At its heart and core, the traditional archery contest, as distinct from the bi-annual contests sponsored by the Zhou kings, was a social occasion.¹⁵⁵ There was a formal host, a principal guest, and a master of ceremonies. Once participants in the contest had assembled, the master of ceremonies would oversee the division of the group into two teams. Three leather targets were set up at distances increasing in difficulty. Each team would be divided into three groups according to skill level. Each participant would then pair up with a member of the opposing team in the same skill class. During each round, three pairs of adversaries in their respective classes would take shots, four arrows at a time. When a shot hit the target, a point was scored for the team of the archer who shot it, provided it was the target designated for his skill level. The arrows would then be collected and the next six participants would enter the field. There would be a total of three rounds for each pair before the final tally was taken and victory declared to the team with the most points. Such were the bare mechanics of the contest.¹⁵⁶

The aesthetic embellishments that decorated the bare mechanics are too numerous and detailed to recount. Meticulous attention was paid to the music played, the proper handling of implements, the proper direction in which objects and participants were to face, the sequence of entry and exit, the seating arrangements, and much else. Furthermore, as a large-scale social event, a generous amount of wine was consumed. The time and attention devoted to the etiquette of drinking: rinsing the glasses, pouring the wine, and toasting one another, easily matched or exceeded the time and attention devoted to the actual business of the sport. The *Songs* relates the scene in lively verse, with commentary sharply critical of those who became too drunk at the contests.¹⁵⁷

Properly run, the archery contest was a highly refined aesthetic event. On the shooting field, contestants carried out movements to the accompaniment of various musical scores. The set pieces of music (*yue* 樂) were themselves designed to promote and express the enjoyment (*le* 樂) of the contest itself.¹⁵⁸ It is recorded that Confucius found the choreographed syncopation to be among the most challenging aspects of the contest. He relished the challenge: "How is an archer to shoot? How is an archer to listen? Releasing the shot in perfect time with the musical note; moreover, to shoot without missing the center of the target. Only one of consummate virtue can do this! Someone not as consummate cannot be relied on to hit the mark (*zhong* 中)."¹⁵⁹ As Derk Bodde suggests, "Elegance [during the contest] was apparently judged to be as important as the actual skill in hitting the mark."¹⁶⁰ Archery, it seems, became identified in early China with male elegance generally.¹⁶¹

For Amy Olberding and Linda Zagzebski, elegance in comportment plays an important role in exemplarist ethics.¹⁶² As Olberding writes: "Grace, decorum, poise [and] naturalness are part of virtuous activity at its best, serving to convey to others that in doing what one ought, one also does what one wishes, or what reaches to one's convictions and dispositions."[163] The archery contest, then, was considerably more than just an archery contest. It was a social event that showcased the refinement, elegance, and resolute commitment (zhi 志) of its participants. It promoted ritual propriety, civility, and taught one how to win and lose. Moreover, it fostered camaraderie among competing parties. It is significant that the competition was between teams and not between individuals. Victory and defeat extended to groups, not to lone archers; and in the end, the experience transcended even team affiliations. For at the close of the contest, in a final show of camaraderie, the winning side would humble itself to the losing side by serving up one last cup of wine. In a closing ceremony, each pair of archers would approach a platform on which the winner would stand while the loser sat to receive his cup. Once the wine was consumed, the two participants would exchange courtesies before yielding to the next pair.

This component of the contest deeply impressed Confucius. He regards the gesture as symbolic of how exemplary persons ought to behave in all contentious situations. As he says: "Exemplary persons are not contentious, except when they must be, as in the archery contest. Ascending the hall, they bow and defer to others; and together on descent, they drink a salute. This is how exemplary persons compete."[164] Thus, even in the midst of contention, there is virtue in grace, humility, civility, and camaraderie. In fact, any number of virtues: decorum, community-mindedness, fairness, as well as the good-natured enjoyment of oneself in the company of others, are all embodied in the Confucian archery contest.

The centrality of such social virtues reveals a lot about ethics in this tradition, as well as about what "moral self-reflection" means. As Confucius suggests, if one fails to hit the mark, there should be no ill will toward the winning party. Nor, incidentally, should one seek to readjust the target, for as the *Annals of Lü Buwei* says: "When an archer shoots and fails to hit the mark, if he just resets the target, how is he going to improve himself at hitting the mark (zhong 中)?"[165] Instead, when an archer fails to hit the mark, the proper response is self-reflection (zifan 自反). As Mencius says: "Archers make sure [their stance] is correct (zheng 正) before letting the arrow fly. If one fails to hit the target, one does not blame the winners, but rather turns back (fan 反) to find the reason in oneself."[166]

The archery metaphor tells us a lot about what Mencius regards as the "object" of moral self-reflection, that to which one "returns" when the mark is missed. As it turns out, Confucian self-reflection is not a survey of motives in private psychological space, nor is it a review of reasons for or against acting on some impulse, nor is it coming to realize the directives of some moral apparatus "inside" the self. Since the arena in which ethical actions "hit or miss" is wholly within the social realm, self-reflection in the face of moral transgression amounts to considering how genuinely associated one is in the "field" of ethics itself.

Recall that, for the Confucians, archery involves two things: skill in "positioning," to ensure proper aim, and strength in "discharge," to ensure that an arrow reaches the target. Mencius likens wisdom (*zhi* 智) to the first element and sagacity (*sheng* 聖) to the second.[167] As Mencius also suggests, associated humanity (*ren* 仁) correlates with the element of positioning (*ju* 居).[168] Thus, in the archery metaphor, associated humanity is where one "returns" when one fails to hit the mark. It is the "position" from which one's stance can be evaluated for its correctness (*zheng* 正). Mencius teaches, accordingly, that if one fails to effectively express concern for others, one must turn to examine one's own associated humanity (*ren* 仁).[169] Similarly, when one is treated inconsiderately, it is to one's own associated humanity that one must turn.[170] Just as one would expect in a role-based model, the "object" of self-reflection is the presence or absence of *human association*. To reflect on the "self," in other words, is to reflect on the quality and sincerity of one's relationships with *other people*.

As Mencius sees it, if on self-reflection (*zifan* 自反) one finds oneself sincere and committed in one's associated living, then one can trust the appropriateness (*yi* 義) of the acts and judgments "discharged" (*you* 由) from that position. In the Confucian estimation, so long as one remains correctly "positioned" with respect to others in associated life, one cannot stray far from the mark. As Confucius says: "If one's resolute commitment (*zhi* 志) is set on associated humanity (*ren* 仁), one can do no wrong."[171] Likewise, when it comes to passing judgment, Confucius says that, "Only the person of associated humanity (*ren*) can be approving or disapproving of others."[172] Mencius provides a vivid account of what Confucian self-reflection looks like in the latter instance:

> In the event that someone treats her in an unacceptable manner, the exemplary person will turn to herself and say: "I must be lacking in associated humanity (*ren*) and be without ritual form (*li* 禮); otherwise, how could such things happen to me?" If, upon self-reflection, she finds herself established in human association and not lacking in ritual form, and yet the unacceptable behavior continues, she will turn to herself and say: "I must have failed to show this person loyalty (*zhong* 忠)." If, upon self-reflection, she finds that she has shown loyalty to this person, and yet the

unacceptable behavior continues, she will conclude: "This person is unruly. As such, how can he be distinguished from an animal? What can one do about an animal?"[173]

As prescribed by the archery metaphor, the "archer" in this case first turns to seek the reason for ethical misfire in the self. Once she determines that her "position" is firm, she has confidence that the shot "discharged" from that position is both wise and appropriate.

As suggested in the *Mencius*, sincere self-reflection (*zifan* 自反) is something that can lend one tremendous courage and strength in the face of adversity. Here, the courage (*yong* 勇) of Confucius is cited as exemplary. Confucius is

Figure 5.1. *John Dewey*, by Edwin B. Child, 1929. This painting, featuring Dewey with a statue of a Chinese sage, hangs in the Dewey Memorial Lounge on the campus of the University of Vermont. Getty Images.

reported as having said that, if he finds himself upright and well-poised upon self-reflection, he would go forward "even if thousands of people opposed him."[174] Such "strength" in discharge correlates to the second component of the archery metaphor: the unyielding conviction and perseverance befitting of the sage, a distant but achievable goal.[175]

Sagehood aside, it is well established in the tradition that for most people becoming correctly "positioned" remains of primary concern in ethical experience. Confucius suggests as much, as do other classical sources.[176] Having proper ethical sensibilities is fundamental. Such wisdom (*zhi* 智) begins with adopting the correct stance, one that is "positioned" in the Confucian *dao* 道. Without wisdom at the beginning, the "strength" of one's conviction is irrelevant, since the shot is likely to miss the mark. As Mencius puts it: "Exemplary persons draw back the bow, and they stand (*li* 立) squarely in *dao* before letting the arrow fly. Those who are able, do the same."[177] For Mencius, *dao* is the moral "field," the arena of human goodness wherein targets are developed, aims are taken, and shots are released. To be firmly positioned in this *dao* is the only way that one will ever hit the mark (*zhong* 中). There are, in other words, no moral hermits in the Confucian tradition. The "field" of ethical experience, like the "field" of the traditional archery contest, is thoroughly *social*—populated not with separate, numerically distinct "individuals" but with role-bearing participants engaged in communal activity supported and ennobled through ritual-custom (*li* 禮).

As such, the archery contest reflects the nature of associated humanity (*ren* 仁) itself. The two ideas, in fact, are regarded as equivalent. As Mencius says: "Associated humanity (*ren*) is like archery,"[178] and as the "Meaning of Archery" teaches: "Archery is the *dao* 道 of associated humanity (*ren*)."[179] As for what *ren* signifies to Mencius: "Associated humanity (*ren*) is what it means to be 'human' (*ren* 人) and to accord with this and teach it is *dao*."[180] The moral *dao* is thus bound up with the human community. For the early Confucians, as for Dewey: "All morality is social," not because it ought to be, but just because it is.[181] Without *other people*, there would be no ethics. Similarly, without *archery contests*, there would be no targets, no aims, no hits, and no misfires.

As such, associated humanity (*ren* 仁) is not so much a privately cultivated "virtue" as a function of one's integration in interpersonal relationships—a measure of how integrated the self is with *other people* in loyal and sympathetic relationships. As Mencius explains: "Everything is here with us. There is no greater joy than inspecting one's own person and finding it well integrated (*cheng* 誠). To conduct oneself in a way that consistently puts oneself in the place of others (*shu* 恕): this is the shortest route to associated humanity (*ren*)."[182] Like the early Confucians, Dewey also regards "sympathy" as the key to moral understanding. "To put ourselves in the place of others," Dewey writes, "is the surest way to attain objectivity of moral knowledge." For him, sympathy "is the tool, *par excellence*, for resolving complex problems."[183]

But how is this tool used? Famously, Confucius suggests that his entire *dao* 道 is bound together with "one thread"—loyalty (*zhong* 忠) and sympathy (*shu* 恕).[184] One is immediately struck by the oddity that the "one thread" consists of *two* things, but the point is that these are integrated functions in Confucian ethics. Self-reflection (*zifan* 自反) in the face of ethical difficulty means not only reflecting on one's level of *loyalty*, but also on one's level of *engagement*, i.e., on one's degree of associated humanity (*ren* 仁). This means relying on one's active intercourse with others for the wisdom to know what is appropriate (*yi* 義). As the early Confucians see it, the firmer one is positioned (*ju* 居) in associated life, the more attuned one is to the feelings and demands of *other people*—the only real factor in morality.

According to the archery metaphor, there are qualities of conduct and attitude that make for excellence in the Confucian tradition. Poise, civility, elegance, decorum, community-mindedness, sincerity, and camaraderie might suggest itself as a tentative list, but the inventory of concrete "virtues" is probably endless. This ought not concern us. Systematically enumerating "*the* virtues" is not a very feasible philosophical assignment; plus, it risks shifting focus away from what is more important. "The mere idea of a catalogue of different virtues," Dewey writes, "commits us to the notion that virtues may be kept apart, pigeon-holed in water-tight compartments," when in fact, "virtuous traits interpenetrate one another; this unity is involved in the very idea of integrity of character."[185] The key perhaps is to recognize, as the Master suggests, that all virtues are bound together with "one thread." The existential integration of its dual functions is the locus of the moral self. Loyalty (*zhong* 忠) and sympathy (*shu* 恕) interpenetrate existentially in the resolute commitments (*zhi* 志) of actual people in real communities. Morality happens nowhere else.

Amy Olberding gets this. As she astutely observes, the *Analects* sports a distinct "look and feel" as a philosophical text. Its atmospheric qualities, she writes, include the "sense of philosophical activity happening on the fly, an intellectual account of morality developing within a narrative about a community of people who are most decidedly themselves traversing the mix and muddle of morally complicated lives."[186] We too are these people. The "field" in which moral experience occurs is forever one in which flesh-and-bone human beings live together in real time, with all their needs and desires, pains and pleasures, hopes and fears on the table. To show loyalty (*zhong* 忠) in one's relationships, to have sympathy (*shu* 恕) for others, and to model one's self on those who command admiration and deference—this does the work of a thousand ethical theories (*yan* 言). For at least 250,000 years, human capabilities for loyalty, sympathy, and peer modeling have co-evolved with our innate capacities for deepening and expanding our life activities as associated beings. All this time, the emerging "field" of human association (*ren* 仁) has been the only "foundation" that morality has ever had—and it remains the only one that it ever needs.

In chapter 6, we turn to Mencius to better understand those aspects of human nature (*renxing* 人性) through which our moral capacities are realized. Alongside recent findings in evolutionary biology, scholars are increasingly aware of how empirically well-grounded Mencius' teachings on human nature are. Once again, however, specific readings hamper and obscure this fact through over-reliance on "out of gear" concepts. Thus, we need to contend once again with the "Heaven's plan" reading of Confucianism—further challenging the Greek-medieval inferences that commentators bring to their readings of the *Mencius*. This proves to be a worthwhile assignment, for it enables us to look closely at evidence that illuminates the meaning of *tian* 天 in early Confucianism, and to reflect carefully on the status of normative and religious claims about human nature (*renxing*) in the absence of intelligent design theorizing. All of this and more will occupy us in chapter 6.

6

Humans and Nature

> Aristotle's concept of final cause had always been responsible for difficulty, but the harm was compounded when the idea was adopted by theologians and made an instrument to serve the interests of religion . . . To justify the existence of a final cause people will resort to all manner of ridiculous arguments.
>
> —John Dewey, National Peking University, November 1919

Naturalizing Heaven

Dewey's library contained a copy of Lionel Giles' 1942 translation of the *Mencius*. It was a gift from Hu Shih. Its title page was inscribed as follows:

> I present this new translation of *The Book of Mencius*, which has for over two thousand years taught the Chinese intelligentsia how to live and act.[1]

Indeed. As Donald J. Munro has recently observed, the *Mencius* is one of a small number of ancient texts that still serve as actual guides for living and acting. Thus, as Munro argues, it is important that we continue to update our readings of it—not only in light of emerging research about its origins, but also in light of our present needs and circumstances.

In a thoughtful essay entitled "Mencius and an Ethics of the New Century," Munro argues that recent theories in the evolutionary sciences regarding the biological basis of altruism and infant bonding might lend credence to Mencius' philosophy of human nature. Such theories, says Munro, support Mencius' contention that certain moral concepts derive from something that is "inborn." What such naturalistic theories do not address, however, is whether or not such instincts are also "founded on something transcendental," and by this he means the suggestion that human nature is derived from a supernatural "Heaven" (*tian* 天).² As Munro explains, Mencius' philosophy is relevant precisely because the "foundation of [its] ethics lies *not* in a supernatural being or realm." While some Chinese thinkers regarded *tian* as a supernatural entity, Munro observes that "Mencius did not."³ Thus, Munro suggests that contemporary philosophers who draw inspiration from the *Mencius* do well to "filter out" such "religious" accretions in order to focus on the original, more scientifically viable features of Mencius' philosophy. Such features, he surmises, "will survive [such a] sifting to become for the new century the essence of the *Mencius* text, separated from what will then be disregarded as the dross."⁴

Irene Bloom's response to Munro is required reading. She reminds us that in fulfilling this challenge we must not disregard *tian* 天 altogether. She submits that when Mencius speaks of "Heaven"—and as she notes, "the word *tian* in Mencius may in most cases be more aptly translated as 'Nature' rather than 'Heaven'"—he is giving expression to a "deep yet un-testable sense for what the world is like—and why—and to an equally un-testable sense for what we can make it through our efforts." For Bloom, *tian* represents something central to the *Mencius*: a deeper sense of connectedness and continuity, something that is not necessarily empirical but that cannot be wholly discarded without relinquishing the spiritual essence of the text. "[Such an] un-testable but undeniable sense of being part of a whole," she writes, "is not something [that] should be filtered out."⁵

Philip J. Ivanhoe agrees. He suggests, however, that the disagreement between Bloom and Munro may not run very deep. Much depends, he observes, on how one understands *tian* 天. According to Ivanhoe, the idea that our "evolutionary past has woven us inextricably into Nature" and that we "continue to receive much of our most powerful inspiration and most profound satisfaction from [Nature]" resonates with features of "Heaven" as found in the *Mencius*, features that suggest the "interconnection" between the human experience and the natural world. These features, Ivanhoe suggests, are present in the text and are "worth retaining and savoring."⁶

Ivanhoe enters this debate in an awkward position. He is the principal exponent of the "Heaven's plan" reading of the *Mencius*, a reading that stands in tension with the "evolutionary past" that he makes reference to. For Ivanhoe, Mencius' Heaven is "an agent with a plan for the world," one that formulates and sets in motion a "design" for the human race.⁷ Heaven, he submits, is a caring, supernatural Deity that fashions "human nature" with our best interests in mind. Heaven, he writes, "has arranged things in the world in such a way that for each thing there is a proper role and function." Accordingly, there is a divine plan in the world that "human beings can and must come to understand" (even though this plan is only "vague and loosely defined" in the text).⁸ Not unlike God in the Bible, the Heaven that Ivanhoe attributes to the *Mencius* commands affairs in the human domain, such that humans must "obey Heaven" and "fulfill Heaven's grand design for us and for the world."⁹

Such ideas are precisely those that Munro encourages us to "filter out." Not only do they not reflect Mencius' actual position, they are "out of gear" by modern standards and have no role to play in contemporary philosophical discourse. The time has come to "disregard them as the dross."

Here, I concur with Munro. I also join Bloom, however, in suggesting that updating our readings of the *Mencius* invites us to recover something important in the text. As Bloom maintains, while *tian* 天 in the *Mencius* is usually better translated as "Nature" rather than "Heaven," it remains central to the text's religious vision.¹⁰ Again, scholars agree that *tian* is an idea that evolves during the Warring States period, moving from a more supernatural notion to one more naturalistic in content. Where on the spectrum the *Mencius* lies (assuming that it occupies only one position) is largely a matter of conjecture. As Franklin Perkins notes, it is "remarkably difficult" to determine the nature of *tian* in the *Mencius*,¹¹ and despite the boldness of his intelligent design inferences, even Ivanhoe acknowledges that the *Mencius* provides only a "vague sketch" of what *tian* actually means.¹² Thus, each commentator hazards an educated guess. In recent decades, however, the situation has changed in ways that tilt the beam against the "Heaven's Plan" reading. The influx of new archeological evidence, along with the increasing volume and quality of philosophical research, enables us to make better-educated guesses.

As we have seen, Ivanhoe's reading of the Confucian tradition is conceptually informed by Western virtue ethics. Within this framework, the notion that "Heaven has a plan for human beings" is functionally equivalent to the Scholastic notion that God formulates such a plan.¹³ Such conceptions fortify the fixed, normative status of "human nature" and thus secure a teleological basis for human flourishing (*eudaimonia*).

In the case of the *Analects*, the need/wish to ground Western-style virtue ethics in the text is what actually motivates "human nature" inferences, because the text is explicit in providing no basis for such inferences. In the *Mencius*, however, the case is different. Not only is there a theory of human nature, but it relates to Nature/Heaven (*tian* 天) in a manner that lends itself quite easily to Greek-medieval inferences. Human nature (*renxing* 人性) in the *Mencius* possesses a natural structure (*ti* 體) the parts of which have natural functions (*guan* 官). It features four nascent impulses or "sprouts" (*duan* 端) that are identifiable as virtues: empathy (*ren* 仁), appropriateness (*yi* 義), ritual propriety (*li* 禮), and wisdom (*zhi* 智). Mencius relies on a verse from the *Songs* to underscore that human nature is inclined towards such behaviors as a rule. "'*Tian* produces the teeming masses," we learn, "and where there is a thing there is a rule (*ze* 則)." For Mencius, to become properly human is to actively cultivate such proclivities and to thereby provide assistance to *tian*. As the text explains: "One who fully expresses one's feelings (*xin* 心) realizes one's nature (*xing*). Realizing one's nature, one realizes *tian* (*zhitian* 知天). By preserving one's feelings and nourishing one's nature, one serves *tian* (*shitian* 事天)."[14]

Even the most qualified Sinologists will make Greek-medieval inferences at this point. James Legge illustrates such reasoning rather well. "By the study of ourselves we come to the knowledge of Heaven, and Heaven is served by obeying our Nature," he submits. "It is much to be wished," however, "that instead of the term Heaven, vague and indefinite, Mencius had simply said 'God,'" but the message remains the same. "I can get no other meaning from this paragraph," Legge confesses—"the 'preservation' [of our *xin* 心] is the holding fast what we have from Heaven [*tian* 天], and the 'nourishing' [of our *xing* 性] is the acting in harmony therewith, so that the 'serving Heaven' is just being and doing what *It* has intimated in our constitution to be *Its* will concerning us."[15] Ivanhoe follows such inferences move-for-move. He likewise concludes that we must "obey Heaven" and "fulfill Heaven's grand design for us and for the world."[16] The resulting "Heaven's plan" is one that "human beings can and must come to understand."[17] As Ivanhoe sees it, "Heaven" ensures that the "virtues" are inscribed in our divinely ordained natures.

It must be understood that such readings are *inferred* from the *Mencius* rather than stated in the text. As Franklin Perkins notes, the idea that all things proceed according to some "higher plan" in the *Mencius* is a "common view among Western interpreters, but [Mencius] never says anything like it."[18] The fact that the statement is made rather than found is plain in Legge's translations. Whenever Mencius speaks of *tian* "producing" humankind (e.g., *tianzhishengcimin* 天之生此民), Legge over-translates the phrase as "Heaven's plan in producing humankind."[19] In the Chinese text, however, there is no word indicating any "plan." Rather, it is inferred from *tian* that there must be some "plan." Ivanhoe introduces this notion just as Legge does—not with any specific textual citation, but through sheer inference.

There are a number of intersecting issues here, and not all of them need to be treated thoroughly. There are the perennial questions about how *tian* 天 relates to Warring States theism in general. Is *tian* an anthropomorphic deity? How does it act in the world? Does it transcend the world? How are human beings and gods/spirits related in early China? At this juncture, such questions can be bracketed out for two reasons. First, there are treatments available that are better than anything I might provide.[20] Second, evidence in the *Mencius* is so conflicting and/or insufficient that such questions are not easily answered from within the text. At present, the more pressing question is whether or not *tian*—however it is conceived in the *Mencius*—realizes a divine, benevolent "plan" in producing "human nature," as James Legge and Philip J. Ivanhoe maintain. The answer to this question directly impacts the genetic and normative status of *xing* 性 in the *Mencius*. It also reveals how compatible *tian* is with the more naturalistic reading of the text that Donald J. Munro and Irene Bloom advocate. If Munro and Bloom are right, such questions hold more than antiquarian interest for us.

Where to begin? Recall that Confucius once remarked that if one wishes to acquaint oneself with species of trees one should consult the *Songs*. If one wishes to become acquainted with species of *tian* 天 one might do the same. The term occurs 170 times in the *Songs* and its meaning covers a broad spectrum. Some instances refer simply to the "sky" or to the "heavenly blue" above. Others are emotional interjections, like "Oh Mother, *tian*!" and "Oh, distant azure heavens!"[21] But primarily, the term serves to focus a range of religious emotions representative of our common hopes and fears, prone as we are before precarious and inscrutable forces beyond our control. Mencius indeed draws from the *Songs* to remind us that, "*tian* produces the teeming masses, and where there is a thing there is a rule." Other *tian*-related passages, however, register more ominous truths: "*tian* produces the teeming masses," we read, "but what it mandates (*ming* 命) is not faith-worthy (*feichen* 匪諶)." Indeed, if there is one overriding message in the *Songs* it is that *tian* has no special regard for the human good.

The iron rule, however, remains in effect—*Seek and ye shall find*. Those looking for Heavenly goodness in the *Songs* will note exceptions. *Tian* 天 sometimes bestows its blessings on deserving people, and it can illuminate (*ming* 明) our path—breaking light (*dan* 旦) as our journey unfolds. But in general, *tian* is simply indifferent to our needs. It is described as uncooperative (*buyong* 不傭), unfair (*buping* 不平), without pity (*budiao* 不弔), and unkind (*buhui* 不惠). It torments the innocent, and it inflicts death and disorder for no reason. Such arbitrariness prompts the lament, "*tian* actually *did this*" (*tianshiweizhi* 天實為之)—what can be said about it?" Is there some higher, benevolent "plan" behind it all? The text states clearly that there is not. "*Tian* is a sick force (*jiwei* 疾威)," we are told, "without any concern (*fulu* 弗慮) and without any plan (*futu* 弗圖)."[22] Remember—Confucius himself is said to have edited the *Songs*. The capricious indifference of *tian* there exhibited led inexorably to its naturalization in the early Confucian tradition.

While Xunzi lies at the end of that road, the unsteadiness of Mencius' faith in the goodness of *tian* 天 is already palpable. This feature is showcased in some of the more recent, evidentially thicker studies of the *Mencius*—studies that pose significant challenges to the more thinly defended "Heaven's plan" reading, according to which Mencius retains a steadfast "faith in Heaven's commitment to the good."²³ Through more scrupulous textual analysis, Michael J. Puett demonstrates that, "Mencius distinguishes between what is right and what [*tian*] actually does."²⁴ This is not to say that Mencius does not prudently defer to *tian* and to the fates that it mandates (*tianming* 天命).²⁵ Mencius' final position, as Puett explains, is that one "must side with [*tian*] and do so without resentment."²⁶ This falls well short, however, of endorsing everything that *tian* does—and hardly does it signal faith in some benevolent "plan." One can accept misfortune and tragedy without resentment and still not believe that it happened for any good reason. Franklin Perkins arrives at a similar conclusion. He provides a series of detailed analyses of episodes and encounters in the *Mencius* that demonstrate how Mencius' appeal to *tian* repeatedly "explains why things did *not* work out the way they should." As he observes: "To take [*tian*] as good thus requires reading these passages as meaning the opposite of what they say."²⁷ Indeed—defenders of "Heaven's plan" in the *Mencius* must do this in the Panglossian sense and then some.²⁸

Spiritualizing Nature

The fact that the "Heaven's plan" reading of the *Mencius* is problematic should help to mitigate the shock of Donald J. Munro's suggestion that we finally "disregard it as the dross." As Irene Bloom suggests, thinking of *tian* 天 as "Nature" rather than "Heaven" remains truer to both the spirit and the letter of the text, provided that one understands that *tian* gives expression to a deep sense of continuity and connection with the cosmos. As Bloom says, the relationship between the human experience (*ren* 人) and *tian* is central to the religious vision of the *Mencius*. It suggests, she writes, "what the world is like—and why," and indicates "what we can make it through our efforts." *Tian* in the *Mencius*, according to Bloom, reveals to us "how we are located in a larger human context, [and] what difference we can make in the world."²⁹

As I have maintained throughout these volumes, arguments in favor of particular readings of classical texts are never *only* arguments about the truth and accuracy of an interpretation; they are also arguments about *importance* and *meaning*—claims about what is at stake, and why anyone should care. What attracts me to Bloom's reading (in addition to its historical accuracy) is the premium it places on human effort and significance. The "Heaven's plan" reading more than fails to provide such things—it positively takes them away. In objecting to supernaturalism in general, and to divine providence in particular, Dewey explains how this is so. Whenever values that have "grown up in the matrix of human relations" are projected into a "supernatural and other-worldly locus," the transferal "[obscures] their real nature and [weakens] their force."[30] The idea that all human goods—ideals that have taken shape over the ages in struggle, persistence, and sacrifice—are all just "Heaven's plan for human beings" is degrading to human experience. The corollary idea that any good that one might do amounts to "obeying Heaven" diminishes and cheapens the natural value of human goodness. When all human striving reduces to "Thy will be done," then "the very possibility of human dignity [becomes] dependent upon compliance with something transcendent"—an idea that, as Roger T. Ames argues, "is repugnant."[31] It falsifies and distracts from the human condition. When every good in human experience is one that "fulfills Heaven's grand design for us and for the world," then human experience counts for nothing.

That is not all. While the notion that "Heaven/God" plans everything for the best might prove therapeutic for the broken, it becomes disastrous as a general social attitude. As Dewey suggests, it encourages passivity in the face of evil and is "too easy a way out of difficulties." For it "leaves matters in general just about as they were before; that is, sufficiently bad so that there is additional support for the idea that only supernatural aid can better them."[32] Such is the mindset that sends "thoughts and prayers" in the face of human tragedy, rather than rolling up one's sleeves and determining what intelligent measures can be taken to prevent such tragedies from happening again. As such, the notion that "Heaven has a plan for human beings" manages to insult intelligence twice. First, it insults intelligence by being preposterous. Second, it encourages us to abdicate intelligence as a resource for ameliorating the human condition. Ideas like "Heaven's plan" are thus the apogees of anti-intellectualism. Discarding empiricism altogether, they teach us that what is happening is not actually happening because what is really happening is under the command of a divine, invisible force. As Irene Bloom understands better than most, *tian* 天 in the *Mencius* is fully about the natural world and "what we can make it through our efforts." There is nothing alien or unnatural about human effort and intelligence in the cosmos. Through such powers, as Mencius suggests, we realize our own natures (*xing* 性) and provide service to *tian* in the process.[33]

The focus for thinkers like Dewey and Mencius is squarely on the possibilities that reside in the human experience. As Bryan W. Van Norden rightly observes, "Dewey [is] a surprisingly Mencian thinker," in that he has an "almost naïve faith in human nature."[34] This is true because Dewey and Mencius each think that it is better to risk faith in "human nature" than in a so-called "Heaven" that is not faith-worthy (*feichen* 匪諶). When Dewey imagines the possibilities of human intelligence, he pictures a vast untapped resource. As he tells an audience at Nanjing Teacher's College: "Human intelligence is something like a rich vein of minerals somewhere in China, still waiting to be discovered and mined."[35] Likewise, texts like the *Mencius* and *Focusing the Familiar* elevate human potential to spirit-like status, such that "Heaven" itself becomes a glass ceiling for humans (*ren* 人) to surpass. Michael J. Puett's thesis is exactly that: "The tension in Mencius is not with the world but with Heaven [*tian* 天]. Or, more particularly, it is between Heaven and the divine potentials of humans."[36]

Both for Dewey and for Mencius, the human experience is a religious enterprise. Confronted with such a proposition, Philip J. Ivanhoe expresses a concern that is mirrored among cultural conservatives in the West: namely, that failing to recognize (or infer) some overriding "faith" in the goodness of "Heaven," risks reducing Confucianism to a form of "secular humanism."[37] Preventing such readings is a legitimate concern, but to insist on "faith" where it does not exist is the wrong preventative measure. The best way to prevent Confucianism from being misread as "secular humanism" is to recognize that Confucian philosophy dissolves the "Sacred/Secular" dualism altogether. As Herbert Fingarette observes, "instead of being diversion of attention from the human realm to another transcendental realm," Confucian religiousness operates *genuinely* as a "dimension of all truly human existence."[38] If this is true, then Confucian "secular humanism" is a contradiction in terms.

Some who read Dewey superficially also mistake him for a "secular humanist" or an "atheist," but he never describes himself in such terms—in fact, he goes out of his way to avoid such associations. The primary reason that Dewey uses the word "God" in *A Common Faith* is that he wishes to disassociate himself from any "militant" or "aggressive" atheism that defines itself against a "supernaturalism" to which religious experience is ceded.[39] Dewey denies the assumption—common to theists *and* atheists—that supernaturalism and religious experience must stand or fall together. Again, the point is to *overcome* the "Sacred/Secular" dualism. The difficulty here is that this particular dualism is bound up with a whole "brood and nest" of dualisms in the Western tradition.[40] Such dualisms snap into place whenever one assesses, for instance, a more naturalistic reading of the *Mencius*.

Thus, reactions to the present reading can be anticipated. "Self-divinization" in the face of cosmic conditions indifferent and recalcitrant—is this not Sartrean existentialism? "Man is nothing but what he makes of himself," Jean-Paul Sartre tells us. Since the "Heaven's plan" reading is being rejected, another voice is heard between the lines. "[So] embarrassing that God does not exist," Sartre mocks. "For there disappears with Him all possibility of finding values in an intelligible Heaven."[41] Before you know it, the present reading is dismissed as what Bryan W. Van Norden describes as "postmodern Confucianism."[42]

Such labels are misguided. The more one reads Dewey, the more adolescent Sartre sounds. As Raymond D. Boisvert explains, with respect to the "religious attitude," the difference between Dewey and Sartre hinges on how their respective philosophies understand the status of "dependence and support" in the human enterprise.⁴³ "The essentially unreligious attitude," Dewey tells us, "is that which attributes human achievement and purpose to man in isolation from the world of physical nature and his fellows."⁴⁴ What this means is that, for Dewey, the *un*-religious attitude (e.g., Sartre's) is an outlook that is positively delusional. As Mary Midgley observes, Sartre regards the human as a "spontaneous, independent force, completely detached from all natural motives and capable of opposing them all."⁴⁵ This severs humanity from Nature (*tian* 天) and considers nihilism an actual possibility.

For Dewey, as for pragmatic naturalists generally, such detached nihilism is not possible for the sentient human being. As Sandra B. Rosenthal explains: "For all pragmatists, the irreducibly meaningful behavior of the human organism in interaction with its natural environment is the foundation of the noetic unity by which humans are bound to their world."⁴⁶ We *know* our world as one with value and meaning because we experience it as such *all the way down*—grounded in our pre-reflective somatic and biological experiences. As Mark Johnson argues: "*meaning reaches deep down into our corporeal encounter with our environment.*"⁴⁷ The human being thus emerges, as Rosenthal says, "[into] a universe rich with ontologically real value-laden qualities that span the gamut of the rich fullness of human existence, qualities that themselves emerge in the interactive contexts of humans with the universe in which they are enmeshed."⁴⁸

Such a vision, which is central to Dewey's philosophical outlook, is one that Irene Bloom identifies with *tian* 天 in the *Mencius*—and as she maintains, "Nature" is better than "Heaven" in describing it. For Dewey, the "spiritual life" gets its "surest and most ample guarantees" when its values are "implicated in the working processes of the universe" rather than in some supernatural entity or realm that is superordinate and detached. Religious values become *real* when they are "buoyed up by the forces which have developed nature," and the religious life becomes *vital* when it is lived "not as an individual but as an organ in maintaining and carrying forward the universal process."⁴⁹ Such sensibilities lie at the heart of what the "continuity between Nature and the human" (*tianrenheyi* 天人合一) means in the Confucian tradition.

As we have seen, Dewey was skittish about using the word "humanism" for good reason. Given its associations, he figured that it would never escape the "Sacred/Secular" dualism. Dewey does sign the "Humanist Manifesto" in 1933, but he rejects "Humanism" itself as a religious position. "A humanistic religion," he warns, "if it excludes our relation to nature, is pale and thin, as it is presumptuous, when it takes humanity as an object of worship."[50] For Dewey, to separate human experience from Nature (*tian* 天) construes it falsely and renders it impotent. Postulating a supernatural "Heaven/God" however, *also* construes human experience falsely and renders it impotent. The solution is not to replace the supernatural "Heaven/God" with the "Human." The solution is to *naturalize* "Heaven/God," recover the spiritual quality of Nature (*tian*), and then restore its continuity (*yi* 一) with the human experience. Irene Bloom gets this, and that is why she was reluctant to follow Donald J. Munro in completely "filtering" *tian* out of the *Mencius*. Such a move can only obscure the religious quality of the text, and such a quality is central to what it teaches.

In the end, regardless of what evidence we have, *tian* 天 is irreducibly complex in early Confucianism. I do not know of anyone who is sanguine in understanding it. As David L. Hall and Roger T. Ames suggest, since so many conflicting features orbit around the term, "we must really question the appropriateness of using 'concept' language to discuss [it]."[51] *Tian* is perhaps more emblematic than conceptual, more symbolic than literal. Nevertheless, it is clearly identified with a kind of *agency*—frequently anthropomorphic—that can and does act in the world. It appears like the "spirit of the age," or the "collective will of society," weighing in to pronounce its mandate (*ming* 命) and change the course of events. As Ni Peimin observes, such ideas reflect how it came to be understood that *tian* "immanently exhibited itself in popular consensus" like a "projection of the will of the people."[52] In today's world, things like "approval ratings" and the "mood in the country" register similar sociopolitical effects. When 700,000 people descend upon Washington, D.C., one feels that *tianming* 天命 is shifting. The difficulty is coming to understand how such large-scale agencies actually work.

Mozi maintains that *tian* 天 has definite intentions (*zhi* 志) and that it makes such intentions clear (*ming* 明).[53] For Mencius, the matter is more ambiguous. *Tian* does not speak (*buyan* 不言) but instead manifests itself through happenings in the world. Its agency, Mencius says, is diffuse: "What is done without a doer is *tian*," and it duplicates the larger social collective: "What the people see and hear are the eyes and ears of *tian*."[54] He maintains a clear distinction between *tian* and human beings (*ren* 人), but they also seem to overlap in power and function, such that while political legitimacy is presented as the business of *tian*, it is also said that: "No one becomes ruler without winning the hearts of the people."[55]

Reading Dewey alongside such statements, one is reminded of his debate with Walter Lippmann over the status and efficacy of "the public." Dewey argues that "the public" actually exists, both as a conjoint agency that has *effects* and as a complex entity that can be *affected*.⁵⁶ The ontological status of such an entity, however, is far from self-evident. Mencius' view that "the people" (*min* 民) are the "eyes and ears of *tian* 天" is similarly obscure. Reflecting his early Hegelian influences, Dewey denies that human thought is an individual matter originally or by production. "It comes to us from others," he writes, "by education, tradition, and the suggestion of the environment." Accordingly, says Dewey: "'*It* thinks' is a truer psychological statement than 'I think.'"⁵⁷ The manner in which *tian* transcends individuals and yet expresses the efficacy of the people (*min*) suggests a similar dynamic.

Recent archeological finds help us to better position Mencius among a range of Warring States views on the goodness and efficacy of *tian* 天.⁵⁸ The *Guodian* 郭店 text, *Failure and Success According to the Times* (*Qiongdayishi* 窮達以世) sheds light specifically on the relationship between *tian* and human activity in this period, with vocabulary that parallels what we find in the *Mencius*. The document opens with the following observation:

> There is *tian* and there are people. Between them there is a difference. By examining the difference one understands how to proceed. If one has the people but not the right age (*shi* 世), then even those of quality will not proceed effectively. Yet, if the age is right, what difficulties could there be?⁵⁹

For Mencius too, "success and failure" (*qiongda* 窮達) depends on circumstances beyond the resolute commitment (*zhi* 志) of particular persons.⁶⁰ Reflecting, then, on the failure of Duke Ping of Lu to call upon his services, Mencius relates that: "When a person proceeds effectively something facilitates it. When a person is hindered, something interrupts it. Proceeding effectively and being hindered are not within a person's control (*neng* 能). That it did not come to pass (*yu* 遇) that I would meet the Marquis of Lu is a matter of *tian*."⁶¹ Like the *Mencius* itself, *Success and Failure According to the Times* identifies what "comes to pass" (*yu*) with *tian*,⁶² thus forging a conceptual link between the "age" (*shi*) in which one lives and the "forces" that hinder or facilitate successful action: in other words, with *tian*.

Dirk Meyer contributes an extensive analysis of *Success and Failure According to the Times*, further demonstrating that it exhibits nothing like the "faith" that Philip J. Ivanhoe ascribes to the *Mencius*. Confirming Michael J. Puett's thesis instead, Meyer finds that the text is premised on an "intrinsic tension between Heaven and Man," and that it delivers something like a "guide to dealing with life's imponderables as caused by Heaven," without any assurance that such imponderables are going according to "plan" or are even intentional.⁶³ Reflecting on what it means to consider the "age" (*shi* 世)

when discussing *tian* 天 in this connection, Pang Pu 庞朴 draws the following conclusion:

> (*Tian* in the Guodian strips) is a force beyond the human being that humans can neither anticipate nor control—yet must accept. It is an opportunity that comes and goes or appears in cycles, and it is the conditions under which one prospers if one grasps it and declines if one loses it, but it cannot be commanded. It is an environment people yield to fearfully and rely on to survive. Hence, what was then called "*tian*" took on a special meaning. Using modern concepts, it is actually the social context, social conditions, social opportunities, or simply put, social forces.[64]

As such, *tian* comes to mean the "times" (*shi*) in which one lives. As Meyer observes: "[*tian*] and the times [*shi*] are given equal structural significance, and either of them can be substituted for the other."[65] In light of such evidence, it becomes most plausible that when Mencius alludes to the agency of *tian* that he understands this as the sort of "collective will" that we identify with public interest, acceptance, and censure in the present age (*shi*): notions that transcend individuals yet maintain continuity with human activities.[66] For Dewey, such notions of large-scale "public" agency are invaluable in democratic discourse—plus, they are "in gear" with naturalistic assumptions. In defending their viability, Dewey begins with "electrons, atoms, and molecules" and observes that: "conjoint, combined, associated action is a universal trait of the behavior of things," and that "such action has results."[67]

While much of this remains speculative (evidence keeps coming in), documents like *Failure and Success According to the Times* enable us to update our understanding of *tian* 天 in the *Mencius* with some confidence. We are better able to see how the agency of things like "Society" or "Nature" broadly construed might have been conceived as large-scale forces (*tian*) that mandate the conditions (*ming* 命) under which things in the world can or cannot come to pass (*yu* 遇). Such mandates must be recognized and accepted. For better or for worse, there is only so much that the individual can do in the face of them and the rest is up to *tian*.[68] While recognizing and accepting that which is beyond one's control (*neng* 能) is a sign of wisdom, it does not require or imply faith in "Heaven's plan." Again, as Puett argues: "Mencius distinguishes between what is right and what [*tian*] actually does."[69] This is not to say that Mencius does not defer to *tian* and to its mandates (*ming*).[70] His final position, as Puett says, is that "we must side with [*tian*] and do so without resentment."[71] This, however, is more like prudence than piety on Mencius' part. It is wise to accept without resentment that which cannot be different.

The result, as Puett observes, is a creative tension in the *Mencius* that is not easily resolved. Like Confucius, Mencius clearly "stands in awe of mandated conditions (*ming* 命)" and he seeks to "understand" them.[72] One must not disregard conditions, nor misjudge them. Mencius does not, however, always see fit to capitulate to conditions as they stand. He reserves a discretionary prerogative that belongs to human beings in every age. Mencius explains:

> There is nothing that is without mandated conditions (*feiming* 非命). One goes along with and accommodates only those conditions that are proper to accept. Thus, one who comes to understand such conditions will not go on standing beneath a wall on the verge of collapse. One who dies after bringing *dao* 道 to optimal term has lived within conditions properly. One who dies in fetters and chains has not.[73]

Bringing *dao* to optimal term is more important than passively accepting every condition that forces mandate (*tianming* 天命). If the wall is about to collapse, then *get out of the way*. The early Confucians are not, as Mozi suggests, passively fatalistic. Mencius maintains that given conditions (*ming*) are just that—*given conditions*. Such conditions need to be worked with or around in order to achieve the optimal course (*dao*). Often, it is not advisable or simply impossible to resist the "mandates of Nature/Society/Heaven" (*tianming*). If *tian* ensures anything, however, it is that the conditions that obtain are *exactly* the conditions that obtain. With this understood, we turn our attention once again to the topic of human nature (*renxing* 人性).

Understanding Human Nature

There are patterns that reoccur in nature. One such pattern is the *rachis*. In plants, the rachis is the axis or "shaft" from which green leaves shoot out to absorb light. In vertebrate animals, the vertebrae that encase the spinal cord form a rachis, a middle column from which the bones of the rib cage reach around to protect the heart and lungs. The feather type common to most modern birds has a rachis running up its center, wherefrom countless vanes emerge with tiny barbs that lock onto one another giving the feather its silky stiffness. Cereal grains like buckwheat, rye, and barley are also supported by a rachis from which the spikes of grain protrude.

Of barley (*mou* 麰) there are thirty-one varieties, mostly wild. In the wild varieties, the rachis is *tender*, such that a dense stand of barley thrashes under a circling wind. Occasionally, a recessive allele in one of two genes will result in a barley stalk having a *tough* rachis, a mutation that is maladaptive and scarce in the wild.[74] Such a stalk stands out as odd among its fellows. For human purposes, however, it is the tough rachis that makes reaping, threshing, and sowing easier, resulting in ears that are less prone to shattering. Thus, this mutant form was selected for human domestication, a process that began some ten thousand years ago in the Fertile Crescent.

It would take time for domesticated barley to become what it is today. Because humans cannot digest the cellulose in the husks, domestication would include the development of grains from which the glumes fall away easily. Two-row and six-row barleys were followed by naked grain varieties.[75] Eventually, domesticated barley made its way into China's temperate zones. Its thousand-year journey along the Tibetan Plateau composes a fascinating chapter in evolutionary history.[76] Once in China, barley would continue to evolve. As Gerhard Fischbeck notes, "Spontaneous hybridization between different types of cultivated barley as well as with accompanying weedy forms of [wild barley] probably allowed a multitude of barley genotypes to survive within mixed stands that differed in morphological as well as in physiological traits." Such diversity furthered the evolution of domesticated barley, which was "subjected to the forces of natural selection for adaptation to the prevailing growing conditions [in China]."[77]

Mencius likens human beings to stands of barley, and argues on this basis that it is arbitrary to think that humans do not likewise constitute a type (*lei* 類). "Let barley seeds be sown and covered with soil," he writes, "the ground being the same, and the time of planting the same, it grows rapidly—and in due seasonal course, it ripens." This is true. Stalks also vary in quality. As Mencius observes: "Though there are differences in the yield, this is due to differences in the fertility of the soil, the nourishment of the rain, and the human effort invested." Indeed, human investment is especially important in ensuring the quality of domesticated barley. Stem diseases like take-all and eyespot, and foliar diseases like net blotch and mildew will occur if intelligent measures are not taken. Plus, there are dozens of viruses that can spread through a barley stand if farmers are incautious. Such outcomes, however, are preventable. Mencius' point is that barley exhibits a type (*lei*) and that "things of the same type exhibit commonalities." This is true of every organic form that we know anything about. Thus, as Mencius asks: "Why would anyone doubt this only when it comes to human beings?"[78]

At this juncture, readers must choose between interpretive routes. One route understands the barley example by making a series of essentialist inferences—*because human beings are like barley, they possess an inborn, end-driven teleological nature that never changes and has no history*. Given our cognitive predispositions, this is the majority route. It certainly is among readers who are influenced by Greek-medieval thinking and by readers like Zhu Xi whose understandings have been shaped by Buddhist polemics in China. The more imaginative route, however, pauses to consider whether or not thinkers like Mencius might have, subtly perhaps, worked their way *around* common sense—maybe even arriving at a philosophical standpoint more congenial to contemporary scientific understandings. Evidence for this is indirect, but at least it can be drawn from classical Chinese sources.

What would "human nature" be like if Mencius challenged teleological common sense, presuming instead that organic forms exhibited directional order (*de* 德) but acted without presumption with respect to outcome or aim (*weierbushi* 為而不恃)? What would it be like if he assumed that organic growth was mutually engendering (*yunyunxiangsheng* 芸芸相生)? What would it be like if he understood that maturation (*cheng* 成) involved not an inner potential (*dunamis*) but rather the propensity (*shi* 勢) shored up in an organism-environment circuit? What would it be like if he understood types (*lei* 類) to be more like analogical groupings than Greek-medieval species essences? What would it be like if Dan Robins and A. C. Graham are correct, and the nature (*xing* 性) of a thing amounts to the way it behaves when it "behaves that way spontaneously,"[79] a "spontaneous development in a certain direction rather than [its] origin or goal?" As Graham says, this would involve "the interdependent becoming integral rather than the realization of an end."[80] *In sum, what would it be like if Mencius thought more like a Warring States philosopher and less like Aristotle?* As an intellectual matter, if one seriously entertains this possibility, then one must forego the Greek-medieval route and choose the more imaginative route in reading the *Mencius*.

As Dewey knew personally, challenging Greek-medieval assumptions touches a nerve, and this is no less true in *Mencius* studies. The present reading will be labeled "controversial" or "postmodern" and resisted by some. Readers can speculate for themselves why this is so, but it is likely connected to the fact that, as Lee Yearly observes: Confucianism "makes claims on both our scholarly attention and our personal allegiances."[81] As Munro reminds us, the *Mencius* is a text that still matters to people. To defend an alternative reading of the *Mencius* is to defend an alternative worldview. That being true, I have made plain my own allegiances. Within the framework of intra-cultural philosophy, I maintain that it is the cultural responsibility of philosophers to question ideas that are "out of gear" with our best scientific understandings. This must be done, however, while attending to *cultural context*—both one's own and that of the historical traditions with which one works. The "Heaven's plan" reading, as I have argued, relies more on Greek-medieval inferences than on textual support, and it is now challenged by thicker and better-evidenced Sinological treatments. Thus, it has become questionable by purely scholarly standards.

I also believe, however, that to argue that "Heaven" created human beings in accordance with some "grand plan" is maladaptive by our own cultural and intellectual standards. Thus, we have a double incentive to reject the "Heaven's plan" reading. What remains is a theory of human nature (*renxing* 人性) that is not divinely created, but rather, as Irene Bloom argues, fundamentally "biological in the broad sense of that term."[82] It is one that retains what Mencius calls the natural structure (*ti* 體) and natural functions (*guan* 官) of organic form.[83] There is no question that *tian* 天 mandates (*ming* 命) what human nature (*renxing*) is for Mencius. But as Bloom suggests, it is more accurate to understand *tian* as "Nature" rather than "Heaven" in this connection. The crucial thing, in any case, is to base one's understanding on principles that are demonstrably operative in early Chinese natural philosophy. When Bryan W. Van Norden and others read the *Mencius* based on the premise that all things are "structured teleologically by a quasi-theistic entity," they are choosing the alternate route to the one taken here.[84]

To resist the Greek-medieval route and adopt the more imaginative (and, incidentally, more scientifically viable) route does not mean denying "human nature" altogether. Contemporary evolutionary biologists like Marjorie Grene and David Depew, for instance, "have no trouble acknowledging the existence of a human nature, characterized by a species-specific array of highly plastic and variable traits."[85] That said, from the standpoint of evolutionary theory, there is no reason to expect that any whole set of traits will be perfectly consistent and exclusive to each species. As Edward O. Wilson reminds us, "human nature is just one hodge-podge out of many conceivable." Scores of human-exhibited traits are shared with other mammals—possessing four limbs (*siti* 四體) for instance. Other traits are distinct in equipping us to associate with conspecifics. As Wilson observes: "It is inconceivable that human beings could be socialized into the radically different repertories of other groups such as fishes, birds, antelopes, or rodents."[86] Confucius notes the same. "I cannot congregate socially (*tongqun* 同群) with birds and beasts," he says. "If I am not among other humans, then with whom should I associate?"[87]

The resulting picture of "human nature," one that has evolved through human association, retains the natural structure (*ti* 體) and natural functions (*guan* 官) of organic form, neither of which (as Darwin teaches) necessitate final ends. *Tian* 天 mandates (*ming* 命) what human nature is for Mencius—that is to say, natural processes have produced in us a set of habits and proclivities; and as the concept of *xing* 性 entails, there is no superordinate purpose or "end" (*telos*) involved in their expression. In this respect, Mencius' outlook is consistent with evolutionary biology. In fact, as Donald J. Munro suggests, Mencius' substantive position on human nature is remarkably strong by this standard. His theory features four nascent impulses: empathy (*ren* 仁), appropriateness (*yi* 義), propriety (*li* 禮), and wisdom (*zhi* 智). Each of these corresponds to features of human behavior that we have only recently begun to better understand.

Ren 仁 is commonly translated as "benevolence" in the *Mencius*, but one needs to understand the genealogy of this translation before adopting it. James Legge aligned himself theologically with the Presbyterian bishop, Joseph Butler (1692–1752). Butler devoted his philosophical talents to attacking Deism and to refuting the "egoism" of Thomas Hobbes, who in his *Leviathan* (1651) argued that human nature was essentially self-interested. In sermons such as "Upon The Love Of Our Neighbor," Butler argues that "benevolence"—the desire to promote the general happiness of humankind—is an innate virtue of human nature as created by God. "Human nature is so constituted," proclaims Butler, "that every good affection implies love of itself . . . Thus, to be *righteous* implies in it the love of righteousness; to be *benevolent*, the love of benevolence."[88] Legge believed that the teachings of Bishop Butler were divinely prefigured in the *Mencius*, according to which "Heaven is served by obeying our Nature."[89] The ideas of Butler were thus inscribed directly into Legge's translation of the text.

Mencius' advice to self-doubting rulers, for instance, is pure Butler: "Let the prince be benevolent (*ren* 仁) and all his acts will be benevolent, let the prince be righteous (*yi* 義), and all his acts will be righteous."[90] Mencius' doctrine of human nature was, according to Legge, "as nearly as possible, identical with that of Bishop Butler," and since Butler maintained that, "there is a natural principle of benevolence in man," Legge translated *ren* in the *Mencius* as "benevolence."[91] This particular translation, along with its Butler connection, remains serviceable within the "virtue ethics" paradigm and produces results accordingly.[92]

As we have seen, *ren* 仁 can be understood as something like "associated humanity" in the *Analects*, a general term for the quality of being properly "human" such that this is an inherently social enterprise. While the usage of the term evolves and narrows in the *Mencius*, it is prudent to retain some continuity with this earlier meaning. *Ren* remains, for Mencius, a resolutely social concept. It is identified with "caring for others," "excluding no one from care," and not being able to "bear" the suffering of others.[93] Unlike Confucius, Mencius offers a straightforward definition of the term—it is "the feeling of sympathy for [another's] suffering" (*ceyinzhixin* 惻隱之心).[94] Dewey counts "sympathy" among the "social emotions," and presents it as such to his Beijing audience in 1919. "Sympathy is the core of social unity," he explains, "it is the adhesive force which holds people together. It is the basis of cooperation; it is what makes people enjoy and suffer together."[95]

Such pro-social instincts, according to Mencius, extend from feelings of commiseration that are deeply rooted in our native motor and autonomic responses. His famous example is the "Child at the Well."[96] Should one see a child about to fall into a well (or, say, a toddler meandering behind a parked car as the reverse lights pop on), one is immediately filled with alarm, distress, and concern for the safety of the child. Such an immediate response has nothing to do with gaining favor, winning praise, or agonizing over the thought of a soon-to-be injured child. Such higher-order cognitive operations are preceded and eclipsed by an immediate, other-regarding *concern*. The primatologist Frans de Waal regards Mencius' "Child at the Well" example to be an excellent illustration of how emotional contagion occurs in core structures of the brain while more advanced mechanisms occur at the outer shell. "There exists a rich literature on human empathy and sympathy that, generally, agrees with the assessment of Mencius that impulses in this regard come first and rationalizations later," explains de Waal.[97] Mencius is on solid empirical ground here.

While debates continue in the relevant fields, we have some basic theories about how feelings of commiseration evolved through natural selection. This can be discussed within the framework of the "evolution of helping," from kin selection, to reciprocal altruism, and other related developments.[98] From a Confucian perspective, what is important to note is that contemporary theories of evolutionary ethics often begin with kin selection—i.e., with *family feeling*. So, when Confucius describes family feeling as the "root of associated humanity" (*renzhiben* 仁之本), he is also on solid empirical ground.[99]

Like all pro-social instincts, kin selection involves helping others at personal cost. Such behavior is not a human invention. "Helping," in fact, is a fundamental feature of life-processes in general. Life amounts to continued *growth*, and at the molecular level each organism is a vehicle through which growth continues into subsequent generations; in other words, each organism that reproduces is "helping" the species. Each life sacrifices itself to its own line of genetic transmission. In the interim, willingness to help others at personal cost varies in relation to genetic relatedness. The evolutionary reasoning is expressed in "Hamilton's rule."[100] Let "r" stand for genetic relatedness, "B" stand for recipient benefit, and "C" stand for cost to the help-provider. Behavior in which $rB > C$ can be expected to be favored by natural selection. The "C" threshold goes up as the "r" increases. Nuclear families normally share 50 percent of their genetic material, whereas first cousins share 12.5 percent and third cousins once removed share .391 percent. Cost bearing instincts correlate accordingly. Highly social creatures, such as honeybees, share as much as 75 percent of their genetic material. The stingers with which honeybees defend their hives can thus be discharged at high cost: massive abdominal ruptures that kill them. Mammalian parents are often willing to risk their lives to defend their kin, but they are not *structurally* evolved so as to automatically die in the process. Apparently, only when $r = 75$ will Nature (*tian* 天) allow that to happen.

Now, what about the "Child at the Well" episode? Mencius presumes that the child is not related to the onlooker, so kin selection is not the driver here. Where do such automatic sympathetic responses come from? One answer lies in the logic of "reciprocal altruism." In his now classic paper, "The Evolution of Reciprocal Altruism," Robert L. Trivers provides a mathematical model demonstrating how altruistic behavior "can be selected for even when the recipient is so distantly related to the organism performing the altruistic act that kin selection can be ruled out."[101] Here, it is the uniform *exchange* of altruistic acts that favors it for selection. In becoming common practice, acts that are of small cost to the giver and great benefit to the receiver benefit everyone in the long run.

Once again, such behaviors do not wait upon humans to be realized. Birds give warning calls to other birds to alert them to danger. Why? Because birds that found themselves in areas *without* callers have been selected against relative to birds in areas that had them. Primates regularly engage in reciprocal social grooming. Why? Because primates with fewer ectoparasites live longer, and they cannot find the bugs and remove them alone. There is nothing strange or even remarkable about such things if one remembers, as de Waal reminds us, that living things "are social to the core." "Our bodies and minds are not designed for life in the absence of others," he writes.[102] The logic of altruism has helped to shape the body-mind that humans *have*, and such body-minds experience emotional contagion and involuntary sympathy to an unusually high degree. As Trivers argues, "the emotion of sympathy has been selected to motivate altruistic behavior as a function of the plight of the recipient of such behavior." In other words: "The greater the potential benefit to the recipient, the greater the sympathy and the more likely the altruistic gesture."[103]

Some philosophers will take what is here first-order material and convert it into a "problem" through second-order analysis. "Is altruism really *altruistic*?" they will ask, "or is altruism actually *egotistic*?" If so-called "altruism" temporarily reduces one's fitness but ensures one's own success in the long run, does this not mean that "altruism" is ultimately self-interested? Such questions misfire because they bifurcate what is not bifurcated in the first instance. This, in fact, underscores one of the problems with "benevolence" as an English translation of *ren* 仁. The term already stands in opposition to the "egoism" of Hobbes, thus evoking elements peculiar to a historical debate in English moral philosophy. This obscures the fact that Mencius' thinking, while similarly themed, diverges in its core assumptions. As Dewey notes, the main assumption in the English debate is that the "[human] psychological structure contains two sets of motive springs, termed respectively self-love and benevolence." This distinction is lodged within a broader dualistic framework "arising from a separation of the individual from social relations," which as Dewey observes, "has no basis in fact."[104]

In Mencius' thinking, it is important to recognize that neither egoism nor altruism is *motivating* the "Child at the Well" response. That is the whole point of the example. As Dewey explains, "Psychologically speaking, our native impulses and acts are neither egoistic nor altruistic; that is, they are not actuated by *conscious* regard for either one's own good or that of others. They are rather direct responses to situations."[105] One jumps at the sight of a child in danger not because one wishes to gain social advantage or garnish praise (i.e., more "egotistic" motives), nor because one would be sincerely pained by the sound of the injured child (i.e., more "altruistic" motives). One jumps to save the child because one is human (*ren* 人), and humans have a spontaneous "feeling of sympathy for [another's] suffering" (*ceyinzhixin* 惻隱之心).[106] Properly understood, the "Child at the Well" response is not even a "moral" response—it is simply the discharge of *dao* 道-activity. In such cases, as Dewey says, "there is a natural response to a particular situation, and one lacking in moral quality as far as it is wholly unreflective, not involving the idea of *any* end, good or bad."[107] When moral reflection *does* get up and running, the last thing Mencius wants to see is "egoism" or "altruism" emerging as a distinct, theoretical basis for "moral motivation." Once such bases exist, we have the likes of Yang Zhu "refusing to pluck a single hair from his body to save others" and Mozi "rubbing his body raw from head to toe" to do the same.[108]

While humans display altruistic/empathetic tendencies spontaneously, they also display tendencies to cheat the reciprocal system. Given the evolutionary advantage of the former, however, psychological adaptations have evolved to regulate such transgressions. "Natural selection," argues Trivers, "will rapidly favor a complex psychological system in each individual regulating both his own altruistic and cheating tendencies and his responses to these tendencies in others."[109] Accordingly, the second trait that Mencius identifies with human nature is *yi* 義, which he associates with both "feelings of shame and dislike" (*xiuwuzhixin* 羞惡之心).[110] Zhu Xi identifies the first element (shame) with "being ashamed about what is not good in oneself" and the second (dislike) with "hating what is not good in others."[111] Not surprisingly, such notions: shame, dislike, judgment of others, and redress of wrongs, are all on Donald E. Brown's list of human universals.[112]

Oddly, one still finds the term *yi* 義 translated into English as "righteousness," another Victorian-era relic derived from Bishop Butler that provides continuity for some commentators but only obscures the meaning of the Chinese term. *Focusing the Familiar* provides definitions of *ren* 仁 and *yi* that underscore their distinct associations in this branch of Confucianism: "Associated humanity (*ren*) means conducting oneself as a human being, wherein devotion to kin is most important," whereas "appropriateness (*yi*) means doing what is fitting (*yi* 宜), wherein esteeming those of superior quality is most important."[113] Within the framework of evolutionary biology, *ren* expresses instincts that arise in systems of altruistic behavior (kin selection being first) and *yi* 義 expresses the approbation (and blame) that regulates such systems. "Feelings of shame and dislike" (*xiuwuzhixin* 羞惡之心) regulate behavior by detecting when something is not "right" (*yi* 宜). It is noteworthy that examples in the *Mencius* often have to do with food procurement—something that is necessary to sustaining the life of the individual organism. One does not, for instance, hunt birds with charioteers who break the rules; stomach goose meat inadvertently consumed from an unfairly compensated household; eat food intended as a funeral offering; or accept food when offered in a demeaning manner.[114]

In the latter instance, Mencius offers a rationale that underscores how powerful such pro-social instincts can be: "I desire life, and I also desire appropriateness (*yi* 義), but if I cannot satisfy both simultaneously, I will give up life and choose appropriateness."[115] Thus we have Confucian moral paragons like Bo Yi and Shu Qi who elect to starve to death rather than eat the rice of a violent and unjust government.[116] From the standpoint of ethical egoism, such behavior makes no sense. From an evolutionary standpoint, however, such "moral stands" are comprehensible. Refusing food on principle incurs immediate cost to an individual organism—perhaps even starvation. Such behavior "helps," however, by reinforcing regulatory impulses selected to sustain the advantages of reciprocal altruism at the species-level.

To imagine that "Heaven's plan" or "God" created us uniquely with such "moral" impulses makes humans feel special—but Nature (*tian* 天) does not bear this out. "Human morality," as Mary Midgley observes, "is not a brute anomaly in the world."[117] Even rats display inhibitions when confronted with the pain of others.[118] In the primate world, such pro-social instincts are well documented. Rhesus monkeys will refuse to pull a chain that delivers them food if it shocks a companion at the same time.[119] As Frans de Waal reports: "One monkey stopped pulling for five days, and another one for twelve days after witnessing shock delivery to a companion. These monkeys were literally starving themselves to avoid inflicting pain upon one another."[120]

The difference between monkeys and humans is a matter of degree. With larger brain capacities, humans are able to register how accepting food improperly offered or procured inflicts harm on others more indirectly—whether by disregarding fair play in hunting, perpetuating unjust social or economic conditions, or by impacting the health of the environment. In such cases, intelligent humans also hesitate before "pulling the chain." As for the monkeys, it is hard to know whether or not they experience "feelings of shame and dislike" (*xiuwuzhixin* 羞惡之心) when they pull the chain or watch others pull it. My uneducated guess is that monkeys *do* experience such feelings—dimly perhaps—toward themselves and toward others. What distinguishes humans (*ren* 人) is that such feelings are more structurally refined, more highly developed, and better communicated in the species.

This brings us to Mencius' third trait of human nature, *li* 禮. As outlined in *Focusing the Familiar*, this trait is defined as that which gives rise (*sheng* 生) to functions that pertain (1) to how devotion to kin and others is distributed, and (2) to how esteem for superior persons is ranked.[121] Strictly speaking, the core sensibilities involved here are not the *creations* of the ritual order. Rather, such "distribution" and "ranking" are sourced in the values of altruism and its regulatory adaptations, respectively. Mencius is right, then, to describe *li* as something that "sections and embellishes" (*jiewen* 節文) a more primitive stratum of other-regarding concern and appropriateness (*renyi* 仁義) that is already there.[122]

Rather than focusing on the more ceremonial aspects of ritual-custom, Mencius focuses on ritual propriety (*li* 禮) as a trait associated in different contexts with feelings of deference (*cirangzhixin* 辭讓之心) and feelings of reverence (*gongjingzhixin* 恭敬之心)[123]—two distinct species of admiration that one might have toward others. As Linda Zagzebski explains, admiration is an emotion directed at human excellences of all kinds, but one that divides naturally into admiration for "natural" vs. "acquired" excellences.[124] This would explain why Mencius associates *li* with two distinct forms of admiration: *deference* and *reverence*. Such emotions stabilize human communities veridically (within kin systems) and horizontally (in peer groupings) respectively, with moral exemplarism being the rule.

The treatment of *li* 禮 in the *Mencius* is more psychological in content than what one finds in the *Analects*, wherein more emphasis is placed on the formal (*wen* 文) aspects of ritual-custom. Mencius' treatment remains compatible, however, with that of the Master. As Erving Goffman suggests, expressions of deference and reverence are ritualized functions that permeate our everyday lives. Opportunities to affirm the ritual order in overtly "formal" or ceremonial ways are relatively rare. Simple everyday gestures of deference and reverence, however, while sometimes regarded as "empty" because they "last but a brief moment [and] involve no substantive outlay," serve to sustain the entire field in which ritual order operates. "The gestures which we sometimes call empty," Goffman writes, "are perhaps in fact the fullest things of all."¹²⁵ *Li* for Mencius is a feeling (*xin* 心) rather than a set of formalities, but such feelings need to be there when formalities begin.

Since sustaining such feelings (*cunxin* 存心) is Mencius' primary focus,¹²⁶ he is less interested in following the rules of ritual-custom (*li* 禮) to the letter. This comes through clearly in the text. According to ritual-custom, one is not supposed to touch the hand of one's sister-in-law—but if she is *drowning*, of course one pulls her out of the water. "Only an animal would not pull her out," Mencius says.¹²⁷ There is also the interesting question of whether or not ritual-custom (*li*) is more important than biological imperatives such as eating (*shi* 食) and sex (*se* 色). One of Mencius' students, Wuluzi, is asked about this and answers that observing ritual-custom is more important. "OK," the interlocutor says, "but what if by following ritual one dies of hunger or fails to secure a wife?" Wuluzi is unsure how to answer and consults Mencius. His answer is in keeping with Confucian situational ethics. Mencius suggests to him that things must be weighed (*quan* 權) properly. In some instances, biological imperative is the more important thing and ritual-custom is inconsequential. Sometimes it's the opposite. One would not forcibly grab food out of the hands of one's brother, for instance, nor take a sexual partner by force.¹²⁸ As Mencius sees it, one must adapt to particular circumstances in following ritual-custom by "weighing" the situation through reflective intelligence.¹²⁹

This brings us to the last of the "four sprouts," *zhi* 智. This term is normally translated as "wisdom," which is serviceable enough so long as its meaning is understood within the context of Chinese thinking and not as a Greek-medieval analogue. As discussed in chapter 5 of volume one, wisdom in early China can be thought of as the opposite of stupidity, the quality exhibited in the "Man from Song" stories. As such, wisdom involves intelligence in means-end deliberation (*ming* 明), aiming always to sustain continuity between the two. Accordingly, wisdom is distinguished from theoretical inflexibility in *Mencius* 5B.1. Here, three figures are compared with Confucius who differs from them in being more timely (*shi* 時). As Kwong-loi Shun explains, "Unlike these three, who adhered to fixed policies concerning when to serve in government, Confucius was a sage who was timely—he took or stayed in office, hastened or delayed his departure, all according to the circumstances."¹³⁰ Hastening or delaying activity *without* regard to circumstances tracks on to the two signature failures in Chinese instrumental reasoning: "Shoot pulling" and "Stump watching." As Mencius suggests, without timeliness (*shi*), wisdom is liable to result in mindless routine as well as forcing situations that call for active patience (*wuwei* 無為). He had a favorite saying about the latter error.

"One might be clever, but it is better to take advantage of the propensity of circumstances (*shi* 勢). One might have a garden hoe, but it is better to wait for the season (*shi* 時) to arrive."[131]

As Bryan W. Van Norden notes, "skill in means-end deliberation" is associated with wisdom in passages such as *Mencius* 1B.3.[132] We also saw how Mencius relates wisdom to "skill" in the archery metaphor, such that it involves having the proper "stance" to discern what is appropriate (*yi* 義) in specific situations.[133] As Kwong-loi Shun notes: "in archery, proper aim is not a matter of following rigid rules but requires an ability to adjust one's aim according to the circumstances, such as wind direction."[134] Such situational awareness and discernment accords naturally with the human trait of *sapientia* and it belongs to *Homo sapiens* by definition. Our species triumphed over others in our genus by adapting to our environments more intelligently and wisely. As such, *zhi* 智 is a feature of human nature.

Thus, Mencius provides us with scientifically viable insights into human nature. Over the course of evolutionary history, our species has indeed evolved four distinct capacities: empathy (*ren* 仁), appropriateness (*yi* 義), ritual propriety (*li* 禮), and wisdom (*zhi* 智). Donald J. Munro is correct to suggest that such features are consistent with human nature from an evolutionary perspective. The next step is to build upon this analysis to address one of the signature issues in Mencius' philosophy.

The Goodness (*shan* 善) of Human Nature

Dewey became familiar with the early Chinese debate over the goodness of human nature prior to visiting China. Jiang Menglin had written a dissertation under his supervision that featured an extensive discussion of the debate within the context of his topic, "The Principles of Education in China."[135] During his "Ethics" lectures in Beijing, Dewey evokes the Chinese debate and decides to weigh in. He reconstructs its positions as follows:

> Some Chinese philosophers take the stand that human nature is inherently good, and that humans become evil only through contamination by an evil environment. Others contend that human nature is inherently evil, and that it must be corrected and restrained by imposition of social codes. Still others maintain that human nature is neither good nor evil, but that it is neutral. They compare it with water, which can run to the east or to the west, depending on the topography. Those who support the inherent goodness of human nature disagree with those who hold

that it is inherently evil, because it becomes naturally good just as water can naturally run downhill. This is the logical argument in philosophy that bears directly on our consideration of morals. We must know whether, and to what extent we can trust human instinct. If instincts are good, how can we cultivate them; and if they are bad, how can we control them?[136]

The debate that Dewey refers to plays itself out initially in the pages of the *Mencius* and later in the pages of the *Xunzi*. It is generally agreed, however, that the terms of the debate change between these two texts.

As A. C. Graham observes, the treatment in the *Xunzi* "starts from a conception of human nature quite different from Mencius', and for a western reader much easier to grasp."[137] For Xunzi, the inclinations of one's nature (*xing* 性) is distinguished from artifice (*wei* 偽), which involves conscious exertion upon a raw material. Thus, "human nature" is likened to a "warped piece of wood that must be steamed and straightened out on a pressing frame."[138] Such a conception is easier for Western readers to understand, perhaps, because it is fundamentally dualistic. It lends itself easily to the "Nature/Nurture" distinction. As Philip J. Ivanhoe observes, such a "re-formation" model is reliant on metaphors of craftsmanship, whereas Mencius' "development" model is reliant on metaphors of botanical growth.[139] The latter approach is closer to Dewey's own and does not succumb as easily to the "Nature/Nurture" dualism. It is Mencius' more "developmental" approach that we will be interested in reconstructing here.

Debates over the goodness of human nature concentrate in a cluster of passages in the "Gaozi" chapter of the *Mencius*. Here, an interlocutor named "Gaozi" introduces a number of postulates regarding human nature and Mencius and his followers refute them one-by-one, resulting in something that reads like a debate manual.[140] The polemical context behind these arguments needs to be understood in order to appreciate what is actually happening. By his own admission, Mencius enters into debate (*bian* 辯) reluctantly, only to counter the teachings of those he reviles.[141] He intends to do so with expediency— "just to get the pigs back in the fold."[142] Mencius maintains that his primary adversaries, the Mohists and Yangists, are "animals."[143]

Here, I think, he tips his hand. When Mencius assigns a trait to "human nature" in direct correspondence with a Confucian virtue, it would be naïve not to read this as corollary to his belief that non-Confucians are less than "human." There is nothing dispassionate about Mencius' theory of human nature. It is initiated and devised solely to defeat his adversaries. All the while his intentions are clear: he means to defend the tradition of the Confucian sages. He does so in the face of spreading, viable alternatives to that tradition. It is important to recognize that, within the context of this debate, the claim that Confucian virtues belong to "human nature" is also a claim that Confucian virtues are qualitatively "human" (*ren* 人). Thus, saying that such a nature lends itself to goodness (*shan* 善) amounts to providing *normative* guidance in addition to any *factual* content that it might contain. In its native context, Mencius' "theory of human nature" amounts to a position on the goodness of the *Confucian tradition*. It is forwarded, as Irene Bloom says, "less as a theory than as an argument."[144]

Such an admission is neither scandalous nor fatal to the cause of Mencius. It is only a more direct way of expressing what we already know: that Mencius' theory of human nature is presented as support for those goods that he thinks are important. Such an admission does not require us to deny the existence of human nature, nor does it require us to drop the claim that Confucian-friendly impulses are innate to human nature and actually tend toward goodness (*shan* 善). All that needs to be refigured is the relationship between the Confucian tradition and the facts about human nature.

For Mencius, the two virtually overlap. He ascribes a colossal role, for instance, in the development of human nature to the historical Confucian sages, far exceeding anything supportable by evolutionary biology. According to Mencius' account, it was the legendary Xie (Minister of Education under Shun) who taught our pre-human ancestors the "five relationships" (*renlun* 人倫) that originally separated humans from animals.[145] This work is described in Promethean terms. In setting Xie to task in educating our predecessors, Shun told him to "Encourage them, lead them, reform them, and correct them. Assist them—give them wings. Enable them to realize themselves (*zide* 自得)."[146]

Defenders of the "Heaven's plan" reading will be quick to suggest that intelligent design was at work even here: that the sages were able to realize Confucian culture by being the first to realize their pre-programmed, "Heavenly-endowed" natures to perfection.[147] There is, however, a "chicken and egg" problem that hampers the logic of such a reading. If, as Philip J. Ivanhoe suggests, the sages were those whose "moral sprouts were able to mature"[148] and such maturity "requires a certain kind of environment,"[149] then which came first—the perfectly realized sage, or the environment necessary for that realization: an environment that the sages themselves were the first to establish? Such a "chicken and egg" problem is resolved by understanding the Xie story metaphorically in terms more consistent with evolutionary theory. As Dewey suggests: "The chicken precedes the egg. But this particular egg may be so treated as to modify the future type of chicken."[150] Let us understand the contributions of the sages to culture as representing the vast human experience from which our natures emerge—an experience that may not trace back to specific individuals, but that does trace back through *nothing but* individuals. This vast history is part of what *tian* 天 represents, for as Mencius says (echoing Confucius) the sages "modeled themselves after *tian*" (*zetian* 則天).[151] Sages are thus understood to have operated as co-equals with Nature (*tian*) in creating the conditions for human experience, contributing to the forces shaping human nature over time. Like barley, humans have a history. If we allow the legendary sages to represent major developments in that history—and it appears in Confucianism that they already *do*—then we arrive at a reading that is intellectually defensible.

As for the Chinese debate over the "goodness" of human nature, Dewey weighs in as follows. "There is a degree of truth in the view which holds that human nature is inherently good," he submits. For "if human nature were absolutely evil, it could not become good even under the influence of the most favorable environment." Thus, "there has to be a basis upon which human goodness can develop." He is sympathetic, however, with the other side. "Those who hold that human nature is inherently evil argue that if it were good, there would be no necessity for education," and the obvious need for education "substantiates their view."[152]

As Dewey sees the matter, "both viewpoints have flaws." The basic problem is that each considers certain instincts to *be* "good" or "not good" in abstraction from the context of development. "Instincts are the raw material of education," Dewey says: "they are neither good nor evil, but can *become* either, depending on the treatment we accord them." He continues:

> To be more specific, wherein lies the good or evil of instincts? The fact is merely that some instincts lend themselves more readily to training for goodness than do some others. For example, it is easier to produce goodness from love, sympathy, kindness, and selflessness, than it is from fear, anger, and so on. But they all have the same basic moral value; the difference lies in the use to which we put them. There is no single instinct which cannot be cultivated to produce goodness; and there is none that cannot be perverted to produce evil.

To demonstrate, Dewey discusses how "anger" can become righteous in the face of injustice, and how "kindness" can perpetuate sloth and pity when misplaced. His point is that moral growth is not about "good" or "bad" instincts *per se*, but rather about "giving positive direction to the instincts so that their operation produces desirable results."[153]

It is important to see how Dewey's treatment of the debate plays itself out in relation to the original Chinese arguments. He initially presents the controversy in terms consistent with the "reformation" model operative in the *Xunzi*. The initial question is whether or not human nature is "inherently" good or bad. Dewey finds such positions to be flawed. His resolution involves adopting a more "developmental" model akin to what one actually finds in the *Mencius*. Recognizing the importance of Dewey's own transition can help to ensure that our analysis of Mencius' position remains properly formulated. Mencius never says that human nature is "inherently good." The oft-quoted slogan, "Human nature is inherently (*ben* 本) good," comes not from the *Mencius* but from Zhu Xi's twelfth-century commentary.[154] This fact was unknown to Dewey, and it remains often overlooked by those only casually familiar with the *Mencius*. Once we "set aside the explanations of the Song Confucians," as Chen Lai suggests, we will begin to understand that Nature's mandate (*tianming* 天命) for Mencius does "not entail that human nature is good."[155]

But why even speculate? Mencius' position is plain in the text. In *Mencius* 6A.6, he is presented with three positions on the "goodness" of human nature:

1. Human nature is neither "good" (*shan* 善) nor "not good" (*bushan* 不善).

2. Human nature "can become good" (*keyiweishan* 可以為善) or "not good."

3. Some people have a "good" nature and others have a "not good" nature.

Given these options, Mencius is asked what *he* means by saying that "human nature is good" (*xingshan* 性善) and whether or not he thinks the other two positions are wrong. Mencius responds as follows: "In terms of our actual responses (*qing* 情), we can *become* good (*keyiweishan*). This is what I mean by saying 'good.' As for whether or not one becomes not good (*bushan*), this cannot be blamed on one's raw capacities (*cai* 才)."[156] Thus, Mencius affirms the second position but with the added provision that there really *are* natural, pro-social instincts to be worked with in human nature. Thus, like Dewey, Mencius stops short of saying that "human nature is *inherently* good" because the mere presence of such instincts alone does not determine that outcome.

Here, it is important to properly understand the "developmental" model. How such development occurs is where the question of teleology enters. In reconstructing Mencius' argument, Dewey (and others) are mistaken when they relate the idea that human nature is "inherently good" (which is *not* in the *Mencius*) to the image of water running downhill (which is). The analogy of water running downhill must be understood within Mencius' own "developmental" framework, in which the nature (*xing* 性) of human beings is not inherently good but rather "can become good."

At this juncture, it is critical to resist making Greek-medieval inferences and to understand this analogy squarely within the framework of Chinese natural philosophy. As Dan Robins argues, when ideas such as "It is the *xing* 性 of water to run downhill" are encountered, *xing* is not the subject of predication. Rather, it is the water and not its *xing* that runs downhill. Water behaves in that particular *way* when it is not disturbed, and *xing* is descriptive of such *ways* of behaving. As Robins explains: "It is a thing's *xing* to have some characteristic just in case the thing has that characteristic naturally, and it is a thing's *xing* to behave in some way only if it behaves that way spontaneously."[157] This is not teleology, because there is no superordinate "end" that is causally operative. Rather, there is simply water, a compound that has ways of behaving spontaneously. *How* it behaves (e.g., it might freeze, evaporate, boil, etc.) is a function of how supporting conditions shape (*xing* 形) its activities within existential configurations that have the propensity (*shi* 勢) to trigger such responses. These responses, in transaction with specific environments, emerge as the directional order (*de* 德) of the water in its course (*dao* 道) of development.

Since common sense inclines so strongly toward bifurcating "Means/Ends" in such instances, commentators accustomed to Greek-medieval readings of the *Mencius* will be slow to embrace Dan Robins' approach. Biases against such thinking have proven to be persistent.[158] Since *xing* 性 can be mentally abstracted from embedded activity it *will* be abstracted. The "end" that a given process happens to reach will then be relocated to the beginning and made part of a "nature" that is ontologically distinct from the "nurture" that draws it out. This is what Dewey calls "*the* philosophical fallacy." Chinese natural philosophy provides a way around this fallacy, and such thinking should be deferred to when reading the *Mencius*. Scholars who opt for the alternative route, treating *xing* in the *Mencius* as a "teleological trajectory" along Greek-medieval lines—as Aaron Stalnaker argues a sort of "moral destiny" that involves "a set of teleological natural tendencies"—do so only by neglecting to incorporate the principles of Chinese natural philosophy into their discussions.[159]

Studies that continue this practice now overlook a growing body of evidence against them. Over the past quarter century, newly recovered materials have shed considerable light on the meaning of *xing* 性 in the Warring States period. Franklin Perkins demonstrates that such evidence helps us to recognize that *xing* in early Confucian discourse "does not offer a teleology" because the term is not about "shifting something from potential to actual being but rather channeling an actually existing force into various directions."[160] Liang Tao, who also engages these newly recovered materials, reconstructs the relationship between *xing* and life/growth (*sheng* 生) and reaches a similar conclusion. "What the ancients described as *xing* is not an abstract essence or definition," he writes, "rather, it is direction, trend, activity, process. It is something dynamic and not static."[161] As fresh evidence continues to mount, work remains to be done on *xing* in early Chinese texts. Scholars breaking ground in this area should recognize the intra-cultural significance of their labors. Liberating *xing* from Greek-medieval inferences not only helps us to better understand texts like the *Mencius*, it also helps us to manage the "return wave" and get our own thinking "back in gear."

Some may continue to miss this opportunity. Bryan W. Van Norden, for instance, working squarely within the "virtue ethics" paradigm, maintains that early Chinese thinkers held that water has a "normal, healthy course of development" because they ascribed a *xing* to it.[162] As readers, we are here presented with a choice. Either ancient Chinese water is a completely alien substance—incommensurable with any water that we know—or Van Norden misunderstands *xing* in the *Mencius*. Surely it's the latter. In terms of fluid dynamics, water is isotropic. Dan Robins' theory covers it perfectly—and within the framework of Chinese natural philosophy it is plainly the superior account.

Naturally, Confucian virtue ethicists are free to continue testing Greek-medieval inferences in the *Mencius*. Each "quart bowl" in Chinese philosophy has something to offer. Larger segments of the field, however, are eager to move on. It may have taken us a few generations to realize it, but the water analogy is not about "teleological trajectories." The debate is about whether or not water has a spontaneous tendency to behave in certain ways under specific conditions. Mencius maintains that under the "right" conditions (i.e., positioned on an incline), water flows downwards. By the same token, under the "right" conditions (i.e., in a robust Confucian society), human nature has the tendency to become good (*shan* 善). If this does not happen, blame is not to be placed on our actual responses (*qing* 情) but on whatever conditions prevented our better inclinations from being realized.

Logically, *xing* 性 is not the subject of predication in this process—it is not a "thing" to be reified and ascribed essential (or fixed) attributes. Instead, it describes how something is presently disposed to behave spontaneously (*ziran* 自然)—nothing more, and nothing less. It manifests itself as a set of "rules" (*ze* 則) for how things behave, much the same way that the term *ze* is a grammatical connective indicating the conditional relation.

Such thinking is consistent with the Chinese logic of types (*lei* 類) as outlined in chapter 3 of the previous volume. Operationally speaking, types amount to *if-then* propositions that "are not about the individuals of the kind, but about a relation of characteristic traits which determine the kind."[163]

Types are determined according to a chosen standard (*fa* 法), each representing some characteristic "way" that a thing behaves in interaction with other things. As texts like the *Huainanzi* make clear, everything in the universe is implicated with everything else. "Acorns become oak trees" under conditions favorable to oak trees—that is the "way" (*dao* 道) of the acorn. This *way* of behavior can be stated in propositional form: *if* an acorn is provided with adequate soil, nourishment, light, water, and so on, *then* it becomes an oak tree. There are other propositions that are true of the acorn under different conditions, and those are also a function of its *xing* and *dao*. As Dewey says: "Concrete things have *ways* of acting, as many ways of acting as they have points of interaction with other things."[164] The directional order or potential (*de* 德) of the thing in *every* case, as Dewey suggests, implies a "progressively increasing diversification of a specific thing in a particular direction" and not a teleological force "immanent within a homogenous something and leading it to change."[165]

Having now better understood *xing* 性, there remains a missing link in Mencius' philosophy. By itself, *xing* is not a moral concept. Cholera germs also have a *xing*. If Mencius maintains the goodness of human nature (*renxing* 人性) there must be a broader normative framework in place. As it currently stands, one might charge that Mencius' reasoning is ultimately circular: he projects onto human nature qualities derived from his cultural tradition, and then he uses that "nature" (*xing*) to argue that the tradition itself is natural and good. Some independent, normative criterion is required to explain *why* certain Confucian-related promptings in our *xing* are important to develop. This problem will be taken up in chapter 7. As a preliminary step, however, the idea of "normality" needs to be considered.

Nature and Normality

Quoting the *Songs*, Mencius suggests that "*tian* 天 produces the teeming masses and where there is a thing there is a rule (*ze* 則). The firm-hold and steadiness of humankind lies in being fond of this admirable power (*de* 德)."[166] What does this mean? How do species-level regularities translate into how things behave normally or as a rule? Reflecting on who counts as "human" (*ren* 人) in the *Mencius*, Bryan W. Van Norden suggests that this category would include "humans who are within the broad bounds of normality for their species."[167] This is problematic on a few levels. In addition to being a controversial notion in modern biology, the idea that normality is "bounded" at the species-level rests on meta-theoretical assumptions that are not demonstrably operative in early China.

As Dale Goldhaber explains, there are two basic schools of thought on "norms" at the biological level. One is the "nativist" approach and the other the "systems" approach. The nativist approach presumes that we can cleanly partition the variance in biological processes once we "disentangle the many variables that might influence a particular behavior and examine the relative influence of each variable on the outcome behavior independently of the influence of all other variables."[168] In such an approach, genotype is treated as something independent that places limits on the "environment," which operates as a separable, additive causal influence determining the phenotype. Considered in isolation from its environment, the genotype is thus assigned a "reaction range" that is deemed "normal," similar to what Van Norden calls the "bounds of normality" for creatures like us.

The problem is that "normal reaction ranges" have no ontological standing apart from environmental conditions, so there is really no way to factor the environment *out*. Here, Dewey is vindicated. In contemporary genetics: "The concept that phenotype represents the consequences of genotype-environment interactions is universal and relates to all living organisms."[169] As we saw in chapter 2 of volume one, Chinese natural philosophy is based on a similar set of assumptions. Nevertheless, commentators regularly assume that Mencius *must* have held nativist assumptions. As a result, positions get attributed to him that are startlingly programmatic and sometimes ridiculous.[170]

With "norms" not residing strictly on the organism side, some turn to the environment side hoping that through analysis of the statistical composite of pressures that selected our traits we might lock down a "normal" set of conditions that resemble as closely as possible "*the* environment" to which we are adapted. Norms of reaction to such a "natural" environment might then be considered "normal" for creatures like us.

From an evolutionary standpoint, this is also unworkable. As David J. Buller reminds us, "to say that a trait is 'adapted to' or 'designed for' a particular environment is simply shorthand for saying that the trait was *selected over alternative traits* in that environment." Selection is just one factor in this process, combined with "mutation, recombination, genetic drift, and migration into and out of populations." While each nature (*xing* 性) reflects the Natural conditions (*tianming* 天命) that produced it, this does not mean that it is ideally suited for *one* particular environment and that such an environment is wholly recoverable. Remember—we humans find ourselves here night-blind, with male nipples, wisdom teeth, and an appendix. Just as we are not complete "naturals" for *this* environment, "there are no principled reasons deriving from evolutionary theory to designate certain environments in a norm of reaction as 'natural environments.'"[171] Note that vestigial structures linger as the insignias of change. In such cases, as Dewey says: "The conditions which originally called the power forth, which led to its 'selection,' under which it got its origin and formation, have ceased to exist, not indeed, wholly, but in such part that the power is now more or less irrelevant."[172]

Zhuangzi keeps us honest here. The "*De* 德 Satisfies the Tally" chapter pushes back against the idea that we should privilege any *single* human form (*xing* 形) as perfectly "normal." Likewise, when nature (*xing* 性) becomes a topic in the "Outer Chapters" of the *Zhuangzi* it is suggested that no *single* human environment should be privileged as perfectly "natural" for our kind either. Some humans in the *Zhuangzi* manage to thrive on icy mountains or in aquatic environments.[173]

The systems approach allows for such concessions. Its meta-theoretical assumptions resemble those developed in early Chinese thought with respect to resonance (*ganying* 感應). According to the systems approach, rather than regard the phenotype as the effect of separable, fixed causal influences, the world is such that "all antecedents influence behavior in an interactive, synergistic, systemic manner," such that "the development of the individual is best considered as the emergent property of a constant interplay between the genome and the environment."[174] In such an approach, discussion of "normal reaction ranges," or what Van Norden calls the "bounds of normality," is replaced with discussion of "reaction norms" in *specific* environments. So, with respect to barley, reaction norms will amount to a graphed function showing that barley with genotype G_1 has height phenotype P_1 in environment E_1, height phenotype P_2 in environment E_2, and so on. As Buller observes: "Nothing in the norm of reaction would identify any particular height as 'natural' for [barley] of that genotype. There are simply different heights that [barley] of that genotype can have under a range of different environmental conditions."[175] As a graphed function, what is considered "normal" is the height that is statistically most frequent.

The rules (*ze* 則) that govern organic development will produce different norms over time, and these will fluctuate along with environmental variables. As we already know: "Orange trees planted south of the Huai River produce mandarin oranges (*ju* 橘), while those planted north of the river produce bitter-fruited oranges (*zhi* 枳)."[176] Each fruit is considered "normal" relative to the environment in which it grows. Even here, however, such norms are "vague" in the Peircean sense. As David Sloan Wilson points out: "Uniformity at the coarsest scale does not imply uniformity at the finer scales."[177] Peirce's "logic of infinitesimals" remains always in effect—it is the tireless gatekeeper that escorts each unit of possibility (*deyi* 得一) through the womb of the Great Continuum (*taiyi* 太一). As we read in *Focusing the Familiar*, the *dao* 道 of Nature-and-Earth can be summed up in one phase: "Since events are never duplicated, their production is unfathomable."[178] Given this inescapable logic, types (*lei* 類) generated from *xing* 性 as well as their "norms" are going to be statistical all the way down.

Thus, Daoist philosophers *should* check any attempt to equate the "normal" with the "normative" when it comes to natures (*xing* 性). Such socially constructed "norms" need to be critically assessed. Zhuangzi is keen on making this point. As he is asked, "Can there be a 'human' who lacks the actual responses (*qing* 情) of a human?" Zhuangzi responds in the affirmative: "Yes. *Dao* 道 gives him that appearance, and Nature (*tian* 天) gives him that form." Then he is asked: "How could a 'human' *not* have the actual responses (*qing* 情) of a human?" Zhuangzi replies: "You misunderstand what I mean by actual responses (*qing*). What I mean when I say that he lacks them is that he does not use his own better/worse preferences to harm his body (*shen* 身). He takes spontaneity (*ziran* 自然) to be normal (*chang* 常) and does not try to *add* anything to the growth process (*sheng* 生)."[179]

This is a cleverly executed exchange.[180] It reveals perfectly how the moment one starts talking about actual responses (*qing* 情) at the human-level one is already thinking in normative terms. Based on *our* preferences, we have in mind what a "normal" human is supposed to be. Zhuangzi shifts attention away from such norms to the integrity of the growth process itself, which has its own rules. Consider again the orange tree. Given its nature (*xing* 性), it spontaneously (*ziran* 自然) gives rise to different fruits in specific environments—bitter-fruit in the north, mandarins in the south. This is normal (*chang* 常) for the tree. Imagine, however, if one of those trees developed a preference for mandarin fruitage. Now, imagine that unlucky specimen gets stuck in the north. Life is miserable for the tree—wanting always to *be* somewhere else *doing* something else. Perhaps it feels "abnormal" because it is not in the south (S). "If only I were in the south," thinks the tree, "then I would be normal (N)." Humans can relate to such mental longings. But consider the reasoning involved: the tree is deducing S > N from ~S > ~N. This is a spectacular logical error. Sadly for us, the ability to perpetuate and institutionalize such errors belongs to humans and not to orange trees.

Nature (*tian* 天) produces things with their own rules (*ze* 則). That is true. The "firm-hold and steadiness" of the human species has been achieved by working within such "rules" to secure and develop tendencies advantageous to its own flourishing. But what makes this good (*shan* 善)? The answer is not going to be found in any "teleological trajectory" associated with *xing* 性. If we wish to save Mencius from circularity in his prescriptive outlook, do justice to recently discovered textual evidence, and also make Mencius relevant in the twenty-first century, we need a normative measure consistent with evolutionary thinking within a systems framework—not an outmoded essentialism housed within a Greek-medieval framework.

This puts a finer point on the challenge posed by Donald J. Munro to the "Heaven's plan" reading of the *Mencius*. In the face of such a challenge, Philip J. Ivanhoe remains concerned. He cautions:

> [We] should be clear that evolutionary theory does not prescribe anything; it only describes the mechanisms of natural selection. We may judge that evolution has led us to become ethically better creatures than we used to be. However, we must not forget that evolution may lead us to become creatures that by our present lights we would judge to be abominations. The point is that any judgment about whether as a species we have improved or will get worse must come from a standard that is independent of the course of evolution itself. This issue needs to be sorted out more clearly by anyone who seeks to support [Mencius'] views with those of evolutionary biology.[181]

I agree. The issue does need to be sorted out more clearly. To that end, two things need to happen. First, we must understand that dismissing the "Heaven's plan" reading does not mean embracing "scientific materialism" or "secular humanism," as Ivanhoe fears. It means abolishing the "Sacred/Secular" dualism altogether. Second, we must be willing as philosophers to embrace any ethical and religious naturalism that classical Confucianism has to offer, even if this means retiring Greek-medieval readings that are more vested and less demanding.

As Irene Bloom suggests, "Nature" rather than "Heaven" carries most of the ethical and spiritual load in the *Mencius*—and as Munro suggests, this should be the focus of contemporary readings. Dewey urges us forward, promising us that values become more real when they are "buoyed up by the forces which have developed nature."[182] Today, it is a profoundly retrograde mindset that resists such inquiries in favor of supernatural explanations. Like "postmodern relativism," such an approach disregards standard conventions of truth and reason and drives a wedge between the Humanities and the natural sciences. While it may be technically permissible to say, as Ivanhoe does, that "on the level of genes or even cells, there are no ethical or aesthetic values, no human nature or culture, no humanity,"[183] this cannot be taken to mean that there are absolute chasms separating "Fact/Value," "Body/Mind," "Science/Religion," and so on as Irving Babbitt and other cultural conservatives contend. Despite his interest in "Oneness," Ivanhoe can be strikingly dualistic in his own philosophical reasonings.[184] Such dualistic thinking inflicts needless lacerations upon culture and only serves to fortify minds that can embrace propositions like, "God created the Earth in six days," and "Heaven has a plan for human beings" but not propositions like, "Anthropogenic activity is disrupting the planet's ecology" and "Humans and apes share a common ancestry."

Modern cultural conservatism, which perpetuates this condition, is based on a wholly unwarranted fear: that somehow natural science by its very nature eats into the face of morality and religion. Getting our thinking "back in gear," however, does not mean reducing one side of our cultural dualisms to the other. Ethics is not going to be converted into *genes*, and religion will not to be reduced to *cells*. Getting ourselves "back in gear" means restoring continuity (*yi* 一) between levels of experience that Nature (*tian* 天) wholly embraces, thereby grounding our ethical and religious values more deeply and securely than they currently are. Irene Bloom thought that Mencius could help us to do this, and I think she was right.

Chapter 7 will address our standing problem. What independent, normative criterion explains *why* certain Confucian-related promptings in our *xing* 性 are important to develop? The Chinese answer, as we will see, lies in the dynamic between harmony (*he* 和) and growth (*sheng* 生). In coming to understand this dynamic, the best strategy is to begin with an examination of the family and its ritual-customs (*li* 禮). Understanding family (*jia* 家) will always be the main entryway into Confucian thinking.

7

Harmony and Growth

> When a newborn infant first drinks milk he is already receiving a sort of education from his mother. From the very moment that a child is born there is not a day without some interplay between natural instincts and the social environment.
>
> —John Dewey, National Peking Academy of Fine Arts, May 1921

Families and Human Nature

The family (*jia* 家) is the primary social environment in which humans take shape. Families bring us into the world. It is curious that all philosophies of human nature do not start with this fact. "We are all born into families," Dewey writes, and from there human experience begins—shaped through association with role-bearing others. "The family," Dewey reminds us, "is something other than one person, plus another, plus another. It is an enduring form of association in which the members of the group stand from the beginning in relations to one another, and in which each member gets direction for his conduct by thinking of the whole group and his place in it."[1] Human life remains social for its entire duration. "Think of any human adult in a concrete way, and at once you must place him in some 'social' context and functional relationship," Dewey writes. It thus becomes "glaringly evident that 'social' stands for properties which are intrinsic to every human being."[2]

As Frans de Waal reminds us, this is not a feature that is unique to *Homo sapiens*. "There never was a point at which we *became* social," he writes. "Descended from highly social ancestors—a long line of monkeys and apes—we have been group living forever."[3] Indeed, it is difficult to imagine *any* mammalian species surviving long without the emergence of pro-social instincts, especially those selected for nurturing and protecting its own offspring. In humans, such mechanisms co-evolved with a complex set of hormones and neurotransmitters resulting in tightly calibrated bonding instincts and emotional ties that unite parents and children for life.

In beholding the *dao* 道 of mother-and-child, one can forgive the philosopher for imagining that some divine choreography must be behind its miracles. William Paley, in his 1802 classic *Natural Theology*, marvels at the means-end coordination exhibited in placental mammals. This can only be "prospective contrivance," he says. First, neither "cookery nor chemistry" can produce the colostrum that provides nutrition, antibodies, cytokines, and the mild laxative perfectly suited to each nursing infant. Such is the very manifestation of intelligent design! Next, there is the mother's care: "inexplicable upon any other hypothesis than that of instinct," but one by which "an animal, formed for liberty, submits to confinement, in the very season when everything invites her abroad."[4]

How could this *not* be evidence of God's grand design for us and for the world? For William Paley, these were sincere reflections. Hardly stern in manner, Paley was a good and cheerful soul who genuinely marveled at the wonders of nature. It is errant analysis, however, that divides the indivisible. Colostrum-and-infant is not something that is "aligned," nor is mother-and-child "contrived" by any outside agency. Ontologically speaking, these are not *two things*. They are *one thing*—expressions of *dao* 道-activity wherein means-and-ends are perfectly coterminous (*yi* 一). To mentally isolate one element and present it as occurring for the sake (*wei* 為) of another amounts to needless reduplication. As Dewey says: "Operations of splitting up [such phenomena] into two parts and then having to unite them again by appeal to causative power are equally arbitrary and gratuitous."[5]

In addition to misunderstanding the maternal process ontologically, human cognition (specifically of the male variety) has a tendency to underrepresent its primacy in other ways. As Joanne D. Birdwhistell argues, Mencius' theory of human nature is "derived in a fundamental, but unacknowledged, way from maternal experience," consistent with how the early Confucians "appropriated the logic, along with certain views and assumptions, of maternal thinking but did not identify them as such."[6] Indeed, the fact that the legendary educator Xie specifically needed to teach (*jiao* 教) our pre-human ancestors about affection between fathers and sons (*fuziyouqin* 父子有親) raises questions about the status of the paternal instinct.[7]

Consider how such instruction registers within the Mencian framework. Human relations (*renlun* 人倫) amount to ritual-customs (*li* 禮) fashioned to section and embellish (*jiewen* 節文) a more primitive substratum of unlearned instinct.[8] But where do such unlearned habits originate? Biologically, maternal instincts are more primitive than paternal instincts—the latter having undergone sexual and other selection over the course of human evolution just as domesticated barley was chosen for the firmness of its rachis. In early China, it was understood that in primitive times children "knew their mothers but not their fathers."[9] This does not mean that contemporary paternal instincts are *un*natural. It only means that they are more recently organized in the species. One still observes this organization at work. Among animals that engage in biparental care of offspring—certain varieties of gerbils, hamsters, and mice, for instance—there is a marked drop in postpartum testosterone levels in males. Human males currently display the same tendency, but its "causes" cannot be traced.[10]

Given how our species has evolved, Confucianism is left with a cultural problem: Even though the mothering instinct is one that never had to be "taught" (*jiao* 教), the family-oriented social order that emerges in the tradition systematically prioritizes male experience as the default human norm. As Birdwhistell observes: "By claiming that men have these and other inborn feelings too, Mencius argues for a cosmic grounding of the patriarchal social virtues that can be developed from these feelings."[11] Regarded as emblematic of the human experience, it is fine to suggest that the legendary sages contributed to the evolution of "human nature" as such. But any suggestion that human civilization is primarily a "male" undertaking would completely distort the ontology of family and human development.

Let's back up and approach the topic of male domesticity from another angle. The cultural foundation of family remains *marriage*, and its status proves instructive. Confucius' views on marriage are difficult to reconstruct with certainty. His own marriage was monogamous, as was customary for commoners in his day. His family background, however, was complicated. Confucius was born in a "wild union" (*yehe* 野合) between an older man and a much younger woman. Confucius never knew his father, who had died by the time he was three years old. His mother soon deserted the paternal clan and raised Confucius with her own relatives. Confucius' mother died young, so when he married at the age of nineteen he had no parents.[12] One can only speculate how such circumstances impacted his later positions on the centrality of family in human development.

Insofar as his loyalties were with the Duke of Zhou, the famous Regent and cultural hero of the Zhou dynasty, Confucius would likely have shown a preference for monogamy but a tolerance for polygamy. Wu Kuo-chen surmises that the curious inclusion of statistics in the *Rituals* detailing the ratio of men to women in the nine regions of the Zhou empire was a strategic move by the Duke to provide cover to an elite class that was not prepared to give up polygamy. The sociopolitical pressure would have been great on the Duke of Zhou, who "might have begun with the idea of taking a more positive stand on monogamy, but upon discovering the disproportionate ratio between men and women, decided to let the matter remain as it had always been, leaving the statistics in the book as a sort of self-justification."[13] Meanwhile, for the common majority, ritual-customs (*li* 禮) were established to facilitate monogamous nuptials between separate bloodlines. As the *Rituals* explains, "The ritual-custom of marriage is intended to bring together (*he* 合) what is best for two surnames."[14] In this context, what is "best" (*hao* 好) is plainly for the women (*nü* 女) to have children (*zi* 子). To that end, the *Etiquette and Ritual* (*Yili* 儀禮) prescribes that males should marry by the age of thirty and females by the age of twenty. Matchmakers were employed to organize regional get-togethers each spring for men and women who had reached those ages but were not yet married.[15]

While the contracting surnames played a central role in the process, the core of each union was ideally a love relationship between principals. The voice of Confucius surfaces in the *Questions of Duke Ai* (*Aigongwen* 哀公問) chapter in the *Rituals* to advocate that love (*ai* 愛) and respect (*jing* 敬) become the foundation of marriage. As the Master says: "Without love, there can be no intimacy (*qin* 親); without respect, there can be no rectitude (*zheng* 正)."[16] In order to sustain the primacy of love and respect, marriages should be inexpensive and not attended by large transfers of wealth. The groom's side was expected to make only token offerings to the bride's family—plus "six wild geese (*yan* 雁) at most." As Wu Kuo-chen observes, "at that time the plains of China abounded with the species; one could acquire any number of them merely for the trouble it took to capture them."[17]

Of course, there is more behind the geese. Very few mammalian species display monogamous behavior (3 to 5 percent) whereas 90 percent of avian species do. Among the latter, geese are noteworthy for their devotion. As studies of the North Atlantic barnacle goose (*Branta leucopsis*) observe: "pair-bond members generally remain together every day, each year, often for life." Such pair bonding appears to be selected in geese due to their constant need for male-female cooperation. "Male assistance is apparently essential for females to acquire enough fat and nutrient reserves to enable breeding attempts," research suggests. Males provide females cover mostly by fending off threats, but barnacle geese pair-bonds work closely together in every phase of the life process protecting their eggs and broods.[18] The role of wild geese as tributes in early Chinese marriage customs is symbolic of such monogamous devotion.

The gesture is significant, because it is difficult to determine whether or not human males are "naturally" monogamous. Among primate species, only about 25 percent display such behavior at all. The anthropological record shows that a mixture of polygyny and monogamy prevails in over 80 percent of cases, whereas monogamy alone prevails in only 17 percent of cases.[19] As

Bernard Chapais suggests, it is difficult to know when and why monogamy developed in human groups without access to data on the social structure of early hominids, but such data is "intrinsically limited by the fact that social patterns leave few traces in the fossil record and the resulting reconstructions are fragmentary."[20] It is generally accepted that chimpanzee-like promiscuity and one-male polygyny preceded monogamy in our hominid ancestors. Monogamy arose later due to costs incurred in evolving organism-environment circuits. New pressures resulted in increased sexual competition, greater difficulty in male provisioning, strains on social cooperation, and the like. One theory calls to mind the "Eat, Drink, Man, Women" (*yinshinannü* 飲食男女) picture of human nature that is observed in the *Rituals*.[21] Richard Wrangham argues that cooking with fire finally led to pair-bonding in humans. Less of the daily diet was consumed on the spot. Thus, finding it more efficient to pool our resources and cook together on a single hearth, the conditions for monogamy were born.[22]

Biological factors also contributed. The evolution of concealed ovulation meant more nonreproductive sex, which lent itself to extended male-female relationships.[23] Meanwhile, generation after generation of sexual selection weighted the gene pool in favor of parentally invested fathers, and cultural evolution further solidified its survival functions. The marriage-based family is now firmly established as the human norm and its advantages are manifest. As Shelley Taylor documents, the health of modern males especially has a tendency to decline precipitously in the absence of pair-bond units typical of marriage.[24] Nature-culture circuits, however, are complicated. Whatever the factors are that led to pair-bonding in *Homo sapiens*, Chapais believes that, "polygyny was thwarted, but the motivation for polygyny was not necessarily selected against." The result, in that case, would be what human history in fact displays: "a preponderance of monogamous unions with a minority of polygynous unions when conditions allowed."[25] This is what one finds in early China, and the Duke of Zhou let the condition stand.

Accordingly perhaps, Confucius' own teachings on marriage are not very specific. Wu Kuo-chen regards this, however, as a philosophical virtue. Remember that in adapting the rituals of the Xia, the Yin altered them; and in adapting the rituals of the Yin, the Zhou altered them. It was presumed that such alteration would continue into the future.[26] Citing this tenet from the *Analects*, Wu concludes that Confucius' general position on ritual-custom (*li* 禮) was that "no social system is perfect; each is devised only to suit its time; and its shortcomings will be discovered as time rolls on, and sooner or later a new system has to be established to take its place, benefitting from the old, but lasting only as long as it is suitable."[27] However precise the Master sometimes was in prescribing specific practices (as we too might be precise), there is nothing in his broader philosophy suggesting that such norms could never change.

Progressive cultural change registers as a threat to the conservative mind. Such change, as we have seen, is projected uncharitably as "the open-ended search for the best form of culture" and the "on-going quest for what is good for creatures like us."[28] Among social conservatives and religious fundamentalists in the United States, such concerns are widespread. When they become consolidated into fears, the resulting social damage is incalculable. Believing that a single ritual-custom (*li* 禮) of marriage is divinely sanctioned, same-sex marriage is opposed. Believing that human nature is set in place through supernatural agency, the theory of evolution is rejected. Believing that one's own culture is perfectly formed and rightly superior, other traditions are denigrated. Believing that scientific inquiries and moral truths are incompatible, scientific facts are denied.

While working in China, Dewey formulated a social philosophy that could challenge the conservative mindset without playing into it. The latter is easy to do. Conservatives imagine themselves to be protecting us from "relativists." Those who oppose the conservative will note that he or she is an "absolutist." The resulting stalemate favors the conservative, for the contest remains framed within the "Absolute/Relative" dualism that the conservative mindset requires. The key, then, is to challenge the notion that "relativists" as defined by the conservative actually exist. One must ask—what *is* a "relativist?" Mencius claims that it is improper to touch one's sister-in-law's hand, but if she is drowning one makes an exception. Does this make Mencius a "relativist?" To weigh up (*quan* 權) the situation while adjudicating right and wrong in a complex world—is that "relativism?" To surmise that changing conditions make better or worse outcomes really possible—is that "relativism?" Presumably, the "relativist" is someone who believes that "anything goes" and that one outcome is just as good as any other. But really, *who* believes this? Such a position belongs to the idiotic. Those who are *called* "relativists" are those who accept the fact that change happens, that situations matter, and that human intelligence cannot be abdicated. Such a pragmatic approach is broadly consistent with a style of thinking well understood in early China— one in which "virtue has no constant model, but is oriented toward what is good (*shan* 善); and what is good has no constant orientation, but accords with what is adequate in a single instance (*xieyukeyi* 協於克一)."[29]

As Sing-nan Fen suggests, to "realize that our value activities as well as our value standards are relational to our other cultural conditions" prepares us to engage with others in the world intelligently (*ming* 明). "This does not imply that we cannot decide which [activity] is better and which is worse," he explains. To the contrary—understanding how value operates in specific contexts is the prerequisite for making intelligent choices. For "until and unless we have these conditions, circumstances, and causes under control, good is abstract and bad is uncontrollable." The so-called problem of "relativism" hinges on how value factors into the relationship between elements that are contingent in human experience and elements that are not. As we saw in our study of "common sense" in chapter 1, however, it is difficult to parse such elements in human behavior and get a clean look at our shared proclivities. As Fen explains: "We cannot establish the much desired or desirable value standard on the basis of these common human nature and/or needs, not because they do not exist, but because values are not concerned with the bare satisfaction of these needs. Rather are they concerned with the cultural ways or cultured ways through which these needs may be satisfied."[30]

Philip J. Ivanhoe's most cogent contribution, in my estimation, relates to what he calls "ethical promiscuity," a position based on the facts of ethical pluralism and that "no single human life or culture can realize all of the values that are possible for creatures like us." Such a view underwrites the values of pluralism and toleration. Ivanhoe recognizes that "ethical promiscuity" requires us to articulate human nature such that its "needs, desires, and capacities" can provide a foundation for judgment in such a framework. He finds that generating such a foundation, however, presents a "complex challenge" and he declines to take it up.[31]

Dewey, for his part, identifies a number of features of human nature that require satisfaction: "interests to be served" and "impulses that have to be expressed." Such features, he notes, result in "fairly universal modes of union and association." Clearly, family and marriage are among such universals, but it is difficult to get a proper inventory of the common needs they satisfy. The evolution of monogamy in humans, as we have seen, is not well understood. Some features of human pair-bonding are likely shared with other animals, while others are surely adaptations to uniquely human conditions. Lacking material evidence, there is no way to know for certain how family units evolved over the past 150,000 years, what selection pressures they answered to, and which of those pressures remain. However such features came to evolve, modern humans are nevertheless family-born creatures by Natural mandate (*tianming* 天命) and generally disposed to take pleasure in such experience. That much we know.

The *value* question concerns how the relative success of the resulting institutions stands to be measured. "Heaven's plan" offers us nothing here. Dewey's ideal, which he establishes in his "Social and Political Philosophy" lectures in Beijing, more closely resembles the Chinese notion of harmony (*he* 和) with respect to the satisfaction of human needs—that is, to "frame in imagination a picture in which there is an equal proportionate development of all these forms of associated life, where they interact freely with one another . . . where in short there is mutual stimulation and support and free passage of significant results from one to another."[32] The best social arrangement is one that optimally *satisfies* and *integrates* a variety of human needs in a particular cultural situation. Within such arrangements, ritual-customs (*li* 禮) operate to *liberate*, *secure*, and *enhance* such values in the social matrix. It goes without saying that there are contingent factors at play—technological, cultural, economic, and so on. As these factors change, so too must our ritual-customs. This was the attitude that Dewey took toward family and marriage in China. His approach was "progressive" in that he believed that the Chinese were able to reflect intelligently on changing conditions in order to improve such institutions for the better. "The better is the good," he writes: "the best is not better than the good but is simply the discovered good."[33]

Our conservative instincts tend to associate the "best" with a pre-formulated state of absolute perfection (usually in the past). Thus, the conservative Confucian might speak of the sages as creating "the *perfect* plan for society," the "*perfect* model" for human development.[34] Such perfection, in addition to being empirically inaccessible, paves the way to despair. Pragmatically, "perfection" means that whatever one does that fails to match the "perfect" standard will always fall short. The "honest conclusion," as Dewey observes, "is pessimism."[35]

Like William James before him, Dewey chose the path of "meliorism" instead. As he explains: "Meliorism is the belief that the specific conditions which exist at one moment, be they comparatively bad or comparatively good, in any event may be bettered. It encourages intelligence to study the positive means of good and the obstructions to their realization, and to put forth endeavor for the improvement of conditions."[36] Such an approach equates the "better" with the "good" and actively pursues it. It avoids despair by making progress. In an imperfect world, there are always things that can be made demonstrably better. Thus, the "progressive" focuses on conditions here and now—knowing that the "better" can always be discovered "from study of the deficiencies, irregularities and possibilities of the actual situation."[37]

In order to understand how this approach relates to Confucian thought, we need to look deeper into how harmony (*he* 和) operates as a normative measure in the human experience. Harmony is not an anthropogenic value; it is a quality that permeates Nature (*tian* 天)—one that is agreeable to humans on a pre-reflective level. Understanding this enables us to make better sense of the normative dimension of Mencius' philosophy.

The Norm of Harmony (*he* 和)

It had a mouth and two eyes that were staring right back at him. Three million years ago, wandering around in search of food or sex, the *Australopithecus africanus* came across a red jasper stone that eerily resembled a human face. Known today as the "Makapansgat pebble," the *Australopithecus* carried it at least 20 miles from where it was found to a cave in South Africa. There, researchers found it in the 1920s amid the remnants of bone and fire. Paleolithic hominids had a penchant for collecting eye-catching shells, fossilized coral, and the odd-looking stone when it pleased them. In Maine we do the same thing. My kids and I walk along the beach and look down, collecting sea glass or interesting shells and pebbles. They all end up in a big jar in the living room.

Aesthetic appreciation is one of the most primitive human capacities, and it appears to predate *Homo sapiens* in the genus *Homo*. As Dewey sees it, the origin of aesthetic experience lies deep in our biological natures. Upon the "Potter's Wheel of Nature" the qualities of rhythm and symmetry pervade the organic process. "While man is other than bird or beast," Dewey observes, "he shares basic vital functions with them and has to make the same basal adjustments." Along with such adjustments come two core intuitions—"balance" and "rightness." For Dewey, "Art is thus prefigured in the very process of living."[38] Scholars like Mark Johnson and Richard Shusterman argue persuasively that somatic experience grounds our aesthetic sensibilities, and that such sensibilities inform our logical, moral, and spiritual sensibilities.[39] Indeed, this is one area in which contemporary philosophy is catching up with Dewey. "We need a Dewey for the twenty-first century," writes Johnson. "That is, *we need a philosophy that sees aesthetics as not just about art, beauty, and taste, but rather as about how human beings experience and make meaning. Aesthetics concerns all of the things that go into meaning—form, expression, communication, qualities, emotion, feeling, value, purpose, and more.*"[40] In short, we need a philosophy in which qualities like balance and rightness inform how we conceive of culture and its values.

Confucianism has a lot to offer here, so long as its normative dimension is properly understood. Recall our concern about the potential circularity in Mencius' thinking—i.e., that he identifies qualities of his cultural tradition with those in human nature and *vice versa*. While there may be some circular referencing in Mencius' account, he does not commit the fallacy of circular reasoning. Mencius does not use the qualities of human nature to account for the tradition from which they are deduced. If, however, one believes that a Heavenly-endowed "human nature" somehow precedes the advent of Confucian culture and accounts for its very emergence, then there is a "chicken and egg" problem. That need not concern us here, because Mencius never makes such a claim. What he claims instead is that, in inaugurating Confucian culture, the sages were the first to "apprehend in our feelings what is commonly so," and by this he means that they were the first to realize the norms of pattern (*li* 理) and rightness (*yi* 義). Together, Mencius says, these two qualities bring satisfaction to all humans.[41]

This strengthens Mencius' position considerably, because from a strictly evolutionary standpoint one could argue that the "four sprouts" (*siduan* 四端) do not have any particular normative force. Altruism/empathy, shame/blame, deference/reverence, and intelligence are *factual* conditions of human nature—they are survival adaptations on par with other biological processes. In order to measure how they become good (*shan* 善) one needs recourse to something that obtains independently of them.

Pattern (*li* 理) and rightness (*yi* 義) point the way. These qualities are generic enough to encompass multiple species of aesthetic value, including those expressed in cultures all over the world—Confucian, Mayan, American, Yoruban, and so on. For Mencius, such qualities are realized in Confucian culture as inaugurated by the sages. The evidence that such qualities appeal to us on a pre-reflective level can be drawn from our shared human nature, which Mencius evokes with reference to our common musical, culinary, and other aesthetic experiences. As he famously asks: "Palates are similar in their preferences, why not our feelings as well?"[42] Such analogies serve to underscore not only the generality of our common aesthetic sensibilities, but also their *vagueness*. Such analogies serve, in other words, as a corrective to overly programmatic readings of cultural-level phenomena. Thus, while it is true that all humans recognize delicious food, this does not mean that there is a single, "perfect cuisine" the recipes for which are written into "Heaven's Cookbook." That would be silly. What we get instead is a variety of delicious cuisines—Sichuan, Italian, Ethiopian, Japanese, and so on, each of which satisfy the generic features of the human palate with what is locally available and artfully developed—a sort of "culinary promiscuity," if you will. Human language emerges through a similar dynamic. Its use and related structures are common to *Homo sapiens*, but this does not mean that any one language is pre-figured or "innate." Each language is "shaped by broad historical events" that render it comparable to other languages while also being singular and unique.[43]

Human experience thus cooperates with Nature (*tian* 天) in generating particular cultural forms from a common nature. The Chinese sages, as Mencius recognizes, "modeled themselves after Nature" (*zetian* 則天) in doing so. Rather than realizing some pre-programmed "design" or "plan," which is nowhere suggested in the *Mencius*, the sages realized the qualities of pattern (*li* 理) and rightness (*yi* 義), resulting in a set of cultural technologies that are comparable to what we find in other cultures but also uniquely Confucian. This is consistent with the idea that the sages invented (*zuo* 作) Confucian culture by "lifting" or "causing to rise" (*qi* 起) patterns inherent in the world in a manner that retained the "continuity between Nature and the human" (*tianrenheyi* 天人合一).[44] The so-called Si-Meng 思孟 lineage of Confucianism, which traces from the *Mencius* through *Focusing the Familiar* regards human experience accordingly—as *co*-creative alongside Nature. Sages are those who get the most out of their nature as human beings (*jinrenzhixing* 盡人之性), thus forming a "triad" (*san* 參) with terrestrial and cosmic forces. They become the "compliments of Nature" (*peitian* 配天) in the process.[45]

In the field of Chinese philosophy, the extent to which this reading is embraced corresponds to the degree to which its normative measure is understood. As Chenyang Li argues, much contemporary scholarship distorts or simply overlooks the concept of harmony (*he* 和). In the "Confucian virtue ethics" genre, for instance, entire books are written that do not mention the term even once. Often in such cases, the notion is already reduced to something not worth mentioning. As Li says, it is regarded as "presupposing a fixed grand scheme of things that pre-exists in the world to which humanity has to conform."[46] The entire message of early Confucianism is thus obscured—reduced to the decree to "obey Heaven."

Harmony (*he* 和), however, is indispensable to any adequate understanding of early Confucian thinking. It is the unspoken *meta*-norm that informs Mencius' claim that pattern (*li* 理) and rightness (*yi* 義) bring pleasure to all humans. As illustrated in the soup analogy, harmony entails the achievement of an optimally unified, optimally varied order that most fully expresses the worth of its constituents. The harmony of a soup is measured by the degree to which it succeeds in incorporating its raw materials (*zhi* 質) in an aesthetically pleasing way. This entails both the achievement of an order (*li*) as well as the satisfaction of meaningful inclusion *within* that order—that is, the feeling of "significance" or "rightness" (*yi*).

Here, the term *yi* 義 is suggestive. In this context, it means more than moral appropriateness. As Bernhard Karlgren notes, the term is cognate with *yi* 宜, "fitting," and it also denotes "sense" and "signification."[47] In pairing such rightness (*yi* 義) with pattern (*li* 理), Mencius displays his understanding that neither rightness nor significance can be achieved in a vacuum. Without the function of form (*wen* 文) meaning will never emerge, and thus the *value* of an experience will never register. As Dewey says: "Form is a character of every experience that is *an* experience."[48] Arguably, such a sensibility underwrites Confucius' entire philosophy of culture and education.

Harmony (*he* 和) is also what accounts for the centrality of family in the Confucian tradition. The *Songs* relates how closely the two are related:

> Dishes may be abundant. And wine consumed to the limit.
> But when brothers are in attendance.
> This is harmony (*he*), joy, and happiness.
>
> Happy union of wife and children: it is the melody of lutes.
> But when brothers are joined.
> The harmony and joy (*le* 樂) are profound.
>
> It is fitting (*yi* 宜) to have a home and a family.
> It is a joy to have a wife and children.
> As soon as one considers it, it is just as soon the case.[49]

Knowing that family experience is a contingent product of human evolution, one cannot defend its "goodness" simply by saying that it is "human nature" to take pleasure in such experience. Even though this is *true*, it would be a form of circular reasoning. Remember, this is the challenge that Philip J. Ivanhoe poses to those like Donald J. Munro who hope to link Mencius' philosophy to evolutionary biology—i.e., the challenge to produce a "standard that is independent of the course of evolution" through which practices can be normatively assessed.[50] Ivanhoe answers this challenge by grounding the *telos* of human nature in "Heaven's plan," thus alleviating the need for Mencius to address the question philosophically. If Mencius is going to be relevant in the twenty-first century, however, we need to give him a better reading than that.

Having worked steadily at the intersection of classical American and Chinese philosophies for decades, Robert C. Neville generates a theory of harmony that fits the bill. It articulates "four transcendental features" that account for its normative force: "form or pattern," "multiplicity of components," "existential relations," and "value achieved."[51] One need only recall the soup analogy to get at Neville's reasoning. "A harmony is an *achievement* of having things together which would be separate without the harmony, or which would be together in a different way with another harmony," he writes. "This achievement is a value. If the harmony is achieved without loss of the achievements of otherwise separate components, it is a net gain."[52] In a harmonious soup, value registers in the fact that the onion is *better* in the soup and the soup is *better* with the onion. As Chenyang Li documents, the term harmony (*he* 和) has always been associated with the mixing together of different things—all the way back to the Bronze Scripts,[53] and there is never any question that harmony is a good. In Chinese philosophy, bringing things together productively (*shan* 善) is better than not doing so.

This is not hard to fathom. For Neville as for Mencius, we are talking here about a core intuition. "Is it not part of our common aesthetic sense that a harmony is *good*, all else being equal?" asks Neville. "Furthermore, do we not say that an arrangement of things is better if it is more harmonious? The greater the harmony, the greater the value."[54] Neville recognizes in Dewey a similar normative sensibility, which he associates with the Chinese notions of focus (*zhong* 中) and pattern/coherence (*li* 理). "For Dewey," Neville writes, "the unity in the self is an achievement, not a guaranteed starting point. Every living person has a kind of biological harmony, and people work to achieve a unity of consciousness, of emotions, of areas of attention to various parts of life, [and] finally of a spirit that somehow comprehends and unifies itself with the quality unifying the universe."[55] In this respect, it is hard to think of a philosopher more congenial to Si-Meng Confucianism than Dewey.

As Neville recognizes, in certain Western traditions, "there is a great temptation to let norms slip into relativism." This is because norms have been grounded in supernatural agencies that have become philosophically untenable. Such is the risk of "Heaven's plan." Thinkers like Dewey, however, "who do develop an objectivist ground for norms do so by means of aesthetic motifs more closely allied to East Asia than by means of decree models."[56] Neville here provides us with additional assurance that abandoning the "Heaven's plan" reading brings us *closer* to East Asian thinking, and that doing so is not going to result in "relativism."

Again, understanding *he* 和 is the key. As Neville says: "There are two principal factors in the structure of a harmony—complexity and simplicity. *Complexity* is the diversity of kinds of things included within the harmony; it is subject to degrees, and the minimal degree is homogeneity."[57] Thus, as Confucius says, the exemplary person chooses harmony over homogeneity (*heerbutong* 和而不同).[58] Such a preference values the continuance of creative growth over inertia and stagnation. *Simplicity*, Neville explains, is "the character of organization within the harmony whereby the togetherness of components constitutes a new reality within which the components are harmonized."[59] The Spring and Autumn period historian Shi Bo 史伯 helps to confirm that Neville's understanding of harmony is consistent with early Chinese thinking. As Shi Bo writes: "Harmony (*he*) actually grows (*sheng* 生) things, whereas sameness (*tong* 同) causes them to discontinue. To bring different things into equilibrium (*ping* 平) is what harmony means. This enables things to extend lushly (*fengchang* 豐長) and returns them (*guizhi* 歸之) [to growth]."[60]

Presented with such an image of "flourishing," it is tempting to evoke *eudaimonia* and to revert to the standard, Greek-medieval inferences about organic form. As we have seen, however, Chinese natural philosophy operates under a different set of assumptions. Only when approached from a Chinese philosophical perspective does Shi Bo's account of growth lend insight into how botanical thinking in early China informs Mencius' understanding of human development. In Mencius' understanding (as we will see) it is not with Aristotle but with Dewey that the connections really crackle.

The Meaning of Growth

As Sarah Allan observes, the *Mencius* is a text that is "grounded in the root metaphor of water and the plant life that it nourishes."[61] Confucian virtue ethicists likewise note the centrality of botanical metaphors in the text. As Bryan W. Van Norden observes, the *Mencius* "often uses plant metaphors to explicate human flourishing and cultivation."[62] Rather than being literary embellishments, Philip J. Ivanhoe notes that such metaphors foreground certain "subtle and distinctive" features of its philosophy.[63] The problem is that "Confucian virtue ethics" too often ends up being devoid of many of those features. The inference drawn from the text's botanical metaphors is that Mencius' account of human development implies a pre-determined schema: what Ivanhoe calls "a teleological view about the flourishing of human nature expressed in an ideal or paradigmatic model of what it is to be human."[64] Such inferences need to be defended, and the only way to defend them is to analyze how botanical life was most often understood in classical Chinese philosophical texts. Mencius is not, after all, using *Greek* metaphors. Allan's work on water and plant imagery in early China is the kind of research needed to back up the claim that Mencius' chosen metaphor implies a teleological worldview akin to what one finds in Aristotle and Aquinas.

Allan's work undermines the "virtue ethics" reading. Like that of Dan Robins, her account of *xing* 性 is carefully formulated and precise. *Xing*, she explains, evokes "the potential contained by a seed or the first shoots of a seedling to become a fully developed plant." That is all. As Robins says, there is no demonstrable basis upon which to proceed from there to "[regard] the concept of *xing* as essentially tied to species natures."[65] Allan likewise resists the postulation of such a nature when discussing *xing*, describing those who nourish human nature to its fullest extent as "unusual specimens of humankind." To designate predetermined ends in the process, she suggests, "erroneously projects ideas from a transcendent scheme upon the Chinese immanent worldview."[66]

Neglecting Chinese natural philosophy distorts one's understanding of Warring States philosophical traditions almost automatically. Insofar that it eschews such investigations, "Confucian virtue ethics," as Liu Liangjian says, "remains nothing more than a negative image of Confucianism in the mirror of virtue ethics." Western-trained virtue ethicists overlook the fact that pre-Qin authors do not regard *xing* 性 as an "intrinsic, unchanging nature," but rather, as Liu writes: "It was precisely the opposite case for them." *Xing*, he explains, was about "growing daily and maturing daily" in a manner that is neither "readymade nor determined," representing an "imperfective process of perfecting [one's *xing*] at every moment."[68] Such *growth*—not the *telos* of Greek-medieval metaphysics—is what botanical metaphors in the *Mencius* stood for in their original context.

Such processes reveal their natures less alongside Greek-medieval analogues and more alongside contemporary systems and process-oriented approaches. As we saw earlier, Giuseppe Longo and Maël Montévil argue that *biological temporal organization* is a feature of all living things. Things that grow "organize" themselves into unique trajectories that are irreversible and non-iterative.[69] Every phase in such a process is defined, as Dan Robins suggests, by what the thing is *currently doing*.[70] The agency involved is one of *extended critical transition*, such that *xing* 性 is always "poised" at criticality—in a "permanent 'transition,' conceived as an ongoing or *extended* and *critical* transition."[71] In Liu Liangjian's words, *xing* is always in the process of "becoming and pending completion."[72]

The environment in which such processes take shape (*xing* 形) is one in which *enablement* is operative. What is *enabled* is the annulment (*fan* 反) of an organism's own store of possibilities. In systems theory, this is conceptually challenging at the micro-level because "*every point* of the evolution/development space is near a critical point." For early Chinese thinkers, this reflects the immensity (*da* 大) of space itself, which even at the more limited scale of pertinent observables is infinitely dense. What organic phase space is dense with are symmetry groups of equilibrium states that pass into one another. Remember—all living things are moving on the "Potter's Wheel of Nature," and upon its surface there is only one rule: *keep moving or die*. With criticality extended to every point in the system (even cell mitosis exhibits *anti-entropy*), the growth process (*sheng* 生) is one of continually restored equilibrium—a rhythmic, discursive process of attaining the one (*deyi* 得一).

As Longo and Montévil observe, "The dense set of symmetry groups may be potentially infinite, but, of course, an organism (or a species) explores only finitely many of them in its life span, and only viable ones."[73] The directional order (*de* 德) of each organism is expressed in this process. Texts like Chapter 51 of the *Daodejing* and the "Short Preface" (*xiaoxu* 小序) to the *Songs* provide us with thoughtful and discerning accounts of how organic growth was understood in the Warring States period. In keeping with the

Figure 7.1. One of several photographs in John Dewey's collection depicting the young people he encountered while travelling in China. John Dewey collection, Special Collections Research Center, Morris Library, Southern Illinois University–Carbondale.

understated power (*de*) of infancy and childhood, these accounts stress situated growth and are explicitly non-teleological: "*Dao* 道 produces them, and *de* rears them: grows them, nurtures them, structures them, matures them, nourishes them, and protects them. Things are generated but are not beholden (*buyou* 不有). They act but without presumption (*bushi* 不恃). They grow but without being directed by any outside force (*buzai* 不宰). This is what is referred to as their mysterious *de*."

The most conservative (i.e., least radical) hermeneutical approach is to treat the *Mencius* within this general conceptual framework unless textual documentation, including recently unearthed archeological evidence, compels us to do otherwise. It does not. The botanical and horticultural metaphors that "virtue ethics" commentators observe, then, ought to be understood within the framework of Warring States natural philosophy.

As Bryan W. Van Norden rightly notes, the "sprouts" to which Mencius refers are not "tips" but rather the germinal beginnings of organic processes. "These metaphors," he writes, "are important for conveying [Mencius'] notion that we naturally have only incipient dispositions toward virtue, and that these dispositions require cultivation in order to grow into mature virtues."[74] That our native-born "sprouts" need to be cultivated or educated (i.e., *educare*—"drawn out" or "reared") is a central idea in Si-Meng Confucianism. As *Focusing the Familiar* states: "What Nature mandates is called a disposition (*xing* 性). To follow/lead (*shuai* 率) this disposition is called *dao* 道.[75] Cultivating *dao* is called education (*jiao* 教)."[76] Within the broader framework of early Chinese natural philosophy, it is important to recognize that none of this implies or requires anything like a Greek-medieval teleological framework.

When requisite adjustments are made, the question that critics throw at Dewey naturally arises: "To what end should one be cultivating oneself?" If we are to abandon Greek-medieval teleological reasoning along with the more radical "Heaven's plan" reading, how then are we to normatively assess the outcome of human development in the *Mencius*?

We are now able to consider such questions alongside the recently discovered Warring States text, *Dispositions Arise from Mandated Conditions* (*Xingzimingchu* 性自命出). Most scholars associate this text with the Si-Meng lineage, although its intellectual affiliation remains unclear.[77] Whatever its affiliation, the text opens with an intriguing proposal: "Generally speaking, while people have dispositions (*xing* 性), their feelings (*xin* 心) have no resolute commitment (*zhi* 志). This waits upon things and events, and only then arises. It waits upon inclination, and only then enters into action. It waits upon the formation of cultural habits (*xi* 習), and only then becomes fixed."[78] Such a statement, vague as it is, might be relevant across the Confucian spectrum, as it essentially reiterates the Master's own position: "Human beings are similar in their natures (*xing*), but vary with respect to their cultural practices (*xi*)."[79] In Scott Cook's assessment of the text, "its main focus is on the need for education—through the codified traditions of the [Confucian classics] and, above all, music—in order to properly mold our nature and give it order and direction." This is not, however, a "blank slate" approach. As Cook explains, the text emphasizes how "these forms of education ultimately and necessarily derive from human nature itself, thus suggesting that the capacity for goodness is somehow intrinsic within us to begin with, but it also explicitly describes our nature—or rather the heart-mind [*xin*] that contemplates for it—as lacking any definite direction and thus, in another sense, as value-neutral."[80]

Philosophically, one has to be grateful for the ambiguity that such Chinese accounts display. Every time one tries to apply some conventional dualism to the tradition, the tradition pushes back. In coming to understand texts like the *Mencius* and *Dispositions Arise from Mandated Conditions*, our instinct is to partition "Nature/Nurture" so we know where to place the normative emphasis. Such attempts, however, are always thwarted. This is the key, in fact, to understanding Irene Bloom's "biological" reading of the *Mencius*. "Though Mencius obviously contemplated the effects of environment on human development," she writes, "he would almost certainly have resisted a classic Western distinction between 'nature' versus 'nurture,' precisely because his conception [of *xing* 性] was developmental rather than essentialist, dynamic rather than static."[81] As Bloom reads the "Gaozi" debates, Mencius distinguishes his position from what she calls "narrow biologism" and "strong environmentalism." The former locates everything about us in our initial conditions, while the latter locates everything about us in our surroundings.[82] Each position relies on a sharp "Nature/Nurture" distinction.

For those doing contemporary work in early Chinese philosophy, the fact that we have a philosopher in Mencius keen enough to resist the "Nature/Nurture" dualism is something to advertise. In a 2014 survey, a number of working scientists were asked: "Which scientific ideas should be retired?" Many returned with the opinion that: "the familiar distinction between nature and nurture has outlived its usefulness."[83] This aspect of Mencius' philosophy should be plainly articulated and foregrounded as we make the text relevant for the twenty-first century. At present, this is hardly an idle philosophical detail. As Dale Goldhaber argues, the "Nature/Nurture" debate "has done more harm than good, both in terms of our conceptual understanding of the course of development and in terms of the inappropriate policy and practice recommendations that have flowed from such a flawed perspective."[84] Here is another instance in which we need to get "back in gear" and where early Chinese thought is ready to assist.

But let us return to the question at hand. Having abandoned teleology and "Heaven's plan," how are we to measure goodness (*shan* 善) in the process of human growth in the Confucian tradition? If harmony (*he* 和) is the operative norm, then what is the *end*? We know how such questions play themselves out in Daoism. "Knowledge" wanders north to ask them and then comes away empty. *Dao* 道 is precisely the continuity between means-and-ends, and it dissolves the moment one starts asking about it in end-related terms. But how does one convert this outcome into something useful, like policy recommendations or institutional reforms?

Perhaps we need to take a step back. In reality, the question of *the* "end" for human experience is too large a question to ask or to answer. What kind of response could one possibly expect to receive? Based on the present reading of Confucianism, why not go ahead and make harmony (*he* 和) the "end" for human beings. There. *Now* what? We have seen how it might work in a "Confucian democracy." The aim of such a system would be *greater* inclusiveness, *more* participation, *better* communication, and a host of other concrete goods. Excellent—now we have some practical work to do, and each task will be undertaken (hopefully) with an intelligent (or *ming* 明) "end-in-view" wherein means-and-ends are coterminous. If you prefer, now go ahead and switch the ultimate end from harmony to "Happiness." What changes? It seems to me that persistence in the demand for clarity on *the* "end" of human development is actually an insistence that there be a predetermined schema, i.e., what Philip J. Ivanhoe calls "an ideal or paradigmatic model of what it is to be human."[85] The corollary, then, is that "progress" can only be made when we fill out *that* schema.

Dewey discovered the fallacy of such thinking early in his philosophical career. In an 1893 article, "Self-Realization as the Moral Ideal," he criticizes the notion that self-cultivation entails a "fixed *schema* or outline, while realization consists in the filling up of this *schema*." Dewey demonstrates instead that "the self [is] always a concrete *specific* activity," and therefore "self and realization" are identical.[86] His reasoning closely parallels that of Mencius. First, Dewey argues that in ethical development the term "capacity" represents not what something *may be*, but rather what something *is*. Capacity (*cai* 才) is similarly a technical term in the *Mencius*, such that to say that human nature is "good" (*shan* 善) means that it can become good because it *has* that capacity.[87] In another instance, Mencius teaches that when axes cut down all the trees on Ox Mountain, it looks as though it never had any "wood" (*cai* 材). Likewise, when humans fail to nourish their ethical capacities (*cai* 才), they *lose* those capacities and revert back to being animals. Such people "look as though they never had (*you* 有) such capacities (*cai*) to begin with."[88] They used to have them, but now they are gone.

Philosophically, the key here is that having (*you* 有) a capacity is not understood as a state that one *might* enter. It is an existential state that one is either *in* or *not in*. The next step in Dewey's reasoning is to conclude accordingly that: "To *realize* [a] capacity is to act concretely, not abstractly." How could it be otherwise? One does not realize an existential capacity (*cai* 才) in the *future*. On this basis, Dewey challenges the postulation of a preexisting, schematic, or paradigmatic "self" that one realizes in the *future* through ethical "capacities." As he argues: "To realize capacity means to make the special act which has to be performed an activity of the entire *present* self—so far is it from being one step towards the attainment of a remote ideal self."[89] Such a dynamic is consistent with *xing* 性 as here understood.

In rejecting the "ideal or paradigmatic model" of the Confucian self, we must remember that it is Mencius, after all, who evokes the stupidity of the Man from Song for projecting an ideal future-end and "pulling" at his sprouts to reach it.[90] If Mencius were to evoke this image and simultaneously maintain that there exists "an ideal or paradigmatic model of what it is to be human," then that would be the height of stupidity—the gold standard. But *nowhere* does he suggest that there is such an ideal schema to be realized. Confucian virtue ethicists introduce this notion unilaterally. Mencius instead preserves the metaphor of botanical growth, which in the classical Chinese tradition does not evoke a fixed, teleological end-state.

The aspect of virtue ethics most prominent in early China is not that which aligns with Aristotelian essentialism but rather with the Stoic *diathesis homologoumenê*—i.e., the dispositional state in which doing what is virtuous is not done for the sake (*wei* 為) of something else. As Mencius points out, virtuous conduct is something that emerges (*you* 由) from Shun, he does not put it into practice (*xing* 行).[91] In such an exemplarist-virtue ethics, Shun is not "filling in" some preexisting model—he *is* the model. Mencius is pretty clear here: "[The virtues of] propriety and appropriateness emerge (*you* 由) by issuing out from (*chu* 出) persons of quality."[92] All of this is captured in Mencius' own botanical reasoning. The moral "sprouts" need to be brought to fruition (*shi* 實)—but more specifically, they need to be *filled out* so as to be brought to fruition (*chongshi* 充實).[93] There is no "Process/Product" dualism here, just as there is no such "Process/Product" dualism in the directional order (*de* 德) of a plant or tree.

The flourishing nature, for Mencius, "gets the most" (*jin* 盡) out of its capacities.[94] As Dewey argues, this always occurs in the *present*. "To realize capacity does not mean, therefore, to act so as to fill up some presupposed ideal self. It means to act at the height of action, to realize its full meaning."[95] This encompasses what Shi Bo calls "extending lushly" (*fengchang* 豐長) when harmony (*he* 和) is struck between one's disposition (*xing* 性) and the environment in which one grows. In fact, Mencius assures us that such flourishing *will* happen as one's better nature emerges. Filling out (*chong* 充) one's "sprout-like" capacities to be a productive member of one's family, community, and world is like "catching fire."[96] For him, to do this through situated growth *rather* than according to some abstract doctrine (*yan* 言) or schema is the only way to ensure such flourishing. Growth must remain rooted to its source (*ben* 本) in order to receive adequate nourishment. Students of the *Mencius* know perfectly well how Mencius would respond to the virtue ethicists' "ideal or paradigmatic model of what it is to be human." Such a fixed doctrine is compared to rainwater that collects in wooden hollows—it stays around for a while, but soon stagnates, evaporates, and nourishes nothing.[97] When such abstractions are placed aside, sage-like growth can actually occur, and the more "right" (*yi* 義 or *yi* 宜) that growth is—i.e., the more *dao* 道-like it becomes—the more flood-like energy (*qi* 氣) fuels it.[98] Mencius teaches accordingly that once one witnesses a sage in action, "it is difficult to appreciate doctrines (*yan*)." He can hardly make his opposition to abstract, paradigmatic "schema" clearer.[99]

Not so clear is why "Confucian virtue ethics" goes against the grain and postulates paradigmatic or schematic models of human development in the first place. Intra-cultural philosophy remains self-aware enough to know, however, that what is at issue here is more than fidelity to the text. In all such cases, there are cultural values and cognitive biases at work. I am willing to join Henry Rosemont Jr. in bracketing out the textual evidence for a moment (while still insisting that it is on my side) and posing the interpretive issue as a normative question.[100] Let us ask: is it *better* for people to think that there is "an ideal or paradigmatic model of what it is to be human?"

In "Self-Realization as the Moral Ideal," Dewey argues persuasively that postulating the "schema" of such an ideal self is a bad idea. His argument, in fact, is one that locates him well within the broader parameters of virtue ethics. There is, Dewey explains, a "natural history" to the bifurcation of the self into "real" and "ideal" elements. There are standards that we wish to live up to as individuals and as societies, and there is the realization that we fail to measure up. The problem is that we commit "the fallacy of hypostatizing into separate entities what in reality are simply two stages of insight on our part." We externalize some "ideal self" and then imagine that the cultivation of our characters is for the sake (*wei* 為) of *that* self. This invites the kind of externalization (*wai* 外) that hinders the development of virtue in any *dao* 道-based philosophy. The key to virtuous behavior, as Dewey says, "consists in not degrading any required act into a mere means toward an end lying outside itself, but in doing it for its own sake, or, again, in doing it *as self*." That such a conception is *better* than the one that postulates a preexisting schema hinges on the psychological dispositions involved. There is something disturbing about people who do "good" for others in service to something that has nothing to do with the beneficiaries. If one acts in accordance with some "paradigmatic model of what it is to be human" then one realizes one's "ideal self" so defined. As Dewey sees it, however: "The only reason for performing any moral act is then *for* this self . . . I do not believe it possible to state this theory in a way which does not make action selfish in the bad sense of selfish."[101]

This returns us to the topic of "ultimate ends" in human life. We have seen once again that insisting on them is counterproductive to any *dao* 道-oriented approach. The only "ends" compatible with *dao*-activity are those that work *within* the means-end circuit as "ends-in-view." This means that "the end is no longer a terminus or limit to be reached. It is the active process of transforming the existent situation." Such ends, which are the only ones that the "Way of Nature" (*tiandao* 天道) ever exhibits, ought to be sufficient for the good life. As Dewey says: "The ever-enduring process of perfecting, maturing, refining is the aim of living."[102] Introducing "ultimate ends" or schemata goes against the natural process of growth and development, which is what organic life normally (*chang* 常) exhibits. As Dewey suggests, to imagine "growth" as what occurs for the sake (*wei* 為) of something beyond itself introduces a "false idea of growth or development." Growth is then "regarded as *having* an end, instead of *being* an end."[103]

This is a revealing statement. Dewey is actually quite clear about what the "end" of human development is. "Growth itself is the only moral 'end,'" he writes.[104] Along the same lines, when Shi Bo says that, "Harmony (*he* 和) actually grows things, whereas sameness causes them to discontinue," he is establishing *he* 和 as a normative measure. Harmony enables things to "extend lushly" (*fengchang* 豐長) by returning them to growth.[105] For Dewey and for Chinese thinkers, ensuring growth is the "ultimate good." If you don't like such reasoning, then stop growing and see how you like that.

Family Experience and Non-Dualism

With such an "ultimate good" in mind, let us return to the family (*jia* 家). We now observe its complex features: specific institutions of family and marriage are historically contingent; yet, they are simultaneously human universals that have evolved to satisfy a range of concrete goods. "Growth" is the most generic of these goods. It is not uncommon today to hear that marriages fall apart because one party is prevented from "growing" or because both parties "grow apart." It is often said that, "Half of all marriages in the United States end in divorce." Fortunately, this is a myth. In the 1970s and 1980s the divorce rate approached 45 percent in the U.S. Since then, it has steadily dropped to its current rate of about 15 percent. Among these numbers, there are clear correlations between socioeconomic wellbeing and marital success.[106] Couples with restricted access to education, economic security, affordable housing, childcare, and other basic necessities have a harder time making their marriages work.

One of the hallmarks of modern political conservatism is to decry the breakdown of "traditional" institutions like marriage and family while simultaneously eroding the socioeconomic conditions that enable them to succeed. Mencius understood that this was like "climbing a tree in search of a fish." He knew that economic security was necessary in order for people to have secure feelings (*hengxin* 恆心) and that parents and children could not be properly cared for without access to social goods and services.[107] Mencius was a strong advocate of a state-sponsored village school system, maintaining that vigorous support for public education was necessary to secure the support of the people.[108] He proposed economic policies to ensure that people would not incur debt while carrying out their filial duties, thus endorsing a family-based economic system proposed by King Wen, one ensuring that the material needs of kin would be provided for.[109] He took active stands on land and tax reform and prescribed strategies to increase food production. As Mencius asks: "When food is as plentiful as fire and water, then who among the people will exhibit anything but altruism/empathy (*ren* 仁)?"[110] Unlike modern conservatives (who sometimes appeal to the *Mencius* in support of their positions),[111] Mencius did not believe that the social good resulted simply from "following human nature." As Howard J. Curzer ably demonstrates, social order in the *Mencius* was to be nurtured into being by a broad range of progressive-minded socioeconomic policies—policies that Mencius regarded as the exercise of benevolent government.[112]

With this, one is compelled to ask: According to the *Mencius*, is it human nature that makes Confucian society good, or is it the benevolent socioeconomic policies that Mencius prescribes that make it so? Every effort must be made to resist the "Nature/Nurture" dualism behind this question. Remember—the power of Mencius' vision is that it avoids extremes by not reducing to either "narrow biologism" (basic nature) or "strong environmentalism" (external conditioning). This calls to mind Confucius' own resistance to approaches that reduce self-cultivation to either raw material (*zhi* 質) or refinement (*wen* 文) when in fact once cultivation begins "*zhi* is no different from *wen*, and *wen* is no different from *zhi*."[113] That there is a similar blending process at work in the *Mencius* is made evident by the fact that alongside the botanical metaphors we find the aesthetic ones, culinary and musical. The key to overcoming the "Nature/Nurture" dualism is to realize, as Shi Bo teaches, that harmony (*he* 和) brings dynamic elements into balance (*ping* 平) so that growth ensues.

Let us now try to better understand culture by examining more precisely how human experience emerges on the nature-nurture continuum. As we know, not every structural element functions equally at every stage in the evolutionary process. Vestigial structures linger from past adaptations, while a range of homologous structures become deposited rather accidentally across the biosphere. Humans and cats both have eyes, for instance, and the basic arrangement of bones in human limbs is similar to that in other tetrapods. Mencius is keen to specify what he means by human nature (*renxing* 人性) amidst this panoply of features. He explains:

> The relationships between mouth and taste, eyes and color, ears and sound, nose and smell, and the four limbs and physical repose: these are a matter of natural disposition (*xing* 性), and something about them has the quality of being mandated (*ming* 命). Exemplary persons do not consider these as their natures (*xing*). The relationships between altruism/empathy (*ren* 仁) and the parent/child relation, appropriateness (*yi* 義) and the ruler/

subject relation, ritual propriety (*li* 禮) and the guest/host relation, wisdom (*zhi* 智) and the person of quality, and the sages and the course of Nature: these are [also] mandated (*ming* 命), but something about them has the quality of natural disposition (*xing*). Exemplary persons do not consider these as being mandated (*ming*).[114]

As Bryan W. Van Norden observes, Mencius is interested here in distinguishing which aspects of human nature require human effort for their cultivation and which aspects do not.[115] Those that *do* require intelligent cultivation on the human level are properly regarded as "human nature" and trace back to the cultural innovations of the sages, i.e., those that correspond to the "four sprouts" (*siduan* 四端) that have been identified and fortified over the course of human history.

Again, Mencius is on solid empirical ground here. Altruism and empathy, admiration and shame, infant bonding, sociality, etc. are capacities (*cai* 才) that we now share. Since the tradition gives no content-specific definitions of what each "sprout" is destined to become, I see no reason to suppose that Mencius did not have a basically accurate idea of the variability involved. Like any eco-morphological process (think of the orange tree), such "sprouts" will as a rule (*ze* 則) result in different phyla according to *how* and *where* they are nurtured and grown. Should one succeed in untangling and isolating the resulting habits (*habitus*) into discreet, self-standing, readily-defined "moral virtues" (good luck with that), one would note some generic similarities between "fortitude" in northern Siberia and El Salvador.

Since humans exhibit such a wide range of shared capacities, it is difficult to say which ones become implicated in the development of specific cultural habits and why. As Dewey reminds us, such "original native tendencies" are based on "the original connections of neurons in the central nervous system," so "instead of their being a small number sharply marked off from one another, [they] are of an indefinite variety, interweaving with one another in all kinds of subtle ways."[116] There are one-hundred-billion neurons percolating in the developing human brain. That's a lot of sprouts. No matter how widely we thus come to vary in our cultural habits, however, there can be no doubt that they originate in a largely shared human nature. As Dewey explains: "Habits as organized activities are secondary and acquired, not native and original. They are [however] outgrowths of unlearned activities which are part of [the human] endowment at birth."[117] Once again we hear the echo of the Master: "Human beings are similar in their natures (*xing* 性), but vary with respect to their cultural practices (*xi* 習)."[118]

The "four sprouts" thus represent vague impulses that particular cultures isolate and cultivate into habits. Broad-based similarities in the selection and development of such instincts would present strong evidence for their adaptive value. Since generic patterns associated with marriage and family are human universals, such patterns and their concomitant dispositions are likely to represent highly successful adaptations. Understanding the status of each element here is important for understanding the teachings of the *Mencius*. Mencius makes it clear that whatever full-blown virtues develop *from* the "four sprouts" are not native to human nature (*renxing* 人性) in any inalienable, essentialist sense. After all, even the sprouts can be lost.[119] Virtuous habits begin, however, *as* "sprouts" (or, as Dewey says, as "outgrowths") of activities that are unlearned and typically present at birth.

Such inborn and unlearned (*buxue* 不學) activities, according to Mencius, are related to those associated with family affection (*qin* 親) and its related instincts. Moral habits and attitudes "grow out" (*da* 達) from one's family-born activities.[120] Mencius explains that, "serving one's parents is bringing associated humanity to fruition; respecting one's elder brothers is bringing appropriateness to fruition," and so on.[121] The resulting fruits (*shi* 實) of family-centered moral development issue from transactions that occur between one's initial conditions and one's family environment—a blending together of nature-and-nurture.

In reading the *Mencius*, readers need to decide for themselves the degree to which Mencius' thinking exhibits a kind of "folk essentialism." One potential (not to mention disturbing) sign of such thinking is that Mencius suggests that those who fail to develop Confucian-related virtues are "animals."[122] This suggests that, in Mencius' mind, individuals who stray from family-centric development are not merely different but deviant. Is *this*, however, sufficient evidence for "folk essentialism?" Our willingness to ascribe essentialist assumptions to Mencius should be weighed against evidence in cognitive science suggesting that, while common among children across cultures, such assumptions vary among adults in different cultural groups. If there is indeed a "sprout" for essentialist thinking, it matures differently in different environments.

I side with Irene Bloom in noting that Mencius' theory of human nature "appears to have been developed less as a theory than as an argument."[123] On that basis, I find Mencius' "Human/Animal" distinction to be rhetorical rather than based on essentialist categories *per se*, "folk" or otherwise. Again, his principal intention is to defend the Confucian tradition. Having decided that to be properly "human" (*ren* 人) means developing Confucian habits, he puts his adversaries on the defensive by calling them "animals." This is an unsavory philosophical move, but it is more of a problem for those who ascribe Aristotelian-style essentialism to the *Mencius*. For if such a reading is correct, then Mencius de-humanizes his adversaries on an ontological rather than rhetorical level. This is not to suggest that either move is acceptable, but the latter is more remediable. In any event, it is quite unclear what evidence there would be for ascribing Aristotelian-style essentialism to Mencius. The very idea that a person might go from being "human" to *not* being "human" more or less guarantees that Mencius did not think of human nature (*renxing* 人性) in Aristotelian terms.

As I see it, the *Mencius* is best understood based on what Edouard Machery calls a "nomological" theory of human nature. Whereas essentialist theories are rooted in folk biology and project a "set of properties that are separately necessary and jointly sufficient for being a human," nomological theories assemble sets of properties normally possessed as a result of contingent but shared conditions. As Machery observes, "The nomological notion of human nature inverts the Aristotelian relation between nature and generalization. For Aristotle, the fact that humans have the same nature explains why many generalizations can be made about them," whereas in nomological theories, "the fact that many generalizations can be made about humans explains in which sense there is a human nature."[124] Thus understood, to say that "humans all have" (*renjieyou* 人皆有) certain traits or dispositions—e.g., the "four sprouts," the inability to bear (*ren* 忍) certain indignities, parental concern, and so on,[125] does not mean that one might not encounter the odd human who does *not* have such things. Such traits are neither necessary nor jointly sufficient for making someone "human." Having them does not define class membership. Instead, such attributions are general statements about populations. The nomological approach is more consistent with a Warring States logic that uses standards (*fa* 法) in designating types (*lei* 類) for practical purposes. Human nature, thus understood, does not track onto any fixed "essence." As a result: "Human nature is not normative; there is nothing wrong in *not* having the properties that are part of human nature."[126]

If such thinking is allowed to serve as the *factual* basis for Mencius' thinking, then his *normative* claims about human nature (*renxing* 人性) are more easily isolated and defended without evoking the kind of supernatural and/or unverifiable claims that Donald J. Munro encourages us to "disregard as the dross." As we have seen, Mencius is most interested in designating family-centered experience as *the* criterion for being "human." As he says: "If one is not engaged in family affection, then one cannot be called 'human.'"[127] This position is rendered more forcefully in the newly discovered *Six Positions* (*Liuwei* 六位) document, which states: "Sharing family affection (*qin* 親) with one's close and distant relatives: being human lies solely in this (*weiqirensuozai* 唯其人所在). Engage (*de* 得) in this affection and the human makes itself present (*ju* 舉). Disengage from this affection and the human ceases to be (*zhi* 止)."[128] Let us try to understand this important statement both factually and normatively. Then, let us see if we can't collapse the "Fact/Value" dualism altogether.

From the *factual* standpoint, one can say that family experience is a common trait for *Homo sapiens*. From an evolutionary perspective, it has clear survival advantages and is stabilized by deep biological underpinnings. The family experience is thus "normal" for humans. In the systems approach, however, to say that a particular nature-nurture circuit is "normal" is to say that it is statistically most frequent. As we know, "Nature (*tian* 天) produces the teeming masses and where there is a thing there is a rule (*ze* 則)."[129] Given the natural history of *Homo sapiens*, its reaction norms respond well spontaneously to family nurturing because other survival-related functions have co-evolved alongside such nurturing. Should families suddenly pass out of existence, with all children relocated to the anonymous rearing pens of the *kallipolis*, then *that* nature-nurture circuit and its uncertain effects would be the new "normal." The *Six Positions* statement would then become *factually incorrect*.

Remember that, as David J. Buller observes: "Nothing in the norm of reaction would identify any particular height as 'natural' for [the barley]."[130] There are simply different heights that it will have under different conditions. If a virus reaches epidemic proportions in a species of barley, then it becomes "normal" and "natural" for that population to exhibit diseased features. Like it or not, genetics alone cannot underwrite the more robust, *normative* notions of "normal" and "natural" used in common speech. Bryan W. Van Norden, in briskly asserting that his reading of the *Mencius* holds up well in light of evolutionary biology, seems strangely unaware of this.[131]

In the midst of pointing out the *factual* elements in human nature, Mencius explains that, "If one is not engaged in family affection, one cannot be called 'human,'" which is meant to be a *normative* claim.[132] He has, after all, already identified Confucian virtues as "good" (*shan* 善) and stated that they take shape within the family.[133] Even though such capacities (*cai* 才) biologically speaking are simply *there*, without the cultural medium of family to register their significance and provide them support their emergence as human-level virtues is not very promising. Family affection must be operative from the start, providing nourishment, direction, and meaning to our native instincts. As Dewey observes:

> In the life of the individual, instinctive activity comes first. But an individual begins life as a baby, and babies are dependent beings.

Their activities could continue at most for only a few hours were it not for the presence and aid of adults with their formed habits ... [Babies] owe to adults the opportunity to express their native activities in ways which have meaning ... In short, the *meaning* of native activities is not native; it is acquired. It depends upon interaction with a matured social medium.[134]

Again, the "four sprouts" are vague, innate impulses that are selected and reinforced within a cultural medium and subsequently cultivated into habits. It is a biological fact that humans generally possess them as capacities (*cai* 才).[135] Strictly speaking, however, this is not what makes us qualitatively "human." The "four sprouts" are simply traits that humans generally have (*you* 有), "just as we have four limbs."[136] What actually makes us "human" is the lived experience of being born into family-centered environments and *thereby* having our "four sprouts" chosen, activated, and developed among a welter of untutored impulses. This should not be mistaken for the "Gaozi" position that human nature is like "swirling water" that goes in whatever direction it is channeled.[137] Human nature has *genuine* tendencies toward altruism/empathy, praise/blame, deference/admiration, and intelligence. If functioning families and other supporting cultural technologies fail to enable the growth of such capacities, however, then humans never develop these "sprouts" and revert to being "animals" (*shou* 獸). As Mencius sees it, the margin for error here is slight (*xi* 希).[138]

Thus, there are both *factual* and *normative* dimensions to Mencius' theory of human development, and distinctions can be made in terms of "Nature/Human" as necessary. The key philosophical move, however, is to collapse this dualism and to restore continuity (*yi* 一) to the nature-nurture circuit, such as Dewey does when he subsumes the "Nature/Human" dualism under the category of "culture." While we often find *ourselves* making distinctions between biological "facts" and cultural "values," there is no "Fact/Value" schism in the operations of Nature itself (*tiandao* 天道). Likewise, in human experience, there are no discrete causal chains the nature of which are exclusively "biological" or "cultural." In the systems approach, these are not ontologically separable domains. As Dale Goldhaber explains, rather than regard the phenotype as the effect of such partitioned influences, our world is really one wherein "all antecedents influence behavior in an interactive, synergistic, systemic manner," such that "the development of the individual is best considered as the emergent property of a constant interplay between the genome and the environment."[139]

This premise, that human experience is both natural-and-cultural in its emergence, underlies Dewey's "cultural naturalism." As Dewey notes: "As [humans] enter into distinctively human associations strictly organic properties are modified and even transformed," such that "there is something more in any family association than bare physiological factors." Often, this transformation is so profound "that it has indeed led to the belief in the intrusive intervention of unnatural and supernatural factors in order to account for the differences between the animal and the human."[140] Such inferences, however, are wholly unwarranted. Notions such as "Heaven's plan" are their trace. By *not* making such unwarranted inferences, focus is permitted to remain on the harmonies (*he* 和) achieved in transactional processes as they actually occur within the nature-culture circuit. As we saw in chapter 3 of this volume, this is the approach to social philosophy that Dewey initiates in his "Social and Political Philosophy" lectures in Beijing. Focusing on continuities of the natural-and-human in social situations is necessary if there is to be intelligent means-end reflection on the harmonies sustained in such circuits. As Shi Bo suggests, it is harmony (*he*) that actually grows (*sheng* 生) things. The balance (*ping* 平) achieved within such circuits enables energies (*qi* 氣) to coalesce and extend themselves. The goal of human development always remains the same: to "get the most out of our natures" (*jinxing* 盡性) within such circuits. Normative guidance is provided by what in our feelings (*xin* 心) is commonly so—i.e., our innate preference for pattern (*li* 理) and rightness (*yi* 義).

The special attention that Confucians pay to the family now makes sense. Family experience exhibits a depth in this respect that is simply not found in other cultural institutions. As Roger T. Ames and Henry Rosemont Jr. observe, "[family] is ordinary and everyday yet at the same time is arguably the most extraordinary aspect of the human experience."[141] Families grant in-coming members significance (*yi* 義) while they are still in the womb. The family-borne child receives a meaningful identity—a personal share (*shenfen* 身份) in a larger whole from the very start. One enters by default into relations with role-bearing others, and through taking on roles one becomes an integral member in cultural patterns (*li* 理) that both precede and result from such integration. "Welcome to the world," indeed.

Meaning and significance (*yi* 義) positively *streams* from such tightly adjusted nature-nurture circuits. Over the course of human history, brand new values have been introduced through the growth and embellishment sponsored by the family (*jia* 家). As Robert C. Neville observes, families "not only make possible the existence and education of human infants but they also make possible human relations of affection, care, and nurture that have nothing to do with infancy."[142] Indeed, family experience has evolved such as to be formative to the human experience generally. Our family experiences largely make us who we are. Research on human brain development, for instance, suggests that, "differences in the pattern of early maternal-infant interactions can initiate long-term developmental effects that persist into adulthood," and that is only the beginning of the influence.[143] When a family is dysfunctional, children almost invariably carry problems into adulthood; and there is solid truth in Leo Tolstoy's observation, that "every unhappy family is unhappy in its own way."[144]

Given its central role in human development, no public expense should be spared in ensuring that families are positioned to succeed. As Dewey observed in China, the family (*jia* 家) is particularly susceptible to the winds of change—industrial, socioeconomic, cultural, technological, etc.—that can upset the efficacy of its operative ritual-customs (*li* 禮). There is also ample evidence, however, of the resilience of families. Given its evolutionary advantages, along with the considerable depth of its roots, family (*jia* 家) is easily the supplest of all human institutions. No two families are exactly alike, and the institution adapts itself from generation to generation almost seamlessly. What remains steady throughout all such changes, however, is the norm of harmony (*he* 和) that measures its goodness.

Culture and Adaptation

Whatever "human nature" actually is, we can say with confidence that it is the result of successful adaptations to selection pressures over time. The so-called "Stone Age Mind" thesis proposes that, "the [human] mind is a set of information-processing machines that were designed by natural selection to solve adaptive problems faced by our hunter-gatherer ancestors."[145] The standard corollary to this view is that the mind has distinct "cognitive modules" that pick up environmental cues and then map them onto adaptive habits that became set during the Pleistocene epoch. The limits of this thesis are increasingly being recognized in the field of evolutionary cognitive science. As Peter J. Richerson and Robert Boyd explain, according to the "Stone Age Mind" theory, cultures are not really "transmitted." Rather, children come pre-equipped with "a variety of preconceptions about how the physical, biological, and social world works, and these preconceptions shape how they use experience to learn about their environments." As Richerson and Boyd suggest: "[Stone Age Mind] scholars are surely right in stating that every form of learning, including social learning, requires an information-rich innate psychology, and that much of the adaptive complexity we see in cultures around the world stems from this information." But reducing culture to a series of inferences constrained by Stone Age modules "is a big mistake."[146]

We have already considered how strongly innate tendencies toward teleological reasoning, essentialism, and the like can impact cultural development.

Indeed, Dewey prepares his own tentative list of cognitive universals in *Logic: The Theory of Inquiry*. He includes "Things," "Natural Kinds," "Teleological Ends," and "Ranks and Hierarchies."[147] He did not see such predispositions, however, as determining individual cultures. While appreciating the enormous role of primitive "common sense," both Dewey and William James would resist the idea that our brains contain a fixed suite of adaptive mechanisms that arose *only* during the Pleistocene epoch. For one thing, this would cut science and philosophy out of the game. Remember that, for Dewey, philosophy is a genetic-functional activity *within* culture that operates as the critical and constructive mode *of* each culture. In *Knowing and the Known*, this twofold nature becomes understood as continuous *via* its analysis as "*trans*-actional" and as expressive of on-going life-activities. Common sense, in its cognitive mode, stands for "direct active participation in the transactions of living" prior to any philosophical reflection.[148] As such, common sense indexes a whole, lived situation—one in which organism-and-environment operate in unbroken equilibrium. Like any equilibrium state, common sense undergoes adjustment in the course of stabilization. As currently operative, one's common sense has *already* evolved in some way from its native state in transaction with the environment in which it operates. This can continue under the influence of science and/or philosophy. Such common sense, for Dewey, serves as the ballast against which scientific and philosophical activities are leveraged. This means that common sense is stable but never truly *static* in human cognition.

One problem that the "Stone Age Mind" and "Heaven's plan" theses share is that each envisions human nature as preceding the emergence of culture, which is then regarded as the by-product of a more-or-less finished human nature. Stephen M. Downes and others disagree, maintaining that "human behavior is a result of evolutionary processes both *much older* and *more recent* than the Pleistocene," meaning that it is not so easy to establish a single, threshold "human nature" through which cultures are then realized.[149] As Richerson and Boyd observe, that latter, more linear approach "neglects the inevitable feedback between the nature of human psychology and the kind of social information that this psychology should be designed to process."[150] Here, Dewey would heartily agree. The "fundamental fallacy" of such thinking, he believes, "is its dualism; that is to say, its separation of activities and capacities from subject matter."[151] Of course, the "Heaven's plan" thesis is guiltier of such dualism than the "Stone Age Mind" thesis, which at least bases its notion of human nature on evolutionary principles. In any case, the larger point is that "over the evolutionary long haul, culture has shaped our innate psychology as much as the other way around."[152] Since, as Frans de Waal says, humans are and always have been "social to the core," it is exceedingly difficult to tease nature-and-culture apart such that the former can be understood as a necessary and sufficient condition for the emergence of the latter.¹⁵³ Methodologically in such cases, as Dewey suggests: "We have to get away from the influence of belief in bald single forces."¹⁵⁴ Systems-oriented approaches are empirically stronger here.

One lurking question is whether or not "human nature" can change. Nominally speaking, Mencius thought that it could *be* changed, because if certain "sprouts" are neglected then they are irretrievably lost. At that point, one goes from having one kind of nature (*xing* 性) to having another.¹⁵⁵ One would think that, if *Homo sapiens* continue to survive for another 200,000 years, then the species would undergo evolutionary change as a matter of course. If that happens, then human nature would change. Precisely *when* it changes into something that is no longer "human nature" is a question that sails on the Ship of Theseus.

Dewey keeps his own inquiry closer to practical concerns.¹⁵⁶ On one level, he suggests, human nature does *not* change: "I do not think it can be shown that the innate needs of [humans] have changed since [humans] became [humans] or that there is any evidence that they will change as long as [humans are] on the earth." Dewey lists such "needs" as those for food and water, meaningful activity, social cooperation, aesthetic experience, and the like. "Whether my particular examples are well chosen or not," he writes, "does not matter so much as does recognition of the fact that there are some tendencies so integral a part of human nature that the latter would not be human nature if they changed."¹⁵⁷ The actual *pattern* of human nature, however, is expressed within the matrix of culture. In this respect, human nature *does* change. Dewey explains that: "While certain needs in human nature are constant, the consequences they produce (because of the existing state of culture—of science, morals, religion, art, industry, legal rules) react back into the original components of human nature to shape them into new forms."¹⁵⁸ So, to the question "Does Human Nature Change?" Dewey's answer is "Yes and No." As Donald J. Munro sees it, this is the premodern Confucian response as well. As he explains: "from one perspective, human nature is not changeable," but from another perspective, "Confucians believed people are enormously receptive to education."¹⁵⁹

Positing unchanging elements in human nature is one step in developing a mature philosophical position on the matter. It is not the final step. As Dewey understands it, "after the fact is recognized that there is something unchangeable in the structure of human nature," the problem is "the inference we draw from it."¹⁶⁰ We suppose that there are fixed routes and arrangements through which human needs *must* be satisfied, when in fact native human nature can be channeled rather "promiscuously" and develop in numberless directions and thrive.¹⁶¹

William James observes such variability in his essay, "The Moral Equivalent of War." Warfare has long satisfied human nature. In ancient times, "to hunt a neighboring tribe, kill the males, loot the village and possess the females, was the most profitable, as well as the most exciting, way of living."[162] Dewey acknowledges that "combative instincts" are a "constituent part of human nature," but in cases of violent warfare he says, "social conditions and forces have led, almost forced, these 'instincts' into this channel." There are menaces greater than our neighbors upon which we might train our "combative instincts." We can band together to fight global injustice, gun violence, or climate change, to name a few. It is possible, Dewey thinks, to reshuffle the manner in which our shared instincts are satisfied so as to secure a more harmonious (he 和) and intelligent (ming 明) society. In the process, there is no avoiding unchanging "human nature"—it is "the factor which in one way or another is always interacting with environing conditions in production of culture."[163] Dewey's point is that when it comes to *how* human beings actually behave, "whatever the sociological causes, they are affairs of tradition, custom, and institutional organization, and these factors belong among the changeable manifestations of human nature, not among the unchangeable elements."[164]

Properly understood, Dewey's position on human nature is that it is developmentally continuous—it both *changes* and *does not change*. Out of necessity, we introduce "Nature/Nurture" distinctions as we reflect upon the desirability of specific outcomes and work intelligently to fortify or reconstruct them. Actual human development, however, is always such that *zhi* 質 is no different from *wen* 文 and *wen* is no different from *zhi*—just as Confucius says.[165] Ontologically, the process of human development is not bifurcated into "Nature/Nurture." As Irene Bloom suggests, Mencius teaches the same "precisely because his conception of [*xing* 性] was developmental rather than essentialist, dynamic rather than static."[166]

Thus, we must be cautious when introducing "Nature/Nurture," "Biology/Culture," or "Fact/Value" distinctions into the *Mencius*. We introduce such distinctions with good enough intentions—we wish to know where to place the normative emphasis. Thinking that there is a single key to be found, however—either in Mencius' specific teachings about "human nature" or in his specific sociopolitical prescriptions—misses the larger point. The contributions of the *Mencius* are methodological as much as substantive. While Mencius' teachings on the "four sprouts" can be empirically defended, the notion that "human nature" is a fourfold structure cannot be. Likewise, while the agricultural policies of King Wen were brilliant in their time, such policies are impractical in our own. There are surely more than *four* promising inclinations in human nature that are capable of becoming good (*keyiweishan* 可以

為善)¹⁶⁷ and it is our responsibility to identify and support such inclinations alongside the "four sprouts" in ways that are practical today.

Our conservative tendency is to balk at such heavy lifting. Nostalgia for ancient theories of "human nature," however, cannot be allowed to substitute for the more difficult undertaking of doing in our time what Mencius did in his own. As Dewey suggests, our more nostalgic views "about the inherent make-up of human nature [tend to neglect] the fundamental question of how its constituents are stimulated and inhibited, intensified and weakened; how their pattern is determined by interaction with cultural conditions."¹⁶⁸ For Dewey, productive integration within nature-human circuits is precisely what culture is concerned with. As he explains in the 1949 "Re-Introduction" to *Experience and Nature*, replacing the term "experience" with "culture" was meant to foreground "that the *standing problem* of Western philosophy throughout its entire history has been the connection-and-distinction of what on one side is regarded as *human* and on the other side as *natural*."¹⁶⁹ The bilateral relation of "connection-and-distinction" between human-level and natural-level phenomena is what culture comes to signify. Intra-cultural philosophy is mindful of the fact that it works at the nature-human intersection and attempts to proceed accordingly.

As we have seen, there is a rich history of disagreement in early China about the relationship between humans and nature. After much debate, the position that finally achieves prominence is that there is "continuity between Nature and the human" (*tianrenheyi* 天人合一).¹⁷⁰ While textual evidence makes it difficult to reconstruct Warring States debates in linear terms, the Si-Meng line of Confucianism so received, which culminates in *Focusing the Familiar*, is the school most committed to securing productive circuits between the human experience and Nature (*tian* 天). The key to securing such cultural circuits is the naturalization of education (*jiao* 教) in the Confucian tradition. Education is presented in *Focusing the Familiar* as something that accords with our natures (*xing* 性) and thus amounts to our *dao* 道.¹⁷¹ The *Dispositions Arise from Mandated Conditions* document concurs. Nature itself mandates that human nature (*renxing* 人性) be educated.¹⁷²

Donald J. Munro considers the mandate to be educated as one of the most relevant features of Mencius' philosophy, one that "makes it consistent with the actual human condition." For Munro, "the Mencian portrait combines the confidence in education that goes along with belief in malleability, with the belief that there is also an inborn or fixed basis for some social behavior."¹⁷³ Because human nature (*renxing* 人性) is developmental rather than static, dynamic rather than fixed, education *must* occur—and this for better or for worse. Dewey agrees with the Confucians here. Once the more dynamic features of human nature are understood, "the question will not be whether it is capable of change, but *how* it is to be changed under given conditions. This problem is ultimately that of education in its widest sense."[174]

Mencius is particularly interested in the mechanics of education. He teaches that there are five modes by which to instruct others: exerting influence, developing virtues, nurturing talents, answering questions, and enabling self-reform.[175] He also explains that parents must not educate their own children. "Educators must resort to correction," he explains, "and when that does not work, one ends up losing one's temper."[176] Such is not appropriate within the family. From an evolutionary perspective, there are other reasons that children are best educated outside the home. Home schooling involves a range of limitations and biases that result in over-weighted vertical cultural transmission, which is detrimental to social growth. As Richerson and Boyd note, many parents have the mistaken belief that they contribute importantly to their children's education. "Behavior genetic studies indicate," however, "that most of the similarity between the personality traits of parents and children is due to genetic inheritance, not vertical transmission."[177] Anecdotally, we know that it is not uncommon for parents and children to have radically different values and attitudes. Confucians recognize the same. As the Master says: when one's father dies, "to refrain from reforming his *dao* 道 for three years is to be filial (*xiao* 孝)."[178] Three years is not that long. Deference is to be shown, but the subtext here is that if we follow the previous generation for too long the *dao* of tradition suffers.

In contrast to such thinking, the "Stone Age Mind" and "Heaven's plan" theses each have some rationale for underplaying the extent to which education (*jiao* 教) substantively contributes to the human experience. There are good reasons, however, to reject such theses and embrace the Confucian thesis instead. Richerson and Boyd's conjecture for why social learning and culture as we know it proliferated so rapidly over the last 11,500 years provides it an empirical explanation. Data gathered from a 2-mile-deep ice core drilled from a glacier in Greenland during the 1990s gives us a record of climatic changes during the end of the Pleistocene epoch, which corresponds with the end of the last ice age as well as with a formative period in the evolution of human behavior. Data shows that between ca. 70,000 and 10,000 BCE the global climate fluctuated rapidly and extremely before evening out to the relative stability that it has displayed during the Holocene epoch. Before 10,000 BCE, "sharp spikes lasting a century or less are common in the Greenland record." Such dramatic fluctuations in climate are unthinkable today (so far), but our brains evolved in the midst of them and retain capacities selected as a result of such radical swings. The thesis is that rapidly fluctuating environments favored an increase in behavioral flexibility and social learning, and this contributed to the emergence of human cultures. "If we are right," Richerson and Boyd write, "culture is adaptive because it can do things that genes cannot do for themselves." Their central claim is that: "Because cumulative cultural evolution gives rise to complex adaptations much more rapidly than natural selection can give rise to genetic adaptations, complex culture was particularly suited to the highly variable Pleistocene environments."[179]

If it is true that human culture is an adaptive force capable of out-pacing the protracted crawl of biological evolution, then there are ironies to observe. As Dewey flatly states: "The force of lag in human life is enormous."[180] Here, in another iteration of the "out of gear" thesis, he again observes that we are suffering "cultural lag" given that "the last century has seen more changes in the conditions under which people live and associate than occurred in thousands of previous years."[181] Thus arises the following puzzle: If human culture is such a dynamic and adaptive power, then why are its resulting customs and traditions not more nimble?

In addressing this question, one needs to properly identify the factors involved. As Dewey observes, "It is precisely custom which has greatest inertia, which is least susceptible of alteration; while instincts are most readily modifiable through use, most subject to educative direction."[182] Compared to standing customs and traditions, human nature (*xing* 性) is *positively dynamic* in the equation of human culture—place *any* newborn in *any* culture and he or she will come to embody that culture and speak its language. That is an astounding degree of plasticity. Equal to the force of such spontaneous adaptation, however, is the force of established cultural habits (*xi* 習). Once cultural attitudes are adopted, they change only gradually. Human nature indeed exhibits enormous flexibility; but as Dewey says, it is wrong to think that "patterns of desire, belief, and purpose do not have a force comparable to the momentum of physical objects once they are set in motion, and comparable to the inertia, the resistance to movement, possessed by the same objects when they are at rest. Habit, not original human nature, keeps things moving most of the time, about as they have moved in the past."[183] So spins what William James refers to as the "enormous fly-wheel of society, its most precious conservative agent."[184]

With this we have established the perennial contest that Dewey identifies in his lectures on "Social and Political Philosophy"—the battle between the "radical" who mistakes plasticity in human nature (*xing* 性) for fluidity in *custom*, and the "conservative" who mistakes stability in custom (*xi* 習) for fixity in *human nature*. The more pragmatically minded "progressive" avoids both mistakes. Alongside Confucius, the progressive recognizes that cultural refinement (*wen* 文) and raw nature (*zhi* 質) are equal ingredients in the social order. When it comes to bringing them together productively, the Confucian and the progressive rely on intelligence (or *ming* 明) rather than preconceived schema. He or she realizes that to radically seize upon a predetermined *end* or to conservatively preserve some expired *means* are two species of the same stupidity—"Shoot pulling" in the one case and "Stump watching" in the other. The way to sustain *dao* 道 in the world is to begin with existing conditions and to find a way to foster their *growth*. This means actively selecting what is good (*zeqishanzhe* 擇其善者) and securing it in a manner that retains continuity between means-and-ends (*dao*). Thus, both the Confucian and the progressive advocate a "gradualist" approach to social reform, one that neither abruptly forces change nor allows stagnation to continue.

The goal, as always, is to achieve and preserve harmony (*he* 和). Again—this is what actually grows (*sheng* 生) things by bringing nature-and-nurture circuits into balanced equilibrium (*ping* 平) so that things can extend lushly (*fengchang* 豐長). Socially, the democratic ideal of growth is that all members of a community find meaning/significance (*yi* 義) in a dynamic, well-ordered whole (*li* 理). This is what human beings desire by nature. As Confucius observes: "When harmony prevails, there is no lack of people."[185] Who would *not* want to join a community in which each one enjoys one's own share (*fen* 分) while appreciating one another's contributions to the value shared by being together? Dewey came away from China with a clear vision of what such a society looks like: "From the standpoint of the individual, it consists in having a responsible share according to capacity in forming and directing the activities of the groups," and "from the standpoint of the groups, it demands liberation of the potentialities of members of a group in harmony with the interests and goods which are common."[186] This is the ideal of harmony (*he*). As we have seen, Dewey's approach to its realization is one of "meliorism," thus avoiding the "Optimism/Pessimism" extremes between which the "radical" and "conservative" invite us to swing.

Further developing Dewey's approach, Scott R. Stroud introduces what he calls "orientational meliorism," a model that encompasses not only *how* we might change the world for the better but also how we regard the world as we do so. To paraphrase Stroud, there are three basic aspects to the melioristic project: (1) end-in-view, (2) means, and (3) unit of change.[187] We must have some notion of the change we wish to make, how we intend to make it, and what unit or "vector" enables it to be made. Stroud alerts us to the fact that such determinations are not made in a vacuum. There is an operative situation, which is how the subject relates to experience or activity at the most general level. This is what he identifies as "orientation," and he identifies three elements within it. Paraphrasing again, these are: *first*, the world (ontological), *second*, value (axiological), and *third*, viable paths of action (actional).[188] As Stroud observes: "Such orientations are not necessarily consciously held and noticed at all times; as habitual ways of thinking (like habits of the body) they often operate without conscious acknowledgement."[189] Stroud focuses most of his "orientational" efforts on one of Dewey's central concerns: shifting focus *away* from fixed ends toward an "attention to the present, concrete situation in all of its richness."[190] Such an orientation is key to both the acceptance of Dewey's form of meliorism and its actual practice.

The habits that prevent us from assuming such "orientational meliorism" are largely cultural. Recall the "primitive mindset" and the wholeness that it expresses through its "hunting vocation." In prehistoric times, there was not much desire or need for hominids to go beyond their present activities to secure some greater meaning "in the clouds," as Dewey says.[191] The Daoist primitivist is correct in noting that with the advent of human culture, something changed. According to Richerson and Boyd, the evolution of horizontal cultural transmission resulted in an explosion of adaptive techniques and proposals. Culture proliferated alongside the processes by which social learning expanded beyond the vertical bounds of family and clan to include those more "culturally" qualified—*teachers, experts, priests, doctors, heroes, prophets, technicians, philosophers*, and so on. The human mind, along with its spoken and written languages, evolved to accommodate the transmission of newly adaptive ideas from such varied sources. There was, however, a design tradeoff being made. While we became good at generating and sharing *good* ideas, we also became adept at generating and sharing *bad* ones. Richerson and Boyd take a particular interest in certain religious ideas, many of which "seem to be good for people's mental health and for creating strong communities," but which also have us "playing host to sometimes spectacularly pathological cultural variants."[192]

The idea that "Heaven has a plan for us and for the world" belongs squarely in the pathological category. It is maladaptive however one looks at it. First, it is seductive. Like refined sugar, it gives us something that we want all at once without the normal labor that goes into securing it. Thus it becomes the ultimate recipe for *passivity*—granting endless "moral holidays" as the fate of the world is left in more powerful hands. Second, it diminishes the constructive human role in developing culture, tending thereby to augment the kind of tribalism that divides the cultural "us," for whom "Heaven has a plan," from the cultural "them" for whom it does not. Such ideas continue to inflict tremendous harm on the human species, and they set us positively against the "Way of Nature" (*tiandao* 天道). Philosophically, the early Confucians are far more sophisticated than this, and as a result their religious insights are deeper and truer. In chapter 8, we explore how this is so. Also, we experiment with connecting Dewey's religious sensibilities to aspects of early Chinese thought. Once having done this, we will bring these volumes to a close.

8

Integration and Religiousness

> I have spoken in many places throughout China, and wherever I go, I sense an atmosphere of optimism and freshness of outlook and viewpoint. Seeing you here today and sensing your aspirations and your optimism is a heartwarming experience for me.
>
> —Dewey, First Normal School, Fujian Province, April 1921

Integration (*cheng* 誠) and Adjustment

One of the signature contributions of Greek-medieval thought to Western civilization is its explication of the "transcendentals." Rather than growing passé, terms like unity (*unum*), goodness (*bonum*), truth (*verum*) and beauty (*pulchro*) remain central categories through which we reflect on human values that are deep and enduring.[1] Such notions continue to inspire and reward philosophical inquiry. One naturally envisions (or simply feels) such qualities whenever integration (*integritas*) is realized, such that unity, goodness, truth, and beauty converge in actual harmonies. Naturally, vocabularies vary from culture to culture, but the felt qualities of "harmony" and "integration" speak to us on a level that does not reduce to any specific cultural tradition. As universals, such qualities reveal our common heritage and aspirations.

As Henry Rosemont Jr. reminds us in his essay, "An Un-integrated Life is Not Worth Living," while ontological, cosmological, and theological claims differ among world religions, such differences "obscure the fact that the spiritual instructions for disciplines of self-cultivation are very similar in all of them."[2] Indeed, while an astonishing array of religious practice is generated within the matrix of culture, only the most hardened nominalist would deny that a kindred integrity is present in the Shabbat Meal, the Rōhatsu Sesshin, the Holy Eucharist, the Morning Pūjā, and the Daily Salah. However disparate such practices are, each expresses something about what human existence truly means. Such religious expressions are among those that strike, as Dewey says, "below the barriers that separate human beings from one another."³

Dewey found himself drawn to East Asian spirituality. Visiting morning chants in a Buddhist temple in Nanjing, he found it "more hypnotic than Catholic mass, more soothing to the nerves," and as he told his children: "If I were near, I would go in every day."⁴ Where does one look to find those features of religious experience that can be felt over-and-across cultures? What exactly *is* "religious experience"?

Over the course of corresponding with his friend John Graves in the summer of 1949, Dewey refined his notion of culture as the matrix in which human experience was communicated and where cross-cultural commonalities would register. Graves reiterated what Dewey already knew: "We must reach 'down' in order to find the common reality by which one culture can communicate with another," which is "better than reaching 'up' to the non-existent heavens."⁵ *Down* into our shared biological natures is where we must look in order to find those features that, as Irene Bloom says, give us that "deep yet un-testable sense for what the world is like—and why" and that deliver to us that "undeniable sense of being part of a whole."⁶ For both Bloom and Dewey, relinquishing the supernatural "Heaven" does nothing to diminish the religious quality of human experience—it rather restores it.

Tracing the evolution of Dewey's own natural piety, Steven C. Rockefeller links it to his encounter with Daoism. As Rockefeller explains: "Dewey's natural piety is suggested by his use of the mother image in describing nature," and upon encountering Daoism, Dewey was drawn to what he called its "remarkable exhibition of piety towards nature."⁷ While Dewey "did not explicitly develop this Daoist emphasis in his later writings on natural piety," Rockefeller notes that "it remained consistent with his mature idea of a sense of dependence on nature" in his post-China writings.⁸ It is difficult to establish with certainty that Daoism directly influenced Dewey's religious thought—but no matter. The connections between Dewey's naturalistic spirituality and Chinese sensibilities lend themselves to mutual illumination almost automatically. What impressed Dewey about East Asian spirituality was that, rather than focusing primarily on morality, it centers in his words on "the *aesthetic* element in its broadest sense," allying itself with "quiet, calm appreciation of the beauties of nature, literature and art."⁹ As Rockefeller explains, Dewey "well understood that achievements of a deep, enduring adjustment in life involves more than a moral faith and ethical activism fundamental as these are in his view." For Dewey, moral faith is a *species* of adjustment that is grounded in life-processes that run deeper into Nature (or *tian* 天). As Rockefeller notes, the "feelings of harmony, belonging to a whole, and peace" that accompany moral faith are equally present in philosophical insight, aesthetic experience, and mystical experience when these are attended by the same kind of core-level adjustments.¹⁰

In coming to understand this form of religiousness, one can begin with Si-Meng Confucian cosmology or with Dewey's aesthetics and arrive at the same basic insight. As developed in *Focusing the Familiar*, the word integration (*cheng* 誠) emerges as a term of art in describing the process of fully realizing (*jin* 盡) the natural dispositions (*xing* 性) of things. As a discursive process, integration defines the character of transactions that come to have aesthetic quality in their consummate phases. The text explains:

> Integration (*cheng*) is self-consummating, and its course is self-directing. Integration is an thing/event (*wu* 物) carried from beginning to end. Without such integration, nothing happens. This is why exemplary persons value integration. But integration is not limited to the consummation (*cheng* 成) of personhood alone—it is how everything becomes consummated. To consummate oneself is to become associated in one's living (*ren* 仁). To consummate an event is to achieve its realization. [Integration] is the quality/directional order (*de* 德) of a natural disposition (*xing*)—the *dao* 道 of coordinating (*he* 合) the inner-and-outer (*neiwai* 內外). Thus, whenever [integration] takes place, it is aesthetically right (*yi* 宜).[11]

As early as his "Reflex Arc" essay, Dewey came to recognize that units of organic behavior involve "adjustment" in the form of an integrated coordination between the "inside" of the organism and the "outside" of its environment.[12] This insight eventually led him to recognize that such discursive processes take on aesthetic quality to the degree that their transactional courses—from beginning to end—mark a "consummation and not a cessation." As presented in *Art as Experience*, such events become individuated in the "developing movement towards [their] own consummation," thereby assuming the character of being "integral." As *Focusing the Familiar* observes, self-consummating integration by its very nature displays the quality of aesthetic rightness. Dewey observed the same.

Integration is a feature of the world that operates at all levels. As Dewey explains, the "mutual adaptation" of self-and-world results in "felt harmony" whenever transactions between them are brought to integral consummation even in the most ordinary of circumstances. One might experience a moment of aesthetic satisfaction poking at a campfire, working in a lab, or loading the dishwasher. The potential for such felt harmony in the course of normal activity (*yong* 庸) is at the heart of Dewey's understanding of religious experience. For when aesthetic experience becomes most pronounced, it "accentuates [the] quality of being a whole and of belonging to the larger, all-inclusive whole which is the universe in which we live." The religious feeling that comes with such integration does not cause one to transcend "the world" but rather plunges one deeper into it. As Dewey explains: "We are, as it were, introduced into a world beyond this world which is nevertheless the deeper reality of the world in which we live in our ordinary experiences."[13] Such religious experience reveals to us the deeper features of reality—features that are continuous with the world here and now. For Dewey, such a religious sensibility "[attaches] itself to the possibilities of nature and associated living," and thereby "[manifests] piety towards the actual."[14]

From the Chinese perspective, actual life-activities grow (*sheng* 生) through phases of agitation and equilibrium (*dongjing* 動靜); this occurs as each newly achieved state balances (*ping* 平) the forces of *yin* 陰 and *yang* 陽 energies on the great "Potter's Wheel of Nature." Emerging in the process are organic forms (*xing* 形) each of which possesses unity, goodness, truth, and beauty, manifesting a unique integrity (*cheng* 誠) as each directional order (*de* 德) finds its own consummation (*cheng* 成). Such forms realize oneness (*deyi* 得一) as units of possibility against an infinite continuum of possibilities (*taiyi* 太一). If spontaneity (*ziran* 自然) were not active, none of this would be happening—but it is active, and it is happening. The world to which we belong sustains within its own coherence (*li* 理) multiple levels of harmony (*he* 和) that continue to sponsor the annulment (*fan* 反) of possibilities in an endless process (*dao* 道). An unimaginable series of contingencies have resulted in the dispositions (*xing* 性) of things as we currently find them. By their very nature, each of these dispositions registers struggle, survival, and growth—a kind of ongoing intelligence (*ming* 明) that has achieved and sustains means-end continuity in its own particular *dao*-activity.

The human contribution amounts to the ability to integrate such dispositions through further acts of intelligence and to "educate" (*educare*) them so as to secure richer, deeper, and more inclusive harmonies. *Focusing the Familiar* distinguishes the natural intelligence that stems from *dao* 道-activity from that which results from human-level education (*jiao* 教)—but it also restores their continuity, thus making human culture at home in the universe. As the text says: "Intelligence that arises from integration (*cheng* 誠) is attributed to natural disposition (*xing* 性), while integration that arises through intelligence (*ming* 明) is attributed to education (*jiao* 教). But wherever there is integration there is intelligence, and wherever there is intelligence there is integration."[15] Thus, while organic-form intelligence and human-level intelligence are executed differently, their status in the universe is the same.[16]

The human enterprise thus lies wholly within Nature (or *tian* 天) and accords with the generic features that characterize it. Among these features is what Chenyang Li calls "deep harmony," the tendency to arrive at multi-scalar equilibrium with "difference and creative tension" factored in and "without a pre-set order" guiding things.¹⁷ All of our successes and failures, triumphs and struggles, hopes and fears, are integrated within such patterns (*li* 理) as they intersect and evolve in Nature (*tian*). In the overall harmony of the cosmos, events at smaller scales correlate with rhythms at larger scales in ways that we can scarcely comprehend—with change occurring in all directions (*xiang* 相). There is peace to be had in realizing this. As Dewey says, "Through the phases of perturbation and conflict, there abides the deep-seated memory of an underlying harmony, the sense of which haunts life like the sense of being founded on a rock."¹⁸ Through every phase of change, toward the better or the worse, harmony (*he* 和) remains the cosmological constant—the condition for the possibility of there even *being* orders that change for the better or the worse. If harmony were not operative, nothing would be happening—but it is operative, and things are happening. Among the things that are happening is each one of *us*. Each human life in real time—a singular and astronomically remote opportunity to develop an allotted set of capacities (*xingming* 性命) within a specific set of mandated conditions (*tianming* 天命).

Focusing the Familiar thus begins with the premise that "What Nature mandates is a natural disposition" (*tianmingzhiweixing* 天命之謂性). In this instance, what Nature mandates has the quality of availing itself to growth and development. Human nature, in other words, is to be furthered along and improved upon through education.¹⁹ As in the *Mencius*, this involves the process of getting the most (*jin* 盡) out of what is given and thus realizing the capacities present in one's nature. Sagehood is described as a process of bringing one's disposition as well as that of other things into harmony on the most inclusive and broadest scale possible. This is always the working ideal in Confucianism. Those who realize this ideal become almost "god-like" in stature. The text explains:

> Only those most fully integrated (*zhicheng* 至誠) into the world are able to get the most out of their natures (*jinxing* 盡性). Getting the most out of one's nature, one is then able to get the most out of the natures of others. Getting the most out of the natures of others, one is then able to get the most out of the natures of things and events. Getting the most out of the natures of things and events, one can assist in the transforming and nourishing processes of Nature-and-Earth. Assisting in the transforming and nourishing processes of Nature-and-Earth, one becomes the third member in a triad with both.⁹²

At this apex of co-creativity, humans become the "counterparts of Nature" (*peitian* 配天). Elsewhere, they are simply equated with Nature (*tian* 天).²⁰

Sages performed this role in the distant past, and according to Mencius, anyone can become a sage. Sagacity means nothing more than getting the most (*jin*) out of conditions as they stand and achieving the optimal degree of pattern (*li* 理) and rightness (*yi* 義) available in one's circumstances.

There is no preexisting, schematic, or perfect "self" waiting in the future that the sage proceeds to realize. Rather, "the *whole* self is an ideal, an imaginative projection," as Dewey teaches. This is understood when Dewey's positive account of "imagination" is recalled. "The healthy imagination," Dewey writes, "deals not with the unreal, but with the mental realization of what is suggested. Its exercise is not a flight into the purely fanciful and ideal, but a method of expanding and filling in what is real."[21] As Mencius suggests, each person is capable of becoming a sage. The process is only initiated, however, when the capacity (*cai* 才) to do so is taken not as a given or guarantee but as an opportunity to grow and expand the depth and breadth of one's actual connections. Each allotted lifespan (*ming* 命) is an opportunity to do so.

Thus, the religious dimension of sagehood in the Confucian tradition is revealed not through the operation of some presumptive "end" but through the function of imagination. As Dewey reminds us: "The idea of a thoroughgoing and deep-seated harmonizing of the self with the Universe (as a name for the totality of conditions with which the self is connected) operates only through imagination." The "end" is not already *there*, driving the process of its own realization. That makes little philosophical sense and offers not much actual meaning. Rather, "taking sagehood as an ideal," as Stephen C. Angle tells us, "means striving to improve oneself. It means committing oneself to being on the road to sagehood." Precisely because achieving sagehood involves harmony (*he* 和), the road cannot be mapped out in advance. It needs to be creatively "articulated" in the process of walking it. This is where imagination plays its critical role. "With imagination," Angle writes, "we can see and achieve new points of balance" along the way.[22]

In Chinese natural philosophy, we know that balance (*ping* 平) involves encountering agitations (*dong* 動) that call for *adjustment*. For both Dewey and William James, such "adjustment" is the key to religious experience. For James, it involves "harmoniously adjusting ourselves" to orders that lie invisibly beyond us, as well as the more private integration of our psychologically "divided selves."[23] For Dewey, it involves "a fulfillment that reaches to the depth of our being—one that is an adjustment of our whole being with the conditions of existence."[24] Within the framework of Dewey's "cultural naturalism," such fulfillment at the human-level is rooted in our biological histories. This is also the case with "integration."[25] For organisms generally, integration and adjustment "lend deep and enduring support to the processes of living"[26] and their desirability is genetically established. In human consciousness, the "loss of integration with environment and recovery of union" registers emotionally, and such feelings sow the seeds of our aesthetic and religious sensibilities.[27] Emergent, human-level structures and functions fall in and out of balance with the conditions that sustain them, and commensurable cycles of satiation-need, pleasure-pain, and serenity-anxiety are thus experienced. Such responses, which are enhanced along with the complexity of their subject matters, retain continuity with primitive structures in the human brain and central nervous system. How could it be otherwise? Again, this is not "reductionism" so long as the principle of continuity (*yi* 一) is properly understood.[28]

The idea that human-level experience involves bi-lateral "adjustments" in a dynamic matrix of conditions recalls the "tension" with Nature (*tian* 天) that Michael J. Puett detects in Mencius' philosophy.[29] It is easy to miss the bi-lateral nature of this tension in the *Mencius*, just as it is easy to overlook the same in Dewey's writings. Dewey explains that adjustment is a compound term that signifies *two* aspects that differ in terms of the facts entailed and the responses involved. First, there is *accommodation*, which entails that "there are conditions we meet that cannot be changed." Second, there is *adaptation*, which entails that we "re-act against conditions and endeavor to change them to meet our wants and demands."[30] Mencius likewise understands our relation to Nature's mandate (*tianming* 天命) as one that involves both *accommodation* and *adaptation*. As Puett argues, Mencius does not advise us to invariably accept whatever *tian* does.[31] "One goes along with and accommodates only those conditions that are proper to accept," says Mencius.[32] If the wall is about to collapse, then *get out of the way*. To charge Mencius with "fatalism" or to identify him as one who simply "obeys Heaven" attributes only *accommodation* to his position and is thus a mistakenly one-sided reading.

A similarly one-sided reading is sometimes attributed to Dewey. John Lachs, for instance, takes issue with what he regards as Dewey's overly enthusiastic approach to "growth," which he feels downplays the fact that not every situation invites our adaptive reconstruction. Lachs suggests that "intelligent pragmatists have to be stoics from time to time," and in certain situations, "we are better advised to accept what cannot be changed and thereby reduce frustration and pain."[33] Scott R. Stroud points out that Dewey's compound notion of adjustment already addresses Lach's concern. "Adaptation," Stroud notes, "is only *half* of what Dewey means by adjustment to an environment."[34] It ignores *accommodation*. As Dewey teaches: "There are conditions we meet that cannot be changed," and we thus "modify our own particular attitudes in accordance with them."[35] Thus, neither Dewey nor Mencius succumbs to the "Fatalism/Voluntarism" trap. Each is *realistic* in accepting some circumstances and not accepting others. In each tradition, discerning which conditions to accept and which to reject can be understood as the work of intelligence (or *ming* 明).

This work is rarely easy, but at least the applicable prayer is simple enough to remember: "*God, grant us the serenity to accept things that cannot be changed, the courage to change things that can be, and the wisdom to know the difference.*"

Recovering the Forfeiture

As *Focusing the Familiar* reminds us, the Chinese world is a haunted one. "The power of the gods and spirits is profound," we read. "Looking we do not see them, and listening we do not hear them. Yet, they embody things and cannot be bracketed out."[36] Believing in such paranormal phenomena does not automatically signal supernaturalism. As Philip J. Ivanhoe explains: "While these various entities were thought to be of a 'higher' order, they were never conceived of as supernatural in the sense of existing in a realm distinct from and independent of the world in which we live. Rather, they were viewed as more powerful and ethereal members of the ordinary world."[37] Strictly speaking, such paranormal beliefs are not *wholly* inconsistent with Dewey's naturalism. Such naturalism would simply insist that if ghosts and spirits *do* exist then a natural account of their existence is available even if we do not currently have it. There is no scientific *knowledge* one way or the other regarding ghosts, so the proposition that they *might* exist is not entirely "out of gear" with what we otherwise know to be true. William James is well known for keeping an open mind about the possibility of ghosts—Dewey, not so much. Dewey did, however, declare himself "agnostic" on the question in a 1928 survey by the *New York Times*. Dewey observed simply that "psychical researchers [have] not come up with significant scientific evidence in support of the idea."[38]

Dewey's main gripe with the world of spirits is that, as commonly entertained, the afterlife is a bad idea to keep promoting. Like other humanistic-leaning thinkers, Dewey recognizes that there is a "fatal back-kick inherent in the position that life here loses all ethical meaning and basis if there is not personal immortality," and that stressing such a future existence results in "the morally and socially injurious consequences of putting practical preoccupation with another world in place of active interest in this one."[39] John Stuart Mill observes the same. He worries about "those who are so wrapped up in self that they are unable to identify their feelings with anything which will survive them, or to feel their life prolonged in their younger contemporaries and in all who help to carry on the progressive movement of human affairs." Such souls, observes Mill, "require the notion of another selfish life beyond the grave, to keep up any interest [in the present one]."[40]

One noteworthy thing about Chinese ghosts, however, is that they retain their own "active interest" in the present world because, as Ivanhoe suggests, they never really leave it. This might mitigate some of Dewey's and Mill's concerns. The widespread belief in ghosts among Chinese people (at least 87 percent of college students in Taiwan believe in ghosts)[41] does not make them take "this world" less seriously—arguably it causes them to take it even *more* seriously. In any case, Dewey does not expect people to stop believing in ghosts. As he indicates in *Unmodern Philosophy*, distinguishing between the "ordinary and extraordinary" is a universal psychological trait in humans, forming "the common matrix out of which emerged all the world's philosophies." We must remember, however, that for Dewey these two regions only marked out "by way of anticipation what are later called the natural and the supernatural." In the primitive mind, the ordinary-and-extraordinary "overlapped and blended," such that there was "no sharp division between heaven and earth [as] separated sources or realms."[42] Dewey's naturalism, properly understood, seeks to restore such primitive continuity. Nature (or *tian* 天) encompasses both the ordinary-and-extraordinary with nothing "supernatural" left over.

Once this is realized—*genuinely* realized and not merely understood—the religious dividends are enormous. As Dewey says: "[Humans] do not throw away their belief in the most valuable things of life unless they feel themselves possessed of a sure way to regain the lost treasure and more."[43] Dewey's argument in *A Common Faith* unfolds accordingly: it is formulated to recover what has been needlessly forfeited to the supernatural. The "Supernatural/Natural" dualism erects two separate regions, and over time the more valuable of life's treasures have been granted supernatural status and stowed accordingly. As Dewey observes, this process involves an intellectual conversion that is more a consequence of Greek-medieval metaphysics than of any empirically justifiable operation. It is taken for granted that the supernatural region transcends "the world" and thus stands outside of time and change. Once something is located *there*, it becomes eternal and spiritual.

Dewey uses "Justice" as an example. Justice is a *real quality* "embedded in the makeup of the actually existing world," one that is genuinely realized through our efforts. We value Justice so much that we count it among the attributes of an all-powerful and eternal God. Having done so, it takes its place among "antecedently existing actualities" the perfect realization of which is fixed as the alpha and omega of God's plan.[44] But once such status is asserted, why bother fighting for Justice in *this* world? God already *guarantees* its realization in the next. Such an assurance only obscures and devalues the actual status and operations of Justice.

As Steven C. Rockefeller observes, Dewey is an "American Feuerbach."[45] Like Ludwig Feuerbach, Dewey recognizes that the qualities attributed to the supernatural God are mental amalgams that dialectically synthesize the spiritual essence of the human experience with an "essence of Nature which is different."⁴⁶ We perform such mental operations as a form of self-preservation or perhaps for other "therapuetic" reasons, but this only alienates us from the genuine source of religious experience, which is the *one and only natural world* to which we belong. We thus become estranged from the natural forms of meaning and satisfaction that accrue as we work to secure values and to realize ideals in the world as it is.

In one of his more Hegelian moments, Dewey forecasts in *A Common Faith* a dialectical process by which the inherent contradiction of such estrangement gives way to the restoration of the natural status of religious experience. In the "first stage," human experience is understood to be so corrupt that only supernatural qualities can save it. In the "second stage" (which Dewey thinks is the current stage), liberal theologians begin to note that qualities found in human experience are akin to those values that we deem distinctively religious. In the "third stage," it is realized that "the values prized in those religions that have ideal elements are idealizations of things characteristic of natural association, which have then been projected into a supernatural realm for safe-keeping and sanction."⁴⁷ With this realization, the "Supernatural/Natural" dualism is overcome and continuity between the ideal-and-actual is restored. What is crucial to recognize is that, in the process of dialectically collapsing this dualism, *nothing of value is lost*. Whatever is actually *real* does not suddenly become *un*real just because we stop projecting a fabricated dualism upon it. The universe remains as it is, imbued with all the religious qualities that it ever actually had—only now we do not presume that such qualities belong to some separate, supernatural realm from which "the world" is somehow removed. True religiousness is thus restored.

In what Dewey calls the "third stage," religion becomes a partner with culture, which generates "connections-and-distinctions" between humans-and-nature for a whole range of human interests: artistic, scientific, educational, political, philosophical, spiritual, and so on. The stubbornness of the "Supernatural/Natural" dualism is what prevents culture from fully realizing this function. The obstacle is not in the universe, but in our selves. *We* want somehow to distinguish that part of us which is merely "animal nature" from that which is *super*-natural and properly "human." Again, Dewey understood that Chinese thinkers had already identified and overcome this problem: "the constant and unifying problem of Western philosophy throughout its whole career," which is "the relation [by] way of distinction-and-connection of what at a given period and in a given area has been taken [up as] *natural* on one side and as *human* on the other."⁴⁸ As Dewey writes: "It is my impression that those who created [Chinese] philosophy have been steadily aware that the problem with which they were concerned is of the kind just stated than have the Westerners, who have been so preoccupied with the then-and-there urgent phase of the problem as not to have seen the forest because of the trees."⁴⁹ Texts like *Focusing the Familiar* record the considerable advances that Chinese philosophers made early on in their tradition—both by naturalizing human spirituality and by establishing the "continuity between Nature and the human" (*tianrenheyi* 天人合一).

Dewey's amateur Sinologist friend, W. R. Houston (we met him in chapter 5 of volume one), detected the resulting connection between Dewey's religiousness and Confucian philosophy straight away. "It's some years since I read your fine statement in *A Common Faith*, but I often think of it," Houston writes. "It isn't far from being a broader version of Master Kong's [Confucius'] insight into the worth of human relationships."⁵⁰ Once again, Houston is right on the mark. Like Dewey, Confucius had nothing to say about paranormal phenomena (*guai* 怪).⁵¹ He focused instead on the human dimension of religious practice.⁵² The Master advised deference toward the ghosts and spirits,⁵³ but like Dewey he discouraged us from thinking too much about the afterlife. Asked by Zilu about death, Confucius replies: "Not yet understanding life, how can one understand death?"⁵⁴

Indeed, death only begins to make sense once life is understood. At this stage in our inquiry, perhaps the question can be broached. Against the infinite nothingness (*wu* 無) at the base of things, what *is* a human life? On the cosmological level, each life-process realizes one unit of possibility against the Great Continuum (*taiyi* 太一). In this respect, Alfred North Whitehead is especially clear-headed about what being here (*you* 有) as opposed to not being here (*wu*) really means. He writes:

> We cannot understand the flux which constitutes our human experience unless we realize that it is raised above the futility of infinitude by various successive types of modes of emphasis which generate the active energy of a finite assemblage. The superstitious awe of infinitude has been the bane of philosophy. The infinite has no properties. All value is the gift of finitude which is the necessary condition for activity.⁵⁵

Dewey agrees with Whitehead that our philosophical obsession with the "infinite" is religiously unfruitful. As Whitehead suggests, the God to whom "infinity" is attributed is a God that has nothing to do with value or activity. We stand rather dumb before the no-thing (*wu*) from which all things originate. As Chapter 1 of the *Daodejing* teaches, the finite order that we witness here (*you*) is the true "Mother" of the ten thousand beings.

Dewey's apathy toward the God of infinity and nothingness is a matter of record. In 1927, he received an unsolicited manuscript from an eclectic high school teacher and former Baptist minister who was living in Honolulu. The book, *Man and His God*, was written under conditions practically divine: "I wrote this book while looking out on the widest stretch of wind-swept ocean that man can face," the author relates. "Like a half-bent bow an iridescent bay spreads over seven miles of rainbow sea from Diamond Head to the bold dome of Koko Head."[56] *Man and His God* deftly explores the idea of God as the mystical, infinite source of all such miracles and touches on topics ranging from quantum physics to Yoga. Dewey was open to things like quantum physics and Yoga, but the overall tone of the book disagreed with him. "I have received and read your manuscript, and I hardly know what to say," Dewey replies back. He explains that the book is eloquent and competent but that he feels no sympathy with it, "and I use sympathy here in an emotional rather than intellectual sense," he adds. Dewey admits that he has no substantive refutation of the book's premise that God is the infinite, mystical source of the universe—but that is not the issue. "[It] doesn't touch me," he writes, "it's not what religion means to me, and religion to my mind is much more important than God, who is the outgrowth of religion not its basis." Religious approaches that probe the mysteries of the infinite "leave me cold," Dewey writes. "When they are finished I have so much physics, and no religion." He is not passing judgment on the author. "For all I know this is my own limitation," Dewey writes. "You, and many others, perhaps most, get what I may call without meaning a disrespect a religious kick out of the mystery behind the physical universe. I get my kick somewhere else."[57]

Dewey's "kick" comes from what Whitehead refers to as the "active energies of finite assemblages" *here* and *now*. While such finite assemblages cannot be fully understood without reference to the infinite, *they themselves* are the true bearers of activity and value. These qualities cannot be derived from any separate, divine source. Such bifurcations only confuse things. "The idea of a double and parallel manifestation of the divine, in which the latter has superior status and authority," Dewey writes, "brings about a condition of unstable equilibrium."[58] The universe can be understood cosmologically as a triadic process (1-2-3) that provides the conditions for the possibility of value—but the resulting value is *here* and *now*, not at some other time or place. The world's better poets direct us to this truth. As Walt Whitman writes: "*There was never any more inception than there is now, nor any more youth or age than there is now; and will never be any more perfection than there is now, nor any more heaven or hell than there is now.*"[59] Reality is not somewhere else waiting to happen. Such thinking invariably manifests itself in psychological agitation and loss of spiritual focus.

Alternately, the true religious life is one that remains sharply focused on the ordinary world (*zhongyong* 中庸). As *Focusing the Familiar* teaches, preserving such focus is the *dao* 道 of the sage, and it is an exalted path to forge: "Like flowing water it sends out nourishment to the myriad beings— so towering, it reaches to the extremities of Nature (*tian* 天). So great is its immensity!" The text explains that the sage invests *entirely* in this world, attending to every article of ritual-custom (*li* 禮) and etiquette (*yi* 儀) with the utmost care and attention. Here, *Focusing the Familiar* further challenges the more programmatic accounts of the Confucian way. The text states clearly that there is no fixed "schema" to the resulting path—in other words, that *dao* does not "congeal" (*ning* 凝) until a sage with the requisite virtue (*de* 德) breaks it forward. As the text explains: "It waits for the person, and then it is trodden" (*daiqirenranhouxing* 待其人然後行). That *this* ongoing world is the locus of *dao*-in-the-making is precisely why exemplary persons take it so seriously. This is why "extending to the broadest expanse and exhausting every micro-detail, they maximize the elevation of intelligence (*ming* 明) and focus on the ordinary world (*zhongyong*)."[60]

It is important to remember that, on the cosmological level, it is not the Great Continuum (*taiyi* 太一) that sponsors order. Rather, harmony (*he* 和) and coherence (*li* 理) do that. As David L. Hall points out, an infinite storehouse of implicate possibilities running into one another results not in "order" but in the "sum of all orders" which is *chaos*.[61] While chaos (*hundun* 混沌) *allows* orders to emerge, the keeper of order is the harmony of the universe at any point in time—an existential configuration that stores (*zang* 藏) possibilities such that their annulment (*fan* 反) results in what is actually here (*you* 有). This further explains why leapfrogging over "the world" to embrace "the infinite" or nothingness (*wu* 無) only distances one from the source of human meaning and value. Every attainment of unity (*unum*), goodness (*bonum*), truth (*verum*) and beauty (*pulchro*) is grounded in the integration (*integritas*) of finite assemblages in actual harmonies. The tendency, again, is to abstract such axiological features from "the world" and to metaphysically convert them for eternal stowage somewhere else. In the Platonic tradition, such formal patterns (*wen* 文) are separated from raw material (*zhi* 質) and converted into ideas (*eidos*) that transcend their instantiations. Such bifurcation cannot occur, however, without diminishing the value that resides precisely in the continuity (*yi* 一) between form-and-matter.

As Sing-nan Fen observes, "It has been very unfortunate in the history of thought that, when philosophers talked about patterns, they did not take into full recognition that patterns are always patterns of *relations*, for patterns would have no specific content unless the relatedness of the parts within the pattern were specified."[62] As Robert C. Neville says, the unity of the relations *is* the value, which is "resident in the harmonic structure of a thing, including each of the concrete components harmonized."[63] Fen wholly concurs: "A relation would have no significance unless the relations organized themselves into a pattern," and "unless it conveys a pattern of relation, it is not significant, and thus not meaningful."[64] Recalibrating religious sensibilities so as to appreciate the fact that value resides *only* in concrete relations recovers the forfeiture that we have surrendered to the supernatural realm. Culturally, we can no longer afford such a forfeiture. Dewey and the Chinese help us to take it back.

Ideals and the Actual

As we have seen, Dewey shows little interest in the God of infinite perfection that we commonly associate with the mysteries of creation and eternity. Given its "remoteness and abstractness," William James is similarly numb to this God, showing more interest in the scruffier God who labors alongside us "in the dust of our human trials."[65] Dewey also has sympathy for this God, and he gives a subtle account of its function in relation to religious faith.

In order to understand Dewey's ideas of God and faith, it is important to recognize that by collapsing the "Supernatural/Natural" dualism one does not thereby collapse the *relations* between its residual natural elements. Under the "Supernatural/Natural" dualism, ideals were metaphysically hypostatized and removed from "the world." When these operations were performed, "faith" amounted to believing in the existence of the hypostatized entities. For Dewey, such "intellectual faith" actually evinces a lack of "*moral* faith," which is the faith that is truly "religious." Once the "Supernatual/Natural" dualism is collapsed, ideals no longer exist as already realized actualities—i.e., there are no *things* out there to "believe" in. Faith *itself* thus becomes the substance (*hypostasis*) of things hoped for, the evidence of things not seen. With this, faith becomes both "religious" and "moral." Ideals continue to operate as they always have—as modalities of the *real*. In Chinese terms, they exist as genuine *possibilities* stored (*zang* 藏) in what is actually here (*you* 有).

The only way to apprehend such possibilities, Dewey teaches, is through *imagination*. "An ideal is not an illusion because imagination is the organ through which it is apprehended," he reminds us. "For *all* possibilities reach us through the imagination."[66] Again, imagination for Dewey "deals not with the unreal, but with the mental realization of what is suggested."[67] Such possibilities are suggested in anything that remains open to further growth: e.g., in an existential disposition (*xing* 性) the nature of which is uncultivated, or in present capacities (*cai* 才) the outcomes of which have yet to be determined. Just as in the Confucian tradition, religiousness for Dewey can only be realized through such modalities.

Dewey finds it remarkable that human experience is guided by unseen ideals. It is astounding that "things unrealized in fact come home to us and have power to stir us." He is so in awe of this fact that he is willing to give the name "God" to the function that enables it—namely, the function by which "ideal possibilities [are] unified through imaginative realization and projection" amidst actual conditions, which are then improved upon by "the action that gives [the ideals] coherence and solidity." As Dewey explains, "It is this *active* relation between ideal and actual to which I would give the name 'God.'"⁶⁸ Of course, Dewey does not insist that such a name be used. One can call it whatever one wants. His main point is that there is a function in the universe that enables humans to imagine better futures while ensuring that, as such futures become realized, the Way (*dao* 道) congeals (*ning* 凝) underfoot. Without this being the case, the religious life is unthinkable. "I would use God to denote *those* forces," writes Dewey, "which at a given time and place are actually working for the better."⁶⁹ Such a God remains "connected with all the natural forces and conditions—[humans] and human association—that promote the growth of the ideal and further its realization."⁷⁰ Any life that remains actively engaged with such forces takes on religious quality.

To celebrate Dewey's ninetieth birthday in 1949, a conference was held in his honor at the University of Illinois, Urbana. Sing-nan Fen delivered a talk entitled, "Dewey's Philosophy as a Program of Action." He reiterated Dewey's position that philosophy becomes a form of escapism when it concerns itself with "problems about another world," and that philosophers too often evoke "abstract terms such as God, Reality, Truth, [and] Spirit in order to evade responsibility for vital and crucial issues."⁷¹ To illustrate Dewey's ideas about the unification of the ideal-and-actual, Fen introduced his audience to Tao Xingzhi. In all likelihood, those assembled had never heard of him.

Tao Xingzhi was born in 1891 in a rural village in Anhui with the given name Wenjun 文濬. His father was a farmer and sold pickles and his mother was illiterate. Out of four children, Tao and his sister were the only ones to survive. When he was five years old, Tao entered a private school near his village and undertook ten years of study to prepare for the imperial exams. The system would be abolished in 1905, effectively closing his school. Tao then entered a local missionary school, but that school also closed in 1908. Now seventeen years old, Tao decided that he wanted to pursue medicine— a decision that he ascribed to the loss of his two siblings to childhood illnesses. He borrowed money from teachers, friends, and family, and travelled to Hangzhou to sit for matriculation exams at a prestigious Medical College run by missionaries. Tao passed the exams, but he was denied admittance to the college because he was not a Christian. He would eventually enroll at Nanjing University.⁷²

In Nanjing, Tao Xingzhi discovered the philosophy of Wang Yangming, the neo-Confucian philosopher who stressed that rectifying the world relied upon the "continuity of knowledge-and-action" (*zhixingheyi* 知行合一). Tao was so taken with Wang's philosophy that he changed his name to Zhixing 知行, "knowledge-and-action," which over time he changed to Xingzhi 行知, "action-and-knowledge," reflecting his evolving sensibilities regarding their relation. Toward the end of his studies at Nanjing, Tao was introduced to the "social gospel" and declared himself a Christian—but he showed no interest in theology or in churches. Christian moral teachings served only to solidify his understanding of the proactive humanism of Wang Yangming. Tao believed that if "God's kingdom" were to be realized on earth, its sole cause would be human perseverance and commitment in the world.[73] Christian morality and Confucian humanism thus fused in his mind, and his life assumed a resolute purpose (*zhi* 志) that only intensified as he moved forward.

Once again borrowing money, Tao Xingzhi attended the University of Illinois to begin doctoral studies in 1914. He began his coursework in Political Science, but was soon introduced to Dewey's philosophy and abruptly switched gears, transferring to Teacher's College in 1915. Tao spent two years at Teacher's College, and under the influence of Dewey and others his life purpose began to crystalize. Tao decided to devote his energies to improving education for the Chinese people. He returned to Nanjing in 1917 (never completing his dissertation) with the firm conviction that education was the means through which China would achieve social, economic, cultural, and spiritual renewal. His aspirations were not set low. He aimed for "the miracle of eliminating illiteracy among 200 million people in ten years."[74]

Officialdom in Nanjing received Tao Xingzhi with mixed enthusiasm, but he had allies among prominent figures, including Dewey's other students. Important among these was Zhang Boling 張伯苓, who had recently returned from Teacher's College to found Nankai University in 1919. That very year, John and Alice Dewey arrived in Nanjing and Tao served as their host and coordinator, translating all of Dewey's public lectures during their visit. Tao also wrote his own articles and served in a variety of official capacities on behalf of educational reform. Along with Dewey, he was closely involved in preparing the "School Reform Decree" of 1922, which laid the groundwork for a transition away from the imperial exam system.[75]

In November 1923, Tao Xingzhi had a religious experience. He had recently co-founded the "Society for the Promotion of Popular Education" in Nanjing, and while working in the countryside he impulsively picked up a traditional cotton jacket, skullcap, and peasant shoes. He had been wearing Western-style outfits since his student days. When he put on the traditional clothing, something clicked at the core of his being. He wrote to his sister, "I felt completely a Chinese and felt much closer to people in general." While he was grateful to have received an international education, there was something about the "foreign upper-class air" among his peers that had produced in Tao an inner conflict. He was himself a peasant boy, and he had yet to reconcile that aspect of himself with the man he had become. Somehow, putting on the clothing triggered a core readjustment. He likened the moment to what Buddhists call "enlightenment" (*juewu* 覺悟) and described its effects as follows: "It was like the Yellow River bursting its dikes. I flowed back toward the path of the common Chinese."76

Having rediscovered his own spirit, Tao Xingzhi retired his Western outfits and threw his energies even more fully into his work. In 1927, his

Figure 8.1. Tao Xingzhi wearing the traditional Chinese clothing that he had come to prefer, date unknown.

efforts culminated in the establishment of the "Experimental Village Normal School" at Xiaozhuang 曉莊 in Jiangsu province, founded with the intent of preparing a new generation of teachers to transform the state of rural education.[77] Tao had become increasingly convinced that China's future relied on bottom-up, grassroots activism. Top-down, ideological movements were too prone to controversy in a political system so desperately unstable. He placed his hope in the individual teachers who passed through Xiaozhuang. As the school grew in size it became a *de facto* center for village renewal, providing space for agricultural forums, cultural events, and community meetings. In 1929, Dewey's colleague, William H. Kilpatrick, visited Xiaozhuang and was deeply impressed. He praised Tao as a pioneer in rural education and community renewal.[78]

Tao Xingzhi did what he could to keep Xiaozhuang above politics, but that was difficult to do in the existing climate. By 1930, the Chinese Communist Party had become a serious threat to the Nationalist government. Some of Tao's students expressed communist sympathies, and several people associated with the school (including Tao himself) participated in anti-Japanese demonstrations, which were seen as recruiting tools for the communist movement. Also, due to the activity of bandits in the area, Tao needed to provision his school with modest weaponry, and this required alliances with regional powers. With Chiang Kai-shek now in power, the Guomindang moved in 1930 to purge China of pro-communist groups as well as "future" pro-communist groups which it called "becoming-red elements." Tao's school was identified as the latter and forced to close in 1930. Tao was compliant but expressed defiance. "The school does not have a door," he wrote, "so it cannot be shut down. Only if one could shut down society, could he shut down Xiaozhuang."[79] Tao initially fled to Japan to avoid arrest, but he soon returned to China and based himself in the French concession in Shanghai where he would be safe from prosecution.[80]

From there, Tao Xingzhi initiated the "Little Teacher System," an enormously popular rural education program through which schoolchildren were taught how to improve their own literacy by serving as tutors to illiterate adults. Tao also founded a school for orphans.[81] His efforts had gained traction and literacy rates steadily improved. Dewey wrote to Tao in 1944, assuring him that he was "glad to know [his] health remains good and that [his] educational work goes on, even under the difficult conditions."[82] As the Chinese civil war intensified, however, conditions became increasingly difficult for Tao. While he never joined the Communist Party, he had developed Marxist sympathies and decided to join the Democratic League. He had also written critically against the Nationalist government. In 1946, right-wing assassins murdered two prominent members of the Democratic League, and Tao learned that he was next on the list to be killed.

His immediate reflex was to work more vigorously. So, that's what he did. Within two weeks of learning that assassins were pursuing him, Tao Xingzhi suffered a stroke and died. He was fifty-six years old. Upon learning of his death, Dewey and Kilpatrick sent a cablegram from New York. "We honor Dr. Tao for his unsurpassed and heroic devotion in behalf of a better education for the common people of China," they wrote. A memorial for him was held at Teacher's College.[83] Dewey was heartened in 1947 to receive an update from the director of one of Tao's schools that the work of his "beloved Chinese student" continued in spite of his untimely death.[84]

As Sing-nan Fen told the audience in Urbana, Tao Xingzhi "was one of the best students that Dewey could ever have had."[85] What made him such a good student was that Tao did what Dewey hoped that his Chinese students would do—not copy or parrot his teachings, but change and adapt them creatively to their own environments. Tao experienced limitations in Dewey's pedagogical theories and adjusted his practices (and his own theories) accordingly. Such adjustments are reflected in his decision to take what was then the all-purpose Dewey slogan, "Education is Life" (*jiaoyujishenghuo* 教育即生活), and reverse it—such that "Life is Education."[86] Rather than envision the school as an environment that passes naturally into life experience, Tao found that life experience *is* the school in rural China. Society itself is the "living book" (*huoshu* 活書) that schools must teach. The school is the extension and conduit of the community. Just as Dewey had refined his theories in light of his own experiences at the Lab School in Chicago, Tao refined his theories in light of his own experiences in rural China.

Tao Xingzhi further embodied Dewey's teachings by realizing that philosophy must, as Sing-nan Fen argues, engender "struggle for a better state in this world."[87] By taking on the struggle of improving the lives of those less fortunate, Tao lived what Dewey would call a life that was "religious in quality." As Dewey writes in *A Common Faith*: "Any activity pursued in behalf of an ideal end against obstacles and in spite of threats of personal loss because of conviction of its general and enduring value is religious in quality."[88] Tao remains an enduring exemplar of such goodness and truth.

The confluence of Dewey's religious sensibilities with his activism precludes the identification of such goodness (*bonum*) and truth (*verum*) with any static, already realized Being (*ens*). In this way, Dewey stands opposed to traditions that seek to prove that "[such] things are not ideal but are real—real not *as* meanings and ideals, but as existential being."[89] Such thinking, for Dewey, separates the ideal from reality and from nature and thus erects dualisms where none exist. As he explains:

> [What] I have been criticizing is the *identification* of the ideal with a particular Being, especially when that identification makes

necessary the conclusion that this Being is outside of nature, and what I have tried to show is that the ideal itself has roots in natural conditions; it emerges when the imagination idealizes existence by laying hold of the possibilities offered to thought and action.[90]

Having embraced the philosophy of Wang Yangming, it makes sense that Tao Xingzhi and others like him would also find Dewey's approach attractive. Each thinker collapses the dualism between ideals and the actual by focusing on concrete activities that improve the world.

In noting the overlap between Wang Yangming and Dewey, Warren G. Frisina forwards what he calls a "radical" reading of the former. Frisina's reading, however, strikes me as rather sensible. Frisina proposes that, when considering the "continuity of knowledge-and-action" (*zhixingheyi* 知行合一), we should take Wang literally and seriously. Thought and action *really are* one thing, and "those of us who fall short of sagehood fail to recognize the unity." Thus, as Frisina sees it, sages are not those who *achieve* the "complete integration of knowledge and action"—for as he argues, "that already exists." The sage instead is one who *recognizes* that thought-and-action is continuous and lives accordingly. "The knowledge associated with Confucian sagehood is always a form of action, a creative response to the world's prompting," writes Frisina. What the world prompts from us is a compound response: see-the-ideal-in-the-actual-and-*act*-to-realize-it. As always, the normative measure for such action is harmony (*he* 和). As Frisina writes: "The cultivation of more complicated harmonic patterning is the ontological task undertaken by the Confucian sage."[91]

Mencius teaches that anyone can become a sage. "The sage is the same type (*lei* 類) as we are," he writes. Barley seeds provide an analogy in making his point. "Let barley seeds be sown and covered with soil, the ground being the same, and the time of planting the same, it grows rapidly—and in due seasonal course, it ripens."[92] The Confucian tradition does not, however, maintain that all people are born with the same inherent *probability* of ripening into illustrious sages. As Edward Slingerland observes: the Master recognizes a "hierarchy of natural ability" when it comes to such realization.[93] Sagehood comes naturally for some, while others have to work at it. Some sages flourish grandly, while others remain modest and anonymous. Some sages appear when the time is ripe, while others arrive before their time.

Given the peculiar logic of barley seeds, Mencius' analogy works rather well. Barley seeds are not, in fact, identical in their strength and fitness. Like many plants, barley produces seeds that vary in size according to their position in the inflorescence or fruit. Seeds at the center of the flower are larger and more robust than seeds at the base and top. Studies have been done to determine why natural selection has not resulted in a reduction in size variance in favor of larger seeds. Since the larger seeds flourish more easily, why aren't all barley seeds large? As B. E. Giles explains, the key question is whether position effect in the inflorescence (which is a spatial quality) contains genetic variation that is available for selection. This is a tricky question, but he concludes that it does supply such information. Evidence suggests that, "position effects are inherited, that variation in their organization and expression exists, and that a seed of any size can regenerate the size distribution." This last point affords some perspective. As Giles finds, "Position effects are the agents creating these size distributions and they *ensure* that seed size variation is produced every generation." Why is this so? Because "seeds of different sizes germinate, grow, and reproduce at different rates in the same environment," suggesting that, "seed size variation could be advantageous in randomly varying environments."[94]

There is sense to be made from this. If humans really *are* like barley seeds, then each person *is* capable of becoming a sage in some environment with a certain degree of natural fitness. Not everyone is born to move Nature-and-Earth in their own time, but each person can play a role at some level. Among the objectives of an individual life is to find that role and to realize it. As Dewey says, each of us must "[throw] into the moving unbalanced balance of things our puny strength," knowing that "such thought and effort is one condition of the coming into existence of the better."[95] In the broader scheme of things, we do not always see how our better thoughts and actions improve the world. We must realize, however, that even our small seeds produce fruit with larger seeds down the line, and those seeds can result in magnificent things. Remember—it was a pickle farmer in Anhui who nurtured the boy who transformed rural China.

Communion and the Human Spirit

Dewey cleaned out his office in 1919 before he left for Asia. Some boxes would not be reopened until 1928, seven years after he returned. Once Dewey finished sorting through those boxes, the wastebasket in his office was full. M. Hasley Thomas, who worked in the philosophy library adjacent to Dewey's office, secretly rummaged through Dewey's trash before the evening custodian arrived and pulled out a sheaf of poetry written by the philosopher. In 1939, when Herbert Schneider took possession of Dewey's office, he also found a "mess of loose scraps of poetry" stuffed in Dewey's desk. These also ended up in the wastebasket—and once again in Thomas' possession. Thomas quietly had the poetry preserved in the Columbiana Collection, where it came to light only after Dewey's death.[96]

Few people knew that Dewey wrote poetry. Apparently, he lacked confidence in his abilities and kept the hobby to himself. He did share his poetry with a select group of friends, e.g., the novelist and literary critic Waldo Frank. Frank recorded his impressions. "At heart [Dewey] is a Christian and a poet: a Christian who will accept no written gospel," he writes. Dewey, says Frank, wanders through the world "modest as a saint, wistful as an adolescent," and even "his driest work is [built] on a mystic faith." Had Dewey not chosen the academic route, Frank estimates that he "would have been a great religious poet."[97]

William Wordsworth had a profound effect on Dewey's philosophical outlook in his formative years. He never completely shed the romantic mysticism that Wordsworth imparted.[98] Much of Dewey's own poetry, similarly, would explore the larger cosmos and our role within it. One poem, "Creation," begins with a vision of undisturbed vacuity, reminiscent of early Chinese creation accounts. Dewey begins with "arid spaces as yet unsown of sun . . . Unchanging, garbed in pallid cloth of grey." Without cause or reason, "Her grey to maddened multicolor grew," and "Life, unloosing his large lusts" came to proliferate—"With breathless reek of untemper'd love of change." Whereas "virgin Time" once stood still in "blank aloofness," the arrival of Life imbued its arcs and cycles with new meanings—"Till emptied of Life's love of changing life, Time was won to love of feeble things that die, And turned to tender care of all that grows." The human experience, with its "dim hazy arts," contributes itself to the cosmos like an "Earth-born dust rising in the air," becoming "Dancing dust motes in their upper flight." The continuity between the human-and-cosmos is felt distinctly but strangely: "Whereby some mystic magic sense, Crept into the minds of men below, So that phantom things stood immense, 'Gainst where heav'n and earth together grow." As the human drama continues to unfold, the "enduring womb of God" remains replete with possibilities—"Woven of undreamed dreams, purposes unthought, Deeds undone, unfelt fears, and dooms unboded." All things rise and fall as the "Mystic mother, in her patience endless, And unconquerable, makes them her own."[99]

Such imagery underscores what Steven C. Rockefeller notes is the striking affinity between Dewey's natural piety and Chinese religiousness.[100] Again, there is no evidence of direct influence.[101] Dewey's poetry reflects his own interests and sensibilities above all. Yet, like classical Daoism and Confucianism, his work squarely rebukes the notion that life requires a divine, teleological "plan" in order to have meaning. As Dewey asks in verse: "Suppose there's no plan at all, But things chanced as did befall, Shall I frown in offish censure, Because it's all a vast adventure?" *No*, answers the poet. "Not till flowers smell foul to me, And the briar rose is unfair to see." Natural values as they become focused in ordinary things are genuine and they suffice. Dewey cannot identify with those who insist that there must be a "Heavenly plan" behind it all, nor with those who lament the fact that there is not. "Ask me not to join your wail, Till loving friendships pass and fail, Till wintery winds do lose their glee, And singing birds no more are free." There is ample goodness (*bonum*) and beauty (*pulchro*) in concrete human relationships and in our communion with Nature (*tian* 天). From the cosmos, Dewey asks only to enjoy such wonders in real time: "Great God, I thee implore, A little help to lend—I do not ask for much, A little space in which to move, To reach, perchance to touch, A little time in which to love, A little hope that things which were, Again may living stir—A future with an op'ning door." The meaning of human life does not rest in any static eternity. Its meaning is encountered in the present, through actually sharing in the process of bringing more unity (*unum*), goodness (*bonum*), truth (*verum*), and beauty (*pulchro*) into the world. As Dewey observes: "That this world which subtly mingled is, Shall ever better come to be—till man knows, That such growth of better is his sole bliss, Lovelier too than lovely mystic rose."[102]

As John Herman Randall observes, Dewey's religiousness hinges on the importance of "shared experience."[103] In his private poetry, this feature shines through. Dewey wonders at the emergence of "sharing" itself as a capacity realized in the cosmos: "Not as bars between but as the world set free, Have things thus grown to be a me and thee, Sharing no longer an unknown motion." He reflects, for example, on the closeness of his relationship with his daughter Jane. "When Janey moves to or fro, My thoughts in like motions go . . . sad or glad I like to think, I'm bound to her by every link, And while she plays and runs so free, Tied tight to her my heart strings be." Through his poetry, Dewey would also cope with the deaths of two children. John and Alice lost two young sons (2½ yrs. and 8 yrs.) to illnesses.[104] Dewey finds perspective in the midst of such unimaginable grief: "To us you came from out of dark . . . Not ours you were but lent . . . To make dark life sweet and white, Not ours you were, but God's own loan . . . our aching arms vainly strove to touch. And hold our own, God's blessed loan."[105] The image of the beloved as a "loan" is a poignant one, acknowledging both the generosity and the impermanence of *dao* 道. It foregrounds the urgency of cultivating the habits of love—to augment and appreciate the experiences that we are blessed enough to share with one another while we are here (*you* 有).

Stories in the *Zhuangzi* evoke a variety of responses. Personally, I have always found the story of Zhuangzi losing his wife to be uniquely moving. When his wife died, Zhuangzi was observed celebrating and singing rather than properly mourning her passing. Huishi questions this seemingly irreverent behavior, and Zhuangzi responds as follows:

> When she first died, how could I not grieve like anyone else? But then I considered her beginnings and the time before she lived. Not only before she lived, but before she had taken shape (*xing* 形). Not only before she had taken shape, but before she had life-energy (*qi* 氣). In the midst of that mysterious jumble, a transformation occurred and there was energy! Those energies transformed, and she took shape! That shape transformed, and she lived! Now, there has been another transformation and she is dead. It's like the progression of the four seasons: spring, summer, fall, winter. She now lies resting in the Vast Chamber. If I were to go running *after* her crying and sobbing, it would be as if I myself had not entered deeply (*tong* 通) into her allotted lifespan (*ming* 命). So I stopped.[106]

I realize that my rendition of the final line is unusual and probably wrong. As a strictly philosophical gloss, however, it is not wholly implausible, nor is it inconsistent with more standard translations.[107] Let me explain.

Zhuangzi's response to the death of his wife reflects a larger conception of his relation to the world and to the inescapable conditions of life and its limits (*ming* 命). As always, the touchstones for Zhuangzi are continuity and context. "Heaven, earth, and I live side-by-side (*bing* 並)," he explains. "The myriad beings and I form a continuity (*yi* 一)."[108] Zhuangzi's equanimity at the loss of his wife is grounded in his recognition that living amounts to transactions in a shared world. When living things become intimately involved, the result is shared experience—the greatest of human goods. Like all living organisms, human beings grow side-by-side. Such growth has its seasons, and to spend one's life with another person is to enter into, "connect with," and become intimately familiar with (*tong* 通) a particular lifespan as it develops and realizes its apportioned limits (*ming*). Perhaps Zhuangzi identifies with his wife in this intimate way, and he feels grateful for the life that he was fortunate enough to share and to witness. There is no need to go running *after* something that remains with you—something that has become part of you. Zhuangzi's reflections direct him to the miraculous fact that his wife was ever there at all—that *she* emerged from that mysterious, jumbled continuum that generates *everything*. What greater miracle could there be?

Alice Dewey died in the summer of 1927. Condolences poured in, and over the weeks that followed Dewey responded to the messages. Like Zhuangzi, his primary sentiment was gratitude for having had Alice as a life partner. He reflected on "how many and how close knit are the ties which are formed in sharing all the vicissitudes of life."[109] Dewey found renewed treasure in the enduring friendships and family that he and Alice had created together. "Our friends have been very kind and have brought the sense of the abiding Good very close," he writes. "I have been very fortunate in having five children and as many grandchildren, and I realize as I never did before how fortunate I am compared to those who [are] really left alone."[110] While Alice was gone, Dewey did not think of her death in terms of what he had lost but rather of what he had gained. "I do not feel that I have a right to complain. Over forty years we were together and Alice has made my life more than anything else." Indeed, when one life fully enters into (*tong* 通) another, the resulting growth can never be reversed. Dewey understood that what Alice gave to him, "will stay with me during the not many years that remain."[111] Alice was gone, but through him she would continue.

With typical discernment, Dewey's poems illuminate the great matters. In "To Death," he writes: "Endure, my love. The noises pass; the stir recedes. To me the silence comes, As I pass within thy spacious night, To more than rest, at one with thee."[112] Indeed, there is no passing out of the cosmos. Every atom is here to stay. As the *Zhuangzi* muses, our loosened energies might someday transform (*hua* 化) into a rat's liver or the arm of a bug. Perhaps the flesh of our bodies will feed the vultures of the sky or the crickets of the earth.[113] In "Two Births," Dewey recognizes the same. "No thief is Nature but mother, Whose power shall not lack, To turn me in time to clean brother, Worm and sister flower and laden air, To feed the tender sprouting plants, Till in their mingled life I share, And in new measures tread creation's dance." Our energies belong forever to the cosmos—"wondrous food for the mysterious life, With which the world, our God, is rife."[114] Among twentieth-century thinkers, Dewey is rare in that he displays little existential anxiety—no dark moods, no fretting over his own mortality. Privately he confides that he enjoys "the peace which passes all understanding," and claims to have had "no emotional disturbance for many years, since substantially I am resting on bedrock."[115]

What was this bedrock upon which Dewey stood? Zhuangzi discovered equanimity in the realization that "the myriad things and I form a continuity (*yi* 一)."[116] Dewey likewise secures peace in realizing the continuity of things. "I believe that the great obstacles are the multitude of matters," he writes, "mind and body, man and the world, [etc.], in which the man of action and the thinker have cooperated however unconvincingly in setting up fixed barriers." Dewey sums up his philosophical mission as follows:

> I have done what I could to break down these barriers by showing that facts show there are no such separations and that they

lead to false conclusions and harmful results . . . I believe that I could do the best I can do by means of helping people to see the continuities and the movements of connections where in the mind of most, [men and women] of action as well as thinkers, divisions and fixities exist . . .

You ask me, in effect, how I got the experience of oneness which is the source of emotional peace. Well, I got it first by "Intuition" based on experience, a few typical ones. Then I got it by discriminating thought, hard work too, in examining in large number the current dualisms and resolving them into "dynamic" continuities.[117]

Dewey's stress on the continuity (or *yi* 一) of things is what makes him such a productive source of connections within East Asian philosophy. Also, as these volumes attest, his thinking readily evokes the insights of both Daoism and Confucianism, reminding us that such "schools" are not as incompatible as we like to imagine. Chinese intellectual history is not about choosing between "Daoism" and "Confucianism." Rather, it is about *syncretism*—drawing freely from traditional sources and creating something new. By rendering nature-and-culture continuous, Dewey facilitates such syncretism and helps us to appreciate the compatibility of Daoism and Confucianism—or at least, he helps us to recognize where specific philosophical differences lie. Dewey's piety toward nature blends seamlessly into his own "moral faith," which is the social expression of that same natural piety. Such nature-culture continuity, for Dewey, affords a "just sense of nature as the whole of which we are parts, while it also recognizes that we are parts that are marked by intelligence and purpose, having the capacity to strive by their aid to bring conditions into greater consonance with what is humanly desirable."[118] Human goods take shape just as natural goods do, being in no constitutive sense "unnatural." Human goods, as the Confucians recognize, are active capacities (*cai* 才) that reside along with the natural dispositions (*xing* 性) of things.

As expressions of Nature (*tian* 天), the capacities that reside in things are not to be liberated by divine fiat and there is no divine plan underwriting their realization. Dewey understood that such an "intellectual readjustment" would come as a shock to some people—for "there is undoubted loss of joy, of consolation, of some types of strength" in the realization that "Heaven's plan" doesn't exist.[119] There is no responsible choice, however, but to ground our spiritual and moral lives in light of the truth as we know it. However "therapeutic" it might be to believe otherwise, there is no "grand scheme" in the cosmos that is arranged with our happiness in mind. Still, for Dewey, "every act may carry within itself a consoling and supporting consciousness of the whole to which it belongs and which in some sense belongs to it." Such consciousness delivers no assurance of any particular success. Such expectations need to be relinquished. We do ourselves no favors, however, by swinging to the opposite extremes of nihilism or Sartrean existentialism. "There is a conceit fostered by perversion of religion which assimilates the universe to our personal desires," Dewey observes—"but there is also a conceit of carrying the load of the universe from which religion liberates us."[120]

Dewey's point is that we neither delegate our destinies to the universe nor hoist upon ourselves responsibility for *its* destiny. We are but one factor in the cosmos—an unimaginably small one at that. But as Dewey reminds us: "Within the flickering inconsequential acts of separate selves dwells a sense of the whole which claims and dignifies them."[121] Ultimately, what Dewey called "Togetherness" is the final truth.[122] We are *together* with everything here (*you* 有)—and that is the ineradicable mystical fact. This fact does not need to dawn on us all at once in a pivotal moment of rapture. "On the contrary," Dewey writes, "there is every reason to suppose that, in some degree of intensity, [such insights] occur so frequently that they may be regarded as normal manifestations that take place at certain rhythmic points in the movement of experience."[123] Arriving at some mutual understanding, expressing reciprocal concern, engaging in a joint undertaking, laughing with a friend—moments arise in the normal course of living that remind us of our underlying *togetherness*.

Personally, Dewey could refer back to a particular experience through which he permanently secured this insight. At the unconfident age of nineteen, he took a job as a high school teacher in Oil City, Pennsylvania. There, he continued reading and tried his early hand at philosophical writing. Alone one evening, he had what he later described to Max Eastman as a "mystical experience." Dewey had difficulty putting it into words. He described it as a sudden feeling—a penetrating realization—that *"everything that's here is here, and you can just lie back on it."*[124] He never lost that feeling.

What gives our lives meaning—what gives *anything* meaning—is that it is connected to other things. Realizing the fact of connectedness is essential to the religious life. "Whether or no we are, save in some metaphorical sense, all brothers," Dewey writes, "we are at least all in the same boat traversing the same turbulent ocean. The potential religious significance of this fact is infinite."[125] The fact of "Togetherness" makes integration possible and ensures that moral and religious progress is made through enlarging our sympathies. Again—as Mencius says: "Everything is here with us. There is no greater joy than inspecting one's own person and finding it well-integrated (*cheng* 誠). To conduct oneself in a way that consistently puts oneself in the place of others (*shu* 恕): this is the shortest route to associated humanity (*ren* 仁)."[126]

Sympathy, then, is the key to both moral and spiritual experience. As Dewey writes: "It is sympathy which carries thought out beyond the self and which extends its scope [until] it approaches the universal as its limit." Teachers as different as Confucius and Jesus have recognized that sympathy is the only rule. Dewey concurs. "To put ourselves in the place of others," he writes, "is the surest way to attain objectivity of moral knowledge."[127] Associated living in pursuit of the resultant goods may or may not be the meaning of life—but it undeniably provides us with meaning *in* life, and its conditions unite us with forces beyond ourselves. As Dewey says: "The community of causes and consequences in which we, together with those not born, are enmeshed is the widest and deepest symbol of the mysterious totality of being the imagination calls the universe."[128]

Long after we are gone, the universe will continue. Some astrophysicists believe that it is shaped like a three-dimensional torus—basically, an outwardly circulating doughnut. If one were to stand at the center, the view would be unusual. Looking forward, we would see our backs; to our right, our left profiles; upwards, the bottoms of our feet.[129] Every moment enters into rotation on the cosmic doughnut, the destiny of which is anybody's guess. "The mystery," Dewey understood, "is that the world is as it is—a mystery that is the source of all joy and all sorrow, of all hope and fear, and the source of development both creative and degenerative."[130]

Chinese thinkers provide us with profound insights into what it means for events to actually occur in the world—i.e., for processes to take shape through phases that are generative (*qian* 乾) and degenerative (*kun* 坤) with respect to functional equilibrium. For the Chinese thinker, *dao* 道 expresses the discursive unity (*yi* 一) that is sustained when means-ends are working together. As organic creatures, we recognize innately that such harmonies are preferable to secure. On this basis, human experience adds to the multitude of harmonious experiences in the universe. As Confucius reminds us, "It is human experience that broadens *dao*, not *dao* that broadens human experience."[131] The parameters that enable growth (*sheng* 生) through harmony (*he* 和) are not of our design; they characterize the "Way of Nature" (*tiandao* 天道) itself. We broaden this cosmic process by working *within* such parameters, cultivating events of novel goodness (*bonum*) and beauty (*pulchro*)—*lights that never were on sea or land*.

It is important to realize that *dao* 道 has no preference for our harmonies or for any particular harmonies. As Confucius suggests, the universe is not in the business of broadening *us*. By its very nature, *dao* has no fixed end (*telos*). Properly understood, this does not negate the meaning of our finite experiences—in fact, it contributes to the conditions under which such meaning is secured. *Dao* yields to the *actual generation* of meanings in the world. If *dao* had its own "ultimate meaning," then that meaning would supplant and supersede the world's meanings. Instead, the gift of meaning is given to the world *constantly* and *unreservedly* in all shapes and sizes—wherever connections are made. To dismiss such gifts because they are not the "ultimate gift" is the most puerile ingratitude imaginable. For the well-adjusted person, the meaning of living is found in the process of discovering more meaning through living, and in appreciating the sheer wonder of being able to do so. Demanding to know *the* "ultimate meaning" or "final end" of human life is yet another expression of "*the* philosophical fallacy"—expecting something in the midst of a process that can arrive only at the end. But as Dewey and Don Quixote both knew, the road is better than the Inn. "If it is better to travel than to arrive," writes Dewey, "it is because traveling is a constant arriving," whereas "arrival that precludes further traveling is most easily attained by going to sleep or dying."[132]

By contrast, to be *awake* and *alive* is to contribute thoughts-and-actions to a process that is *ongoing*—to participate in what Dewey describes as "the energetic, unflagging, unceasing creation of an ever-present new road upon which we can walk together."[133] Philosophy has an important role to play on this "human road" (*rendao* 人道). Given its genetic-functional character—situated *in* a culture as well as being the critical and constructive mode *of* that culture—it maintains both the vehicles and the lanes as the human experience moves forward. In one respect, Dewey writes, "The chief task of those who call themselves philosophers is to help get rid of the useless lumber that blocks our highways of thought, and strive to make straight and open the paths that lead to the future."[134] In another respect, philosophy is what ensures that our mental vehicles are not so far "out of gear" that they cannot reliably get us through the curves and interchanges that we face. Philosophy's function in culture is to survey, critique, and sometimes *replace* the assumptions upon which we act, such that we make our way forward with greater intelligence (*ming* 明) and perseverance.

Such work needs doing, because once our ideas get stuck "out of gear" they become useless in securing present ends no matter how hard we push them. Jiang Menglin shares a story that underscores how Dewey felt about such cases:

> In the scenic Western Hills of Peking, one summer afternoon, Professor John Dewey, Dr. Hu Shih, and I watched a Sisyphus beetle pushing a tiny mud ball up the slope. It pushed first with forelegs, then with hind legs, and then with its side legs. The ball rolled up and up until some mishap occurred which set it rolling down to where it started with the diminutive Sisyphus riding on it. He repeated the process but met with the same failure. Again

and again he tried. We admire his perseverance, said both Hu Shih and I. Yes, but his lack of intelligence is regrettable, said John Dewey.[135]

The slope upon which we push is one whose angles and contours are shaped by forces against which our pre-Darwinian assumptions no longer gain traction. As long as our methods of securing progress remain based on such outmoded tools—e.g., discrete substances, fixed ends, essential natures, "Heaven's plan," etc.—we will get only so far before tumbling backwards again. We need ideas that are more intelligent (*ming* 明): ideas that can better withstand empirical scrutiny and that work more effectively alongside the forces driving change in the present age. Intra-cultural philosophers remain mindful of this charge and search the world over for such ideas.

Our work is badly needed. The challenges that we face today are extremely serious. Problems like climate change, mass extinction, social polarization, and political dysfunction have become so acute that it is difficult to know where to begin. This is where philosophy usually starts. Moving to the cultural front lines, we must help to identify and combat out-moded conceptual schemes that hamper the realization of our better thoughts and actions. In order to do this, philosophers need to remain *awake* and *alive* to the actual challenges. The lure to fall asleep or to find escape grows stronger as the human prospect dims, but such therapeutic remedies are no strategy. We have the resources to solve our problems. Remember that human intelligence is a force of Nature (*tian* 天), one that "after millions of years of errancy has found itself as a method"—and as Dewey says, "it will not be lost forever in the blackness of night." Having evolved in us to secure our precious goods, intelligence (*ming* 明) connects us to the "Way of Nature" (*tiandao* 天道) and by its lights our directive is clear. We must, as Dewey says: "*bend every energy and exhibit every courage so that these precious goods may not even be temporarily lost but be intensified and expanded here and now.*"[136]

Returning to China

We arrive at the end of a very long study. Given its elephantine nature, the foregoing discussion is hard to steer to a proper close. I'd like to end, however, as I began—by further restoring the human dimension of our subject matter. Whatever else these volumes do, I hope they will have succeeded in reminding us of the Chinese students whose lives Dewey changed and whose activities shaped his thinking in return. For me, this human element has more than once reinforced my determination to see this project through. To those of us committed to building upon the Dewey-China connection, these stories are a reminder that we are part of a larger intra-cultural situation the evolution of which encompasses lives other than our own. The aspirations, efforts, and hardships of those who came before make our work possible. My intention, then, is to bookend these volumes by putting into historical context the cultural situation in which we currently find ourselves.

More than anything, Dewey wanted to see China one last time before he died. Jiang Menglin, by then a senior government official, visited Dewey while he was vacationing in Key West in the spring of 1945. "[Jiang] gained two pounds in his four days here," Dewey boasted.[137] In addition to eating and catching up, they apparently hatched plans for Dewey to make a return trip to China. That winter, he received an official invitation from the Chinese government "as a guest of Chinese universities [to] make survey of our problems."[138] Dewey was thrilled. As he wrote to Arthur Bentley: "I had a wonderful time in China twenty-five years ago and there is nothing I would like more before I die than to renew acquaintance with China and my old Chinese friends."[139] He was eighty-six years old. "I don't know if it's a crazy scheme or not," he admitted. At least, he said, his doctors "didn't believe anything would happen [there] that might not happen here." But no matter, Dewey was determined to go. "I had such an experience when I was in China that on the whole I'd rather see it again even for a short time than any other one thing I know of—so I hope it isn't as crazy as it may look to be."[140]

Friends and family were concerned. "I was amazed by the news that John Dewey will travel to China," Felix Kaufmann wrote. "Let me hope that he will have the best facilities for his journey and that he will not stay away from this country too long."[141] Dewey began to refuse invitations in anticipation of his departure.[142] Jane Dewey was completely against her father going. "She thinks it's a crazy idea," Dewey said.[143] Meanwhile, the Chinese Embassy telegraphed from Washington, D.C., with instructions:

AIRMAIL SPECIAL DELIVERY PASSPORTS OF YOURSELF AND SECRETARY FOR MILITARY PERMITS STOP PLEASE ALSO START IMMEDIATLEY INNOCULATIONS FOR SMALL POX TYPHUS TYPHOID CHOLERA YELLOW FEVER TETANUS AND PLAGUE STOP.[144]

The gears were in motion. "I hope it will not be too hard on him," Bentley wrote.[145] "Am preparing immunizations to go to China," Dewey told a friend, "have priorities [for military flight] but no date. Sometime this month if possible."[146] He waited for further instructions. "No further details about China trip," he told Albert Barnes; meanwhile, "shall be a 'walking drug store.'"[147]

Misgivings continued to mount. "I suppose you are all eager to go to China," Barnes wrote back, "but, don't quote me, I hope it falls through."[148] Joseph Ratner was also concerned. He asked Dewey why he was going back to China. The ostensible reason was that he was going to contribute further to China's educational reform, but Ratner wasn't buying it. Most likely, he thought, Jiang Menglin knew that "the old man would like to see China again before he died." Plus, according to Ratner's account, the doctors were more apprehensive about the China trip than Dewey was letting on. Dewey figured that they had not given him a good enough reason *not* to go, except that he was an old man. "But Joe, I'm an old man wherever I am," he protested.[149]

Dewey continued to wait for instructions. "Nothing new or settled about China," he wrote to Barnes, "save have had some inoculations and after a day and a half have recovered."[150] The Chinese Ministry of Finance sent him $5,000 for travel expenses.[151] Days passed and the prospects for an impending departure dimmed. "It now looks as if on various counts I'll be advised to postpone the visit to China till September. Transportation, weather, and university conditions in China should all be better at that time." It didn't matter. Dewey wanted only to make the trip. "I shan't be sorry to wait," he said.[152] In the months that followed, Dewey kept his schedule arranged accordingly.[153] September came and went, and prospects for his departure did not improve. Dewey's second trip to China would never materialize. He returned the $5,000 forwarded by the Chinese Ministry of Finance.[154]

That November, Dewey received Sing-nan Fen's letter of introduction. "I never heard of him before," Dewey told Bentley. Fen included a number of his essays, and Dewey was instantly impressed. "The first few pages are a clearer statement than any I've ever made," he told Bentley. Dewey sent Bentley the essays and responded to Fen on the same day.[155] "I think the first page of your paper is the finest statement of my basic principles that I've ever read," Dewey told him—"You have a firm grasp." His praise was sincere: "I can't quite get over my surprise that you got my basic principles so adequately," Dewey writes; "it took me a long time to arrive at them." Dewey could not wait to learn more about his new Chinese acquaintance: "Where were you educated in China? How long have you been at the University of Chicago? What sort of atmosphere—intellectual, etc.—do you find there? What are your plans?"[156] Dewey had made a new philosophical friend. "I hope to see you soon," Dewey wrote. "My phone is AT 9-6392."[157]

The story of Sing-nan Fen's initial visit to Dewey's apartment and how that "disaster" marked the beginning of their friendship was told at the outset of volume one. The intellectual affinities that Fen and Dewey shared and how these surfaced in their letters and essays have been traced since. Between them, however, there formed some deeper connection—something singular,

Figure 8.2. John Dewey in 1946 sitting under a Chinese scroll in his Manhattan apartment. This was the year that Dewey hoped to make his return trip to China. JHU Sheridan Libraries/Gado/Getty Images.

even spiritual. Dewey described Fen's companionship and his insights into his own thought as "an unexpected gift from the God of Fortune."[158] Really—what were the chances that a Chinese student would learn Dewey's ideas completely on his own, make it to America, and then befriend the philosopher in his final years? Fen was as grateful as Dewey for the resulting communion. "On the eve of my father's ninety-first birthday, I am sending this greeting," Fen wrote to Dewey in 1951. "The greeting is not conventional, for it is from the one whose life course is shaped by the one who is greeted. By greeting you, my dear father, I am celebrating my own life."[159]

Chinese history took a dramatic turn on October 1, 1949. Jiang Menglin, who by then had fled to Taiwan, visited Dewey again in Key West and briefed him on the situation. Dewey relayed to Sing-nan Fen the situation in the newly founded People's Republic. "The academic casualties seem to have begun," Dewey told him. "Feng Youlan has repudiated his previous writings and promised to follow the Marxist line hereafter."[160] Criticism of Hu Shih, who was by then in Taiwan, had commenced in earnest.

Dewey returned to New York in the spring of 1950. With establishments like the Shanghai Café newly opened, he resumed his Chinese dinners. One evening in particular was significant for the seriousness of its discussion. As James Farrell remembers:

> There's one touching incident. One of the last times I saw John I went to have dinner with him and the children and Robbie [his second wife]. We went to a Chinese restaurant with a Chinese couple. The young man had been influenced by John's writings. He was going back to China to teach Deweyism. John sort of felt that he might endanger his life. John was really very touched, and tried to convince the young Chinese not to go back.[161]

This young man was Zhu Qixian 朱启贤. Given his personal history, Zhu had no misgivings about returning to China after the Communist victory. He had two brothers who fought in the Liberation army, and he had personally attended forums with Mao Zedong in Yenan in 1938 and 1942. It was the negative attention thereby attracted from the Nationalist government that prompted Zhu to leave China in 1943 to study at Columbia.[162] While Dewey was already retired from teaching, Zhu studied Dewey's writings and the two became friends. While at Columbia, Zhu also came to know Qiu Chun 邱椿, one of Dewey's former students (1922–1924) and now Professor of Education at Beijing Normal University. Qiu held a visiting lecturership in the United States between 1944 and 1946, and in 1945 Zhu and Qiu were invited together to Dewey's apartment for cocktails and conversation.[163]

Zhu Qixian's dissertation, completed in 1949, would be on *The Development of Sun Yat-sen's Philosophical Thought*—a politically innocuous topic, but Dewey nevertheless remained concerned about his plan to return. As he wrote to Sing-nan Fen: "Zhu Qixian expects to go back to Beijing to teach in the University there—I think he is too naïve to realize what he is getting into or is likely to encounter teaching under the present conditions."[164] Zhu, however, trusted that he could return to China and safely promote a Dewey-inspired social and educational program. Sadly, as we will see, Dewey's concerns about Zhu's wellbeing were justified.

Dewey enjoyed his Chinese dinners as long as he could, but irregularity began to set in. When Sing-nan Fen brought his fiancée to meet Dewey in New York in 1951, the meeting took place in Dewey's apartment because he was too weak to join them at the restaurant.[165] By cruel historical coincidence, Dewey's reputation in China was being destroyed just as his own physical health declined. Criticism of Dewey began as early as 1950, and by 1951 it had become a steady stream of viciousness. The flow crested with the 1951 pamphlet, "An Introduction to the Criticism of Dewey" (*Duweipipanyinlun* 杜威批判引論).[166]

Many of Dewey's devoted students and followers had already fled the scene. Those who remained were being pressured into making public recantations. Recall that at the end of part I of this volume (as Dewey was leaving the port of Qingdao) mention was made of Chen Heqin and his "Living Education" approach. Chen was the founder of the Gulou Kindergarten in Nanjing, and his journal *Living Education* was inspired by Dewey's ideas. Soon after the Communists took power, Chen became a "personalized target" of the party.[167] It began when the National Ministry of Education established its own journal, *People's Education* in the summer of 1950. *People's Education* immediately proceeded to criticize *Living Education* for being a Dewey-inspired periodical. Chen issued a statement inviting readers to assist its editors in identifying and correcting their specific errors, but such conciliatory gestures only went so far.[168] The pressure on Chen was unrelenting. By the autumn of 1951, Chen felt compelled to issue an extensive self-criticism and to denounce Dewey personally:

> As one who has been most poisoned by his reactionary educational ideas, and as one who worked hardest and longest to help spread his educational ideas, I now publicly accuse that great fraud and deceiver in the modern history of education—*John Dewey!*[169]

Living Education began reprinting self-critiques that had already appeared in *People's Education* and was soon enough dissolved.

Between 1951 and 1952, Chen Heqin would "participate" in eleven discussion meetings in major cities during which he would express his self-criticism and then endure hours of further critique and interrogation.[170] In his efforts to become rehabilitated, Chen introduced what came to be known as the "Three Gunshots" (sanqiang 三槍), a slogan that represented the three fatal errors in Dewey's educational philosophy: (1) Growth as the only end, (2) the Child-centered curriculum, and (3) Learning through doing.[171] Chen would write his own book attacking Dewey in 1956.[172] In Dewey's final years, the words "malicious," "ridiculous," "reactionary," "fallacy," "sly," "dirty," and "ugly" came to be associated with Dewey and with his influence in China.[173] American pragmatism was similarly maligned, likened to a "rotten rat which has spread its plague far and wide."[174]

With the founding of the People's Republic, Hu Shih's reputation would also be swiftly attacked. He was identified as one of the "running dogs" of imperialism that needed to be chased out of all intellectual consideration. The rationale for attacking Hu was multifaceted. As Jerome B. Grieder explains, Hu served as proxy for the "archetypical returned student" whose revolutionary consciousness was infected by bourgeois sympathies picked up while studying in the United States. It mattered not so much *what* one had studied or with whom, but rather that one retained some identification with American intelligentsia. Hu would be cast as such an international "type" through critiques that were almost completely *ad hominem*. According to his revolutionary critics, Hu never cared about China but only about his own global reputation; thus, he was portrayed as an "exhibitionist" and a "show-off" in addition to being a pragmatist and a pro-Western imperialist. The idea of attacking Hu, according to Grieder, was "not so much to discredit his conclusions as to cast doubt on his motives."[175] This effectively put all returned students on notice: *Serve the revolution or receive the same treatment.*

The anti-Hu campaign took a disturbing turn in 1950, when Hu Shih's own son produced an "open letter" denouncing his father as an "enemy of the people."[176] Hu trusted that his son was coerced into writing the letter, and he felt this only confirmed the personal as opposed to intellectual nature of the campaign against him. By 1955, there were eight volumes of purge literature against Hu circulating in China. Regarding such attention as evidence of his intellectual stature, Hu kept a collection of the writings in his study.[177] He deeply regretted the animus that his relation with Dewey had prompted against his teacher, but Hu retained a broader historical perspective. "I have brought upon my head and the head of my beloved teacher and friend, John Dewey, years of violent attack and millions of words of abuse and condemnation," Hu wrote, "[but] these same millions of words of abuse and condemnation have given me a feeling of comfort and encouragement—a feeling that Dewey's two years and two months in China were not entirely in vain . . . and that Dewey and his students have left in China plenty of 'poison,' plenty of antiseptic and antitoxin, to plague the Marxist-Leninist slaves for many, many years to come."[178] Hu would remain a prominent figure in Taiwan until his death in 1962.

Zhu Qixian's trajectory would be different, becoming a painful snapshot of the fate of thousands of gifted and dedicated Chinese intellectuals under Maoist rule. Dewey's attempt in the Chinese restaurant to dissuade Zhu from returning to China would be unsuccessful. This, however, was soon irrelevant. Zhu, who was the founder of the New York City branch of the Democratic League, faced deportation in 1950 for organizing an event to celebrate the founding of the People's Republic of China. He had wanted to return to China, and now the American government gave him no alternative. Zhu was given a hero's welcome when he returned to his homeland. He was even received in Beijing by Mao Zedong himself at an event that was covered in the *People's Daily*.[179] Zhu immediately assumed a teaching position at Beijing Normal University alongside Qiu Chun, Dewey's other former student with whom he had shared cocktails in Dewey's apartment less than five years earlier.

Zhu Qixian and Qiu Chun were patriots. They supported the Chinese government, but they were inclined to buck the ideological trend. Zhu rose to defend Dewey during a public "Repudiate Dewey" forum in 1955.[180] He was also critical of the involvement of the Communist party in school affairs. With the arrival of the "Anti-Rightist" campaign in 1957, Zhu would be singled out for interrogation. Students actively debated whether or not Zhu was a "rightist." It was noted that he had been deported from the United States (a positive), but it was also noted that he had stated that Communist Party committee members at his university were "ignorant" (*wuzhi* 無知) and "unprofessional" (*waihang* 外行).[181] During his interrogation, Zhu defended not only himself but also his senior colleague Qiu, who had been wrongly accused of various misdeeds, exonerated, but never publically cleared of wrongdoing. Qiu's family continued to be publically ostracized, and he suffered serious health problems as a result.[182]

Sadly, the struggles of the "Anti-Rightist" campaign foreshadowed greater troubles to come. Intellectuals like Zhu Qixian and Qiu Chun would not survive the Cultural Revolution (1966–1976)—one of China's greatest tragedies, as frenzied brigades of "Red Guards" persecuted their seniors who they suspected of harboring counterrevolutionary sentiments. Qiu was labeled a "reactionary intellectual" and "struggled" (*pidou* 批鬥) to death in 1966. Zhu would be persecuted to death two years later at the age of fifty-eight. It is estimated that over one million people died during the Cultural Revolution, while many thousands more were imprisoned, displaced, disenfranchised, harassed, and publically humiliated.

Sing-nan Fen managed to remain in America. He eventually left Howard University and after a few temporary positions ended up at the University of Nebraska where he enjoyed a long teaching career. He spent the last five years of his life living with his daughter Ruth and two grandchildren in Minneapolis, Minnesota, where he died on May 26, 2011. It is remembered that he "loved his family, children, dancing, reading, and continued swimming daily at the Midtown YMCA until he was 94."[183] Fen was a much younger man on that June morning in 1952 when he read of Dewey's death in *The Washington Post*. Devastated, he travelled from Washington, D.C., to New York City to be there for the memorial service of his beloved American "father." He took part in the mourning and was "treated as one of the family members."[184]

Dewey's passing, unfortunately, did nothing to slow the anti-Dewey campaign that was underway in China. It continued for several more years, as Dewey's positions were distorted and twisted into apologies for *status quo* capitalism, negations of scientific method, and schemes to keep the working class ignorant.[185] Even Tao Xingzhi, who Mao Zedong had once described as a "great people's educator," was caught up in the anti-American wave and labeled a bourgeois liberal element.[186] A pamphlet appeared in 1952 entitled, "A Critique of Tao Xingzhi's Educational Thought," maligning Tao and his American connections.[187] Any thinker or movement associated with Dewey would be targeted with "anti-imperialist" fervor. Eradication was swift and effective. With the "anti-Rightest" campaign followed by the Cultural Revolution, those who might have defended Dewey like Zhu Qixian and Qiu Chun were persecuted or otherwise silenced. With his defenders disappearing from the scene, overt criticism of Dewey made less and less sense. By the mid-1970s, his name was hardly mentioned. "*Duwei* 杜威," had all but vanished in China.

This adds poignancy to the present. Dewey is currently enjoying a robust comeback in Mainland China. His rehabilitation began in the 1980s, a period which saw the loosening of ideological constraints generally. Rebounds such as these tend to begin indirectly. In Dewey's case, it was the rehabilitation of Tao Xingzhi that paved the way. As early as 1981, scholarship appeared that re-evaluated Tao's educational thought, noting that he had borrowed only selectively from Dewey and that Mao Zedong initially had good things to say about Tao and his work in rural China.[188] Arguably, Mao didn't really have any deep philosophical problems with Dewey either. He attended some of Dewey's lectures during 1919–1921 and was even entrusted by a newspaper in Hunan to take notes for publication. Citing such connections, some have argued that Dewey's philosophy influenced Mao's early thinking.[189] This is hard to establish—but in any case, it became safe in the 1980s for Chinese thinkers to suggest that Dewey was worth reconsidering.[190]

Such developments were not occurring in a vacuum. With the death of Mao Zedong, the arrest of the "Gang of Four," and the rise of Deng Xiaoping, China was adjusting course. The "Four Modernizations"—agriculture, industry, defense, and science/technology—now set the national agenda. Education was recognized once again as vital to China's growth, and teaching reclaimed its status as "the most glorious profession under the sun."[191] Dewey emerged independently for reconsideration in 1982, his philosophy being that year's special topic at the annual conference of the "Chinese Association for Research on the History of Education" (*Zhongguo Jiaoyushi Yanjiuhui* 中国教育史研究会). With the Cultural Revolution fresh in everyone's mind, there emerged a belated appreciation for Dewey as a moderate force for reform in modern China. He was someone who had feared the annihilation of Chinese tradition and had warned against going to ideological extremes—be they "radical" or "conservative." Dewey was no longer misrepresented as an agent of "radical individualism," but rather recognized for having had an overall balanced view of society and the individual.[192]

Once again, "Science" and "Democracy" had become catchwords in China. Dewey's stock rose accordingly. In 1988, there would be a nationwide symposium on Dewey's thought in Chengdu with sixty participants and thirty papers delivered.[193] Progressive thinking was back in vogue, and Chinese students once again took the lead. Demanding journalistic integrity, economic justice, and the freedom to associate, up to one million activists occupied Tiananmen Square in the spring of 1989. On June 4th, the government moved in to clear the square of protesters. The scene abruptly changed. The Chinese government blamed the United States for influencing and supporting the demonstrators.[194] The Chinese Communist Party responded with its own campaign to strengthen China's national culture. In the aftermath of June 4th, "Nationalism" would become the primary value to which "Science" and "Democracy" were subordinate.

While Dewey might have been sidelined after Tiananmen, this did not occur. As Barbara Schulte documents, there was a brief reversion to anti-Dewey criticism but it did not last for long. Dewey was simply too valuable a resource for Chinese intellectuals still looking for "a way out of the Bermuda triangle of state, society, and individual," one in which there would ideally be a "harmonization" of all three.[195] As we saw earlier in chapter 4, scholars like David L. Hall and Roger T. Ames, Sor-hoon Tan, and Joseph Grange have worked to establish philosophical connections between Dewey's philosophy of democracy and classical Confucianism—capitalizing on an emerging intra-cultural context in which the rehabilitation of the latter is going hand-in-hand with Dewey's resurgence in the Chinese academy. We are living out this experiment today, and its results are yet to be determined.

Liu Fangtong, founder of Fudan University's "Center for Dewey Studies" (*Duweiyanjiuzhongxin* 杜威研究中心), sees Dewey's current Chinese resurgence in cyclical terms. Having now corrected the misunderstandings and distortions made of Dewey during the Communist era, Liu extends to his Chinese readers a re-invitation. "In a certain sense," he writes, "we are back to the starting line similar to that of the May Fourth Movement, having gone around in a big circle."[196] Indeed, as we observe the centennial anniversary of Dewey's visit to China, harmonizing the triangle of state-society-individual remains the standing challenge. Modern China remains exactly as Dewey knew it: "the world's greatest kaleidoscope."[197] With one full turn of the cylinder, Dewey and his ideas are being repositioned in the complex dynamic of its history—and this time, China's future implicates us all.

Conditions are in place for Dewey to contribute significantly to this future. Under the leadership of Liu Fangtong, the "Center for Dewey Studies" at Fudan completed in 2015 the translation of the entire 37-volume *Collected Works of John Dewey* into Chinese, an achievement that involved nearly one hundred scholars and translators from twenty universities and institutions and took eleven years to complete. The work has been highly acclaimed, and it is universally recognized for its rigor and precision. Another milestone was reached in 2004, when Yuan Gang, Sun Jiaxiang, and Ren Bingqiang assembled the most complete collection of Dewey's "China lectures" to date: *Dewey's Collected Lectures in China*,[198] a collection that goes well beyond the set that Robert W. Clopton and Tsuin-chen Ou assembled at the University of Hawai'i in the 1970s. At present, Chinese readers have unprecedented access to Dewey's thoughts and ideas.

Dewey has returned to China—and this time, his presence is bound up not with the rejection of China's philosophical heritage but with its recovery. Accordingly, this is *the* moment for American philosophers to engage with Chinese thought, to welcome it into the Western academy, and to use it as Dewey says—to forge "*specific* philosophical relationships" given the problems that we face. The Chinese side is ready to engage. As Sun Ning relates in the Spring 2018 issue of *Dewey Studies*, the "Center for Dewey Studies" at Fudan University, "with strong support from the government," is eager to "enhance international communication between Chinese scholars and scholars from all over the world."[199] This new era of philosophical engagement between Dewey and Chinese thought will create opportunities for bilateral development and reciprocal growth, just as their encounter did a century ago.

Today, such reciprocal growth is most urgently needed. The basic argument in these volumes is that selectively assimilating classical Chinese thought can assist us in getting our thinking "back in gear," and that intra-cultural philosophy can facilitate this process. The ultimate rationale for the present undertaking is that "out of gear" thinking currently poses genuine dangers to the human enterprise. Hu Shih credits Dewey with alerting him to the importance of dealing with such crises when they arise. Hu writes:

> It is from Professor Dewey that I have learned that the most sacred responsibility of a [human] life is to endeavor to *think well*. To think sluggishly, to think without strict regard to the antecedents and consequences of thought, to accept ready-made and unanalyzed concepts as premises of thinking, to allow personal factors unconsciously to influence one's thinking, or to fail to test one's ideas by working out their results is to be intellectually irresponsible. All the greatest discoveries of truth, and all the greatest calamities in history, depend upon this.[200]

It is this "sacred responsibility" that precludes intra-cultural philosophy from being content to merely study the past. It must seek to locate and to assimilate resources that can better guide us as we prepare for the future.

Tao Xingzhi likens such assimilation to the grafting of trees: "One kind of tree branch can be grafted onto another kind and make the foliage thicker, the flowers more beautiful, and the fruit sweeter. If we graft knowledge derived from other people's experience onto the knowledge produced from our own experience, then our knowledge will branch out widely, and our lives will be [fuller]."[201] Such organic "grafting" between philosophical strands is what intra-cultural philosophy is all about. Dewey foreshadows this method in his "On Philosophical Synthesis," the inaugural essay in *Philosophy East and West*. While time prevented him from playing a larger role in the burgeoning East-West philosophy movement, it is not too late for us to recover this unique vision and to proceed.

I have said more than enough. At this juncture, F. S. C. Northrop's remarks at the Third East West Philosophers' Conference in 1959 set the agenda more credibly than I can. So, with Northrop's words I close: "Dewey's method," he said, "[requires] that we stop talking so much about what a marvelous philosopher Dewey was and get down to the hard, philosophically analytic labor of determining the precise assumptions of our conflicting cultural customs and beliefs and then of proposing a constructive philosophical solution to the problems confronting us today."[202] If these volumes contribute anything to such labors, then I am satisfied.

Notes

Interlude

1. Nostalgia for Shanghai Café lives on NYC foodie blogs. The original proprietor died in the late 1980s and the restaurant closed in the early 1990s.
2. "Return to Shanghai It's a Sino of the Times: Delectable Dumplings Whet Appetite for Regional Style," *New York Daily News*, August 28, 1996.
3. "New Yorkers Embrace a Little Shanghai Specialty," *New York Times*, January 13, 1999.
4. Cremin (1975): 1–2.
5. *Correspondence* (03860), Sabino Dewey to Lucy Dewey, January 19, 1919.
6. "Criteria for Judging Systems of Thought," Clopton and Ou (1973): 86.
7. *Correspondence* (10745), Alice Chipman Dewey to Dewey Children, April 1, 1919.
8. *Correspondence* (03898), John and Alice Chipman Dewey to Dewey Children, May 1–2, 1919.
9. *Correspondence* (10762), Alice Chipman Dewey (?) to Dewey Children, June 7, 1919. It is unclear if this refers to John or Alice, but it could apply to either.
10. *Correspondence* (03913), Lucy Dewey to John Dewey, April 4–6, 1920.
11. *Correspondence* (03916), John Dewey to Dewey Family, April 11, 1920.
12. *Correspondence* (03946), John Dewey to Dewey Children, October 26, 1920.
13. *Correspondence* (09621), John Dewey to Hu Shih, March 6, 1940.
14. Dalton (2002): 205.
15. *Correspondence* (09845), Dale Carnegie to John Dewey, July 7, 1942.
16. Breslin (2013): 413.
17. Experiments done with bitter compounds such as 6-n-propylthiouracil suggest that about 25% of people register nothing when it touches their palates. See: McQuaid (2015): 58.
18. Breslin (2013): 409.
19. McQuaid (2015): 49, 411, 416.
20. Insight adopted from Richerson and Boyd (2005): 135.
21. *Mencius* 7A.1, Bloom (2009): 144, Mengzi 孟子 (1995): 336.

Chapter 1

1. *Analects* 17.2, Ames and Rosemont (1998): 203.
2. *Analects* 5.13, Ames and Rosemont (1998): 98.
3. Brown (1999): 382.
4. See: Pinker (2002): 435–39.
5. "On Philosophical Synthesis," LW 17: 35.
6. Fen (1961): 92.
7. Slingerland (2008): 15.
8. Pinker (2002): 411–12.
9. *Art as Experience*, LW 10: 250.
10. *Reconstruction in Philosophy*, MW 12: 85.
11. *Democracy and Education*, MW 9: 77.
12. "Contributions to *Cyclopedia of Education*," MW 7: 286.
13. Pinker (2002): 19, 23, 67.
14. Dewey does not enter directly into debates in the field of Anthropology, but he does distinguish his position explicitly from Benedict's, explaining that: "I hold that no adequate philosophy can be formed without taking into account [human] participation in nature, and the contributions to physical and physiological aspects of nature by that contribution." See: *Correspondence* (14843), John Dewey to J. Oliver Buswell Jr., December 8, 1946.
15. *Democracy and* Education, MW 9: 80–81.
16. *Freedom and Culture*, LW 13: 75–76, 77.
17. *Correspondence* (15818), John Dewey to Arthur F. Bentley, January 24, 1950.
18. *Human Nature and Conduct*, MW 14: 45, 107.
19. *Class Lectures of John Dewey*, "Principles of Education (1902)," 2.634.
20. Johnson (2006): 54.
21. *Analects* 17.2, Ames and Rosemont (1998): 203.
22. *Logic: The Theory of Inquiry*, LW 12: 28, 30, 26.
23. *Unmodern Philosophy*, Dewey and Deen (2012): 318.
24. *Logic: The Theory of Inquiry*, LW 12: 48, 66.
25. "Re-Introduction to *Experience and Nature*," LW 1: 331.
26. As it does for "doing-undergoing." See: *Unmodern Philosophy*, Dewey and Deen (2012): 325. Dewey relies on hyphens with greater frequency in his later works, inserting them into words like "*trans*-action" to emphasize bilateral relation. See: *Knowing and the Known*, LW 16: 54.
27. "Re-Introduction to *Experience and Nature*," LW 1: 331–32.
28. *Unmodern Philosophy*, Dewey and Deen (2012): 329, 293.
29. Steiner (2013): 140.
30. *Unmodern Philosophy*, Dewey and Deen (2012): 216.
31. "Body and Mind," LW 3: 27.
32. *Unmodern Philosophy*, Dewey and Deen (2012): 316, 317.

33. *John Dewey Papers*, 102/56/16: 2.
34. *John Dewey Papers*, 102/57/8: 3.
35. Pinker (2002): 436.
36. *Pragmatism*, James and Kuklick (1987): 593–98.
37. *Human Nature and Conduct*, MW 14: 65–66.
38. *Pragmatism*, James and Kuklick (1987): 596.
39. Watson (1968): 77, Zhuangzi 莊子 (1994) 上: 185.
40. *Experience and Nature*, LW 1: 227.
41. *Unmodern Philosophy*, Dewey and Deen (2012): 219, 228.
42. *Human Nature and Conduct*, MW 14: 45.
43. *Psychology: Briefer Course*, James and Myers (1992): 173.
44. Hall and Ames (1995): 169, 178.
45. Bryan W. Van Norden, for instance, cites specific passages in *Anticipating China* in support of his claim that, for Hall and Ames, "the Chinese and Western philosophical traditions are essentially incommensurable." Van Norden provides no analysis of the passages that he cites and he misunderstands what they actually say. Hall and Ames identify pragmatism with "[acceding] to the incommensurability of discourses whenever there is a lack of common conventions to which all parties of a dispute appeal," but there is no claim that the Chinese and Western traditions comprise such a discourse *tout court*. The claim made, in fact, is that such incommensurability (were it to exist) would not really matter to cross-cultural philosophers, since "inter-theoretical engagements lead to real changes" regardless. The discussion is meant to distinguish Hall and Ames' "pragmatic" approach from that of "transcendental monism" which *would* stall in the face of incommensurable discourse were it ever encountered. Hall and Ames' argument is meant to delegitimize the so-called "problem of incommensurability." The argument is subtle, but its concluding *reductio* is not. Hall and Ames clearly dismiss the incommensurability thesis. As they write: "One really does not quite know what to make of the arguments that demonstrate the impossibility of radical translation. They have a certain logical cogency. But their persuasiveness is of the type possessed by arguments to the effect that bumble bees cannot fly." See: Van Norden (2007): 16, and Hall and Ames (1995): 153–54, 171–79.
46. "On Philosophical Synthesis," LW 17:35–36.
47. *Unmodern Philosophy*, Dewey and Deen (2012): 334–35.
48. "What Humanism Means to Me," LW 5: 263.
49. "Contributions to *Cyclopedia of Education*," MW 7: 214.
50. Rockefeller (1991): 451.
51. "What Humanism Means to Me," LW 5: 265–66.
52. *Reconstruction in Philosophy*, MW 12: 179.
53. "Contributions to *Cyclopedia of Education*," MW 7: 217.
54. American conservatives continue to hoist such charges on Dewey.
55. *Correspondence* (13667), John Dewey to Corliss Lamont, September 6, 1940.
56. *Correspondence* (13676), Corliss Lamont to John Dewey, September 12, 1940.
57. *Correspondence* (13677), John Dewey to Corliss Lamont, September 14, 1940.

58. *Democracy and Education*, MW 9: 298.
59. "Dualism and the Split Atom," LW 15: 200.
60. *Correspondence* (14290), John Dewey to Lyle K. Eddy, April 19, 1949.
61. Cosmides and Tooby (1997): 83–92.
62. Downes (2009): 93–101.
63. Cosmides and Tooby (1997): 84, 91.
64. *Pragmatism*, James and Kuklick (1987): 560, 561.
65. "[And] how different must be the worlds in the consciousness of ant, cuttlefish, or crab!" James adds. See: *Principles of Psychology*, James (1910): Vol. 1, 289.
66. *Pragmatism*, James and Kuklick (1987): 562, 566.
67. For a study of dogs in particular, see: Miller, et al. (2009).
68. *Pragmatism*, James and Kuklick (1987): 567.
69. *Unmodern Philosophy*, Dewey and Deen (2012): xiv, xli.
70. *Logic: The Theory of Inquiry*, LW 12: 67.
71. "Résumé of Four Lectures on Common Sense, Science and Philosophy," LW 6: 424–32 and *Logic: The Theory of Inquiry*, LW 12: 67–68.
72. *Logic: The Theory of Inquiry*, LW 12: 68–69, 101.
73. *Logic: The Theory of Inquiry*, LW 12: 76–77 and *Unmodern Philosophy*, Dewey and Deen (2012): 4.
74. *Logic: The Theory of Inquiry*, LW 12: 100.
75. *The Quest for Certainty*, LW 4: 72.
76. *Logic: The Theory of Inquiry*, LW 12: 101, 70.
77. *Periphyseon*, Eriugena and Sheldon-Williams (1997): 611.
78. Zhang (2010): 93.
79. *Knowing and the Known*, LW 16: 247, 246–48.
80. *Experience and Nature*, LW 1: 244.
81. *Logic: The Theory of Inquiry*, LW 12: 101.
82. See: Gelman (2003).
83. *Knowing and the Known*, LW 16: 100.
84. Cf. *The Quest for Certainty*, LW 4: 159.
85. See: chapter one in volume one, pp. 14–17.
86. Cremin (1975): 1–2.
87. *Knowing and the Known*, LW 16: 242.
88. *Knowing and the Known*, LW 16: 101–02.
89. *Knowing and the Known*, LW 16: 242, 101–02, 245n.4, 244–45, italics added.
90. *Experience and Nature*, LW 1: 318.
91. *Knowing and the Known*, LW 16: 255–56, italics added.
92. *Knowing and the Known*, LW 16: 244.
93. *Logic: The Theory of Inquiry*, LW 12: 71–72.
94. *Correspondence* (10791), John Dewey to Jack C. Lamb, June 18, 1948, italics added.
95. *Knowing and the Known*, LW 16: 254.
96. As William James says: "Common sense is *better* for one sphere of life, science for another, philosophic criticism for a third; but whether either be *truer* absolutely, Heaven only knows." See: *Pragmatism*, James and Kuklick (1987): 569.

97. *Knowing and the Known*, LW 16: 255.

98. "The idols of the human spirit, innate and imposed," Bacon and Vickers (2002): 228.

99. *Reconstruction in Philosophy*, MW 12: 95.

100. *Correspondence* (14735), John Dewey to Kurt H. Wolff, October 15, 1948.

101. *Correspondence* (14740), Kurt H. Wolff to John Dewey, November 5, 1948.

102. *Correspondence* (14742), John Dewey to Kurt H. Wolff, November 12, 1948.

103. *Correspondence* (14742), John Dewey to Kurt H. Wolff, November 12, 1948.

104. During his correspondence with Lamb in the summer of 1948, Dewey was in Hubbards, Nova Scotia, writing the first article. Two months after corresponding with Wolff in the autumn of 1948, Dewey was in Key West, Florida, finishing the second. See: *Textual Commentary*, LW 16: 548–52.

105. This is well expressed in 1938's *Logic: A Theory of Inquiry*: "Science is no longer an organization of meanings and modes of action that have their presence in the meanings and syntactical structures of ordinary language. Yet scientific conclusions and techniques have enormously altered the common sense relation of [human beings] to nature and to fellow [human beings]. It can no longer be believed that they do not profoundly react to modify common sense, any more than it can now be supposed that they are but an intellectual organization of the latter." See: *Logic: A Theory of Inquiry*, LW 12: 102.

106. "Has Philosophy a Future?" and "Philosophy's Future in Our Scientific Age: Never Was Its Role More Crucial," LW 16: 358–82.

107. "Has Philosophy a Future?" LW 16: 365.

108. *The Quest for Certainty*, LW 4: 159.

109. *Theaetetus* 150c1–3, Plato and Cooper (1997): 167.

110. *The Quest for Certainty*, LW 4: 159.

111. "Appendix: Dewey's Reply to Albert G.A. Balz," LW 16: 288–89.

112. Thereby making intra-cultural communication the ideal context in which to use the ontologically neutral, problem-oriented logic of Dewey's 1938's *Logic: The Theory of Inquiry*.

113. *Correspondence* (10973), Joseph Ratner to John Dewey to Kurt H. Wolff, June 26, 1949.

114. *Correspondence* (10902), John D. Graves to John Dewey, March 24, 1949.

115. *Correspondence* (10937), John Dewey to John D. Graves, May 23, 1949.

116. *Correspondence* (14293), John Dewey to Lyle K. Eddy, June 29, 1949.

117. *Correspondence* (11001), John Dewey to John D. Graves, July 30, 1949.

118. *Correspondence* (07263), John Dewey to Joseph Ratner, August 9, 1949.

119. *Correspondence* (11023), John D. Graves to John Dewey, August 4, 1949.

120. *Correspondence* (11024), John D. Graves to John Dewey, August 8, 1949.

121. *Correspondence* (11044), John Dewey to John D. Graves, August 24, 1949.

122. *Correspondence* (11054), John Dewey to John D. Graves, August 27, 1949.

123. *Correspondence* (13806), John Dewey to Sing-nan Fen, September 18, 1949.

124. *Correspondence* (15875), John Dewey to Arthur F. Bentley, August 4, 1950.

125. *Correspondence* (07341), John Dewey to Joseph Ratner, August 30, 1950.

126. *Correspondence* (07339), John Dewey to Joseph Ratner, August 5, 1950.

127. This letter is lost. See: *Correspondence* (12377), Charles A. Moore to John Dewey, December 6, 1950.
128. *Correspondence* (12268), Paul Arthur Schilpp to John Dewey, October 13, 1950.
129. *Correspondence* (13521), John Dewey to Paul Arthur Schilpp, October 28, 1950.
130. *Correspondence* (13522), John Dewey to Paul Arthur Schilpp, November 8, 1950.
131. *Correspondence* (14755), John Dewey to Gérard Deledalle, November 10, 1950.
132. *Correspondence* (12377), Charles A. Moore to John Dewey, December 6, 1950.
133. *Correspondence* (13523), John Dewey to Paul Arthur Schilpp, January 1, 1951.
134. Dewey had a few articles that he had been working on in his final years, health permitting. "On Philosophical Synthesis," however, was the only piece to be written *and* published during this final period.
135. *John Dewey Papers*, 59/10, 2pp. holo notes, green ink, 2/19/51.
136. "On Philosophical Synthesis," LW 17: 35.
137. *Correspondence* (15892), John Dewey to Arthur F. Bentley, January 18, 1951.
138. *Correspondence* (12753), Sing-nan Fen to John & Roberta Lowitz Grant Dewey, August 6, 1951.
139. *Correspondence* (20413), Lyle K. Eddy to Arthur F. Bentley, August 16, 1951.
140. *Correspondence* (14206), John Dewey to Boyd H. Bode, September 22, 1951.
141. *Correspondence* (10889), Adelbert Ames, Jr. to John Dewey, February 7, 1949.
142. *Correspondence* (12219), Joseph Ratner to John Dewey, September 9, 1950.
143. Fen (1952): 21.
144. "*How, What,* and *What For* in Social Inquiry," LW 16: 449–50.
145. Fen (1952): 21.
146. "*How, What,* and *What For* in Social Inquiry," LW 16: 452–53.
147. Fen (1952): 20, 23.
148. *Theory of Valuation*, LW 13: 208, 243.
149. Fen (1952): 24–25.
150. "The Field of Value," LW 16: 354.
151. Fen (1952): 25.
152 "The Field of Value," LW 16: 344.
153. Johnson (2006): 54.
154. Fen (1952): 23.
155. "The Field of Value," LW 16: 357.
156. *Mencius* 7B: 36, Bloom (2009): 164–65.
157. *Theory of Valuation*, LW 13: 227.
158. Fen (1952): 25.
159. "The Field of Value," LW 16: 346.
160. Fen (1952): 28.
161. "The Field of Value," LW 16: 355.
162. Fen (1952): 32.

163. See: *Correspondence* (12103), Matthew Lippman to John Dewey, May 17, 1950, and *Correspondence* (13989), John Dewey to Boyd H. Bode, May 18, 1950.
164. *Correspondence* (10893), Joseph Ratner to John Dewey, February 16, 1949.
165. *Correspondence* (14090), John Dewey to Max C. Otto, February 14, 1951.
166. *Correspondence* (14686), John Dewey to Emmanuel G. Mesthene, June 9, 1950.
167. *Correspondence* (03723), John Dewey to Joseph Ratner, February 25, 1949.
168. Fen (1952): 25.
169. Fen (1951): 387.
170. Fen (1952): 25.
171. Dewey (1989): 44.

Chapter 2

1. *Democracy and Education*, MW 9: 5–6.
2. Clopton and Ou (1973): 184.
3. *Experience and Education*, LW 13: 22.
4. *Analects* 7.25, Ames and Rosemont (1998): 116.
5. *Analects* 16.13, Ames and Rosemont (1998): 200–01.
6. *Analects* 17.10, Ames and Rosemont (1998): 206.
7. *Analects* 7.1, 7.20, 7.5, and 3.14, Ames and Rosemont (1998): 85, 111–12, 115.
8. *Analects* 7.18, 17.18, 7.27, 15.11, and 10.8, Ames and Rosemont (1998): 115, 117, 137, 187, 208.
9. *Analects* 9.5, Ames and Rosemont (1998): 127.
10. *Analects* 17.11, Ames and Rosemont (1998): 206.
11. *Analects* 8.8, Ames and Rosemont (1998): 122.
12. *Analects* 17.9, Ames and Rosemont (1998): 206.
13. *Analects* 13.5, Ames and Rosemont (1998): 163.
14. *Analects* 2.11, Ames and Rosemont (1998): 78.
15. We are told, for instance, of Confucius' favorite student Yan Hui: "Being told one thing, he realizes ten." *Analects* 5.9, Ames and Rosemont (1998): 97.
16. *Analects* 3.8, Ames and Rosemont (1998): 83–84.
17. *Analects* 1.15, Ames and Rosemont (1998): 75.
18. Ames and Rosemont stress the performative function of *zhi* 知 in such contexts. See: Ames and Rosemont (1998): 55.
19. Schaberg (1999): 339.
20. Lewis (1999): 150.
21. Schaberg (1999): 337.
22. *Analects* 2.2, Ames and Rosemont (1998): 76.
23. *Analects* 12.1, Ames and Rosemont (1998): 152.
24. *Analects* 6.27, 12.15, Ames and Rosemont (1998): 109, 157.
25. *Analects* 6.18, Ames and Rosemont (1998): 107–08.
26. *Analects* 11.1, Ames and Rosemont (1998): 142.

27. *Analects* 12.8, Ames and Rosemont (1998): 155.
28. *Analects* 14.44, Ames and Rosemont (1998): 183.
29. *Analects* 4.14, Ames and Rosemont (1998): 92.
30. "Dance and sport are activities in which acts once performed spontaneously in separation are assembled and converted from raw, crude material into works of expressive art." See: *Art as Experience*, LW 10: 69.
31. *Pragmatism*, James and Kuklick (1987): 535. This illustration has been re-purposed.
32. *Analects* 3.8, Ames and Rosemont (1998): 83–84.
33. Li (2014): 1.
34. See: Van Norden (2011): 154 and Ivanhoe (1993): 646–47.
35. Li (2014): 23–34.
36. Legge (2000) Vol. 5: 684.
37. The original "Iron Chef" (料理の鉄人 *Ryōri no Tetsujin*) was launched in 1993 and immediately became a hit in Japan. It stopped production in 1999. It became popular internationally, distributed *via* the Food Network, and soon inspired other programs of its kind.
38. *Analects* 12.16, Ames and Rosemont (1998): 157.
39. Legge (1967) Vol. 1: 414, Liji 禮記 (1998) 上: 410.
40. In this respect, early Confucianism aligns with the *Daodejing* in Warring States China. Unlike the Huang-Lao and Legalist movements, its understanding of order is not a top-down, transcendent conception but rather a bottom-up, emergent conception. See: Chapter 3 in Volume One.
41. *Analects* 1.12, Ames and Rosemont (1998): 74.
42. *Analects* 3.4, Ames and Rosemont (1998): 82–83.
43. *Analects* 19.14, Ames and Rosemont (1998): 221.
44. *Analects* 7.32, Ames and Rosemont (1998): 118.
45. *Analects* 3.23, Ames and Rosemont (1998): 88.
46. They address this in terms of the primacy of "aesthetic order" in the *Analects*. See: Hall and Ames (1987): 131–38, 165–67.
47. *Analects* 13.23, Ames and Rosemont (1998): 168–69.
48. *Analects* 8.8 and 13.26, Ames and Rosemont (1998): 122, 169.
49. Ni (2016): 105.
50. Chow (1960): 293.
51. For an overview of the Exam system, see: Miyazaki (1981), a work aptly titled *China's Examination Hell*.
52. *Correspondence* of John Dewey (10756), John Dewey to Dewey Children, May 18, 1919.
53. Clopton and Ou (1970): 307.
54. Bieler (2004): 43–44.
55. Correspondence of John Dewey (10754), John Dewey to Dewey Children, May 13, 1919.
56. Grieder (1970): 45.
57. "Progress," MW 10: 234–43.

58. Hu (1962): 768.
59. Hu (1963): 8, 39.
60. Hu (1963): 63, 131, 181.
61. Gu (2001): 589.
62. *Xinjiaoyu* 新教育 1(3), April 1919.
63. Clopton and Ou (1973): 238.
64. Keenan (1977): 12, 247.
65. It should be noted that different factions of the Chinese left viewed the student uprising differently. Some in the "New Culture" movement disapproved of such "political" action, arguing that "cultural" reform must take priority. This is how Hu Shih felt. See: Chow (1960): 1–15.
66. Tan (2003): 14.
67. "Chinese National Sentiment," MW 11: 215.
68. *Correspondence* of John Dewey (04888), John Dewey to John Jacob Coss, November 15, 1920.
69. *Correspondence* (10759), John Dewey to Dewey Children, June 1, 1919.
70. *Correspondence* (03910), John Dewey to Dewey Children, June 10, 1919.
71. Guo (2004): 63.
72. Clopton and Ou (1973): 188.
73. Ni (2016): 107–08.
74. *Analects* 15.39, Ames and Rosemont (1998): 192.
75. *Analects* 13.9, Ames and Rosemont (1998): 164.
76. *Mencius* 3A.3, Bloom (2009): 51, Mengzi 孟子 (1995): 114.
77. *Analects* 7.7, Ames and Rosemont (1998): 112.
78. Confucius himself was from a humble background, but hardly was he destitute. He had tremendous respect for students who excelled in the face of serious hardship. Here as elsewhere, his favorite student was Yan Hui. See: Ni (2016): 5–6, *Analects* 6.11, 11.19, Ames and Rosemont (1998): 106, 146.
79. Rosenlee (2006): 152–53.
80. Knoblock (1988): 206, Xunzi 荀子 (1995): 71.
81. Rosenlee (2006): 77–79, 115.
82. For Aristotle, "The male is by nature superior, and the female inferior; and the one rules, and the other is ruled; this principle, of necessity, extends to all mankind." See: *Politics* 1254b.13–15, Aristotle and McKeon (2001): 1132.
83. Hall and Ames (1998): 97.
84. Birdwhistell (2007): 89–109.
85. Rosenlee (2006): 159, 154.
86. See: Slingerland (2003) and Van Norden (2008), respectively. There remain a variety of workable, gender-neutral alternatives in the literature, such as "Exemplary Person," "Noble Person," and "Exemplary Individual," in Tan (2003), Sim (2007), and Bloom (2009), respectively.
87. Chow (1960): 257.
88. Witke (1967): 137–41.
89. See: Yuan, et al. (2004): 687–771.

90. Hall (2005) 144–48.
91. Clopton and Ou (1970): 250, 145.
92. Grieder (1970): 54.
93. See: Twanmoh (1966) for a detailed account of Hu Shih's interests and activities in this area.
94. Hu (1934): 50.
95. Ho (1991): 95.
96. Wang (2005): 265–67.
97. Ho (1991): 111.
98. Hu (1934): 51.
99. Grieder (1970): 75–76.
100. Clopton and Ou (1970): 287.
101. "The Sequel of the Student Revolt," MW 12: 25.
102. Hu (1934): 57.
103. Clopton and Ou (1973): 212.
104. Hu (1934): 46.
105. Grieder (1970): 82–83.
106. *Analects* 7.1, Ames and Rosemont (1998): 111.
107. Tan (2004): 82.
108. Legge (1967) Vol. 2: 100, Liji 禮記 (1998) 下: 617.
109. *Analects* 7.34, Ames and Rosemont (1998): 118–19.
110. Tan (2004): 82.
111. Hu (2013): 12, 79, 80.
112. *Analects* 2.15, Ames and Rosemont (1998): 79.
113. Clopton and Ou (1970): 98.
114. Clopton and Ou (1970): 285.
115. Clopton and Ou (1970): 197.
116. *Analects* 5.20, 15.31, Ames and Rosemont (1998): 100, 190.
117. Slingerland (2003): 186.
118 *Analects* 13.5, Ames and Rosemont (1998): 163.
119. Clopton and Ou (1970): 109.
120. *Analects* 2.11, Ames and Rosemont (1998): 78.
121. *Analects* 7.8, Ames and Rosemont (1998): 112.
122. Clopton and Ou (1973): 212–13.
123. Clopton and Ou (1973): 52–53.
124. *Experience and Education*, LW 13: 5, 10, 51.
125. *Analects* 7.20, Ames and Rosemont (1998): 115.
126. *Analects* 7.28, Ames and Rosemont (1998): 117.
127. *Analects* 7.22, Ames and Rosemont (1998): 115.
128. Ni (2009): 314.
129. *German Philosophy and Politics*, MW 8:182.
130. "Introduction," LW 14: xiii.
131. Kirk (1952): 245.

132. Babbitt (1919): 388.
133. Babbitt (1956): 42.
134. Kirk (1952): 247.
135. Babbitt (1956): 74.
136. Kirk (1952): 245–46.
137. Babbitt (1956): 119.
138. Mei (1941): 112.
139. See: "Appendix: Chinese Primitivism," in Babbitt (1919): 395–98.
140. Aldridge (1993): 332, 335.
141. Mei Guangdi to Hu Shih, December 26, 1915, quoted from: Wang (2005): 257.
142. Zhu (2004): 42.
143. Aldridge (1993): 334.
144. Manchester and Shepard (1941): 50, 115–16.
145. Ong (2004): 74.
146. Wu (2004): 13.
147. Eastman (1941): 681–82.
148. "Syllabi: History of Education," LW 17: 170–71.
149. Babbitt (1922): 91.
150. "The Influence of Darwinism on Philosophy," MW 4: 13.
151. Clopton and Ou (1970): 79, 110, 112.
152. Clopton and Ou (1970): 77.
153. Clopton and Ou (1973): 216.
154. Clopton and Ou (1970): 45.
155. Hu (1963): 63, 131, 181.
156. Hu (1934): 72.
157. Quoted from: Kwok (1965): 100.
158. Kwok (1965): 33–58.
159. Kirk (1952): 245.
160. "Introduction: The Relevance of John Dewey's Thought," LW 17: xviii.
161. Clopton and Ou (1973): 216.
162. Remer (1920): 267.
163. Randall (1939): 93.
164. *Analects*, 2.11, Ames and Rosemont (1998): 78.
165. Smith (1981): 2.
166. Sigurðsson (2015): 26–31.
167. *Analects* 6.17, Ames and Rosemont (1998): 107.
168. *Analects* 1.12, Ames and Rosemont (1998): 74.
169. Yao (2000): 282.
170. Richardson and Boyd (2005): 8–9.
171. Democracy and Education, MW 9: 6–7.
172. *Analects* 2.23, Ames and Rosemont (1998): 81.
173. "Old China and New," MW 13: 95.

174. Clopton and Ou (1973): 188.
175. "New Culture in China," MW 13: 114.
176. Wang (2007): 122.

Chapter 3

1. *Correspondence* (10965), John Dewey to John D. Graves, June 20, 1949.
2. *Correspondence of John Dewey* (04884), John Dewey to John Jacob Coss, April 22, 1920.
3. Dewey (1989): 42.
4. *Correspondence of John Dewey* (04898), John Dewey to F. C. S. Schiller, July 18, 1922.
5. Smith (1985): 256.
6. This is the thesis of Wang (2007), an excellent introduction to Dewey's China experience and one that provides inspiration for the present work.
7. Dewey (1989): 42.
8. *Correspondence* (03899), (10762), and (10772), Alice Chipman Dewey to Dewey Children, May 3, 1919; Alice Chipman Dewey (?) to Dewey Children, June 7, 1919 and July 8, 1919.
9. *Correspondence* (10759), John Dewey to Dewey Children, June 1, 1919.
10. *Correspondence* (10776), John Dewey to Dewey Children, July 19, 1919.
11. Clopton and Ou (1970): 37.
12. Keenan (1977): 49.
13. *Correspondence* (04102), John Dewey to Albert C. Barnes, September 12, 1920.
14. *Correspondence* (05029), Johnson Yuan to Bertrand Russell, October 6, 1920.
15. Wang (2007), 27, 45–46.
16. Ding (2007): 158.
17. "Federalism in China," MW 13: 152.
18. "Chinese National Sentiment," MW 11: 223.
19. "Introduction," LW 7: xxii.
20. Gronda (2015): 59.
21. "Contributions to *Cyclopdia of Education*," MW 6: 413–14.
22. *Class Lectures of John Dewey*, "Part III Psychology of Ethics," c1.1.1351.
23. *Class Lectures of John Dewey*, "Principles of Education (1902)," 2.593, 2.632.
24. *Human Nature and Conduct*, MW 14: 58.
25. "Transforming the Mind of China," MW 11: 210.
26. *Class Lectures of John Dewey*, "Ethical Theory (Spring 1926), Sidney Hook notes," 2.2243.
27. *Correspondence* (03491), John Dewey to Herbert W. Schneider, January 3, 1921.
28. "Is China a Nation?" MW 13: 74–75.
29. "Transforming the Mind of China," MW 11: 207.
30. "Chinese National Sentiment," MW 11: 216.
31. "A Parting of the Ways for America," MW 13: 170.

32. Fallace (2011): 137.
33. See: "Interpretation of Savage Mind," MW 2: 39–52.
34. Gronda (2015): 63–65.
35. Fen (1952): 20.
36. Gronda (2015): 51, 67.
37. Extended English summaries of these four articles were prepared at the University of Hawai`i in the late 1960s. See: "Abstracts of *Kaizō* Articles," and "Textual Commentary," MW 13: 433–42, 506.
38. "Some Factors in Mutual National Understanding," MW 13: 262–71.
39. See for example: Frisina (2002), Grange (2004), Hall and Ames (1999), Tan (2003), Wen (2009).
40. As a rhetorical strategy, both Hu Shih and Jiang Menglin defended Dewey's theories of education with appeals to Confucius, Mencius, and Wang Yangming. See: Sizer (1966), pp. 397–99.
41. Sim (2009) pp. 91, 89.
42. Sim (2009): 89n.33, see also: *Ethics*, MW 5: 300.
43. Quoted from: Sim (2009): 97.
44. Quoted from: Keenan (1977): 63, see also: Sim (2009): 98.
45. Sim (2009): 97.
46. *Correspondence* (10779), John Dewey to Dewey Children, August 4, 1919.
47. The timeline for the part II revisions are related in a letter that Dewey wrote to Tufts from China, see: *Correspondence* (07207), John Dewey to James H. Tufts, February 23, 1921.
48. Chiang (1920): 21–22.
49. Chiang (1947): 271.
50. See: Clopton and Ou (1973): 43–44.
51. Keenan (1977): 129–30.
52. Clopton and Ou (1985): 208.
53. Keenan (1977): 47.
54. Clopton and Ou (1970): 635–41.
55. Schulte (2012): 87–88.
56. *Correspondence* (03877), (10746), (10745), John Dewey to Dewey Children, February 22, 1919, John Dewey to Dewey Children, April 1, 1919, Alice Chipman Dewey to Dewey Children, April 1, 1919.
57. *Correspondence* (03877), John Dewey to Dewey Children, February 22, 1919.
58. *Correspondence* (10752), Alice Chipman Dewey to Dewey Children, April 19, 1919.
59. *Correspondence* (10743), Alice Chipman Dewey to Dewey Children, March 14, 1919.
60. *Correspondence* (03899), Alice Chipman Dewey to Dewey Children, May 3, 1919.
61. "Transforming the Mind of China," MW 11: 210. Dewey related this impression again in correspondence, observing that the Chinese were "very human." See: *Correspondence* (05022), John Dewey to Wendell T. Bush, November 13, 1919.

62. *Correspondence* (03899), Alice Chipman Dewey to Dewey Children, May 3, 1919.

63. *Correspondence* (03899), Alice Chipman Dewey to Dewey Children, May 3, 1919.

64. *Correspondence* (03558), John Dewey to Dewey Children, June 27, 1919.

65. "The American Scholar," Emerson and Ziff (1982): 92.

66. *Correspondence* (10774), John Dewey to Dewey Children, July 17, 1919.

67. "What Holds China Back," MW 12: 52, 55.

68. "Old China and New," MW 13: 93.

69. "What Holds China Back," MW 12: 52.

70. "Chinese National Sentiment," MW 11: 223.

71. "What Holds China Back," MW 12: 52.

72. "Chinese National Sentiment," MW 11: 220.

73. "What Holds China Back," MW 12: 52–53.

74. "Old China and New," MW 13: 106.

75. "Chinese National Sentiment," MW 11: 219–20.

76. "What Holds China Back," MW 12: 52, 53, 55–56.

77. Cooley (1909): 23–31.

78. *The Public and Its Problems*, LW 2: 260, 262, 295–96, 316, 367–68, 371.

79. Lamont and Farrell (1959): 87–90, edited for brevity.

80. Wang (2007): 87.

81. Ames and Rosemont (2011): 18.

82. "On Philosophical Synthesis," LW 17: 35–36.

83. Frega (2015): 98.

84. Keenan (1977): 13, italics added.

85. Chiang Yung-chen, private communication, February 6, 2017.

86. See: Dewey (2015).

87. Chiang Yung-chen would disagree, maintaining that, "Dewey did not stray much from his prepared notes to elaborate and digress," and that most discrepancies stem from alterations that Hu Shih later made. Roberto Frega, however, sees it differently: "We can safely make the assumption that Dewey did not read the text he prepared to his audience, as it is clear that this text was not written to be read but rather as a basis for the talk." I tend to think that both processes occurred. Dewey elaborated on his notes in an ad-lib manner, and Hu elaborated on the resulting transcriptions as he re-wrote them for publication. These are not mutually exclusive propositions. See: Chiang (2015): 75 and Frega (2015): 107.

88. Clopton and Ou (1973): 44.

89. Chiang (2015): 75, 95, *passim*.

90. For instance, at one juncture, we find Dewey speaking in a scolding tone toward the student movement, and this is not what he would have done. Hu Shih, however, believed that the student movement was an impertinent distraction from genuine cultural reform—thus the scolding. Some of Dewey's statements regarding language reform also sound unusually strident. For example, Dewey is recorded as saying: "Some classical scholars vehemently oppose this idea on the ground that *baihua* 白話 is so simple that anyone can learn it, and if it should become the language of

instruction, *guwen* 古文 would become obsolete, and the advantage they now enjoy because of their ability to read it would disappear!" It is hard to imagine Dewey weighing in on this topic so forcefully and with such confidence. See: Wang (2005): 30–40 and Clopton and Ou (1970): 241.

    91. Dewey's "China lectures" have recently been recompiled and reissued in China. See: Yuan, et al. (2004). The collection also includes thirteen talks and lectures by Alice and Lucy Dewey.

    92. The notes for lectures I–IV comprise a natural set, and X–XII and XVI another. The first set (I–IV) will be considered presently, and the latter set will be taken in up chapter 4.

    93. Dewey (2015): 7, 8.
    94. Dewey (2015): 9, 10.
    95. Clopton and Ou (1973): 58.
    96. Dewey (2015): 12, 15, italics, in this instance, is what was underlined by hand.
    97. Dewey's 1915 "Progress" article (MW 10: 234–43) approximates the present argument, and he never doubted the continuity between human activities and material conditions.
    98. Dewey (2015): 16.
    99. Dewey (2015): 18, 19.
    100. Dewey (2015): 16.
    101. Clopton and Ou (1973): 68–70.
    102. Dewey (2015): 19.
    103. "Chinese National Sentiment," MW 11: 220.
    104. "Old China and New," MW 13: 104.
    105. See: volume one, pg. 188.
    106. "Contributions to *Cyclopdia of Education*," MW 6: 413–14.
    107. "The New Leaven in Chinese Politics," MW 12: 42.
    108. *Analects* 2.3, Ames and Rosemont (1998): 76.
    109. "The New Leaven in Chinese Politics," MW 12: 42–43.
    110. "The New Leaven in Chinese Politics," MW 12: 47.
    111. Dewey (2015): 20.
    112. Dewey (2015): 22.
    113. Dewey (2015): 22.
    114. Dewey (2015): 23.
    115. Dewey (2015): 24.
    116. Feedback loops develop here. The conservative mind needs there to be "radical individuals" against whom it struggles. So-called "relativists" serve this purpose.
    117. Dewey (2015): 25.
    118. *Analects* 7.28, Ames and Rosemont (1998): 117.
    119. Dewey (2015): 25.
    120. Frega (2015): 104.
    121. "Syllabus: Social Institutions and the Study of Morals," MW 15: 246.
    122. Such discussions do not reappear again until 1949, in the "Re-Introduction to *Experience and Nature*," LW 1: 331–32 and "Dewey's Reply to Albert G. Balz," LW 16: 288.

123. *Correspondence* (15892), John Dewey to Arthur F. Bentley, January 18, 1951.
124. *The Public and Its Problems*, LW 2: 260–61, commas inserted.
125. As for communities of interest without political organization, Confucius says: "Just being filial is carrying out the work of government" (*Analects* 2.21). As for patterns of association exemplified in the family, Confucius says: "Concentrating on the root, i.e. the family, [social order] grows from there" (*Analects* 1.2). As for customs sufficing in place of legislation, Confucius says: "Lead with *li* 禮 rather than law" and "get rid of court cases altogether" (*Analects* 2.3 and 12.13). See: Ames and Rosemont (1998): 71, 76, 80, 157.
126. *The Public and it Problems*, LW 2: 261.
127. *Human Nature and Conduct*, MW 14: 54.
128. Again, in his China writings, Dewey routinely uses the word "customs" when referring to *li* 禮. See: "Chinese National Sentiment," MW 11: 215, 223 and "New Culture in China" and "Chinese Resignations," MW 13: 114, 209. As Sor-hoon Tan observes, "customs," for Dewey, "if not exactly equivalent to *li* 禮, are akin to or at least overlap with them." See: Tan (2011): 475.
129. *Human Nature and Conduct*, MW 14: 54.
130. *Democracy and Education*, MW 9: 304.
131. Clopton and Ou (1985): 68, 71.
132. *Human Nature and Conduct*, MW 14: 58.
133. *The Public and Its Problems*, LW 2: 296.
134. "Chinese National Sentiment," MW 11: 219–20, "Transforming the Mind of China," MW 11: 214.
135. *The Public and Its Problems*, LW 2: 367.
136. Edel (2001): 104, 108.
137. *Ethics*, MW 5: 72.
138. *Ethics*, LW 7: 65.
139. Clopton and Ou (1970): 295.
140. *The Public and Its Problems*, LW 2: 327.
141. Clopton and Ou (1973): 73, c.f. Dewey (2015): 20. This is foreshadowed in *Reconstruction in Philosophy*, MW 12: 196, but it becomes more fully developed in the Beijing lectures.
142. Hall and Ames (1999): 198.
143. *Individualism Old and New*, LW 5: 67.
144. Edel (2001): 136.
145. *Individualism Old and New*, LW 5: 86.
146. *Individualism Old and New*, LW 5: 86.
147. Martin (2002): 393.
148. *Individualism Old and New*, LW 5: 75.
149. *Analects* 1.12, Ames and Rosemont (1998): 74.
150. *Individualism Old and New*, LW 5: 81.
151. Hsu (2016).
152. Gallup Poll, May 19, 2016. See: http://www.gallup.com/poll/191645/americans-support-gay-marriage-remains-high.aspx.

153. Dewey (2015): 20–25.
154. Sim (2009): 91.
155. Ivanhoe (2007): 213, 219.
156. *Analects* 2.23, Ames and Rosemont (1998): 81.
157. Li (2014): 31–32, 124–27.
158. Ni (2016): 54.
159. Bockover (2008): 197.
160. Olberding (2012): 67.
161. *Analects* 12.1, Ames and Rosemont (1998): 152.
162. *Analects* 12.24, Ames and Rosemont (1998): 160.
163. *Analects* 1.12, Ames and Rosemont (1998): 74.
164. "Psychology and Work," LW 5: 239.
165. *The Public and Its Problems*, LW 2: 250.
166. "The Inclusive Philosophic Idea," MW 3: 43.
167. *The Public and Its Problems*, LW 2: 250, italics added.
168. "The Inclusive Philosophic Idea," MW 3: 44.
169. *Freedom and Culture*, LW 13: 66.
170. "Interview with Roger T. Ames," *Confucius Institute Magazine* 39.4 July, 2015, pg. 6/10.
171. Graham (1989): 19.
172. Waley (1938): 27.
173. *Analects* 17.21, Ames and Rosemont (1998): 208–10.
174. Knoblock (1988): 206, Xunzi 荀子 (1995): 71.
175. Knoblock (1990): 104, Xunzi 荀子 (1995): 164.
176. Knoblock (1988): 206, Xunzi 荀子 (1995): 71.
177. *Analects* 17.2, Ames and Rosemont (1998): 203.
178. *Experience and Nature*, LW 1: 141, 144.
179. *Art as Experience*, LW 10: 249, italics added.
180. *Experience and Nature*, LW 1: 132–33.
181. *Psychology: Briefer Course*, James and Myers (1992): 173.
182. "What Makes a Life Significant?" James and Myers (1992): 862.
183. *Experience and Nature*, LW 1: 157.
184. Ames (2009): 266.
185. *Ethics*, LW 7: 450.
186. Coontz (2005): 15, 306.
187. *State vs. Richard Oliver*, Supreme Court of North Carolina, Raleigh: 70 N.C. 60. January, 1874, Decided.
188. Legge (1967): Vol. 1, 457, Liji 禮記 (1998) 上: 452.
189. Rosenlee (2006): 123.
190. Chow (1960): 257–59.
191. "Anti-Naturalism in Extremis," LW 15: 59.
192. *Reconstruction in Philosophy*, MW 12: 146.
193. *Analects*, 2.11, Ames and Rosemont (1998): 78.
194. *Democracy and Education*, MW 9: 85.

195. *Analects* 7.20, Ames and Rosemont (1998): 115.
196. *Analects* 11.20, Ames and Rosemont (1998): 146.
197. *Reconstruction in Philosophy*, MW 12: 138.
198. Li (2014): 1.
199. *Nicomachean Ethics*, 1172a.3–9, Aristotle and McKeon (2001): 1093.
200. *Individualism Old and New*, LW 5: 80–81.
201. *Ethics*, LW 7: 450.
202. *Liberalism and Social Action*, LW 11: 31.
203. *The Public and Its Problems*, LW 2: 368.
204. Cua (1989): 214–20.
205. *Experience and Nature*, LW 1: 158.
206. Dewey (2015): 44.

Chapter 4

1. See: *Nicomachean Ethics* 1131a.33, Aristotle and McKeon (2001): 1007 and Li (2014): 122.

2. Li (2014): 143–47.

3. Early on in Plato's *Republic*, Socrates asks how one gives "justice to things" (*dikaiosunē*) and who is qualified to give each thing its "proper due." Such moments in the philosophical corpus mark with unusual clarity the historical divergence of the Greek and Chinese approaches. Plato's answer is that it is the expert in the relevant art (*technē*) who is best suited to adjudicate "the right" wherever the principles of that art obtain. Knowing (*episteme*) such principles and applying them case-by-case is what judiciousness comes to mean. The kind of *dao* 道-activity prioritized in the Chinese tradition, however, more closely resembles a knack (*empeiria*) than an art. It is not a form of casuistry commensurate with what we commonly find in the Greek-medieval tradition. Rather, it involves the ability to weigh (*quan* 權) situations in a discretionary sense so as to get the optimal result out of them. This renders rightness (*yi* 義) a relational rather than a static term. Of course, there are exceptions in each tradition. Contrarians like Mozi and Gaozi insist that *yi* is a fixed standard that "emerges from Heaven" (*zitianchu* 自天出) or is otherwise external (*wai* 外) to particular situations. Such exceptions prove the rule. More mainstream thinkers like Confucius and Mencius mean to distinguish rightness (*yi*) from such transcendent principles. See: *Republic* 332a–e, Plato and Cooper (1997): 976–77, Mozi and Johnston (2010): 244–45, *Analects* 4.10, Ames and Rosemont (1998): 91, *Mencius* 4A.17 and 6A.4, Bloom (2009): 82, 122.

4. Zangwill (1932): 33, 184–85.

5. Szuberla (1995): 3.

6. The "Melting Pot" became one of Henry Ford's favorite ideas. Three years after Zangwill's play premiered, Ford revolutionized American industry with the Ford Model "T." Immigrants began flocking to Detroit for jobs on the assembly lines. The "Sociological Department" of the Ford Motor Company was established in 1914 to facilitate their assimilation into American life. Through the "Ford English School,"

immigrants learned to speak English and to practice "proper" American habits in areas such as food preparation, etiquette, hygiene, and manners. Upon graduation from the Ford English School, a ceremony was held in which the students would wear costumes reflecting their native lands and one-by-one descend into an enormous stage-prop "Melting Pot," only to emerge in Western suits waving little American flags. The "Melting Pot" idea thus fit hand-in-hand with industrialization in the United States. Industries like the Ford Motor Company were not only mass-producing automobiles, they were mass-producing "Americans." Ford's demographic proclivities as well as his racial and ethnic preferences did not go unnoticed on the world stage. He is the only American deemed worthy of praise in Hitler's *Mein Kampf*.

7. "The Principle of Nationality," MW 10: 289, capitalization added.
8. "Universal Service as Education," MW 10: 183–85, 188, italics added.
9. "Nationalizing Education," MW 10: 204.
10. "Universal Service as Education," MW 10: 188–89.
11. Whitman (2007): 39.
12. While Whitman the *poet* sang the song of America, Whitman the man had mixed feelings about New York City's swelling immigrant populations. Between 1845 and 1855, three million foreigners came to American shores. Culturally speaking, the American *ethos* was never exactly "*pro*-foreigner"—and Whitman was nothing if not an American. Responses to the cultural influx in Whitman's day ranged from the jingoistic nativism of the "Know-Nothings" to the "outreach" of Tammany Hall, which leveraged welfare assistance to new arrivals to bolster its own voter rolls. In Whitman's prose writings, his nativist sympathies come through, and he was not without his prejudices. However, "if he was a nativist," biographer David Reynolds writes, "he was one with a difference." As a poet, Whitman remained wholly beyond ethnic prejudice: "Pleased with the native and pleased with the foreign . . . pleased with the old, and pleased with the new." As a person, however, he identified as someone born and raised in the United States. The resulting paradox is one that lies at the heart of the American experience. See: Reynolds (1995): 98–99, 150–53, Whitman and Schmidgall (1999): 44.
13. Whitman (2007): 67.
14. Reynolds (1995): 309.
15. *Some Problems of Philosophy*, James and Kuklick (1987): 1057.
16. *A Pluralistic Universe*, James and Kuklick (1987): 776.
17. *Some Problems in Philosophy*, James and Kuklick (1987): 1046–047.
18. Kallen (1915): 194, 217.
19. *Correspondence* (03222), John Dewey to Horace M. Kallen, March 31, 1915.
20. "The Principle of Nationality," MW 10: 289.
21. "Nationalizing Education," MW 10: 206.
22. *German Philosophy and Politics*, MW 8: 203.
23. Pratt (2002): 19–20, 103–06, 124.
24. *Correspondence* (15121), John Dewey to Catherine B. Wurster on behalf of the "Common Council for American Unity," April 4, 1949.
25. "Nationalizing Education," MW 10: 202.
26. *Democracy and Education*, MW 9: 26.

27. "Nationalizing Education," MW 10: 204–06.
28. *Correspondence* (21234), Sidney Hook to J. Christopher Eisele, May 15, 1974.
29. In 1956, the 84th Congress of the United States adopted "In God We Trust" as the official U.S. motto, in violation (one would assume) of the Establishment Clause of the First Amendment. Its constitutionality was first challenged in *Aronow vs. United States* in 1970, but the motto was upheld by the Court of Appeals for the Ninth Circuit. Given this precedent, subsequent challenges have not gone very far. *E Pluribus Unum* remains our "un-official" motto.
30. Mozi and Johnston (2010): 131–65.
31. *Analects* 1.2, Ames and Rosemont (1998): 71.
32. "Tenth Fragment," Allen (1966): 41.
33. "Moretum," Virgil and Wilstach (1884), Vol. 1: 123.
34. The objection that "dysfunctional families" exist only begs the question. Families become dysfunctional precisely when they fail to realize the normative measure of harmony (*he* 和).
35. Tan (2003): 60.
36. Kallen (1915): 219.
37. *The Public and Its Problems*, LW 2: 347.
38. "Our Un-Free Press," LW 11: 272.
39. "Radio's Influence on the Mind," LW 9: 309.
40. "The Crucial Role of Intelligence," LW 11: 344.
41. The Federal Communications Commission (FCC) implemented the "Mayflower Doctrine" in 1941, which required broadcasters to "provide full and equal opportunity for the presentation to the public all sides of public issues." This doctrine was replaced by the more robust "Fairness Doctrine" in 1949, which outlined in detail how broadcasters must provide adequate reply time to opposing viewpoints. The "Fairness Doctrine" was eliminated in 1987 under the Reagan Administration. Two corollary rules remained in place: the "Personal Attack Rule" and the "Political Editorial Rule." These were suspended (rather suspiciously) one month before Election Day in 2000. They were officially scrubbed under the George W. Bush Administration.
42. *Individualism Old and New*, LW 5: 82.
43. *Analects* 17.14, Ames and Rosemont (1998): 207.
44. See: Chan and Robinowitz (2006).
45. "China Employs Two Million Microblog Monitors State Media Says," *BBC News*, October 4, 2013.
46. Wallas (1914): 3.
47. *The Public and Its Problems*, LW 2: 323–24, 327.
48. "Creative Democracy: The Task Before Us," LW 14: 230.
49. *The Public and Its Problems*, LW 2: 328, italics added.
50. "Vocational Education and the Labor Problem," Clopton and Ou (1970): 64.
51. *The Public and Its Problems*, LW 2: 261–62.
52. "The Meaning of Democracy," Clopton and Ou (1970): 83.
53. "Creative Democracy: The Task Before Us," LW 14: 226.
54. *Ethics*, MW 5: 520–21.

55. *Democracy and Education*, MW 9: 368. The hyphens are added in give-and-take for consistency. Dewey eventually comes to use them when he identifies "give-and-take" with how democracies are governed. See: *Correspondence* (19905), John Dewey to To Whom it May Concern, June 25, 1941.
56. "The Principle of Nationality," MW 10: 288.
57. *Ethics*, LW 7: 50, 349.
58. *The Public and Its Problems*, LW 2: 332, 371.
59. *Individualism Old and New*, LW 5: 82.
60. "Democracy and Education in the World Today," LW 13: 303.
61. Hall and Ames (1999): 49.
62. Tan (2003): 6–9.
63. Grange (2004): xv.
64. *Analects* 14.6, Ames and Rosemont (1998): 172.
65. *Analects* 14.23, Ames and Rosemont (1998): 177.
66. Grange (2004): xvii, 2, 18.
67. Hall and Ames (1999): 96.
68. Tan (2003): 16.
69. Hall and Ames (1999): 91.
70. Hall and Ames (1999): 97.
71. Tan (2003): 14, capitalization and backslash added.
72. Grange (2004): 70.
73. Tan (2003): 29.
74. Hall and Ames (1999): 112.
75. *The Public and Its Problems*, LW 2: 329.
76. Grange (2004): 67.
77. Hall and Ames (1999): 124.
78. Tan (2003): 162–67.
79. Hall and Ames (1999): 202.
80. *The Public and Its Problems*, LW 2: 329.
81. Tan (2003): 102, italics added.
82. *The Public and Its Problems*, LW 2: 329–30.
83. "Philosophy and Democracy," MW 11: 50, 53.
84. "Freedom, Equality, Individualism, and Education in American Democracy," Clopton and Ou (1970): 13.
85. Edel (2001): 134.
86. Clopton and Ou (1973): 154.
87. It is unfortunate that Dewey's notes for this particular lecture, in which he discusses Mencius, were not among the cache recently recovered from the Hu Shih archives.
88. Meng (1981): 96–97.
89. Chan (1963): 86–87.
90. *Mencius* 4A.5, Bloom (2009): 76, Mengzi 孟子 (1995): 171.
91. *The Public and Its Problems*, LW 2: 368.
92. Hall and Ames (1999): 132.

93. Myall (2012): 4.
94. "In Maine, A Common Language Connects French Canadians, African Immigrants," *National Public Radio*, broadcast on March 27, 2017.
95. Grange (2004): 95–96.
96. Dewey (2015): 25.
97. Yuan, et al. (2004): Vol. 1: 44 and "Essentials of Democratic Politics," Clopton and Ou (1973): 90.
98. Dewey (2015): 25. Dewey here uses the term "*inter*-action," but I have taken the liberty of updating his vocabulary to "*trans*-action" to reflect his ultimate position.
99. "The Relationship Between Democracy and Education," Clopton and Ou (1973): 94.
100. Tan (2003): 196.
101. *Mencius* 2A.3, Bloom (2009): 33, Mengzi 孟子 (1995): 69.
102. *Mencius* 7A.13, Bloom (2009): 146, Mengzi 孟子 (1995): 345.
103. Dewey (2015): 27–28.
104. *Analects* 1.2, Ames and Rosemont (1998): 71.
105. *Analects* 13.3, Ames and Rosemont (1998): 162.
106. Hall and Ames (1999): 158.
107. Dewey (2015): 26.
108. *Analects* 7.28, Ames and Rosemont (1998): 117.
109. Wu (1981): 71.
110. Ni (2016): 88.
111. *Analects* 15.5, Ames and Rosemont (1998): 185.
112. Dewey (2015): 30.
113. Tan (2003): 156.
114. Dewey (2015): 32.
115. Hall and Ames (1999): 113.
116. Dewey (2015): 39.
117. Dewey (2015): 39–40.
118. Grange (2004): 109.
119. Dewey (2015): 40.
120. Dewey (2015): 40.
121. Clopton and Ou (1973): 151–52, 154.
122. Tan (2003): 72–75.
123. Clopton and Ou (1973): 159, 163.
124. Clopton and Ou (1973): 164–68.
125. Hu (1963): 9.
126. Winchester (2008): 172, 259–60, Sivin (2015).
127. Sivin (2015): 6, 11, 13.
128. Sivin (2015): 3–6.
129. Gardiner (2007): 136.
130. Glossing the character *ge* 格 as "arriving" (*zhi* 至) is one of the central elements of Zhu Xi's interpretation. What are these "things" that are being arrived at? Dewey would call them "facts."

131. Graham (1989): 134.
132. Hu (1934): 72.
133. Clopton and Ou (1973): 169.
134. Clopton and Ou (1973): 168–71.
135. Dewey (2015): 41.
136. Dewey (2015): 41.
137. Hall and Ames (1999): 205.
138. *Analects* 16.13, Ames and Rosemont (1998): 200–01.
139. *Analects* 17.10, Ames and Rosemont (1998): 206.
140. Dewey (2015): 41, hyphens added for in "give-and-take" for consistency.
141. Grange (2003): 51, 66.
142. *Analects* 12.1, Ames and Rosemont (1998): 152.
143. Dewey (2015): 41.
144. *Analects* 13.5 and 17.9, Ames and Rosemont (1998): 163, 206.
145. "The New Paternalism," MW 11: 118.
146. Dewey (2015): 42.
147. Hall and Ames (1999): 138.
148. Along the way, let us remember that the landscape continues to change. Fox News for instance, at the time of writing, remains the most watched cable news network in the United States according to Nielsen ratings. The median age of its viewership, however, is *sixty-eight*. David is a younger generation with its own stones and slings, and against this generation such aging Goliaths will have diminishing power. New media is rapidly positioning itself to take over the news mantle, and hopefully the essence and integrity of news will be restored in the process.
149. *The Public and Its Problems*, LW 2: 347.
150. "Context and Thought," LW 6: 9–10.
151. *Analects* 2.11, Ames and Rosemont (1998): 78.
152. Dewey (2015): 43.
153. Grange (2004): 52.
154. Frisina (2002): 169.
155. *The Public and Its Problems*, LW 2: 350.
156. Dewey (2015): 44.
157. *The Public and Its Problems*, LW 2: 350.
158. *Correspondence* (03964), John Dewey to Dewey Family, July 25, 1921.
159. *Correspondence* (03936 and 03943), Lucy Dewey to Dewey Family, July 28, 29, 1921.
160. Keenan (1977): 65–66.
161. Clopton and Ou (1973): 23.
162. Ho (1991): 141–45.
163. Tillman (2013): 217.
164. *Correspondence* (04723), John Macrae to John Dewey, October 3, 1921.
165. Bieler (2004): 209.
166. *Columbia Spectator*, October 14, 1921: 1–3; October 15, 1921: 3.
167. Veazie (1961): 1.

168. Feng (1948): 539.
169. Feng (2000): 52.
170. See: Feng (1924).
171. Feng (2000): 112–18, italics added.
172. Feng (1948): 540.
173. "Textual Commentary," LW 1: 402–02.
174. Wang (2007): 122–23.
175. Meng (1981): 113, 43–144.
176. *Correspondence* (04953), John Dewey to Evangeline Walker Andrews, June 10, 1926: n.1.
177. Bieler (2004): 236.
178. *Correspondence* (03135): Lucy Dewey Brandauer to Dewey Family, October 27, 1924.
179. *Correspondence* (03146): Lucy Dewey Brandauer to Dewey Family, January 12–13, 1925.
180. *Correspondence* (03110): Eliza H. Kendrick to Alice Chipman Dewey, January 25, 1924.
181. *Correspondence* (03112): Grace Li to Alice Chipman Dewey, February 1, 1924.
182. *Correspondence* (05622): T. Y. Wang to John Dewey, July 20, 1927.
183. See, for instance: Clopton and Ou (1983): "Appendix," 225–63, Keenan (1977), Kuang (1994): Ch. 3, Ching (1985), and Gu (2015).
184. Gu (2015).
185. Martin (2002): 326.
186. *Analects* 1.12, Ames and Rosemont (1998): 74.
187. *Analects* 17.21, Ames and Rosemont (1998): 208–10.
188. Olberding (2011): 154, 159. As Olberding explains, factors such as higher childhood mortality rates, lower life expectancy rates, and the foundational role of family in the larger social order, shaped Warring States attitudes toward the deaths of relatives.
189. *Analects* 2.23, Ames and Rosemont (1998): 81.
190. See: "Actors Fill in at Family Funerals: Chinese Mourners Hiring Professionals to Wail Loudly as Traditional Ritual Dictates," *Daily Mail*, April 6, 2014.
191. Moirology, however, is in fact an ancient practice that is exhibited in several cultures. As God says in *Jeremiah* 9:17: "Call for the mourning women, that they may come."
192. Hu (1919): 709–23.
193. *Analects* 3.4, Ames and Rosemont (1998): 82–83.

Chapter 5

1. Washington (1988): 9, 12, 14, 19.
2. *Analects* 10: 2, 4, 10, Ames and Rosemont (1998): 134–35, 138. Translation is Ames and Rosemont's.

3. Angle (2014): 238–40.
4. See: Yu (2007): 82.
5. Van Norden (2007): 21, 101, 117, 126–33.
6. "On Philosophical Synthesis," LW 17: 36.
7. While not alone in applying foreign categories to Chinese thinkers, Van Norden is notably prolific in doing so. As critics observe, in his presentation of the Chinese philosophical tradition, "All Chinese thinkers are interpreted in terms of Western philosophical doctrines," which negatively affects the "interpretive precision" of his readings. See: Lau (2015): 523.
8. Ni (2017): 222–29.
9. Ni (2016): 60.
10. Van Norden (2007): 2, 6.
11. *Physics* 192b.8–193b.22, Aristotle and McKeon (2001): 236–38.
12. *Nicomachean Ethics* 1098a.15–20, Aristotle and McKeon (2001): 943.
13. *Summa Theologica* Pt. 1 Q. 44, Art. 4, Aquinas (1948): 232.
14. *Compendium of Theology*, Pt. 1 Ch. 137, "Fortuitous Events," Aquinas (1947): 146.
15. Van Norden (2007): 126.
16. Slingerland (2001): 119.
17. *Analects* 17.2, 5.13, Ames and Rosemont (1998): 98, 203.
18. Van Norden (2007): 126.
19. Ivanhoe (2007): 213–15.
20. Graham (1989): 17.
21. Eno (1990): 96, italics added.
22. Perkins (2014): 48.
23. Ivanhoe (2007): 213–15, italics added.
24. Slingerland (2001): 118, italics added.
25. *Mozi* 48.14, Mozi and Johnston (2010): 688–89.
26. Fraser (2016): 228.
27. Keightley (2014): 63.
28. *Analects* 3.12, Ames and Rosemont (1998): 85.
29. *Analects* 7.21, Ames and Rosemont (1998): 115.
30. *Analects* 16.8, 20.3, Ames and Rosemont (1998): 198, 229.
31. Puett (2002): 98.
32. *Analects* 5.13, Ames and Rosemont (1998): 98.
33. Slingerland (2003): 44.
34. Ivanhoe (2002a): 129.
35. *Analects* 7.24, Ames and Rosemont (1998): 116.
36. Ivanhoe (2002a): 129–30.
37. Ivanhoe (2002a): 127–28.
38. Nivison (1966): 141.
39. Ivanhoe (2002a): 129–30.
40. Sim (2007): 47, 141, italics added.
41. Clopton and Ou (1985): 131.

42. Clopton and Ou (1985): 132.
43. Olberding (2008): 625.
44. Zagzebski (2013): 204.
45. *Summa Theologica* Q. 61, Art. 4, Aquinas (1948): 848.
46. Zagzebski was invited to outline her theory as part of "The Gifford Lectures" in 2015 and presents it in monograph form in Zagzebski (2017). See: http://www.giffordlectures.org/lectures/exemplarist-virtue-theory.
47. Zagzebski (2004): 45, Zagzebski (2017): 30–59.
48. See: Putnam (1975): 196–207, 215–71 and Kripke (1980): 106–55.
49. Zagzebski (2013): 198–99.
50. Olberding (2008): 627.
51. Olberding (2012): 42.
52. Zagzebski (2017): 17, 91.
53. *Ethics*, LW 7: 180.
54. Olberding (2012): 24.
55. Pappas (2008): 11.
56. Alexander (2004): 248.
57. "The Postulate of Immediate Empiricism," MW 3: 158–64, italics added.
58. "Experience and Philosophical Method," LW 1: 377.
59. Pappas (2008): 31.
60. *Experience and Nature*, LW 1: 34, 200, 352, 389.
61. "Context and Thought," LW 6: 5.
62. "Moral Theory and Practice," EW 3: 97–98, dash and italics added.
63. Pappas (2008): 49.
64. Watson (1968): 152–53.
65. "Moral Theory and Practice," EW 3: 102.
66. *Reconstruction in Philosophy*, MW 12: 180.
67. *Analects* 5.3, 8.1, 11.5, 14.9, 15.7, Ames and Rosemont (1998): 95, 120, 142–43, 173, 185–86.
68. Other passages that demonstrate "exemplarism" include *Analects* 3.22, 6.2, 6.8, 6.15, 8.21, 11.3, 11.18, 11.24, 13.8, 14.12, 18.1, 18.8, 18.11, and 19.16, although this is only a partial list.
69. *Analects* 4.17, Ames and Rosemont (1998): 92–93. The Ames/Rosemont translation is largely adopted here.
70. *Analects* 7.22, Ames and Rosemont (1998): 115–16.
71. Slingerland (2001): 119.
72. *Logic: The Theory of Inquiry*, LW 12: 169.
73. "Experience, Knowledge and Value: A Rejoinder," LW 14: 31, italics added.
74. Pappas (2008): 120.
75. *Logic: The Theory of Inquiry*, LW 12: 170.
76. *Freedom and Culture*, LW 13: 83–84.
77. *The Public and Its Problems*, LW 2: 250.
78. *Ethics*, LW 7: 323.
79. *Analects* 5.13, Ames and Rosemont (1998): 98.

80. Li (2014): 10.
81. *Analects* 17.2, Ames and Rosemont (1998): 203.
82. *Human Nature and Conduct*, MW 14:78.
83. *Analects* 1.12, 3.23, and 7.32, Ames and Rosemont (1998): 74, 88, 203.
84. *Freedom and Culture*, LW 13: 77–78.
85. Olberding (2012): 58–59.
86. Van Norden (2007): 101.

87. Space is limited here, so the reader should consult Olberding's work directly. Of particular interest is her discussion of the *Analects*' "silences," which underscores that what Confucian virtue ethics finds lacking in the text amounts to positive evidence of its exemplarism. See: Olberding (2008): 633–36.

88. Ames (2011): 169.
89. Ames and Rosemont (1998): 27.
90. Ames (2011) and Rosemont (2015).
91. *Analects* 1.2, Ames and Rosemont (1998): 71.
92. *Reconstruction in Philosophy*, MW 12: 193.
93. Dewey (2015): 20–25.
94. *Ethics*, LW 7: 227.
95. Ames and Rosemont (2011): 19.
96. Ames (2011): 193.
97. *Analects* 13.3, Ames and Rosemont (1998): 162.
98. Ames and Rosemont (2011): 19.
99. Ivanhoe (2008): 39–40, 44, italics added.
100. Moeller and D'Ambrosio (2017): 19–30.
101. Ivanhoe (2008): 38.
102. Rosemont (2008a): 393–97.

103. In fact, "virtue ethics" has become such a vague category among philosophers that, as Stephen C. Angle suggests, it might as well cover the entire range. That fact, however, also makes the "virtue ethics" designation not a very useful one. See: Angle (2014): 251.

104. Ames and Rosemont (2011): 35.
105. Van Norden (2007): 6.
106. Olberding (2008): 625 and Olberding (2012): 2, 96–99.
107. Slingerland (2011): 1.
108. See: Bullock (2011): 57, Yangzi 楊子 (1983): 卷三.一.
109. Jun (2013): 114, 118.
110. *Mencius*, 5B.1, Bloom (2009): 110–11, Mengzi 孟子 (1995): 261.

111. This can be compared to the principles of archery in the Zen tradition, wherein all elements of the shot "flow together without a break." See: Herrigel (1981): 43, 61.

112. *Mencius*, 7A.33, Bloom (2009): 151–52, Mengzi 孟子 (1995): 364.
113. Lewis (1999): 162–63.
114. Tillich (1957): 10.
115. Lewis (1999): 162, 329.

116. *Analects* 11.26, Ames and Rosemont (1998): 148–51.
117. Tillich (1957): 8–9.
118. As it says in the "Meaning of Archery," *Sheyi* (射義) chapter of the *Rituals*: "moral character is observed" (*guande* 觀德) through the archery contest. See: Legge (1967), Vol. 2: 446, Liji 禮記 (1998) 下: 985.
119. The "Six Arts" are: Ritual, Music, Archery, Charioteering, Calligraphy, and Mathematics.
120. See: Legge (1967), Vol. 1: 471–72, Liji 禮記 (1998) 上: 473. Here, the gender exclusivity of archery is made painfully clear: "Males take up archery and females do not" (*nansheniifou* 男射女否). The birth of a female was heralded not with an archery bow but with a handkerchief hung on the right side of the door.
121. Fong (1988–1989): 11.
122. Selby (2000): 65.
123. *Mencius*, 3A.3, Bloom (2009): 53, Mengzi 孟子 (1995): 115.
124. In the *Book of Documents* (*Shangshu* 尚書) the "conviction of the shot" (*shezhiyouzhi* 射之有志) appears as a metaphor. See: Legge (2000), Vol. 2: 231.
125. *Mencius*, 6A.20, Bloom (2009): 131, Mengzi 孟子 (1995): 309.
126. Legge (1967), Vol. 2: 450–51, Liji 禮記 (1998) 下: 991.
127. Cheng (2004): 131–32.
128. *Ethics*, LW 7: 291.
129. Legge (1967), Vol. 2: 451, Liji 禮記 (1998) 下: 991.
130. *Analects* 12.11, Ames and Rosemont (1998): 156.
131. *Ethics*, LW 7: 228, italics added.
132. Ames and Rosemont (2009): 11.
133. *The Public and Its Problems*, LW 2: 368.
134. *Ethics*, LW 7: 117, 197–98.
135. Keating (1964): 28, 29, 30.
136. *Democracy and Education*, MW 9: 206.
137. *Mencius*, 6A.4–5, Bloom (2009): 122–23.
138. *Democracy and Education*, MW 9: 111.
139. Keating (1964): 27.
140. *Analects* 6.20, Ames and Rosemont (1998): 108.
141. Ames and Rosemont (2011): 76.
142. Ni (2018): 193.
143. *Nicomachean Ethics*, 1094a.22–25, Aristotle and McKeon (2001): 935.
144. Recall Mencius' debate with Gaozi. "Respecting the elderly," likewise, is not a self-standing end or goal to be reached without regard to means. Such ends are rather "ends-in-view," ends that are coterminal with the means by which they are realized. See: volume one, pp. 189–191.
145. *Human Nature and Conduct*, MW 14: 155–56.
146. *Ethics*, LW 7: 278.
147. *Human Nature and Conduct*, MW 14: 160, italics added.
148. *Democracy and Education*, MW 9: 112–13.
149. Knoblock and Riegel (2000): 216.

150. Zhuangzi offers up the following statement: "Some archers, without initially taking aim, still 'hit the mark' and we call them good archers. There! Everyone in the world is a Master Archer Yi. Is this acceptable?" Huizi replies: "Okay!" The point, I think, is that ethical living can be pretty hit-or-miss, and some people manage very well without trying at all. Watson (1968): 267, Zhuangzi 莊子 (1994) 下: 695.

151. *Quest for Certainty*, LW 4: 209.

152. McCartney (1926), 140, italics added. See also: McCartney (1940): 537–41.

153. I trust that this is not what the early Confucians meant by "aiming at the father target."

154. Legge (1967), Vol. 2: 449.

155. By some accounts, there were four main types of archery contests, and they varied in function. See: Selby (2000): 50–51.

156. According to tradition, the archery contest was an event institutionalized by the Duke of Zhou and held according to instructions recorded in ritual texts. It is difficult to ascertain the accuracy of the tradition or the precise historicity of the received texts. One can, however, learn a lot about the contest from available descriptions. My brief account is reconstructed from the "Ritual Observances of the District-Level Archery Meeting," *Xiangsheli* (鄉射禮) and "Great Archery Meeting," *Dashe* (大射) chapters in the *Rituals*, see: Steele (1917), Vol. 1: 74–121; 150–88, and "The Meaning of Archery," *Sheyi* (射義) chapter in the *Liji* 禮記, see: Legge (1967), Vol. 2: 446–53. I also draw from K. C. Wu's insightful account of the ancient contest. See: Wu (1982): 437–44.

157. One section reads: "When the guests have drunk too much, they shout out and become obnoxious. They disorder the dishes. They keep dancing in a fantastic manner. Thus, when they have drunk too much, they become insensible to their errors. With their caps on one side, as if falling off, they keep on dancing and will not stop. If, when they have drunk too much, they just took leave, both they [and their hosts] would be happy. But remaining after they are drunk is what is called 'doing injury to virtue.' Drinking is a good institution, but only when there is good deportment in it." See: Legge (2000), Vol. 4: 395–400. See also: Waley (1960): 296. The translation here is a slightly modified hybrid of the Legge and Waley translations.

158. Legge (1967), Vol. 2: 447–48, Liji 禮記 (1998) 下: 984–85. The character, 樂, means both "music" and "enjoyment" and is used to signify both in the text.

159. Legge (1967), Vol. 2: 453, Liji 禮記 (1998) 下: 993.

160. Bodde (1991): 293.

161. The connection between archery and displays of male elegance that stretched beyond the parameters of the archery contest is evident in the *Songs*:

Hey-ho! So handsome and accomplished! Magnificent in stature!
What elegance in his high forehead! What motion in his beautiful eyes!
What skill in the swift movement of his feet!
What a master of archery.

See: Legge (2000), Vol. 4, 161 and Waley (1960): 22. The translation here is a slightly modified hybrid of the Legge and Waley translations.

162. Zagzebski (2017): 86.
163. Olberding (2012): 91.
164. *Analects* 3.7, Ames and Rosemont (1998): 83.
165. Knoblock and Reigel (2000): 101.
166. *Mencius* 2A.7, Bloom (2009): 36, Mengzi 孟子 (1995): 76. See also: Hall and Ames (2001): 94–95.
167. *Mencius* 5B.1, Bloom (2009): 111, Mengzi 孟子 (1995): 261.
168. *Mencius* 7A.33, Bloom (2009): 151–52, Mengzi 孟子 (1995): 364.
169. *Mencius* 4A.4, Bloom (2009): 76, Mengzi 孟子 (1995): 170.
170. *Mencius* 4B.28, Bloom (2009): 92, Mengzi 孟子 (1995): 226–27.
171. *Analects* 4.4, Ames and Rosemont (1998): 89.
172. *Analects* 4.3, Ames and Rosemont (1998): 89.
173. *Mencius* 4B.28, Bloom (2009): 92–93, Mengzi 孟子 (1995): 226–27.
174. *Mencius*, 2A.2, Bloom (2009): 29, Mengzi 孟子 (1995): 57.
175. For a discussion of the attainment of sagehood and its status as a "distant goal" in early Confucianism, see: Rosemont (2008b): 157–58.
176. Confucius subordinates "strength" in the archery metaphor. As he says: "In archery, the concern is not to pierce the leather target. This is because the strength of archers is not the same. Such is the ancient way." This is echoed in the "Ritual of the District Archery Meeting," *Xiangsheli* (鄉射禮) chapter of the *Etiquette and Ritual* (*Yili* 儀禮) which suggests that archery is all about "Ritual in shooting, not piercing the target" (*lishebuzhupi* 禮射不主皮). Once divided into groups, archers were not expected to reach targets beyond their current strength. With practice, however, their strength could increase. This was understood as an orderly process wherein "position" is of first importance and "strength" is something that comes gradually. See: *Analects* 3:16, Ames and Rosemont (1998): 86.
177. *Mencius*, 7A.41, Bloom (2009): 154, Mengzi 孟子 (1995): 372.
178. *Mencius* 2A.7, Bloom (2009): 36, Mengzi 孟子 (1995): 76.
179. Legge (1967), Vol. 2: 452, Liji 禮記 (1998) 下: 993.
180. *Mencius* 7B.16, Bloom (2009): 159, Mengzi 孟子 (1995): 389.
181. *Human Nature and Conduct*, MW 14: 16, 217, 219.
182. *Mencius* 7A.4, Bloom (2009): 144, Mengzi 孟子 (1995): 339.
183. *Ethics*, LW 7: 270.
184. *Analects* 4.15, Ames and Rosemont (1998): 92.
185. *Ethics*, LW 7: 257.
186. Olberding (2012): 188.

Chapter 6

1. *Correspondence*, Research Tools, Identifications, "Hu Shih."
2. Munro (2002): 305–07.
3. Munro (2005): 72, 85, italics added.
4. Munro (2002): 305–06.

5. Bloom (2002): 100–01.
6. Ivanhoe (2004): 263.
7. Ivanhoe (2004): 217; see also: Ivanhoe (2000): 17–18, 22.
8. Ivanhoe (2007): 216 and Ivanhoe (1997): 156.
9. Ivanhoe (2000): 18, 20.
10. Bloom (2002): 100.
11. Perkins (2014): 116.
12. Ivanhoe (2002b): 59.

13. The intelligent design theory that Ivanhoe attributes to Mencius, while explicated only thinly, differs from the kind of Deism that one associates with thinkers like William Paley. It is grounded more firmly in Greek-medieval principles. Aquinas reasons that providence must be present wherever there is evidence of final causality exhibited in things that lack intelligence. It is important to recognize that Aquinas' reasoning, unlike that of the modern Deist, begins with the presence of finality in non-cognitive nature (the Aristotelian premise). The latter, so-called "teleological argument" finds design in nature and thus postulates an intelligent "maker"—an argument from analogy that relies on mechanistic assumptions rather than teleological assumptions. The "Heaven's plan" outlook that Ivanhoe attributes to early Confucianism most closely resembles Aquinas' argument for "Divine Providence." For a helpful summary of Aquinas' distinct line of argument, see: Wippel (2000): 410–13.

14. *Mencius* 2A.6, 6A.6, 6A14–15, 7A.1, Bloom (2009): 35–36, 123–24, 129–30, 144, Mengzi 孟子 (1995): 74, 289, 303–05, 336.

15. Legge (2000), Vol. 2: 448–49, italics added.
16. Ivanhoe (2000): 18, 20.
17. Ivanhoe (2007): 216.
18. Perkins (2014): 118.
19. See: Legge (1970): 363, 370, italics mine.

20. Michael J. Puett provides a thorough, critical review of secondary literature on such questions. Readers should also consult the primary sources that he discusses directly. See: Puett (2002): 5–26.

21. Legge (2000): Vol. 4: 73–74, 183–84.
22. Legge (2000): Vol. 4: 255, 628, 641, 503, 312, 313, 311, 325, 312, 559, 340, 528, 65–66, 326.
23. Ivanhoe (2007): 217.
24. Puett (2002): 139.
25. See, for instance: *Mencius* 4A.7, Bloom (2009): 76–77.
26. Puett (2002): 140.
27. Perkins (2014): 122–23.

28. The classic example is *Mencius* 2B.13. Here, with palpable frustration, Mencius laments the lag of *tian* 天 in bringing order to the world. One of his disciples, Chong Yu, reminds him that he himself had said in the past that one "must not complain against *tian*." Mencius snaps back, "That was then; this is now" (*biyishiciyishiye* 彼一時此一時也). Philip J. Ivanhoe argues in a 1988 paper that this response can and should be understood to serve as a "testament to Mencius' enduring faith in Heaven's plan."

This paper provides a helpful overview of the issue, but its conclusion relies again on sheer inference rather than on textual or philosophical evidence. The passage under discussion involves an apparent discrepancy. In saying, "That was then; this is now," Mencius registers frustration with affairs at Qi. But then, at the end of the passage, he seems to come around and decide that he is OK with what occurred. Ivanhoe argues that there are two possible ways to reconcile these elements. First, Mencius might be "talking himself out of his initial feeling of distress." Second, he might mean in the first statement that, "This time is the same as *that* time [when Confucius had a similar experience]." Ivanhoe prefers the second interpretation, although it is more of a grammatical stretch. What is important to recognize is that, in either case, Ivanhoe never *proves* that Mencius has "faith in the goodness of Heaven's plan." Under either proposed solution, the discrepancy is just as easily resolved by having Mencius arrive at a more stoic acceptance of whatever *tian* does, for better or for worse (the view of Michael J. Puett and others). The notion that Mencius instead displays "faith in the *goodness* of Heaven's plan" is the sheer inference. Decades later, Ivanhoe still finds *Mencius* 2B.13 "quite vexing" and expresses uncertainty with his own interpretation. Compounding such uncertainty would have to be the fact that his reading conflicts with what we know about Warring States philosophies. During this period, Confucians are criticized not for their steadfast "faith in Heaven's plan," but for what others perceive as their religious skepticism and fatalism. It is the Mohists, not the Confucians, who are known for having faith in the goodness of "Heaven's will" (*tianzhi* 天志). Ivanhoe, however, claims that Mencius has "faith" in the goodness of what happened in Qi because it "followed Heaven's will." Again, this is sheer inference on Ivanhoe's part. He provides no textual support for this claim, and indeed there is none. The phrase "Heaven's will" (*tianzhi*) appears nowhere in the *Mencius*. See: Ivanhoe (1988): 158, 160, *passim*, Ivanhoe (2007): 217n.12.

29. Bloom (2002): 100–01.
30. *A Common Faith*, LW 9: 47.
31. Ames (2002): 74.
32. *A Common Faith*, LW 9: 32.
33. *Mencius* 7A.1, Bloom (2009): 144.
34. Van Norden (1993): 343.
35. Clopton and Ou (1985): 8.
36. Puett (2002): 143.
37. Ivanhoe (2007): 219.
38 Fingarette (1972): 17.
39. *A Common Faith*, LW 9: 3, 36.
40. "Introduction: *Reconstruction as Seen Twenty-Five Years Later*," MW 12: 271.
41. Kaufmann (1956): 291, 294.
42. This vague, derisive label is used by Van Norden (and Philip J. Ivanhoe) and is normally reserved, with little explication, for David L. Hall and Roger T. Ames. Edward Slingerland engages in similar labeling when he identifies Hall and Ames (1987) with "Sartrean existentialism," even though Sartrean existentialism is considered and

explicitly rejected in that work. See: Van Norden (2007): 324–25, Ivanhoe (2002b): 6–7, Slingerland (2001): 97, Hall and Ames (1987): 74–80.
  43. Boisvert (2003): 224.
  44. *A Common Faith*, LW 9: 18.
  45. Midgley (1994): 8.
  46. Rosenthal (2003): 231.
  47. Johnson (2007): 25.
  48. Rosenthal (2003): 231.
  49. "Evolution and Ethics," EW 5: 53.
  50. *A Common Faith*, LW 9: 36.
  51. Hall and Ames (1998): 243.
  52. Mozi and Johnston (2010): 233–77.
  53. *Mencius* 5A.5, Bloom (2009): 103–04, Mengzi 孟子 (1995): 248–49.
  54. Ni (2017): 42.
  55. *Mencius* 4B.16, Bloom (2009): 89, Mengzi 孟子 (1995): 211.
  56. *The Public and Its Problems*, LW 2: 257–58.
  57. *Human Nature and Conduct*, MW 14: 216, italics added.
  58. From the Shanghai Museum collection, the *Triadic Virtue* (*Sande* 三德) manuscript maintains a fairly traditional view of "Heaven" as a force that intervenes when malfeasance occurs (including environmental abuse: denuding hilltops, damming rivers, overtaxing soil, etc.). As Scott Cook explains, the text suggests that, "Moral reckoning is not merely an inevitable consequence of the inherent order of things, but that our deeds directly beckon the conscious intervention of Heaven above." Meanwhile, the *Rongchengshi* 容成氏 manuscript, which is devoted to the history of dynastic succession (an area in which "Heaven's mandate" traditionally plays a large role), evokes *tian* 天 not at all. The text "is not interested in the mandate of heaven," explains Sarah Allan. "This lack of interest in the role of heaven is further evidence of a historical paradigm which recognized material progression, be it good or bad, and loss of faith in the idea of a spiritually transferred mandate." One would be reluctant in this period to call one view more "mainstream" than the other. Mencius seems to fall somewhere in the middle. He believes that *tian* is a responsive force, but he displays no "faith" that it leans toward the good. See: Cook (2010): 109, Allan (2010): 78.
  59. Li: (2002): 86.
  60. *Mencius* 7A.9, Bloom (2009): 145–46.
  61 *Mencius* 1B.16, Bloom (2009): 26, Mengzi 孟子 (1995): 51.
  62. Li (2002): 86.
  63. Meyer (2012): 55, 56.
  64. Pang (1999): 27.
  65. Meyer (2012): 58.
  66. At one juncture, Ivanhoe also entertains the idea that "Heaven" might be understood as "a kind of collective will." See: Ivanhoe (2007): 217n.11.
  67. *The Public and Its* Problems, LW 2: 250, 257.
  68. See, for instance, *Mencius* 1B.14, Bloom (2009): 25.

69. Puett (2002): 139.
70. See, for instance, *Mencius* 4.A7, Bloom (2009): 76–77, Mengzi 孟子 (1995).
71. Puett (2002): 140.
72. *Analects* 16.8 and 20.3, Ames and Rosemont (1998): 198, 229.
73. *Mencius* 7A.2, Bloom (2009): 144, Mengzi 孟子 (1995): 337.
74. Hillman and Davies (1990): 166–67.
75. Zohary and Hopf (1993): 63.

76. Radiocarbon analysis of seventy ancient barley grains in and around the region, together with DNA and ancient textual records, reveals that barley switched from a winter to a winter/summer crop as farmers pushed its cultivation higher into the mountains. By the time it reached China, the genetic makeup of barley "had been altered so that flowering was no longer triggered by day length, allowing it to be planted in both spring and fall." See: Liu (2017).

77. Fischbeck (2002): 2.
78. *Mencius* 6A.7, Bloom (2009): 125, Mengzi 孟子 (1995): 297.
79. Robins (2011): 32.
80. Graham (1991): 287–88.
81. Yearly (2003): 137–38.
82. Bloom (1997): 32n.19.
83. *Mencius* 6A.14-15, Bloom (2009): 129–30. See also: Ivanhoe (2000): 19–20.
84. Van Norden (2004): 168.
85. Grene and Dupew (2004): 335.
86. Wilson (1978) 9–11.
87. *Analects* 18.6, Ames and Rosemont (1998): 214.
88. Butler (1850): 145, italics added.
89. Legge (2000), Vol. 2: 448 n.1.
90. Legge (2000), Vol. 2: 310–11.
91. Legge (1970): 60, 64, see also: 56–57.

92. Working within this paradigm, Lee Yearly finds that *ren* 仁 "resembles Butler's understanding of benevolence, and benevolence is clearly the best rendering of the term." David S. Nivison also evokes Bishop Butler in making sense of ethics in the *Mencius*. As one might expect, insights generated within this paradigm have a parochial feel. One is initially intrigued, for instance, when Bryan W. Van Norden suggests that Mencius' virtue ethics "provides a radical alternative to the Aristotelian and Thomistic paradigms most often evoked." How "radical" is this alternative? "Of Mencius' four cardinal virtues," he writes, "benevolence, righteousness, wisdom, and ritual propriety—only one, wisdom, corresponds even vaguely to anything in the Aristotelian list of virtues." His assumption is that the Chinese and Greek-medieval models are structurally identical and differ only in incidental content. The so-called "interesting questions" generated through such an approach excite little curiosity in the field. "For instance," Van Norden asks: "Why doesn't courage appear on Mencius' list of cardinal virtues?" See: Yearly (1990): 38, Nivison (1996): 114, Van Norden (1996): 2, 283n.2, and Van Norden (2003): 108.

93. *Mencius* 1A.7, 4B.28, 7A.46, 7B.31, Bloom (2009): 7–8, 92, 155, 163.

94. *Mencius* 6A.6, Bloom (2009): 124, Mengzi 孟子 (1995): 289.
95. "Social Emotion," Clopton and Ou (1985): 95.
96. *Mencius* 2A.6, Bloom (2009): 35.
97. De Waal (2006): 39, 49–52.
98. Joyce (2006): 19–40.
99. *Analects* 1.2, Ames and Rosemont (1998): 71.
100. See: Joyce (2006): 20–21.
101. Trivers (1971): 35.
102. De Waal (2006): 5.
103. Trivers (1971): 49.
104. "Contributions to *Cyclopedia of Education*," MW 6: 367–68.
105. *Ethics*, LW 9: 293.
106. *Mencius* 6A.6, Bloom (2009): 124, Mengzi 孟子 (1995): 289.
107. *Ethics*, LW 9: 294.
108. *Mencius* 7A.26, Bloom (2009): 150, Mengzi 孟子 (1995): 358.
109. Trivers (1971): 48.
110. *Mencius* 6A.6, Bloom (2009): 124, Mengzi 孟子 (1995): 289.
111. See: Van Norden (2007): 264 and Shun (1997): 60. Van Norden and Shun each maintain that Zhu Xi's interpretation "cannot be correct" because the term for "dislike" (*wu* 惡) is also used with respect to one's own errant behavior in the *Mencius*. Such usages are not mutually exclusive. One can be ashamed of another person, so feelings of shame and dislike can always go both ways.
112. Pinker (2002): 439.
113. Hall and Ames (2001): 100–01.
114. *Mencius* 3B.1, 3B.10, 4B.33, 6A.10, Bloom (2009): 61–62, 71–72, 95–96, 127–28.
115. *Mencius* 6A.10, Bloom (2009): 127, Mengzi 孟子 (1995): 298.
116. See: Ziporyn (2009): 59n.10.
117. Midgley (1994): 3.
118. Church (1959).
119. See: Wechkin and Masserman et al. (1964).
120. De Waal (2006): 29.
121. Hall and Ames (2001): 100–01.
122. *Mencius* 4A.27, Bloom (2009): 84, Mengzi 孟子 (1995): 196.
123. *Mencius* 2A.6, 6A.6, Bloom (2009): 35, 124, Mengzi 孟子 (1995): 74, 289.
124. Zagzebski (2017): 39.
125. Goffman (1967): 277–78.
126. *Mencius* 4B.28, Bloom (2009): 92, Mengzi 孟子 (1995): 226.
127. *Mencius* 4A.17, Bloom (2009): 82, Mengzi 孟子 (1995): 187.
128. *Mencius* 6B.1, Bloom (2009): 132, Mengzi 孟子 (1995): 310.
129. Van Norden (2008): 159.
130. Shun (1997): 66.
131. *Mencius* 2A.1, Bloom (2009): 28, Mengzi 孟子 (1995): 54.
132. Van Norden (2007): 277.

133. *Mencius* 5B.1, Bloom (2009): 111.
134. Shun (1997): 68.
135. Chiang (1924): 37–50.
136. "Morality and Human Nature," Clopton and Ou (1985): 78–79.
137. Graham (1989): 246.
138. Knoblock (1994): 151, Xunzi 荀子 (1995): 482.
139. Ivanhoe (2000): 33.

140. The identity and pedigree of "Gaozi" remains a mystery. My guess is that there is no "Gaozi" and that *gao* 告 (which means to "accuse" or "say") stands in generically for the "Accuser" or "Speaker" in a debate situation. Thus, the "Gaozi" passages actually *do* serve as a debate manual for Mencius' followers. Accordingly, there is no single, coherent "Gaozi" position. This is pure speculation on my part.

141. *Mencius* 3B.9, Bloom (2009): 68, Mengzi 孟子 (1995): 154.
142. *Mencius* 7B.26, Bloom (2009): 162, Mengzi 孟子 (1995): 402.
143. *Mencius* 3B.9, Bloom (2009): 70, Mengzi 孟子 (1995): 155.
144. Bloom (1994): 44.
145. The five relations are: Ruler-Subject, Father-Son, Husband-Wife, Elder Brother-Younger Brother, and Friend-Friend.
146. *Mencius* 3A.4, Bloom (2009): 57, Mengzi 孟子 (1995): 122.

147. In this connection, Philip J. Ivanhoe describes the sages as the "paragons of human development" whose pre-programmed natures matured to create "the perfect plan for society," providing the "perfect model" for human development. See: Ivanhoe (1990): 480–82.

148. Ivanhoe (2002b): 112.
149. Ivanhoe (2000): 22.

150. *Human Nature and* Conduct, MW 14: 68. This is not an exact quote. Dewey uses the word "hen" instead of "chicken."

151. *Mencius* 3A.4, Bloom (2009): 57, Mengzi 孟子 (1995): 122.
152. Clopton and Ou (1985): 79–80.
153. Clopton and Ou (1985): 81–82, italics added.
154. Van Norden (2007): 28–29.
155. Chen (2010): 43.
156. *Mencius* 6A.6, Bloom (2009): 123–24, Mengzi 孟子 (1995): 289.
157. Robins (2011): 32.

158. Roger T. Ames notes the fate of A.C. Graham's final interpretation of *xing* 性, which was "either misunderstood or ignored" in favor of less taxing essentialist readings. Ames (2018): 199.

159. Stalnaker's comparison of Mencius, Augustine, and Xunzi on the topic of "human nature" demonstrates both the care with which we undertake such projects in the post-Hall and Ames epoch and the stubborn fact that our comparative *tertium* continue to shape our readings despite our best efforts. Stalnaker wishes to use "human nature" vaguely as a "bridge concept" for cross-cultural purposes. In doing so, he equates human nature with a "natural course of development," converts this by common sense into teleology, and then reads it back into the *Mencius*. His intention,

however, is the right one: "to achieve a high level of historical faithfulness to my sources, as interpreted within their specific contexts." See: Stalnaker (2005): 210, 218.
    160. Perkins (2010): 19.
    161. Liang and Lambert (2009): 185.
    162. Van Norden (2007): 282.
    163. *Logic: The Theory of Inquiry*, LW 12: 255.
    164. *Reconstruction in Philosophy*, MW 12: 167.
    165. "The Subject Matter of Metaphysical Inquiry," MW 8: 11.
    166. *Mencius* 6A.6, Bloom (2009): 124, Mengzi 孟子 (1995): 289.
    167. Van Norden (2007): 221.
    168. Goldhaber (2012): 38.
    169. Baye, et al. (2011): 59–60.
    170. Philip J. Ivanhoe, for instance, proposes a "thought experiment" imagining how Mencius would respond to the complete annihilation of the "Confucian cultural memory"—a reduction of human history to zero. Through this experiment, he means to assess how much cultural content, for Mencius, is the result of "accumulated experience and reflection" and how much would remain "accessible to a dedicated and reflective individual" as native content. Ivanhoe concludes that the "rationally constructed social order based upon universally available human institutions" is one that "could be easily reconstructed" were the Chinese to begin their cultural history over again from scratch. If I understand Ivanhoe correctly, he is suggesting that flesh-and-blood human experience in dynamic environments plays no role whatsoever in the advent of social and cultural order for Mencius. No part of Confucian culture is contingent. Such a view is absurd in light of modern genetics and anthropology. As Steven Pinker argues: "An infinite range of behavior can be generated by finite combinatorial programs in the mind," and "none of these forces can be understood without taking into account the thought processes of flesh-and-blood people." The historical experience of "flesh-and-blood people" explains why cultural traditions are comparable but not identical. Could Mencius (or anyone) really think otherwise? See: Ivanhoe (1990): 481, Pinker (2002): 36, 71.
    171. Buller (2005): 46–47.
    172. "Evolution and Ethics," EW 5: 45.
    173. See: Watson (1968): 33, 200, 204–05.
    174. Goldhaber (2012): 43–44.
    175. Buller (2005): 45.
    176. Jun (2013): 144–45n.28.
    177. Wilson (1994): 224.
    178. Hall and Ames (2001): 106–07. This is Hall and Ames' translation.
    179. Watson (1968): 75–76, Zhuangzi 莊子 (1994) 上: 181–82.
    180. Readers do well to consult Kim-chong Chong's reading of this passage. It is similar to the one here, but better articulated. See: Chong (2016): 88–94.
    181. Ivanhoe (2004): 262.
    182. "Evolution and Ethics," EW 5: 53.
    183. Ivanhoe (2004): 262.

184. In his article, "Of Geese and Eggs: In What Sense Should We Value Nature as a System," for instance, Ivanhoe takes up the question posed in the article's subtitle. While the origin and nature of life remains a matter of conjecture, he begins by introducing a sharp distinction between the "chemical processes" that gave birth to life and the "living cells" that mark its origin. With this distinction in place, he submits that: "While life is clearly worth valuing, it is not at all clear that we do or should value the chemical processes that resulted in the generation of life here on Earth or elsewhere." The argument proceeds from there. Taking as his point of departure Holmes Rolston, III's *biophilia* hypothesis, i.e., that "the value we see in productive organic process [is] intimately connected with the unique path evolution took here upon Earth," Ivanhoe attempts to gauge the extent to which such valuation is truly a valuing of pre-organic nature or simply a valuing of life as we know it. He performs a "thought experiment," imagining that, were we to encounter life on another planet, we *would* value the system in which it occurs. "Organic productive processes occurring on alien worlds have the *potential* to produce and sustain all the things we in fact value." Thus, for Ivanhoe, they are appropriate objects of "wonder, awe, and reverence." Closer to home, however, Ivanhoe reaches the opposite conclusion with respect to pre-organic chemical processes here on Earth: these have no "value" *per se*. "Although these chemical reactions *can* produce life," he explains (italics mine), "they do not sustain it in the way natural organic systems sustain the life within them," with life as we know it remaining the benchmark valuative reference. Ivanhoe is thus "not sure that we actually do, can, or should value the chemical processes that bring forth life" on our planet. There is a glaring inconsistency in Ivanhoe's reasoning. He equivocates "potential" (for the alien world) and "can" (for Earth), which, logically speaking is an identical criterion in terms of conferring value regardless of whether the term designated is a "system" or "process." This equivocation tracks onto the dualism that he introduces at the outset of his argument, which runs headlong to its conclusion: namely, we do and should value *life*—but we can disregard things like oxygen and carbon. See: Ivanhoe (2010): 69, 75, 77.

Chapter 7

1. *Ethics*, LW 7: 12, 299.
2. "The Crisis in Human History," LW 15: 211.
3. De Waal (2006): 4, italics added.
4. Paley (2006): 136, 164, 169.
5. *Experience and Nature*, LW 1: 195, 196, 210.
6. Birdwhistell (2007): 3, 30.
7. *Mencius* 3A.4, Bloom (2009): 54–59, Mengzi 孟子 (1995): 122.
8. *Mencius* 4A.27, Bloom (2009): 84, Mengzi 孟子 (1995): 196.
9. Watson (1968): 327, Zhuangzi 莊子 (1994) 下: 849.
10. More specifically, male parental caregiving "correlates" with lower testosterone levels, and within evolving organism-and-environment circuits influences are

always mutual (*xiang* 相). What cannot be "causally" determined, then, is whether male caregivers tend to have lower testosterone levels or whether caregiving tends to lower male testosterone levels. As this complex nature-culture equation gets written, it would be hard to argue from any essentialist perspective that the process is being driven by some universal, perfectly calibrated "human nature" generative of *eudiamonia*, as postpartum hormonal changes continue to correlate with higher rates of clinical depression in both males and females. See: Saxbe (2017).

11. Birdwhistell (2007): 133.
12. Huang (2013): 3-4.
13. Wu (1982): 420-41.
14. Legge (1967), Vol. 2: 428, Liji 禮記 (1998) 下: 964.
15. See: Wu (1982): 421.
16. Legge (1967), Vol. 2: 264, Liji 禮記 (1998) 下: 801.
17. Wu (1982): 425.
18. Black (2001): 640, 642-43.
19. Otherwise stated, with respect to humans: "Approximately 85 percent of societies in the anthropological record permit men to marry multiple wives." See: Henrich, et al. (2012): 657 and Chapais (2013): 54.
20. Chapais (2013): 52.
21. Legge (1967), Vol. 1: 380, Liji 禮記 (1998) 上: 376.
22. See: Wrangham (2009), Chapter 7, *passim*.
23. Geary and Flinn (2001): 7.
24. Taylor (2002): 120-29.
25. Chapais (2013): 59.
26. *Analects* 2.23, Ames and Rosemont (1998): 81.
27. Wu (1982): 426-27.
28. Ivanhoe (2007): 219.
29. Legge (2000), Vol. 3: 217-18.
30. Fen (1952): 23, 24-25.
31. Ivanhoe (2009): 314, 326n.24.
32. Dewey (2015): 16.
33. *Human Nature and Conduct*, MW 14: 193.
34. Ivanhoe (1990): 480-82, italics added.
35. *Human Nature and Conduct*, MW 14: 193.
36. *Reconstruction in Philosophy*, MW 12: 181-82.
37. *Human Nature and Conduct*, MW 14: 199.
38. *Art as Experience*, LW 10: 19, 30.
39. See: Johnson (2007) and Shusterman (2008).
40. Johnson (2007): 212.
41. *Mencius* 6A.7, Bloom (2009): 125-26, Mengzi 孟子 (1995): 292.
42. *Mencius* 6A.7, Bloom (2009): 125-26, Mengzi 孟子 (1995): 292.
43. Pinker (2002): 69-72, see also: Pinker (2004): 6.
44. C.f. Puett (2001): 22-25.
45. Hall and Ames (2001): 105, 112-13.

46. Li (2014): 1.
47. Karlgren (1974): 85.
48. *Art as Experience*, LW 10: 142.
49. Legge (2000), Vol. 4: 252–53.
50. Ivanhoe (2004): 262.
51. Neville (2016): 44.
52. Neville (1981): 81.
53. Li (2014): 23–27.
54. Neville (1981): 81.
55. Neville (1991): 148.
56. Neville (2000): 127.
57. Neville (1981): 81.
58. *Analects* 13.23, Ames and Rosemont (1998): 168–69.
59. Neville (1981): 81.
60. *Guoyu* 國語, *Zhengyu* 鄭語, see: Guoyu 國語 (1959): 186.
61. Allan (1997): 131.
62. Ivanhoe (2013): 31.
63. Van Norden (2007): 38.
64. Ivanhoe (2013): 29.
65. Robins (2011): 48n.30.
66. Allan (1997): 108, 135.
67. Legge (2000) Vol. 4: 64–65.
68. Liu (2013): 66, 72–73.
69. Longo and Montévil (2014): 76.
70. Robins (2011): 37, italics added.
71. Longo and Montévil (2014): 161, 165.
72. Liu (2013): 73.
73. Longo and Montévil (2014): 173.
74. Van Norden (2007): 217.
75. As David L. Hall and Roger T. Ames note, Karlgren identifies *shuai* 率 with both "following" and "leading." See: Hall and Ames (2001): 116n.4 and Karlgren (1957): 136. The ambiguity is appropriate, as *xing* 性 is simultaneously what one *is* and what one *becomes* in the process.
76. Hall and Ames (2001): 89.
77. See: Cook (2012): 678–86 for a discussion of these issues. I was initially confident that the text belonged squarely within the Si-Meng school. At the time of writing, I am not so sure.
78. Cook (2012): 697–98.
79. *Analects* 17.2, Ames and Rosemont (1998): 203.
80. Cook (2012): 667.
81. Bloom (2002): 99–100.
82. See: Bloom (1994): 33–38 and Bloom (1997): 26–27.
83. See: "Time to Retire the Simplicity of Nature vs. Nurture," *Wall Street Journal*, January 24, 2014.
84. Goldhaber (2012): 141.

85. Ivanhoe (2013): 29.
86. "Self-Realization as the Moral Ideal," EW 4: 43.
87. *Mencius* 6A.6, Bloom (2009): 124, Mengzi 孟子 (1995): 289.
88. *Mencius* 6A.8, Bloom (2009): 126, Mengzi 孟子 (1995): 294–95.
89. "Self-Realization as the Moral Ideal," EW 4: 49, italics added.
90. *Mencius* 2A.2, Bloom (2009): 30–31, Mengzi 孟子 (1995): 58.
91. *Mencius* 4B.19, Bloom (2009): 89, Mengzi 孟子 (1995): 214.
92. *Mencius* 1B.16, Bloom (2009): 26, Mengzi 孟子 (1995): 51.
93. *Mencius* 7B.25, Bloom (2009): 161–62, Mengzi 孟子 (1995): 397.
94. *Mencius* 6A.6, Bloom (2009): 123–24, Mengzi 孟子 (1995): 289.
95. "Self-Realization as the Moral Ideal," EW 4: 49.
96. *Mencius* 2A.6, Bloom (2009): 35–36, Mengzi 孟子 (1995): 289.
97. *Mencius* 4B.18, Bloom (2009): 89, Mengzi 孟子 (1995): 213.
98. *Mencius* 2A.2, Bloom (2009): 30, Mengzi 孟子 (1995): 58.
99. I discuss this more extensively in Behuniak (2005): 37–41.
100. See: Rosemont (2008a): 393–97.
101. "Self-Realization as the Moral Ideal," EW 4: 51–53.
102. *Reconstruction in Philosophy*, MW 12: 181.
103. *Democracy and Education*, MW 9: 55.
104. *Reconstruction in Philosophy*, MW 12: 181.
105. *Guoyu* 國語, *Zhengyu* 鄭語, see: Guoyu 國語 (1959): 186.
106. "The Divorce Surge is Over, but the Myth Lives On," *New York Times*, December 2, 2014.
107. *Mencius* 1A.7, 3A.3, Bloom (2009): 10, 51, Mengzi 孟子 (1995): 15, 114–15.
108. *Mencius* 1A.3, 7A.14, Bloom (2009): 3–4, 146, Mengzi 孟子 (1995): 5–6, 346.
109. *Mencius* 3A.3, 4A.13, 7A.22, Bloom (2009): 51–54, 80–81, 148–49, Mengzi 孟子 (1995): 114–15, 182, 354.
110. *Mencius* 7A.23, Bloom (2009): 149, Mengzi 孟子 (1995): 355.
111. See: Chaves (2003) and Kalb (2015).
112. Curzer (2012).
113. *Analects* 12.8, Ames and Rosemont (1998): 155.
114. *Mencius* 7B.24, Bloom (2009): 161, Mengzi 孟子 (1995): 396.
115. Van Norden (2008): 189–90.
116. *Democracy and Education*, MW 9: 68.
117. *Human Nature and Conduct*, MW 9: 65.
118. *Analects* 17.2, Ames and Rosemont (1998): 203.
119. *Mencius* 6A.8, Bloom (2009): 126–27, Mengzi 孟子 (1995): 295.
120. *Mencius* 7A.15, Bloom (2009): 147, Mengzi 孟子 (1995): 349.
121. *Mencius* 4A.27, Bloom (2009): 84, Mengzi 孟子 (1995): 196.
122. *Mencius* 3B.9, Bloom (2009): 70, Mengzi 孟子 (1995): 155.
123. Bloom (1994): 44.
124. Machery (2008): 65–66.
125. *Mencius* 2A.6, 3B.3, 6A.6, Bloom (2009): 35, 63–64, 123–24, Mengzi 孟子 (1995): 74, 140, 289.
126. Machery (2008): 66, italics added.

127. *Mencius* 4A.28, Bloom (2009): 85, Mengzi 孟子 (1995): 197–98.
128. Li (2002): 131.
129. *Mencius* 6A.6, Bloom (2009): 124, Mengzi 孟子 (1995): 289.
130. Buller (2005): 45.
131. Van Norden maintains (without much elucidation) that replacing the "details" of Mencius' position as he understands it with evolutionary biology would leave his virtue ethics reading of the *Mencius* intact, even though the "details" as he understands them include both teleological and intelligent design reasonings. Were it as easy as Van Norden suggests to substitute an evolutionary model of human nature for one divinely ordained and teleological, then one would have expected Judeo-Christian civilization to absorb Charles Darwin in stride. See: Van Norden (2007): 345–46.
132. *Mencius* 4A.28, Bloom (2009): 85, Mengzi 孟子 (1995): 197–98.
133. *Mencius* 4A.27, 6A.6, 7A.15, Bloom (2009): 84, 124, 147, Mengzi 孟子 (1995): 196, 289, 349.
134. Dewey, *Human Nature and Conduct* (MW 9: 65).
135. *Mencius* 6A.7, Bloom (2009): 125–26, Mengzi 孟子 (1995): 292.
136. *Mencius* 2A.6, Bloom (2009): 35, Mengzi 孟子 (1995): 74.
137. *Mencius* 6A.2, Bloom (2009): 121, Mengzi 孟子 (1995): 282–83.
138. *Mencius* 4B.19, Bloom (2009): 89, Mengzi 孟子 (1995): 214.
139. Goldhaber (2012): 43–44.
140. "The Inclusive Philosophical Idea," LW 3: 48.
141. Ames and Rosemont (2009): 1.
142. Neville (2002): 37.
143. Kolb and Gibb (2011): 273.
144. Tolstoy (2006): 1.
145. Cosmides and Tooby (1997): 83.
146. Richerson and Boyd (2005): 44–45.
147. *Logic: The Theory of Inquiry*, LW 12: 68–69, 101.
148. *Knowing and the Known*, LW 16: 244.
149. Downes (2009): 93.
150. Richerson and Boyd (2005): 12.
151. *Democracy and Education*, MW 9: 70.
152. Richerson and Boyd (2005): 4.
153. De Waal (2006): 5.
154. *Freedom and Culture*, LW 13: 90.
155. This is the message of the "Ox Mountain" passage. See: *Mencius* 6A.8, Bloom (2009): 126–27, Mengzi 孟子 (1995): 294–95.
156. Dewey's most concise statement on this topic is his essay, "Contrary to Human Nature," LW 14: 258–61.
157. "Does Human Nature Change?" LW 13: 286–87.
158. *Freedom and Culture*, LW 13: 142.
159. Munro (2005): 55.
160. "Does Human Nature Change?" LW 13: 287.

161. Again, in his work on "ethical promiscuity," Philip J. Ivanhoe notes the same. As Ivanhoe writes: "No single human life or culture can realize all of the values that are possible for creatures like us." See: Ivanhoe (2009): 314.
162. "The Moral Equivalent of War," James and Kuklick (1987): 1281.
163. *Freedom and Culture*, LW 13: 75.
164. "Does Human Nature Change?" LW 13: 288–89.
165. *Analects* 12.8, Ames and Rosemont (1998): 155.
166. Bloom (2002): 99–100.
167. *Mencius* 6A.6, Bloom (2009): 124, Mengzi 孟子 (1995): 289.
168. *Freedom and Culture*, LW 13: 83.
169. "Re-Introduction to *Experience and Nature*," LW 1: 331.
170. Puett (2001): 3.
171. Hall and Ames (2001): 89.
172. *Dispositions Arise from Mandated Conditions* states that: "An ox born will grow. A goose born will spread its wings. It is *xing* 性 that causes this to happen. However, for a human, it is the result of education." The deeper meaning, however, is not so easy to decipher. As Scott Cook explains, "the line in question here is crucial to our understanding of the nature of human nature and the precise role of learning in this text, but we are unfortunately left to only guess at the meaning." One assumes that "education" is to humans what "spreading wings" is to birds, but there is more than one way to understand this analogy, or possibly metaphor. See: Cook (2012): 702–03.
173. Munro (2005): 85.
174. "Does Human Nature Change," LW 13: 293. Italics added, and Dewey writes "of how" and the "of" has been removed from the quote.
175. *Mencius* 7A.40, Bloom (2009): 154, Mengzi 孟子 (1995): 371.
176. *Mencius* 4A.18, Bloom (2009): 82, Mengzi 孟子 (1995): 188.
177. Richerson and Boyd (2005): 156.
178. *Analects* 4.20, Ames and Rosemont (1998): 93.
179. Richerson and Boyd (2005): 131–47.
180. *Human Nature and Conduct*, MW 14: 77.
181. *Freedom and Culture*, LW 13: 97.
182. *Human Nature and Conduct*, MW 14: 76–77.
183. "Does Human Nature Change?" LW 13: 291–92.
184. *Psychology: Briefer Course*, James and Myers (1992): 145.
185. *Analects* 16.1, Ames and Rosemont (1998): 194–96.
186. *The Public and Its Problems*, LW 2: 327.
187. Stroud (2011): 139.
188. Stroud (2006): 292.
189. Stroud (2011): 142.
190. Stroud (2006): 297.
191. *Freedom and Culture*, LW 13: 174.
192. Richerson and Boyd (2005): 167–68.

Chapter 8

1. For a direct introduction to St. Thomas' writings on the transcendentals, see: Aquinas and Anderson (1997): 45–98. For an insightful discussion of the inclusion of "Beauty" in the thirteenth century, see: Eco (1986): 17–27.

2. Rosemont (2008b): 154.

3. *Art as Experience*, LW 10: 275.

4. Quoted from Rockefeller (1991): 319. Rockefeller's citation appears to be errant. I was unable to find the original source for this quotation.

5. *Correspondence* (11023), John D. Graves to John Dewey, August 4 1949.

6. Bloom (2002): 100–01.

7. Rockefeller (1991): 499. See also: "As the Chinese Think," MW 13: 224.

8. Rockefeller (1991): 501.

9. "Some Factors in Mutual National Understanding," MW 13: 265.

10. Rockefeller (1991): 491.

11. Hall and Ames (2001): 106.

12. "The Reflex Arc Concept in Psychology," EW 5: 96–109.

13. *Art as Experience*, LW 10: 42, 47, 50, 199.

14. *The Quest for Certainty*, LW 4: 244.

15. Hall and Ames (2001): 105.

16. Such compact reasoning may require a bit more elucidation. The idea here is that natural dispositions have a kind of "integrity" from which means-end coordination or intelligence spontaneously issues. The hen, for instance, is disposed to set on her eggs "by nature." The intelligence thus exhibited results from the fact that the "end" is thoroughly integrated into the "means." For humans, however, there is a range of technological options available. We can, for instance, produce or augment the integration of things through directed intelligence *via* education, which is the inverse of what the hen is doing. We can use our intelligence to *produce* integration, whereas for the hen its own integration *manifests* its intelligence. The point is that, regardless of how "intelligence" is exhibited in Nature, it is always attended by "integration" and *vice versa*. Human intelligence and hen intelligence are exercised differently, but the one is no less "natural" than the other. This represents, I believe, the ultimate response to Daoist critiques from the standpoint of Si-Meng Confucianism.

17. Li (2014): 23.

18. *Art as Experience*, LW 10: 23.

19. Hall and Ames (2001): 89, 116–17n.4 and 6.

20. Hall and Ames (2001): 112–13.

21. *How We Think*, MW 6: 310–11.

22. Angle (2009): 21, 65.

23. *Varieties of Religious Experience*, James and Kuklick (1987): 55, 158, 454–55.

24. *Art as Experience*, LW 10: 23.

25. As S. Morris Eames observes: "On the pragmatic naturalist's view of adjustment, sometimes the term 'integration' is used as a synonym." See: Eames (1977): 14.

26. *A Common* Faith, LW 9: 12.

27. *Art as Experience*, LW 10: 20–21.
28. Recall that for Dewey continuity "precludes reduction of the 'higher' to the 'lower' just as it precludes complete breaks and gaps," meaning that human-level operations "*grow out of* organic activities, without being identical with that from which they emerge." See: *Logic: The Theory of Inquiry*, LW 12: 26, 30.
29. Puett (2002): 134–44.
30. *A Common Faith*, LW 9: 12.
31. Puett (2002): 139.
32. *Mencius* 7A.2, Bloom (2009): 144, Mengzi 孟子 (1995): 337.
33. Lachs (2005): 96.
34. Stroud (2011): 147.
35. *A Common Faith*, LW 9: 12.
36. Hall and Ames (2001): 96.
37. Ivanhoe (2007): 212.
38. Rockefeller (1991): 488–89.
39. "Review of Intimations of Mortality," LW 11: 426.
40. "The Utility of Religion," Mill (1998): 119.
41. See: "In Taiwan, Those who Believe in Ghosts (Just about Everyone) Brace for a Long Spirit Month," *Los Angeles Times*, July 23, 2006.
42. *Unmodern Philosophy*, Dewey and Deen (2012): 4.
43. "Reconstruction," EW 4: 102.
44. *A Common Faith*, LW 9: 16.
45. Rockefeller (1991): 216.
46. Feuerbach (1873): 47.
47. *A Common Faith*, LW 9: 48.
48. *John Dewey Papers*, 102/56/16: 2.
49. *John Dewey Papers*, 102/57/8: 3.
50. *Correspondence* (09883), W. R. Houston to John Dewey, February 19, 1943.
51. *Analects* 7.21, Ames and Rosemont (1998): 115.
52. *Analects* 3.12, Ames and Rosemont (1998): 85.
53. *Analects* 6.22, Ames and Rosemont (1998): 108.
54. *Analects* 11.12, Ames and Rosemont (1998): 144.
55. "Mathematics and the Good," Schilpp (1951): 674.
56. Jernegan (1927): 77.
57. *Correspondence* (04929), John Dewey to Prescott Ford Jernegan, February 23, 1927.
58. *A Common Faith*, LW 9: 49.
59. Whitman (2007): 22.
60. Hall and Ames (2001): 108–09.
61. Hall (1982): 140, 177, 189, 195, 199, 209–10, 228, 240.
62. Fen (1953): 210, italics added.
63. Neville (1989): 62.
64. Fen (1953): 210–11.
65. *Pragmatism*, James and Kuklick (1987): 518.

66. *A Common Faith*, LW 9: 30.
67. *How We Think*, MW 6: 310–11.
68. *A Common Faith*, LW 9: 30, 34.
69. *Correspondence* (03535), John Dewey to Scudder Klyce, May 29, 1915.
70. *A Common Faith*, LW 9: 34.
71. Fen (1950): 82, 87.
72. Tao's life story is well documented. See: Brown (1987): 120–38 and Bieler (2004): 285–87.
73. Brown (1987): 125.
74. Tao (1925): 143.
75. Keenan (1977): 65–66, Brown (1987): 132.
76. Kuhn (1959): 170.
77. Brown (1987): 133.
78. Bieler (2004): 286.
79. Tao (1930): 119.
80. Zhu (2015): 26.
81. Bieler (2004): 286.
82. *Correspondence* (16416), John Dewey to Tao Hsing-chih, June 10, 1944.
83. Bieler (2004): 287.
84. *Correspondence* (10570), H. C. Chen to John Dewey, September 23, 1947.
85. Fen (1950): 83.
86. Kuhn (1959): 183.
87. Fen (1950): 82.
88. *A Common Faith*, LW 9: 19.
89. *Experience and Nature*, LW 1: 310.
90. *A Common Faith*, LW 9: 33.
91. Frisina (2002): 75, 83.
92. *Mencius* 6A.7, Bloom (2009): 125, Mengzi 孟子 (1995): 292.
93. Slingerland (2003): 196, see also: *Analects* 7.20, 16.9, Ames and Rosemont (1998): 115, 199.
94. Giles (1990): 241, 247–48.
95. *Experience and Nature*, LW 1: 314.
96. Dewey and Boydston (1977): x–xii.
97. Frank (1926): 15–16.
98. Rockefeller (1991): 65–69.
99. Relying on "Creation" and related fragments, see: Dewey and Boydston (1977): 35–44.
100. Rockefeller (1991): 317, 499–501.
101. It should be noted, however, that Dewey wrote "Creation" during the period that he was overseeing Hu Shih's dissertation (1916–1917). This provided him with an occasion to learn more about Chinese philosophy.
102. Assembled from various verses and fragments, see Dewey and Boydston (1977): 7, 49, 60.
103. Randall (1940).

104. Rockefeller (1991): 231.
105. Culled from various verses and fragments, see: Dewey and Boydston (1977): 30, 56, 73–74.
106. Watson (1968): 191–92, Zhuangzi 莊子 (1994) 上: 494–95.
107. Standard translations of the closing line, 自以為不通乎命, follow somewhere along the lines of Burton Watson's: "It would show that I don't understand anything about fate."
108. Watson (1968): 43, Zhuangzi 莊子 (1994) 上: 80.
109. *Correspondence* (04942), John Dewey to Eleanor Allen Thomas, July 27, 1927.
110. *Correspondence* (04903), John Dewey to Edwin A. Burtt, August 14, 1927.
111. *Correspondence* (05437), John Dewey to George Herbert and Helen Castle Mead, July 27, 1927.
112. Dewey and Boydston (1977): 29.
113. Watson (1968): 84, 361, Zhuangzi 莊子 (1994) 上: 208, 下: 927.
114. Dewey and Boydston (1977): 30–31.
115. *Correspondence* (04694), John Dewey to Scudder Klyce, May 13, 1927 and *Correspondence* (04749), John Dewey to Scudder Klyce, October 18, 1927.
116. Watson (1968): 43, Zhuangzi 莊子 (1994) 上: 80.
117. *Correspondence* (04751), John Dewey to Scudder Klyce, October 21, 1927.
118. *A Common Faith*, LW 9: 18.
119. "Religion and Our Schools," MW 4: 168.
120. *Human Nature and Conduct*, MW 14: 227.
121. *Human Nature and Conduct*, MW 14: 227.
122. Dewey and Deen (2012): 334–35.
123. *A Common Faith*, LW 9: 26.
124. Eastman (1941): 673.
125. *A Common Faith*, LW 9: 56.
126. *Mencius* 7A.4, Bloom (2009): 144, Mengzi 孟子 (1995): 339.
127. *Ethics*, LW 7: 270.
128. *A Common Faith*, LW 9: 56.
129. Lachièze-Rey (2003): 22, and MSG 7.30.17.
130. "Time and Individuality," LW 14: 112.
131. *Analects* 15.29, Ames and Rosemont (1998): 190.
132. *Human Nature and Conduct*, MW 14: 195.
133. *Freedom and Culture*, LW 13: 188.
134. "From Absolutism to Experimentalism," LW 5: 160.
135. Jiang (1947): 257.
136. *Liberalism and Social Action*, LW 11: 65.
137. *Correspondence* (10139), John Dewey to W. R. Houston, April 29, 1945.
138. *Correspondence* (10233), T. V. Soong and Chiang Monlin to John Dewey, November 15, 1945.
139. *Correspondence* (15550), John Dewey to Arthur F. Bentley, February 2, 1946.
140. *Correspondence* (10302), John Dewey to W. R. Houston, March 16, 1946.
141. *Correspondence* (20110), Felix Kaufmann to Arthur F. Bentley, March 16, 1946.

142. *Correspondence* (20699), John Dewey to Otto Lous Mohr, March 17, 1946.
143. *Correspondence* (07138), John Dewey to Joseph Ratner, March 25, 1946.
144. *Correspondence* (10308), Chinese Embassy to John Dewey, March 26, 1946.
145. *Correspondence* (19979), Arthur F. Bentley to Felix Kaufmann, March 28, 1946.
146. *Correspondence* (09439), John Dewey to Corinne Chisholm Frost, April 1, 1946.
147. *Correspondence* (04525), John Dewey to Albert C. Barnes, April 2, 1946.
148. *Correspondence* (04526), Albert C. Barnes to John Dewey, April 4, 1946.
149. *Correspondence* (16673), Joseph Ratner to Frances Davenport, April 4, 1946.
150. *Correspondence* (04527), John Dewey to Albert C. Barnes, April 5, 1946.
151. *Correspondence* (10297), Chinese Ministry of Finance to John Dewey, April 8, 1946.
152. *Correspondence* (15559), John Dewey to Arthur F. Bentley, April 10, 1946.
153. *Correspondence* (04530), John Dewey to Albert C. Barnes, June 13, 1946.
154. *Correspondence* (10470), C. S. Li to John Dewey, January 28, 1947.
155. *Correspondence* (15624), John Dewey to Arthur F. Bentley, November 10, 1946.
156. *Correspondence* (13259), John Dewey to Sing-nan Fen, November 10, 1946. Punctuation and editing has been added here for clarity.
157. *Correspondence* (05736), John Dewey to Sing-nan Fen, May 1, 1947.
158. *Correspondence* (13815), John Dewey to Sing-nan Fen, October 31, 1950.
159. *Correspondence* (12272), Sing-nan Fen to John Dewey and Roberta Lowitz Grant Dewey, October 15, 1951.
160. *Correspondence* (13810), John Dewey to Sing-nan Fen, March 13, 1950. Note: different transcriptions of the original letter have incorrect spellings of Feng's name.
161. Lamont and Farrell (1959): 127–28.
162. Information gathered from Internet webpage maintained by the grandchild of one of Zhu's siblings. See: http://chuansong.me/n/1196519452473.
163. *John Dewey Papers*, "Reminiscences of Dewey: Mr. T. C. Ou," 81/14, audio recording.
164. *Correspondence* (13810), John Dewey to Sing-nan Fen, March 13, 1950. Note: different transcriptions of the original letter have incorrect spellings of Zhu's name.
165. "Life with 'Father,'" by Sing-nan Fen, March 19, 1985. Included in folder, *Correspondence* (13804), John Dewey to Sing-nan Fen, March 22, 1949.
166. Cao (1951).
167. Fernandez (2001): 90n.39.
168. Tillman (2013): 216–18.
169. See: Hu (1962): 767. It should be noted that this source incorrectly states that Chen's confession against Dewey occurred in 1955. It first occurred in 1950 and was published in 1951. See: Clopton and Ou (1985): 259.
170. Tillman (2013): 217.
171. Clopton and Ou (1985): 259–61.
172. Chen (1956).

173. Su (1995): 312.
174. Chan (1968): 564.
175. Grieder (1970): 359–60, 366.
176. Chan (1968): 552n.6.
177. Grieder (1970): 366–67.
178. Hu (1962): 769.
179. Information gathered from Internet webpage maintained by the grandchild of one of Zhu's siblings. See: http://chuansong.me/n/1196519452473.
180. Zhu (2013), Vol. 2: 279.
181. Information gathered from Internet webpage maintained by the grandchild of one of Zhu's siblings. See: http://chuansong.me/n/1196519452473.
182. Zhu (2013), Vol. 1: 262–63.
183. "Fen, Sing-Nan," *Lincoln Journal Star*, June 29, 2011.
184. "Life with 'Father,'" by Sing-nan Fen, March 19, 1985. Included in folder, *Correspondence* (13804), John Dewey to Sing-nan Fen, March 22, 1949.
185. Schulte (2012): 94–97.
186. Zeng (1988): 88.
187. Pan (1952).
188. See: Chen (1981).
189. Lu (2009): 137.
190. Schulte (2012): 100–02.
191. Guo (2004): 69.
192. Schulte (2012): 99–100, 103–04.
193. Zhan (1989): 99.
194. See: "Beijing Blames America for Tiananmen Protests," *Washington Post*, May 31, 1999.
195. Schulte (2012): 105.
196. Quoted in Sun (2007): 121–22.
197. *Correspondence* (03910), John Dewey to Dewey Children, June 10, 1919.
198. Yuan, et al. (2004).
199. Sun (2018) 104, 105, the word "the" has been deleted twice.
200. Hu (2013): 95.
201. Quoted from Keenan (1977): 103.
202. Northrop (1962): 527. The original quote reads rather inelegantly. For clarity's sake, I have inserted a comma, changed a "the" to an "our," and changed an "of" to a "to."

Works Cited

Aldridge, A. Owen (1993). "Irving Babbitt In and About China." *Modern Age*, Summer 1993: 332–39.
Alexander, Thomas (2004). "Dewey's Denotative-Empirical Method: A Thread Through the Labyrinth." In *The Journal of Speculative Philosophy* (18.3): 248–56.
Allan, Sarah (1997). *The Way of Water and Sprouts of Virtue*. Albany: State University of New York Press.
Allen, Reginald E. (1966). *Greek Philosophy: Thales to Aristotle*, Third Edition. New York: The Free Press.
Ames, Roger T. (2002). "Mencius and a Process Notion of Human Nature." In *Mencius: Contexts and Interpretations*. Edited by Alan K. L. Chan. Honolulu: University of Hawai`i Press, 72–90.
———. (2009). "Becoming Practically Religious: A Deweyan and Confucian Context for Rortian Religiousness." In *Rorty, Pragmatism, and Confucianism*. Edited by Yong Huang. Albany: State University of New York Press, 255–76.
———. (2011). *Confucian Role Ethics: A Vocabulary*. Honolulu: University of Hawai`i Press.
———. (2018). "Reconstructing A. C. Graham's Reading of Mencius on *Xing* 性: A Coda to "The Background of the Mencian Theory of Human Nature" (1967)." In *Having a Word With Angus Graham at Twenty-Five Years into his Immortality*. Edited by Carine Defoort and Roger T. Ames. Albany: State University of New York Press, 185–213.
Ames, Roger T., and Henry Rosemont, Jr. (1998). *The Analects of Confucius: A Philosophical Translation*. New York: Ballantine Books.
———. (2009). *The Chinese Classic of Family Reverence: A Philosophical Translation of the* Xiaojing. Honolulu: University of Hawai`i Press.
———. (2011). "Were the Early Confucians Virtuous?" In *Ethics in Early China: An Anthology*. Edited by Chris Fraser, Dan Robins, and Timothy O'Leary. Hong Kong: Hong Kong University Press, 17–39.
Angle, Stephen C. (2009). *Sagehood: The Contemporary Significance of Neo-Confucian Philosophy*. Oxford: Oxford University Press.
Aquinas, St. Thomas, and James F. Anderson (1997). *An Introduction to the Metaphysics of St. Thomas Aquinas*. Washington, DC: Regnery Publishing, Inc.

Aquinas and Vollert, Cyril (1947). *Compendium of Theology.* St. Louis: Herder.
Aquinas, St. Thomas. (1981). *Summa Theologica.* Vol. 1–5. Allen, TX: Christian Classics.
Aristotle, and McKeon, Richard (2001). *The Basic Works of Aristotle.* New York: Modern Library.
Babbitt, Irving (1919). *Rousseau and Romanticism.* Boston: Houghton Mifflin Company.
———. (1922). "Humanistic Education in China and the West." *The Chinese Student's Monthly,* Vol. 12, Nov. 1921–June 1922: 85–91.
———. (1956). *Literature and the American College: Essays in Defense of the Humanities.* Chicago: Gateway Editions.
Bacon, Francis, and Brian Vickers (2002). *Francis Bacon: The Major Works.* Oxford: Oxford University Press.
Baughman, M. D. (1958). *Teacher's Treasury of Stories for Every Occasion.* Englewood Cliffs, NJ: Prentice-Hall.
Baye, Tesfaye, and Tilahun Abebe, et al. (2011). "Genotype-Environment Interactions and Their Translational Implications." *Personalized Medicine,* 8(1): 59–70.
Behuniak, James, Jr. (2005). *Mencius on Becoming Human.* Albany: State University of New York Press.
———. (2008). "Confucius on Form and Uniqueness." In *Confucius Now: Contemporary Accounts with the Analects.* Edited by David Jones. Chicago: Open Court, 49–57.
———. (2011a). "Naturalizing Mencius," *Philosophy East and West,* 61(3): 492–515.
———. (2011b). "Hitting the Mark: Archery and Ethics in Early Confucianism," *Journal of Chinese Philosophy* 37(4): 588–604.
Bieler, Stacey (2004). *"Patriots" or "Traitors"? A History of American-Educated Chinese Students.* New York: M. E. Sharpe, Inc.
Birdwhistell, Joanne D. (2007). *Mencius and Masculinities: Dynamics of Power, Morality, and Maternal Thinking.* Albany: State University of New York Press.
Black, Jeffery M. (2001). "Fitness Consequences of Long Term Pair-Bonds in Barnacle Geese: Monogamy in the Extreme." *Behavioral Ecology,* 12(5): 640–45.
Bloom, Irene (1994). "Mencian Arguments on Human Nature (Jen-hsing)." *Philosophy East and West,* 44(1): 19–53.
———. (1997). "Human Nature and Biological Nature in *Mencius.*" *Philosophy East and West,* 47(1): 21–32.
———. (2002). "Biology and Culture in the Mencian View of Human Nature." In *Mencius: Contexts and Interpretations.* Edited by Alan K. L. Chan. Honolulu: University of Hawai'i Press, 91–102.
———. (2009). *Mencius.* New York: Columbia University Press.
Bockover, Mary (2008). "The *Ren Dao* of Confucius: A Spiritual Account of Humanity." In *Confucius Now: Contemporary Encounters with the Analects.* Edited by David Jones. LaSalle, IL: Open Court, 189–205.
Bodde, Derk (1991). *Chinese Thought, Society, and Science.* Honolulu: University of Hawai'i Press.
Boisvert, Raymond D. (2003). "What is Religion? A Pragmatist Response." In *Pragmatism and Religion.* Edited by Stuart Rosenmaum. Urbana: University of Illinois Press, 209–28.

Breslin, Paul A. S. (2013). "An Evolutionary Perspective on Food and Human Taste." *Current Biology*, 23(9): 409–18.
Brown, Donald E. (1999). "Human Universals." In *The MIT Encyclopedia of the Cognitive Sciences*. Edited by Robert A. Wilson and Frank C. Keil. London: MIT, 382–83.
Brown, Hubert O. (1987). "American Progressivism in Chinese Education: The Case of Tao Xingzhi." In *China's Education and the Industrialized World: Studies in Cultural Transfer*. Edited by Ruth Hayhoe and Marianne Bastid. New York: M. E. Sharpe, 120–38.
Buller, David J. (2005). "Adapting Minds: Evolutionary Psychology and the Persistent Quest for Human Nature." In *Arguing About Human Nature: Contemporary Debates*. Edited by Stephen M. Downes and Edouard Machery (2013). New York: Routledge Press, 35–63.
Bullock, Jeffrey S. (2011). *Yang Xiong: Philosophy of the Fa Yan, A Confucian Hermit in the Han Imperial Court*. Highlands: Mountain Mind Press.
Butler, Joseph (1850). *The Whole Works of Joseph Butler*. London: William Tegg and Co.
Cao, Fu (1951). *Duweipipan yinlun* 杜威批判引論. Beijing: Independently Published.
Chan, Philip A. and Robinowitz, Terry (2006). "A Cross-Sectional Analysis of Video Games and Attention Deficit Hyperactivity Disorder Symptoms in Adolescents." *Annals of General Psychiatry*, 5(16): 1–10.
Chan, Lien (1968). "Chinese Communism versus Pragmatism: The Criticism of Hu Shih's Philosophy, 1950–1958." *The Journal of Asian Studies*, 27(3): 551–70.
Chan, Wing-Tsit (1963). *A Sourcebook in Chinese Philosophy*. Princeton, NJ: Princeton University Press.
Chen, Hancai (1981). "*Qianxi Tao Xingzhi yu Duwei jiaoyusixiang de benzhiqubie* 浅析陶行知与杜威教育思想的本质区别, *Hunan Shifan Daxue Xuebao* 湖南师范大学, 4. https://wenku.baidu.com/view/cb973c05a6c30c2259019e94.html
Chapais, Bernard (2013). "Monogamy, Strongly Bonded Groups, and the Evolution of Human Social Structure." *Evolutionary Anthropology*, 22: 52–65.
Chaves, Jonathan (2003). "Confucianism: The Conservatism of the East." *The Intercollegiate Review*, 38(2): 44–50.
Chen, Heqin (1956*). Pipan Duwei fan dong jiaouuxue de zhexue jichu* 批判杜威反動教育學的哲學基礎. Shanghai: Xin zhishi chubanshe.
Chen, Lai (2010). "The Guodian Bamboo Slips and Confucian Theories of Human Nature." *Journal of Chinese Philosophy*, 37(s1): 33–50.
Cheng, Chung-ying (2004). "A Theory of Confucian Selfhood: Self-Cultivation and Free Will in Confucian Philosophy." In *Confucian Ethics: A Comparative Study of Self, Autonomy, and Community*. Edited by Kwong-loi Shun and David B. Wong. Cambridge: Cambridge University Press, 124–47.
Chiang, Monlin (1920). "*Hewei Xinsixiang* 何謂新思想," *Guodushidaizhi Sixiangyujiaoyu* 過渡時代之思想與教育, 1920 (1): 21–22.
———. (1924). *A Study in Chinese Principles of Education*. Shanghai: The Commercial Press.
———. (1947). *Tides from the West: A Chinese Autobiography*. New Haven, CT: Yale University Press.

Chiang, Yung-chen (2015). "Appropriating Dewey: Hu Shi and his Translation of Dewey's 'Social and Political Philosophy' Lecture Series in China." *European Journal of Pragmatism and American Philosophy*, 7(2): 71–97.

Ching, Julia (1985). "China's Response to Dewey." *Journal of Chinese Philosophy*, 12(3): 261–81.

Chong, Kim-chong (2016). *Zhuangzi's Critique of the Confucians: Blinded by the Human.* Albany: State University of New York Press.

Chow, Tse-tsung (1960). *The May Fourth Movement: Intellectual Revolution in Modern China.* Cambridge, MA: Harvard University Press.

Church, Russell M. (1959). "Emotional Reactions of Rats to the Pain of Others." *Journal of Comparative and Physiological Psychology*, 52(2): 132–34.

Clopton, Robert, and Tsuin-chen Ou (1970). *John Dewey: Additional Lectures in China, 1919–1921.* Special Collections, Hamilton Library, University of Hawai`i.

———. (1973). *John Dewey: Lectures in China, 1919–1920.* Honolulu: University of Hawaii Press.

———. (1985). *John Dewey: Lectures in China, 1919–1920, On Logic, Ethics, Education, and Democracy.* Taipei: Chinese Culture University Press.

Conn, Peter (1998). *Pearl S. Buck: A Cultural Biography.* Cambridge: Cambridge University Press.

Cook, Scott (2010). "'San De' and Warring States Views on Heavenly Retribution." *Journal of Chinese Philosophy*, 37(s1): 101–23.

———. (2012). *The Bamboo Texts of Guodian: A Study and Complete Translation.* Ithaca, NY: Cornell East Asia Series.

Cooley, Charles H. (1909). *Social Organization.* New York: Charles Scribner's Sons.

Coontz, Stephanie (2005). *Marriage, A History: from Obedience to Intimacy: How Love Conquered Marriage.* New York: Viking.

Cosmides, Leda, and Tooby, John (1997). "Evolutionary Psychology: A Primer." In *Arguing About Human Nature: Contemporary Debates.* Edited by Stephen M. Downes and Edouard Machery. New York: Routledge Press, 83–92.

Cremin, Lawrence A. (1975). "Public Education and the Education of the Public." *Teachers College Record*, 77(1): 1–12.

Cua, Antonio S. (1989). "The Concept of *Li* in Confucian Moral Theory." In *Understanding the Chinese Mind: The Philosophical Roots.* Edited by Robert E. Allison. Oxford: Oxford University Press, 209–35.

Curzer, Howard J. (2012). "Benevolent Government Now." *Comparative Philosophy*, 3(1): 74–85.

DeWaal, Frans (2006). *Primates and Philosophers: How Morality Evolved.* Edited by Stephen Macedo and Josiah Ober. Princeton, NJ: Princeton University Press.

Dewey, Jane M. (1989). "Biography of John Dewey." In *The Philosophy of John Dewey.* Edited by Paul Arthur Schilpp and Lewis Edwin Hahn. La Salle, IL: Open Court, 3–45.

Dewey, John (2015). "Lectures in Social and Political Philosophy." *European Journal of Pragmatism and American Philosophy*, 7(2): 7–44.

Dewey, John, and Arthur F. Bentley (1964). *John Dewey and Arthur F. Bentley: A Philosophical Correspondence, 1932–1951.* Edited by Sidney and Jules Altman. New Brunswick, NJ: Rutgers University Press.
Dewey, John, and Jo Ann Boydston (1977). *The Poems of John Dewey.* Carbondale: Southern Illinois University Press.
———, et al. (2008). *The Collected Works of John Dewey, Early Works*, Vols. 1–4. *Middle Works*, Vols. 1–15. *Late Works*, Vol. 1–17. Carbondale: Southern Illinois University Press.
Dewey, John, and Philip Deen (2012). *Unmodern Philosophy and Modern Philosophy.* Carbondale: Southern Illinois University Press.
Dewey, John, and Samuel Myer (1984). *Types of Thinking: Including A Survey of Greek Philosophy.* New York: Philosophical Library.
Ding, Zijiang (2007). "A Comparison of Dewey's and Russell's Influences on China." *Dao*, 6(2): 149–65.
Downes, Stephen M. (2009). "The Basic Components of the Human Brain Were Not Solidified During the Pleistocene Epoch." In *Arguing About Human Nature: Contemporary Debates.* Edited by Stephen M. Downes and Edouard Machery (2013). New York: Routledge Press, 93–101.
Eames, S. Morris (1977). *Pragmatic Naturalism: An Introduction.* Carbondale: Southern Illinois University Press.
Eastman, Max (1941). "John Dewey." *The Atlantic Monthly*, December, 1941: 671–84.
Eco, Umberto (1986). *Art and Beauty in the Middle Ages.* New Haven, CT: Yale University Press.
Edel, Abraham (2001). *Ethical Theory and Social Change: The Evolution of John Dewey's Ethics: 1908–1932.* London: Transaction Publishers.
Emerson, Ralph Waldo, and Larzer Ziff (1982). *Ralph Waldo Emerson: Selected Essays.* Harmondsworth, Middlesex, UK: Penguin Press.
Eno, Robert (1990). *The Confucian Creation of Heaven: Philosophy and the Defense of Ritual Mastery.* Albany: State University of New York Press.
Fallace, Thomas D. (2011). *Dewey and the Dilemma of Race: An Intellectual History 1895–1922.* New York: The Teacher's College Press.
Fen, Sing-nan (1950). "Dewey's Philosophy as a Program of Action." In *Essays for John Dewey's Ninetieth Birthday.* Edited by Kenneth D. Benne and William O. Stanley. Urbana: College of Education, University of Illinois, 82–87.
———. (1951). "On Being and Being Known." *Journal of Philosophy* 48(12): 381–87.
———. (1952). "The Contribution of Cultural Relativism to Cultural Reconstruction." *Educational Theory*, 2(1): 20–32.
———. (1953). "Meaning and Existence." *Journal of Philosophy*, 50(7): 206–16.
———. (1961). "Education as Growth of Environmental Consciousness." *Educational Theory*, 11(2): 85–92.
Feng, Youlan (1926). *A Comparative Study of Life Ideals.* Shanghai: The Commercial Press, Ltd.

———. (1948). "Chinese Philosophy and a Future World Philosophy." *The Philosophical Review*, 57(6): 539–49.

———. (2000). *The Hall of Three Pines: An Account of My Life*. Honolulu: University of Hawai'i Press.

Fernandez, Jeanette Ford (2001). *Mao's Prey: The History of Chen Renbing, Liberal Intellectual*. New York: Routledge.

Feuerbach, Ludwig (1873). *The Essence of Religion*. Amherst, NY: Prometheus Books.

Fingarette, Herbert (1972). *Confucius: The Secular as Sacred*. Prospect Heights, IL: Waveland Press, Inc.

Fischbeck, Gerhard (2002). "Contribution of Barley to Agriculture: A Brief Overview." In *Barley Science: Recent Advances from Molecular Biology to Agronomy of Yield and Quality*. Edited by Gustavo A. Slafer, et al. New York: Food Products Press, 1–14.

Fong, Mary H. (1988–1989). "The Origin of Chinese Pictorial Representation of the Human Figure." *Artibus Asiae*, 49 (1/2): 5–38.

Frank, Waldo (1926). "The Man Who Made Us What We Are." *New Yorker* (2): 15–16, May 22, 1926.

Fraser, Chris (2016). *The Philosophy of the Mozi: The First Consequentialists*. New York: Columbia University Press.

Frega, Roberto (2015). "John Dewey's Social Philosophy: A Restatement." *European Journal of Pragmatism and American Philosophy*, 7(2): 98–127.

Frisina, Warren G. (2002). *The Unity of Knowledge and Action: Toward a Non-Representational Theory of Knowledge*. Albany: State University of New York Press.

Gardiner, Daniel K. (2007). *The Four Books: The Basic Teachings of the Later Confucian Tradition*. Indianapolis, IN: Hackett Publishing Company, Inc.

Geary, David C., and Mark V. Flinn (2001). "Evolution of Human Parental Behavior and the Human Family." *Parenting: Science and Practice*, 1(1–2): 5–61.

Gelman, S. A. (2003). *The Essential Child: Origins of Essentialism in Everyday Thought*. New York: Oxford University Press.

Giles, B. E. (1990). "The Effects of Variation in Seed Size on Growth and Reproduction in the Wild Barley *Hordeum vulgare ssp. Spontaneum*." *Heredity*, 64: 239–50.

Goffman, Erving (1967). "Interaction Ritual: Deference and Demeanor." In *Readings in Ritual Studies*. Edited by Ronald L. Grimes. Upper Saddle River, NJ: Prentice Hall, 268–79.

Goldhaber, Dale (2012). *The Nature-Nurture Debates: Bridging the Gap*. Cambridge: Cambridge University Press.

Graham, A. C. (1989). *Disputers of the Tao: Philosophical Argument in Ancient China*. La Salle, IL: Open Court.

———. (1991). "Reflections and Replies." In *Chinese Texts and Philosophical Contexts: Essays Dedicated to Angus C. Graham*. Edited by Henry Rosemont, Jr. La Salle, IL: Open Court, 267–322.

Grange, Joseph (2004). *John Dewey, Confucius, and Global Philosophy*. Albany: State University of New York Press.

Grene, Marjorie, and David Dupew (2004). *The Philosophy of Biology: An Episodic History*. Cambridge: Cambridge University Press.

Grieder, Jerome B. (1970). *Hu Shih and the Chinese Renaissance: Liberalism in the Chinese Revolution, 1917–1937*. Cambridge, MA: Harvard University Press.

Gronda, Roberto (2015). "What Does China Mean for Pragmatism: A Philosophical Interpretation of Dewey's Sojourn in China (1919–1921)." *European Journal of Pragmatism and American Philosophy*, 7(2): 45–70.

Gu, Edward X. (2001). "Who was Mr. Democracy? The May Fourth Discourse of Popular Democracy and the Radicalization of Chinese Intellectuals (1915–1922)," *Modern Asian Studies*, 35(3): 589–621.

Gu, Hongliang (2015). *Shiyongzhuyi de wudu: Duweizhixue dui Zhongguoxiandaizhixue de yingxiang* 实用主义的误读: 杜威哲学对中国现代哲学的影响. Guilin: Guangxi Normal University Press.

Guo, Shibao (2004). "China as a Contesting Ground for Ideologies: Examining the Social and Ideological Forces that influence China's Educational System." *Canadian Journal of University Continuing Education*, 30(1): 55–77.

Guoyu 國語 (1959). *Guoyu*國語. Shanghai: Commercial Press, Ltd.

Hall, David. L. (1982). *Eros and Irony: A Prelude to Philosophical Anarchism*. Albany: State University of New York Press.

Hall, David L., and Roger T. Ames (1987). *Thinking Through Confucius*. Albany: State University of New York Press.

———. (1995). *Anticipating China: Thinking through the Narratives of Chinese and Western Culture*. Albany: State University of New York Press.

———. (1998). *Thinking from the Han: Self, Truth, and Transcendence in Chinese and Western Culture*. Albany: State University of New York Press.

———. (1999). *The Democracy of the Dead: Dewey, Confucius, and the Hope for Democracy in China*. Chicago, IL: Open Court.

———. (2001). *Focusing the Familiar: A Translation and Philosophical Interpretation of the Zhongyong*. Honolulu: University of Hawai'i Press.

———. (2003). *Dao De Jing: A Philosophical Translation: "Making this Life Significant."* New York: Ballantine Books.

Hall, Irene (2005). *The Unsung Partner: The Educational Work and Philosophy of Alice Chipman Dewey*. Harvard University, Graduate School of Education Dissertation. UMI No. 3176333.

Henrich, Richard, and Robert Boyd, et al. (2012). "The Puzzle of Monogamous Marriage." *Philosophical Transactions of the Royal Society*, B (367): 657–69.

Herrigel, Eugen (1981). *Zen in the Art of Archery*. New York: Vintage Books.

Hillman, Gordon C., and M. Stuart Davies (1990). "Measured Domestication Rates in Wild Wheats and Barley under Primitive Cultivation, and their Archeological Implications." *Journal of World Prehistory*, 4: 157–222.

Hsu, Elizabeth (2016). "French Artist Jacques Picoux Dies After Fall from Building." *Focus Taiwan*, Oct. 17, 2016. http://focustaiwan.tw/news/asoc/201610170006.aspx.

Hu, Shih (1919). "*Wo dui Sangli de Gaige* 我對喪禮的改革," in *Hushiwencun* 胡適文存, 1–4集Taipei: *Yuandongtushugongsi* 遠東圖書公司, 709–23.

———. (1934). *The Chinese Renaissance: The Haskell Lectures 1933*. Chicago: University of Chicago Press.

———. (1962). "John Dewey in China." In *Philosophy and Culture: East and West*. Edited by Charles A. Moore. Honolulu: University of Hawai'i Press, 762–69.
———. (1963). *The Development of the Logical Method in Ancient China*. New York: Paragon Books.
———. (2013). *English Writings of Hu Shih: Literature and Society (Volume One)*. New York, NY: Springer.
Huang, Yong (2013). *Confucius: A Guide for the Perplexed*. New York: Bloomsbury Academic.
Ivanhoe, Philip J. (1988). "A Question of Faith: A New Interpretation of *Mencius* 2B.13." *Early China*, 13: 153–95.
———. (1990). "Thinking and Learning in Early Confucianism." *Journal of Chinese Philosophy*, 17(4): 473–93.
———. (1993). "Zhuangzi on Skepticism, Skill, and the Ineffable *Dao*." *Journal of the American Academy of Religion*, 61(4): 639–54.
———. (1996). "Was Zhuangzi a Relativist?" In *Essays on Skepticism, Relativism, and Ethics in the Zhuangzi*. Edited by Paul Kjellberg and Philip Ivanhoe. Albany: State University of New York Press, 196–214.
———. (1997). "Human Beings and Nature in Chinese Thought." In *A Companion to World Philosophies*. Edited by Eliot Deutsch and Ron Bontekoe. Oxford: Blackwell Publishing, 155–64.
———. (2000). *Confucian Moral Self-Cultivation*, Second Edition. Indianapolis, IN: Hackett Publishing Company, Inc.
———. (2002a). "Whose Confucius? Which *Analects*?" In *Confucius and the Analects: New Essays*. Edited by Bryan W. Van Norden. Oxford: Oxford University Press, 119–133.
———. (2002b). *Ethics in the Confucian Tradition: The Thought of Mengzi and Wang Yangming*. Indianapolis, IN: Hackett Publishing Company.
———. (2004). "Interpreting the *Mengzi*." *Philosophy East and West*, 54(2): 249–63.
———. (2007). "Heaven as Source for Ethical Warrant in Early Confucianism." *Dao*, 6(3): 211–20.
———. (2008). "The Shade of Confucius: Social Roles, Ethical Theory, and the Self." In *Polishing the Chinese Mirror: Essays in Honor of Henry Rosemont Jr.* Edited by Marthe Chandler and Ronnie Littlejohn. New York: Global Scholarly Publications, 34–49.
———. (2010). "Of Geese and Eggs: In What Sense Should We Value Nature as a System?" *Environmental Ethics* 32: 67–78.
———. (2013). "Virtue Ethics and the Chinese Confucian Tradition." In *Virtue Ethics and Confucianism*. Edited by Stephen C. Angle and Michael Slote. New York: Routledge, 28–46.
James, William, and Bruce Kuklick (1987). *William James: Writings, 1902–1910*. New York: The Library of America.
James, William, and Gerald E. Myers (1992). *William James: Writings 1878–1899*. New York: The Library of America.

Jernegan, Prescott F. (1927). *Man and his God*. Palo Alto, CA: Mayfield.
John Dewey Papers, 1858–1970. Special Collections, Morris Library. Southern Illinois University, Carbondale.
Johnson, Mark (2006). "Mind Incarnate: From Dewey to Damasio." *Daedalus*, 135(3): 46–54.
———. (2007). *The Meaning of the Body: Aesthetics of Human Understanding*. Chicago: The University of Chicago Press.
Joyce, Richard (2006). *The Evolution of Morality*. Cambridge: The MIT Press.
Jun, Wenren (2013). *Ancient Chinese Encyclopedia of Technology: Translation and Annotation of the Kaogong Ji (the Artificer's Record)*. New York: Routledge.
Kalb, James (2015). "The Left vs. Human Nature." *Crisis Magazine*, March 27, 2015. http://www.crisismagazine.com/2015/left-vs-human-nature
Kallen, Horace (1915). "Democracy Versus the Melting Pot." *The Nation* (100): 2590, Feb. 18, 25, 1915: 190–94, 217–20.
Karlgren, Bernhard (1957). *Grammata Serica Recensa*. Stockholm: The Museum of Far Eastern Antiquities.
———. (1974). *Analytic Dictionary of Chinese and Sino-Japanese*. New York: Dover Publications
Kaufmann, Walter (1956). *Existentialism from Dostoevsky to Sartre*. New York: Meridian Books.
Keating, James W. (1964). "Sportsmanship as a Moral Category." *Ethics*, 75(1): 25–35.
Keenan, Barry (1977). *The Dewey Experiment in China: Educational Reform and Political Power in the Early Republic*. Cambridge, MA, Harvard University Press.
Keightley, David N. (2014). *These Bones Shall Rise Again: Selected Writings on Early China*. Edited by Henry Rosemont, Jr. Albany: State University of New York Press.
Kirk, Russell (1952). "The Conservative Humanism of Irving Babbitt." *Prairie Schooner*, 26(3): 245–55.
Knoblock, John (1988). *Xunzi: A Translation and Study of the Complete Works*. Vol. 1. Stanford, CA: Stanford University Press.
———. (1990). *Xunzi: A Translation and Study of the Complete Works*. Vol. 2. Stanford, CA: Stanford University Press.
———. (1994). *Xunzi: A Translation and Study of the Complete Works*. Vol. 3. Stanford, CA: Stanford University Press.
Knoblock, John, and Jeffery Riegel (2000). *The Annals of Lü Buwei*. Stanford, CA: Stanford University Press.
Kolb, Bryan, and Robbin Gibb (2011). "Brain Plasticity and Behavior in the Developing Brain." *Journal of the Canadian Academy of Child and Adolescent Psychology*, 20(4): 265–76.
Kripke, Saul A. (1980). *Naming and Necessity*. Cambridge, MA: Harvard University Press.
Kuang, Qizhang (1994). "Pragmatism in China: The Deweyan Influence." Dissertation. Michigan State University, Department of Educational Administration. UMI: 9605897.

Kuhn Philip A. (1959). "T'ao Hsing-Chih, 1891–1946, An Educational Reformer." *Papers on China*, 13: 163–95.

Kwok, D. W. Y. (1965). *Scientism in Chinese Thought: 1900–1950*. New Haven, CT: Yale University Press.

Lachièze-Rey, Marc (2003). "Cosmic Topology." https://arxiv.org/pdf/gr-qc/9605010.pdf.

Lachs, John (2005). "Stoic Pragmatism." *Journal of Speculative Philosophy*, 19: 95–106.

Lamont, Corliss (1959). *Dialogue on John Dewey*. New York: Horizon Press.

Lau, Po-Hei (2015). "Introduction to Chinese Philosophy." *Journal of Chinese Philosophy*, 41(3–4): 521–23.

Legge, James (1967). *Li Chi: Book of Rites*, Vol. 1 and 2. New Hyde Park, NY: University Books.

———. (1970). *The Works of Mencius*. New York: Dover Publications, Inc.

———. (2000). *The Chinese Classics*, Vol. 1–5. Taipei: SMC Publishing Inc.

Lewis, Mark Edward (1999). *Writing and Authority in Early China*. Albany: State University of New York Press.

Li, Chenyang (2014). *The Confucian Philosophy of Harmony*. New York: Routledge Press.

Li, Ling (2002). *Guodian Chujian Jiaoduji* 郭店楚簡校讀記. Beijing: Beijing University Press.

Liang, Tao, and Andrew Lambert (2009). "Mencius and the Tradition of Articulating Human Nature in Terms of Growth." *Frontiers of Philosophy in China*, 4(2): 180–97.

Liji 禮記 (1998). *Liji Jinzhujinyi* 禮記今註今譯, Vol. 1 (上) and Vol. 2 (下). Taipei: The Commercial Press, Ltd.

Liu, Fantong (1997). "*Daixu: Chongxinrenshi he pingjia Duwei* 代序：重新认识和评价杜威." In *Xinjuigerenzhuyi: Duwei Wenxuan* 新旧个人主义：杜威文选. Translated by Sun Youzhong, et al. Shanghai: Shanghai University Press.

Liu, Liangjian (2013). "Virtue Ethics and Confucianism: A Methodological Reflection." In *Virtue Ethics and Confucianism*. Edited by Stephen C. Angle and Michael Slote. New York: Routledge, 66–73.

Liu, Xinyi (2017). "Journey to the East: Diverse Routes and Variable Flowering Times for Wheat and Barley en route to Prehistoric China," *PLOS ONE* (2017). https://phys.org/news/2017-11-ancient-barley-high-road-china.html.

Longo, Giuseppe, and Maël Montévil (2014). *Perspectives on Organisms: Biological Time, Symmetries, and Singularities*. Springer: Lecture Notes on Morphogenesis.

Lu, Guoqi (2009). "*Lun Duwei dui Mao Zedong zaoqijiaoyusixiang de yingxiang* 论杜威对毛泽东早期教育思想影响." *Xue Linxiangilun* 学理论, 5 (2): 136–37.

Machery, Edouard (2008). "A Plea for Human Nature." In *Arguing About Human Nature: Contemporary Debates*. Edited by Stephen M. Downes and Edouard Machery (2013). New York: Routledge Press, 64–70.

Manchester, Fredrick, and Odell Shepard, eds. (1941). *Irving Babbitt: Man and Teacher*. New York: G. P. Putnam's Sons.

Martin, Jay (2002). *The Education of John Dewey: A Biography*. New York: Columbia University Press.

McCartney, Eugene S. (1926). "Folklore of Marksmanship." *The Classical Journal*, 22(2): 140–41.
———. (1940). "Marvelous Feats of Archery." *The Classical Journal*, Vol. 35(9): 537–41.
McQuaid, John (2015). *Tasty: The Art and Science of What we Eat*. New York: Scribner.
Meng Chih (1981). *Chinese American Understanding: A Sixty-Year Search*. New York: China Institute in America.
Mengzi 孟子 (1995). *Mengzi Jinzhujinyi* 孟子今註今譯. Taipei: The Commercial Press, Ltd.
Meyer, Dirk (2012). *Philosophy on Bamboo: Text and the Production of Meaning in Early China*. Leiden: Brill.
Midgley, Mary (1994). *The Ethical Primate: Humans, Freedom and Morality*. London: Routledge.
Mill, John Stuart (1998). *Three Essays on Religion*. Amherst, NY: Prometheus Books.
Miller, Holly, Cassie D. Gipson, Aubrey Vaughan, Rebecca Rayburn-Reeves, and Thomas R. Zentall (2009). "Object Permanence in Dogs: Invisible Displacement in Rotation Task." *Psychonomic Bulletin & Review*, 16(1): 150–55.
Miyazaki, Ichisada (1981). *China's Examination Hell: The Civil Service Examinations of Imperial China*. New Haven, CT: Yale University Press.
Moeller, Hans-Georg, and Paul J. D'Ambrosio (2017). *Genuine Pretending: On the Philosophy of the Zhuangzi*. New York: Columbia University Press.
Mozi, and Johnston, Ian (2010). *The Mozi: A Complete Translation*. New York: Columbia University Press.
Munro, Donald J. (2002). "Mencius and an Ethics of the New Century." In *Mencius: Contexts and Interpretations*. Edited by Alan K. L. Chan. Honolulu: University of Hawai'i Press, 305–15.
———. (2005). *A Chinese Ethics for the New Century: The Ch'ien Mu Lectures in History and Culture, and Other Essays on Science and Confucian Ethics*. Hong Kong: The Chinese University Press.
Myall, James (2012). "Franco-Americans in Maine: Statistics from the American Community Survey." Prepared for the Franco-American Taskforce. Sept. 26, 2012. http://www.maine.gov/legis/opla/JamesMyallFATFReport.pdf
Neville, Robert C. (1981). *Reconstruction of Thinking*. Albany: State University of New York Press.
———. (1989). *Recovery of the Measure: Interpretation and Nature*. Albany: State University of New York Press.
———. (1991). *Behind the Masks of God: An Essay Towards Comparative Theology*. Albany: State University of New York Press.
———. (2000). *Boston Confucianism: Portable Tradition in the Late-Modern World*. Albany: State University of New York Press.
———. (2002). *Religion in Late Modernity*. Albany: State University of New York Press.
———. (2016). *The Good is One, its Manifestations Many: Confucian Essays on Metaphysics, Morals, Rituals, Institutions, and Genders*. Albany: State University of New York Press.

Ni Peimin (2009). "How Far is Confucius an Aristotelian? Comments on May Sim's *Remastering Morals with Aristotle and Confucius*." *Dao*, 8(3): 311–19.

———. (2016). *Confucius: The Man and the Way of Gongfu*. Lanham, MD: Rowman and Littlefield.

———. (2017). *Understanding the* Analects *of Confucius*. Albany: State University of New York Press.

———. (2018). "Does Confucianism Need a Metaphysical Theory of Human Nature?" In *Appreciating the Chinese Difference: Engaging Roger T. Ames on Methods, Issues, and Roles*. Edited by Jim Behuniak. Albany: State University of New York Press, 183–201.

Nivison, David S. (1966). *The Life and Thought of Chang Hsüeh-ch'eng (1738–1801)*. Stanford, CA: Stanford University Press.

———. (1996). *The Ways of Confucianism: Investigations in Chinese Philosophy*. Edited by Bryan W. Van Norden. LaSalle, IL: Open Court.

Northrop, F. S. C. (1962). "Comparative Philosophy and Science in Light of Comparative Law." In *Philosophy and Culture East and West: East-West Philosophy in Practical Perspective*. Edited by Charles A. Moore. Honolulu: University of Hawai`i Press.

Noble, Denis (2014). "Foreword." In *Perspectives on Organisms: Biological Time, Symmetries, and Singularities*. By Giuseppe Longo and Maël Montévil (2014). Springer: Lecture Notes on Morphogenesis, vii–x.

Ohlson, Kristin (2016). "Everything Worth Knowing about Animal Intelligence." *Discover Magazine*, July/August, 2016. http://discovermagazine.com/2016/jul-aug/animal-intelligence.

Olberding, Amy (2008). "Dreaming of the Duke of Zhou: Exemplarism in the *Analects*." *Journal of Chinese Philosophy*, 35(4): 625–39.

———. (2011). "I Know Not 'Seems': Grief for Parents in the *Analects*." In *Mortality in Traditional Chinese Thought*, edited by Amy Olberding and Philip J. Ivanhoe. Albany: State University of New York Press, 153–75.

———. (2012). *Moral Exemplars in the* Analects: *The Good Person is That*. New York: Routledge.

Ong, Chang Woei (2004). "Which West Are You Talking About? Critical Review: The Unique Model of Conservatism in Modern China." *Humanitas*, 12(1–2): 69–82.

Paley, William (2006). *Natural Theology*. Oxford: Oxford World Classics.

Pan, Kaipei (1952). *Tao Xingzhi Jiaoyusixiang de Pipan* 陶行知教育思想的批判. Beijing: Independently Published.

Pang, Pu (1999). "*Kong-Mengzhijian Guodianchujianzhong de Rujiaxinxingshuo* 孔孟之間郭店楚簡中的儒家心性說." In *Guodian Chujian Yanjiu* 郭店楚簡研究. Edited by Jiang Guanghui. Liaoling Province Education Publishing Company, Series in Chinese Philosophy, Vol. 20: 22–35.

Pappas, Gregory Fernando (2008). *John Dewey's Ethics: Democracy as Experience*. Bloomington: Indiana University Press.

Perkins, Franklin (2010). "Recontextualizing *Xing*: Self-Cultivation and Human Nature in the Guodian Texts." *Journal of Chinese Philosophy*, 37(s1): 16–32.

———. (2014). *Heaven and Earth are Not Humane: The Problem of Evil in Classical Chinese Philosophy*. Bloomington: Indiana University Press.

Pinker, Steven (2002). *The Blank Slate: The Modern Denial of Human Nature*. New York: Penguin Group.
———. (2004). "Why Nature and Nurture Won't Go Away." *Daedalus*, 133(4): 5–17.
Plato, John M. Cooper (1997). *Plato: Complete Works*. Indianapolis, IN: Hackett Publishers.
Pratt, Scott (2002). *Native Pragmatism: Rethinking the Roots of American Philosophy*. Bloomington: Indiana University Press.
Puett, Michael J. (2001). *Ambivalence of Creation: Debates Concerning Innovation and Artifice in Early China*. Stanford, CA: Stanford University Press.
———. (2002). *To Become a God: Cosmology, Sacrifice, and Self-Divinization in Early China*. Cambridge, MA: Harvard University Press.
Putnam, Hilary (1975). *Mind, Language and Reality: Philosophical Papers*, Volume Two. Cambridge: Cambridge University Press.
Randall, John Herman, Jr. (1939). "Dewey's Interpretation of the History of Philosophy." In *The Philosophy of John Dewey*. Edited by Paul A. Schilpp. LaSalle, IL, Open Court, 77–102.
———. (1940). "Religion of Shared Experience." In *The Philosopher of the Common Man: Essays in Honor of John Dewey to Celebrate His Eightieth Birthday*. Edited by Horace M. Kallen. New York: G. P. Putnam's, 106–45.
Remer, C. F. (1920). "John Dewey in China." *Millards Review of Far East*, July 3, 1920: 266–68.
Reynolds, David S. (1995). *Walt Whitman's America: A Cultural Biography*. New York: Vintage Books.
Richardson, Peter J., and Boyd, Robert (2005). *Not By Genes Alone: How Culture Transformed Human Evolution*. Chicago: University of Chicago Press.
Robins, Dan (2011). "The Warring States Concept of *Xing*." *Dao*, 10(1): 31–51.
Rockefeller, Steven C. (1991). *John Dewey: Religious Faith and Democratic Humanism*. New York: Columbia University Press.
Rosemont, Henry, Jr. (2008a). "An Unintegrated Life is Not Worth Living." In *Confucius Now: Contemporary Encounters with the Analects*. Edited by David Jones. La Salle, IL: Open Court, 153–65.
———. (2008b). "Responses to Contributors." In *Polishing the Chinese Mirror: Essays in Honor of Henry Rosemont Jr*. Edited by Marthe Chandler and Ronnie Littlejohn. New York: Global Scholarly Publications, 352–402.
———. (2015). *Against Individualism: A Confucian Rethinking of the Foundations of Morality, Politics, Family, and Religion*. Lanham, MD: Lexington Books.
Rosenlee, Li-Hsiang Lisa (2006). *Confucianism and Women: A Philosophical Interpretation*. Albany: State University of New York Press.
Rosenthal, Sandra (2003). "Spirituality and the Spirit of American Pragmatism: Beyond the Theism-Atheism Split." In *Pragmatism and Religion*. Edited by Stuart Rosenbaum. Urbana: University of Illinois Press, 229–42.
Saxbe, Darby (2017). "Dads Can Feel Postpartum Depression Too, with Startling Testosterone Changes." *The Washington Post*, Sept. 23, 2017.
Schaberg, David (1999). "Song in the Historical Imagination in Early China," in *Harvard Journal of Asiatic Studies* 59(2): 305–61.

Schilpp, Paul Arthur, ed. (1951). *The Philosophy of Alfred North Whitehead.* New York: Tudor Publishing Company.

Schulte, Barbara (2012). "The Chinese Dewey: Friend, Fiend, and Flagship." In *The Global Reception of John Dewey's Thought: Multiple Refractions Through Time and Space.* Edited by Rosa Bruno-Jofré and Jürgen Schriewer. New York: Routledge: 83–115.

Scotus, John Eriugena, and I. P. Sheldon-Williams (1997). *Basic Issues in Medieval Philosophy: Selected Readings.* Edited by Richard N. Bosley and Martin Tweedale. Peterborough, Ontario: Broadview Press.

Selby, Stephen (2000). *Chinese Archery.* Hong Kong: Hong Kong University Press.

Shun, Kwong-loi (1997). *Mencius and Early Chinese Thought.* Stanford, CA: Stanford University Press.

Shusterman, Richard (2008). *Body Consciousness: A Philosophy of Mindfulness and Somaesthetics.* Cambridge: Cambridge University Press.

Sigurðsson, Geir (2015). *Confucian Propriety and Ritual Learning: A Philosophical Interpretation.* Albany: State University of New York Press.

Sim, May (2007). *Remastering Morals with Aristotle and Confucius.* Cambridge: Cambridge University Press.

———. (2009). "Dewey and Confucius on Moral Education." *Journal of Chinese Philosophy,* 36(1): 85–105.

Sivin, Nathan (2005). "Why the Scientific Revolution Did Not Take Place in China—Or Didn't It?" Revised version of 1982 article first published in *Chinese Science* 5:45–66. http://ccat.sas.upenn.edu/~nsivin/scirev.pdf.

Sizer, Nancy F. (1966). "John Dewey's Ideas in China 1919 to 1921." *Comparative Education Review,* 10(3): 390–403.

Slingerland, Edward (2001). "Virtue Ethics, the 'Analects,' and the Problem of Commensurability." *The Journal of Religious Ethics,* 29(1): 97–125.

———. (2003). *Confucius: Analects, with Selections from Traditional Commentaries.* Indianapolis, IN: Hackett Press.

———. (2008). *What Science Offers the Humanities: Integrating Body and Culture.* New York: Cambridge University Press.

———. (2011). "Metaphor and Meaning in Early China." *Dao,* 10(1): 1–30.

Smith, Douglas C. (1981). "John Dewey and Free China." *Taiwan Today,* July 1, 1981.

Smith, John E. (1985). "Pragmatism at Work: Dewey's Lectures in China." *Journal of Chinese Philosophy,* 12(3): 231–59.

Stalnaker, Aaron (2005). "Comparative Religious Ethics and the Problem of 'Human Nature.'" *The Journal of Religious Ethics,* 33(2): 187–224.

Steele, John (1917). *The Yili or Book of Etiquette and Ceremonial,* Vol. 1 and 2. London: Probsthain & Co.

Steiner, Pierre (2013). "The Nature of the Modern Mind: Some Remarks on Dewey's Unmodern Philosophy and Modern Philosophy." *European Journal of Pragmatism and American Philosophy,* 5(1): 140–54.

Stroud, Scott R. (2006). "Pragmatism and Orientation." *The Journal of Speculative Philosophy,* 20(4): 287–307.

———. (2011). *John Dewey and the Artful Life: Pragmatism, Aesthetics, and Morality*. University Park: The Pennsylvania State University Press.
Su, Zhixin (1995). "A Critical Evaluation of John Dewey's Influence on Chinese Education." *American Journal of Education*, 103(3): 302–25.
Sun, Ning (2018). "Research Note: The Dewey Center at Fudan University." *Dewey Studies*, 2(1): 103–105.
Sun, Youzhong (2007). "The Trans-Pacific Experience of John Dewey," *The Japanese Journal of American Studies*, 18: 107–24.
Szuberla, Guy (1995). "Zangwill's The Melting Pot Plays Chicago." *Melus*, 20(3): 3–20.
Tao, Xingzhi (1925). "China." In *Educational Yearbook of the International Institute of Teacher's College, Columbia University, 1924*. New York: Columbia University.
———. (1930). "*Huxiao xuanyan* 護校宣言," in *Jingbao* 警報, Oct. 17, 1930.
Tan, Sor-hoon (2003). *Confucian Democracy: A Deweyan Reconstruction*. Albany: State University of New York Press.
———. (2011). "The *Dao* of Politics: *Li* (Rituals/Rites) and Laws as Pragmatic Tools of Government." *Philosophy East and West* 61(3): 468–91.
Taylor, Shelly (2002). *The Tending Instinct: Women, Men, and the Biology of our Relationships*. New York: Henry Holt and Company.
Tillich, Paul (1957). *Dynamics of Faith*. New York: Harper Collins.
Tillman, Margaret Mih (2013). "Precocious Politics: Preschool Education and Child Protection in China, 1903–1953." Dissertation, Department of History, University of California, Berkeley, Spring 2013.
Tolstoy, Leo (2006). *Anna Karenina*. New York: Bantam Books.
Trivers, Robert L. (1971). "The Evolution of Reciprocal Altruism." *The Quarterly Review of Biology*, 46(1): 35–57.
Twanmoh, Harriet Chien-ming (1966). *Hu Shih and Female Emancipation in China*. Australia National University. Open Access Theses (Masters). https://openresearch-repository.anu.edu.au/handle/1885/123806
Van Norden, Bryan W. (1993). "Book Review: *John Dewey and American Philosophy*." *Philosophy East and West*, 43(2): 341–43.
———. (1996). "Introduction." In *The Ways of Confucianism: Investigations in Chinese Philosophy*. Edited by Bryan W. Van Norden. LaSalle, IL: Open Court, 1–13.
———. (2003). "Virtue Ethics and Confucianism." In *Comparative Approaches to Chinese Philosophy*. Edited by Bo Mou. Burlington, VT: Ashgate, 99–121.
———. (2004). "The Virtue of Righteousness in Mencius." In *Confucian Ethics: A Comparative Study of Self, Autonomy, and Community*. Edited by Kwong-loi Shun and David B. Wong. Cambridge: Cambridge University Press, 148–82.
———. (2007). *Virtue Ethics and Consequentialism in Early Chinese Philosophy*. Cambridge: Cambridge University Press.
———. (2008). *Mengzi, with Selections from Traditional Commentaries*. Indianapolis, IN: Hackett Press.
———. (2011). *Introduction to Classical Chinese Philosophy*. Indianapolis, IN: Hackett Press.
Veazie, Walter B. (1961). "John Dewey and the Revival of Greek Philosophy." *University of Colorado Studies: Series in Philosophy* (2): 1–10.

Virgil and Wilstach (1884). *The Works of Virgil*. Vol. 1. Translated by John Augustine Wilstach. New York: Houghton Mifflin and Company.
Waley, Arthur (1938). *The Analects of Confucius*. New York: Vintage Books.
———. (1960). *The Book of Songs*. New York: Grove Press.
Wallas, Graham (1914). *The Great Society: A Psychological Analysis*. New York: The Macmillan Company.
Wang, Jessica Ching-Sze (2005). *John Dewey in China: To Teach and To Learn*. Albany: State University of New York Press.
Washington, George (1988). *George Washington's Rules of Civility and Decent Behavior in Company and Conversation*. Boston: Applewood Books.
Watson, Burton (1968). *The Complete Works of Chuang Tzu*. New York: Columbia University Press.
Wechkin, Stanley, and Jules Masserman, et al. (1964). "'Altruistic' Behavior in Rhesus Monkeys." *The American Journal of Psychiatry*, 121: 584–85.
Wen, Haiming (2009). *Confucian Pragmatism as the Art of Contextualizing Personal Experience and World*. New York: Rowman & Littlefield.
Whitman, Walt (2007). *Leaves of Grass: The Original 1855 edition*. Mineola, NY: Dover Publications, Inc.
Whitman, Walt, and Gary Schmidgall (1999). *Walt Whitman: Selected Poems, New Edition*. New York: St. Martin's Griffen.
Wilson, David Sloan (1994). "Adaptive Genetic Variation and Human Evolutionary Psychology." *Ethology and Sociobiology*, 15: 219–35.
Wilson, Edward O. (1978). "On Human Nature." In *Arguing About Human Nature: Contemporary Debates*. Edited by Stephen M. Downes and Edouard Machery (2013). New York: Routledge Press, 7–23.
Winchester, Simon (2008). *The Man Who Loved China*. New York: Harper Collins.
Wippel, John F. (2000). *The Metaphysical Thought of Thomas Aquinas: From Finite Being to Uncreated Being*. Washington, DC: The Catholic University of America Press.
Witke, Roxanne (1967). "Mao Tse-tung, Women and Suicide in the May Fourth Era." *The China Quarterly*, 31: 128–47.
Wrangham, Richard (2009). *Catching Fire: How Cooking Made Us Human*. New York: Basic Books.
Wu, K. C. (1982). *The Chinese Heritage*. New York: Crown Publishers.
Wu, Xuezhao (2004). "The Birth of a Chinese Cultural Movement: Letters Between Babbitt and Wu Mi." *Humanitas*, 12(1–2): 6–25.
Xunzi 荀子 (1995). *Xunzi Jinzhujinyi* 荀子今註今譯. Taipei: The Commercial Press, Ltd.
Yangzi 揚子 (1983). *Yangzi Fayan* 揚子法言. Taipei: Chung Hwa Book Company, Ltd.
Yao, Xinzhong (2000). *An Introduction to Confucianism*. Cambridge: Cambridge University Press.
Yearly, Lee H. (1990). *Mencius and Aquinas: Theories of Virtue and Conceptions of Courage*. Albany: State University of New York Press.
———. (2003). "Confucianism and Genre: Presentation and Persuasion in Early Confucian Thought." *Journal of Ecumenical Studies*, 40(1/2): 137–52.

Yu, Liyuan (2007). "Making Sense of Cross-Cultural Dialogue: Comments on the Papers of Tang Yijie and Roger Ames." In *Dialogue of Philosophies, Religions, Civilization in the Age of Globalization*. Edited by Zhao Dunhua. Washington, DC: The Council for Research in Values and Philosophy.

Yuan, Gang, Sun Jiaxing, and Ren Bingqiang (2004). *Minzhizhuyi yu xiandaishehui: Duwei zaihuajiangyanji* 民治主义与现代社会: 杜威在华讲演集, Vol. 1 (上) and Vol. 2 (下). Beijing: Peking University Press.

Zagzebski, Linda (2010). "Exemplarist Virtue Theory." *Metaphilosophy*, 41(1–2): 41–57.

———. (2013). "Moral Exemplars in Theory and Practice." *Theory and Research in Education*, 11(2): 193–206.

Zagzebski, Linda Trinkaus (2004). *Divine Motivation Theory*. Cambridge: Cambridge University Press.

———. (2017). *Exemplarist Moral Theory*. Oxford: Oxford University Press.

Zangwill, Israel (1932). *The Melting Pot: Drama in Four Acts*. New York: Macmillan Company.

Zeng, Zida (1988). "A Chinese View of the Educational Ideas of John Dewey." *Interchange*, 19(3–4): 85–91.

Zhan, Xufang (1989). "Changes in the Attitude of Chinese Philosophical Circles towards Pragmatism." *Studies in Soviet Thought*, 38(1): 99–104.

Zhang, Xianglong (2010). "Comparison Paradox, Comparative Situation and Interparadigmaticy: A Methodological Reflection on Cross-Cultural Philosophical Comparison." *Comparative Philosophy*, 1(1): 90–105.

Zhu, Shoutong (2004). "Chinese Reactions to Babbitt: Admiration, Encumbrance, Vilification." *Humanitas*, 12(1–2): 26–45.

Zhu, Qian (2015). "Tao Xingzhi's Non-Communist Mass Education Movement in 1930's China." *Review of History and Political Science*, 3(1): 25–32.

Zhu, Zheng (2013). *Fanyoudouzhengquanshi* 反右斗争全史, Vol. 1 and 2. Independently Published.

Zhuangzi 莊子 (1994). *Zhuangzi Jinzhujinyi* 莊子今註今譯, Vol. 1 (上) and 2 (下). Taipei: The Commercial Press, Ltd.

Ziporyn, Brook. (2009). *Zhuangzi: The Essential Writings with Selections from Traditional Commentaries*. Indianapolis, IN: Hackett Press.

Zohary, Daniel, and Maria Hopf (1993). *Domestication of Plants in the Old World*. Oxford: Oxford University Press.

Index

A Key to the Language of America, 129
Acorns to Oak Trees
   and its status as if-then proposition, 237
Adjustment
   and accommodation and adaptation, 287
   and integration, 281–288
   and its meaning for James and Dewey, 286
Agamemnon, 198
Alexander, F. Matthias
   and the Alexander technique, 13
Alexander, Thomas M.
   and the denotative method, 181
Allan, Sarah
   and botanical metaphors in early China, 256
   and *tian* 天, 355n.58
   and *xing* 性, 256
American Frontier, 113
American Nationality
   and democracy, 127–132
   and Dewey, 130–132
   and *E Pluribus Unum*, 133–134
   and the enemy within, 130
   and give-and-take, 138
   and the ideal of welcoming strangers, 129
   and immigration, 129–132, 134, 145–146, 341n.12
   and Kallen, 127–128, 134
   and Whitman, 125–126

Ames, Roger T. *See also* Hall, David L. and Roger T. Ames
   and Graham on *xing* 性, 358n.158
   and *li* 禮, 119
   and *ren* 仁, 117
   and role ethics, 187–190, 194
   and *tian* 天 in the *Mencius*, 213
Ames, Roger T. and Henry Rosemont Jr.
   and the asymmetrical bias in comparative philosophy, 98
   and family, 271
   and role ethics, 187–190
Analytic Philosophy
   and its impact in China, 87
   and its lack of vitality, 38–39
   and value inquiry, 38
Angle, Stephen C.
   and Confucian virtue ethics, 170, 349n.102
   and sagehood, 286
Animals
   and association for Confucius, 222
   and Confucian critique, 231, 267–268
   and the evolution of moral sense, 225, 227–228
   and the human in early China, 61, 117–118
   and human-level experience, 12–13, 61, 152
   and humans as social, 225, 243–244
Annals of Lü Buwei, 197
   and archery and self reflection, 200

392 / Index

Aquinas, St. Thomas, 173, 256
  and *beatitudo*, 170
  and fortitude, 179
  and human nature and God's plan, 172, 353n.13
Archeological Finds
  and Chinese philosophy, 209, 217–218, 235–236, 355n.58
Archery
  and the Chinese Archery contest, 199–200, 351n.155–156
  and its status as a Confucian metaphor, 190–198, 352n.175
  and Confucian self-reflection, 200–203
  and *ren* 仁, 203
  and gender in early China, 350n.119
  and male elegance in early China, 351n.160
  and the Western tradition, 198
  and wisdom in Confucianism, 230
  and Zen Buddhism, 349n.110
  and the *Zhuangzi*, 351n.149
Aristotle, 161, 185, 256
  and American readings of the *Analects*, 76
  and the archery metaphor, 196
  and comparisons with Confucius, 75–76, 171, 176–177, 196
  and comparisons with Mencius, 267–268
  and Dewey on human relationships, 121–122
  and essentialism, 61, 70–71, 267–268
  and *eudaimonia*, 170, 194–195
  and gender, 331n.82
  and human nature and virtue, 172
  and just proportion, 124
  and substance, 21, 70–71
Artificer's Record
  on bow making, 190–191
Artists
  and the news media, 158
Associated Humanity. See *Ren* 仁

Association
  and Chinese cosmology, 121
  and Dewey's thought, 116–117, 137, 146–147, 185–186
  and moral self-reflection, 200–203
Asymmetry
  and comparative philosophy, 98

Babbitt, Irving, 78, 90, 154, 241
  biographical, 72–76
  and his critique of Dewey, 161–162
  and Mei Guangdi, 64, 71–74
  and new humanism, 15, 64, 72
Bacon, Francis
  and the four idols, 27
Barley
  and its status as a metaphor in the *Mencius*, 220–221, 233, 300–301
  and its nature as a plant, 219–220, 239, 244–245, 269, 300–301, 356n.76
Barnes, Albert
  and his correspondence with Dewey, 87, 311–312
Benedict, Ruth
  and the autonomy of culture, 6, 16
  and Dewey, 324
Bentley, Arthur
  and his correspondence with Dewey, 31–32, 311
Birdwhistell, Joanne D.
  and Confucianism and gender, 61, 244, 245
Black, Dora, 87
Blank Slate. See Human Nature
Bloom, Irene, 165
  and argument in the *Mencius*, 232, 267
  and nature/nurture in the *Mencius*, 259–260, 275
  and *renxing* 人性 in the *Mencius*, 222
  and *tian* 天 in the *Mencius*, 208–211, 212, 213, 215, 216, 222, 241–242, 282

Boas, Franz
   and his influence, 6
Bockover, Mary
   and *ren* 仁, 115
Body
   and the purely physical, 8, 13
Boisvert, Raymond D.
   and Dewey and Sartre, 215
Boxer Rebellion, 55
   and the Boxer indemnity fund, 55, 73, 162
Boyd, Robert. *See* Richardson, Peter J. and Robert Boyd
Brown, Donald E.
   and human nature, 3–4, 12, 36, 184, 226
Buddhism. *See also* Zen Buddhism
   and going against the stream, 18
Buller, David J.
   and biological norms, 238–239, 269
Burroughs, John, 16
Butler, Joseph, 227
   and Confucian virtue ethics, 223, 356n.92

Cai Yuanpei
   and Dewey in China, 59
Center for Dewey Studies
   and Fudan University, 320
Chaos
   and the source of value, 293
Chapais, Bernard
   and human male monogamy, 246–247
Chen, Duxiu
   and his article in *La Jeunesse*, 58
Chen, Hengzhe
   and language reform, 65
Chen, Heqin
   biographical, 159–160, 315–316
   and Communist China, 315–316
Chen, Lai
   and the *Mencius* and human nature, 234

Cheng, Chung-ying
   and *zhi* 志, 193
Cheng Brothers
   and Confucius, 175
Chiang, Kai-shek, 298
Chiang, Yung-chen
   and the newly discovered Dewey notes, 100–101
   and the translation of Dewey's lectures, 336n.87
China Institute
   and Dewey, 55, 162
   and Meng Chih, 162
China Lectures (Dewey)
   and the conservative/radical split, 69
   and cross-cultural ethics, 178, 230–231
   and Dewey's newly discovered notes, 99–101, 109
   and progress, 57
   and social/political philosophy, 59, 99–108, 114, 146–159, 188, 249–250, 271, 278–279
   and their number and scope, 59, 86
   and the translation process, 99–101, 147, 336n.87
Chong, Kim-chong, 359n.180
Classic of Family Reverence, 66
   and role ethics, 187
Classic of Music, 66
Climate Change
   and climate change denial, 76
   and the evolution of culture, 277–278
Clopton, Robert W., 147, 320
Coherence
   and democracy, 132
   and *gewu* 格物, 154
   and pattern in aesthetic experience, 252–253
   and science in China, 77
   and wholeness in Chinese cosmology, 126
Common Sense
   and continuity, 16–25

Common Sense *(continued)*
   and its status as culturally universal and specific, 19, 249, 273
   and Dewey, 19–25, 273
   and its status as genetic-functional, 23–25
   and intra-cultural philosophy, 17–25
   and James, 17–18, 273
   and science, 18–20, 25
   and its status as transactional, 24–25

Communication
   and community, 142–143, 146–148, 159
   and Dewey's thought, 118–119, 146–147
   and give-and-take, 155
   and across and over cultures, 30, 31, 33, 90–91
   and ritual-custom, 119, 122, 155–156

Confucian Democracy: A Deweyan Reconstruction, 139

Confucius
   and American readings of the *Analects*, 76
   and the archery contest, 198, 199, 200, 352n.175
   and comparisons with Aristotle, 75–76, 171, 176–177, 196
   and courage, 202–203
   and creativity, 46–47, 66, 68–70
   and death, 291
   and education, 43–53, 60–61, 67–70
   and enjoyment, 196
   and his family background, 245–246
   and harmony, 50–52, 279
   and human experience, 308
   and human nature, 3, 7, 118, 171, 172–177, 186, 266
   and law *vs.* ritual-custom, 105, 338n.125
   and learning *vs.* thinking, 67–70
   and marriage, 246–247
   and moral cultivation, 183
   and moral exemplarism, 182–183
   and music, 52–53
   and non-human animals, 222
   and the one thread, 204
   and personal growth, 140, 186–187
   and his status as a progressive, 60, 70, 81–82, 120–121, 247–248
   and the rectification of names, 148
   and ritual-custom, 47–50, 52, 105, 115–116, 156, 164
   and the *Songs*, 45–47, 156
   and teleology, 171
   and *tian* 天, 173–174
   and the timely sage, 229
   and tradition, 69–70, 80, 115, 120–121, 277
   and *zhi* 志, 192

Connection-and-Distinction
   and common sense, 17, 23
   and cultural consequences, 34–35
   and culture for Dewey, 8–12, 30, 78, 90–91, 109, 276, 290
   and intra-cultural inquiry, 13–14, 276

Conservatism
   and Babbitt, 71–73
   and Chinese culture, 90, 92, 95–96
   and Confucianism, 65–66, 68, 81, 114–115
   and the culture wars, 71, 241–242
   and Dewey in China, 88, 90
   and education, 44, 68
   and the erosion of family, 264
   and the fear of progress, 248
   and nostalgia towards human nature, 276
   and perfection, 250
   and postmodern relativism, 70–71, 241–242
   and the radical, 102, 107–108, 113, 248, 278–279, 337n.116
   and readings of the *Analects*, 76, 81
   and relativism, 120, 248, 337n.116
   and Republican China, 53–54

Continuity
   and Chinese culture, 95
   and common sense, 16–25

and culture, 80
and *dao* 道-activity, 244
and Dewey, 7, 13, 367n.28
and Dewey and Zhuangzi, 304–306
and emotional peace, 305–306
and intra-cultural philosophy, 13–14
and knowledge-and-action, 158, 296, 300
and Nature-and-the-human, 11–12, 72, 79, 140, 215, 253, 276, 291
and nature-culture circuits, 102
and religiousness, 305–308
and self-and-body, 10
Cook, Scott
and *Dispositions Arise from Mandated Conditions*, 259, 365n.172
and *tian* 天, 355n.58
Cooley, Charles Horton
and the face-to-face turn in Dewey's thought, 97
Coontz, Stephanie
and marriage, 119–120
Cosmic Doughnut, 308
Cosmides, Leda
and James, 17
and the stone age mind, 17
Creationism. *See* Religious Fundamentalism
Cremin, Lawrence
biographical, 23, xi–xii
Cua, Antonio S.
and *li* 禮, 122
Cultural Revolution, 317, 319
Culture
and cultural relativism, 34–40
and Dewey, 4, 7–12, 15, 25, 78, 90–91, 117
and evolution, 272–273, 277–278
and Graves, 30–31
and nature, 3–41, 90, 101–102, 108, 265–267, 270–271
and the return wave, 26–29
Curzer, Howard J.
and the *Mencius* on government, 265

Custom
and Dewey, 88–89, 91–96, 110–113, 138, 278, 338n.128
and its material disruption, 104–105, 111, 152

D'Ambrosio, Paul
and sincerity and authenticity, 189
Dai, Zhen
and Confucius, 176
Dao 道-Activity
and the child at the well, 226
and ends, 263–264
and giving things their proper due, 340n.3
and human communication, 118, 122
and non-dualism, 195, 196, 244, 284
and ritual-custom, 80
Daodejing
and cosmology, 291
and governance, 149
and organic growth, 257–258
Darwinism, 71, 72, 222. *See also* Evolution
and China, 56
and Hu Shih, 56
Daxue. *See Great Learning*
de Waal, Frans
and animals and moral sense, 227
and animals as social, 225
and humans as social animals, 243, 273–274
and Mencius' child at the well example, 224
Death
and the continuity of things, 305
and human meaning, 291–292
and Zhuangzi's wife, 303–305
Deism, 223, 353n.13
Democracy
and American nationality, 127–132
and classical liberalism, 150–151
and Confucian thought, 139–146, 156, 260

Democracy *(continued)*
  and democratic realism, 109–110
  and Dewey, 93, 122, 123–159
  and the great community, 137
  and harmony, 132, 134, 137
  and Republican China, 59
  and its status as a way of life, 137–138
Democracy of the Dead: Dewey, Confucius, and the Hope for Democracy in China, 139
Deng, Xiaoping, 319
Denotative Method
  and Dewey, 181
  and moral philosophy, 183–184
Depew, David
  and human nature, 222
Dewey, Alice, 85, 86, 93, 95, 159, 303, 304–305
  and Chinese students in America, 162–163
  and feminism in China, 62
  and ritual form in Japan, 94
Dewey, Jane, 303
  and Dewey and China, 86
  and Dewey's return to China, 311
Dewey, Lucy, 159, 162
  and feminism in China, 62
  and Grace Wu, 63
Dewey's Collected Lectures in China, 320
Ding, Zijiang
  and analytic philosophy in China, 87
Directional Order
  and growth, 185, 257–258
  and the process/product dualism, 262
Dispositions Arise from Mandated Conditions
  and its pedigree, 362n.77
  and *xing* 性 and human development, 259, 276, 365n.172
Dissertation on Roast Pig, 37
Don Quixote, 309
Downes, Stephen M.
  and evolution and human nature, 273

Downes, Steven M.
  and human cognition, 17
Drew, Dora May, 74

E Pluribus Unum, 130
  and its status as an American ideal, 133–134
  and "In God We Trust," 342n.29
Eames, S. Morris
  and adjustment in pragmatic naturalism, 366n.25
East-West Philosophers' Conference, 57, 321
Eastman, Max
  and Dewey and mysticism, 307
  and Dewey in the classroom, 74–75
Edel, Abraham
  and Dewey and custom, 88, 111
  and Dewey and Mencius, 144
  and the individual for Dewey, 112
Education
  and American nationality for Dewey, 129–132, 134
  and *educare*, 155, 276–277, 284
  and home schooling, 277
  and human nature, 276–277
  and the imperial exam system, 53–55
  and learning *vs.* thinking, 67–70
  and Mencius, 264, 277
  and reforms in Republican China, 159
  and tradition, 45, 53
  and transmission, 43–44, 80
  and *xing* 性 in Si-Meng Confucianism, 259, 284–286
Einstein, Albert, 71
Embracing the One
  and intelligence, 82
Emerson, Ralph Waldo, 125
  and experience, 95
Empathy. *See* Ren 仁
Ends
  and ends-in-view, 197, 263

and being external to activity, 184
and flourishing, 194–195, 260–264
Eno, Robert
  and *tian* 天 in the *Analects*, 173
Equality
  and Dewey, 142–144
Eriugena, John Scotus
  and analysis, 20–21, 22
Espionage/Sedition Acts, 156
Essentialism
  and common sense, 267
Etiquette and Ritual, 94
  and archery, 352n.175
  and marriage, 246
Eudaimonia. *See* Flourishing
Evolution. *See also* Darwinism
  and altruism, 224–226
  and the barley plant, 219–220
  and biological norms, 238–239
  and culture, 80, 272–273, 277–278
  and Daoism, 58
  and the evolution of helping, 224
  and final ends, 185
  and human nature, 272–274, 277–278
  and language reform, 66
  and the paternal instinct, 244–247
Evolution and Ethics
  and Hu Shih, 56
Exemplarist Ethics
  defined, 178–182
  and its advantage over virtue ethics, 177, 187, 349n.86
  and Confucianism, 178, 182–183, 187
Experience
  and Dewey's cultural turn, 9–10
  and Emerson, 95

Face-to-Face
  and connectedness, 145
  and Dewey's thought, 97–98, 110, 111, 137, 138
Failure and Success According to the Times
  and *tian* 天, 217–218

Faith
  and imagination, 294–295
  and moral faith, 294
Fallace, Thomas D.
  and Dewey in China, 89
Family. *See also* Fatherhood, Marriage, Nation as Family
  and the community of interest, 148
  and Confucian role ethics, 187–188
  and the evolution of altruism, 224–226
  and factual and normative dimensions, 269–272
  and give-and-take, 138
  and growth, 264–265, 270
  and harmony, 133–134, 254
  and hereditary rule in China, 148
  and home schooling, 277
  and human experience, 271–272
  and human nature, 243–250, 267, 268–269
  and kin-based emotions, 133, 243–244
Faraday, Michael, 71, 72
Farrell, James
  and his Chinese dinner with Dewey, 314
Fatherhood
  and Confucian moral targets, 193–194
  and human nature, 244–247, 360–361n.10
  and the rectification of names, 148
Feminism
  and Confucianism, 60–62, 331n.86
  and Dewey in China, 62
  and the male default in Confucian ethics, 244–245
  and the May Fourth Movement, 62–63, 108, 188
  and the status of women in China and America, 103–104, 106, 108
Fen, Sing-nan, 39, xi
  biographical, 33–34, 315, 318

Fen, Sing-nan *(continued)*
  and communion with Dewey, 312–314
  and his correspondence with Dewey, 31, 315
  and cultural relativism, 34–40, 67, 90, 248–249
  and Dewey and intercultural philosophy, 4
  and the ideal-and-actual, 295, 299
  and patterns and relations, 293–294
  and Tao Xingzhi, 299
Feng, Youlan
  and Communist China, 314
  and Dewey, 160–161
  and his dissertation, 161
Feuerbach, Ludwig, 289
Fingarette, Herbert
  and the sacred/secular distinction in Confucianism, 214
Fischbeck, Gerhard
  and the evolution of barley, 220
Five Practices, 66
Flourishing
  and Chinese natural philosophy, 255–256, 260–264
  and Confucius, 187
  and ethical enjoyment, 194–195
  and human association, 122, 185–186
  and virtue ethics, 170, 185
Flower, Elizabeth
  and Dewey and custom, 88
Focusing the Familiar, 66, 288
  and human potential, 214, 285–286
  and integration, 283, 285
  and naturalizing spirituality, 291, 292–293
  and the production of things, 239
  and *ren* 仁 and *yi* 義, 227
  and *xing* 性 and education, 259, 276, 284–286
Fong, Mary H.
  and the archery contest, 192
Food
  and Dewey, xi–xiii
  and metabolic processes, xiii–xiv
  and taste, xiv, 323n.17
Force
  and moral *vs.* political force, 147–150
  and state force, 147
Ford, Henry
  and the melting pot ideal, 340–341n.6
Fox News, 345n.148
Frank, Waldo
  and Dewey's mysticism, 302
Fraser, Chris
  and the Mohist critique of Confucians, 174
Fraternity
  and Dewey, 142–144
Frega, Roberto
  and Dewey in China, 99
  and Dewey's China lectures, 109
  and the translation of Dewey's lectures, 336n.87
Frisina, Warren G.
  and the continuity of knowledge-and-action, 158
  and Wang Yangming, 300

Gardner, Daniel K.
  and *gewu* 格物, 153
Gelman, Susan
  and essentialist assumptions, 22
Gewu 格物. *See* Investigation of Things
Ghosts, 288–289
Giles, B. E.
  and barley seeds, 301
Give-and-Take
  and Dewey's thought, 137–138
  and mind, 155
God. *See* Faith
Goffman, Erving
  and ritual, 228–229
Goldhaber, Dale
  and the nature/nurture dualism, 260, 270
  and the systems-approach in biology, 238

Graham, A. C.
  and the Confucian debate over human nature, 231
  and *gewu* 格物, 154
  and *ren* 仁, 117
  and *tian* 天 in the *Analects*, 173
  and *xing* 性, 221, 358n.158
Grange, Joseph, 319
  and classical liberalism, 150
  and Confucian democracy, 139–146
  and engagement in Confucianism, 158
  and *li* 禮 and communication, 155–156
Graves, John
  and his correspondence with Dewey, 30–31, 282
Great Learning, 66
  and its impact on Dewey, 144–145, 151
  and the investigation of things, 153–154
Great Society, 136–137
Green Ink Pages, 33
Grene, Marjorie
  and human nature, 222
Grieder, Jerome B.
  and Hu Shih, 316
Gronda, Roberto
  and Dewey in China, 88, 90
Growth
  and Confucian governance, 147, 149
  and Dewey and Confucius, 140
  and family, 264–265
  and harmony, 255–256, 264, 279, 284
  and marriage, 264
  and its status as a moral end, 185, 263–264
  and ritual-custom, 122
  and *xing* 性, 235–236, 257, 261–262
Gu, Hongliang
  and Dewey in China, 163
Guojia 國家. *See* Nation as Family

Habit
  and Dewey, 266
  and James, 278
Hall, David L.
  and chaos, 293
Hall, David L. and Roger T. Ames, 319
  and aesthetic *vs.* logical order, 53
  and Confucian democracy, 139–146
  and Confucian individuals, 112
  and cultural vagueness, 14
  and democracy and news media, 157
  and *li* 禮, 155
  and the rectification of names, 148
  and sexism and Confucianism, 61
  and *tian* 天, 216
  and Western liberal democracy, 150
Hamilton's Rule, 224
Harmony
  and Chinese philosophy, 50–51, 121, 124, 133–134, 186, 284–285
  and complexity and simplicity, 255
  and democracy, 132, 134, 137
  and Dewey's thought, 112, 113, 249–250
  and family, 133–134, 254
  and growth, 255–256, 279
  and the indifference of *dao* 道, 308–309
  and intelligence, 115
  and its status as a norm, 81, 111–112, 115, 124, 126, 146, 186, 251–256, 260
  and ritual-custom, 52, 80, 111–112, 115, 116, 164
  and the soup analogy, 50–51, 67, 133–134, 186, 253, 254
  and value, 67, 80, 124, 254–256, 293
He 和. *See* Harmony
He, Yan
  and Confucius, 175
Heaven's Plan, 205, 255, 259, 260
  and the over-translation of *tian* 天, 210

Heaven's Plan *(continued)*
    and the chicken and egg problem,
        232–233
    and Chinese natural philosophy,
        165–166
    and Confucian conservatism, 114–115
    and Confucius' ethics, 182–183
    and cultural maladaptation, 222, 280,
        310
    and degradation of the human,
        212–213, 280
    and Ivanhoe, 173–176, 208–209
    and intelligence, 213
    and intellectual readjustment, 306
    and absurdity, 154, 213
    and its irrelevance to moral
        judgment, 115, 184, 249, 254
    and more recent scholarship,
        211–212, 221–222
    and Slingerland, 174, 183
    and teleology, 353n.13
    and education in culture, 273, 277, 280
    and its status as an inference,
        218–219, 271
Heraclitus
    and the one and many, 133
Heredity
    and Dewey, 6
Hermeneutics
    and intra-cultural philosophy, 171–172
    and the iron rule, 171, 174, 177, 211
    and reading the *Mencius*, 258
Hitting the Mark
    and aesthetic sensibility, 255
    and Confucian value, 187
    and human association, 200–203
    and pleasure, 195
    and resolute commitment, 196–197
Hobbes, Thomas, 150
    and egoism, 223, 225
Hood, Robin, 198
Hook, Sidney
    and Dewey and cultural pluralism,
        132

    and Dewey and *The Two Cultures*,
        78–79
Houston, W. R.
    and Dewey and Confucian
        religiousness, 291
Hu Shih, 54, 151, 309, xiii
    biographical, 55, 56–59, 71, 73, 165
    and the student uprising in China,
        335n.40, 336n.90, xiii
    and Communist China, 314, 316–317
    and Darwinism, 56
    and Dewey on thinking, 321
    and Dewey's copy of the *Mencius*,
        207
    and Dewey's lectures, 101, 147
    and Dewey's political philosophy, 93
    and his dissertation, 57, 77–78, 152,
        368n.101
    and feminism, 62–63
    and funeral rituals, 165
    and the Hu Shih archives, 100–101
    and language reform in China, 63–66
    and science in China, 77–78, 152,
        154
Huainanzi, 237
Human Nature
    and aesthetic appreciation, 251–253,
        281–282
    and blank slate theories, 5–6, 12, 184,
        259
    and Brown, 3–4, 12, 36, 184, 226
    and Confucius, 3, 7, 118, 171,
        172–177
    and debates about its goodness, 3–4,
        184–185, 230–237
    and developmental *vs*. reformation
        models, 232, 234–235
    and Dewey, 5–12
    and early Confucianism, 3, 16, 149
    and education, 276–277
    and evolutionary biology, 222–223,
        272–273
    and family, 243–250, 268–269
    and homologous structures, 265–266

and kin-based emotions, 133, 224
and Mencius, 37, 207–211, 219–230, xiv
and morality, 223–230
and the naturalistic fallacy, 36
and the paternal instinct, 244–247
and Pinker, 5
and political philosophy, 149–150
and its status as raw material, 186
and its status as shared, 3–4, 180, xiii–xiv
and virtue ethics, 172–173, 179, 185
and whether it can change, 274–276
Humanism
  and the cultural right and left, 15
  and Dewey, 15–16, 71, 78–79, 215–216
  and early Confucianism, 175
  and James, 12–13
  and new humanism, 15, 64, 72
Humanism and America, 15, 64
"Humanist Manifesto"
  and Dewey, 16, 215–216
Hundred Days of Reform, 54
Hunting Vocation
  and wholeness, 195, 280
Huxley, T. H., 56
Hyphenated Americanism, 123, 125
  and Dewey, 131–132
Hyphens
  and Dewey, 324n.26

Imagination
  and faith, 294–295
  and self cultivation, 286
Immigration. *See* American Nationality
Imperial Exam System
  and Chinese history, 53–55
  and Dewey, 55, 68
  and language reform in China, 63–64
  and Mei Guangdi, 64
Incommensurability
  and cultural difference, 17
Individualism
  and the American character, 125–126
  and Confucianism, 92, 112
  and Dewey's social philosophy, 93, 105–108, 110–113, 138, 143–144
  and equality, 143–144
  and give-and-take, 138
  and the great disconnect, 140
  and the lost individual, 112–113, 121
  and role ethics, 187–190
Inherent Ethical Scheme
  and harmony, 50, 67
  and responsibility, 77
  and its status as therapeutic, 50, 76, 306
Instrumentalism
  and intelligence, 182, 184
  and theories, 182, 184
Integration
  and adjustment, 281–288
  and aesthetic experience, 281–283
  and intelligence, 284, 366n.16
Intelligence
  and customs, 110–113
  and flexibility, 38
  and future projections, 82
  and harmony, 115
  and Heaven's plan, 213
  and instrumentalism, 182
  and integration, 284, 366n.16
  and the intelligent sage, 66
  and Nature, 310
  and progressivism, 77
  and the radical/conservative dualism, 105, 108, 113
  and ritual for Mencius, 229
Internet Age. *See* Technology
Intra-cultural Philosophy
  and bias, 98, 189, 263
  and common sense, 17–25
  and continuity, 13–14, 276
  and its status as culturally situated, 9
  and the *dao* 道 of culture, 39
  and essentialism, 37
  and hermeneutics, 171–172, 177
  and human nature, 3–41

Intra-cultural Philosophy (continued)
   and importance, 177
   and life-activity, 25
   and postmodernism, 4–5, 12, 13
   and the return wave, 29
Investigation of Things
   and connectedness, 145–146, 157
   and science in China, 78, 153–154, 344n.130
   and Wang Yangming, 56
Iron Chef, 330n.37
   and harmony, 51
Iron Rule of Hermeneutics. *See* Hermeneutics
Ivanhoe, Philip J., 217
   and *Analects* 5.13, 175–176
   and botanical metaphors in the *Mencius*, 256
   and the Chinese commentarial tradition, 176
   and Confucian conservatism, 114–115
   and his critique of role ethics, 189–190
   and his debate with Rosemont, 189–190
   and dualistic thinking, 240–241, 360n.184
   and ethical promiscuity, 249, 365n.161
   and evolution and human nature, 241–242, 254
   and Heaven's plan, 114–115, 165, 173–176, 208–209, 353–354n.28
   and human nature in the *Mencius*, 210, 241
   and Mencius as nativist, 359n.170
   and paradigmatic model of the human, 256, 261–264
   and perfection in human development, 358n.147
   and postmodern Confucianism, 354–355n.42
   and reformation *vs.* development models of human nature, 231
   and sages and human nature, 232
   and secular humanism, 214, 241–242
   and spirits in early China, 288–289
   and *tian* 天, 208–212, 355n.66

James, William
   and adjustment, 286
   and common sense, 17–18, 20, 326n.96
   and evolutionary psychology, 17–18
   and God, 294
   and habit, 278
   and human nature, 275
   and humanism, 12
   and his influence, 6
   and meliorism, 250
   and the paranormal, 288
   and pluralism, 126–127
   and sport, 49
   and what makes life significant, 119
Jesus, 308
Jiang, Menglin, 54, 314, 335n.40
   and Dewey's return to China, 311, 312
   and his dissertation, 230
   and the five Confucian relationships, 92
   and human relationships, 92–93
   and his story about Dewey in China, 309–310
John Dewey, Confucius, and Global Philosophy, 139
Johnson, Mark
   and the body and aesthetic experience, 251
   and culture and value pluralism, 7, 36
   and meaning and the body, 215
Johnston, Reginald, 86

Kallen, Horace, 159
   and democracy and the melting pot, 127–128, 134
   and the face-to-face turn in Dewey's thought, 97

Karlgren, Bernhard
    and *yi* 義, 253
Kaufmann, Felix
    and Dewey's return to China, 311
Keating, James W.
    and sport, 195
Keenan, Barry, 92, 93
    and Dewey in China, 87, 99–100, 101
Kilpatrick, William H., 298, 299
Kirk, Russell
    and Babbitt and Dewey, 72–73
    and his attitude toward Dewey, 78
Knowledge
    and Chinese cosmology, 158
    and realization, 46
Kripke, Saul
    and direct reference semantics, 179–180
Kuo, Ping-wen, 162

La Jeunesse, 58
    and feminism in Republican China, 62
    and language reform in China, 65
Lachs, John
    and Dewey and adjustment, 287
Lamb Meat
    and environmental cost, 35
Lamb, Jack
    and his correspondence with Dewey, 26
Lamont, Corliss
    and Dewey and humanism, 16
Language. *See also* Communication
    and the human difference, 118–119
Language Reform
    and evolution, 66
    and Republican China, 63–66, 336–337n.90
Le Rencontre, 146
Leaves of Grass, 125–126
Legalism
    and its opposition in early China, 149
Legge, James
    and the foundations of Confucian virtue ethics, 170
    and human nature in the *Mencius*, 210
    and the influence of Butler, 223
Lei 類. *See* Types (Species)
Leviathan, 223
Lewis, Mark Edward
    and the *Songs*, 47
    and *zhi* 志, 192
Li 理. *See* Coherence
Li 禮. *See* Ritual-Custom
Li-Hsiang, Lisa Rosenlee
    and Confucian feminism, 61–62
Li, Chenyang
    and harmony, 50, 67, 115, 121, 124, 186, 253, 254, 284–285
Liang, Tao
    and *xing* 性, 235–236
Liberty
    and Dewey, 142–144
Life
    and common sense transactions, 25
    and human life as body-mind, 11
    and the meaning of life, 308–309
Liji 禮記. *See Rituals*
Lippman, Walter, 216
    and democratic realism, 109–110
    and the public, 136–137
Literary Revolution. *See* Language Reform
Literature and the American College, 72
Liu, Fangtong
    and the Center for Dewey Studies, 320
Liu, Liangjian
    and Confucian virtue ethics, 257
Liuwei 六位. *See Six Positions*
Locke, John, 150, 161
Longo, Giuseppe and Maël Montévil
    and the systems theory of organism, 257

Machery, Edouard
    and the nomological theory of human nature, 268

Makapansgat Pebble, 251
Man and His God, 292
Mao, Zedong, 314, 317, 318, 319
    and Dewey, 318
    and feminism, 62
Marriage. *See also* Family
    and Confucius, 245–246
    and Dewey, 119
    and divorce rates, 264
    and growth, 264
    and its history, 119–120, 267, 361n.19
    and same-sex marriage, 81–82, 107–108, 113–115
Martin, Jay
    and the individual for Dewey, 113
Mather, Cotton, 129
May Fourth Movement, 68, 73, 105, 139, 144
    and China at present, 320
    and Dewey, 58–59, 105–106, 188
    and feminism, 62–63, 188
    and its status as an object lesson, 40, 81
    and science, 152
    and the student uprising in China, 335n.40, 336n.90
Mead, Margaret
    and the autonomy of culture, 6
Mei Guangdi
    biographical, 64–65, 71–74
    and Babbitt, 64, 71–74
Mei, Yibao
    and Dewey and Confucius, 79
Meliorism
    and James, 250
    and orientational meliorism, 279–280
    and progress, 250
Melting Pot
    and its status as an American Ideal, 125, 134
    and Dewey's critique, 125, 128
    and the Ford Motor Company, 340–341n.6
    and Zangwill's *The Melting Pot*, 124–125
Mencius 孟子, 118
    and adjustment to conditions, 219, 287
    and archery and ethics, 191–192, 200–203
    and authoritarian government, 147
    and capacity (*cai* 才), 261, 266
    and the child at the well, 224–226
    and comparisons with Aristotle, 267–268
    and connectedness and *ren* 仁, 307
    and Chinese natural philosophy, 221
    and courage, 202–203
    and economics, 60, 264–265
    and education, 264, 276–277
    and ends as external, 195
    and family-born activities, 267, 268–272
    and feelings of shame and dislike, 227–228
    and flood-like energy, 262
    and flourishing, 262
    and folk essentialism, 267
    and the four sprouts, 209, 223–230, 252, 262, 266–268, 275–276
    and the Gaozi chapters, 231, 260, 350n.143, 358n.140
    and the goodness of human nature, 230–237
    and human nature, 37, 209–210, 219–230, 251–252, 265–266, 268–272, 274, xiv
    and human potential, 214, 261–262
    and its influence on Dewey, 144–145
    and moral self-reflection, 200–203
    and the nature/nurture dualism, 260, 265
    and ritual propriety, 228–229
    and sagehood, 66, 191, 262, 285–286, 300
    and *tian* 天, 207–212, 216–219, 237, 355n.58

and wisdom, 191, 229-230
and *zhi* 志, 191-192
Meng, Chih
  biographical, 144, 161-162
  and the China Institute, 162
  and Dewey, 144
Meyer, Dirk
  and *tian* 天, 217-218
Midgley, Mary
  and animals and moral sense, 227
  and Sartrean existentialism, 215
Mill, John Stuart
  and the afterlife, 288
Millard's Review of the Far East, 79
Ming 明. *See* Intelligence
Modernization
  and Dewey in China, 79
  and Westernization, 140-141
Moeller, Hans-Georg
  and sincerity and authenticity, 189
Mohism, 226, 231
  and Confucian fatalism, 219
  and Confucian religiousness, 174
  and fixed standards, 340n.3
  and impartial concern, 132-133
  and pragmatism, 58
  and *tian* 天, 216
Moirology, 164-165, 346n.191
Montévil, Maël. *See* Longo, Giuseppe and Maël Montévil
Moore, Charles A.
  and *Philosophy East and West*, 32-33
Morality. *See also* Exemplarist Ethics, Inherent Ethical Scheme, Role Ethics, Virtue Ethics
  and the Confucian archery metaphor, 190-198
  and gender in Confucianism, 61-62
  and the goodness of human nature, 3-4, 184-185, 230-237
  and growth, 185
  and human nature, 223-230
  and moral *vs.* political force, 147-150
  and pre-theoretical admiration, 179-180
  and progressivism, 71
  and the purpose of moral philosophy, 180-181, 182
  and the return wave, 26-28, 29
  and self-reflection, 200-203
  and situations, 183-184, 188-189
  and its status as social, 198-205
  and sympathy, 203-204, 223-224, 308
  and theoretical foundations, 172
More, Paul Elmer
  and new humanism, 15
Munro, Donald J., 165, 221, 268
  and Confucianism and education, 274, 276-277
  and Mencius and evolutionary biology, 223, 230, 241, 254
  and tian 天 in the *Mencius*, 207-209, 212, 216
Munroe, Paul, 162
Music
  and Confucius, 52-53
Mystery
  and Dewey, 116, 308

Narragansett Tribe
  and *wunnégin*, 129
Nation as Family
  and the Chinese ideal, 132-134, 139
  and the community of interest, 148
  and hereditary rule in China, 148
Naturalistic Fallacy
  and human nature, 36
Nature
  and harmony, 251-256, 284-285
  and humans as co-creative, 252-253, 284-286
  and intelligence, 310
  and normality, 237-242
  and religiousness, 215-216, 281-294
  and the supernatural, 289-290, 294
  and the translation of tian 天, 208, 209, 212, 215, 222, 241

Nature/Nurture Dualism
  and Chinese natural philosophy, 259–260
  and cultural evolution, 80, 275
  and its need to be retired, 260
Needham, Joseph
  and the "Needham Question," 153
Neville, Robert C.
  and family, 271
  and harmony, 254–255
  and relations and value, 293
New Culture Movement
  and Dewey, 86–87
  and Republican China, 58, 74, 331n.65
  and self-determination in marriage, 120
News Media
  and the artist, 158
  and Dewey's thought, 156–159
  and the meaning of "news," 157
Ni Peimin
  and Confucius and Aristotle, 196
  and Confucian education, 53
  and Confucius and the past, 70, 149
  and the *gongfu* 功夫 reading of the *Analects*, 171
  and *tian* 天, 216
  and *ren* 仁, 115
Nivison, David S.
  on Mencius, 356n.92
  on Zhang Xuecheng, 176
Northrop, F. S. C.
  on Dewey, 321

Object Permanence
  and humans and animals, 18
Observing the Small
  and intelligence, 82, 108
Oil City Episode
  and Dewey's mysticism, 307
Olberding, Amy
  and the *Analects*, 204
  and Confucian exemplarist ethics, 178–183, 190
  and elegance and exemplarism, 199–200
  and flourishing in the *Analects*, 187
  and mourning in early China, 164
  and *ren* 仁, 115–116
Orange Trees
  and form-environment continuity, 239–240
Ou, Tsuin-chen, 147, 320
  and Dewey in China, 58

Paley, William
  and intelligent design, 244, 353n.13
Pang, Pu
  and *tian* 天, 218
Pappas, Gregory Fernando
  and Dewey and moral philosophy, 181
Peirce, Charles Sanders
  and the logic of infinitesimals, 239
Perkins, Franklin
  and Heaven's plan in the *Mencius*, 210
  and *tian* 天 in the *Analects*, 173
  and *tian* 天 in the *Mencius*, 209, 212
  and *xing* 性, 235
Phantom Public, 110
Philosophical Fallacy, The, 194, 235, 309
  and Chinese thought, 235
  and theory construction, 181
Philosophy
  and the human way, 309
  and science and common sense, 29, 273
Philosophy East and West, 32–33
Picoux, Camille, 113–114, 115
Pinker, Steven
  and human nature, 5, 359n.170
  and postmodernism, 15
Pivot of *Dao* 道
  and intelligence, 34–35
Plato, 43, 109, 293
  and doing justice to things, 340n.3

Pluralism
  and the American character, 126–134
  and James, 126–127
Poetry
  and Dewey, 301–305
Postmodernism
  and conservatism, 70–71
  and humanism, 15
  and the postmodern relativist, 70–71
  and Slingerland, 4–5, 13, 15, 16, 70
Pratt, Scott L.
  and the origins of American philosophy, 129
Primitivism
  and modern thought patterns, 89, 280
Process Philosophy
  and responsibility, 76
Progressivism
  and Confucius, 60, 65–66, 69–70
  and Dewey's "Progress" article, 56–57, 64, 337n.97
  and education, 44
  and intelligence, 77, 102, 278–279
  and Legalism, 58
  and meliorism, 250, 279–280
  and the *Mencius*, 264–265
  and morality, 71
  and readings of the *Analects*, 76
  and social philosophy, 102–105, 108, 250, 278–279
  and tradition in China, 69, 95
Public (Publicity)
  and agency, 216–217
  and agency of change, 134–135
  and democracy, 150–151
  and news media, 156–159
  and science, 154–155
Public Opinion, 109
Puett, Michael J., 353n.20, 354n.28
  and Confucius and ritual, 175
  and human potential in the *Mencius*, 214, 287
  and *tian* 天 in the *Mencius*, 212, 218–219, 287

Putnam, Hilary
  and direct reference semantics, 179–180

Qiongdayishi 窮達以世. *See* Failure and Success According to the Times
Qiu, Chun, 318
  biographical, 314, 317
Quality/Form Dynamic, 275
  and cultivation of personhood, 48, 50, 67, 81, 93, 116, 265
  and Dewey in Asia, 94–95
  and education, 45–46, 67–68
  and harmony, 50–53, 80

Radio
  and Dewey, 135
  and federal regulations, 135, 342n.41
Randall, John Herman
  and Dewey and religiousness, 303
  and Dewey in China, 79
  and the face-to-face turn in Dewey's thought, 98
Ratner, Joseph
  and Dewey and culture, 30
  and Dewey and philosophy, 38–39
  and Dewey's return to China, 312
  and Sing-nan Fen, 34
Reconstruction
  and Dewey in China, 77, 79, 87
  and ritual-custom, 69, 108, 113
Reconstruction (*Kaizō* 改造), 90, 91
Rectification of Names
  and Confucian government, 148
  and Hu Shih, 57–58
  and moral problems, 188–189
Relativism
  and absolutism, 38, 248
  and the assumption of cognitive privilege, 183–184
  and conservatism, 120, 248
  and cultural relativism, 35–36, 248–249
  and postmodernism, 5–6, 16
  and virtue ethics, 172–173, 183

Religious Fundamentalism
   and cognitive habits, 76
   and the fear of progress, 248
Religiousness
   and actualizing ideals, 294–301
   and Confucianism, 214
   and connectedness, 307
   and continuity, 305–308
   and God for Dewey, 214
   and human nature, 281–282
   and integration, 281–288
   and naturalism, 215–216
   and naturalism vs. supernaturalism, 288–294
   and shared experience, 303–305
Ren 仁
   defined, 114–116, 223–226
   and benevolence, 223, 225–226
   and democracy, 137
   and Dewey's thought, 147
   and empathy/sympathy, 223–224
   and its relation with archery, 203
   and growth, 133, 140
   and li 禮, 156
   and moral self-reflection, 200–203
   and political vs. moral force, 147–150
Ren Bingqiang, 320
Resolute Commitment
   and bow making, 191
   and hitting the mark, 196–197
   and its primacy in Confucian ethics, 191–194
   and Tillich on faith, 192
Return Wave
   and culture, 26–29, 71
Rhythm
   and the potter's wheel of nature, 251, 257
Richardson, Peter J. and Robert Boyd
   and the evolution of culture, 80, 272, 273, 277–278, 280
Rights
   and first and second generation rights, 142

Ritual-Custom
   and communication, 119
   and dao 道-activity, 80
   and Dewey on custom, 88, 110–113
   and educative, 47–52, 155
   and harmony, 52, 110–113, 115, 116
   and its function, 47–50, 81, 116, 122
   and its material disruption, 104–105, 111, 152
   and reconstruction, 69–70
   and ritual propriety for Mencius, 228–229
   and social grammar, 119, 155
   and tradition, 96–97
   and Xunzi, 61, 118
Rituals, 245
   and Confucian education, 44–45, 47–49
   and the intelligent sage, 66
   and marriage, 120, 246, 247
Robins, Dan
   and xing 性, 221, 235, 236, 256, 257
Rockefeller, Steven C.
   and Dewey and Daoism, 282, 302
   and Dewey and religiousness, 282, 289–290, 302
Role Ethics
   defined, 187–189
   and its advantage over virtue ethics, 177
   and the Confucian archery metaphor, 194
   and Confucianism, 187–190
   and Dewey on Confucian role ethics, 178
   and its debate with virtue ethics, 189–190
Rolston, Holmes, 360n.184
Romero, Father Óscar
   and fortitude, 179–182
Rongchengshi 容成氏
   and tian 天, 355n.58
Roosevelt, Theodore, 124
   and hyphenated Americanism, 123

Rosemont Jr., Henry, 263. *See also*
Ames, Roger T. and Henry
Rosemont Jr.
and his debate with Ivanhoe, 189–190
and religiousness, 281
and role ethics, 187–190
Rosenthal, Sandra B.
and value in pragmatic naturalism, 215
Rousseau, Jean-Jacques, 150
Rules of Civility and Decent Behavior in Company and Conversation, 169–170
Russell, Bertrand
and his visit to China, 87

Sagehood
and the barley seed metaphor, 300–301
and cultural creation, 232–233, 253
and focus on the ordinary world, 293
and imagination, 286
and the *Mencius*, 285–286
and moral courage, 202–203
and Si-Meng Confucianism, 285
Same-Sex Marriage, 154
and cultural progress, 81–82
and social philosophy, 107–108
and Taiwan, 113–115
Sande 三德. See *Triadic Virtue*
Sartre, Jean-Paul
and nihilism, 214–215, 307
Schaberg, David
and the *Songs*, 46–47
Schilpp, Paul Arthur
and *Library of Living Philosophers*, 32
Schneider, Herbert, 301
and the face-to-face turn in Dewey's thought, 97–98
Scholarly Review, 74
Schulte, Barbara
and Dewey and Communist China, 319
and Dewey in China, 93

Science
and Chinese thought, 77–78, 152–154
and common sense, 18–20, 25, 273, 327n.105
and Dewey, 71
and Republican China, 77
and the return wave, 26–29
Second Opium War, 54
Serenity Prayer, 288
Shanghai Café, 314, 323n.1, xi–xii
Shen 身
and the body-self relation, 10
and the cultivation of personhood, 45, 144–145
Shen, Kuo
and science in China, 153
Shi Bo
and harmony and growth, 255–256, 262, 265, 271
Shijing 詩經. See *Songs*
Shoot Pulling
and its status as form of stupidity, 261, 279
and timeliness, 229–230
Shun, Kwong-loi, 357n.111
and archery and wisdom, 230
and Confucius as timely, 229
Shusterman, Richard
and the body and aesthetic experience, 251
Si-Meng 思孟 Confucianism
and Dewey, 255
and the growth of character, 258–259
and human co-creativity, 253
and religiousness, 283
and Daoist critiques, 366n.16
and *xing* 性 and education, 276–277
Sigurðsson, Geir
and tradition in Chinese thought, 79–80
Sim, May
and Confucian conservatism, 114–115
and Confucian virtue ethics, 176–177
and Dewey and Confucius, 91–93

Sing-nan Fen
  biographical, xi
Sino-Japanese War, 54
Situation
  and moral problems, 183–184, 188–189
  and orientational meliorism, 279–280
Sivin, Nathan
  and science in China, 152–153
Six Positions
  and family and human nature, 268–269
Sleeper, R. W.
  and Dewey and science, 71
Slingerland, Edward
  and *Analects* 5.13, 175
  and Confucian learning, 68
  and Confucian virtue ethics, 172–173, 183
  and Heaven's plan, 174
  and *junzi* 君子 as gentleman, 62, 331n.86
  and metaphor in Chinese thought, 190
  and postmodernism, 5, 13, 15, 16, 70
  and sagehood, 300
  and Sartrean existentialism, 354–355n.42
Smith, John E.
  and Dewey in China, 86
Snow, C. P.
  and *The Two Cultures*, 16, 78–79
Social Philosophy (Dewey). *See* China Lectures (Dewey)
Socrates, 180
  and wisdom as guide to life, 29
Songs
  and the archery contest, 199, 351n.156, 351n.160
  and education, 44–47, 65–66
  and harmony and family, 254
  and organic growth, 257
  and *tian* 天, 211, 237
Sport
  and non-instrumental enjoyment, 195–196
  and the quality/form dynamic, 49–50, 330n.30

St. Paul
  and anger, 17
Stalnaker, Aaron
  and the teleological reading of the *Mencius*, 235, 358–359n.159
Steiner, Pierre
  and Dewey and mental phenomena, 10
Stone Age Mind Thesis, 17, 272, 273, 277–278
Stroud, Scott R.
  and Dewey and adjustment, 287
  and orientational meliorism, 279–280
Stump Watching
  and its status as form of stupidity,, 279
  and timeliness, 229–230
Stupidity
  and future projections, 82
  and the importance of the standard, 39
  and the Man from Song, 261
  and social philosophy, 278–279
Sun Ning
  and the Center for Dewey Studies, 320
Sun, Jiaxiang, 320
Sun, Yat-sen, 56
  and Dewey, 56
Supernaturalism
  and naturalism, 154
Systems Theory
  and Chinese natural philosophy, 256–258
  and nature-and-culture, 274
  and the organism, 238–239, 257, 269

Tan, Sor-hoon, 319
  and Confucian democracy, 139–146
  and Confucianism and creativity, 66
  and human nature and Confucianism, 149
  and Mencius and government, 147
  and nation as family in China, 134

Tao, Xingzhi, 54
  biographical, 295–299
  and Communist China, 318
  and cultural communication, 321
  and example of religiousness, 299
Taylor, Shelley
  and human males and marriage, 247
Technology
  and Chinese history, 141
  and the Internet age, 136
  and media technologies, 134–135
  and the organism-technology circuit, 135
  and the return wave, 28, 29
Teleology
  and Chinese natural philosophy, 221, 235–237, 256–264
  and common sense, 19
  and Confucius' teachings, 171
  and the eradication of final cause, 20, 185, 353n.13
  and readings of *xing* 性, 235–237, 256–257
Tell, William, 198
Thomas, M. Hasley, 301
Three Gunshots, 316
Tian 天. See also Heaven's Plan, Nature
  and the *Analects*, 173–174
  and its indifference, 211–212
  and its evolution in early China, 174–176
  and the *Mencius*, 207–212, 216–219
  and Nature, 208, 209, 212, 215
  and social forces, 216–219
  and the Songs, 211
Tianming 天命
  and Confucius, 175
  and the forces of the age, 217–219
  and the *Mencius*, 212, 219
Tillich, Paul
  and faith and ultimate concern, 192
Togetherness
  and Dewey, 14, 126, 307
Tolstoy, Leo
  and unhappy families, 272

Tooby, John
  and James, 17
  and the stone age mind, 17
Tradition
  and Chinese thought, 79–82
  and its comparison to ship at sea, 82
  and the *dao* 道 of tradition, 40, 77–82, 95–96, 108, 115, 120–121
  and Dewey and Confucius, 91–92
  and education, 45, 53
  and progressivism, 69–70, 120–121
  and ritual-custom, 96–97
Tragic Split
  and Dewey, 16
Transaction
  and common sense, 24–25
  and life-activity, 23–24, 30
Transcendentals
  and Greek-medieval thought, 281
Triadic Virtue
  and *tian* 天, 355n.58
Trivers, Robert L.
  and reciprocal altruism, 225–226
Truman Show, 108
Tseng, Ching-chao, 114, 115
Tufts, James
  and custom, 111
Two Cultures, 16, 78–79
Types (Species)
  and early China, 236–237
  and their status as statistical, 239–240

Ulysses, 198

Value
  and cultural relationism, 35–36, 67, 248–249
  and finite relations, 291, 293–294
  and harmony, 67, 80, 124, 254–256
  and the here and now, 292
  and nihilism, 214–215, 307
  and organic systems, 360n.184
  and valuation, 35–38
  and value pluralism, 7, 36

Van Norden, Bryan W., 357n.111
  and botanical metaphors in the *Mencius*, 256, 258
  and Confucian virtue ethics, 170–173, 176, 177, 187, 190, 356n.92
  and Dewey and Mencius, 213
  and human nature in the *Mencius*, 222, 266
  and interpretive precision, 347n.7
  and *junzi* 君子 as gentleman, 62, 331n.86
  and methodological pluralism, 172, 190
  and his misreading of Hall and Ames, 325n.45
  and postmodern Confucianism, 214, 354–355n.42
  and species-level norms, 237–238, 239, 269
  and teleological reading of *xing* 性, 222, 236, 364n.131
  and wisdom in the *Mencius*, 230
Virgil
  and *E Pluribus Unum*, 133
Virtue Ethics
  and the Confucian archery metaphor, 194–195
  and Confucianism, 165, 169–177, 187, 209, 236, 256–257, 261–262, 356n.92
  and Dewey on moral development, 263–264
  and the enumeration of the virtues, 204
  and human nature, 172–173, 179, 185
  and its debate with role ethics, 189–190
  and Scholastic theology, 179
  and the vagueness of the term, 349n.102
  and for Van Norden, defined, 170

Waley, Arthur
  and *ren* 仁, 117
Wallas, Graham
  and *The Great Society*, 136–137

Wang, Jessica Ching-Sze, 161
  and Dewey and China, 83, 98, 334n.6
Wang, Yangming
  and the continuity of knowledge-and-action, 56
  and Hu Shih, 56
  and the investigation of things, 56
  and knowledge-and-action, 296, 300
Washington, George, 169–170
Weber, Ralph
  and the *terium comparationis*, 23
Welcoming Strangers (*Wunnégin*), 129
Whitehead, Alfred North
  and human meaning, 291–292
Whitman, Walt, 159
  and the American character, 125–126
  and American immigration, 341n.12
  and the here and now, 292
Wild Geese
  and monogamy, 246
Williams, Roger
  and Native Americans, 129
Wilson, David Sloan
  and biological norms, 239
Wilson, Edward O.
  and human nature, 222
Wisdom
  and the Man from Song, 229
  and Mencius, 219, 229–230
  and timeliness, 229–230
Wolff, Kurt
  and correspondence with Dewey, 27–28
Wordsworth, William
  and his impact on Dewey, 302
Wrangham, Richard
  and monogamy and cooking, 247
Wu, Grace, 63
Wu, Kuo-chen
  and Confucius and marriage, 247
  and polygamy in early China, 245–246
Wu, Zhihui
  and materialism in China, 78

Wuxing 五行. See *Five Practices*

Xiaojing 孝經. See *Classic of Family Reverence*
Xing 性. *See also* Human Nature
  and Chinese natural philosophy, 235–240, 256–259
  and current Sinological research, 235–236
  and norms, 237–241
Xingzimingchu 性自命出. See *Dispositions Arise from Mandated Conditions*
Xunzi 荀子
  and human nature, 231, 234
  and humans and animals, 61, 118
  and *tian* 天, 174, 211

Yang Zhu, 226, 231
Yang, Xiong
  and archery and ethics, 190
Yao, Xinzhong
  and Confucian education, 80
Yearly, Lee
  and Confucianism, 221
  and *ren* 仁, 356n.92
Yen, Fu, 56
Yili 儀禮. See *Etiquette and Ritual*
Yuan, Gang, 320
Yuan, Shikai, 56
Yueji 樂記. See *Classic of Music*

Zagzebski, Linda
  and elegance and exemplarism, 199
  and exemplarist ethics, 178–181, 348n.46
  and types of admiration, 228

Zangwill, Israel
  and *The Melting Pot*, 124–125
Zen Buddhism
  and archery, 349n.110
Zhang, Boling, 296
Zhang, Xianglong
  and the comparison paradox, 21
Zhang, Xuecheng
  and Confucius, 176
Zhengming 正名. See *Rectification of Names*
Zhi 志. See *Resolute Commitment*
Zhi/Wen 質文 Dynamic. See *Quality/Form Dynamic*
Zhong 中. See *Hitting the Mark*
Zhongyong 中庸. See *Focusing the Familiar*
Zhu, Qixian, 318
  biographical, 314–315, 317
Zhu, Xi, 221
  and Confucius, 175–176
  and *gewu* 格物, 154
  and the goodness of human nature, 234
  and shame and dislike, 226, 357n.111
Zhuangzi 莊子
  and the archery metaphor, 198, 351n.149
  and the continuity of things, 304, 305
  and his wife's death, 303–305
  and norms and organic form, 239–240
  and the optimal human standpoint, 13
Zuozhuan 左傳
  and harmony and soup, 50–51

www.ingramcontent.com/pod-product-compliance
Lightning Source LLC
Chambersburg PA
CBHW020119240426
43673CB00038B/532